The Revolutionary Atlantic

The Revolutionary Atlantic

Republican Visions, 1760–1830
A Documentary History

RAFE BLAUFARB

New York   Oxford
OXFORD UNIVERSITY PRESS

Oxford University Press is a department of the University of Oxford. It furthers the University's objective of excellence in research, scholarship, and education by publishing worldwide. Oxford is a registered trade mark of Oxford University Press in the UK and certain other countries.

Published in the United States of America by Oxford University Press
198 Madison Avenue, New York, NY 10016, United States of America.

For titles covered by Section 112 of the US Higher Education Opportunity Act, please visit www.oup.com/us/he for the latest information about pricing and alternate formats.

Library of Congress Cataloging-in-Publication Data

Names: Blaufarb, Rafe, editor.
Title: The revolutionary Atlantic : Republican visions, 1760–1830 : a
    documentary history / Rafe Blaufarb.
Description: New York, NY : Oxford University Press, 2017. | Includes
    bibliographical references.
Identifiers: LCCN 2016049650 | ISBN 9780199897964 (pbk.)
Subjects: LCSH: Atlantic Ocean Region—Politics and government—18th
    century—Sources. | Atlantic Ocean Region—Politics and government—19th
    century—Sources. | United States—History—Revolution,
    1775–1783—Sources. | France—History—Revolution, 1789–1799—Sources. |
    Revolutions—History—18th century. | Revolutions—History—19th century.
Classification: LCC D299 .R47 2017 | DDC 909/.0982107—dc23 LC
    record available at https://lccn.loc.gov/2016049650

9 8 7 6 5 4 3 2 1

Printed by Webcom, Inc., Canada

TABLE OF CONTENTS

ACKNOWLEDGMENTS   xiii

ABOUT THE AUTHOR   xv

MAP 1: THE ATLANTIC IN 1763   xvi

MAP 2: THE ATLANTIC IN 1830   xviii

INTRODUCTION   1

Chapter 1   **The Enlightenment**   7
I. The Giants   8
    1. John Locke, *Two Treatises of Government*   8
    2. Montesquieu, *The Spirit of Laws*   14
    3. Voltaire, *Handy Philosophic Dictionary*   17
    4. Denis Diderot, "Political Authority"   19
    5. Jean-Jacques Rousseau, *The Social Contract*   21
II. History and Political Theory   27
    6. Henry de Boulainvillier, *History of the Ancient Government
       of France*   27
    7. Jacob-Nicolas Moreau, *Lessons in Morality, Politics and Public
       Law Drawn from the History of Our Monarchy*   28
    8. Gabriel Bonnot de Mably, *Observations on the History
       of France*   30
III. Enlightenment and Revolution   34
    9. Guillaume-Joseph Saige, *The Citizen's Catechism*   35

Chapter 2   **The Strains of Empire**   40
I. Spain   40
    1. Alexander Von Humboldt on New Spain (Mexico)   41
    2. Economic Complaints   43

3. Exploitation and Corruption: The View from the Top 46

4. Exploitation and Corruption: The View from Below 48

5. First Stirrings of Revolution (1799) 49

II. France 51

6. Taxing Saint-Domingue (1763–1764) 51

III. Great Britain 55

7. Royal Proclamation on the Western Territories (October 7, 1763) 56

8. Grievances of Western Settlers 57

9. Reaction to the Quebec Act (1775) 59

10. Adam Smith on Colonial Taxation (1776) 63

11. A New Colonial Order (1764) 66

12. Resistance: "The New York Petition to the House of Commons" (1764) 68

13. Resistance: The Irish House of Commons (December 13, 1763) 72

14. Resistance: The Jamaican House of Assembly (1769–1783) 73

Chapter 3 **Origins of the American Revolution 79**

I. Repealing the Stamp Act (1766) 79

1. Parliamentary Debate over the Withdrawal of the Stamp Act (January 1766) 80

2. Parliamentary Testimony of Benjamin Franklin (February 13, 1766) 83

II. Conflict Intensifies (1766–1774) 89

3. Samuel Adams, *The Rights of the Colonists* (1772) 89

4. A Climate of Paranoia 91

5. More Paranoia 93

III. On the Brink (1774–1775) 97

6. The Continental Congress's Declaration and Resolves (1774) 98

7. Edmund Burke, *Speech on Conciliation with America* (March 22, 1775) 101

IV. Imperial Shockwaves 111

8. The View from Jamaica (1774) 111

9. The View from Ireland (1776) 115

V. The Breaking Point (1775–1776) 116

10. Declaration of the Causes and Necessity of Taking Up Arms (June 1775) 116

11. Thomas Paine, *Common Sense* (1776) 121

12. Charles Inglis, *The True Interest of America Impartially Stated* (1776) 126

13. Declaration of Independence (July 4, 1776)   130

14. Loyalist Declaration of Dependence (1781)   133

Chapter 4   **Winning American Independence   139**

I. Race, Slavery, and the War   140

1. Lord Dunmore's Proclamation (November 7, 1775)   140

2. John Laurens Recommends Recruiting Slaves   141

3. Alexander Hamilton's Response to the Idea   143

4. George Washington's Reaction   144

5. Slave Petition for Freedom to the Massachusetts Legislature
(January 13, 1777)   145

6. Pennsylvania Abolishes Slavery (1781)   146

II. Native Americans and the American Revolution   147

7. Oneida Declaration of Neutrality (1775)   148

8. Continental Congress Seeks Iroquois Neutrality
(July 13, 1775)   148

III. Loyalists   151

9. Lafayette Describes the American Revolution as a
Civil War   152

10. Loyalist Song: "The Rebels"   152

11. Show the Loyalists No Mercy (1779)   154

IV. A Government for Independent America   156

12. John Adams, *Thoughts on Government*
(April 1776)   156

13. Articles of Confederation (1777)   160

V. The Constitution of 1787   165

14. James Madison, *Vices of the Political System of the
United States* (April 1787)   166

15. The Problem of Slavery and Representation   168

16. The Constitution (1787)   171

VI. Ratifying the Constitution   180

17. James Madison, *Federalist Number 10*   180

18. *Antifederalist Number 17*   186

19. Virginia Declaration of Rights (1776)   189

20. Bill of Rights   191

21. George Washington's Farewell Address (1796)   192

Chapter 5   **Origins of the French Revolution   197**

I. Resistance to the Parlements   198

1. Remonstration of the Parlement of Paris Against the Acts of
Violence Committed Against the Different Parlements
(December 26, 1763)   199

2. The Royal Session Known as the "Session of Flagellation"
(March 3, 1766)   201

3. Remonstrations Leading to the Maupeou Coup
(December 1770–January 1771)   203

4. Remonstration of the *Cour des Aides* (May 6, 1775)   205

II. Alternate Pathways to Reform   209

5. Marquis de Mirabeau, *Memoir on Provincial Estates*   210

6. Anne-Robert-Jacques Turgot, *Memoir on Municipalities*   212

7. Jacques Necker, *Account Given to the King* (1781)   217

III. The Pre-Revolution (1787–1788)   220

8. The Assembly of Notables (1787)   220

9. Parlement's Remonstration Against the Stamp Tax
(July 26, 1787)   223

IV. Radicalization and the Shifting Alignment of Political
Conflict   224

10. *Deliberation to be Taken by the Third Estate in all the
Municipalities of the French Kingdom* (1788)   225

11. Parlement's Denunciation of the *Deliberation to be Taken*
(December 16, 1788)   226

12. Abbé Sieyes, *What is the Third Estate?* (January 1789)   227

13. Memoir of the Princes (December 12, 1788)   233

14. Result of the Council on the Composition of the
Estates-General (December 27, 1788)   234

V. The Nation Speaks   235

15. Cahier of the Clergy of Rouen   235

16. Cahier of the Nobility of Rouen   239

17. Cahier of the Third-Estate of Rouen   243

18. Cahier of the Barrel-Makers of Rouen   248

19. Cahier of Le Val de la Haye   248

Chapter 6   **The French Revolution   250**

I. From Estates-General to the National Assembly   250

1. Arthur Young, *Travels in France* (1789)   251

II. Dismantling the Old Regime   256

2. A Wigmaker Recounts the Great Fear at Cremieu (1789)   257

3. The Marquis d'Agoult Describes the Night of August 4th   259

4. Decree of August 10, 1789   260

III. The New Regime . . . and Its Limits   262

5. Declaration of the Rights of Man and the Citizen
(August 26, 1789)   262

6. Olympe de Gouges, *The Rights of Women*
(September 1791)   264

7. Maximillian Robespierre, Speech Against Property
Qualifications to Exercise the Full Rights of Citizenship
(April 1791)   266

8. Abbé Grégoire, *Motion in Favor of the Jews*
(December 23, 1789)   268

IV. The Church's Place in the New Regime   271

9. The Constitutionality of Corps: Le Chapellier
(October 31, 1789)   272

10. The Clerical Position: Archbishop Boisgelin
(October 31, 1789)   272

11. The Civil Constitution of the Clergy (July 12, 1790)   275

V. Reaction to the Revolution   277

12. Edmund Burke, *Reflections on the Revolution in
France* (1790)   277

13. Thomas Paine, *Rights of Man* (1791)   279

VI. Revolution and Counter-revolution   282

14. The Jacobin Crusade   282

15. The King's Flight (June 21–22, 1791)   284

VII. War   287

16. The Declaration of War (April 20, 1792)   287

17. The Brunswick Manifesto (July 25, 1792)   288

18. The *Marseillaise* (1792)   290

19. Decree for the Levy en Masse (August 23, 1793)   291

VIII. The Republican Revolution   292

20. Saint-Just, *Republican Institutions* (1794)   292

21. Maximillian Robespierre, *The Principles of Political
Morality* (1794)   294

22. *Declaration of the Rights of Man and Citizen* (1793)   297

IX. The Directory   299

23. Drafting the Directorial Constitution (1795)   300

24. Inaugural Message of the Directory to the French People
(November 5, 1795)   302

25. Doctrine of Gracchus Babeuf   303

X. The Brumaire Coup and Consulate   304

26. Consular Address to the French People
(November 19, 1799)   304

27. The Concordat (1802)   305

28. The Civil Code (1804)   307

XI. The Empire   310

29. The Motion to Make Bonaparte a Hereditary Ruler
(April 30, 1804)   310

30. Napoleon's New Nobility (1807)   311

31. Why the French Submitted to Napoleon's Rule   312
XII. The Restoration   313
   32. Louis XVIII's Constitutional Charter (1814)   314
   33. Reactionary Europe (1820)   315
   34. Great Britain and European Reaction   316

Chapter 7 **Toward the Haitian Revolution   318**
I. Abolitionist Sentiment in Pre-Revolutionary France   319
   1. The Society of the Friends of the Blacks   319
II. The Beginning of the French Revolution   320
   2. The Planters' Fears of Revolutionary Radicalism   321
   3. Planter Grievances and Aspirations   322
   4. A Planter Pamphlet   324
   5. Divisions Among Whites   326
   6. The Atlantic Merchants Weigh In   326
   7. The Colonial Order Rips Itself Apart   329
III. Free People of Color   331
   8. The Free People of Color Enter the Scene   331
   9. The Abbé Grégoire Intervenes   334
IV. The Assembly Debates Equality for the Free People of Color   336
   10. The Colonial Committee's Initial Approach
      (March 1790)   336
   11. Abbé Grégoire, *Letter to the Lovers of Humanity*
      (October 1790)   338
   12. The Debate Over Race and Citizenship (1791)   341
V. The Slave Revolt (August 1791)   357
   13. The Jamaicans React (November 1, 1791)   358
   14. The French Reaction: The Political Right   358
   15. The French Reaction: The Political Left   361

Chapter 8 **Emancipation and Independence   369**
I. Emancipation   369
   1. Sonthonax's Emancipation Proclamation
      (August 29, 1793)   370
   2. The National Convention Ratifies Emancipation
      (February 4, 1794)   372
II. Post-Emancipation   374
   3. Polverel's Labor Regulations (1793–1794)   375
   4. Toussaint Louverture's Labor Regulations
      (October 12, 1800)   377
   5. Toussaint's Constitution (May 9, 1801)   379
III. Napoleon's Expedition   382

6. The Fate of Louisiana 383

7. The Fate of the French Expedition 386

IV. Defining the Meaning of Independence 389

8. Declaration of Independence and Abjuration of the French Nation (1804) 389

9. A Black Republic (April 1804) 392

10. Foreign Reactions to Haitian Independence 396

11. African American Reactions 397

V. Independent Haiti 399

12. Haiti in 1807 399

13. Haiti in 1826 404

14. Colonial Fears of Haiti 408

15. Haiti As Sanctuary 409

Chapter 9 **The Struggles for Latin American Independence 415**

I. Forerunners of Independence 416

1. Count de Aranda's Secret Report to King Carlos III 416

2. Juan Pablo Viscardo y Guzman, *Letter to the Spanish Americans* (1810) 418

3. Francisco de Miranda, Draft Constitution for Spanish America (late 1790s) 421

II. The Napoleonic Wars and Latin American Independence 422

4. Proclamation of King Joseph to the Spanish Americans (October 2, 1809) 423

5. Francisco Martinez Marina, *Theory of the Cortes* (1813) 424

6. Colonial Representation in the Cortes (1810) 427

7. Manifesto to the Mexican People from Their Representatives to the Cortes (November 6, 1813) 431

III. Declaring Independence 432

8. Venezuelan Declaration of Independence (July 5, 1811) 432

9. Argentinian Independence Implied (1811) 436

10. Mexican Declaration of Independence (November 6, 1813) 438

IV. Mexican Independence (1810–1815) 438

11. Excommunications of Hidalgo (September 24, 1810) 439

12. Hidalgo's Manifesto Against His Excommunication 441

13. José Morelos, *Sentiments of the Nation* (September 14, 1813) 442

V. The Rise, Fall, and Rebirth of Latin American Independence 444

14. Bolivar's Proclamation of War to the Death (June 15, 1813) 445

15. Bolivar's Jamaica Letter (September 6, 1815)   446

16. Bolivarian Naval Dominance (1818)   454

17. Roussin, "Report on Venezuela and New Granada"
    (July 30, 1820)   455

18. State of Revolution in South America (1817–1818)   457

Chapter 10   **The Contours of Independence   462**

I. A New World of Republics?   463

1. Bolivar, "Angostura Address" (February 15, 1819)   463

II. Mexico Achieves Independence   476

2. Address of Colonel Quiroga to Ferdinand VII
   (January 7, 1820)   477

3. Plan of Iguala (February 24, 1821)   478

III. Brazilian Independence   480

4. Manifesto of the Prince Regent to the People of Brazil
   (August 1, 1822)   481

IV. Latin American Independence and the Atlantic Powers   486

5. Circular of Spain to the European Governments
   (December 10, 1817)   486

6. Canning's Memorandum to the Cabinet on Spanish American Policy (November 15, 1822)   491

7. The "Polignac Memorandum" (October 23, 1823)   497

8. Monroe Doctrine (December 2, 1823)   500

9. Latin American Criticism of the Monroe Doctrine   501

10. Bernardo Monteagudo, "Essay on the Need for a General
    Federation between the Hispano-American States"
    (1824)   502

CONCLUSION   506

ACKNOWLEDGMENTS

This book began in early 2011 with an email from Charles Cavaliere, Executive Editor at Oxford University Press. Charles opened with an apology for contacting me out of the blue and then proceeded to ask if I might be interested in writing a primary source reader on the French Revolutionary Atlantic. I told Charles that the basic idea seemed good, but that the scope of the project was too narrow. Given that recent research had highlighted the interconnectedness of the different "national Atlantics," I responded, intellectual honesty seemed to demand a transnational approach. Market calculations reinforced this conclusion. Although there were many excellent primary source readers on each of the great Atlantic revolutions (the American, French, Haitian, and Latin American), nothing had as yet been published bringing them all together. We agreed to expand the scope of the project, and I (slowly) got down to work. This volume is the result.

All translations are my own, unless otherwise noted. But because I am a specialist in the French Revolution, I relied heavily on the advice of colleagues with expertise in the other major revolutions. Consequently, the list of those to whom I owe a debt of acknowledgement is long. For help with the American Revolution, I thank Andrew Frank, Woody Holton, Maya Jasanoff, Katherine Mooney, and Jon Parmenter. For advice on the Haitian Revolution and the related issue of slavery, I turned to Kelly Brignac, John Garrigus, Philippe Girard, Rebecca Hartkopf-Schloss, Sue Peabody, and Cecile Vidal. For help with the Latin American chapters, I benefited from the advice of Matt Brown, Scott Eastman, Peter Hicks, and Jaime Rodriguez O. For his help on the Enlightenment chapter, I wish to thank my former colleague Darrin McMahon. I also wish to thank Marjolein Kars and Wim Klooster for their advice on the Dutch Atlantic and Sylvie Kleinman for her help with the Irish perspective on the Age of Revolution. I also thank the wonderful group of undergraduate and graduate research assistants who helped me identify and transcribe documents—Daniel Arenas, Erik Lewis, Marina Ortiz, Richard Siegler, and Nicholas Stark. I could not have finished without them. Finally, I wish to thank Charles Cavaliere for thinking of me for this project and guiding it to completion. I also wish to thank Willem Klooster, Clark University; Alyssa Sepinwall, California State University — San Marcos; Rebecca Hartkopf Schloss, Texas A & M University; and Jordan Dym, Skidmore University for their support and wonderful endorsements of this book. And, finally, I wish to thank Sophia Rosenfeld, University of Virginia; Alyssa Goldstein Sepinwall, California State University, San Marcos; Dayo Nicole Mitchell, University of Oregon; J. P. Short, University of Georgia; Steven Soper, University of Georgia; and Gregory Brown, University of Nevada, Las Vegas, who shared their helpful feedback with me.

ABOUT THE EDITOR

R afe Blaufarb is the Ben Weider Eminent Scholar Chair and Director of the Institute on Napoleon and the French Revolution at Florida State University. He is the author of four monographs, four primary source readers, and more than a dozen journal articles. His most recent publications are *Inhuman Traffick: The International Struggle Against the Transatlantic Slave Trade* (Oxford University Press, 2014) and *The Great Demarcation: The French Revolution and the Invention of Modern Property* (Oxford University Press, 2016).

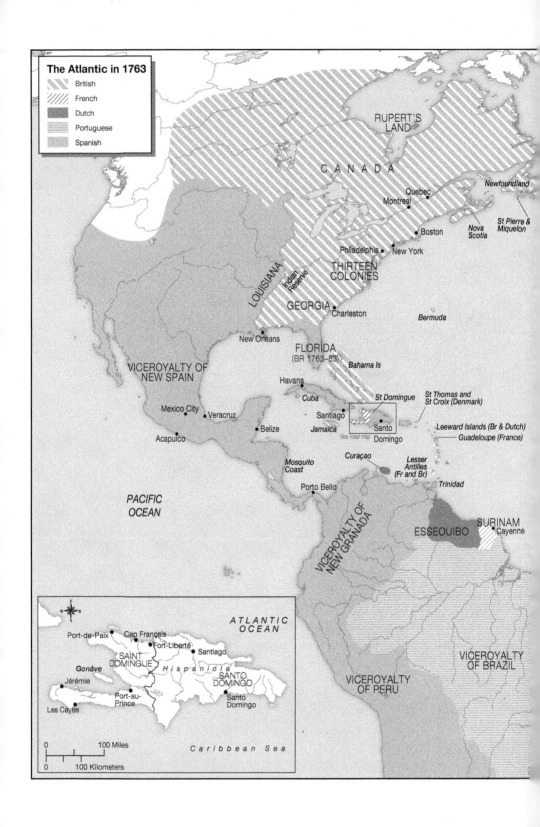

The Atlantic in 1763

- British
- French
- Dutch
- Portuguese
- Spanish

RUPERT'S LAND

C A N A D A

Quebec
Montreal
Newfoundland
St Pierre & Miquelon
Nova Scotia
Boston
Philadelphia • New York
THIRTEEN COLONIES
LOUISIANA
Indian Reserve
GEORGIA
Charleston
Bermuda
New Orleans
FLORIDA (BR 1763–83)
Bahama Is
VICEROYALTY OF NEW SPAIN
Havana
Cuba
St Domingue
St Thomas and St Croix (Denmark)
Mexico City • Veracruz
Santiago
Santo Domingo
See inset map
Leeward Islands (Br & Dutch)
Acapulco
Belize
Jamaica
Guadeloupe (France)
Mosquito Coast
Curaçao
Lesser Antilles (Fr and Br)
Trinidad
Porto Bello
PACIFIC OCEAN
VICEROYALTY OF NEW GRANADA
ESSEQUIBO
SURINAM
Cayenne
VICEROYALTY OF BRAZIL
VICEROYALTY OF PERU

ATLANTIC OCEAN

Port-de-Paix
Cap Français
Fort-Liberté
Santiago
SAINT DOMINGUE
Hispaniola
SANTO DOMINGO
Gonâve
Jérémie
Port-au-Prince
Santo Domingo
Les Cayes

0   100 Miles
0   100 Kilometers

Caribbean Sea

GREAT BRITAIN

DENMARK

London

HOLLAND

Paris

FRANCE

AUSTRIA

Bordeaux

ITALY

PORTUGAL   SPAIN

Madrid

OTTOMAN
EMPIRE

Lisbon

Seville

Azores

Cadiz

NORTH
ATLANTIC
OCEAN

MOROCCO

Canary Is

AFRICA

Cape Verde
Islands

St Louis
Gorée
Fort James

Timbuktu

Niger R.

HAUSA

SEGU

NUBA

OYO

ASANTE   BENIN

Lagos

Elmina   Accra

Fernando Po

DUTCH
BRAZIL
(1630–54)

SOUTH
ATLANTIC
OCEAN

Congo R.

LUBA

Recife

Luanda

LUNDA

Bahia

St Helena

Rio de Janeiro

0

1200 Miles

0

1200 Kilometers

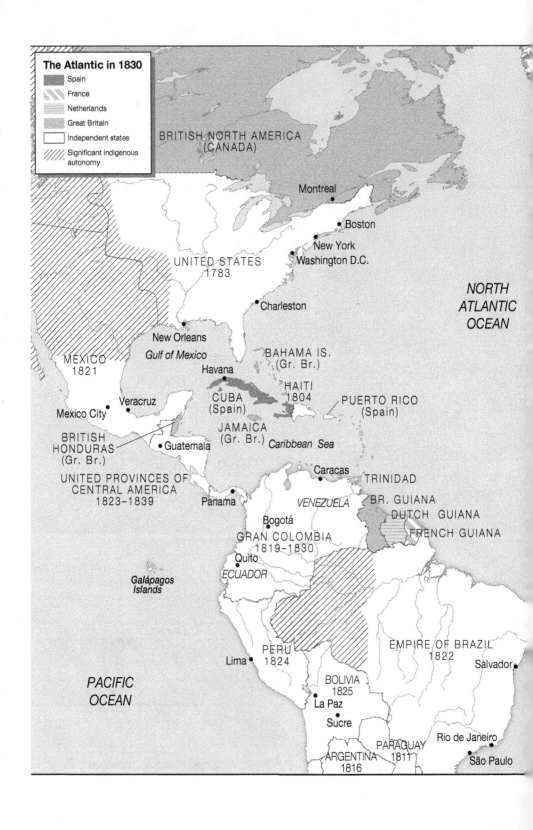

The Atlantic in 1830

- Spain
- France
- Netherlands
- Great Britain
- Independent states
- Significant indigenous autonomy

BRITISH NORTH AMERICA
(CANADA)

Montreal

Boston

New York
Washington D.C.

UNITED STATES
1783

Charleston

NORTH
ATLANTIC
OCEAN

New Orleans
Gulf of Mexico

MÉXICO
1821

Havana

BAHAMA IS.
(Gr. Br.)

HAITI
1804

Veracruz

CUBA
(Spain)

PUERTO RICO
(Spain)

Mexico City

JAMAICA
(Gr. Br.) *Caribbean Sea*

BRITISH
HONDURAS
(Gr. Br.)

Guatemala

UNITED PROVINCES OF
CENTRAL AMERICA
1823–1839

Panama

Caracas

TRINIDAD

BR. GUIANA

DUTCH GUIANA

VENEZUELA

FRENCH GUIANA

Bogotá

GRAN COLOMBIA
1819–1830

Quito

ECUADOR

*Galápagos
Islands*

PACIFIC
OCEAN

PERU
1824

Lima

EMPIRE OF BRAZIL
1822

Salvador

BOLIVIA
1825

La Paz

Sucre

Rio de Janeiro

PARAGUAY

ARGENTINA 1811
1816

São Paulo

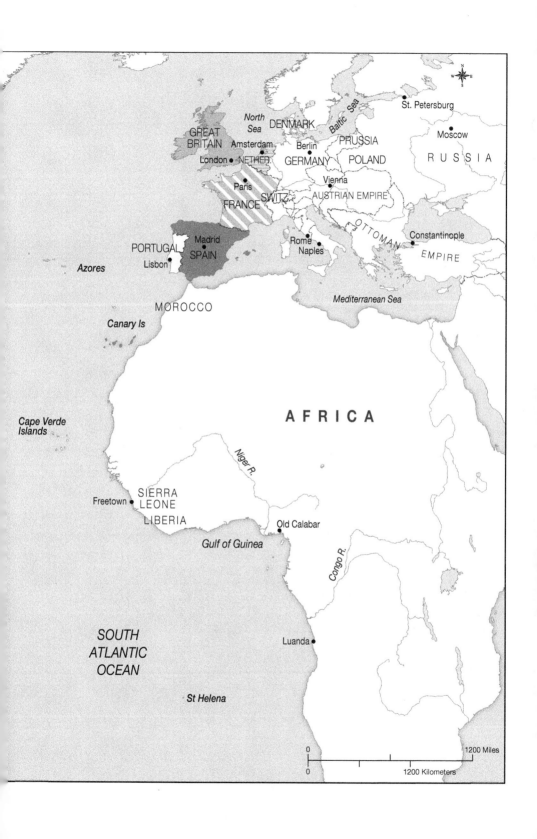

Introduction

The premise of this book—that a republican revolutionary movement transformed the political culture of the Atlantic world during the period 1760s–1830s—owes a debt to R. R. Palmer's notion of an "Age of Democratic Revolution." In 1959, Palmer introduced this idea in the first volume of a two-volume book on *The Age of Democratic Revolution*. In its first pages, Palmer defined what he meant by "democratic revolution." He cautioned that he did not mean his (and still less our) contemporary sense of political democracy, for it was "not primarily the sense of a latter day in which universality of suffrage became a chief criterion of democracy." Nor did it refer to the egalitarianism of social democracy or communism. Instead, Palmer defined the social content of democratic revolution as "a new feeling for a kind of equality, or at least a discomfort with older forms of social stratification and formal rank." Politically, it was a "movement against the *possession*[1] of government, or any public power, by any established, closed, or self-recruiting groups of men."[2] Those who pursued these aims were the democratic revolutionaries. They called their opponents aristocrats. Edmund Burke captured their understanding of political power in 1790 when he asserted that "we hold, we transmit our government and our privileges, in the same manner in which we enjoy and transmit our property. . . . In this choice of inheritance, we have given to our frame of polity the image of a relation in blood." In response, the globetrotting republican Thomas Paine dismissed "the idea of hereditary legislators" as an absurdity no less ridiculous than "hereditary judges," "hereditary juries," "hereditary

---

[1]My emphasis. The word *possession*, I think, is the critical term that exposes what was at issue in the age of revolutions. Before those revolutions, public power was considered a legitimate form of private property. The fundamental transformation the revolution operated was to exclude public power from the category of property. I develop this argument in *The Great Demarcation: The French Revolution and the Invention of Modern Property* (New York: Oxford University Press, 2016).

[2]R. R. Palmer, *The Age of the Democratic Revolution: A Political History of Europe and America, 1760–1800* (Princeton, NJ: Princeton University Press, 1959), vol. 1, 4–5.

1

mathematicians," "an hereditary wise man," or "an hereditary poet."[3] Their famous exchange encapsulates what was at stake in the revolutionary age.

Although he was clear that the Democratic Revolutions did not involve twentieth-century notions of political and social democracy, Palmer emphatically believed that, in their own historical context, they were radical, transformational, and foundational. He also insisted on their fundamental unity. Although he understood that the various revolutions of Europe and the Americas "arose everywhere out of local, genuine, and specific causes," he nevertheless saw them as "part of one great movement." In insisting on their essential unity, Palmer was neither ignoring nor minimizing their differences. Instead, his concept of a unified "Age of Democratic Revolution" was intended "to set up a larger framework, or conceptual structure, in which phenomena that are admittedly different, and even different in very significant ways, may yet be seen as related products of a common impulse."[4]

With some important changes, in this volume, I borrow Palmer's understanding of democratic revolution. It is based on the notion that the last decades of the eighteenth century saw a relatively coherent revolutionary movement begin to sweep through large, European-held or influenced parts of the globe. I agree with Palmer that the essence of this movement was a "new feeling for a certain kind of equality" and the rejection of formal political privilege and hereditary public power. I do not, however, accept Palmer's ideas uncritically. Since the publication of *The Age of Democratic Revolution*, a persuasive body of scholarship on the "Atlantic Revolutions" has exposed its exclusions and suggested ways in which its approach to the revolutionary age might be broadened.[5] These criticisms inform this book.

The critics' main objection is that Palmer's conception of the Age of Democratic Revolution leaves out the revolutions of the Global South, notably those of Haiti and Latin America, and also excludes subaltern groups within the North American and European revolutions. These "silences and omissions," the "absence of indigenous peoples," and the "neglect of subaltern subjects" are the main weakness of Palmer's portrait of the revolutionary movements.[6] I agree with these criticisms, and they determined the scope of this book. Half of its main (i.e., nonintroductory) chapters are dedicated to the Haitian and Latin American

---

[3] Edmund Burke, *Reflections on the Revolution in France* (Garden City: Anchor Books, 1973), 45; and Thomas Paine, *The Rights of Man* (Garden City, Anchor Books, 1973), 321.

[4] Palmer, *Age of the Democratic Revolution*, vol. 1, 9.

[5] Critics have paid less attention, however, to how Palmer's vague definition of the movement's ideological content might be sharpened. To describe it merely as a "new feeling for a certain kind of equality" and a rejection of "the possession of government, or any public power, by any established, closed, or self-recruiting groups of men" does not do justice either to its originality or profound ramifications. Moreover, much more could be said about the intellectual roots of this novel ideology, a question Palmer barely raises.

[6] Michael A. McDonnell, "Rethinking the Age of Revolution," *Atlantic Studies* 13, no. 3 (2016): 303, 305, and 308.

revolutions, and the themes of gender equality, racial equality, and anti-slavery run through its pages.

At the same time, however, the book retains Palmer's fundamental argument that a coherent revolutionary movement swept through much of the Atlantic world during the latter part of the eighteenth century. By emphasizing the movement's coherence, I am not suggesting that it diffused outward from center to periphery. Nor am I downplaying the fact that people in different localities launched revolutionary movements on their own initiative, for their own reasons, and for their own ends. Rather, I share Palmer's view that "revolutionary aims and sympathies existed throughout Europe and America. They arose everywhere out of local, genuine, and specific causes. . . . They were not imported from one country to another."[7] Recognizing the unity of the revolutionary movement does not have to translate into Eurocentrism or a diffusionist model.

While redressing exclusions and silences and while acknowledging local contexts and initiatives, we must be careful not to lose sight of the big picture: that in the latter decades of the eighteenth century, a "framework, or conceptual structure" coalesced in the Atlantic world within which "equality [became] a prime social desideratum."[8] During the revolutionary period, the concept of equality itself expanded and acquired new meanings: equality between colonials and metropolitans, between nobles and commoners, between different religions, between members of the same trade. For some it came to mean equality between men and women, between different races, and even equality of wealth. These more capacious meanings of equality were strongly resisted and often repressed. Because of this, it is somewhat misleading to describe the Atlantic revolutions as "democratic." Palmer, of course, was fully aware that they were not democratic in the modern sense and warned readers not to take it in that way.[9] Yet the meaning of the term has now expanded so far beyond its late eighteenth-century sense that it is probably advisable to avoid confusion by replacing it. Another reason for doing so is that most revolutionaries would not have described themselves as democratic, an epithet that evoked demagoguery and mob rule. For these reasons, I have chosen to describe the revolutionary movements as republican, a term that emphasizes the publicness of political power toward which they all strove.

The most remarkable—and, in the long term, most consequential—characteristic of the republican revolutionary movement was the elasticity of its other, complementary aim: equality. Here is where the subaltern actors absent from Palmer's account—indigenous peoples, women, slaves, serfs, and the urban

---

[7]Palmer, *Age of the Democratic Revolution*, vol. 1, 7. David Armitage and Sanjay Subrahmanyam, however, characterize Palmer's viewpoint as "strikingly Eurotropic, if not quite Eurocentric" and his conception of revolutionary change as "diffusionist." "Introduction: The Age of Revolutions, c.1760–1840 – Global Causation, Connection, and Comparison," in *The Age of Revolutions in Global Context, c.1760-1840*, eds. David Armitage and Sanjay Subrahmanyam (Basingstoke, UK: Palgrave Macmillan, 2010), xvii–xviii, xxix.

[8]Palmer, *Age of the Democratic Revolution*, vol. 2, 573.

[9]Ibid. 4.

poor—come to the fore. By probing, pushing, and challenging the limits of equality, their revolutionary action activated the expansive potential of the concept. That was their fundamental contribution. To be sure, few pursued truly universal equality. Whereas some elite American women denounced the tyranny of men and asked their legislators to give them legal equality, they said nothing about the inequalities generated by private property. The small group of French revolutionaries who wanted to abolish private property recoiled at the idea of female citizenship. Virtually all Haitians wanted an end to slavery, but none is known to have advocated female political participation. Few of the Spanish Americans who fought for independence felt comfortable with religious toleration. It is true that there were a handful of figures, such as Jacques-Pierre Brissot, Olympe de Gouges, and the Abbé Grégoire, who saw these different inequalities and exclusions as symptoms of the same underlying evil and fought them all with equal passion. But they were the exceptions. Nonetheless, in the long term, the aggregate effect of distinct groups of subaltern actors struggling to achieve equality for themselves transformed the idea of equality itself. Through their actions, republican revolution ultimately became democratic revolution.

The marginalized, excluded, oppressed, and enslaved produced almost no tracts or theoretically developed explanations of their aims and aspirations.[10] Writing works of political theory was the monopoly of the men of European descent who dominate Palmer's account. But the subaltern revolutionaries gave concepts that—in the books of the Lockes, Montesquieus, and Rousseaus—had relatively limited scope, a good, hard stretching. They did not accomplish this through the written word. This is what gave the concept of equality its expansive dynamic. It is this dynamic that leads Palmer's critics to demand the inclusion of the silenced, excluded, and erased actors of history and thus redress "the many lived inequalities of the past and present."[11] In carrying out this agenda, however, we must not lose sight of the elite-derived, republican ideal of equality that subalterns appropriated and transformed through their actions. It was precisely the conjunction of elite theory and subaltern action that unleashed its viral potential.

Because our political culture continues to resonate to the expansive egalitarian dynamic unlocked in the late eighteenth century, it is difficult to set an end point to the Age of Revolutions. In contrast, it is relatively easy to identify its beginning. In the last ten years, a scholarly consensus on this has emerged: an imperial crisis that peaked during the Seven Years' War set in motion the train of events that would spark the American, French, Haitian, and Latin American revolutions.[12] But there is no agreement on when the revolutionary age ended.

---

[10]Michel-Rolph Trouillot has addressed the problem of archival power and the silences it creates in his *Silencing the Past: Power and the Production of History* (Boston: Beacon Press, 1995).

[11]McDonnell, "Rethinking the Age of Revolution," 308.

[12]Jeremy Adelman, "An Age of Imperial Revolutions," *American Historical Review* 113, no. 2 (April 2008), 319–340; Armitage and Subrahmanyam, "Introduction," xii–xxxii; and Sarah Knott, "Narrating the Age of Revolution," *William and Mary Quarterly* 73, no. 1 (January 2016), 29–30.

Palmer's "Age of Democratic Revolution" was over by 1800. In contrast, David Armitage and Sanjay Subrahmanyam's "Age of Revolutions" extends to 1840. And for François Furet, who was admittedly only concerned with the French Revolution, it continued until the 1880s.[13] Early iterations of this book ventured far into the nineteenth century, with chapters on the movement to abolish the slave trade and then slavery itself, on socialism, on the rise of universal manhood suffrage, and finally on the campaign for women's suffrage. All of these causes first appeared during the revolutionary movements of the late eighteenth century; and although they only bore fruit a century or more later, they can reasonably be considered part of the revolutionary age. However, they had to be cut from this book because it was already too long. Perhaps someone will write a sequel to it dedicated to those, and still other, issues.

I begin this volume with two short introductory chapters. In chapter 1, I offer selections from some of the most influential political writings of the eighteenth-century Enlightenment. These include classic passages from Locke, Montesquieu, and Rousseau as well as less-familiar (and never-before translated) writings by Mably, Moreau, and Saige. Ranging from justifications of monarchy and aristocracy to republican manifestos, this sample of famous and obscure political pieces offers a wide survey of eighteenth-century political thought. In chapter 2, I feature documents illuminating the forces that strained the great empires of the Atlantic world. I show the efforts of these imperial states to extract more and more resources from the people they ruled and the resistance they provoked. This second introductory chapter illustrates how the political concepts introduced in the first chapter were used to articulate this resistance and traces the evolution of these conflicts from simple struggles over taxes into constitutional crises.

The main part of the book, consisting of eight chapters, examines the American, French, Haitian, and Latin American revolutions in detail. Two chapters are devoted to each of these four major revolutions, the first on its origins and the second on its unfolding and aftermath. Because of constraints on length, I do not treat the smaller revolutions of the time in this volume. Some, however, such as the Spanish liberal triennium of 1820–1823, appear when they intersect significantly with one of the four major revolutions.

In selecting primary documents to include, I deliberately chose to emphasize those containing explicit political ideas. I made this decision for two reasons: one intellectual, the other pedagogical. Pedagogically, I believe that the role of a primary source reader is to support the course narrative. It can do this by providing documents illustrative of events such as eyewitness accounts of the Battle of Yorktown, the taking of the Bastille, or San Martín's crossing of the Andes. But textbooks, films, paintings, songs—and the instructor's own narration—can often describe events more effectively than the printed word. A more distinctive contribution primary sources can make

[13]Palmer, *Age of Democratic Revolution*; Armitage and Subrahmanyam, *Age of Revolutions*; and François Furet, *Revolutionary France, 1770–1880*, trans. Antonia Neville (Oxford, England: Blackwell, 1995).

is to open a window on the aspirations, motivations, concepts, assumptions, and feelings—in a word, the mental universe—of historical actors. That is the most effective way primary sources can be used to complement the course narrative and stimulate discussion. Given that the subject of this book is republican revolution, a primarily political phenomenon (albeit with cultural, social, and other sweeping consequences), it is only natural that the documents focus on political ideas.

Intellectually, my decision to emphasize political documents reflects my belief in the unique—and uniquely significant—ideological content of the revolutionary republican project.[14] It is not at all clear that the late eighteenth century was an unprecedentedly revolutionary age. Human history is full of revolution—not to mention war, urban riot, rural jacquerie, and all other kinds of upheaval. These were all part of the American, French, Haitian, and Latin American revolutions, but they are not what make those revolutions distinctive or historically significant. Kings had been overthrown before, aristocracies had been toppled, the poor and oppressed had risen in violent revolt, empires had crumbled, and new polities had arisen upon their ruins. None of this is what makes the four great revolutions truly great. What sets them apart from all of the other revolutions in world history and makes them especially significant is their ideological content. There is no doubt that these revolutions were full of violence and trauma. There is no doubt that they wrought enormous social change, much of it unforeseen by the revolutionaries themselves. But beneath the Sturm und Drang of revolutionary events was a common ambition to create a new kind of polity, never before seen in world history, based on equal citizenship, uniform law, the "privateness" of property, and the "publicness" of political power. This republican vision was the great, lasting legacy of the Age of Revolution.

---

[14]Palmer, *Age of Democratic Revolution*, vol. 2, 573.

CHAPTER 1

The Enlightenment

The Enlightenment was an intellectual and cultural movement within Europe and the Atlantic world during the eighteenth century. Because that century culminated in a series of major revolutions, contemporary observers and scholars in the following centuries believed that there was a causal connection between the Enlightenment and the Age of Revolution. Hostile eyewitnesses to the French Revolution regarded the Enlightenment as a deliberate plot to overthrow monarchy, aristocracy, and, above all, religion. Subsequent scholars rejected the idea of a conspiracy but continued to see the Enlightenment as a cause of the revolutions. For some, it was an ideological program against tradition; for others it was a class ideology directed against the feudal aristocracy by the bourgeoisie; and for still others it represented the triumph of modern individualism. What all these interpretations had in common was the assumption that the Enlightenment was a revolutionary program.

Scholars began to challenge this assumption in the mid-twentieth century, and it has now been abandoned. Although most Enlightenment thinkers shared an emphasis on the power of rational thought to perfect man and society, they agreed on little else. When it came to politics, the diversity of their opinions was pronounced. Some advocated a rationalized bureaucratic absolutism, others constitutional monarchy, others aristocratic monarchy, and still others republicanism. Moreover, scholars now believe that there was no unitary Enlightenment movement but rather a variety of national or regional Enlightenments, each drawing on and responding to local contexts. The new picture of the Enlightenment that has emerged is that of a changing climate of culture and opinion that took different forms at different times and places. As this new image has evolved, the old notion of the Enlightenment as "blueprint of revolution" has been rejected.

The question of the relationship between Enlightenment and Revolution is today an open one. The notion of a direct causal link is no longer tenable, but that does not mean that Enlightenment political thought had no impact on revolutionary aspirations and actions. You will find that many of the concepts featured in this section's documents recur again and again in the following chapters. Was the Enlightenment no more than a general faith in humanity and confidence that the world could be made better? Was it a discourse—an underlying verbal structure unconsciously driving revolutionary thought, expression, and action? Was it a toolbox of concepts that revolutionary actors could dip into as they needed? Scholars do not agree on the answer to these questions. It is for you to make up your own mind.

I. The Giants

In this section, I offer a selection of excerpts from the greatest political writings of the Enlightenment period. Their authors were leading figures of the movement and through their persons and actions, defined what it meant to be an Enlightenment philosopher. Their political thinking shared some common characteristics but hardly constituted a coherent political program. Indeed, in some important ways, the political theories of these men—Locke, Montesquieu, Rousseau, and others—were incompatible with one another. Nonetheless, these writings collectively inspired the revolutionary generation without, however, providing it with a formal program for revolutionary action.

1. JOHN LOCKE, *TWO TREATISES OF GOVERNMENT*[1]

Although he predated the eighteenth-century Enlightenment by several generations, John Locke (1632–1704) had an important influence on its political thinking. An English physician and philosopher who wrote on a broad range of subjects, Locke is best-remembered for his Two Treatises of Government, *a work that established the modern theory of representative government. It was once thought that Locke wrote this work as a defense of the Glorious Revolution of 1688, the English political revolution that confirmed the supremacy of Parliament over the Crown. But it is now known that Locke wrote it earlier as a general critique of and remedy for absolutist government. Starting from the premise that the purpose of government was to protect the individual's "natural rights" of life, health, liberty, and possessions, Locke re-envisioned the state as a contract between the governed and the government in which the former essentially ruled themselves through representatives.*

The natural liberty of man is to be free from any superior power on earth, and not to be under the will or legislative authority of man, but to have only the law of nature for his rule. The liberty of man in society, is to be under no other legislative power, but that established, by consent, in the commonwealth; nor under the

[1]John Locke, *Two Treatises of Government* (London: Whitmore and Fenn, 1821), 205–206, 209–213, 259–264, 269–272, 294–295, 300–311, 316–322, 370–378.

dominion of any will, or restraint of any law, but what that legislative shall enact, according to the trust put in it. . . .

Freedom of men under government is, to have a standing rule to live by, common to every one of that society, and made by the legislative power erected in it; a liberty to follow my own will in all things, where the rule prescribes not; and not to be subject to the inconstant, uncertain, unknown, arbitrary will of another man: as freedom of nature is, to be under no other restraint but the law of nature.

This freedom from absolute, arbitrary power, is so necessary to, and closely joined with a man's preservation, that he cannot part with it, but by what forfeits his preservation and life together: for a man, not having the power of his own life, cannot, by compact, or his own consent, enslave himself to any one, nor put himself under the absolute, arbitrary power of another. . . .

Chapter V. Of Property

Though the earth, and all inferior creatures, be common to all men, yet every man has a property in his own person: this no body has any right to but himself. The labour of his body, and the work of his hands, we may say, are properly his. Whatsoever then he removes out of the state that nature hath provided, and left it in, he hath mixed his labour with, and joined to it something that is his own, and thereby makes it his property. It being by him removed from the common state nature hath placed it in, it hath by this labour something annexed to it, that excludes the common right of other men: for this labour being the unquestionable property of the labourer, no man but he can have a right to what that is once joined to it. . . .

The chief matter of property being now not the fruits of the earth, and the beasts that subsist on it, but the earth itself; as that which takes in and carries with it all the rest; I think it is plain, that property in that too is acquired as the former. As much land as a man tills, plants, improves, cultivates, and can use the product of, so much is his property. He by his labour does, as it were, inclose it from the common.

Chapter VII. Of Political or Civil Society

Man being born, as has been proved, with a title to perfect freedom, and an uncontrouled enjoyment of all the rights and privileges of the law of nature, equally with any other man, or number of men in the world, hath by nature a power, not only to preserve his property, that is, his life, liberty and estate, against the injuries and attempts of other men: but to judge of, and punish the breaches of that law in others. . . . But because no political society can be, nor subsist, without having in itself the power to preserve the property, and in order therunto, punish the offences of all those of that society: there, and there only is political society, where every one of the members hath quitted this natural power, resigned it up into the hands of the community in all cases that exclude him not from appealing for protection to the law established by it. And thus all private judgment of every particular member being excluded, the community comes to be umpire, by settled standing rules, indifferent, and the same to all parties. . . . Those who are united into one body, and have a common established law and judicature to appeal to, with authority to decide controversies between them, and punish offenders, are in civil society one with another: but those who have no such . . . are still in the state of nature.

And thus the commonwealth comes by a power to set down what punishment shall belong to the several transgressions which they think worthy of it, committed amongst the members of that society, (which is the power of making laws) as well as it has the power to punish any injury done unto any of its members, by any one that is not of it, (which is the power of war and peace); and all this for the preservation of the property of all the members of that society, as far as is possible. . . . Wherever therefore any number of men are so united into one society, as to quit every one his executive power of the law of nature, and to resign it to the public, there and there only is a political or civil society. . . .

Hence it is evident that absolute monarchy, which by some men is counted the only government in the world, is indeed inconsistent with civil society, and so can be no form of civil government at all: for the end of civil society, being to avoid, and remedy those inconveniencies of the state of nature, which necessarily follow from every man's being judge in his own case, by setting up a known authority, to which every one of that society may appeal . . . and which every one of the society ought to obey; wherever any persons are, who have not such an authority to appeal to, . . . those persons are still in the state of nature; and so is every absolute prince, in respect of those who are under his dominion.

For he being supposed to have all, both legislative and executive power in himself alone, there is no judge to be found, no appeal lies open to any one, who may fairly, and indifferently, and with authority decide, and from whose decision relief and redress may be expected of any injury or inconveniency, that may be suffered from the prince, or by his order: so that such a man, however intitled, Czar, Grand Seignor, or how you please, is as much in the state of nature, with all under his dominion, as he is with the rest of mankind: for wherever any two men are, who have no standing rule, and common judge to appeal to on earth, for the determination of controversies of right betwixt them, there they are still in the state of nature. . . .

Chapter VIII. Of Beginning of Political Societies

Men being, as has been said, by nature, all free, equal, and independent, no one can be put out of this estate, and subjected to the political power of another, without his own consent. The only way whereby any one divests himself of his natural liberty, and puts on the bonds of civil society, is by agreeing with other men to join and unite into a community, for their comfortable, safe, and peaceable living one amongst another, in a secure enjoyment of their properties, and a greater security against any, that are not of it. This any number of men may do, because it injures not the freedom of the rest; they are left as they were in the liberty of the state of nature. When any number of men have so consented to make one community or government, they are thereby presently incorporated, and make one body politic, wherein the majority have a right to act and conclude the rest. . . .

And thus every man, by consenting with others to make one body politic under one government, puts himself under an obligation to every one of that society, to submit to the determination of the majority, and to be concluded by it; or else this original compact, whereby he with others incorporates into one society, would signify nothing. . . .

For if the consent of the majority shall not, in reason, be received as the act of the whole, and conclude every individual; nothing but the consent of every individual can make any thing to be the act of the whole: but such a consent is next to impossible ever to be had. . . .

Whosoever therefore out of a state of nature unite into a community, must be understood to give up all power, necessary to the ends for which they unite into society, to the majority of the community, unless they expressly agreed in any number greater than the majority. And this is done by barely agreeing to unite into one political society, which is all the compact that is, or needs be, between the individuals, that enter into, or make up a commonwealth. And thus that, which begins and actually constitutes any political society, is nothing but the consent of any number of freemen capable of a majority to unite and incorporate into such a society. And this is that, and that only, which did, or could give beginning to any lawful government in the world.

Chapter IX. Of the Ends of Political Society and Government

If man in the state of nature be so free, as has been said; if he be absolute lord of his own person and possessions, equal to the greatest, and subject to no body, why will he part with his freedom? . . . To which it is obvious to answer, that though in the state of nature he hath such a right, yet the enjoyment of it is very uncertain, and constantly exposed to the invasion of others: for all being kings as much as he, every man his equal, and the greater part no strict observers of equity and justice, the enjoyment of the property he has in this state is very unsafe, very unsecure. This makes him willing to quit a condition, which however free, is full of fears and continual dangers: and it is not without reason, that he seeks out, and is willing to join in society with others . . . for the mutual preservation of their lives, liberties, and estates, which I call by the general name, property. . . .

Chapter X. Of the Forms of a Commonwealth

The majority having, as has been shewed, upon men's first uniting into society, the whole power of the community naturally in them, may employ all that power in making laws for the community from time to time, and executing those laws by officers of their own appointing: and then the form of the government is a perfect democracy: or else may put the power of making laws into the hands of a few select men, and their heirs or successors; and then it is an oligarchy: or else into the hands of one man, and then it is a monarchy: if to him and his heirs, it is an hereditary monarchy: if to him only for life, but upon his death the power only of nominating a successor to return to them an elective monarchy. And so accordingly of these the community may make compounded and mixed forms of government, as they think good. And if the legislative power be at first given by the majority to one or more persons only for their lives, or any limited time, and then the supreme power to revert to them again; when it is so reverted, the community may dispose of it again anew into what hands they please, and so constitute a new form of government: for the form of government depending upon the placing of the supreme power, which is the legislative, it being impossible to conceive that an inferior power should prescribe to a superior, or any but the supreme make laws, according as the power of making laws is placed, such is the form of the commonwealth. . . .

Chapter XI. Of the Extent of the Legislative Power

The great end of men's entering into society, being the enjoyment of their properties in peace and safety, and the great instrument and means of that being the laws established in that society; the first and fundamental positive law of all commonwealths is the establishing of the legislative power. . . . This legislative is not only the supreme power of the commonwealth, but sacred and unalterable in the hands where the community have once placed it: nor can any edict of any body else, in what form soever conceived, or by what power soever backed, have the force and obligation of a law, which has not its sanction from that legislative which the public has chosen and appointed: for without this the law could not have that, which is absolutely necessary to its being a law, the consent of the society, over whom no body can have a power to make laws, but by their own consent, and by authority received from them. . . .

Though the legislative . . . be the supreme power in every commonwealth, yet:

First, it is not nor can possibly be absolutely arbitrary over the lives and fortunes of the people: for it being but the joint power of every member of the society given up to that person or assembly, which is legislator, it can be no more than those persons had in a state of nature before they entered into society, and gave up to the community. . . . A man, as has been proved, cannot subject himself to the arbitrary power of another; and having in the state of nature no arbitrary power over the life, liberty, or possession of another, but only so much as the law of nature gave him for the preservation of himself, and the rest of mankind; this is all he doth, or can give up to the commonwealth, and by it to the legislative power, so that the legislative can have no more than this. Their power, in the utmost bounds of it, is limited to the public good of the society. It is a power that hath no other end but preservation, and therefore can never have a right to destroy, enslave, or designedly to impoverish the subjects. . . .

Secondly, the legislative, or supreme authority, cannot assume to itself a power to rule by extemporary arbitrary decrees, but is bound to dispense justice, and decide the rights of the subject by promulgated standing laws, and known authorized judges. . . .

Thirdly, the supreme power cannot take from any man any part of his property without his own consent: for the preservation of property being the end of government, and that for which men enter into society, it necessarily supposes and requires, that the people should have property, without which they must be supposed to lose that, by entering into society, which was the end for which they had entered into it. . . .

It is true, governments cannot be supported without great charges, and it is fit every one who enjoys his share of the protection should pay out of his estate his proportion for the maintenance of it. But it still must be with his own consent, i.e. the consent of the majority, giving it either by themselves, or their representatives chosen by them: for if any one shall claim a power to lay and levy taxes on the people, by his own authority, and without such consent of the people, he thereby invades the fundamental law of property, and subverts the end of government: for what property have I in that, which another may by right take, when he pleases, to himself? . . .

Chapter XIII. Of the Subordination of the Powers of the Commonwealth

Though in a constituted commonwealth . . . there can be but one supreme power, which is the legislative, to which all the rest are and must be subordinate, yet the legislative being only a fiduciary power to act for certain ends, there remains still in the people a supreme power to remove or alter the legislative, when they find the legislative act contrary to the trust reposed in them: for all power given with trust for the attaining an end, being limited by that end, whenever that end is manifestly neglected, or opposed, the trust must necessarily be forfeited, and the power devolve into the hands of those that gave it, who may place it anew where they shall think best for their safety and security. And thus the community perpetually retains a supreme power of saving themselves from the attempts and designs of any body, even of their legislators, whenever they shall be so foolish, or so wicked, as to lay and carry on designs against the liberties and properties of the subject. . . .

It may be demanded here, what if the executive power, being possessed of the force of the commonwealth, shall make use of that force to hinder the meeting and acting of the legislative, when the original constitution, or the public exigencies require it? I say, using force upon the people without authority . . . is a state of war with the people, who have a right to reinstate their legislative in the exercise of their power. . . . In all state and conditions, the true remedy of force without authority, is to oppose force to it. The use of force without authority always puts him that uses it into a state of war, as the aggressor, and renders him liable to be treated accordingly. . . .

Chapter XIX. Of the Dissolution of Government

The usual, and almost only way whereby this union is dissolved, is the inroad of foreign force. . . .

Besides this overturning from without, governments are dissolved from within.

First, when the legislative is altered. Civil society, being a state of peace, amongst those who are of it, from whom the state of war is excluded by the umpirage which they have provided in their legislative . . . it is in the legislative, that the members of a commonwealth are united, and combined together into one coherent living body. . . . Therefore, when the legislative is broken, or dissolved, dissolution and death follows: for the essence and unity of the society consisting in having one will, the legislative, when once established by the majority, has the declaring, and as it were keeping of that will. The constitution of the legislative is the first and fundamental act of society, whereby provision is made for the continuation of their union, under the direction of persons, and bonds of laws, made by persons authorized thereunto, by the consent and appointment of the people, without which no one man, or number of men, amongst them, can have authority of making laws that shall be binding to the rest. When any one or more, shall take upon them to make laws, whom the people have not appointed so to do, they make laws without authority, which the people are not therefore bound to obey; by which means they come again to be out of subjection, and may constitute themselves a new legislative, as they think best, being in full liberty to resist the force of those, who without authority would impose any thing upon them. . . .

When the government is dissolved, the people are at liberty to provide for themselves, by erecting a new legislative, differing from the other, by the change of persons, or form, or both, as they shall find it most for their safety and good: for the society can never, by the fault of another, lose the native and original right it has to preserve itself.

2. MONTESQUIEU, *THE SPIRIT OF LAWS*[2]

Charles-Louis de Secondat, Baron de Brède et de Montesquieu (1689–1755) was a French nobleman, feudal lord, magistrate, and philosopher. His most influential work of political theory was the massive The Spirit of Laws. *Although Montesquieu addressed the same fundamental problem as Locke—how to moderate the power of government—his approach was historical and comparative. Montesquieu was keenly aware of the differences between countries and cultures and never claimed that there was a single model of limited government applicable to all. But several general elements of good government emerge from his analysis. One was the notion that the most effective way of limiting the power of government was to separate executive, legislative, and judicial authority. When combined with Locke's insistence on representative government, Montesquieu's separation of powers constituted a formidable check (too formidable for some) on the unbridled growth of government power.*

Of the Relations of Laws to the Nature of Monarchical Government
The intermediate, subordinate, and dependent powers constitute the nature of monarchical government; I mean of that in which a single person governs by fundamental laws. . . . These fundamental laws necessarily suppose the intermediate

---

[2] *The Spirit of Laws*, Baron De Montesquieu. *The Spirit of Laws* was first published in 1748. This excerpt is from the 1890 translation (New York: The Colonial Press), vol. 1, Book II, 15–18, 25, 53–57, 113–116.

channels through which the power flows: for if there be on the momentary and capricious will of a single person to govern the state, nothing can be fixed, and, of course, there is no fundamental law.

The most natural, intermediate and subordinate power is that of the nobility. This in some measure seems to be essential to a monarchy, whose fundamental maxim is, no monarch no nobility; no nobility, no monarch. . . .

There are men who have endeavored in some countries in Europe to suppress the jurisdiction of the nobility, not perceiving that they were driving at the very thing that was done by the Parliament of England. Abolish the privileges of the lords, the clergy and cities in a monarchy, and you will soon have a popular state, or else a despotic government.

The courts of a considerable kingdom in Europe have, for many ages, been striking at the patrimonial jurisdiction of the lords and clergy. We do not pretend to censure these sage magistrates; but we leave it to the public to judge how far this may alter the constitution. . . .

It is not enough to have intermediate powers in a monarchy: there must also be a depositary of the laws. This depositary can only be the judges of the supreme courts of justice, who promulgate the new laws, and revive the obsolete. The natural ignorance of the nobility, their indolence and contempt of civil government, require that there should be a body invested with the power of reviving and executing the laws, which would be otherwise buried in oblivion. The prince's council are not a proper depositary. They are naturally the depositary of the momentary will of the prince, and not of the fundamental laws. Besides, the prince's council is continually changing; it is neither permanent nor numerous; neither has it a sufficient share of the confidence of the people. . . .

Despotic governments, where there are no fundamental laws, have no such kind of depositary. . . .

Of the Principle of Monarchy

A monarchical government supposes, as we have already observed, pre-eminences and ranks, as likewise a noble descent. Now, since it is the nature of honor[3] to aspire to preferments and titles, it is properly placed in this government.

Ambition is pernicious in a republic. But in a monarchy it has some good effects; it gives life to the government, and is attended with this advantage, that it is in no way dangerous, because it may be continually checked.

It is with this kind of government as with the system of the universe, in which there is a power that constantly repels all bodies from the centre, and a power of gravitation that attracts them to it. Honor sets all the parts of the body politic in motion, and by its very action connects them; thus each individual advances the public good, while he only thinks of promoting his own interest.

---

[3]In a previous section, Montesquieu defined honor as "the prejudice of every person and rank."

True it is, that philosophically speaking it is a false honor which moves all the parts of the government; but even this false honor is as useful to the public as true honor could possibly be to private persons. . . .

In what Manner the Laws are in relation to their Principle in Monarchies

As honor is the principle of a monarchical government, the laws ought to be in relation to this principle.

They should endeavor to support the nobility, in respect to whom honor may be, in some measure, deemed both child and parent.

They should render the nobility hereditary, not as a boundary between the power of the prince and the weakness of the people, but as the link which connects them both. . . .

The land of the nobility ought to have privileges as well as their persons. The monarch's dignity is inseparable from that of his kingdom; and the dignity of the nobleman from that of his fief.

All these privileges must be peculiar to the nobility, and incommunicable to the people, unless we intend to act contrary to the principle of government, and to diminish the power of the nobles together with that of the people. . . .

Of the Excellence of a Monarchical Government

Monarchy has a great advantage over a despotic government. As it naturally requires there should be several orders or ranks of subjects, the state is more permanent, the constitution more steady, and the person of him who governs more secure. . . .

In the commotions of a despotic government, the people, hurried away by their passions, are apt to push things as far as they can go. The disorders they commit are all extreme; whereas in monarchies matters are seldom carried to excess. The chiefs are apprehensive on their own account; they are afraid of being abandoned, and the intermediate dependent powers do not choose that the populace should have too much the upper hand. It rarely happens that the estates of the kingdom are entirely corrupted: the prince adheres to these; and the seditious, who have neither will nor hopes to subvert the government, have neither power nor will to dethrone the prince. . . .

As people who live under a good government are happier than those who without rule or leaders wander about the forests, so monarchs who live under the fundamental laws of their country are far happier than despotic princes who have nothing to regulate, neither their own passions nor those of their subjects. . . .

It is in monarchies that we behold the subjects encircling the throne, and cheered by the irradiancy of the sovereign; there it is that each person filling, as it were, a larger space, is capable of exercising those virtues which adorn the soul, not with independence, but with true dignity and greatness.

Of the Corruption of the Principle of Monarchy

As democracies are subverted when the people despoil the senate, the magistrates, the judges of their functions, so monarchies are corrupted when the prince insensibly deprives societies or cities of their privileges. In the former case the multitude usurp the power, in the latter it is usurped by a single person. . . .

Monarchy is destroyed when a prince thinks he shows a greater exertion of power in changing than in conforming to the order of things; when he deprives some of his subjects of their hereditary employments to bestow them arbitrarily upon others; and when he is fonder of being guided by fancy than judgment.

Again, it is destroyed when the prince, directing everything entirely to himself, calls to the state his capital, the capital to his court, and the court to his own person.

Finally, it is destroyed when the prince mistakes his authority, his situation and the love of his people, and when he is not fully persuaded that a monarch ought to think himself secure, as a despotic prince ought to think himself in danger.

The principle of monarchy is corrupted when the first dignities are marks of the first servitude, when the great men are deprived of public respect, and rendered the low tools of arbitrary power.

It is still more corrupted when honor is set up in contradiction to honors, and when men are capable of being loaded at the very same time with infamy and with dignities.

It is corrupted when the prince changes his justice into severity. . . .

Again, it is corrupted when mean and abject souls grow vain of the pomp attending their servitude, and imagine that the motive which induces them to be entirely devoted to their prince exempts them from all duty to their country.

3. VOLTAIRE, *HANDY PHILOSOPHIC DICTIONARY*[4]

Voltaire, whose real name was François-Marie Arouet (1694–1778), set the model of the Enlightenment philosopher. If we can speak of an Enlightened style, it was Voltaire who defined it. Although he was a prolific author in many genres, he never wrote a work of political theory. He did, however, contribute significantly to eighteenth-century thinking about liberty. Of course liberty had been a central concept for both Locke and Montesquieu. They, however, tended to define it rather narrowly as the right of property. Voltaire broadened the notion of individual liberty to encompass what might be called liberty of the mind. He was passionately committed to freedom of thought (in both religious and political matters) and to the right of individuals to express those thoughts. Voltaire thus placed the issue of individual

---

[4]First published in 1764. This translated excerpt is from J. H. Robinson, *Readings in European History* (Boston: Ginn, 1906), vol. 2, 380–382.

rights squarely on the agenda of the eighteenth century. The following are entries from his Handy Philosophical Dictionary, *illustrating Voltaire's hostility toward the control he felt the Catholic Church exercised over peoples' minds.*

Law

No law made by the Church should ever have the least force unless expressly sanctioned by the government. It was owing to this precaution that Athens and Rome escaped all religious quarrels.

Such religious quarrels are the trait of barbarous nations. . . .

The civil magistrate alone may permit or prohibit labor on religious festivals, since it is not the function of the priest to forbid men to cultivate their fields.

Everything relating to marriage should depend entirely upon the civil magistrate. . . .

Lending money at interest should be regulated entirely by the civil law, since trade is governed by civil law.

All ecclesiastics should be subject in every case to the government, since they are subjects of the state. . . .

No priest can deprive a citizen of the least of his rights on the ground that the citizen is a sinner, since the priest—himself a sinner—should pray for other sinners, not judge them.

Officials, laborers, and priests should all alike pay the taxes of the state, since they all alike belong to the state.

There should be but one standard of weights and measures and one system of law.

Let the punishment of criminals be useful. A man when hanged is good for nothing: a man condemned to hard labor continues to serve his country and furnish a living lesson.

Every law should be clear, uniform, and precise. To interpret law is almost always to corrupt it.

Nothing should be regarded as infamous except vice.

The taxes should never be otherwise than proportional to the resources of him who pays.

Grace

We have been accustomed to think—absurdly enough as it appears—that the Eternal Being never follows special laws, as we lowly human creatures must, but his own general laws, eternal like himself. It never occurred to any of us that God was like a crazy master who gave a fortune to one slave and refused another his necessary food.

Everything from God is grace; he has conferred his grace on the globe we dwell upon by forming it; upon the trees the grace to grow; upon the beasts that of finding food. But if one wolf finds a lamb in his way to make a good meal of, and another wolf is famishing, shall we say that God has shown his special grace to the first wolf? Has he by "preventing" grace been busied in causing one oak to grow preferably to another? . . .

How pitiable to suppose that God is continually making, unmaking, and re-making sentiments in us, and what presumption to think that we are different in this respect from all other beings! Moreover it is only for those who go to confession that all these changes are imagined. A Savoyard or a man from Bergamo shall on Monday have grace to have a mass said for twelve shillings; Tuesday grace will fail him and he will go to the tavern; on Wednesday he will have cooperating grace which will send him away to confession, but without the efficacious grace of perpetual contrition; Thursday it may be a "sufficient" grace which will prove insufficient. God will be continually at work in the head of this man of Bergamo, sometimes strongly, sometimes weakly, without minding any other thing upon earth and without caring what becomes of the inside of Indians or Chinese. . . .

You miserable creatures! Lift up your eyes to the heavens: see the Eternal Artificer creating millions of worlds all gravitating toward one another by general and eternal laws! Behold the same light reflected from the sun to Saturn and from Saturn to us; and amidst this harmony of so many luminous bodies in a course as amazing as swift, amidst this general obedience of all nature, I defy you to believe that God is occupied with conferring versatile grace on Sister Theresa and concomitant grace on Sister Agnes. . . .

4. DENIS DIDEROT, "POLITICAL AUTHORITY"[5]

Like his fellow philosophers, Denis Diderot (1713–1784) was a prolific author of novels and dramas as well as analytical nonfiction. He is best known for overseeing the Encylopédie, *a compendium of knowledge produced with the collaboration of the greatest philosophers, scientists, jurists, and historians of the day. Unlike the bland modern encyclopedia, Diderot's* Encylopédie *tackled controversial subjects and used its entries to offer probing analysis and trenchant critiques of social and political convention. For this reason, it was banned by the French government, although thousands of copies were imported illegally. The following is Diderot's own entry on "political authority."*

No man received from nature the right to command others. Liberty is a gift of heaven, and each individual of the same species has the right to enjoy it. . . . If nature established an authority, it is paternal power: but paternal power has its limits, and in the state of nature it ends as soon as the children are old enough to guide themselves. All other types of authority come from a source other than nature. If we investigate closely, we will recognize that it always comes from one of two sources: either force and violence . . . or the consent of those who have submitted themselves to it by a contract. . . .

[5]Denis Diderot and Jean le Rond d'Alembert, eds., *Encyclopédie*, vol. 1, 898–899. From the University of Chicago ARTFL Encylcopédie Project (Spring 2016 edition), Robert Morrissey and Glen Roe, eds. http://encyclopedie.uchicago.edu.

Power acquired through violence is but usurpation and lasts only as long as the force of he who commands is greater than those who obey; thus, if these latter become stronger and throw off the yoke, they will do it with as much right and justice as the other, who had imposed it on them. The same law that makes authority thus unmakes it; it is the law of the strongest. . . .

Power that comes from the consent of the peoples necessarily supposes conditions which make its use legitimate, useful to society, advantageous to the republic, and fix and restrain it within limits; for man must not and cannot give himself entirely and without reserve to another man because he has a superior master above everything, to whom he belongs entirely. This is God. . . . For the common good and preservation of society, he allows men to establish among themselves an order of subordination . . . but he wants it to be reasonable and measured, not blind and without reserve, so that the creature does not arrogate for himself the rights of the Creator. Any other kind of submission is the true crime of idolatry. . . .

The prince holds from his very subjects the authority he has over them; and this authority is limited by the laws of nature and the state. The laws of nature and the state are the conditions under which they have submitted themselves. . . . One of these conditions is that, having power and authority over them only by their choice and consent, he can never use that authority to annul the act or contract by which he received it; in that case, he would be acting against himself because his authority can only subsist through the title that established it. To annul one is to destroy the other. Thus, the prince cannot use his power . . . without the consent of the nation. . . . If he did otherwise, everything would be null. . . .

Even if hereditary in a family and placed in the hands of a single person, the government is not a private property, but a public one which, consequently, cannot be taken from the people, to whom it belongs essentially and in full property. [The people] thus always grant the lease of it [and] always intervene in the contract that awards its exercise. The state does not belong to the prince, the prince belongs to the state; but it is for the prince to govern in the state because the state chose him for that purpose, because he engaged himself to the peoples to administer affairs and that, for their part, they promised to obey him according to the laws. He who wears the crown can absolutely discharge himself of it if he wants; but he cannot place it on the head of another without the consent of the nation who placed it on his own. In a word, the crown, the government, and public authority are goods of which the body of the nation is the property-owner and of which princes are just usufructaries, ministers, and depositaries. . . .

This deposit is sometimes entrusted to a certain order of society, sometimes to several people chosen from among all the orders, and sometimes to a single person. The conditions of this pact are different from state to state. But everywhere the nation has the right to maintain the contract that it made; no power can change it and, when it ceases to function, [the nation] recovers the right and full liberty to agree upon a new [contract] with whomever and under whatever conditions it wants.

5. JEAN-JACQUES ROUSSEAU, *THE SOCIAL CONTRACT*[6]

Jean-Jacques Rousseau (1712–1778) was a Swiss philosopher whose Social Contract *(1762) is today the Enlightenment's best-known work of political theory. During Rousseau's lifetime, however, he was known primarily for his novels, treatises on education, and autobiographical writings. It was only when prominent French revolutionaries adopted its concepts and vocabulary that the* Social Contract *began to acquire the stature it now enjoys. Rousseau was not the first theorist to envision the formation of political society as the result of a contract between the individuals composing it. But he explored the nature and dynamics of this contract far more intensively than anyone had done before. Moreover, in contrast to Locke and others, Rousseau understood the social contract in purely republican terms. Indeed, his insistence on popular sovereignty was so uncompromising that he rejected the legitimacy of representative government itself.*

Book 1, Chapter 5, "That We Should Always Refer to the First Convention"

When uncivilized men are successively subjugated by an individual, whatever number there may be of them, they appear to me only as a master and his slaves; I cannot regard them as a people and their chief. They are, if you please, an aggregation, but they are not an association; for there is neither public property or a political body amongst them.

A man may have enslaved half the world and yet continue a private individual, if his interest is separate from the general interest and confined to himself alone. . . .

"A people (says Grotius) can give themselves to a king." According to Grotius, then, they are a people before they give themselves to the king. The donation itself is a civil act and supposes a public consultation by an assembly of the people; it will therefore be necessary, before we examine the act by which they elected a king, to enquire into that by which they became a people; for that act, being anterior to the other, is the true foundation of the society.

In fact, if there was no prior convention, where would be (unless the election of the chief was unanimous) the obligation which should bind the lesser number to submit to the choice of the greater? And from whence would a hundred men, who wished to submit to a master, derive the right of binding by their votes ten other men who were not disposed to acknowledge any chief? The law which gives a majority of suffrages the power of deciding for the whole body can only be established by a convention and proves that there must have been at some former period a unanimous will.

---

[6]Jean-Jacques Rousseau, *An Inquiry into the Nature of the Social Contract or Principles of Political Right* (Dublin, Ireland: William Jones, 1791), 22–39 (Book 1) and 49–67 (Book 2).

Book 1, Chapter 6, "Of the Social Compact"

We will suppose that men in a state of nature are arrived at that crisis, when the strength of each individual is insufficient to defend him from the attacks he is subject to. This primitive state can therefore subsist no longer; and the human race must perish unless they change their manner of life.

As men cannot create for themselves new forces, but merely unite and direct those which already exist, the only means they can employ for their preservation is to form by aggregation an assemblage of forces that may be able to resist all assaults, be put in motion as one body, and act in concert upon all occasions.

This assemblage of forces must be produced by the concurrence of many; and as the force and the liberty of a man are the chief instruments of his preservation, how can he engage them without danger and without neglecting the care which is due to himself? This doubt, which leads directly to my subject, may be expressed in these words:

"Where shall we find a form of association which will defend and protect with the whole aggregate force the person and the property of each individual; and by which every person, while united with ALL, shall obey only HIMSELF, and remain as free as before the union?" Such is the fundamental problem of which the Social Contract gives the solution.

The articles of this contract are so unalterably fixed by the nature of the act, that the least modification renders them vain and of no effect. They are the same everywhere and are, everywhere, understood and admitted even though they may never have been formally announced: so that, when once the social pact is violated in any instance, all the obligations it created ceased and each individual is restored to his original rights and resumes his native liberty, as the consequence of losing that conventional liberty for which he exchanged them.

All the articles of the social contract will, when clearly understood, be found reducible to this single point—THE TOTAL ALIENATION OF EACH ASSOCIATE AND ALL HIS RIGHTS TO THE WHOLE COMMUNITY. For every individual gives himself up entirely—the condition of every person is alike; and being so, it would not be the interest of any one to render himself offensive to others. . . .

If, therefore, we exclude from the social compact all that is not essentially necessary, we shall find it reduced to the following terms:

"We each of us place, in common, his person and all his power under the supreme direction of the general will; and we receive into the body each member as an indivisible part of the whole."

From that moment, instead of so many separate persons as there are contractors, this act of association produces a moral collective body composed of as many members as there are voices in the assembly; which from this act receives its unity, its common self, its life, and its will. This public person, which is thus formed by the union of all the private persons, took formerly the name of city, and now takes that of republic or body politic. It is called by its members state when it is passive and sovereign when in activity; and whenever it is spoken of with other bodies of a similar kind, it is denominated power. The associates take collectively the name of people, and separately that of citizens, as participating in the sovereign authority; they are also styled subjects because they are subjected to the laws. . . .

Book 1, Chapter 7, "Of the Sovereign Power"

The sovereign power being formed only of the individuals which compose it, neither has, nor can have, any interest contrary to theirs; consequently the sovereign power requires no guarantee towards its subjects because it is impossible that the body should seek to injure all its members; and we shall see presently that it can do no injury to any individual. The sovereign power, by its nature, must, while it exists, be every thing it ought to be; but it is not so with subjects towards the sovereign power; to which, notwithstanding the common interest subsisting between them, there is nothing to answer for the performance of their engagements, if some means is not found of ensuring their fidelity.

In fact, each individual may, as a man, have a private will, dissimilar or contrary to the general will which he has as a citizen. His own particular interest may dictate to him very differently from the common interest; his mind, naturally and absolutely independent, may regard what he owes to the common cause as a gratuitous contribution, the omission of which would be less injurious to others than the payment would be burthensome to himself; and considering the moral person which constitutes the state as a creature of the imagination because it is not a man, he may wish to enjoy the rights of a citizen without being disposed to fulfill the duties of a subject: an injustice which would, in its progress, cause the ruin of the body politic.

In order therefore to prevent the social compact from becoming a vain form, it tacitly comprehends this engagement, which alone can give effect to the others— That whoever refuses to obey the general will shall be compelled to it by the whole body, which is in fact only forcing him to be free; for this is the condition which guarantees his absolute personal independence to every citizen of the country; a condition which gives motion and effect to the political machine; which alone renders all civil engagements legal; and without which they would be absurd, tyrannical, and subject to the most enormous abuses.

Book 1, Chapter 8, "Of the Civil State"

The passing from a state of nature to a civil state produces in man a very remarkable change, by substituting justice for instinct and giving to his actions a moral character which they wanted before. . . .

A man loses by the social contract his natural liberty and an unlimited right to all which tempts him and which he can obtain. In return he acquires civil liberty and a just right to all he possesses.

That we may not be deceived in the value of these compensations, we must distinguish natural liberty, which knows no bounds but the power of the individual, from civil liberty, which is limited by the general will: and between that possession which is only the effect of force or of first occupancy from that property which must be founded on a positive title.

We may add to the other acquisitions of the civil state that of moral liberty, which alone renders a man master of himself; for it is slavery to be under the impulse of appetite; and freedom to obey the laws.

Book 2, Chapter 2, "That the Sovereignty Is Indivisible"

For the same reason that the sovereignty is inalienable, it is indivisible. For the will is general, or it is not; it is either the will of the whole body of the people or only of a part. In the first case, this declared will is an act of the sovereign power and becomes a law; in the second, it is but a private will or an act of the magistracy, and is at most but a decree.

Politicians not being able to divide the principle of sovereignty, they have divided its object: into force and will, legislative power and executive power; the right of levying taxes, of administering justice, and making war; the internal government of the kingdom and the power of treating with foreigners. But by sometimes confounding all these parts and sometimes separating them, they make of the sovereign power a fantastical being, formed of relative parts; just like a man, composed from many bodies; one of which should lend eyes, another arms, another legs, but nothing more. . . .

Whenever we suppose the sovereignty divided, we deceive ourselves; that the rights which we take for a part of that sovereignty are all subordinate to it, and always suppose a supreme will which is carried into execution by the exercise of those rights.

It is impossible to express how greatly this want of an exact knowledge of the sovereign power has obscured the arguments and conclusions of political writers, when they have attempted to decide on the respective rights of kings and people. . . .

Book 2, Chapter 3, "Whether the General Will Can Err"

It follows from what has been said that the general will is always right and tends always to the public advantage; but it does not follow that the resolutions of the people have always the same rectitude. Their will always seeks the public good, but it does not always perceive how it is to be attained. The people are never corrupted, but they are often deceived and under the influence of deception the public will may err.

There is frequently much difference between the will of all and the general will. The latter regards only the common interest; the former regards private interest, and is indeed but a collection of the wills of individuals; but remove from these the wills that oppose each other and the general will remains. . . .

When cabals and partial associations are formed at the expence of the public, the wills of such meetings, though general with regard to the agreement of their members, are private with regard to the state. . . .When one of these associations becomes so large that it prevails over all the rest, its will domineers; and you have no longer, as the result of your public deliberations, the sum of many opinions dissenting in a small degree from each other; but that of one great dictating dissentient. From that moment, there is no more general will, but the predominating opinion is that of an individual. It is therefore of the utmost importance for obtaining the real will of the public that no partial associations should be formed in a state; and that every citizen should speak his opinion entirely from himself.

Book 2, Chapter 4, "Of the Limits of the Sovereign Power"

If the state or city is only a moral person, the existence of which consists in the union of its members and if its most important care is that of preserving itself, there is a necessity for its possessing a universally compulsive power for moving and disposing each part in the manner most convenient to the whole.

As Nature gives to a man the absolute command of all his members, the Social Compact gives to the political body the same command over the members of which it is formed; and it is this power, when directed by the general will, that bears, as I have said before, the name of SOVEREIGNTY.

But besides the public person, we are to consider the private persons which compose it and whose lives and liberty are naturally independent of it. The point here is to distinguish properly between the respective rights of the citizens and the sovereign power and between the duties which the former have to fulfill in quality of subjects and the natural rights which they ought to enjoy in quality of men.

It is granted that all which an individual alienates by the social compact, of his power, his property, and his liberty, is only a part of that in the use of which the community is concerned; but we must also grant that the sovereign power is the only judge of that which the community may have occasion for.

All the services which a citizen can render to the state must be rendered as soon as the sovereign power demands them; but the sovereign power cannot, on its side, impose any burden on the subject which the interest of the community does not render expedient; neither can it have the inclination to do so. . . .

The engagements which bind us to the social body are only obligatory because they are mutual; and their nature is such that, in fulfilling them, we cannot labour for others without labouring at the same time for ourselves.

Wherefore is the general will always right; and wherefore do all the wills which form the general will invariably seek the happiness of every individual amongst them, if it is not that there is no person who does not appropriate the word each to himself; and who does not think of himself when he is voting for all? Which proves that the equality of right and the idea of justice which it inspires is derived from the preference which each gives to himself, and consequently from the nature of man.

The general will, to be truly such, must be so in its views, as well as its essence; it must be ready to part with every thing to apply it to ALL; and it loses its natural rectitude when it tends towards any one individual object; because then, judging of what is extraneous, it has no fixed principle of equity to guide it. . . .

The generality of the will depends less on the number of voices than on the common interest which unites them; for in this institution each necessarily submits to the conditions which he imposes on others; an admirable union of interest and justice which gives to the common deliberations a character of equity that vanishes in the discussion of all private affairs, for want of a common interest . . .

The social contract establishes amongst citizens such an equality that they are all engaged under the same conditions and must all enjoy the same rights; and that, by the nature of the Pact, all acts of the sovereignty, that is to say, all authentic acts of the general will, oblige or favour all citizens alike; in such a manner as evinces that the sovereign power knows no person but the body of the nation and does not distinguish any one of the members which compose it.

What in reality is this Pact but an act of the sovereignty? It is not a convention between a superior and an inferior, but a convention of the body with each of its members, rendered legal by having the social contract for its basis; equitable because it can have no other object but the general good; and solid because it is guaranteed by the public force and the supreme power.

While subjects are under the government of such conventions only, they obey no person; their obedience is paid to their own proper will; and to enquire how far the respective rights of the sovereign and citizens extend is to talk how far they can engage with themselves each towards all and all towards each.

We see by this that the sovereign power, all absolute, all sacred, all inviolable as it is, neither will or can exceed the bounds of general conventions: that every man may fully dispose of what is left to him of his property and his liberty by these conventions and that the sovereign power never has any right to charge one subject more than another because then the affair would become personal. . . .

These distinctions once admitted, it is evidently false that individuals have made any real renunciation by the social contract. On the contrary, they find their situation, by the effect of that contract, rendered greatly preferable to what it was before; and that, instead of making any alienation, they have only made an advantageous transition from a mode of living unsettled and precarious to one more established and secure; from a state of natural independence to one of liberty; from possessing the power of injuring others to the enjoyment of that protection which secures them from being injured; and from the right of employing that force which others might by the employment of theirs overcome, to the right of benefiting by that aggregate force which is invincible. Their lives even, which they have devoted to the state, are continually protected; and when they are exposed in its defence, what is it but restoring that which they have received from it? What do they do but what they did more frequently and with more danger in a state of nature when, living in continual and unavoidable conflicts, they defended at the peril of their lives the property which was necessary to the preservation of life? ALL, it is true, must fight for their country when their service is requisite, but then no person has occasion to fight for himself as an individual. And is it not gaining a great advantage to be obliged to incur occasionally only a part of that danger for the protection of the state to which we owe our own security, which we must be again exposed to if driven from the social state and depending entirely on our personal force to protect us?

II. History and Political Theory

Not all Enlightenment-era political theorists wrote abstractly as in the manner of Locke, Diderot, and Rousseau. Some preferred instead to present their ideas and debate their opponents through the medium of history. This tendency seems to have been particularly strong in France. There, erudite histories of the Frankish period often concealed powerful arguments for the entire range of political forms, from aristocratic oligarchy to absolute monarchy to democracy. Following are excerpts from three influential political-theoretical histories illustrating these positions.

6. HENRY DE BOULAINVILLIER, *HISTORY OF THE ANCIENT GOVERNMENT OF FRANCE*[7]

Henry de Boulainvillier (1658–1722) was a noble critic of absolutism, which he felt had grown excessively during the reign of Louis XIV. He wrote a number of historical-political works suggesting that reinvigorated nobility was necessary to check royal power and protect the French people from the oppression of the central government. This view influenced aristocratic thinking during the eighteenth century, including that of Montesquieu. This excerpt is from one of Boulainvillier's works on early French history. It was circulated widely in manuscript form during Boulainvillier's lifetime, but it was only published posthumously.

The Franks were originally all free and perfectly equal and independent. . . . They had Kings; but, while we now consider their dignity and power as incompatible with individual liberty, it was not the same then. The Frankish Kings were only Civil Magistrates chosen and appointed by the Cantons to judge disputes between individuals. . . . The People enjoyed real liberty in the personal choice of these Kings.

In addition to their Kings, the Franks sometimes also elected other Chiefs to lead them to war . . . and they chose them without distinction either in the Royal Family or in another one, considering only their valor, talent in the art of war, and reputation. . . .

Thus, it is absolutely contrary to the true character of the ancient Franks to imagine that the Royal power among them was Sovereign, Monarchical, or Despotic over their lives, properties, liberty, honor, or fortune; rather, the Franks were free . . . They were all companions. . . .

The Gauls, who really became the Subjects of the Franks both by the right of conquest and the necessity of obeying the strongest, were not strictly Subjects of

---

[7]Henri de Boulainvillier, *Histoire de l'ancien gouvernement de la France* (La Haye and Amsterdam, Netherlands: Aux dépends de la Compagnie, 1727), vol. 1, 26–39.

the King.... In effect, the right of Lordship and Domicile over [the Gauls] belonged to the Owners of the Lands they inhabited.... [The Gauls] were called ... Serfs or Subjects.... They were not Subjects of the State in general ... and consequently they were not Subjects of the King....

This truth is so established that, according to the custom of the Monarchy, the Third Estate only began to constitute a Corps when, once it had been emancipated by the Lords, it came under the protection of the Kings and sought to become their direct Subjects. This was an enterprise conducted against the obvious right of the Owners of Lands and against the Fundamental Law of the Government....

The Liberty of the Franks having been proven, it is easy to show that after the conquest of Gaul, only they were recognized as Nobles, which is to say Masters and Lords....

To think that the subject Gauls were true Nobles, because the Franks were unknown and barbaric foreigners for whom violence could never gain true Nobility, is not obvious; it was enough that they were victors.... In a word, the Gauls became Subjects while the others remained Masters and independent. If we add to this the long abasement in which the Gauls existed under Frankish domination; their exclusion from military service and civil Charges, their obligation to pay all kinds of taxes ... it is clear that, from the time of the Conquest, the original Franks were true Nobles and the only ones who could have that status, while the entire fate of the Gauls was subject to the will of the Victors.

7. JACOB-NICOLAS MOREAU, *LESSONS IN MORALITY, POLITICS AND PUBLIC LAW DRAWN FROM THE HISTORY OF OUR MONARCHY*[8]

Nicholas Moreau (1717–1803) was Louis XVI's official historian. He was a prolific author whose works all justified absolutist monarchy. For Moreau, strong royal government was necessary to protect the people from the rapaciousness of the feudal nobility.

During one of the most important periods of the French Monarchy, you see the Scepter of Charlemagne pass to the most powerful vassal of the Crown. This name is given to those who had previously been the supreme Magistrates of the Nation, ... depositories of an authority for which they had to give account. In fact, these Offices were hereditary, and, from the reign of Charles the Bald, this abuse became a kind of right. Hugues Capet received the Crown; and we must acknowledge that the revolution that gave it to him was much more harmful to Royal Power than that which had deposed the Merovingians. However, let us make here

---

[8]Jacob-Nicolas Moreau, *Lessons in Morality, Politics and Public Law Drawn from the History of Our Monarchy* (Versailles, France: Imprimerie du département des affaires étrangères, 1773), 77–83 and 123–129.

an important observation. The grand vassals did not partake of sovereignty. They did not say to Hugues Capet, "we will be your equals." They placed him on the Throne of Charlemagne and, by doing so, recognized, at least tacitly, that he was inheriting all the rights of the Household for which they were substituting him. This long-forgotten principle, ultimately recognized by both the Sovereign and Vassals, saved the Monarchy. . . .

Since this time, what was the state of Legislation in France? This important question deserves to be explored in depth. You will see our Kings ignore their power, and perhaps misunderstand the duties they could hardly fulfill. The power of Government changed into the power of property, and this disorder is the greatest plague that can threaten humanity. The same epoch witnessed our Kings stripped of their authority, the annihilation, or if you prefer, the suspension of all political legislation. There was no concertation, for the general government, between the Monarch and the Vassals. Each one saw himself as master in his own territory. They made war upon each other; they concluded treaties; they gave orders to their Subjects. Everything that had previously constituted Public Power seems to have become a dependence and attribute of property. . . . There were no more general Laws, no more Capitularies. We see Charters, given by Kings and Lords, executed within their domains; we see the Peoples enslaved and subjected to barbaric customs, more or less unjust, more or less unreasonable, according to whether the petty despot who governed them was a good or bad master. Legislation only began to reappear in France once our Kings began to free themselves from the obstacles they had received; and the Peoples only recovered their liberty when the Sovereign recovered his rights. [We call] . . . this sort of administration Feudal Government. . . .

Under the reign of [Henri IV], the Government was no longer feudal; for a century, all the obstacles which had hindered the exercise of Royal Power gradually vanished; and after the entire reunion [to the Crown] of the grand fiefs . . . [and] of all the debris of the Public Power, there remained only Justice which was still considered as being attached to the possession of lands. Nonetheless, this type of territorial Magistracy was subordinated to the power of the Monarchy, which could always restrain its excess and correct its abuses. But if the Lords had long ceased to be a type of Sovereign . . . they were still very grand and perhaps too powerful. Their internal divisions, their intriguing, their ambition weakened what remained of authority. During the troubles of the League, they caused so much harm to the State that it became clear that the People's liberty needed the Monarch's authority of the Monarch to be increased. Sully resisted their greed; and they had themselves already prepared their downfall when Richelieu finally struck down their power. . . .

[Under Louis XIII and Richelieu] you will admire the foundations of public liberty laid by the very hand of despotism, so necessary after such long disorder. I say the foundations of public liberty because the great, under-appreciated accomplishment of Cardinal Richelieu was to concentrate on the head of the King alone the power of arms which, attached to the supreme Magistracy during the first two races [the Carolingians and Merovingians] and to the Lordships during the third [Capetians], was still too freely exercised by the Nobility. The new Magistrates entrusted with public power, after our Kings had recovered it entirely, only had civil authority: they administered, they judged, but the title of their Office no longer gave them the power to draw the sword. Provincial Governors, military Officers, even great Lords on their lands, still believed that private violence was permitted. The Minister of Louis XIII proved to them that the right to use force belonged to the Sovereign alone. . . . Interior fortresses disappeared . . . and the common People felt that it finally had a King once it no longer had to fear a multitude of tyrants. Thus did Richelieu, in the civil order, complete the organization of a Political Body much more perfect and much more favorable to liberty than that over which Charlemagne had ruled.

8. GABRIEL BONNOT DE MABLY, *OBSERVATIONS ON THE HISTORY OF FRANCE*[9]

Although he had gone to seminary and taken religious orders, the Abbé de Mably (1709–1785) was not a practicing priest. Rather, he was a philosopher who often chose the medium of history to expound his democratic political theories. The following is an excerpt from one of his many works.

Chapter II, "What was the condition of the Gauls and others peoples subject to the domination of the Franks?"

Nothing tells us how [the Franks] acquired their lands. . . . This silence on such an important matter permits us to guess that they spread randomly across the provinces they had subjugated and, without any rule, took over part of the Gaul's possessions. Lands, houses, slaves, herds, everyone took what he pleased and made his domains more or less considerable according to his greed, force, or credit he enjoyed in his nation.

The Gauls were not reduced to servitude because the Franks knew only liberty. . . . Like the other Germans, they treated their slaves like men; tyranny . . . required notions and techniques of which they were entirely ignorant. But victory made them insolent and brutal; they grew used to insulting the Gauls; and when they wrote their customs and laws, they established a humiliating distinction between them and the vanquished. The Gaul was considered a vile man, his blood judged of less value than a Frank's. . . .

We need only glance at our [ancient Germanic] laws to see the great attachment of the Franks to their natal customs. They were both too ignorant and too

[9]Gabriel Bonnot de Mably, *Observations on the History of France*. (The Company of Booksellers: First published in 1765). This translation is from the 1788 London edition, vol. 1, 143–164, 169–175, 181–183.

fortunate in their enterprises to suspect what they lacked in their new situation. This attachment for the least important customs is the strongest proof that, initially, their government experienced no change in its most essential principles. Always free and forming a true republic, whose prince was just the chief magistrate, the nation reigned as a body over the different peoples who inhabited its conquests. The Champ de Mars [the Frankish national assembly] still assembled; the great leaders still formed the prince's council; and the Gaulish cities were governed like the villages of Germany; the former Grafions, now called dukes or counts, were both captains and judges of the people of their district. . . .

After the Gauls had recovered from their initial terror and became familiar with their masters, they no longer regretted the loss of their former situation [Roman imperial despotism]. . . . They did see some of their properties pass into the hands of the Franks; but they had expected to suffer much greater losses; and what remained to them was enough to console them for what they had lost. Since the pillaging was conducted haphazardly, many citizens did not suffer at all from it and others were compensated by the suppression of the former [Roman] taxes. . . .

All these taxes, that the greed and luxury of the emperors had demanded of their subjects, were forgotten under Frankish government. To support himself, the prince had his domains, free gifts that his subjects gave him at the assembly of the Champs de Mars, . . . and other dues that the law gave him. Instead of a permanently poor society, . . . the Gauls found themselves in a rich state, because liberty and courage were its soul. Since the Franks did not sell their services to the fatherland, they did not dream of buying those of the Gauls. . . . All taxes thus lost their purpose, and subject and master alike were simply obliged to go to war at their own expense when required. . . .

The Gauls had the satisfaction of keeping their national laws, an advantage also enjoyed by the other peoples under Frankish domination. . . . [The Franks] left to the Gauls a great portion of the public authority. . . . At first humiliated, disdained, and treated as the vanquished, the Gauls gradually obtained the privilege . . . of incorporating themselves into the victorious nation and becoming naturalized Franks. After having declared to the prince . . . that he was giving up Roman law to live under [Germanic] law, a Gaul would enjoy the prerogatives specific to the Franks . . . [and] having become a citizen, would be admitted to the assemblies of the Champ de Mars and thus enter into a portion of the sovereignty and administration of the state. . . .

Chapter III, "On the causes which contributed to the ruin of the Franks' democratic government. How the successors of Clovis took over a greater share of authority than that allowed him by Law. Tyranny of the Grandees. Establishment of Seigneuries"

At last having a homeland, lands, and fixed dwellings, the Franks soon began to feel the insufficiency of the Germanic laws.

When they lived from pillage, democracy tempered by the council of grandees and the authority of the prince had given the Franks everything necessary for the safety and progress of a society of brigands. We know that political theorists consider this form of government as the one most capable of enlightening a nation about its interests and sharpening the spirit and courage of its citizens. It would very likely have given rise among the Franks to the qualities and institutions necessary for a rich and established people, if they had worked at firming it up; but no sooner had they established themselves in Gaul than love of liberty ceased to be their guiding passion. Their conquests weakened their government; by giving them different ideas than those they had brought out of Germany, new needs and circumstances gradually detached them from their ancient political principles.

Rather than establishing themselves in one place, the Franks spread across the breadth of their conquests; thus retaining no relation between themselves, the force of the nation seemed to evaporate, the citizens no longer had a single interest. . . . The need to live from pillage had previously attached each individual to the body of the nation, [but] . . . this link no longer remained after the conquest. Each Frank felt he had done enough once he had acquired a property and gave himself over to the pleasure of exploiting his new possessions. . . . The public good was sacrificed to particular interest, and this moral shift announced a revolution in the form of government. . . .

Having become rich, the Franks did not suspect that their riches would tempt the greed of the most powerful among them and that their new needs were but so many chains to strangle them. The government, which tolerated their injustices because it did not know how to repress them and establish order, gave them a dangerous sense of security. The less force the civil laws had over the citizens, the more the Franks should have feared for the loss of their domestic fortune and liberty; but they were still far from seeing that truth. Rather, confusing the most extreme licence with liberty, they thought they would always be free because they could not be repressed; they gave themselves over to greed and their natural laziness and neglected to attend the assemblies of the Champs de Mars, which were no longer held regularly and soon stopped being convoked.

All the authority that the entire body of the nation had enjoyed, now found itself in the council of the prince and grandees, who had until then possessed only executive power. But this nascent aristocracy did not have any solid foundation. . . .

The predecessors of Clovis, and probably this prince himself, tried to gain the respect of the grandees by giving them small presents, such as a warhorse, javelin, or sword. . . . The Merovingian kings, interested in winning them over in order to increase their power . . . imagined a new kind of present more likely to please them; they gave them part of their domain; this is what our ancient texts call *bénéfices* or *fiscs* and what some modern writers have mistakenly confused with what came to be called fiefs. . . .

Whether by lack of knowledge or economy . . . the Franks saw the fortunes that their forefathers had acquired diminish day by day. The prince, who repaired these losses [by distributing *bénéfices*], was no longer a simple minister of the laws. . . . The sons of Clovis, who had subjugated the national council by their gifts, became its master. They took over public power all the more easily . . . because they had kept for themselves the right of taking back at will the *bénéfices* they had granted. . . .

Several grandees, who still kept the former spirit of the nation or who were the richest and most powerful, had the courage and luck to escape the yoke being prepared for them. Whether fearing the forces of the court and the indifference with which the people regarded the decadence of the government, or whether they loved public liberty less than their own elevation, they did nothing in favor of the laws and, to the contrary, profited from the examples of injustice given to them. . . . [They] hoped to become tyrants and asserted rights over their neighbors, who possessed lands with the same independence as themselves. This gave rise to our patrimonial lordships.

Chapter IV, "On the conduct and interests of the different Orders of the State. How the Benefices granted by the Merovingian kings became hereditary. Harm that this innovation did to the authority these Princes had acquired"

The new lords, who had made for themselves independent principalities in the heart of the State, could only firm up their own power by limiting royal authority. . . .

This odious policy succeeded. . . . Outraged at the arbitrary way the prince gave, took back, gave back, and recovered his *bénéfices*, they sought to remedy this abuse. . . . Having made themselves masters of the King thanks to his own gifts, they succeeded in making themselves feared. Assembled at Andély to negotiate peace between Gontran and Childebert, they forced these princes to agree in their treaty that they could no longer recover at will the *bénéfices* they had conferred or would grant in the future. . . . *Bénéfices* were given back to those who had been stripped of them. . . . It is quite likely that the grandees who negotiated these articles of peace believed they had made the *bénéfices* hereditary in the families that possessed them.

This treaty was only good for perpetuating disorder and embittering spirits. Its enemies were the two princes who had contracted it, as well as all who did not then possess *benefice*. . . . A common interest united them against those who had taken most of the domains of the Crown and who, for their part, had to form an alliance and were more determined than ever to defend their new rights. Thus, the heredity, or at least the guaranteed possession, of the *bénéfices* . . . became the principal dynamic of all the movements of the Franks. Violated when circumstances permitted and executed when it was impossible to violate, the Treaty of Andély did not cause a sudden revolution in the state, but made it necessary. . . .

Chapter V, "On the origin of Nobility among the Franks. How this innovation contributed to the abasement of Royal authority and confirmed the servitude of the People"

As long as *bénéfices* were not hereditary, the distinctions awarded to the Frankish nobles were only personal. Their nobility, which was not transmitted by blood, left their children in the common class of citizens. . . .

To the contrary, when the *bénéfices* changed nature and became hereditary, the sons of a *bénéfice*-holder, by the right of birth which summoned them to the succession of their father, found themselves under the trust or loyalty of the king and were either obliged to him or protected by him. Birth gave them a prerogative that was previously acquired only by the oath of fidelity; it began to be thought that they were born as nobles. Always adroit at profiting from its advantages, vanity is even more attentive to extending them on the slightest pretext. These new kinds of nobles believed they were superior to the others, and the idea of nobility that we have today began to take hold; the families of the *bénéfice*-holders . . . formed a separate class, not only from those who had not sworn the oath of loyalty to the prince, but even from families that had been ennobled in the old way. . . . The families of the *bénéfice*-holders formed a distinct order of citizens in the state. . . .

Once there were citizens with particular privileges and had them only because of their birth, they came to despise those who were no longer their equals and began to unite themselves, form a separate body, and have interests distinct from those of both the prince and the people. To the quality of judge, the lords joined that of captains of the men of their lands; or rather, they did not distinguish between functions which, until then, had always been united in the prince, dukes, counts, and other public magistrates of the nation. . . . Because of that, the nobility, equally redoubtable to the people because of its right of justice and to the prince because of the militia it commanded, made itself master of the laws and held in its hands all the force of the state. It required nothing else to ruin royal authority and deprive the Merovingians of all hope of rising again. The lords would have even consolidated their empire over the people if, by moderation, they had habituated it to regard them as legitimate; but, having elevated themselves by violating the law, they did not understand that nothing is stable without its backing, and continued to know other rule than greed, pride, and violence. . . .

III. Enlightenment and Revolution

The political works presented previously in this chapter were not written as interventions in specific political moments or crises. They may have been intended to sway opinion, but only gradually and in a general rather than an immediate sense. In the context of revolutionary crisis, however, the writing of even abstract theory could become a political act. In 1788 in France, on the eve of the Revolution, Enlightenment abstraction and revolutionary immediacy flowed into one. The following excerpt illustrates the blending of Enlightenment and Revolution, as well as the fusion of abstract and historical modes of political theorizing.

9. GUILLAUME-JOSEPH SAIGE,
THE CITIZEN'S CATECHISM[10]

Q. Let us recapitulate the diverse matters we have just discussed and, to begin, what is a political society?

A. It is a collection of men, freely united to work together for their common advantage; and this in virtue of an original contract, which forms the basis of the association.

Q. Can a political society be legitimate if its members have not joined together freely?

A. No, because liberty is essential to man and, having received from nature an absolute power of direction over himself, only the individual has the right to modify his original and natural status. . . .

Q. What is the original contract? Is it essential to the creation of a society?

A. The original contract is a convention of the social body with each of its members, by which it guarantees the protection of all of its forces to maintain the enjoyment of liberty and property; and, by submitting to the absolute empire of the association, the individual promises to use [his liberty and property] only in conformity with the decisions of the general will. This contract gives life and existence to civil society. . . .

Q. What is the goal of the political society?

A. This goal is contained in the definition of the society; it is the general good or common advantage of its members.

Q. How can one attain this goal?

A. By establishing a force which directs the totality of the political machine toward it.

Q. What is this force?

A. Sovereign authority.

Q. Where should it reside?

A. Since the goal of the formation of societies is essentially the happiness of their members, it is a natural consequence that sovereign authority resides in the single will, which cannot depart from the social goal; that is to say, in the will of the body of the citizens, that we call the general will.

Q. From whence comes the necessary tendency of the general will to strive toward the happiness of society?

A. It comes from the love of self, a sentiment which essentially orients each individual toward his own good and necessarily (and for the same reason) directs any collection of individuals toward their common advantage.

Q. How does sovereign authority operate on the political body?

A. This authority is only directed in its action toward a general goal; from this point of view, it is the social body which acts upon itself; . . . and this

---

[10]Guillaume-Joseph Saige, *The Citizen's Catechism*, 1788 edition, 80–99.

is precisely what ensures the essential impartiality and goodness of its decisions; qualities which would no longer be inherent to it if the general tended toward an individual object. . . .

Q. How is the sovereign power formed?

A. It is formed of the aggregate of particular powers that nature gave to each individual over his own being.

Q. But since the social body is composed of individuals and the laws must be applied to them, and since the sovereign authority has only general views, is it necessary to have an agent charged with particularizing these views and applying them to the members of society?

A. This agent exists in each society; it is what we call the executive power or government, and its depositaries are generally called magistrates.

Q. The form of this power, does it vary from society to society, and what are its types?

A. It almost always varies from society to society; and its modifications are very numerous, but we can classify these different variations into three simple forms, whose combinations constitute all the mixed forms. The first occurs when each citizen, or the majority of them, exercise some magisterial functions. We call this Democracy. The second is found wherever the execution of the laws is entrusted to a certain number of chosen citizens; that is Aristocracy. Finally, the third exists when the totality of the executive power is placed in the hands of a unique magistrate; this is monarchical government.

Q. How do magistrates act upon members of society, and what kind of obedience is owed to them?

A. As they are purely the instruments of the general will, the magistrates must only act in its name; consequently, it is only in its name that they have the right to demand obedience from the members of society; and from the moment they depart from its decisions or substitute their own particular wills for it, all citizens can and must refuse to obey their orders, and society has the right to punish them.

Q. Can a society depose its magistrates or wholly change its form of government?

A. It can do both. There is no authority in the political body greater than its own. . . . [Society] established government for its own advantage; consequently, it can destroy it and replace it with another whenever it judges it more useful to attain the great social goal, which is the public welfare. . . .

Q. When, in the social body, a particular will permanently substitutes itself for the general will, what is the result and what effect does that produce on society and its members?

A. The result is the ruin of legitimate sovereignty and the birth of a violent and illegal power, which we call despotism, which is nothing other than a state of war of one or several against a part of the human race, whose liberty they oppress. The effect of this new power is the annihilation of the social contract, the dissolution of society, the freeing of its members from all civil bonds, and their return to the original state in which they are required to recognize no other judges than themselves and no other laws than the eternal laws of nature. . . .

Q. Let us apply to the French constitution these general principles, which pertain to all political societies; and firstly, where does the legislative power reside?

A. It resides in the totality of the nation, composed of the King and the three Orders of the State. . . .

Q. Where does the executive power in France reside, and what is its form?

A. It is shared between the King and a Senate, which we call the Court of France, Parlement, or Court of Paris; therefore, the form [of government in France] is an aristocratic monarchy.

Q. What part of the administration has the nation entrusted to the King?

A. The King finds himself solely invested with all military force, is the Head of State, the first judge of the citizens, the born and perpetual president of the Supreme Senate or Court of Peers; prepares with it all matters that must be brought before the assembly of the Estates; convokes that assembly; is charged with enforcing the laws that are established there, concurrently with the Court of Peers, of which he forms an essential part; and possess these diverse powers by a hereditary right perpetuated by the tacit consent of the nation. . . .

Q. What is the part that finds itself constitutionally placed in the hands of the Parlement?

A. This Senate represents the majesty of the social body when it is not actually assembled; it is charged with defending its rights, overseeing the defense of national liberty and the particular liberty of each individual; counterbalances the royal power, retains it within limits fixed by the laws; is charged with maintaining civil order; is the Supreme tribunal before which are brought in last resort all contestations between citizens, and which sovereignly determines the punishment of all types of crime; finally, this Body legitimates by its cooperation all operations of the supreme magistrate in everything related to internal government.

Q. Who are the members of this Senate?

A. There are two sorts, the Peers or Grandees of the nation, who are the original magistrates of the Parlement and who form its essence; and the Presidents and Councilors who should only be considered as secondary magistrates derived from the first; but who, although inferior in dignity, enjoy together with them all the privileges of this Corps. . . .

Q. When the Throne is vacant, on whom devolves the totality of the executive power?

A. To that part of the administration which, by its nature, always subsists, which is to say, to the Parlement.

Q. Is it in the power of some magistrate, even the King, to annihilate this Senate or one of its parts, or, by his own authority, to deprive one of its members of the place he occupies?

A. As an integral part of the constitution, this body can only be annihilated by the power that formed the constitution, which is to say, by the nation itself; and an enterprise of this sort, undertaken by any authority whatsoever, would be an act of the most violent despotism and an open attack upon the rights of society. Possessing his position by virtue of and under the protection of the laws, each member of the Parliament can only be stripped of it by those very same laws; and the magistrate who would deprive one of these senators of his place or would prevent him from exercising its functions, would render himself, however elevated his dignity, guilty of a very grave abuse of authority, and would consequently deserve to be punished by the supreme authority of the nation.

Q. What are the essential rights of all individuals living in society?

A. Those which derive immediately from the goal of the social institution, which is to say, civil liberty and property.

Q. What is civil liberty?

A. It is independence from all other power than the legislative power, which, residing essentially in the general will, a will that necessarily tends toward the public interest and thus the interest of each individual, gives to all members of the political body the most perfect security imaginable.

Q. Since, in all legitimate constitutions, each citizen must be subject only to the laws and the general will that establishes them, it necessarily follows that no one in the State has the right to deprive a citizen of his independence and that all authority of one individual over another is only legitimate if it derives from the general will?

A. This is incontestable. All acts of an individual will are illegal in the civil State if they do not draw their principle from the legislative authority. To dispose of the life or fortune of an individual independently of the laws; to deprive him of the exercise of his physical liberty; to seek to subject him to particular orders; to forbid him from writing or speaking about the public interest; finally, to remove him in any way from the unique and essential relationship of empire and obedience between the social body and each of its members, to subject him to a particular will . . . all these things are so many attacks against the rights of society, infractions of the original contract, and consequently crimes that require prompt and severe punishment.

Q. What do you mean by property?

A. It is the right that one or several men have to use a thing for their utility or pleasure, and to dispose of it at will.

Q. What are the different types of property?

A. There are two types: natural property and civil property.

Q. What is natural property and where does it come from?

A. Natural property is that which is acquired by purely natural means, outside of the civil state. It comes from the obligation of each man to preserve himself, which, impossible without the means of subsistence, requires each individual to procure for himself the things that can provide him with it and guarantees his possession [of them] from the minute he acquires them.

Q. What is civil property?

A. It is that which owes its origin to the conventions that formed the basis of the political body and which is the portion left to each individual from the general mass of public property; a mass formed by the union of all the natural properties belonging to each of the associates before the formation of the civil state. The preservation of that property being, after liberty, the most important object for each individual and, as it forms a part of his civil existence, is also under the protection of the laws; and any magistrate or individual who attacks it in whole or in part, makes himself guilty of a very marked infraction of the social contract.

Q. Does it not follow from this that any tax imposed on the nation, or part of the nation, independently of the general will is a violation of the right of property?

A. That is a necessary consequence of this principle; add to this that, if the tax is general and takes the form of a law, it is . . . a usurpation of sovereignty. . . .

Q. What is meant by the Commons or Third Estate?

A. The citizens who are neither of the Clergy nor the Nobility; forming the most numerous part of the nation, they consequently form its most important part.

Q. Is its right to attend the Estates General ancient?

A. It is as ancient as the nation and draws its very essence from the political body. In effect, the people, forming the greatest part of the society, should not only participate in legislation, but its own interest should predominate within it. Thus, from the origin of the French Republic, the people always formed the essence and basis of its legislative assemblies. The hereditary Nobility did not exist during those distant times, and the quality of member of the Senate was the only distinction then known, a distinction that was not transmitted to their descendants. Once these magistrates became hereditary through the corruption of government and usurped the right of legislation, the constitution was destroyed, the political body annihilated, and a totally new one was formed, totally dominated by the usurpers. The French will not become a true nation again until the people throws off the yoke of feudal government and recovers it liberty.

CHAPTER 2

The Strains of Empire

The potentially radical ideas elaborated by Enlightenment writers would have made little practical impact without circumstances capable of activating them. Those circumstances were furnished by the strains of imperial warfare. From the mid-seventeenth through the mid-eighteenth century, the European powers fought a succession of increasingly far-flung global wars. Culminating in the decisive British victory over France and Spain in the French-Indian War (1754–1763) or Seven Years' War (1756–1763), these conflicts put enormous pressure on victors and vanquished alike.

The financial costs and other burdens these wars placed on the belligerent powers provoked constitutional crises in those countries and their colonies. The unprecedented scale of these wars led the warring states to adopt unprecedented methods of mobilizing resources. These efforts often jarred with established laws, institutions, traditions, and social interests. Consequently, they stirred up bitter resistance among the populations they targeted. That resistance developed into open revolution in Great Britain's thirteen North American colonies in 1776, in France in 1789, in Saint-Domingue (France's preeminent Caribbean colony) in 1791, and in large parts of Spanish America from 1808 on. Drawing on selected Enlightenment concepts, combining and deploying them in novel ways, and sometimes articulating entirely new ideas, revolutionary movements across the Atlantic world overthrew the European colonial order that had existed before 1763.

I. Spain

By the eighteenth century, it was clear that Spanish power had declined dramatically from the days of the Conquistadors, Charles V, and the Spanish Armada. In Europe, it had long ago lost most of its rich former possessions in the Low Countries and Italy, and Peninsular Spain itself had become a depopulated, economically depressed backwater. In America, the mid-century wars had revealed the vulnerability of the colonies. This was dramatically highlighted during the Seven Years' War when British forces captured Havana, the capital city of the strategically vital Spanish colony of Cuba. After the war, the Spanish government made efforts to reform the state and restore its power. Known as the Bourbon Reforms (after the reigning dynasty of Spain), they focused on extracting more financial and human resources from the American colonies—the one remaining source of potential strength Spain still possessed. For Spain after 1763, the colonies were to be the engine of national revival.

The Bourbon Reforms generated opposition. Attempts to stimulate the colonial economies ran headlong into the opposition of the Cadíz mercantile lobby, which stubbornly defended its monopoly of trade with the Americas. A program to bolster colonial defenses by enlisting people of color in local military forces stoked racial fears among white colonists, both Peninsulars (those born in European Spain) and Creoles (those born in America). And exploitation of the Indians—by requiring the payment of tribute, unpaid labor service, and the forcible purchase of European goods—continued to fuel discontent. Overall, the increasingly direct intervention of the Spanish bureaucracy in local affairs generated resentment and nostalgia for an earlier period of benevolent neglect when Spanish Americans had largely been left to manage their own affairs.

Although revolts occasionally broke out, only two posed a serious threat to Spanish authority. These were the Tupac Amaru rebellion in Peru (1780) and the Comunero revolt in Venezuela (1781). Yet even these were contained, largely by concessions and negotiations. Seemingly the weakest of the European Atlantic powers, Spain showed surprising resiliency in maintaining authority across its sprawling empire. Nonetheless, there was plenty of combustible material in Spanish America. Only a spark was necessary to set it off.

1. ALEXANDER VON HUMBOLDT ON NEW SPAIN (MEXICO)[1]

Alexander Von Humboldt was a German naturalist who travelled widely in Spanish America. His books and essays did much to familiarize eighteenth- and nineteenth-century European readers with that part of the world. Although his primary concern was the geography, flora, and fauna of the Americas, he also commented on the social, economic, and political situation of the Spanish American colonies.

Amongst the inhabitants of pure origin, the whites would occupy the second place, considering them only in the relation of number. They are divided into whites

---

[1]Alexander Von Humboldt, *Political Essays on the Kingdom of New Spain*, trans. John Black (London: T. Davison, 1814), vol. 1, 204–206; and vol. 3, 455–460.

born in Europe, and descendants of Europeans born in the Spanish colonies of America or in the Asiatic islands. The former bear the name of Chapetones or Gachupines, and the second that of Criollos. . . . The Spanish laws allow the same rights to all whites; but those who have the execution of the laws endeavour to destroy an equality which shocks the European pride. The government, suspicious of the Creoles, bestows the great places exclusively on the natives of Old Spain. For some years back they have disposed at Madrid even of the most trifling employments in the administration of the customs and the tobacco revenue. . . . The result has been a jealousy and perpetual hatred between the Chapetons and the Creoles. The most miserable European, without education, and without intellectual cultivation, thinks himself superior to the whites born in the new continent. He knows that, protected by his countrymen, and favoured by chances common enough in a country where fortunes are as rapidly acquired as they are lost, he may one day reach places to which the access is almost interdicted to the natives, even to those of them distinguished for their talents, knowledge, and moral qualities. The natives prefer the denomination of Americans to that of Creoles. Since the peace of Versailles [of 1783, which ended the American Revolution], and, in particular, since the year 1789 [the year of the French Revolution], we frequently hear proudly declared, "I am not a Spaniard, I am an American!" words which betray the working of a long resentment. In the eye of the law every white Creole is a Spaniard; but the abuse of the laws, the false measures of the colonial government, the example of the United States of America, and the influence of the opinions of the age, have relaxed the ties which formerly united more closely the Spanish Creoles to the European Spaniards. A wise administration may re-establish harmony, calm their passions and resentments, and yet preserve for a long time the union among the members of one and the same great family scattered over Europe and America, from the Patagonian coast to the north of California. . . .

The restless and suspicious policy of the nations of Europe, . . . have thrown insurmountable obstacles in the way of such settlements as might secure to these distant possessions, a great degree of prosperity, and an existence independent of the mother country. . . . A colony has for ages been only considered as useful to the parent state, in so far as it supplied a great number of raw materials, and consumed a number of the commodities carried there by the ships of the mother country.

It was easy for different commercial nations to adapt their colonial system to islands of small extent, or factories established on the coast of a continent. The inhabitants of Barbadoes, St. Thomas, or Jamaica are not sufficiently numerous to possess a great number of hands for the manufacture of cotton cloth; and the position of these islands at all times facilitates the exchange of their agricultural produce, for the manufactures of Europe. It is not so with the continental possessions of Spain the two Americas. . . .

The kings of Spain, by taking the title of kings of the Indies, have considered these distant possessions rather as integral parts of their monarchy, as provinces dependent on the crown of Castille, than as colonies in the sense attached to this word since the sixteenth century by the commercial nations of Europe. They early perceived that these vast countries, of which the coast is less inhabited than the interior, could not be governed like islands scattered in the Atlantic Ocean; and from these circumstances the court of Madrid was compelled to have recourse to a less prohibitory system, and to tolerate what it was unable to prevent. Hence a more equitable legislation has been adopted in that country than that by which the greatest part of the other colonies of the New Continent is governed. In the latter, for example, it is not permitted to refine raw sugar; and the proprietor of a plantation is obliged to purchase the produce of his own soil from the manufacturer of the mother country. No law prohibits the refining of sugar in the possessions of Spanish America. If the government does not encourage manufactures, and if it even employs indirect means to prevent the establishment of those silk, paper, and crystal; on the other hand, no decree of the audience, no royal cedula, declares that these manufactures ought not to exist beyond the sea. In the colonies, as well as everywhere else, we must not confound the spirit of the laws with the policy of those by whom they are administered.

Only half a century ago, two citizens, animated with the purest patriotic zeal, the Count de Gijon and the Marquis de Maenza, conceived the project of bringing over to Quito a colony of workmen and artizans from Europe. The Spanish ministry affected to applaud their zeal, and did not think proper to refuse them the privilege of establishing manufactories; but they so contrived to fetter the proceedings of these two enterprising men, that they at last perceived that secret orders had been given to the viceroy and the audience to ruin their undertaking, which they voluntarily renounced. . . . Virtuous men have from time to time raised their voices to enlighten the government as to its true interest; and they have endeavoured to impress the mother country with the idea, that it would be more useful to encourage the manufacturing industry of the Colonies than to allow the treasures of Peru and Mexico to be spent in the purchase of foreign commodities. These counsels would have been attended to if the ministry had not too frequently sacrificed the interests of the nations of a great continent to the interest of a few maritime towns of Spain; for the progress of manufactures in the Colonies has not been impeded by the manufacturers of the peninsula, . . . but by trading monopolists, whose political influence is favoured by great wealth and kept up by a thorough knowledge of intrigue, and the momentary wants of the court.

2. ECONOMIC COMPLAINTS[2]

After the Seven Years' War, Spain looked to the colonial economies to generate the revenue national revival—especially military revival—required. Rather than open the economies of Spanish America to world trade, it sought to enforce trade restrictions

[2]Mariano Moreno, "Extracts from a Representation, addressed to the Viceroy of Buenos Aires," *Mexico in 1827* (London: 1828). [1809] http://web.grinnell.edu/courses/HIS/f01/HIS202-01/Documents/Moreno.html

to ensure that wealth would flow into the Spanish treasury rather than enrich other powers. This restrictive approach to trade, often referred to as mercantilism, was powerfully supported by the merchants of Spain's principal Atlantic port city, Cadíz. Spanish Americans chafed against these trade restrictions.

The resources of the royal treasury being exhausted by the enormous expenditure which has lately been required, Your Excellency, on assuming the reins of government, was deprived of the means of providing for the safety of the provinces committed to your charge. The only mode of relieving the necessities of the country appears to be to grant permission to the English merchants to introduce their manufactures into the town, and to re-export the produce of the interior, by which the revenue will be at once increased, and an impulse given to industry and trade.

Your Excellency possesses powers sufficient for the adoption of any measures that the safety of the country may require, but a natural desire to ensure the result of these measures, by adapting them to the peculiar situation of the viceroyalty, induced Your Excellency to consult the *cabildo* of this city, and the *Tribunal del Real Consulado,* before any definitive resolution was taken.

The intentions of Your Excellency had barely transpired, when several of the merchants manifested their discontent and dissatisfaction. Groups of European shopkeepers were formed in all the public places, who, disguising their jealousy and personal apprehensions under the most specious pretenses, affected to deplore, as a public calamity, the diminution of the profits which they have hitherto derived from the contraband trade. At one time, with hypocritical warmth, they lamented the fatal blow which the interests of the mother country were about to receive, and at another, they predicted the ruin of the colony, and the total destruction of its commerce: others again announced the universal distress that the free exportation of the precious metals would bring upon us, and pretended to feel a lively interest in the fate of our native artisans (whom they have always hitherto despised), endeavoring to enlist in their cause the sacred name of religion, and the interests of morality.

Never, certainly, has America known a more critical state of affairs, and never was any European governor so well entitled as Your Excellency to dispense at once with the maxims of past ages; for if, in less dangerous times, the laws have often been allowed to sleep, when their observance might have checked the free action of the government surely Your Excellency cannot now be condemned for the adoption of a measure, by which alone the preservation of this part of the monarchy can be effected.

Those should be doomed to eternal infamy, who maintain that under present circumstances, it would be injurious either to Spain, or to this country, to open a free intercourse with Great Britain. But even supposing the measure to be injurious, still it is a necessary evil, and one which, since it cannot be avoided, ought at least to be made use of for the general good, by endeavoring to derive every possible advantage from it, and thus to convert it into a means of ensuring the safety of the state.

Since the English first appeared on our coasts, in 1806, the merchants of that nation have not lost sight of the Río de la Plata in their speculations. A series of commercial adventures has followed, which has provided almost entirely for the consumption of the country; and this great importation, carried on in defiance of laws and reiterated prohibitions, has met with no other obstacles than those necessary to deprive the custom house of its dues, and the country of those advantages which it might have derived from a free exportation of its own produce in return.

The result of this system has been to put the English in the exclusive possession of the right of providing the country with all the foreign merchandise that it requires; while the government has lost the immense revenues which the introduction of so large a proportion of foreign manufacturer ought to have produced, from too scrupulous an observance of laws, which have never been more scandalously violated than at the moment when their observance was insisted upon by the merchants of the capital. For what, Sir, can be more glaringly absurd than to hear a merchant clamoring for the enforcement of the prohibitive laws, and the exclusion of foreign trade, at the very door of a shop filled with English goods, clandestinely imported?

To the advantages which the government will derive from the open introduction of foreign goods may be added those which must accrue to the country from the free exportation of its own produce.

Our vast plains produce annually a million of hides, out reckoning other skins, corn, or tallow, all of which are valuable, as articles of foreign trade. But the magazines of our resident merchants are full; there is no exportation; the capital usually invested in these speculations is already employed, and the immense residue of the produce, thrown back upon the hands of the landed proprietors, or purchased at a price infinitely below its real value, has reduced them to the most deplorable state of wretchedness, and compelled them to abandon a labor which no longer repays the toil and expense with which it is attended.

The freedom of trade in America was not proscribed as a real evil, but because it was a sacrifice required of the colonies by the mother country. The events which led to the gradual increase of this exclusive commerce, till it became a monopoly of the Cádiz merchants, are well known. . . .

Is it just that the fruits of our agricultural labors should be lost, because the unfortunate provinces of Spain can no longer consume them? Is it just that the abundant productions of the country should rot in our magazines, because the navy of Spain is too weak to export them? Is it just that we should increase the distress of the mother country, by the tidings of our own critical and vacillating state, when the means are offered to us of consolidating our safety upon the firmest basis? Is it just, that, when the subjects of a friendly and generous nation present themselves in our ports, and offer us, at a cheap rate, the merchandise of which we are in want, and with which Spain cannot supply us, we should reject the proposal, and convert, by so doing, their good intentions to the exclusive advantage of a few European merchants, who, by means of a contraband trade, render themselves masters of the whole imports of the country? Is it just, that when we are entreated to sell our accumulated agricultural produce, we should, by refusing to do so, decree at the same time the ruin of our landed proprietors, of the country, and of society together?

If Your Excellency wishes to diminish the extraction of specie, which has taken place latterly to so great an extent, there is no other mode of effecting it than to open the ports to the English, and thus to enable them to extend their speculations to other objects. It is one of the fatal consequences of the contraband trade, that the importer is absolutely compelled to receive the value of his imports in the precious metals alone. His true interest, indeed, consists in exchanging them at once for articles that may become the objects of a new speculation; but the risks with which the extraction of bulky commodities must be attended, under a system of strict prohibition, induce him to sacrifice this advantage to the greater security which exports in specie afford, and to deprive himself of the hope of new profits, and the country of the sale of its most valuable produce.

Yet the *apoderado* of the Cádiz monopolies maintains, "that a free trade will be the ruin of our agriculture." This luminous discovery is worthy of his penetration. The free exportation of the produce is declared to be detrimental to the interests of the producer! What, then, is to be the mode of encouraging his in his labors? According to the principles laid down by our merchants, the agricultural produce should be allowed to accumulate—purchasers are to be deterred from entering the market, by the difficulties of exporting the articles bought up to countries where they might be consumed; and this system is to be persevered in until, after ruining the landholders by preventing them from disposing of the fruits of their labors, the superfluous produce itself is to be disposed of, in order to fill up the ditches and marshes in the vicinity of the town.

Yes, Sir, this is the deplorable state to which our agriculture has been reduced during the last few years. The marshes around the town have been actually filled up with wheat; and this miserable condition, which forms a subject of lamentation with all true friends to their country, and scandalizes the inhabitants of the whole district, is the natural fate of a province in which, as soon as an inclination is shown to apply a remedy to these evils, men are found daring enough to assert "that by giving value, or, in other words, a ready market, to the agricultural produce, agriculture will be ruined."

3. EXPLOITATION AND CORRUPTION: THE VIEW FROM THE TOP[3]

The Bourbon reforms brought with them the growing presence and intervention of Spanish government bureaucrats. Established Spanish American elites resented these officials because they encroached on their traditional prerogatives. Indians resented their efforts to raise money, notably their use of forced sales of goods (known as repartimientos). In the following document, a petition to the King from the Cuzco municipal council, the author denounces these practices.

---

[3]"Grievances of the Municipality of Cuzco" (1768), in Carlos Daniel Valcarcel, ed., *Coleccion Documental de la Independencia del Peru*, trans. Daniel Arenas, vol.1, book 2, *La Rebelion de Tupac Amaru: Antecedentes* (Lima, Peru: Commission Nacional del Sesquicentenario de la Independencia del Peru, 1971), 3–9.

The long neglect from which the provinces of the extensive kingdom of Peru have suffered is an issue most worthy of Your Majesty's attention. Many things conspire to ruin Peru, and a remedy is urgently required. . . .

When the provinces were rich and filled with resources, royal officials were able to supplement their salaries by lawful profits earned through their good actions, graces, and other things that benefited the provinces. But as time passed and the former abundance grew less and less, they lost these supplementary revenues. Instead, they began to participate in agricultural and business activities that were forbidden to them and to enrich themselves by manipulating the legal system. . . .

Resisting attempts to rein in these abuses, the royal officials shamelessly pursued their business enterprises, deceiving their provincial subjects and profiting from them by forcibly selling them useless goods. Paying little heed to royal ordinances prohibiting these activities, they proceeded with impunity, with no fear of incurring the penalties laid down by the laws and royal commissions.

When an official deigns to travel to his district, he first looks in the capital for goods and merchandise to bring with him to the province. As he generally does not have sufficient capital to buy with cash, the warehouses and stores provide him with these on credit, at above market price. Called "dragons" by honest traders, these unscrupulous dealers thus relieve themselves of useless goods they cannot sell by furnishing them to the officials who, in turn, use them to cheat the Indians. . . . Three wounds are thus inflicted: once in the violence by which the Indians are forced to buy them, then in the useless nature of the goods, and finally in the inflated price with which the officials were forced to obtain them from the "dragons."

To distribute these goods with the greatest accuracy, the new official uses the information acquired by the previous one . . . and thus forms lists of the inhabitants of the towns, their wealth, and their properties. He uses this information to determine the quantity of goods they will have to buy. The official then forces them to take these goods, forbidding any complaints or resistance. Whoever objects to this process is rewarded with prison. There have even been officials who forcibly obtain compliance through violence. Such a case occurred in a town near Cuzco when a Spaniard who tried to resist a second forced purchase that a royal official was imposing upon him received many brutal blows and was thrown into prison where he received no food. Close to death, he was released on the third day. This unfortunate man tried to flee to another town, but died before arriving there. The official hid what had happened by ordering his subordinates to write fraudulent reports indicating that the man had died from falling from a horse. . . . It is under circumstances like these, and even worse, that the officials carry out their forcible sales. Even Indian chiefs, to whom the official entrusts the distribution of the goods within their respective villages, abuse their power. . . . The uselessness of the goods is surpassed only by their poor quality. . . .

It shows the terror and unqualified loyalty of the subjects that they believe that these proceedings reflect the true order and wish of Your Majesty. When they are made to purchase the useless goods, the Indians generally say that they will obey the King who orders them to do so. But later, when their reason (of which they are not lacking) returns, they say: "Wouldn't it be better to double our annual tribute of eight *pesos*, which actually goes to the King, rather than pay the tyrannical official?" . . .

The unequal distribution of these goods, their lack of quality, and the class of people to whom they are given is the greatest of absurdities. When the official forces cloth of Castille and Quito, silks and brocades, thread, needles, and other useless goods upon the Spaniards and mestizos, it can at least be said that these are goods they can actually use. But when he gives these same goods to the Indians, who have absolutely no possibility of using them, it is an abominable act of reckless cruelty. Since their typical garment is a loincloth, with neither shirt nor socks, what use could possibly be served by velvets, chambrays, or the tons of women's stockings to people who do not even use shoes, belts, penknives, or buttons?

Are these goods supposed to be for their consumption? They are certainly no recompense for their work and forced labor on the land. . . .

4. EXPLOITATION AND CORRUPTION:
THE VIEW FROM BELOW[4]

The following document describes the same activities of local royal officials, but from a different perspective. Written by a relatively high-ranking Spanish priest, it supposedly relays in their own words the complaints that his Indian parishioners made to him about the repartimientos.

Father, the royal officials have treated us with such rigor and inhumanity that, after repeatedly forcing us to purchase goods that are totally useless to us, they do not even permit us respite. Consequently, our properties are neglected and their productions are reduced; yet it is these productions which provide subsistence for our families. [The official] sells his goods at very inflated prices. . . . If he does not make enough profit to cover the expenses of his opulence, he punishes us with cruel lashes, even those of us who are governors or chiefs. . . . He throws us into prison and oppresses us with dungeons. . . . He treats us as the most vile serfs and enemies.

The tax collectors employ all rigorous means imaginable to raise revenue. The landlords, for whom we work, could defend us. But instead, they are indifferent to our travails. Far from helping us, they increase our suffering by the growing labor obligations they impose on us. . . . Many of the landlords imitate the officials and make us purchase useless goods. We feel very little difference between the one and the other. . . .

---

[4]"Letter to the King's Confessor from the Dean of the Church of La Paz" (1781), in Valcarel, *Coleccion Documental*, 426–427.

Although we know that this treatment is against the will of our Lord and King, whose royal piety has produced ordinances and documents in our favor, we cannot actually avail ourselves of the remedies they offer. If we go to the officials, they do not understand us because they are ignorant of our language. When we come with some complaint or request, even the most simple matter, they order that we put it in writing. Because of this, and other formalities we are forced to undergo, the cost of these procedures exceeds anything we might gain by them. Besides this, in the presence of the official, we fear the rigorous treatment he usually reserves for us. And even when we do not owe him any money, we are always afraid of appearing before him, precisely so as not to contract new debts. Because of all this, we are always denied justice.

If we appeal to our priests (some of whom favor us) to defend us, this has little effect because many do not understand our language. They consequently leave us to their subordinates who, either out of respect for royal officials or fear of landlords act neither as intermediaries nor as fathers and pastors. . . .

[At this point in the letter, the priest-writer switches to his own voice to offer a series of remedies.]

First, abolish the positions of those royal officials, whose very names are hated by the people, and put in their place judges who, having no personal or particular interest, care only about good government, the administration of justice, and the collection of royal tributes. Prohibit these judges, under the most rigorous penalties, from exercising all commercial activities. . . . Also, prohibit landlords from forcibly selling goods. Order the . . . mentioned judges to zealously execute these measures. End the outrages of the tithe collectors and other persons who take advantage of the miserable condition of the Indians. . . .

5. FIRST STIRRINGS OF REVOLUTION (1799)[5]

Despite the manifold grievances of Spanish Americans and even serious revolts such as those in the early 1780s, there was no movement for independence in Spanish America. Many certainly wanted reforms, but only within the framework of the Spanish monarchy. After the outbreak of the French Revolution in 1789, that began to change. Spanish Americans inspired by the French example began to consider breaking with the mother country and claiming sovereignty for themselves. One of these was Juan Pablo Viscardo y Guzman, a former Jesuit priest whose radical ideas led to his expulsion from the Spanish dominions. Inspired by the French Revolution, he wrote his Letter to the Spanish Americans in 1791 while living as an exile in London. It was disseminated widely in Spanish America and was translated into English and French.

---

[5]William Walton, *The Present State of the Spanish Colonies* (London: Longman, Hurst, Rees, Orme, and Brown, 1810), vol. 2, 341–344.

[The Spanish government] is accustomed to consider our property as an estate which belongs to it. All its study consists in increasing its [power and wealth] at our expense, in always giving the colour of utility to the *mother country*, to the infamous sacrifice of all our rights and of our dearest interests. This logic is that of the highwayman; it justifies the usurpation of the goods of another by the utility which arises from them to the usurper.

The expulsion and ruin of the Jesuits had, according to every appearance, no other motives than the report of their riches: the latter being exhausted, the government, without pity for the disastrous situation to which it has reduced us, wished to aggravate it still further by its new imposts, particularly in South America where, in 1780, it cost Peru so much blood. We should groan still under this this new oppression, if the first sparks of an indignation too long repressed, had not forced our tyrants to desist from their extortions.[6] *Generous Americans of the new kingdom of Grenada!* If Spanish America owes you the noble example of intrepidity, which ought always to be opposed to tyranny, and the new lustre added to its glory, it is in the annals of humanity that we shall see engraven in immortal characters, that your arms protected our countrymen, the poor Indians, and that your deputies stipulated for their interests with the same successful zeal as for your own. . . .

The ministry is far from renouncing its projects of swallowing up the miserable remains of our property; but disconcerted by the unexpected resistance which it experienced . . . , it has changed the means of arriving at its aim, and adopting, when least expected, a system contrary to that which its mistrustful policy had invariably observed, it has resolved to furnish arms to the Spanish Americans, to instruct them in military discipline; it hopes, without doubt, to obtain from the regular American troops, the same assistance which it finds in the bayonets of Spain, to enforce obedience; but thanks to heaven, the corruption of the principles of humanity and of morality is not arrived at its full measure amongst us; never shall we become the barbarous instruments of tyranny, and sooner than stain ourselves with the least drop of the blood of our harmless brothers, we will shed all our own, in defence of our rights and of our common interests.

A powerful navy ready to convey to us all the horrors of destruction, is the other means which our past resistance suggests to tyranny; *this is the necessary support of government, and of the preservation of the Indies*: it is ordained by the decree of the 8th of July, 1787, that the *rents of the Indies (the article of tobacco excepted) prepare funds sufficient for defraying the half or the third of the enormous expenses which the royal navy requires.*

Our settlements on the continent of the New World, even in their state of infancy, and when the power of Spain was in its greatest decline, have always been sheltered from every hostile invasion; and our strength being now much more considerable, it is clear that the increase of the land and sea forces is, in respect to us, an expense as enormous as useless to our defence; thus this formal declaration,

---

[6]A reference to the Comunero Revolt.

announced with so much candour, seems only to indicate that the paternal vigilance of the government for our prosperity, of which to this moment it has afforded us the sweets, intends to give us new proofs of its zeal and its attachment. In consulting the ideas of justice, which one may suppose to belong to every government, we would be tempted to believe, that the funds which we ought to furnish for defraying the enormous expenses of the royal navy, are destined to protect our commerce and to multiply our riches, so that our ports, like those of Spain, are to be free to all nations; and that we shall be at liberty ourselves to visit the most distant regions, there to sell and buy at the first hand: then our treasures will no more issue forth like torrents never to return, but circulating amongst ourselves, they will perpetually increase by industry. . . .

What would Spain and her government say, if we should seriously insist upon the execution of this fine system?

II. France

Like Spain, France was on the losing side in the Seven Years' War. If anything, its sense of decline was even sharper than that of its ally. In part, this was because its fall had been more precipitous. In the late seventeenth century, its ruler, the "Sun King" Louis XIV had made all of Europe tremble. Now after 1763, France found itself humiliated on the European continent and forced to cede its largest colony, Canada, to Britain. Its other vast North American colony, Louisiana, only escaped the same fate because it had been secretly transferred to Spain a few years earlier. More than any other country after the Seven Years' War, France suffered from a deep feeling of national humiliation that would fuel decades of soul-searching, innovative reform, and, in 1789, the Revolution itself.

Unlike Spain, France was a rich, populous, and economically vibrant European country. Although France was able to retain several Caribbean colonies after 1763 (one of which, Saint-Domingue, was on the point of explosive economic growth that would make it the envy of the other European powers), it was primarily a continental power, and it was at home in Europe that its real strength lay. Consequently, its efforts to raise money after 1763 focused on taxation within European France itself. Nonetheless, like the other Atlantic powers, France also took steps to make the colonies contribute.

6. TAXING SAINT-DOMINGUE (1763–1764)[7]

As France's most valuable remaining colonial possession after the debacle of the Seven Years' War, Saint-Domingue was an obvious target for the revenue-hungry French state. In August 1763, France attempted to impose unprecedented new taxes

---

[7]Moreau de Saint-Méry, *Loix et Constitutions de la Partie Françoise de Saint-Domingue* (Paris: Quillau, 1766–1779), vol. 4, 616–617, 644–656. My thanks to Professor John Garrigus for kindly providing this document.

on the colony. The royal government encountered resistance but was able to defuse it through concessions (excusing the colonists from militia service). But once it had secured the colony's assent to the new taxes, it promptly revoked the concessions. Henceforth, Saint-Domingue would have to pay and serve. The following documents recount this process. The first is the formal royal request for a new tax.

"Royal Memoir Requesting a Grant of Four Million" (August 15, 1763)

The diverse events that have occurred in the French colonies of America during the last war, having revealed how little capable they are of resisting and defending themselves, His Majesty has, immediately upon the return of peace, decided, on the one hand, to remedy the vices of their constitutions and, on the other, to make new arrangements to provide them with all possible means of augmenting their agriculture during peacetime and with sufficient forces to be defended in wartime.

His Majesty has had in view principally his Colony of Saint-Domingue, the richest and most important of his possessions. Despite the exhaustion of his finances, he has made the greatest efforts to keep it, and it is only by excessive expenditures that he has succeeded in doing so. The risks that this Colony ran during the last war have made palpable the need to have fortifications in the interior where, in case of need, all the forces can be concentrated, thus taking from the enemy all hope of maintaining himself in this Colony, even after a landing which would be difficult to prevent, given the considerable extent of its coastline.

First, His Majesty designated a certain number of Battalions of French troops, with artillery brigades and engineers, whose proven and recognized talents guarantee both that there will be enough troops to defend Saint-Domingue and that the fortifications to be built there will be well laid out and that the expense of them will not be wasted.

Struck by the need to carry out these arrangements without delay, His Majesty did not even consider the situation of his finances; he began by sending to Saint-Domingue the greatest part of troops, with artillery and engineering officers, and he gave the most precise orders to accomplish the totality of these objects within the year. But His Majesty's precautions would have been in vain, had not he found in the Colony itself some of the resources he requires to meet all these expenses.

The tariffs established at Saint-Domingue are not sufficient to fulfill all these objects; to execute them with all the speed they demand, it is necessary to augment proportionally the quantity of tariffs imposed at Saint-Domingue and to augment their sum to four millions in Saint-Domingue money. However, His Majesty did not want to order this tax in the same manner as in the Windward Isles; he leaves to the Superior Councils of Saint-Domingue the responsibility of determining the augmentations which must be made to raise the four millions that are necessary. . . .

[To approve the request, the two superior councils of the colony were brought together in an extraordinary joint assembly at Le Cap in January 1764. De Montreuil, the governor of the colony, opened the meeting by presenting the royal request.]

De Montreuil, Commander-General: "The King, leaving you the responsibility for determining the augmentations to be imposed on this Colony, is giving you clear proof of his confidence in your justice. I am fully persuaded that you will comply with the intentions of His Majesty with so much eagerness that I will be able to tell him of your zeal and attachment. . . ."

The Intendant: "The attention the King gave to the defense of this Colony during the recent war provides touching proof of his paternal love for his most distant subjects."

"At a time when there was hardly enough to pay for the war in Europe, the most powerful aid, the most experienced Generals were sent to protect and defend us."

"The Metropole made the greatest efforts in our favor, and the enormous expenses that resulted have not diminished the care of the Minister who governs us; through his great foresight and the wisdom of his measures, the Treasuries of France made up for the exhaustion and inadequacy of our own."

"By restoring tranquility and reviving circulation, Agriculture, and Commerce, the return of peace has made His Majesty think it important to take further steps to ensure the conservation and defense of his possessions on this Island, and that, to do so, it was indispensable to raise taxes to the sum of four million pounds per year."

"This is the object of the Memoir we are presenting to you. If, on the one hand, pressing circumstances have forced the best of Kings to ask for new help from his Subjects, on the other, his goodness, by respecting the privileges of the Colonists, entrusts the distribution [of the new tax burden] to the two Superior Courts which represent the Body of Inhabitants. He knows the scope of your knowledge, your zeal (as tireless as disinterested), your love for his person, your ardor for the public good, and he charges you today with the important task of reconciling the needs of his service with those of his People; to raise their taxes, it is true, but to make them less burdensome by a prudent and wise distribution."

"He has already taken the most suitable measures to ensure the happiness of his Subjects of Saint-Domingue and provide them with what concessions he could, whether by establishing the Bureau of Legislation, whether replacing the arbitrary power which previously reigned with the sweetness and justice of municipal administration, whether by returning to the Inhabitants their legitimate liberty by the suppression of the Militia, this difficult burden which, under pretext of the service, has been the source of so many evils. There are no functions more noble or interesting than those entrusted to this august Assembly. The manner in which it fulfills them will ensure it the increasing protection of its Sovereign [and] the love, confidence, and veneration of its fellow Citizens."

[The formal royal request was then read to the Assembly.]

Desmé Dubuisson, Chief Administrator in the Superior Council of Le Cap: "By announcing the unfortunate but necessary responsibility you have to carry out, the spectacle of the reunion of the two Superior Councils must also recall the flattering privilege that our ancestors earned by giving themselves to France, the right of taxing themselves; a right precious not only because of the cause that produced it, but also because of the usefulness that must result from it. Placed between the Prince and his subjects, you have two equally important functions to fulfill. As Sovereign Courts and in virtue of the fundamental Law, by which all imposition must be verified before its collection, you have to register the Royal Memoir, which regulates the quantity of taxes. As the Body representing the Inhabitants, you have, according to the constitution of the Colony, to distribute the sum required by the Sovereign. You will reconcile what you owe to both King and Colony; or rather, since the interests of the Monarch and his Subjects can never be divided, since they are always one, you will accomplish everything by consulting the good of the State."

"It is a principle that public needs are the measure of taxes; and although the augmentation of taxes is unfortunate, it is just to pay them when they have become necessary. We cannot refuse the extraordinary expenses that the number of Troops sent to the Colony has entailed. Taxes must increase in the same proportion; but however great these charges, there is always a sure means of making them less heavy, whether by the objects on which they bear or by the type of tax we establish. This Colony has the singular advantage that you are directed to carry out their distribution. And, what is more, by determining only the sum to be raised, His Majesty appears to be leaving you the liberty to look back over past operations, to examine if they might not have some drawbacks, [to see] if there might not be ways of rendering them more equal or even of substituting other, less onerous [taxes]...."

"What a great reason to be satisfied. What a great consolation and encouragement to the Colonists ... to see that His Majesty seems to unite and link the augmentation of taxes which is being demanded from you, the suppression of the Militia, and the confirmation of the exemption from extraordinary labor service! You know the enormous weight of personal service and extraordinary labor. Experience has shown that these are two of the most redoubtable plagues and that, by their nature, they are not only insurmountable obstacles to the growth of agriculture and population, but also principles destructive to the interior of the Colony. We cannot rejoice too much at the benefit of their suppression; we should thus purchase them with joy. While the King restores the Slaves to agriculture and frees the Masters from the yoke of the Militia, you will hasten to furnish him with the means of forever renouncing these violent contributions, just as useless for his service as ruinous for the Colony."

[On February 4, 1764, the assemblies approved the request, on the condition that they be "perpetually exempted from personal service," from providing the state with the "forced labor service of Negroes," and also from all requisitions of horses, cattle, and carts. Negotiations between the assembly and the royal administrators ensued over exactly which exemptions would be granted in exchange for approving the new tax. As part of the bargaining process (to put pressure on the royal administration), the assembly issued a remonstration to the King. The following are its main articles.]

1. The size of the tax of four millions, a crushing sum at the end of a long and ruinous war, in the course of which the People of this Colony ceaselessly made efforts which exhausted their forces and made them lose almost all the net product of their revenues. [Moreover, the new tax would be] impossible to collect in time of future wars which may occur . . . [and] finally harmful, even during the most sustained period of peace, to the commerce of the Metropole with the Colony both in terms of the enormous debt contracted by the Colony vis-à-vis Commerce, and the immensity of its daily consumption. . . .

2. The necessity in which the Assembly finds itself, given these initial considerations, of ordering the collection of the tax of four millions only provisionally for five years, during which period His Majesty will be convinced of the indispensable necessity . . . of ordering the reduction of the least urgent expenditures, to be able to diminish the amount of the tax. . . .

[In the end, the colony agreed to pay the new tax, and, in return, the royal government agreed to abolish militia service. The Crown, however, reneged on its promise. Militia units, composed largely of free people of color, served heroically in North America during the War of Independence, notably at the Battle of Savannah (1779).]

III. Great Britain

Great Britain was the great victor of the Seven Years' War. The war was a decisive turning point, the culmination of nearly a century of warfare for the dominant position within the Atlantic world. Although its rivals would rearm and get a measure of revenge with the American Revolution, Great Britain in 1763 found itself poised for global hegemony—something it achieved after the definitive defeat of France in 1815. Yet victory came with a high price and challenges of its own. Britain's conquest of French Canada and the Ohio Valley saddled it with the problem of ruling a vast territory peopled by Catholics and Indians. The white, often militantly Protestant, inhabitants of the Britain's thirteen colonies on the Atlantic seaboard coveted the Indians' lands and viewed the Catholics of former French Canada with deep distrust. Managing these tensions caused the British government many headaches after 1763, but even more daunting was the problem of financing the debt that had been incurred during the conflict. Unlike the French state, which had always relied on a domestic land tax to finance itself, Great Britain chose to spare the land and instead draw its revenue from excise taxes and tariffs on colonial trade. After 1763, the British government sought to extend these charges to its Atlantic colonies. In this volume, chapters 3 and 4, on the American Revolution, provide documents illustrating how this policy was received in the thirteen North American colonies. But Great Britain's attempt to raise new revenue from its colonies after 1763 was more than just a North American story. Affecting all British overseas possessions, the postwar drive for new revenue sparked opposition across the entire British Atlantic world.

7. ROYAL PROCLAMATION ON THE WESTERN TERRITORIES (OCTOBER 7, 1763)[8]

The British government worried that the movement of white colonists from the thirteen colonies into the interior lands conquered from France would cause trouble between the newcomers and the Indian inhabitants. Violence had already occurred; and the British government was afraid that if it did not restrict further contact, more serious fighting would break out. To prevent colonists from the Eastern Seaboard from moving onto Indian lands, the British government issued a royal proclamation prohibiting them from entering the interior. This measure was unpopular among certain sectors of the colonial population, especially land speculators.

Whereas We have taken into Our Royal Consideration the extensive and valuable Acquisitions in America, secured to our Crown by the late Definitive Treaty of Peace, concluded at Paris the 10th Day of February last; and being desirous that all Our loving Subjects, as well of our Kingdom as of our Colonies in America, may avail themselves with all convenient Speed, of the great Benefits and Advantages which must accrue therefrom to their Commerce, Manufactures, and Navigation, We have thought fit, with the Advice of our Privy Council. to issue this our Royal Proclamation. . . .

And whereas it is just and reasonable, and essential to our Interest, and the Security of our Colonies, that the several Nations or Tribes of Indians with whom We are connected, and who live under our Protection, should not be molested or disturbed in the Possession of such Parts of Our Dominions and Territories as, not having been ceded to or purchased by Us, are reserved to them or any of them, as their Hunting Grounds. We do therefore, with the Advice of our Privy Council, declare it to be our Royal Will and Pleasure, that no Governor or Commander in Chief in any of our Colonies of Quebec, East Florida. or West Florida, do presume, upon any Pretence whatever, to grant Warrants of Survey, or pass any Patents for Lands beyond the Bounds of their respective Governments, as described in their Commissions: as also that no Governor or Commander in Chief in any of our other Colonies or Plantations in America do presume for the present, and until our further Pleasure be known, to grant Warrants of Survey, or pass Patents for any Lands beyond the Heads or Sources of any of the Rivers which fall into the Atlantic Ocean from the West and North West, or upon any Lands whatever, which, not having been ceded to or purchased by Us as aforesaid, are reserved to the said Indians, or any of them. . . .

And We do hereby strictly forbid, on Pain of our Displeasure, all our loving Subjects from making any Purchases or Settlements whatever, or taking Possession of any of the Lands above reserved, without our especial leave and Licence for that Purpose first obtained.

---

[8]*The London Gazette*, no. 10354 (October 4, 1763).

And We do further strictly enjoyn and require all Persons whatever who have either willfully or inadvertently seated themselves upon any Lands within the Countries above described or upon any other Lands which, not having been ceded to or purchased by Us, are still reserved to the said Indians as aforesaid, forthwith to remove themselves from such Settlements.

And whereas great Frauds and Abuses have been committed in purchasing Lands of the Indians, to the great Prejudice of our Interests. and to the great Dissatisfaction of the said Indians; In order, therefore, to prevent such Irregularities for the future, and to the end that the Indians may be convinced of our Justice and determined Resolution to remove all reasonable Cause of Discontent, We do, with the Advice of our Privy Council, strictly enjoin and require that no private Person do presume to make any purchase from the said Indians of any Lands reserved to the said Indians within those parts of our Colonies where We have thought proper to allow Settlement; but that if at any Time any of the Said Indians should be inclined to dispose of the said Lands, the same shall be Purchased only for Us, in our Name, at some public Meeting or Assembly of the said Indians, to be held for that Purpose by the Governor or Commander in Chief of our Colony respectively within which they shall lie.

8. GRIEVANCES OF WESTERN SETTLERS[9]

Would-be settlers viewed the policies of the British government toward the newly acquired western lands with dismay. They believed that they unfairly favored the Indians and betrayed underlying government hostility toward them. This is a 1764 protest from settlers seeking to move into western Pennsylvania.

Inasmuch as the killing those Indians at Conestogoe Manor and Lancaster has been, and may be, the subject of much Conversation, and by invidious Representations of it, which some, we doubt not, will industriously spread, many unacquainted with the true state of Affairs may be led to pass a Severe Censure on the Authors of those Facts, and any others of the like nature, which may hereafter happen, than think it, therefore, proper thus openly to declare ourselves, and render some brief hints of the reasons of our Conduct, which we must, and frankly do, confess nothing but necessity itself could induce us to, or justify us in, as it bears an appearance of flying in the face of Authority, and is attended with much labour, fatigue and expence.

Ourselves, then, to a Man, we profess to be loyal Subjects to the best of Kings, our rightful Sovereign George the third, firmly attached to his Royal Person,

---

[9]"Declaration of the injured Frontier Inhabitants, of Western Pennsylvania, Together with a brief sketch of grievances the good Inhabitants of the Province labour under" (February 1764), from *Minutes of the Provincial Council of Pennsylvania* (Harrisburg, PA: Theo. Fenn & Co., 1852), vol. 9, 142–145.

Interest, and Government, & of consequence, equally opposite to the Enemies of His Throne & Dignity, whether openly avowed or more dangerously concealed under a mask of falsely pretended Friendship, and chearfully willing to offer our Substance & Lives in his Cause.

These Indians, known to be firmly connected in Friendship with our openly avowed embittered Enemies, and some of whom have, by several Oaths, been proved to be murderers, and who, by their better acquaintance with the Situation and State of our Frontier, were more capable of doing us mischief, we saw, with indignation, cherished and caressed as dearest Friends; But this, alas! is but a part, a small part, of the excessive regard manifested to Indians, beyond His Majesty's loyal Subjects, whereof we complain, and which, together with various other Grievances, have not only enflamed with resentment the Breast of a number, and urged them to the disagreeable Evidence of it they have been constrained to give, but have heavily displeased by far the greatest part of the good Inhabitants of this Province.

Should we here reflect to former Treaties, the exorbitant presents and great Servility therein paid to Indians, have long been oppressive Grievances we have groaned under; and when at the last Indian Treaty held at Lancaster, not only was the Blood of our many murdered Brethren tamely covered, but our poor unhappy captivated Friends abandoned to slavery among the savages, by concluding a Friendship with the Indians, and allowing them a plenteous trade of all kinds of Commodities, without those being restored, or any properly spirited Requisition made of them; How general Dissatisfaction those Measures gave, the Murmurs of all good People (loud as they dare to utter them) to this day declare, and had here infatuated Steps of Conduct, and a manifest Partiality in favour of Indians, made final pause, happy had it been; We perhaps had grieved in silence for our abandoned, enslaved Brethren among the Heathen; but matters of a later Date are still more flagrant Reasons of Complaint. When last Summer His Majesty's Forces under Command of Colonel Bouquet, marched through this Province, and a demand was made by His Excellency General Amherst, of Assistance to escort Provisions, & ca., to relieve that important Post Fort Pitt, yet not one man was granted, although never any thing appeared more reasonable or necessary, as the interest of the Province lay so much at stake, and the standing of the Frontier Settlements, in any manner, evidently depended, under God, on the almost despaired of success of His Majesty's little Army, whose Valour the whole Frontiers with gratitude acknowledge, and as the happy means of having saved from ruin great part of the Province; But when a number of Indians, falsely pretended Friends, and having among them some proved on Oath to have been guilty of Murder since this War begun, when they, together with others, known to be His Majesty's Enemies, and who had been in the Battle against Col. Bouquet, reduced to Distress by the Destruction of their Corn at the Great Island, and up the East branch of Susquehanna, pretend themselves Friends, and desire a Subsistance, they are openly caressed, & the Publick that could not be indulged the liberty of contributing to His Majesty's assistance, obliged, as Tributaries to Savages, to support these Villains, these Enemies to our King & our Country; nor only so, but the hands that were closely shut, nor would grant His Majesty's General a single Farthing against a Savage Foe, have been liberally opened, and the Publick money basely prostituted to hire, at an exorbitant Rate, a mercenary Guard to protect His Majesty's worst Enemies, those falsely pretended Indian friends, while, at the same time, Hundreds of poor distressed Families of His Majesty's Subjects, obliged to abandon their possessions & fly for their lives at least, are left, except a small Relief at first, in the most distressing Circumstances, to starve neglected, save what the friendly hand of private Donations has contributed to their support, wherein they who are most profuse towards Savages, have carefully avoided having any part. When last Summer the Troops raised for Defence of the Province were limited to certain Bounds, nor suffered to attempt annoying our enemies in their Habitations, and a number of brave Volunteers, equipped at their own Expence in September, up the Susquehanna, met and defeated their Enemy, with the loss of some of their number and having others dangerously wounded, not the least thanks or acknowledgement was made them from the Legislature for the confessed Service they had done, nor only the least notice or Care taken of their wounded; Whereas when a Seneca, who, by the Information of many, as well as by his own Confession, had been, through the last War, our inveterate Enemy, had got a cut in his Head, last Summer, in a quarrel he had with his own Cousin, & it was reported in Philadelphia that his Wound was dangerous, a Doctor was immediately employed and sent to Fort Augusta to take care of him, and cure him if possible. To these may be added, that though it was impossible to obtain, through the Summer, or even yet, any Premium for Indian Scalps, or encouragement to excite Volunteers to go forth against them; yet when a few of them known to be the fast friends of our Enemies, and some of them murderers themselves, when these have been struck by a distressed, bereft, injured Frontier, a liberal reward is offered for apprehending the Perpetrators of that horrible Crime of Killing his Majesty's Cloaked Enemies, and their Conduct painted in the most atrocious Colours, while the horrid Ravages, cruel murders, and most shocking Barbarities, committed by Indians on his Majesty's Subjects, are covered over, and excused, under the charitable Term of this being their method of making war. But to recount the many repeated Grievances, whereof we might justly complain, and instances of a most violent attachment to Indians, were tedious beyond the patience of a Job to endure. . . .

9. REACTION TO THE QUEBEC ACT (1775)[10]

Former French Canada (known as Quebec) counted about 80,000 white Catholic inhabitants when it was ceded to Britain in 1763. Because the public practice of Catholicism was illegal in Great Britain and because British Catholics faced official

---

[10]Harold G. Scott, ed., *The Papers of Alexander Hamilton*, vol. 1 (New York: Columbia University Press, 1961), 165–176.

discrimination, the annexation of an overwhelmingly Catholic North American colony posed a problem. In 1775, the British government adopted a flexible, pragmatic solution. It extended civil rights to French Canadian Catholics and permitted them to worship publicly and retain their existing ecclesiastical institutions. Many inhabitants of the thirteen colonies were appalled, seeing in these measures of toleration a plot to impose "Papist" despotism upon them. One of the most paranoid reactions sprang from the pen of Alexander Hamilton.

In compliance with my promise to the public, and in order to rescue truth from the specious disguise with which it has been clothed, I shall now offer a few remarks on the act entitled "An act for making more effectual provision for the government of the province of Quebec in North America"; whereby I trust it will clearly appear that arbitrary power and its great engine, the Popish religion, are, to all intents and purposes, established in that province. . . .

It is . . . provided: "That nothing contained in the act, shall extend, or be construed to extend, to prevent or hinder his Majesty, his heirs and successors, from erecting, constituting, and appointing, from time to time, such courts of criminal, civil, and ecclesiastical jurisdiction, within and for the said province of Quebec, and appointing, from time to time, judges and officers thereof, as his Majesty, his heirs and successors, shall think necessary for the circumstances of the said province."

Here a power of a most extraordinary and dangerous nature is conferred. There must be an end of all liberty where the prince is possessed of such an exorbitant prerogative as enables him, at pleasure, to establish the most iniquitous, cruel, and oppressive courts of criminal, civil, and ecclesiastical jurisdiction; and to appoint temporary judges and officers, whom he can displace and change as often as he pleases. For what can more nearly concern the safety and happiness of subjects, than the wise economy, and equitable constitution of those courts in which trials for life, liberty, property, and religions are to be conducted? Should it ever comport with the designs of an ambitious and wicked minister, we may see an Inquisition erected in Canada, and priestly tyranny hereafter find as propitious a soil in America as it ever has in Spain or Portugal. . . .

Having considered the nature of this bill with regard to civil government, I am next to examine it with relation to religion, and to endeavor to show that the Church of Rome has now the sanction of a legal establishment in the province of Quebec.

In order to do this the more satisfactory I beg leave to adopt the definition given of an established religion by a certain writer who has taken great pains to evince the contrary. "An established religion," says he, "is a religion in which the civil authority engages not only to protect but to support." This act makes effectual provision not only for the protection but for the permanent support of Popery, as is evident from the following clause: "And for the more perfect security and ease of the minds of the inhabitants of the said province, it is hereby declared that his Majesty's subjects, professing the religions of the Church of Rome, in the said province, may have, hold, and enjoy the free exercise of the king's supremacy, etc., and that the clergy of the said Church may hold, receive, and enjoy their accustomed dues and rights," etc. . . .

"Tithes in Canada," it is said, "are the property of the Roman Church; and permitting a tolerated church to enjoy its own property, is far short of the idea of an establishment." But I should be glad to know, in the first place, how tithes can be the property of any but of an established church? And in the next, how they came to be the property of the Romish Church in Canada, during the intermediate space between the surrender of that province to the English and the passing of this act? Nothing can be deemed my property, to which I have not a perfect and uncontrollable right by the laws. If a church have not a similar right to tithes, it can have no property in them; and if it have, it is plain the laws must have made provision for its support, or, in other words, must have established it.

Previous to the surrender of Canada, the Catholic religion was established there by the laws of France; and tithes were, on that account, the legal property of the Church of Rome, and could not be withheld by the laity though ever so much disposed to do it. But after the surrender this circumstance took a different turn. The French laws being no longer in force, the establishment of the Romish Church ceased of course, and with it the property which it before had in tithes.

It is true that the clergy may have continued to receive and enjoy their customary dues, tithes, and other perquisites; but they were not for all that the property of the church, because it had lost its legal right to them, and it was at the discretion of the laity to withhold them, and place them upon a more moderate footing. Their voluntary concurrence was necessary to give their priests a right to demand them as before. But by the late act this matter is again put into its former situation. Tithes are now become the *property* of the church as formerly, because it again has a legal claim to them, and the conditional consent of the people is set aside. Thus we see that this act does not, in fact, permit a tolerated church to enjoy "its own property," but gives it a real and legal property in that which it before held from the bounty and liberality of its professors, and which they might withhold or diminish at pleasure; and this, in the most proper sense, converts it into an establishment. . . .

As to the Protestant religion, it is often asserted that ample provision has been made by the act for its future establishment; to prove which the writer before mentioned has quoted a clause in the following mutilated manner: "It is provided," says he, "that his Majesty, his heirs or successors, may make such provision out of the accustomed dues, or rights, for the encouragement of the Protestant clergy within the said province, as he or they shall, from time to time, think necessary and expedient."

It must excite a mixture of anger and disdain to observe the wretched arts to which a designing administration and its abettors are driven in order to conceal the enormity of their measures. This whole clause, in its true and original construction, is destitute of meaning; and was evidently inserted for no other end than to *deceive* by the *appearance* of a provident regard for the Protestant religion.

The act first declares: "That his Majesty's subjects professing the religious of the Church of Rome may have and enjoy the free exercise of their religion; and that the clergy of the said church may hold, receive, and enjoy their accustomed dues and rights." Then follows this clause: "Provided, nevertheless, that it shall be lawful for his Majesty, his heirs and successors, to make such provision, out of the rest of the said accustomed dues and rights, for the encouragement of the Protestant religion, for the maintenance and support of a Protestant clergy within the said province, as he or they shall, from time to time, think necessary and expedient."

Thus we see the Romish clergy are to have, hold, and enjoy their accustomed dues and rights, and the *rest* and remainder of them is to be applied toward the encouragement of the Protestant religion; but when they had their wonted dues, I fancy it will puzzle the administration, by any effort of political chemistry, to produce the *rest*, or remainder. . . . The Romish priests are to have their accustomed dues and rights; and the *rest* of the said dues and rights is to be dedicated to the encouragement of the Protestant religion. In the above-recited quotation there is a chasm, the words "the *rest* of" being artfully omitted, to give the passage some meaning which it has not in itself. With this amendment, the sense must be that his Majesty might appropriate what portion of the customary revenues of the Romish clergy he should think proper to the support and maintenance of Protestant churches. But, according to the real words of the act, he can only devote "the rest," or remainder, of such revenues to that purpose, which, as I have already shown, is nothing. So that the seeming provision in favor of the Protestant religion is entirely verbal and delusory. . . .

I imagine it will clearly appear, from what has been offered, that the Roman Catholic religion, instead of being tolerated, as stipulated by the treaty of peace, is established by the late act, and that the Protestant religion has been left entirely destitute and unbefriended in Canada. . . .

This act develops the dark designs of the ministry more fully than any thing they have done, and shows that they have formed a systematic project of absolute power.

The present policy of it is evidently this: By giving a legal sanction to the accustomed dues of the priests, it was intended to interest them in behalf of the administration; and by means of the dominion they possessed over the minds of the laity, together with the appearance of good-will toward their religion, to prevent any dissatisfaction which might arise from the loss of their civil rights, and to propitiate them to the great purposes in contemplation—first, the subjugation of the colonies, and afterward that of Great Britain itself. . . .

What can speak in plainer language the corruption of the British Parliament that this act, which invest the king with absolute power over a little world (if I may be allowed the expression), and makes such ample provision for the Popish religion, and leaves the Protestant in such a dependent, disadvantageous situation, that he is like to have no other subjects in this part of his domain, than Roman Catholics, who, by reason of their implicit devotion to their priests, and the superlative reverence they bear those who countenance and favor their religion, will be ready, at all times, to second the oppressive designs of the administration against the other parts of the empire.

10. ADAM SMITH ON COLONIAL TAXATION (1776)[11]

Of even greater concern than the challenges of administering the vast new territories that had been acquired from France was the problem of paying the debts that had been incurred in doing so. After 1763, the government of Great Britain looked to the colonies to pay a greater share. The political economist, Adam Smith, provided it with justification.

In order to render any province advantageous to the empire to which it belongs, it ought to afford, in time of peace, a revenue to the public sufficient not only for defraying the whole expense of its own peace establishment, but for contributing its proportion to the support of the general government of the empire. Every province necessarily contributes, more or less, to increase the expense of that general government. If any particular province, therefore, does not contribute its share towards defraying this expense, an unequal burden must be thrown upon some other part of the empire. The extraordinary revenue, too, which every province affords to the public in time of war, ought, from parity of reason, to bear the same proportion to the extraordinary revenue of the whole empire which its ordinary revenue does in time of peace. That neither the ordinary or extraordinary revenue which Great Britain derives from her colonies, bears this proportion to the whole revenue of the British empire, will readily be allowed. The monopoly, it has been supposed, indeed, by increasing the private revenue of the people of Great Britain, and thereby enabling them to pay greater taxes, compensates the deficiency of the public revenue of the colonies. But this monopoly, I have endeavoured to show, though a very grievous tax upon the colonies, and though it may increase the revenue of a particular order of men in Great Britain, diminishes instead of increasing that of the great body of the people; and consequently diminishes instead of increasing the ability of the great body of the people to pay taxes. The men, too, whose revenue the monopoly increases, constitute a particular order, which it is both absolutely impossible to tax beyond the proportion of other orders, and extremely impolitic even to attempt to tax beyond that proportion, as I shall endeavour to show in the following book. No particular resource, therefore, can be drawn from this particular order.

The colonies may be taxed either by their own assemblies, or by the parliament of Great Britain.

That the colony assemblies can ever be so managed as to levy upon their constituents a public revenue sufficient not only to maintain at all times their own civil

---

[11]Adam Smith, *An Inquiry into the Nature and Causes of the Wealth of Nations*, 9th ed. (London: A. Strahan, 1799), vol. 2, 445–451.

and military establishment, but to pay their proper proportion of the expense of the general government of the British empire seems not very probable. It was a long time before even the parliament of England, though placed immediately under the eye of the sovereign, could be brought under such a system of management, or could be rendered sufficiently liberal in their grants for supporting the civil and military establishments even of their own country. It was only by distributing among the particular members of parliament a great part either of the offices, or of the disposal of the offices arising from this civil and military establishment, that such a system of management could be established even with regard to the parliament of England. But the distance of the colony assemblies from the eye of the sovereign, their number, their dispersed situation, and their various constitutions, would render it very difficult to manage them in the same manner, even though the sovereign had the same means of doing it; and those means are wanting. It would be absolutely impossible to distribute among all the leading members of all the colony assemblies such a share, either of the offices or of the disposal of the offices arising from the general government of the British empire, as to dispose them to give up their popularity at home, and to tax their constituents for the support of that general government, of which almost the whole emoluments were to be divided among people who were strangers to them. The unavoidable ignorance of administration, besides, concerning the relative importance of the different members of those different assemblies, the offences which must frequently be given, the blunders which must constantly be committed in attempting to manage them in this manner, seems to render such a system of management altogether impracticable with regard to them.

The colony assemblies, besides, cannot be supposed the proper judges of what is necessary for the defence and support of the whole empire. The care of that defence and support is not entrusted to them. It is not their business, and they have no regular means of information concerning it. The assembly of a province, like the vestry of a parish, may judge very properly concerning the affairs of its own particular district; but can have no proper means of judging concerning those of the whole empire. It cannot even judge properly concerning the proportion which its own province bears to the whole empire; or concerning the relative degree of its wealth and importance compared with the other provinces. . . . What is necessary for the defence and support of the whole empire, and in what proportion each part ought to contribute, can be judged of only by that assembly which inspects and superintends the affairs of the whole empire.

It has been proposed, accordingly, that the colonies should be taxed by requisition, the parliament of Great Britain determining the sum which each colony ought to pay, and the provincial assembly assessing and levying it in the way that suited best the circumstances of the province. What concerned the whole empire would in this way be determined by the assembly which inspects and superintends the affairs of the whole empire; and the provincial affairs of each colony might still be regulated by its own assembly. Though the colonies should in this case have no representatives in the British parliament, yet, if we may judge by experience, there is no probability that the parliamentary requisition would be unreasonable. The parliament of

England has not upon any occasion shown the smallest disposition to overburden those parts of the empire which are not represented in parliament. The islands of Guernsey and Jersey, without any means of resisting the authority of parliament, are more lightly taxed than any part of Great Britain. Parliament in attempting to exercise its supposed right, whether well or ill grounded, of taxing the colonies, has never hitherto demanded of them anything which even approached to a just proportion to what was paid by their fellow-subjects at home. If the contribution of the colonies, besides, was to rise or fall in proportion to the rise or fall of the land tax, parliament could not tax them without taxing at the same time its own constituents, and the colonies might in this case be considered as virtually represented in parliament.

Examples are not wanting of empires in which all the different provinces are not taxed, if I may be allowed the expression, in one mass; but in which the sovereign regulates the sum which each province ought to pay, and in some provinces assesses and levies it as he thinks proper; while in other, he leaves it to be assessed and levied as the respective states of each provinces shall determine. In some provinces of France, the king not only imposes what taxes he thinks proper, but assesses and levies them in the way he thinks proper. From others he demands a certain sum, but leaves it to the states of each province to assess and levy that sum as they think proper. According to the scheme of taxing by requisition, the parliament of Great Britain would stand nearly in the same situation towards the colony assemblies as the King of France does towards the states of those provinces which still enjoy the privilege of having states of their own, the provinces of France which are supposed to be the best governed.

But though, according to this scheme, the colonies could have no just reason to fear that their share of the public burdens should ever exceed the proper proportion to that of their fellow-citizens at home; Great Britain might have just reason to fear that it never would amount to that proper proportion. The parliament of Great Britain has not for some time past had the same established authority in the colonies, which the French king has in those provinces of France which still enjoy the privilege of having states of their own. The colony assemblies, if they were not very favourably disposed (and unless more skillfully managed than they ever have been hitherto, they are not very likely to be so) might still find many pretences for evading or rejecting the most reasonable requisitions of parliament. A French war breaks out, we shall suppose; ten millions must immediately be raised in order to defend the seat of the empire. This sum must be borrowed upon the credit of some parliamentary fund mortgaged for paying the interest. Part of this fund parliament proposes to raise by a tax to be levied in Great Britain, and part of it by a requisition to all the different colony assemblies of America and the West Indies. Would people readily advance their money upon the credit of a fund, which partly depended upon the good humour of all those assemblies, far distant from the seat of the war, and sometimes, perhaps, thinking themselves not much concerned in the event of it? Upon such a fund no more money would probably be advanced than what the tax to be levied in Great Britain might be supposed to answer for. The whole burden of the debt contracted on account of the war would in this manner fall, as it always has done hitherto, upon Great Britain; upon a part of the empire, and not upon the whole empire. Great Britain is, perhaps, since the world began, the only state which, as it has extended its empire, has only increased its expense without once augmenting its resources. Other states have generally disburdened themselves upon their subject and subordinate provinces of the most considerable part of the expense of defending the empire. Great Britain has hitherto suffered her subject and subordinate provinces to disburden themselves upon her of almost this whole expense. In order to put Great Britain upon a footing of equality with her own colonies, which the law has hitherto supposed to be subject and subordinate, it seems necessary, upon the scheme of taxing them by parliamentary requisition, that parliament should have some means of rendering its requisitions immediately effectual, in case the colony assemblies should attempt to evade or reject them; and what whose means are, it is not very easy to conceive, and it has not yet been explained.

11. A NEW COLONIAL ORDER (1764)[12]

A practical, administratively oriented guide to the new place of the colonies in the postwar empire was provided by Francis Bernard, the governor of Massachusetts.

1. THE Kingdom of *Great Britain* is *imperial;* that is, Sovereign, and not subordinate to or dependent upon any earthly power.
2. In all *imperial* states there resides somewhere or other an absolute power, which we will call the *Sovereignty.*
3. The *Sovereignty* of *Great Britain* is in the *King in Parliament;* that is, in the King, acting with the advice and consent of the *Lords* and the *Commons* (by their Representatives), assembled in the *Parliament* of *Great Britain.*
4. The *King in Parliament* has the sole right of legislation, and the supreme superintendency of the government; and in this plenitude of power, is absolute, uncontrollable, and accountable to none; and therefore, in a political sense, can do no wrong. . . .
9. The kingdom of *Great Britain* has, belonging to and depending upon it, divers external dominions and countries; all which, together with *Great Britain,* form the *British Empire.* Let, therefore, the *British Empire* signify the aggregate body of the *British* dominions, and the *Kingdom of Great Britain* the Island which is the seat of government.
10. The *King in Parliament,* is the sole and absolute Sovereign of the whole *British Empire.*
11. No members of the *British Empire,* other than the *Parliament* of *Great Britain,* can have a right to interfere in the exercise of this Sovereignty,

[12]Governor Francis Bernard, "Principles of Law and Polity, Applied to the Government of the British Colonies in America" (1764), in *Select Letters on the Trade and Government of America and the Principles of Law and Polity, Applied to the American Colonies* (London: T. Payne, 1774), 2nd ed., 71–85.

but by being admitted into the *Parliament,* as *Wales, Chester, and Durham,* have been, and *Ireland* may be.

12. Such an union is not necessary to the generality of the *British* external dominions; but it may be expedient with most of them.

13. The external *British* dominions, without such an union, are subordinate to and dependent upon the *Kingdom* of *Great Britain,* and must derive from thence all their powers of legislation and jurisdiction.

14. Legislation is not necessary to an external and dependent government; jurisdiction is necessary and essential to it. Therefore,

15. A separate legislation is not an absolute right of *British* subjects residing out of the seat of Empire. . . .

16. Where it is granted or allowed, it must be exercised in subordination to the Sovereign power from whom it is derived.

17. No grant of the power of Legislation to a dependent government, whether it comes from the *King* alone, or from the *Parliament,* can preclude the *Parliament* of *Great Britain* from interfering in such dependent government, at such time and in such manner as they shall think fit. . . .

29. The rule that a *British* subject shall not be bound by laws, or liable to taxes, but what he has consented to by his representatives, must be confined to the inhabitants of *Great Britain* only; and is not strictly true even there.

30. The *Parliament* of *Great Britain,* as well from its rights of *Sovereignty* as from occasional exigencies, has a right to make laws for, and impose taxes upon, its subjects in its external dominions, although they are not represented in such *Parliaments.* But.

31. Taxes imposed upon the external dominions ought to be applied to the use of the people, from whom they are raised. . . .

36. The Colonies ought, so far as they are able, to pay the charge of the support of their own Governments, and of their own defence.

37. The Defence of the *American* Colonies, being now almost wholly a sea service, is connected with the defence of trade. Therefore,

38. Duties upon imports and exports, make the most proper funds for the expenses of such defence. And

39. It being the proper business of the *Parliament* of *Great Britain,* to establish and determine the necessary regulations and restrictions of the trade of their external dominions; and the duties upon the *American* imports and exports being interwove with the regulations and restrictions of trade; the imposition of such Duties is the proper business of the *Parliament.* . . .

44. Although the right of the *Parliament* of *Great Britain,* to raise taxes in any part of the *British Empire,* is not to be disputed; yet it would be most advisable to leave the Provincial Legislature to determine the raising of internal taxes. . . .

59. The subjects of the *British Empire,* residing in its external dominions, are intitled to all the rights and privileges of *British* subjects, which they are capable of enjoying.

60. There are some rights and privileges which the *British* subjects, in the external dominions, are not equally capable of enjoying with those residing in *Great Britain.*

61. The right of having a share in the Imperial Legislature, is one of these incapacities in those external dominions, where a representation is impracticable.

62. A Representation of the *American* Colonies in the Imperial Legislature is not impracticable: and therefore,

63. The propriety of a Representation of the *American* Colonies, in the Imperial Legislature, must be determined by expediency only . . .

64. A Representation of the *American* Colonies, in the Imperial Legislation, is not necessary to establish the authority of the *Parliament* over the Colonies. But

65. It may be expedient for quieting disputes concerning such authority, and preventing a separation in future times.

66. The expediency of *American* Legislatures, does not arise from the want of their having Representatives in the Imperial Legislature.

67. If the *American* Colonies had Representatives in *Parliament,* still there would be an occasion for provincial Legislatures, for their domestic economy, and the support of their Governments. But

68. All external Legislatures must be subject to, and dependent on, the Imperial Legislature: otherwise there would be an *Empire* in an *Empire.* . . .

12. RESISTANCE: "THE NEW YORK PETITION TO THE HOUSE OF COMMONS" (1764)[13]

The British government's commitment to making the colonies pay a greater share of their expenditures provoked massive outcry. The thirteen colonies of North America were particularly outspoken in their resistance. The following document is a protest by the assembly of New York against new taxation and the implied change in the constitutional relationship between colony and metropole it implied.

From the year 1683, to this Day, there have been three Legislative Branches in this Colony; consisting of the Governor and Council appointed by the Crown, and the Representatives chosen by the People, who, besides the Power of making Laws for the Colony, have enjoyed the Right of Taxing the Subjects for the Support of the Government.

Under this political Frame, the Colony was settled by Protestant Emigrants from several Parts of *Europe,* and more especially from *Great-Britain* and *Ireland,* . . . The Planters, and Settlers conceived the strongest Hopes, that the Colony had gained a civil Constitution, which so far at least as the Rights and Privileges of the People were concerned, would remain permanent and be transmitted to their latest Posterity.

---

[13]"The New York Petition to the House of Commons," on the website America's Homepage, http://ahp.gatech.edu/ny_petition_1764.html.

It is therefore with equal Concern and Surprise, that they have received Intimations of certain Designs lately formed if possible, to induce the Parliament of *Great-Britain*, to impose Taxes upon the Subjects *here*, by Laws to be passed *there*; and as we who have the Honour to represent them, conceive that this Innovation, will greatly affect the Interest of the Crown and the Nation, and reduce the Colony to absolute Ruin; it became our indispensable Duty, to trouble you with a seasonable Representation of the Claim of our Constituents, to an Exemption from the Burthen of all Taxes not granted by themselves, and their Foresight of the tragical Consequences of an Adoption of the contrary Principle, to the Crown, the Mother Country, themselves and their Posterity.

Had the Freedom from all Taxes not granted by ourselves been enjoyed as a *Privilege*, we are confident the Wisdom and Justice of the *British* Parliament, would rather establish than destroy it, unless by our abuse of it, the Forfeiture was justly incurred; but his Majesty's Colony of *New-York*, can not only defy the whole World to impeach their Fidelity, but appeal to all the Records of their past Transactions, as well for the fullest Proof of their steady Affection to the Mother Country, as for their strenuous Efforts to support the Government, and advance the general Interest of the whole *British* Empire.

It has been their particular Misfortune, to be always most exposed to the Incursions of the *Canadians*, and the more barbarous Irruptions of the Savages of the Desert, as may appear by all the Maps of this Country; and in many ways Wars we have suffered an immense Loss both of Blood and Treasure, to repel the Foe, and maintain a valuable Dependency upon the *British* Crown.

On no Occasion can we be justly reproached for with-holding a necessary Supply, our Taxes have been equal to our Abilities, and confessed to be so by the Crown; for Proof of which we refer to the Speeches of our Governors in all Times of War; and though we remember with great Gratitude, that in those grand and united Struggles, which were lately directed for the Conquest of Canada, Part of our Expenses was reimbursed, yet we cannot suppress the Remark, that our Contribution surpassed our Strength, even in the Opinion of the Parliament, who under that Conviction, thought it but just to take off Part of the Burthen, to which we had loyally and voluntarily submitted: in a Word, if there is any Merit in Facilitating on all Occasions, the publick Measures in the remote Extremes of the national Dominion, and in preserving untainted Loyalty and cheerful Obedience, it is ours; and (with submission) unabused, nay more, well improved Privileges cannot, ought not, to be taken away from any People.

But an Exemption from the Burthen of ungranted, involuntary Taxes, must be the grand Principle of every free State. Without such a Right vested in themselves, exclusive of all others, there can be no Liberty, no Happiness, no Security; it is inseparable from the very Idea of Property, for who can call that his own, which may be taken away at the Pleasure of another? And so evidently does this appear to be the natural Right of Mankind, that even conquered tributary States, though subject to the Payment of a fixed periodical Tribute, never were reduced to so abject and forlorn a Condition, as to yield to all the Burthens which their Conquerors might at any future Time think fit to impose. The Tribute paid, the Debt was discharged; and the Remainder they could call their own.

And if conquered Vassals upon the Principle even of *natural Justice*, may claim a Freedom from Assessments unbounded and unassented to, without which they would sustain the Loss of every Thing, and Life itself become intolerable, with how much Propriety and Boldness may we proceed to inform the Commons of *Great-Britain*, who, to their distinguished Honour, have in all Ages asserted the Liberties of Mankind, that the People of this Colony inspired by the Genius of their Mother Country, nobly disdain the thought of claiming that Exemption as a *Privilege*. They found it on a Basis more honourable, solid and stable; they challenge it, and glory in it as their right. That Right their Ancestors enjoyed in *Great-Britain* and *Ireland*; their Descendants returning to those Kingdoms, enjoy it again: And that it may be exercised by his Majesty's Subjects at Home, and justly denied to those who submitted to Poverty, Barbarian Wars, Loss of Blood, Loss of Money, personal Fatigues, and the Thousand unutterable Hardships. To enlarge the Trade, Wealth, and Dominion of the Nation; or, to speak with the most unexceptionable Modesty, that when as *Subjects*, all have equal Merit; a Fatal, nay the most odious Discrimination should nevertheless be made between them, so Sophistry can recommend to the Sober, impartial Decision of common Sense.

Our Constituents exult in that glorious Model of Government, of which your Hon. House is so essential a Part; and earnestly pray the Almighty Governor of all, long to support the due Distribution of the Power of the Nation in the three great Legislative Branches. But the Advocates for divesting us of the Right to tax ourselves, would by the Success of their Machination; render the Devolution of all civil Power upon the *Crown alone*, a Government more favorable, and therefore more eligible to these *American* Dependences. The supreme Ruler in a Monarchy, even in a despotic Monarchy, will naturally consider his Relation to be, what it is, equal to all his good subjects: An equal Dispensation of Favours will be the natural Consequences of those Views; and the Increase of mutual Affection must be productive of an Increase of the Felicity of all. But no History can furnish an Instance of a Constitution to permit one Part of a Dominion to be taxed by another, and unequal Constitution should be adopted, who, that considers the natural Reluctance of Mankind to burthens, and their inclination to cast them upon the Shoulder of others, cannot foresee, that while the People on one Side of the *Atlantic*, enjoy an Exemption from the Load, those on the other, must submit to the most unsupportable Oppression and Tyranny.

Against these Evils, the Indulgence of the present Parliament, of which we have had such large Experience, cannot provide, if the grand Right to tax ourselves is invaded. Depressed by the Prospect of an endless Train of the most distressing Mischiefs, naturally attendants upon such an Innovation, his Majesty's *American* Subjects, will think it no inconsiderable Augmentation of the Misery, that the Measure itself implies the most severe and unmerited Censure, and is urged, as far as they are acquainted, by no good Reasons of State.

They are unconscious of any Conduct, that brings the least Imputation upon their Love and Loyalty, and whoever has accused them, has abused both the

Colonies and their Mother Country; more faithful Subjects his Majesty has not, in any Part of his Dominions, nor *Britain* more submissive and affectionate Sons.

And if our Contribution to the Support of the Government upon this Continent, or for the Maintenance of an Army, to awe and subdue the Savages should be thought necessary, why shall it be presumed, without a Trial, that we more than others, will refuse to hearken to a just Requisition from the Crown? To Requisitions for Aids salutary to our own Interests? Or why should a more incorrigible and unreasonable Spirit be imputed to us, Than to the Parliament of *Ireland*, or any other of his Majesty's Subjects?

Left to the Enjoyment of our antient Rights, the Government will be truly informed when a Tax is necessary, and of the Abilities of the People; and there will be an equitable Partition of the Burthen. And as the publick Charges will necessarily increase with the Increase of the Country, and the Augmentation or Reductions of the Force kept up, be regulated by the power and temper of our barbarian Enemy, the Necessity for continuing the present Model must appear to be most strongly inforced. –At the remote Distance of the *British* Commons from the sequestered Shades of the interior Parts of this Desert, False Intelligence of the State of the *Indians* may be given; whereas the Vicinity of the Colonies will enable them, not only, to detect all false Alarms, and check all the fraudulent Accounts, but urge them by the never failing Motive of Self-Preservation, to oppose any hostile Attempts upon their Borders.

Nor will the Candour of the Commons of *Great Britain*, construe our Earnestness to maintain this Plea, to arise from a Desire of Independency upon the supreme Power of the Parliament. Of so extravagant a Disregard to our own Interests we cannot be guilty. From what other Quarter can we hope for Protection? We reject the Thought with the utmost Abhorrence; and a perfect Knowledge of this Country will afford the fullest Proof, that nothing in our Temper can give the least Ground for such a Jealousy.

The peaceable and invariable Submission of the Colonies, for a Century past, forbids the Imputation, or proves it a Calumny. What can be more apparent, than that the State which exercises a Sovereignty in Commerce, can draw all the Wealth of its Colonies into its own Stock? And has not the whole Trade of *North-America*, that growing Magazine of Wealth, been from the Beginning, directed, restrained, and prohibited at the sole Pleasure of the Parliament? And whatever some may pretend, his Majesty's American Subjects are far from a Desire to invade the just Rights of *Great-Britain*, in all commercial Regulations. They humbly conceive, that a very manifest Distinction presents itself, which, while it leaves to the Mother Country an incontestable Power, to give Laws for the Advancement of her own Commerce, will, at the same Time, do no Violence to the Rights of the Plantations.

The Authority of the Parliament of *Great-Britain*, to model the Trade of the whole Empire, so as to subserve the Interest of her own, we are ready to recognize in the most extensive and positive Terms. Such a Preference is naturally founded upon her Superiority, and therefore, to assign one Instance, instead of many, the Colonies cannot, would not ask for a Licence to import woolen Manufactures from *France*; or to go into the most Lucrative Branches of Commerce, in the least Degree incompatible with the Trade and Interest of *Great-Britain*.

But a Freedom to drive all Kinds of Traffick in a Subordination to, and not inconsistent with, the *British* Trade; and an Exemption for all Duties in such a Course of Commerce, is humbly claimed by the Colonists from, and connected, in the common Bond of Liberty, with the uninslaved Sons of *Great-Britain.*

For, with Submission, since all Impositions, whether they be internal Taxes or Duties paid for what we consume, equally diminish the Estates upon which they are charged; what avails it to any People, by which of them they are impoverished? Every Thing will be given up to preserve Life; and though there is a Diversity in the Means, yet the whole Wealth of a Country may be as effectually drawn off, by the Exaction of Duties, as by any other Tax upon their Estates.

And therefore, the General Assembly of *New-York,* in Fidelity to their Constituents, cannot but express the most earnest Supplication, that the Parliament will charge our Commerce with no other Duties, than a necessary Regard to the particular Trade of *Great-Britain* evidently demands; but leave it to the legislative Power of the Colony, to impose all other Burthens upon it's own People, which the publick Exigences may require.

Latterly, the Laws of Trade seem to have been framed without an Attention to this fundamental Claim. . . .

The General Assembly of this Colony have no desire to derogate from the Power of the Parliament of *Great-Britain;* but they cannot avoid deprecating the Loss of such Rights as they have hitherto enjoyed, Rights established in the first Dawn of our Constitution, founded upon the most substantial Reasons, confirmed by invariable Usage, conducive to the best Ends; never abused to bad purposes, and with the loss, of Liberty, Property, and all the Benefits of Life tumble into Insecurity and Ruin: Rights: the Deprivation of which, will dispirit the People, abate their Industry, discourage Trade, introduce Discord, Poverty and Slavery; or by depopulating the Colonies, turn a vast fertile, prosperous Region, into a dreary Wilderness; impoverish *Great-Britain,* and shake the Power and Independency of the most opulent and flourishing Empire in the World. . . .

13. RESISTANCE: THE IRISH HOUSE OF COMMONS (DECEMBER 13, 1763)[14]

Less well known than North American resistance to the new imperial fiscal policy is the resistance of the other British colonies and possessions. The following document is a protest issued by the House of Commons of the Kingdom of Ireland against the heavy burden that had been placed on it during the recently concluded war. It resolved the following:

That an humble address be presented to His Majesty, to acknowledge with the utmost Gratitude, His Majesty's most gracious acceptance of our past Services.

---

[14]*The Journals of the House of Commons of the Kingdom of Ireland* (Dublin: Abraham Bradley, 1771), vol. 12, 741–743.

To assure His Majesty of our firm Resolution to pursue such Measures as shall tend most to promote the real Interest and Honour of the Crown. To express the general Satisfaction and Joy with which His Majesty's most gracious declarations . . . were received, "That by the Conclusion of a general Peace, we were at length relieved from those Burthens which were unavoidable during a war. That the situation of Publick Affairs would permit a very considerable diminution of the publick expence, that nothing was to be asked but the continuance of the supplies for the support of the ordinary establishments, and that His Majesty thanked us for our past efforts, without again having recourse to the experienced liberality of Parliament." That from these assurances, we drew the most flattering expectations of reducing the National debt, and relieving the impoverished people from the burthen of those taxes they were so little able to bear; but that these pleasing hopes were soon blasted by the unexpected requisition of supplies, to support a civil establishment, loaded with a long train of pensions, the amount of which, exclusive of the French and Military, exceeded the expence of all the other branches of the civil establishment. . . . That the number of officers upon the military establishment is increased, not only far beyond what it ever was in time of peace, but even beyond what it was in the time of the most dangerous war, and would under any reign by that of His Majesty, raise just apprehensions for the Constitution, not only of this Kingdom, but of Great Britain. . . . That from Principles of Duty and affection to His Majesty, we granted the supplies which were demanded from us in His Majesty's Name, for the support of these several establishments; however unsuitable to the Circumstances of the Kingdom, however insupportable to the People. But though the warmth of our zeal and affection for His Majesty induced us thus liberally to grant those supplies, our duty to him, and those we represent, will not permit us to conceal from His Majesty, or the Publick, the real State and Condition of this Kingdom. . . . The imports, exports, and home consumption of this kingdom are already taxed to the utmost they can bear. That any addition to these taxes, instead of increasing, must lessen the revenue. That nothing now remains to be taxed but our lands, which are already loaded with quit rents, crown rents, composition rents, and hearth money. That if the present establishments are to be continued, the debt of the nation must constantly increase, and in the end prove the utter ruin of the kingdom.

14. RESISTANCE: THE JAMAICAN HOUSE OF ASSEMBLY (1769–1783)[15]

Great Britain possessed a number of slave-based sugar colonies in the Caribbean. Although these faced the prospect of slave revolt or surprise attack by Spanish or French forces based on the neighboring islands (and thus required a strong British military presence to protect them), they too joined in the chorus of protest against the new

---

[15]British National Archives, Colonial Office, series 140, boxes 46 and 57.

imperial fiscal policies. Trouble started soon after the end of the Seven Years' War in a controversy over unprecedented requisitions the former wartime governor had made but refused to reimburse.

"Petition of the House of Assembly to the King" (September 21, 1769)

We, your majesty's most dutiful and loyal subjects, the assembly of Jamaica, with hearts full of the utmost gratitude to your majesty, for that royal and gracious attention which you have, at all times, been pleased to give to the welfare and security of our country, humbly beseech your majesty to believe, that as your subjects of this colony do not yield to those of any other part of your dominions, in a most dutiful attachment to your sacred person and government, so they will, at all times, readily comply with every requisition that shall be made to them, in your majesty's name, which shall be within the reach of their abilities, and consistent with their rights and privileges as free men and Britons; and that they would most cheerfully venture their lives and fortunes, in defence of your majesty's crown, to preserve it in your royal and illustrious family.

Your majesty's lieutenant-governor having, by your express commands, this session, signified to us your majesty's requisition that we should re-pay into the British treasury, a sum of money which was issued from thence, for the island subsistence of your majesty's troops upon this station, during the late intermission of assemblies; and your faithful assembly believing that this measure was advised by your majesty's ministers for want of proper information, and upon a presumption that the faith of our country stands engaged for the same, humbly beg leave, in this our address and representation, to state to your majesty, fully and fairly, the manner in which this money was obtained from the treasury, the use that was made of it by Mr. Lyttleton, our late governor, the nature of our engagements, and of the present requisition, and the reasons which restrain us from complying therewith.

It has appeared to us, by copies of three letters from Mr. Lyttleton, to the lords commissioners of trade and plantations, two of them dated about the month of October 1762, and the other in January 1763, that he had formed a scheme for altering the constitutional and established government of this colony; that he found an insuperable obstruction to it from the assemblies, and from the necessity that there would be for their annual meeting, so long as the troops were subsisted by them; that, in order to get rid of this obstruction, he solicited a privy seal, empowering him to draw upon the treasury of Great Britain for this purpose. . . .

After having solicited this power, and, in confidence of being supported, he sought an occasion of quarreling with the assembly, in 1764, and dissolved it; that assembly had, in the usual course, voted an ample provision for the troops, and actually passed a bill for subsisting one of the regiments, which also passed the council; but it was rejected by the governor, without any cause assigned by him, for such rejection.

The power with which he was thus intrusted by the treasury, was only conditional, in case the assembly did not provide for the troops; the assembly were willing to provide, and did provide, for the troops, but the governor refused the provision; and he never would suffer any assembly, which he afterwards called, to proceed to business, so that it could, not with justice, be imputed to the assembly, that the troops were not provided for; the governor, in soliciting for this power, promised to make no use of it but in case of necessity; there was absolutely no necessity but what he himself occasioned, by refusing the grants of that assembly, and by not suffering those which were afterwards called by him to do business, so that the money was drawn for upon the treasury, against the express condition upon which it was permitted.

The subsistence given by this colony, to such of your majesty's troops as have been stationed here, was, we believe, originally a voluntary grant from ourselves, made upon consideration of the dearness of provisions in this country, and the difficulty of their being able to subsist upon their English pay, and without any requisition from the crown, or previous stipulation on our parts; and it continued upon this footing until the year 1756, when the assembly addressed your royal grandfather, desiring a reinforcement of troops, and promising to make the same provision for them, as had been made for his majesty's 49th regiment; and we do very readily acknowledge, that the public faith of this country is staked and bound to your majesty, for making such provision for the troops here as was at that, or at any other time, provided; but we hope to make it appear to your majesty, that we have, on our parts, faithfully and constantly complied with our engagement, and we have, in many instances, very liberally exceeded.

The provision for subsisting the 49th regiment was always made here, in that regular and constitutional manner, which is observed in granting money to the crown, by every government within your majesty's British dominions; that is, by grants from the people made and appropriated by their representatives, at their annual meetings; and our engagements to your majesty's royal grandfather must have been so taken, and will not now be otherwise understood, by the best of kings.

Permit us to assure your majesty, that the assemblies of this colony have never refused to make the usual provision for the troops, but that the same was always regularly made, whenever we have been permitted so to do; that our late governor, William Henry Lyttleton, esquire, in pursuance of a very destructive scheme which he had formed against the liberties of our country, thought fit to refuse the grants of your people for this purpose, and to subsist the troops by money drawn (we presume to say without any justifiable necessity) from the treasury of Great Britain, and this, sir, is the money now required of us.

The sums raised annually in this colony, for subsisting the troops, and for providing for the other exigencies of your majesty's government, arise principally from a duty upon negroes imported, and from that upon spirituous liquors retailed; and, as these duties expired the 31st day of December 1764, and Mr. Lyttleton dissolved the assembly the 22nd day of December 1764, as has been already said, without suffering them to re-enact the said duties, or make the said provision, and as he never afterwards suffered an assembly to proceed to business so, from that time, till June 1766, when the present lieutenant-governor met his first assembly, these duties were lost to the public, to the amount of more than double the sum that is now required of us; insomuch that, to discharge the debts during that time incurred by the public, we were under the necessity of laying a heavy poll-tax, a tax never imposed but in cases of great emergency, and the effects of it are still felt by the people.

We beg leave most humbly to represent to your majesty, that in this colony we labour under many disadvantages, which our fellow subjects in Great Britain are not exposed to: One of the greatest of these is, that we are at such a distance from your majesty's presence, and by that means, as individuals, in many cases beyond the reach of your royal protection; and our condition would be desperate indeed, if governors could, with convenience to themselves, and with impunity, avoid calling assemblies annually, for it is only from frequent and regular meetings of their representatives, that your majesty's subjects here can hope for protection, or have any security in the time of an ill-designing governor, against every species of outrage and injustice, the assembly being the proper constitutional channel, through which the complaints of your people can, at such a time, be conveyed to your royal ear.

By virtue of the money issued from the British treasury, Mr. Lyttleton was at liberty to pay the troops in what mode he pleased, and he actually did pay them in a mode different from the appropriations for that purpose in the bill which he had rejected, and in a mode less favourable to the troops; and, by having it in his power to subsist the troops in this way, he was enabled to govern without assemblies; Were we to repay this money, it would, we apprehend, open to future governors, an easy method of encroaching upon the assembly's undoubted right of appropriation, and render the very calling of assemblies useless and unnecessary.

It is not, therefore, most gracious sovereign, from the narrow motive of resentment to Mr. Lyttleton, that we do not comply with your majesty's requisition, for that gentleman is now, thanks to your majesty's paternal interposition, removed from a station in which he was oppressing your people; nor is it from any want of attachment to your majesty's royal person and government; but it is because our compliance will establish a precedent which, by enabling future governors to encroach upon the privileges of assembly, and to render the very calling of them useless, would leave the people of this colony without protection or security for any thing; and because we are convinced, as we hope your majesty will be, that, by complying with it, we shall betray our constituents, and leave posterity to the mercy of future administrations, at a time when your majesty (whom God long preserve) shall be no more, and when they may perhaps not enjoy, as we do, the happiness of living under the protection of a patriot king.

[In the end, Jamaica remained loyal to the British Crown during the American Revolution. But the expenses incurred during that war only increased the House of Assembly's frustration with imperial fiscal demands.]

"Petition of the House of Assembly to the King" (February 27, 1783)
We, your majesty's dutiful and loyal subjects, the assembly of Jamaica, most humbly implore your majesty's attention to the concerns of this valuable colony: when we reflect upon the many proofs of loyalty and attachment to your majesty's person and government, which this island has manifested, we are emboldened to submit our petitions to your majesty, with the honest confidence of servants who have deserved attention, and of subjects who hope to receive it.

During the present unhappy war, Sire, this island has been a scene of perpetual alarm: Its known intrinsic value and its consequence to Great Britain; its situation among hostile neighbours; the avowed determination of the court of Spain to attempt the reduction of it; every circumstance, in short, conspired to assure us that Jamaica must be perpetually endangered by the machinations of such formidable adjacent enemies.

The apprehensions of your majesty's subjects were further augmented by comparing the dangers which surrounded them with the means of resistance that remained. Assailed in all parts by confederated enemies, Great Britain was obliged to hope for the safety of this island, more from the approved loyalty of your majesty's subjects than from any fleets or armies which at that time she sent out; we cheerfully submitted to the discipline of militia service; we built and repaired fortifications; we made ample provision for your majesty's forces; and, though harassed, impoverished, and taxed beyond measure, we ventured to incur an enormous island debt, which it will require the heaviest internal taxes to discharge.

Such have been our services, Sire, and such our exertions; yet it was during the height of these services, and in the midst of these exertions, while the means of supporting them were yet to be provided, that a new tax upon our staple was projected.

Your majesty's memorialists and petitions cannot avoid submitting to your majesty that this tax was the more unaccountable, as it was imposed immediately after a dreadful hurricane; which, by carrying desolation over the face of the island, had marked us out as objects of parliamentary charity, while we were objects of parliamentary taxation; thus, Sire, your faithful subjects had the mortification to find both ministers and parliament confederating with the war, and with the elements, to complete their ruin.

Your memorialists and petitioners humbly submit to your majesty that, when the first of our late taxes was imposed, your majesty's then ministers attempted to allay our apprehensions by suggesting that means would be adopted, by giving every discouragement to the importation and vending of foreign produce, and thus preventing a glut of West India produce at market, to remove the pressure of the duties from the planters, to the consumers of sugars. But this hope, if it could be called such, is since taken away by temporary laws which have been passed for a partial suspension of the navigation act.

We beg leave to represent to your majesty that the navigation act, while it limits the trade of the colonies, gives them in return a kind of exclusive preference at the home market, by the great duties which are therein imposed upon foreign

West-India produce; but the temporary laws in question, while they take away this preference, have carefully preserved all the limitations. By the sanction given to neutral flags under these temporary laws, a sanction which gives a latitude even to English vessels to load at St. Domingo, French sugars, unclogged either by enormous freight or enormous insurances, are poured into the ports of Great Britain; and thus, under every disadvantage, we meet with competitors at our own markets, in the very powers against which we have been contending.

Sire, while your majesty's subjects in Jamaica are depressed and neglected, we are obliged to be spectators of the astonishing prosperity of our hostile neighbours. Taxes upon our produce at home, and public and private debts incurred under the impulses of a becoming and honourable loyalty, have brought upon this island a complication of difficulties and misfortunes; while the islands of our neighbouring enemies exhibit nothing but the hurry of unlimited traffic and the splendour of overflowing wealth: St. Domingo and St. Kitts are mortifying contrasts to the state of this unhappy island; in St. Domingo, the policy of France in the management of her colonies is strikingly displayed; under a disreputable surrender to French government, the commerce of St. Kitts is augmented.

Your memorialists and petitioners finally submit to your majesty, whether these growing discouragements to industry may not compel many planters to throw up their estates and abandon the country entirely; and thus, in times of future danger, make the island more defenceless than it has hitherto been? It was under the gentle hand of mild and fostering government that your memorialists and petitioners, and their predecessors, were encouraged to encounter these sultry and unwholesome climes; and we pray your majesty to consider how far it may be advisable, at this time, to give birth to a new spirit of emigration and adventure.

CHAPTER 3

Origins of the American Revolution

The financial strain of the wars of Empire was felt throughout the Atlantic world after 1763, as the imperial powers struggled with war debt and sought to rearm for the expected renewal of fighting. No colony was spared from the efforts to raise revenue, and everywhere those efforts caused friction. But nowhere was the outcome more consequential than in Great Britain's thirteen North American colonies. There, a series of taxes and measures of imperial control were introduced between 1763 and 1776. They were met with American resistance, which usually forced the British government to withdraw the offending measures. The taxes themselves were not particularly heavy. But Americans believed that they violated their historic, constitutional liberties and heralded a despotic turn in metropole–colony relations. With each new crisis, feelings on both sides hardened and ultimately led to war. The rhetoric of liberty, popular sovereignty, and resistance generated during the period of conflict leading up to 1776 would echo across the Atlantic world.

I. Repealing the Stamp Act (1766)

As part of Great Britain's effort to increase colonial revenue, in 1765 it imposed a tax on the paper used for publications and legal documents. Known as the Stamp Act, it was the first tax Britain had ever imposed directly on the internal commerce of its North American colonies. Seeing it as an unprecedented assault on their liberties, the Americans resisted on a massive scale. They formed militant patriot groups known as the Sons of Liberty, shut their businesses rather than comply, and organized protests that sometimes degenerated into riots. Boston was the epicenter of resistance. In the face of this storm of protest, Parliament withdrew the measure in March 1766; but to save face and maintain its rights, it also passed a Declaratory Act reaffirming its unlimited sovereignty over the colonies.

1. PARLIAMENTARY DEBATE OVER THE WITHDRAWAL OF THE STAMP ACT (JANUARY 1766)[1]

The following document is an excerpt from the January 1766 debate in Parliament over the repeal of the Stamp Act. It touched on the fundamental organizing principles of the British Empire and shows that the British themselves were grappling with some of the same constitutional issues as the American colonists. The main participants in the debate were William Pitt, head of the British government, and George Grenville, leader of the opposition and Pitt's bitter rival.

[PITT:] It is my opinion, that this kingdom has no right to lay a tax upon the colonies. At the same time, I assert the authority of this kingdom over the colonies, to be sovereign and supreme, in every circumstance of government and legislation whatsoever. They are the subjects of this kingdom, equally entitled with yourselves to all the natural rights of mankind and the peculiar privileges of Englishmen, equally bound by its laws, and equally participating of the constitution of this free country. The Americans are the sons, not the bastards of England. Taxation is no part of the governing or legislative power. The taxes are a voluntary gift and grant of the Commons alone. In legislation the three estates of the realm are alike concerned, but the concurrence of the peers and the crown to a tax, is only necessary to close with the form of a law. The gift and grant is of the Commons alone. In ancient days, the crown, the barons, and the clergy possessed the lands. In those days, the barons and the clergy gave and granted to the crown. They gave and granted what was their own. At present, since the discovery of America, and other circumstances permitting, the Commons are become the proprietors of the land. The crown has divested itself of its great estates. The church (God bless it) has but a pittance. The property of the Lords, compared with that of the Commons, is as a drop of water in the oceans: and this House represents those Commons, the proprietors of the lands; and those proprietors virtually represent the rest of the inhabitants. When, therefore, in this House we give and grant, we give and grant what is our own. But in an American tax, what do we do? We, your Majesty's Commons of Great Britain, give and grant to your Majesty, what? Our own property? No. We give and grant to your Majesty, the property of your Majesty's commons of America. It is an absurdity in terms.

The distinction between legislation and taxation is essentially necessary to liberty. The Crown, the Peers, are equally legislative powers with the Commons. If taxation be a part of simple legislation, the Crown, the Peers, have rights in taxation as well as yourselves: rights which they will claim, which they will exercise, whenever the principle can be supported by power.

[1]William Cobbett, ed., *The Parliamentary History of England* (London: Hansard, 1813), vol. 16, 97–108.

There is an idea in some, that the colonies are virtually represented in the House. I would fain know by whom an American is represented here? Is he represented by any knight of the shire, in any county in this kingdom? Would to God that respectable representation was augmented to a greater number! Or will you tell him, that he is represented by any representative of a borough—a borough, which perhaps, its own representative never saw. That is what is called, "the rotten part of the constitution." It cannot continue the century; if it does not drop, it must be amputated. The idea of a virtual representation of America in this House, is the most contemptible idea that ever entered into the head of a man; it does not deserve a serious refutation.

The Commons of America, represented in their several assemblies, have ever been in possession of the exercise of this, their constitutional right, of giving and granting their own money. They would have been slaves if they had not enjoyed it. At the same time, this kingdom, as the supreme governing and legislative power, has always bound the colonies by their laws, by her regulations, and restrictions in trade, in navigation, in manufactures, in every thing, except that of taking their money out of their pockets without their consent. . . .

[GRENVILLE:] [T]he disturbances in America . . . began in July, and now we are in the middle of January; lately they were only occurrences, they are now . . . disturbances, tumults, and riots. I doubt they border on open rebellion; and if the doctrine I have heard this day be confirmed, I fear they will lose that name to take that of revolution. The government over them being dissolved, a revolution will take place in America. I cannot understand the difference between external and internal taxes. They are the same in effect, and only differ in name. That this kingdom has sovereign, the supreme legislative power over America, is granted. It cannot be denied; and taxation is a part of that sovereign power. It is one branch of the legislation. It is, it has been exercised, over those who are not, who were not represented. It is exercised over India Company, the merchants of London, the proprietors of the stocks, and over many great manufacturing towns. It was exercised over the palatinate of Chester, and the bishopric of Durham, before they sent any representative to parliament. . . . When I proposed to tax America, I asked the House, if any gentleman would object to the right; I repeatedly asked it, and no man would attempt to deny it. Protection and obedience are reciprocal. Great Britain protects America; America is bound to yield obedience. If not, tell me when the Americans were emancipated? When they want the protection of this kingdom, they are always very ready to ask it. That protection has always been afforded them in the most full and ample manner. The nation has run itself into an immense debt to give them their protection; and now they are called upon to contribute a small share towards the public expence, and expence arising from themselves, they renounce your authority, insult your officers, and break out, I might almost say, into rebellion. The seditious spirit of the colonies owes its birth to the factions in this House. Gentlemen are care-less of the consequences of what they say, provided it answers the purposes of opposition. We were told we trod on tender ground; we were bid to expect disobedience. What was this, but telling the Americans to stand out against the law, to encourage their obstinacy with the expectation of support from hence? . . .

[PITT:] I have been charged with giving birth to sedition in America. They have spoken their sentiments with freedom, against this unhappy act, and that freedom has become their crime. Sorry I am to hear the liberty of speech in this House imputed as a crime. But the imputation shall not discourage me. It is a liberty I mean to exercise. No gentleman ought to be afraid to exercise it. It is a liberty by which the gentleman who calumniates it might have profited. He ought to have profited. He ought to have desisted from his project. The gentleman tells us, America is obstinate; America is almost in open rebellion. I rejoice that America has resisted. Three millions of people, so dead to all the feelings of liberty, as voluntarily to submit to be slaves, would have been fit instruments to make slaves of the rest. I come not here armed at all points, with law cases and acts of parliament, with the statute-book doubled down in dogs-ears, to defend the cause of liberty: if I had, I myself would have cited the two cases of Chester and Durham. I would have cited them, to have shewn, that, even under any arbitrary reigns, parliaments were ashamed of taxing a people without their con-sent, and allowed them representatives. Why did the gentleman confine himself to Chester and Durham? He might have taken a higher example in Wales; Wales, that never was taxed by parliament, till it was incorporated. I would not debate a particular point of law with the gentleman: I know his abilities. I have been obliged to his diligent researches. But, for the de-fence of liberty upon a general principle, upon a constitutional principle, it is a ground on which I stand firm; in which I dare meet any man. The gentleman tells us of many who are taxed, and are not represented—the India company, merchants, stock-holders, manufacturers. Surely many of these are represented in other capacities, as owners of land, or as freeman of boroughs. It is a misfortune that more are not actually represented. But they are all inhabitants, and, as such, are virtually represented. Many have it in their option to be actually represented. They have connexions with those that elect, and they have influence over them. . . . [No minister] ever dreamed of robbing the colonies of their constitutional rights. That was re-served to mark the era of the late administration: not that there were want-ing some, when I had the honour to serve his Majesty, to propose to me to burn my fingers with an American Stamp-Act. With the enemy at their back, with our bayonets at their breasts, in the day of their distress, perhaps the Americans would have submitted to the imposition; but it would have been taking an ungenerous and unjust advantage. . . . I am no courtier of America, I stand up for this kingdom. I maintain, that the parliament has a right to bind, to restrain America. Our legislative power over the colonies is sovereign and supreme. When it ceases to be sovereign and supreme, I would advise every gentleman to sell his lands, if he can, and embark for that country. When two countries are connected together, like England and her colonies, without being incorporated, the one must necessarily govern; the greater must rule the less; but so rule it, as not to contradict the fundamental principles that are common to both.

If the gentleman does not understand the difference between internal and external taxes, I cannot help it; but there is a plain distinction between taxes levied for the purposes of raising a revenue, and duties imposed for the regulation of trade, for the accommodation of the subject; although, in the consequences, some revenue might incidentally arise from the latter.

The gentleman asks, when were the colonies emancipated? But I desire to know, when they were made slaves? But I dwell not upon words. When I had the honour of serving his Majesty, I availed myself of the means of information, which I derived from my office: I speak, therefore, from knowledge. My materials were good. I was at pains to collect, to digest, to consider them; and I will be bold to affirm, that the profits to Great Britain from the trade of the colonies, through all its branches, is two millions a year. This is the fund that carried you triumphantly through the last war. . . . You owe this to America. This is the price that America pays you for her protection. . . .

The Americans have not acted in all things with prudence and temper. They have been wronged. They have been driven to madness by injustice. Will you punish them for the madness you have occasioned? Rather let prudence and temper come first from this side. . . .

Upon the whole, I will beg leave to tell the House what is really my opinion. It is, that the Stamp Act be repealed absolutely, totally, and immediately. That the reason for the repeal be assigned, because it was founded on an erroneous principle. At the same time, let the sovereign authority of this country over the colonies, be asserted in as strong terms as can be devised, and be made to extend to every point of legislation whatsoever. That we may bind their trade, confine their manufactures, and exercise every power whatsoever, except that of taking their money out of their pockets without their consent.

2. PARLIAMENTARY TESTIMONY OF BENJAMIN FRANKLIN (FEBRUARY 13, 1766)[2]

Parliament called a number of witnesses to testify about the effects of the Stamp Act. One of these was the agent for Pennsylvania, Benjamin Franklin.

---

[2]Cobbett, *Parliamentary History*, vol. 16, 137–143, 145–149, 151–152, 155–156, 158–160.

Q. What is your name, and place of abode?

A. Franklin, of Philadelphia.

Q. Are not the colonies, from their circumstances, very able to pay the stamp duty?

A. In my opinion, there is not gold and silver enough in the colonies to pay the stamp duty for one year.

Q. Don't you know that money arising from the stamps was all to be laid out in America?

A. I know it is appropriated by the act to the American service; but it will be spent in the conquered colonies, where the soldiers are, not in the colonies that pay it.

Q. Is there not a balance of trade due from the colonies where the troops are posted, that will bring back the money to the old colonies?

A. I think not. I believe very little would come back. I know of no trade likely to bring it back, I think it would come from the colonies where it was spent directly to England; for I have always observed, that in every colony the more plenty of means of remittance to England, the more goods are sent for, and the more trade with England carried on. . . .

Q. Do you think it right, that America should be protected by this country, and pay no part of the expence?

A. That is not the case. The colonies raised, clothed and paid, during the last war, near 25,000 men, and spent many millions.

Q. Were you not reimbursed by parliament?

A. We were only reimbursed what, in your opinion, we had advanced beyond our proportion, or beyond what might be reasonably expected from us; and it was a very small part of what we spent. Pennsylvania, in particular, disbursed about 500,000*l*., and the reimbursements, in the whole, did not exceed 60,000*l*. . . .

Q. Do not you think the people of America would submit to pay the stamp duty, if it was moderated?

A. No, never, unless compelled by force of arms. . . .

Q. What was the temper of America towards Great Britain before the year 1763?

A. The best in the world. They submitted willingly to the government of the crown, and paid, in all their courts, obedience to the acts of parliament. Numerous as the people are in the several old provinces, they cost you nothing in forts, citadels, garrisons or armies, to keep them in subjection. They were governed by this country at the expence only of a little pen, ink, and paper. They were lead by a thread. They had not only a respect, by an affection for Great Britain, for its laws, its customs and manners, and even a fondness for its fashions, that greatly increased the commerce, Natives of Britain were always treated with particular regard; to be an Old-England man was, of itself, a character of some respect, and gave a kind of rank among us.

Q. And what is their temper now?

A. O, very much altered.

Q. Did you ever hear the authority of parliament to make laws for America questioned till lately?

A. The authority of parliament was allowed to be valid in all laws, except such as should lay internal taxes. It was never disputed in laying duties to regulate commerce. . . .

Q. In what light did the people of America use to consider the parliament of Great Britain?

A. They considered the parliament as the great bulwark and security of their liberties and privileges, and always spoke of it with the utmost respect and veneration. Arbitrary ministers, they thought, might possibly, at times, attempt to oppress them; but they relied on it, that the parliament, on application, would always give redress. They remembered, with gratitude, a strong instance of this, when a bill was brought into parliament, with a clause to make royal instructions laws in the colonies, which the House of Commons would not pass, and it was thrown out.

Q. And have they not still the same respect for parliament?

A. No, it is greatly lessened. . . .

Q. Don't you think they would submit to the Stamp Act, if it was modified, the obnoxious parts taken out, and the duty reduced to some particulars, of small moment?

A. No, they will never submit to it. . . .

Q. What is your opinion of a future tax, imposed on the same principle with that of the Stamp Act, how would the Americans receive it?

A. Just as they do this. They would not pay it.

Q. Have not you heard of the resolution of this House, and of the House of Lords, asserting the right of parliament relating to America, including a power to tax the people there?

A. Yes, I have heard of such resolutions.

Q. What will be the opinion of the Americans on those resolutions?

A. They will think them unconstitutional and unjust.

Q. Was it an opinion in America before 1763, that the parliament had no right to lay taxes and duties there?

A. I never heard any objection to the right of laying duties to regulate commerce; but a right to lay internal taxes was never supposed to be in in parliament, as we are not represented there.

Q. On what do you found your opinion, that the people in America made any such distinction?

A. I know that whenever the subject has occurred in conversation where I have been present, it has appeared to be the opinion of every one, that we could not be taxed in a parliament where we were not represented. But the payment of duties laid by act of parliament, as regulations of commerce, was never disputed. . . .

Q. Considering the resolutions of parliament as to the right, do you think, if the Stamp Act is repealed, that the North Americans will be satisfied?

A. I believe they will.

Q. Why do you think so?

A. I think the resolutions of right will give them very little concern, if they are never attempted to be carried into practice. The colonies will probably consider themselves in the same situation, in that respect, with Ireland; they know you claim the same right with regard to Ireland, but you never exercise it. And they may believe you never will exercise it in the colonies, any more than in Ireland, unless on some very extraordinary occasion.

Q. But who are to be the judges of that extraordinary occasion? Is not the parliament?

A. Though the parliament may judge of the occasion, the people will think it can never exercise such right, till representatives from the colonies are admitted into parliament. . . .

Q. Can any thing less than a military force carry the Stamp Act into execution?

A. I do not see how a military force can be applied to that purpose.

Q. Why may it not?

A. Suppose a military force sent into America, they will find nobody in arms; what are they then to do? They cannot force a man to take stamps who chuses to do without them. They will not find a rebellion; they may indeed make one.

Q. If the act is not repealed, what do you think will be the consequences?

A. A total loss of the respect and affection the people of America bear to this country, and of all the commerce that depends on that respect and affection.

Q. How can the commerce be affected?

A. You will find, that if the act is not repealed, they will take very little of your manufactures in a short time.

Q. Is it in their power to do without them?

A. I think they may very well do without them.

Q. Is it their interest not to take them?

A. The goods they take from Britain are either necessaries, mere conveniences, or superfluities. The first, as cloth, & c. with a little industry they can made at home: the second they can do without, till they are able to provide them among themselves; and the last, which are much the greatest part, they will strike off immediately. They are mere articles of fashion, purchased and consumed, because the fashion in a respected country, but will now be detested and rejected. . . .

Q. Is it their interest to make cloth at home?

A. I think they may at present get it cheaper from Britain, I mean of the same fineness and neatness of workmanship; but when one considers other circumstances, the restraints on their trade, and the difficulty of making remittances, it is their interest to make every thing.

Q. Suppose an act of internal regulations connected with a tax, how would they receive it?

A. I think it would be objected to.

Q. Then no regulation with a tax would be submitted to?

A. Their opinion is, that when aids to the crown are wanted, they are able to be asked of the several assemblies according to the old established usage, who will, as they have always done, grant them freely. And that their money ought not to be given away, without their consent, by persons at a distance, unacquainted with their circumstances and abilities. The granting aids to the crown, is the only means they have of recommending themselves to their sovereign, and they think it extremely hard and unjust, that a body of men, in which they have no representatives, should make a merit to itself of giving and granting what is not its own, but theirs, and deprives them of a right they esteem of the utmost value and importance, as it is the security of all their other rights. . . .

Q. If an excise was laid by parliament, which they might likewise avoid paying, by not consuming the articles excised, would they then not object to it?

A. They would certainly object to it, as an excise is unconnected with any service done . . .

Q. You say they do not object to the right of parliament, in laying duties on goods to be paid on their importation; now, is there any kind of difference between a duty on the importation of goods and an excise on their consumption?

A. Yes, a very material one; an excise, for the reasons I have just mentioned, they think you can have no right to lay within their country. But the sea is yours; you maintain, by your fleets, the safety of navigation in it, and keep it clear of pirates; you may have therefore a natural and equitable right to some toll or duty on merchandizes carried through that part of your dominions, towards defraying the expence you are at in ships to maintain the safety of that carriage. . . .

Q. If the Stamp Act should be repealed, would not the Americans think they could oblige the parliament to repeal every external tax law now in force?

A. It is hard to answer questions what people at such a distance will think.

Q. But what do you imagine they will think were the motives of repealing the Act?

A. I suppose they will think that it was repealed from a conviction of its inexpediency; and they will rely upon it, that while the same inexpediency subsists, you will never attempt to make such another.

Q. What do you mean by inexpediency?

A. I mean its inexpediency on several accounts; the poverty and inability of those who were to pay the tax; the general discontent it has occasioned; and the impracticability of enforcing it. . . .

Q. Do you think the assemblies have a right to levy money on the subject there, to grant to the crown?

A. I certainly think so; they have always done it. . . .

Q. Do they know that by that statute, money is not to be raised on the subject but by consent of parliament?

A. They are very well acquainted with it.

Q. How then can they think that they have a right to levy money for the crown, or for any other than local purposes?

A. They understand that clause to relate to subjects only within the realm; that no money can be levied on them for the crown, but by consent of parliament. The colonies are not supposed to be within the realm; they have assemblies of their own, which are their parliaments. . . .

Q. If the Stamp Act should be repealed, and an act should pass, ordering the assemblies of the colonies to indemnify the sufferers by the riots, would they obey it?

A. That is a question I cannot answer.

Q. Suppose the King should require the colonies to grant a revenue, and the parliament should be against their doing it, do they think they can grant a revenue to the King, without the consent of the parliament of Great Britain?

A. That is a deep question. As to my own opinion I should think myself at liberty to do it, and should do it, if I liked the occasion. . . .

Q. Don't you know that there is, in the Pennsylvania charter, an express reservation of the right of parliament to lay taxes there?

A. I know there is a clause in the charter, by which the King grants that he will levy no taxes on the inhabitants, unless it be with the consent of the assembly, or by an act of parliament.

Q. How then could the assembly of Pennsylvania assert, that laying a tax on them by the Stamp Act was an infringement of their rights?

A. They understand it thus: by the same charter, and otherwise, they are entitled to all the privileges and liberties of Englishmen; they find in the Great Charters, and the Petition and Declaration of Rights, that one of the privileges of English subjects is, that they are not to be taxed but by their common consent; they have therefore relied upon it, from the first settlement of the province, that the parliament never would, nor could, by colour of that clause in the charter, assume a right of taxing them, till it had qualified itself to exercise such right, by admitting representatives from the people to be taxed, who ought to make a part of that common consent.

Q. Are there any words in the charter that justify that construction?

A. The common rights of Englishmen, as declared by Magna Charta, and the Petition of Right, all justify it. . . .

Q. If the Stamp Act should be repealed, would it induce the assemblies of America to acknowledge the right of parliament to tax them, and would they erase their resolutions?

A. No, never.

Q. Is there no means of obliging them to erase those resolutions?

A. None, that I know of; they will never do it, unless compelled by force of arms.

II. Conflict Intensifies (1766–1774)

The repeal of the Stamp Act in 1766 marked only a temporary respite. The Declaratory Act (which Americans mostly overlooked in their joy at the demise of the Stamp Act) was followed in 1767 by the Townshend Acts (which they did not overlook). Imposing import duties on a wide range of products, this measure again sparked massive resistance, including a boycott of British imports. In the face of this opposition, Parliament rescinded the Townshend duties one by one. But as a symbol of its right to tax colonial trade, it kept in place the tax on tea—leading in December 1773 to the Boston Tea Party.

3. SAMUEL ADAMS, *THE RIGHTS OF THE COLONISTS* (1772)[3]

As the dispute between Great Britain and its North American colonies worsened, one of the leading patriots of Boston published an influential pamphlet. Its insistence on the natural rights of the colonists and claim that Parliamentary taxation was theft of their property resonated throughout the colonies.

1st. Natural Rights of the Colonists As Men

Among the natural rights of the Colonists are these: First, a right to life; Secondly, to liberty; Thirdly, to property; together with the right to support and defend them in the manner they can. These are evident branches of, rather than deductions from, the duty of self-preservation, commonly called the first law of nature.

All men have a right to remain in a state of nature as long as they please, and in case of intolerable oppression, civil or religious, to leave the society they belong to, and enter into another.

When men enter into society, it is by voluntary consent and they have a right to demand and insist upon the performance of such conditions and previous limitations as form an equitable original compact.

Every natural right not expressly given up, or, from the nature of a social compact, necessarily ceded, remains.

3d. The Rights of the Colonists As Subjects

A commonwealth or state is a body politic, or civil society of men, united together to promote their mutual safety and prosperity by means of their union.

The absolute rights of Englishmen and all freemen, in or out of civil society, are principally personal security, personal liberty, and private property.

---

[3]Harry Alonzo Cushing, ed., *The Writings of Samuel Adams* (New York: G. P. Putnam's Sons, 1906), vol. 2, 351–359.

All persons born in the British American Colonies are, by the laws of God and nature and by the common law of England, exclusive of all charters from the Crown, well entitled, and by acts of the British Parliament are declared to be entitled, to all the natural, essential, inherent, and inseparable rights, liberties, and privileges of subjects born in Great Britain or within the realm. Among those rights are the following, which no man, or body of men, consistently with their own rights as men and citizens, or members of society, can for themselves give up or take away from others.

First, the first fundamental, positive law of all commonwealths or states is establishing the legislative power. As the first fundamental natural law, also, which is to govern even the legislative power itself, is the preservation of the society.

Secondly, the Legislative has no right to absolute, arbitrary power over the lives and fortunes of the people; nor can mortals assume a prerogative not only too high for men, but for angels, and therefore reserved for the exercise of the Deity alone.

The Legislative cannot justly assume to itself a power to rule by extempore arbitrary decrees; but it is bound to see that justice is dispensed, and that the rights of the subjects be decided by promulgated, standing, and known laws, and authorized independent judges; that is, independent, as far as possible, of Prince and people. There should be one rule of justice for rich and poor, for the favorite at court, and countryman at the plough.

Thirdly, the supreme power cannot justly take from any man any part of his property, without his consent in person or by his representative.

These are some of the first principles of natural law and justice, and the great barriers of all free states and of the British Constitution in particular. It is utterly irreconcilable to these principles and to many other fundamental maxims of the common law, common sense, and reason that a British House of Commons should have a right at pleasure to give and grant the property of the Colonists. . . .

Now what liberty can there be where property is taken away without consent? Can it be said with any color of truth and justice, that this continent of three thousand miles in length, and of breadth as yet unexplored, in which, however, it is supposed there are five millions of people, has the least voice, vote, or influence in the British Parliament? Have they all together any more weight or power to return a single member to that House of Commons who have not inadvertently, but deliberately, assumed a power to dispose of their lives, liberties, and properties, than to choose an Emperor of China? . . . The inhabitants of this country, in all probability, in a few years, will be more numerous than those of Great Britain and Ireland together; yet it is absurdly expected by the promoters of the present measures that these, with their property shall be disposed of by a House of Commons at three thousand miles' distance from them, and who cannot be supposed to have the least care or concern for their real interest; who have not only no natural care for their interest, but must be in effect bribed against it, as every burden they lay on the Colonists is so much saved or gained to themselves. . . .

4. A CLIMATE OF PARANOIA[4]

Samuel Adams had expressed himself in the rational language of Locke and his Enlightenment successors. Other American pamphleteers, however, indulged in paranoid fantasies in which Parliamentary taxation was but the first element of a comprehensive plan to enslave America. The following document is a statement from the New York City Sons of Liberty, issued at the height of the tea crisis.

It is essential to the freedom and security of a free people, that no taxes be imposed upon them but by their own consent, or their representatives. For "what property have they in which another may, by right, take when he pleases to himself?" The former is the undoubted right of Englishmen, to secure which they expended millions and sacrificed the lives of thousands. And yet, to the astonishment of all the world, and the grief of America, the commons of Great Britain, after the repeal of the memorable and detestable stamp-act, reassumed the power of imposing taxes on the American colonies; and, insisting on it as a necessary badge of parliamentary supremacy, passed a bill, in the seventh year of his present majesty's reign, imposing duties on all glass, painters' colors, paper and teas, that should, after the 20th of November, 1767, be "imported from Great Britain into any colony or plantation in America." This bill, after the concurrence of the lords, obtained the royal assent. And thus they who, from time immemorial, have exercised the right of giving to, or withholding from the crown, their aids and subsidies, according to their *own free will and pleasure,* signified by their representatives in parliament, do, by the [Revenue] Act in question, deny us, their brethren in America, the enjoyment of the same right. As this denial, and the execution of that act, involves our slavery, and would sap the foundation of our freedom, whereby we should become slaves to our brethren and fellow subjects, born to no greater stock of freedom than the Americans, the merchants and inhabitants of this city, in conjunction with the merchants and inhabitants of the ancient American colonies, entered into an agreement to decline a part of their commerce with Great Britain, until the . . . act should be totally repealed. This agreement operated so powerfully to the disadvantage of the manufacturers of England that many of them were unemployed. To appease their clamors, and to provide the subsistence for them, which the non-importation had deprived them of, the parliament, in 1770, repealed so much of the revenue act as imposed a duty on glass, painters' colors, and paper, and left the duty on tea, as *a test to the parliamentary right to tax us.* The merchants of the cities of New York and Philadelphia, having strictly adhered to the agreement, so far as it is related to the importation of articles subject to an American duty, having convinced the ministry, that some other measures

---

[4]Thwarting the "Diabolical Project of Enslaving America": "The Association and Resolves of the New York Sons of Liberty" (Dec. 15, 1773). From Hezekiah Niles, ed., *Principles and Acts of the Revolution in America* (Baltimore: William Ogden Niles, 1822), 169–170.

must be adopted to execute parliamentary supremacy over this country, and to remove the distress brought on the East India company, by the ill-policy of that act. Accordingly, to increase the temptation to the shippers of tea from England, an act of parliament passed the last session, which gives the whole duty on tea, the company were subject to pay, upon the importation of it to England, to the purchasers and exporters; and when the company have ten millions of pounds of tea, in their ware-houses exclusive to the quantity they may want to ship, they are allowed to export tea, discharged from the payment of that duty, with which they were before chargeable. In hopes of aid in the execution of this project, by the influence if the owners of the American ships, application was made by the company to the captains of those ships to take the tea on freight; but they virtuously rejected it. Still determined in the scheme, they have chartered ships to bring tea to this country, which may be hourly expected, to make an important trial of our virtue. If they succeed in the sale of that tea, we shall have no property that we can call our own, and then we may bid adieu to our American liberty. Therefore, to prevent a calamity which of all others is the most to be dreadful—slavery, and its terrible concomitants—we, the subscribers, being influenced from a regard to liberty, and disposed to use all lawful endeavors in our power, to defeat the pernicious project, and to transmit to our posterity, those blessings of freedom which our ancestors have handed down to us; and to contribute to the support of the common liberties in America, which are in danger to be subverted, *do*, for those important purposes, agree to associate together, under the name and style of the *sons of New York*, and engage our honor to, and with each other faithfully deserve and perform the following *resolutions, viz.*

1st. *Resolved*, That whoever shall aid, or abet, or in any manner assist, in the introduction of tea, from any place whatsoever, into this colony while it is subject, by a British act of parliament, to the payment of a duty, for the purposes of raising a revenue in America, he shall be deemed an enemy to the liberties of America.

2d. *Resolved*, That whoever shall be aiding, or assisting, in the landing, or carting of such tea, from any ship, or vessel, or shall hire any house, store-house or cellar or any place whatsoever, to deposit the tea, subject to a duty as aforesaid, he shall be deemed an enemy of the liberties of America.

3d. *Resolved*, That whoever shall sell, or buy, or in any manner contribute to the sale, or purchase of tea, subject to a duty as aforesaid, or shall aid, or abet, in transporting such tea, by land or water, from this city until . . . the revenue act shall be totally and clearly repealed, he shall be deemed an enemy to the liberties of America.

4th. *Resolved*, That whether the duties on tea, imposed by this act, be paid in Great Britain or in America, our liberties are equally affected.

5th. *Resolved*, That whoever shall transgress any of these resolutions, we will not deal with, or employ, or have any connection with him.

5. MORE PARANOIA[5]

The following document continues in the same vein. Note the insinuation that the Catholic Church was behind the "settled fix'd plan for inslaving the colonies." These insinuations played on the North American colonists' zealous Protestantism as well as their concern about the recently passed Quebec Act legalizing Catholic practice in Canada.

If we view the whole of the conduct of the ministry and parliament, I do not see how nay one can doubt but that there is a settled fix'd plan for *inslaving* the colonies, or bringing them under arbitrary government, and indeed the nation too. The present parliament have ever been (by all accounts) more devoted to the interest of the ministry, than perhaps ever a parliament were. Now notwithstanding the excellency of the British constitution, if the ministry can secure a majority in parliament, who will come into all their measures, will vote as they bid them; they may rule as absolutely as they do in *France* or *Spain*, yea as in *Turkey* or *India*: And this seems to be the present plan to secure a majority of parliament, and thus enslave the nation with their own consent. The more places or pensions the ministry have in their gift; the more easily they can *bribe* a majority of parliament, by bestowing those places on them and their friends. This makes them erect so many new and unnecessary offices in America, even so as to swallow up the whole of the revenue. The king is not at all the richer for these duties. But then by bestowing these places—places of considerable profit and no labour—upon the children or friends, or dependants of the members of parliament, the ministry can secure them in their interest. This doubtless is the great thing the ministry are driving at, to establish arbitrary government with the consent of parliament. And to keep the people of England still, the first exertions of this power are upon the colonies. If the parliament insist upon the right of taxing the colonies at pleasure, the least we can expect is, to be tax'd as heavily as we can possibly bear, and yet support our lives; for as the members of parliament feel no burdens themselves by what they lay upon us, and are under no danger of losing their places by taxing us, so long as they can persuade the people of England they are lightening their burdens thereby; they are under no motives of interest to abstain from loading us with taxes as heavy as we can possibly groan under. Doubtless they will be cautious enough, to introduce these heavy taxes gradually, lest they excite too great commotions in this country. But let the *right* be once fix'd and established; it will be very easy to keep adding tax to tax; till the loads grow so heavy and are so fast bound, that we can

---

[5]"A Settled Fix'd Plan for Inslaving the Colonies": Ebenezer Baldwin, "An Appendix Stating the Heavy Grievances the Colonies Labor Under . . ." (Aug. 31, 1774). Samuel Sherwood, *A Sermon, Containing, Scriptural Instructions to Civil Rulers and all Free-born Subjects* (New Haven, CT: T. and S. Green, 1774), 67–81.

never shake them off. Nothing most certainly but a principle of justice will keep them from it; and what can we expect from this quarter, when in open defiance of the *English* constitution, they claim a right to tax us, and thus deprive us of our dearest privileges?

In the mean time we must expect our *charters* will fall a sacrifice to these arbitrary claims. Charter governments have long been disagreeable to the powers in Britain. The *free* constitution of these colonies makes them such nurseries of freemen as cannot fail to alarm an arbitrary ministry. They only wait a favourable opportunity to abolish their charters, as they have done that of the Massachusetts-Bay. We know the principle the parliament have adopted and openly profess to act upon, that they have a right to alter or annihilate charters when they judge it convenient. And we may depend upon it, whenever they shall think it can be done without raising too great commotions in the colonies, they will judge it convenient. Some may imagine it was the destroying the tea induced the parliament to change the government of the Massachusetts-Bay. If it was, surely 'tis very extraordinary to punish a whole province and their posterity thro' ages, for the conduct of a few individuals. How soon will a riot or some disorder of a few individuals, afford them a pretext for the like treatment of all the other charter governments. I believe, however, it may be made very evident, that the destroying the tea was not the reason for altering the government of the Massachusetts-Bay; but that it was a fix'd plan long before, and they only waited a colourable pretext for carrying it into execution. . . .

There is great reason to fear the next step will be the vacating all grants and patents of land from the king; that all our landed property may revert to his majesty; to be regranted under such *quit rents and services* as those in power shall see fit to impose: Nor will *this fear* appear chimerical to any one that duly considers what hath been already done, and what the plan is, which the ministry are doubtless pursuing, ... Our fathers when they planted this wilderness, placed equal confidence in the royal word pledged in their charters; as in the patents by which they held their land: and deemed the privileges granted in the former of as much worth; as the property granted by the latter. The principle upon which the parliament proceeded in vacating the Massachusetts charter; will equally warrant them, whenever they shall see fit, to vacate all our grants of lands. . . .

And have we not just grounds to fear that this will not be the completion of their oppressive plan, if the ministry find themselves successful in their first attempts? By the *Quebec-Act* we find the parliament claim a power to establish in *America*, the same arbitrary government that takes place in *France*; to take away trials by juries; to set aside general assemblies; to vest the king with a power to appoint legislative councils etc. Now this act not only respects the *French* inhabitants (who having been long used to slavish subjections, and not knowing the benefit of any other form of government, are possibly well eno' pleased with it, especially as the pill is gilded over with a full establishment of that religion, of which they are such bigotted professors), but it respects thousands of *English*, who have settled there since the conquest, and all such as may settle any where within that vast extended province in future time. By the same right they could establish this form of government over the *English* in Canada, they may do it in the other provinces. . . . Viewing the things that have taken place, is it without foundation that I express my fears, that the British ministry will e'er long find our general assemblies troublesome things, a hindrance to government and the like, and so set them aside, under a notion of their being *inexpedient*, and lodge the whole legislative power in a council appointed by the king? . . . And very likely the ministry may find *juries* equally a bar to the government they mean to establish, and so may persuade the parliament, on the footing of expediency to abolish them likewise.

And when our civil rights and privileges shall have thus fallen a sacrifice to tyranny and oppression, our religious liberties cannot long survive: for where hath it ever been known that civil and ecclesiastical tyranny and despotism have not yet gone hand in hand together. The latter is so necessary to uphold and support the former, that arbitrary princes or ministers of state have ever found their interest in the encouragement of it. And should America be forced to yield in the present struggle for civil liberty, we have no reason to expect but ecclesiastical tyranny, in some shape or other will like a mighty torrent overspread our land. Those princes on this British throne since the reformation, who have been most disposed to trample upon the rights of the people, and to rule in an arbitrary and despotic manner; have ever caressed the papists and shewn a favourable disposition towards the bloody religion of Rome, as that religion is the surest prop to tyranny and despotism. . . . Some late transactions shew a very favourable disposition in the present ministry and parliament towards the religion of Rome; how far they may attempt to introduce it into the English nation both in Britain and the colonies, God only knows. . . .

View now the situation of America: loaded with taxes from the British parliament, as heavy as she can possibly support, our lands charged with the most exorbitant quit-rents, these taxes collected by foreigners, steeled against any impressions from our groans or complaints, with all the rapaciousness of Roman publicans, our charters taken away, our assemblies annihilated, governors and councils, appointed by royal authority without any concurrence of the people, enacting such laws as their sovereign pleasure shall dictate, judges appointed from the same source, without any check from juries carrying their arbitrary laws into execution, the lives and property of Americans is entirely at the disposal of officers more than three thousand miles removed from any power to controul them, armies of soldiers quartered among the inhabitants, who know the horrid purpose for which they are stationed, in the colonies, to subjugate and bear down the inhabitants, who know what a chance they stand for impunity, tho' they commit the greatest excesses. These will be ready, not only to execute every arbitrary mandate of their despotic masters; but self-moved (if like others of their profession) to commit every outrage upon the defenceless inhabitants. Robberies, rapes, murders, etc. will be but the wanton sport of such wretches without restraint let loose upon us. These will be at hand by force and arms to quell every rising murmur, to crush every rising groan or complaint e'er it be uttered. And whenever the iron hand of oppression shall excite opposition or raise insurrections among the people (which will ever be the case under arbitrary and despotic government, till long use has rendered their necks callous and insensible to the galling yoke), blood-thirsty soldiers will be let loose upon them. Those who survive their murdering hands and have the misfortune to be taken captive by them, will soon be dragged, by the sentence of more merciless judges, to the place of estates, families reduced to beggary, orphans crying for bread, and such like scenes of distress. The spirits of the people soon grow depress'd, industry and public spirit die away, learning, virtue and religion are soon extinguished, no comfort or happiness to be enjoyed in social life, every one will be jealous and mistrustful of his nearest friends and neighbours. To such a dreadful state as this, my countrymen, the present measures seem to be swiftly advancing. What free-born Englishman can view such a state of abject slavery as this, tho' at the greatest distance, without having his blood boil with indignation? . . .

Should the colonies refuse to receive the chains prepared for them, and the present measures issue in a hostile rupture between Great Britain and the colonies, which God forbid, and which I wish the ministry may not have in view to pro-mote, see what precautions they have early taken either to ruin us, or force us to subjection. To the Canadians who have been long inured to arbitrary government, and so are become fit tools for inslaving others, they have granted an establish-ment of their religion, the restoration of their former laws, etc. to attach them to their interest; have continued Canada a military government that they may have store of forces at hand; that they may let loose these with all the force of Canada and all the northern tribes of Indians upon our exposed and helpless frontiers. What else can they have in view in trying so much to gratify the French inhabit-ants of that province?

Now if the British parliament and ministry continue resolved to prosecute the measures they have entered upon, it seems we must either submit to such a dreadful state of slavery as hath been shewn will be the probable issue of their measures, or must by force and arms stand up in defence of our liberties. The thoughts of either of which is enough to make our blood recoil in horror. Can any person survey the events that have taken place, and yet remain so stupid as not to be shocked at the dreadful prospect before us? Is there a wretch so unfeeling, as not to feel grieved and affected at the injured and violated liberties of America? Is there that tool of arbitrary power among the free-born sons of America, that will dare hold up his head in defence of such measures as these? If there be any such, I am sure I cannot find it in my heart to wish them worse, than to feel the iron rod of slavery, that is now shook over America, till they are brought to a sounder mind.

Having thus given a brief account of the late acts of the British parliament respecting the colonies, of the grievances the colonies labour under therefrom, and of what the probable consequences of these measures will be, I will very briefly touch upon the last thing proposed viz. what can be done by us in such an alarming crisis. . . . To pray to God for redress is certainly innocent, and happy it is we have heaven to go to, tho' our prayers should be denied on earth. God hath once and again in answer to prayer wrought eminent deliverance for the oppressed. . . . But little will prayer avail us without unfeigned repentance and humiliation before God under the heavy frowns of his righteous providence. We have more reason to be afraid of the vice and wickedness that abounds among us, than of all the arms of Britain. These give us reason to fear lest we have not virtue enough to make use of the properest means of redress, and lest heaven should fight against us. Were a general reformation to take place I make no doubt heaven would find a way for our relief. The present alarming situation of things therefore loudly calls upon us to examine what sins in particular have provoked these calamities, and by this rule will not the enslaving the poor *Africans* in the colonies stand forth in the front of the dreadful catalogue? Are not the colonies guilty of forcibly depriving them of their natural rights? Will not the arguments we use in defence of our own liberties against the claims of the British parliament, equally conclude in their favour? And is it not easy to see there is something retributive in the present judgments of heaven? We keep our fellow men in slavery; heaven is suffering others to enslave us. Again I must mention worldliness, covetousness, selfishness, dishonesty, disobedience to constitutional authority, and many other vices as contained in the dismal train, and for which we need to repent and humble ourselves before God. . . .

But if ever we would hope for redress from the grievances we labour under; 'tis not only necessary that we repent, reform and pray; but that we unitedly prosecute the most firm and prudent measures for the attainment of it. A very little attention must convince every one of the necessity of our being united. If the colonies are divided or the people in the several colonies are very considerably divided, we are undone. Nothing but the united efforts of America can save us: and if united they must have that weight, which gives me the most sanguine hopes of success. It should then be the concern of every one to labour as far as his influence extends, to promote this necessary union. The determinations of the congress of delegates from the several colonies may be deemed the general voice of America. A concurrence with these we should every one labour to promote. If in every particular we should not be entirely suited; yet the dreadful consequences of disunion should make us cautious how we let it be known. The Congress we hear have come into a conclusion that we *import* no British goods. This is a measure for redress, of which we may very safely and easily make trial. We can with a little self-denial do without the superfluities we receive from Britain. This will doubtless be distressing to the Mother Country and may convince them of the necessity of continuing to us our dear bought rights and privileges. No friend of his country can hesitate a moment in such a cause to deny himself to the superfluities of Britain. . . .

III. On the Brink (1774–1775)

By 1774, British North America stood on the brink of war. Isolated acts of violence against the British military had already occurred, notably the attack by a mob on troops that resulted in the Boston Massacre (1770) and the seizure of the patrol boat Gaspee (1772). To punish Boston for the Tea Party (1773), the city was placed under martial law and troops were sent to garrison it. In response, Massachusetts patriots formed militia units. In 1774, the First Continental Congress assembled to deal with the growing crisis. It found itself in a difficult position. On one hand, it believed that the colonists were in the right and encouraged their intransigence. On the other hand, it wanted to find a peaceful solution within the framework of the British Empire. Some British politicians felt the same way—but support for a peaceful resolution of the standoff was becoming increasingly hard to find on both sides.

6. THE CONTINENTAL CONGRESS'S DECLARATION AND RESOLVES (1774)[6]

The following document is the Continental Congress's justification of colonial resistance.

Whereas, since the close of the last war, the British parliament, claiming a power, of right, to bind the people of America by statutes in all cases whatsoever, hath, in some acts, expressly imposed taxes on them, and in others, under various pretences, but in fact for the purpose of raising a revenue, hath imposed rates and duties payable in these colonies, established a board of commissioners, with unconstitutional powers, and extended the jurisdiction of courts of admiralty, not only for collecting the said duties, but for the trial of causes merely arising within the body of a country.

And whereas, in consequence of other statutes, judges, who before held only estates at will in their offices, have been made dependant on the crown alone for their salaries, and standing armies kept in times of peace. And whereas it has lately been resolved in parliament, that by force of a statute, made in the thirty-fifth year of the reign of King Henry the Eighth, colonists may be transported to England, and tried there upon accusations for treasons and misprisions, or concealments of treasons committed in the colonies, and by a late statute, such trials have been directed in cases therein mentioned.

And whereas, in the last session of parliaments, three statutes were made; one entitled, "An act to discontinue, in such manner and for such time as are therein mentioned, the landing and discharging, lading, or shipping of goods, wares and merchandise, at the town, and within the harbor of Boston, in the province of Massachusetts-Bay in New England," and another entitled, "An act for the better regulating the government of the province of Massachusetts-Bay in New England,"

---

[6]"Continental Congress's Declaration and Resolves" (1774), in Worthington Ford, ed., *Journals of the Continental Congress, 1774-1789*, Friday, October 14, 1774 (Washington, DC: Government Printing Office, 1904), vol. 1, 63–73.

and another entitled, "An act for the impartial administration of justice, in the cases of persons questioned for any act done by them in the execution of the law, or for the suppression of riots and tumults, in the province of Massachusetts-Bay in New England," and another statute was then made, "for making more effectual provision for the government of the province of Quebec, etc." All which statutes are impolitic, unjust, and cruel, as well as unconstitutional, and most dangerous and destructive of American rights.

And whereas, assemblies have been frequently dissolved, contrary to the rights of the people, when they attempted to deliberate on grievances; and their dutiful, humble, loyal, and reasonable petitions to the crown for redress, have been repeatedly treated with contempt, by his Majesty's ministers of state.

The good people of the several colonies . . . justly alarmed at these arbitrary proceedings of parliament and administration, have severally elected, constituted, and appointed deputies to meet, and sit in general Congress, in the city of Philadelphia, in order to obtain such establishment, as that their religion, laws, and liberties, may not be subverted. Whereupon the deputies so appointed being now assembled, in a full and free representation of these colonies, taking into their most serious consideration, the best means of attaining the ends aforesaid, do, in the first place, as Englishmen, their ancestors in like cases have usually done, for asserting and vindicating their rights and liberties, declare,

That the inhabitants of the English colonies in North America, by the immutable laws of nature, the principles of the English constitution, and the several charters or compacts, have the following RIGHTS:

Resolved, . . . 1. That they are entitled to life, liberty and property: and they have never ceded to any foreign power whatever, a right to dispose of either without their consent.

Resolved, . . . 2. That our ancestors, who first settled these colonies, were at the time of their emigration from the mother country, entitled to all the rights, liberties, and immunities of free and natural-born subjects, within the realm of England.

Resolved, . . . 3. That by such emigration they by no means forfeited, surrendered, or lost any of those rights. . . .

Resolved, 4. That the foundation of English liberty, and of all free government, is a right in the people to participate in their legislative council: and as the English colonists are not represented, and from their local and other circumstances, cannot properly be represented in the British parliament, they are entitled to a free exclusive power of legislation in their several provincial legislatures, where their rights of representation can alone be preserved, in all cases of taxation and internal policy, subject only to the negative of their sovereign, in such a manner as has been heretofore used and accustomed: But, from the necessity of the case, and a regard to the mutual interest of both countries, we cheerfully consent to the operation of such acts of British parliament, as are bon[a]fide, restrained to the regulation of our external commerce, for the purpose of securing the commercial advantages of the whole empire to the mother country, and the commercial benefits of its respective members; excluding every idea of taxation internal or external, for raising a revenue on the subjects, in America, without their consent.

Resolved, . . . 5. That the respective colonies are entitled to the common law of England, and more especially to the great and inestimable privilege of being tried by their peers of the vicinage, according to the course of that law.

Resolved, 6. That they are entitled to the benefit of such of the English statutes, as existed at the time of their colonization. . . .

Resolved, . . . 7. That these, his Majesty's colonies, are likewise entitled to all the immunities and privileges granted and confirmed to them by royal charters, or secured by their several codes of provincial laws.

Resolved, . . . 8. That they have a right peaceably to assemble, consider of their grievances, and petition the kind; and that all prosecutions, prohibitory proclamations, and commitments for the same, are illegal.

Resolved, . . . 9. That the keeping a standing army in these colonies, in times of peace, without consent of the legislature of that colony, in which such army is kept, is against the law.

Resolved, . . . 10. It is indispensably necessary to good government, and rendered essential by the English constitution, that the constituent branches of the legislature be independent of each other; that, therefore, the exercise of legislative power in several colonies, by a council appointed, during pleasure, by the crown, is unconstitutional, dangerous and destructive to the freedom of American legislation.

All and each of which the aforesaid deputies, in behalf of themselves, and their constituents, do claim, demand, and insist on, as their indubitable rights and liberties, which cannot be legally taken from them, altered or abridged by any power whatever, without their own consent, by their representatives in their several provincial legislatures.

In the course of our inquiry, we find many infringements and violations of the foregoing rights, which, from ardent desire, that harmony and mutual intercourse of affection and interest may be restored, we pass over for the present, and proceed to state such acts and measures as have been adopted since the last war, which demonstrate a system formed to enslave America.

Resolved. . . . That the following acts of parliament are infringements and violations of the rights of the colonists; and that the repeal of them is essentially necessary, in order to restore harmony between Great Britain and the American colonies, viz.

The several acts . . . which impose duties for the purpose of raising a revenue in America, extend the power of the admiralty courts beyond their ancient limits, deprive the American subject of trial by jury, authorize the judges certificate to indemnify the prosecutor from damages, that he might otherwise be liable to, requiring oppressive security from a claimant of ships and goods seized, before he shall be allowed to defend his property, and are subversive of American rights.

Also . . . "An act for the better securing his majesty's dockyards, magazines, ships, ammunition, and stores," which declares a new offence in America, and deprives the American subject of a constitutional trial by jury of the vicinage, by authorizing the trial of any person, charged with the committing any offence described in the said act, out of the realm, to be indicated and tried for the same in any shire or country within the realm.

Also the three acts passed in the last session of parliament, for stopping the port and blocking up the harbor of Boston, for altering the charter and government of Massachusetts-Bay, and that which is entitled, "An act for the better administration of justice, &c."

Also the act passed in the same session for establishing the Roman Catholic religion, in the province of Quebec, abolishing the equitable system of English laws, and erecting a tyranny there, to the great danger (from so total a dissimilarity of religion, law and government) of the neighboring British colonies, by the assistance of those whose blood and treasure the said country was conquered from France.

Also the act passed in the same session, for the better providing suitable quarters for officers and soldiers in his majesty's service, in North-America.

Also, that the keeping a standing army in several of these colonies, in time of peace, without the consent of the legislature of that colony, in which the army is kept, is against the law.

To the grievous acts and measures, Americans cannot submit, but in hopes their fellow subjects in Great-Britain will, on a revision on them, restore us to that state, in which both countries found happiness and prosperity, we have for the present, only resolved to pursue the following peaceable measures:

1. To enter into a non-importation, non-consumption, and non-exportation agreement or association.
2. To prepare an address to the people of Great-Britain, and a memorial to the inhabitants of British America.
3. To prepare a loyal address to his majesty; Agreeable to resolutions already entered into.

7. EDMUND BURKE, *SPEECH ON CONCILIATION WITH AMERICA* (MARCH 22, 1775)[7]

Edmund Burke (1729-1797) was a respected political theorist, statesman, and member of Parliament. He had long opposed the British government's policy toward America, but with no success. Sensing that war was imminent, he made one last attempt to urge conciliation with America—again, to no avail. Fighting began the next month at Lexington and Concord. The following is an excerpt from Burke's speech.

[7]Edmund Burke, Speech on Conciliation with America, ed. C.H. Ward (Chicago and New York: Scott, Foresman, and Company, 1910), pp.48–27.

I mean to give peace. Peace implies reconciliation; and where there has been a material dispute, reconciliation does in a manner always imply concession on the one part or on the other. In this state of things I make no difficulty on affirming that the proposal ought to originate from us. Great and acknowledged force is not impaired, either in effect or in opinion, by an unwillingness to exert itself. The superior power may offer peace with honor and with safety. Such an offer from such a power will be attributed to magnanimity. . . .

The capital leading questions on which you must this day decide are two: First, whether you ought to concede; and secondly what your concession ought to be. On the first of these questions we have gained (as I have just taken the liberty of observing to you) some ground. But I am sensible that a good deal more is still to be done. Indeed, to enable us to determine both on the one and the other of these great questions with a firm and precise judgment, I think it may be necessary to consider distinctly the true nature and the peculiar circumstances of the object which we have before us: because, after all our struggle, whether we will or not, we must govern America according to that nature and to those circumstances, and not according to our own imaginations, not according to abstract ideas of right by no means according to mere general theories of government, the resort to which appears to me, in our present situation, no better than arrant trifling. I shall therefore endeavor, with your leave, to lay before you some of the most material of these circumstances in as full and as clear a manner as I am able to state them.

The first thing that we have to consider with regard to the nature of the object is the number of people in the colonies. I have taken for some years a good deal of pains on that point. I can by no calculation justify myself in placing the number below two millions of inhabitants of our own European blood and color, besides at least 500,000 others, who form no inconsiderable part of the strength and opulence of the whole. . . . Such is the strength with which population shoots in that part of the world. . . .

I put this consideration of the present and the growing numbers in the front of our deliberation, because this consideration will make it evident to a blunter discernment than yours, that no partial, narrow, contracted, pinched, occasional system will be at all suitable to such an object. . . . It will prove that some degree of care and caution is required in the handling such an object; it will show that you ought not, in reason, to trifle with so large a mass of the interest and feelings of the human race. You could at no time do so without guilt; and be assured you will not be able to do it long with impunity.

But the population of this country, the great and growing population, though a very important consideration, will lose much of its weight, if not combined with other circumstances. The commerce of your colonies is out of all proportion beyond the numbers of the people. . . .

The trade with America alone is now within less than 500,000*l*. of being equal to what this great commercial nation, England, carried on at the beginning of this century with the whole world! . . .

In the character of the Americans a love of freedom is the predominating feature which marks and distinguishes the whole: and as an ardent is always a jealous affection, your colonies become suspicious, restive, and untractable, whenever they see the least attempt to wrest from them by force, or shuffle from them by chicane, what they think the only advantage worth living for. This fierce spirit of liberty is stronger in the English colonies, probably, than in any other people of the earth, and this from a great variety of powerful causes; which, to understand the true temper of their minds, and the direction which this spirit takes, it will not be amiss to lay open somewhat more largely.

First, the people of the colonies are descendants of Englishmen. England is a nation which still, I hope, respects, and formerly adored, her freedom. The colonists emigrated from you when this part of your character was most predominant; and they took this bias and direction the moment they parted from your hands. They are therefore not only devoted to liberty according to English ideas and on English principles. Abstract liberty, like other mere abstractions, is not to be found. Liberty inheres in some sensible object; and every nation has formed to itself some favorable point, which by way of eminence becomes the criterion of their happiness. It happened, you know, that the great contests for freedom in this country were from the earliest times chiefly upon the question of taxing. Most of the contests in the ancient commonwealths turned primarily on the right of election of magistrates, or on the balance among the several orders of the state. The question of money was not with them so immediate. But in England it was otherwise. On this point of taxes the ablest pens and most eloquent tongues have been exercised, the greatest spirits have acted and suffered. In order to give the fullest satisfaction concerning the importance of this point, it was not only necessary for those who in argument defended the excellence of the English Constitution to insist on this privilege of granting money as a dry point of fact, and to prove that the right had been acknowledged in ancient parchments and blind usages to reside in a certain body called an House of Commons: they went much further: they attempted to prove, and they succeeded, that in theory it ought to be so, from the particular nature of a House of Commons, as an immediate representative of the people, whether the old records had delivered this oracle or not. They took infinite pains to inculcate, as a fundamental principle, that in all monarchies the people must in effect themselves, mediately or immediately, possess the power of granting their own money, or no shadow of liberty could subsist. The colonies draw from you, as with their life-blood, these ideas and principles. Their love of liberty, as with you, fixed and attached on this specific point of taxing. Liberty might be safe or might be endangered in twenty other particulars without their being much pleased or alarmed. Here they felt its pulse; and as they found that beat, they thought themselves sick or sound. I do not say whether they were right or wrong in applying your general arguments to their own case. It is not easy, indeed, to make a monopoly of theorems and corollaries. The fact is, that they did thus apply those general arguments; and your mode of governing them, whether through lenity or indolence, through wisdom or mistake, confirmed them in the imagination, that they, as well as you, had an interest in these common principles.

They were further confirmed in this pleasing error by the form of their provincial legislative assemblies. Their governments are popular in an high degree: some are merely popular; in all, the popular representative is the most weighty; and this share of the people in their ordinary government never fails to inspire them with lofty sentiments, and with a strong aversion from whatever tends to deprive them of their chief importance.

If anything were wanting to this necessary operation of the form of government, religion would have given it a complete effect. Religion, always a principle of energy, in this new people is no way worn out or impaired; and their mode of professing it is also one main cause of this free spirit. The people are Protestants, and of that kind which is the most adverse to all implicit submission of mind and opinion. This is a persuasion not only favorable to liberty, but built upon it. I do not think, Sir, that the reason of this averseness in the dissenting churches from all that looks like absolute government is so much to be sought in their religious tenets as in their history. Every one knows that the Roman Catholic religion is at least coeval with most of the governments where it prevails, that it has generally gone hand in hand with them, and received great favor and every kind of support from authority. The Church of England, too, was formed from her cradle under the nursing care of regular government. But the dissenting interests have sprung up in direct opposition to all the ordinary power of the world, and could justify that opposition only on a strong claim to natural liberty. Their very existence depended on the powerful and unremitted assertion of that claim. All Protestantism, even the most cold and passive, is a sort of dissent. But the religion most prevalent in our northern colonies is a refinement on the principle of resistance: it is the dissidence of dissent, and the protestantism of the Protestant religion. This religion, under a variety of denominations agreeing in nothing but in the communion of the spirit of liberty, is predominant in most of the northern provinces, where the Church of England, notwithstanding its legal rights, is in reality no more than a sort of private sect, not composing, most probably, the tenth of the people. The colonists left England when this spirit was high, and in the emigrants was the highest of all; and even that stream of foreigners which has been constantly flowing into these colonies has, for the greatest part, been composed of dissenters from the establishments of their several countries, and have brought with them a temper and character far from alien to that of the people with whom they mixed.

I can perceive, by their manner, that some gentlemen object to the latitude of this description, because in the southern colonies the Church of England forms a large body, and has a regular establishment. It is certainly true. There is, however, a circumstance attending these colonies, which, in my opinion, fully counterbalances this difference, and makes the spirit of liberty still more high and haughty than in those to the northward. It is, that in Virginia and the Carolinas they have a vast multitude of slaves. Where this is the case in any part of the world, those who are free are by far the most proud and jealous of their freedom. Freedom is to them not only an enjoyment, but a kind of rank and privilege. Not seeing there, that freedom, as in countries where it is a common blessing, and as broad and general as the air, may be united with much abject toil, with great misery, with all the exterior of servitude, liberty looks, amongst them, like something that is more noble and liberal. I do not mean, to comment on the superior morality of this sentiment, which has at least as much pride as virtue in it; but I cannot alter the nature of man. The fact is so; and these people of the southern colonies are much more strongly, and with an higher and more stubborn spirit, attached to liberty, than those to the northward. Such were all the ancient commonwealths; such were our Gothic ancestors; such in our days were the Poles; and such will be all masters of slaves, who are not slaves themselves. In such a people, the haughtiness of domination combines with the spirit of freedom, fortifies it, and renders it invincible.

Permit me to add another circumstance in our colonies, which contributes no mean part towards the growth and effect of this untractable spirit: I mean their education. In no country, perhaps, in the world is the law so general a study. The profession itself is numerous and powerful, and in most provinces it takes the lead. The greater number of deputies sent to the Congress were lawyers. But all who read, and most do read, endeavor to obtain some smattering in that science. I have been told by an eminent bookseller, that in no branch of his business, after tracts of popular devotion, were so many books as those on the law exported to the plantations. The colonists have now fallen into the way of printing them for their own use. . . .

The last cause of this disobedient spirit in the colonies is hardly less powerful that the rest, as it is not merely moral, but laid deep in the natural constitution of things. Three thousand miles of ocean lie between you and them. No contrivance can prevent the effect of this distance in weakening the government. Seas roll, and months pass, between the order and the execution; and the want of a speedy explanation of a single point is enough to defeat a whole system. You have, indeed, winged ministers of vengeance, who carry your bolts in their pounces to the remotest verge of the sea: but there a power steps in, that limits the arrogance of raging passions and furious elements, and says, "So far shalt thou go, and no farther." Who are you, that should fret and rage, and bite the chains of Nature? Nothing worse happens to you than does to all nations who have extensive empire; and it happens in all the forms into which empire can be thrown. In large bodies, the circulation of power must be less vigorous at the extremities. . . .

Then, from these six capital sources, of descent, of form of government, of religion in the northern provinces, of manners in the southern, of education, of the remoteness of situation from the first mover of government—from all these causes a fierce spirit of liberty has grown up. It has grown with the growth of the people in your colonies, and increased with the increase of their wealth: a spirit, that, unhappily meeting with an exercise of power in England, which, however lawful, is not reconcilable to any ideas of liberty, much less with theirs, has kindled this flame that is ready to consume us.

I do not mean to commend either spirit in this excess, or the moral causes which produce it. Perhaps a more smooth and accommodating spirit of freedom in them would be more acceptable to us. Perhaps ideas of liberty might be desired more reconcilable with an arbitrary and boundless authority. Perhaps we might wish the colonists to be persuaded that their liberty is more secure when held in trust from them by us (as their guardians during a perpetual minority) than with any part of it in their own hands. But the question is not, whether their spirit deserves praise or blame, what, in the name of God, shall we do with it? You have before you the object, such as it is, with all its glories, with all its imperfections on its head. You see the magnitude, the importance, the temper, the habits, the disorders. By all these considerations we are strongly urged to determine something concerning it. We are called upon to fix some rule and line for our future conduct, which may give a little stability to our politics, and prevent the return of such unhappy deliberations as the present. Every such return will bring the matter before us in a still more untractable form. For what astonishing and incredible things have we not seen already! What monsters have not been generated from the unnatural contention! Whilst every principle of authority and resistance has been pushed, upon both sides, as far as it would go, there is nothing so solid and certain, either in reasoning or in practice, that has not been shaken. Until very lately, all authority in America seemed to be nothing but an emanation from yours. Even the popular part of the colony constitution derived all its activity, and its first vital movement, from the pleasure of the crown. We thought, Sir, that the utmost which the discontented colonists could do was to disturb authority; we never dreamt they could of themselves supply it, knowing in general what an operose business it is to establish a government absolutely new. But having, for our purposes in this contention, resolved that none but an obedient assembly should sit, the humors of the people there, finding all passage through the legal channel stopped, with great violence broke out another way. Some provinces have tried their experiment, as we have tried ours; and theirs has succeeded. They have formed a government sufficient for its purposes, without the battle of a revolution or the troublesome formality of an election. Evident necessity and tacit consent have done the business in an instant. So well they have done it, that Lord Dunmore (the accounts is among the fragments on your table) tells you that the new institution is infinitely better obeyed than the ancient government ever was in its most fortunate periods. Obedience is what makes government, and not the names by which it is called: not the name of Governor, as formerly, or Committee, as present. This new government has originated directly from the people, and was not transmitted through any of the ordinary artificial media of a positive constitution. It was not a manufacture ready formed, and transmitted to them in that condition from England. The evil arising from hence is this: that the colonists having once found the possibility of enjoying the advantages of order in the midst of a struggle for liberty, such struggles will not henceforward seem so terrible to the settled and sober part of mankind as they had appeared before the trial. . . .

We suffer as much at home by this loosening of all ties, and this concussion of all established opinions, as we do abroad. For, in order to prove that the Americans have no right to their liberties, we are every day endeavoring to subvert the maxims which preserve the whole spirit of our own. To prove that the Americans ought not to be free, we are obliged to depreciate the value of freedom itself; and we never seem to gain a paltry advantage over them in debate, without attacking some of those principles, or deriding some of those feelings, for which our ancestors have shed their blood. . . .

The temper and character which prevail in our colonies are, I am afraid, unalterable by any human art. We cannot, I fear, falsify the pedigree of this fierce people, and persuade them that they are not sprung from a nation in whose veins the blood of freedom circulates. The language in which they would hear you tell them this tale would detect the imposition; your speech would betray you. An Englishman is the unfittest person on earth to argue another Englishman into slavery.

I think it is nearly as little in our power to change their republican religion as their free descent, or to substitute the Roman Catholic as a penalty, or the Church of England as an improvement. The mode of inquisition and dragooning is going out of fashion in the Old World, and I should not confide much to their efficacy in the New. The education of the Americans is also on the same unalterable bottom with their religion. You cannot persuade them to burn their books of curious science, to banish their lawyers from their courts of law, or to quench the lights of their assemblies by refusing to choose those persons who are best read in their privileges. It would be no less impracticable to think of wholly annihilating the popular assemblies in which these lawyers sit. The army, by which we must govern in their place, would be far more chargeable to us, not quite so effectual, and perhaps, in the end, full as difficult to be kept in obedience.

With regard to the high aristocratic spirit of Virginia and the southern colonies, it has been proposed, I know, to reduce it by declaring a general enfranchisement of their slaves. This project has had its advocates and panegyrists; yet I never could argue myself into any opinion if it. Slaves are often much attached to their masters. A general wild offer of liberty would not always be accepted. History furnishes few instances of it. It is sometimes as hard to persuade slaves to be free as it is to compel freemen to be slaves; and in this auspicious scheme we should have both these pleasing tasks on our hands at once. But when we talk of enfranchisement, do we not perceive that the American master may enfranchise, too, and arm servile hands in defence of freedom? . . .

But let us suppose all these moral difficulties got over. The ocean remains. You cannot pump this dry; and as long as it continues in its present bed, so long all the causes which weaken authority by distance will continue. . . .

If, then, the removal of the causes of this spirit of American liberty be, for the greater part, or rather entirely, impracticable. . . . No way is open, but . . . to comply with the American spirit as necessary, or, if you please, to submit to it as a necessary evil.

If we adopt this mode, if we mean to conciliate and concede, let us see of what nature the concession ought to be. To ascertain the nature of our concession, we must look at their complaint. The colonies complain that they have not the characteristic mark and seal of British freedom. They complain that they are taxed in a Parliament in which they are not represented. If you mean to satisfy them at all, you must satisfy them with regard to this complaint. . . .

You will now perhaps imagine that I am on the point of proposing to you a scheme for a representation of the colonies in Parliament. Perhaps I might be inclined to entertain some such thought; but a great flood stops me in my course. *Opposuit Natura*. I cannot remove the eternal barriers of the creation. . . .

I only wish you to recognize, for the theory, the ancient constitutional policy of this kingdom with regard to representation, as that policy has been declared in acts of Parliament, and as to the practice, to return to that mode which an uniform experience has marked out to you as best, and in which you walked with security, advantage, and honor, until the year 1763.

My resolutions, therefore, mean to establish the equity and justice of a taxation of America by *grant*, and not by *imposition*; to mark the *legal competency* of the colony assemblies for the support of their government in peace, and for public aids in time of war; to acknowledge that this legal competency has had *a dutiful and beneficial exercise*, and that experience has shown *the benefit of their grants*, and *the futility of Parliamentary taxation, as a method of supply*.

These solid truths compose six fundamental propositions. There are three more resolutions corollary to these. If you admit the first set, you can hardly reject the others. But if you admit the first, I shall be far from solicitous whether you accept of refuse the last. I think these six massive pillars will be of strength sufficient to support the temple of British concord. I have no more doubt than I entertain of my existence, that, if you admitted these, you would command an immediate peace, and, with but tolerable future management, a lasting obedience in America. . . .

The first is a resolution "That the colonies and plantations of Great Britain in North America, consisting of fourteen separate governments, and containing two millions and upwards of free inhabitants, have not had the liberty and privilege of electing and sending any knights and burgesses, or others, to represent them in the high court of Parliament." . . .

The second is like unto the first, "That the said colonies and plantations have been made liable to, and bounden by, several subsidies, payments, rates, and taxes, given and granted by Parliament, though the said colonies and plantations have not their knights and burgesses in the said high court of Parliament, of their own election, to represent the condition of their country; by lack whereof they have been oftentimes touched and grieved by subsidies, given, granted, and assented to, in the said court, in a manner prejudicial to the common wealth, quietness, rest, and peace of the subjects inhabiting within the same." . . .

The next proposition is, "That, from the distance of the said colonies, and from other circumstances, no method hath hitherto been devised for procuring a representation in Parliament for the said colonies." . . .

The fourth resolution is, "That each of the said colonies hath within itself a body, chosen, in part or in the whole, by the freemen, freeholders, or other free inhabitants thereof, commonly called the General Assembly, or General Court, with powers legally to raise, levy and assess, according to the several usages of such colonies, duties and taxes towards defraying all sorts of public services." . . .

The fifth resolution is also a resolution of fact, "That the said general assemblies, general courts, or other bodies legally qualified as aforesaid, have at sundry times freely granted several large subsidies and public aids for his Majesty's service, according to their abilities, when required thereto by letter from one of his Majesty's principal Secretaries of State; and that their right to grant the same, and their cheerfulness and sufficiency in the said grants, have been at sundry times acknowledged by Parliament." . . .

I think, then, I am, from those journals, justified in the sixth and last resolution, which is "That it hath been found by experience, that the manner of granting the said supplies and aids by the said general assemblies hath been more agreeable to the inhabitants of the said colonies, and more beneficial and conducive to the public service, than the mode of giving and granting aids and subsidies in Parliament, to be raised and paid in the said colonies. . . .

The question now, on all this accumulated matter, is whether you will choose to abide by a profitable experience or a mischievous theory? whether you choose to build on imagination or fact? whether you prefer enjoyment or hope? satisfaction in your subjects, or discontent? . . .

I do not know that the colonies have, in any general way, or in any cool hour, gone much beyond the demand of immunity in relation to taxes. It is not fair to judge of the temper or dispositions of any man or any set of men, when they are composed and at rest, from their conduct of their expressions in a state of disturbance and irritation. It is, besides, a very great mistake to imagine that mankind follow up practically any speculative principle, either of government or of freedom, as far as it will go in argument and logical illation. We Englishmen stop very short of the principles upon which we support any given part of our Constitution, or even the whole of it together. I could easily, if I had not already tired you, give you very striking and convincing instances of it. This is nothing but what is natural and proper. All government, indeed every human benefit and enjoyment, every virtue and every prudent act, is founded on compromise and barter. We balance inconveniences; we give and take; we remit some rights, that we may enjoy others; and we choose rather to be happy citizens that subtle disputants. As we must give away some natural liberty, to enjoy civil advantages, so we must sacrifice some civil liberties, for the advantages to be derived from the communion and fellowship of a great empire. But, in all fair dealings, the thing bought must bear some proportion to the purchase paid. None will barter away the immediate jewel of his soul. Though a great house is apt to make slaves haughty, yet it is purchasing a part of the artificial importance of a great empire too dear, to pay for it all essential rights, and all the intrinsic dignity of human nature. None of us who would not risk his life rather than fall under a government purely arbitrary. But although there are some amongst us who think our Constitution wants many improvements to make it a complete system of liberty, perhaps none who are of that opinion would think it right to aim at such improvement by disturbing his country and risking everything that is dear to him. In every arduous enterprise, we consider what we are to lose, as well as what we are to gain; and the more and better stake of liberty every people possess, the less they will hazard in a vain attempt to make it more. These are *the cords of man*. Man acts from adequate motives relative to his interest, and not on metaphysical speculations. Aristotle, the great master of reasoning, cautions us, and with great weight and propriety, against this species of delusive geometrical accuracy in moral arguments, as the most fallacious of all sophistry. . . .

It is said, indeed, that this power of granting, vested in American assemblies, would dissolve the unity of the empire. . . . I do not know what this unity means; nor has it ever been heard of, that I know, in the constitutional policy of this country. The very idea of subordination of parts excludes this notion of simple and undivided unity. England is the head; but she is not the head and the members too. Ireland has ever had from the beginning a separate, but not an independent legislature, which, far from distracting, promoted the union of the whole. Everything was sweetly and harmoniously disposed through both islands for the conservation of English dominion and the communication of English liberties. I do not see that the same principles might not be carried into twenty islands, and with regard to America, as far as the internal circumstances of the two countries are the same. I know no other unity of this empire than I can draw from its example during these periods, when it seemed to my poor understanding more united than it is now, or than it is likely to be by the present methods. . . .

My hold of the colonies is in the close affection which grows from common names, from kindred blood, from similar privileges, and equal protection. These are ties which, though light as air, are as strong as links of iron. Let the colonies always keep the idea of their civil rights associated with your government—they will cling and grapple to you, and no force under heaven will be of power to tear them from their allegiance. But let it be once understood that your government may be one thing and their privileges another, that these two things may exist without any mutual relation—the cement is gone, the cohesion is loosened, and everything hastens to decay and dissolution. As long as you have the wisdom to keep the sovereign authority of this country as the sanctuary of liberty, the sacred temple consecrated to our common faith, wherever the chosen race and sons of England worship freedom, they will turn their faces towards you. The more they multiply, the more friends you will have; the more ardently they love liberty, the more perfect will be their obedience. Slavery they can have anywhere. It is a weed that grows in every soil. They may have it from Spain, they may have it from Prussia. But, until you become lost to all feeling of your true interest and your natural dignity, freedom they can have from none but you. This is the commodity of price, of which you have the monopoly. This is the true Act of Navigation, which binds to you the commerce of the colonies, and through them secures to you the wealth of the world. Deny them this participation of freedom, and you break that sole bond which originally made, and must still preserve, the unity of the empire. Do not entertain so weak an imagination as that your registers and your bonds, your affidavits and your sufferances, your cockets and your clearances, are what form the great securities of your commerce. Do not dream that your letters of office, and your instructions, and your suspending clauses are the things that hold together the great contexture of this mysterious whole. These things do not make your government. Dead instruments, passive tools as they are, it is the spirit of the English communion that gives all their life and efficacy to them. It is the spirit of the English Constitution, which, infused through the mighty mass, pervades, feeds, unites, invigorates, vivifies every part of the empire, even down to the minutest member. . . .

In full confidence of this unalterable truth, I now (*quod felix faustumque sit!*) lay the first stone of the Temple of Peace; and I move you,

"That the colonies and plantations of Great Britain in North America, consisting of fourteen separate governments, and containing two millions and upwards of free inhabitants, have not had the liberty and privilege of electing and sending any knights and burgesses, or others, to represent them in the high court of Parliament."

IV. Imperial Shockwaves

The North American colonies were only half of all British colonies in the 1770s. The other thirteen followed the unfolding American crisis with concern. Changes in the imperial relationship with North America might have significant consequences for their own place within the British Empire.

8. THE VIEW FROM JAMAICA (1774)[8]

The Jamaican planter elite had mixed feelings about the growing crisis. On one hand, they shared many of the North Americans' concerns about Parliamentary taxation and the rights of Englishmen. They even felt some of the same paranoia about the "Papism" they felt was creeping into British institutions. But on the other hand, they realized that they were in a distinctly vulnerable situation. Living on an island in the midst of a hostile enslaved population and surrounded by foreign colonies (French and Spanish) eager for revenge for the defeats of the Seven Years' War, they knew that they depended on British power for their continued prosperity and survival.

We, your majesty's most dutiful and loyal subjects, the assembly of Jamaica, having taken into consideration the present critical state of the colonies, humbly approach the throne, to assure your majesty of our must dutiful regard to your royal person

[8]British National Archives, Colonial Office, series 140, box 46.

and family, and our attachment to, and reliance on, our fellow subjects in Great Britain, founded on the most solid and durable basis, the continued enjoyment of our personal rights, and the security of our properties.

That, weak and feeble as this colony is, from its very small number of white inhabitants, and its peculiar situation, from the encumbrance of more than two hundred thousand slaves, it cannot be supposed that we now intend, or ever could have intended, resistance to Great Britain.

That this colony has never, by riots or other violent measures opposed, or per-mitted an act of resistance against, any law imposed on us by Great Britain, though always truly sensible of our just rights, and of the pernicious consequences both to the parent and infant state, with which some of them must be attended; always re-lying, with the most implicit confidence, on the justice and paternal tenderness of your majesty, even to the most feeble and distant of your subjects; and depending, that when your majesty and your parliament should have maturely considered, and deliberated on, the claims of Great Britain and her colonies, every cause of dissatisfaction would be removed.

That, justly alarmed with the approaching horrors of an unnatural contest be-tween Great Britain and her colonies, in which the most dreadful calamities to this island, and the inevitable destruction of the small sugar colonies are involved, and excited by these apprehensions, as well as by our affection for our fellow subjects, both in Great Britain and the colonies, we implore your majesty's favourable recep-tion of this our humble petition and memorial, as well on behalf of ourselves and our constituents, the good people of this island, as on behalf of all other your maj-esty's subjects, the colonists of America, but especially those who labour at present under the heavy weight of your majesty's displeasure, for whom we entreat to be admitted as humble suitors, that we may not, at so important a crisis, be wanting to contribute our sincere and well meant (however small) endeavours, to heal those disorders which may otherwise terminate in the destruction of the empire.

That, as we conceive it necessary, for this purpose, to enter into the different claims of Great Britain and her colonies, we beg leave to place it in the royal mind, as the first established principle of the constitution, that the people of England have a right to partake, and do partake, of the legislation of their country; and that no laws can affect them, but such as receive their assent, given by themselves or their representatives; and it follows therefore, that no one part of your majesty's English subjects, either can, or ever could, legislate for any other part.

That the settlers of the first colonies, but especially those of the elder colo-nies of North America, as well as the conquerors of this island, were a part of the English people, in every respect equal to them, and possessed of every right and privilege at the time of their emigration, which the people of England were pos-sessed of; and, irrefragably, to that great right of consenting to the laws, which should bind them in all cases whatsoever; and who, emigrating at first in small numbers, when they might have been oppressed, such rights and privileges were constantly guaranteed by the crown to the emigrants and conquerors, to be held and enjoyed by them, in the places to which they emigrated, and were confirmed by many repeated solemn engagements, made public by proclamations, under the faith of which they did actually emigrate and conquer; that therefore the people of England had no rights, power, or privilege to give to the emigrants, as these were at the time of their emigration possessed of all such rights, equally with themselves.

That the peers of England were possessed of very eminent and distinguished privileges in their own rights, as a branch of legislature; a court of justice in the dernier resort, for all appeals from the people; and, in the first instance, for all causes instituted by the representatives of the people; but that it does not appear, that they ever considered themselves as acting in such capacities for the colonies; the peers having never, to this day, heard or determined the causes of the colonists in appeal, in which it ever was, and is their duty, to serve the subjects within the realm.

That, from what has been said, it appears that the emigrants could receive nothing from either the peers or the people; the former being unable to communicate their privileges, and the latter on no more than an equal footing with themselves; but that, with the king it was far otherwise; the royal prerogative, as now annexed to and belonging to the crown, being totally independent of the people, who cannot invade, add to, or diminish it, nor restrain or invalidate those legal grants, which the prerogative hath a just right to give, and hath very liberally given, for the encouragement of colonization; to some colonies it granted almost all the royal powers of government, which they hold and enjoy at this day; but to none of them did it grant less, than to the first conquerors of this island; in whole favour it is declared, by a royal proclamation, "that they shall have the same privileges to all intents and purposes, as the free-born subjects of England."

That, to use the name or authority of the people of the parent state, to take away or render ineffectual the legal grants of the crown to the colonists, is delusive and destroys that confidence which the people have ever had, and ought to have, of the most solemn royal grants in their favour, and renders unstable and insecure those very rights and privileges which prompted their emigration.

That your colonists and your petitioners, having the most implicit confidence in the royal faith, pledged to them in the most solemn manner by your predecessors, rested satisfied with their different portions of the royal grants; and having been bred, from their infancy, to venerate the name of parliament, a word still dear to the heart of every Briton, and considered as the palladium of liberty, and the great source from whence their own is derived, received the several acts of parliament of England and Great Britain, for the regulation of the trade of the colonies, as the salutary precautions of a prudent father, for the prosperity of a wide extended family; and, that in this light we received them, without a thought of questioning the right, the whole tenor of our conduct will demonstrate, for above one hundred years: that though we received those regulations of trade from our fellow subjects of England and Great Britain, so advantageous to us, as colonists, as Englishmen, and Britons, we did not thereby confer on them a power of legislating for us, far less that of destroying us and our children, by divesting us of all rights and property.

That, with reluctance, we have been drawn from the prosecution of our internal affairs, to behold with amazement a plan almost carried into execution, for enslaving the colonies, founded, as we conceive, on a claim of parliament to bind the colonists in all cases whatever.

Your humble petitioners have, for several years, with deep and silent sorrow, lamented this unrestrained exercise of legislative power; still hoping, from the interposition of their sovereign, to avert that last and greatest of calamities, that of being reduced to an abject state of slavery, by having arbitrary government established in the colonies; for the very attempting of which, a minister of your predecessors was impeached by a house of commons.

With like sorrow do we find the Popish religion established by law, which by treaty was only to be tolerated.

That the most essential rights of the colonists have been invaded, and their property given and granted to your majesty, by men not entitled to such a power.

That the murder of the colonists hath been encouraged, by another act, disallowing and annulling their trials by juries of the vicinage; and that fleets and armies have been sent to enforce those dreadful laws.

We, therefore, in this desperate extremity, most humbly beg leave to approach the throne, to declare to your majesty, that our fellow subjects in Great Britain, and consequently their representatives, the house of commons, have not a right, as we trust we have shewn, to legislate for the colonies; and that your petitioners, and the colonists, are not, nor ought to be, bound by any other laws, than such as they have themselves assented to, and not disallowed by your majesty.

Your petitioners do therefore make this claim and demand from their sovereign, as guarantee of their just rights, on the faith and confidence of which they have settled, and continue to reside in these distant parts of the empire, that no laws shall be made, and attempted to be forced upon them, injurious to their rights as colonists, Englishmen, or Britons.

That your petitioners, truly sensible of the great advantages that have arisen from the regulations of trade in general, prior to the year 1760, as well to Great Britain and her colonies, as to your petitioners in particular, and being anxiously desirous of increasing the good effects of these laws, as well as to remove an obstacle which is new in our government, and could not have existed on the principles of our constitution, as it hath arisen from colonization, we do declare for ourselves, and the good people of this island, that we freely consent to the operations of all such acts of the British parliament, as are limited to the regulation of our external commerce only, and the sole objects of which, are the mutual advantage of Great Britain and her colonies.

We, your petitioners, do therefore beseech your majesty, that you will be pleased, as the common parent to your subjects, to become a mediator between your European and American subjects, and to consider the latter, however far removed from your royal preference, as equally entitled to your protection and the benefits of the English constitution; the deprivation of which must dissolve that dependance on the parent state, which it is our glory to acknowledge, whilst enjoying those rights under her protection; but, should this bond of union ever be destroyed, and the colonists reduced to consider themselves as tributaries to Britain, they must cease to venerate her as an affectionate parent.

We beseech your majesty to believe, that it is our earnest prayer to Almighty Providence, to preserve your majesty in all happiness, prosperity, and honour, and that there never may be wanting one of your illustrious line, to transmit the blessings of our excellent constitution to the latest posterity, and to reign in the hearts of a loyal, grateful, and affectionate people.

9. THE VIEW FROM IRELAND (1776)[9]

Ireland was the richest, most populous part of the British Empire in the 1770s. Technically not a colony, it was a kingdom (ruled by the same king as England, George III) with a parliament of its own. Most Irish political elites displayed considerably less sympathy toward the American cause than the Jamaica planters. But there were a few opposing Irish voices. One was Hugh Boyd, a Protestant clergyman, who published a strongly pro-American pamphlet in 1776. In the end, however, neither Boyd's pamphlet nor the handful of other, similar writings deflected the Irish Parliament's support for the British Crown. During the American Revolutionary War, Ireland would admirably fulfill its accustomed role within the Empire as source of soldiers, supplies, and revenue for the British military.

Let this country be timely warned. The spirit of despotism is gone forth. Oppression her object, devastation her means, famine, sword, and fire her instruments, even now she ravages the new world. If Heaven, for ultimate purposes beyond human reach, permit success to the oppressor; and if that mighty continent must sink to slavery, can this little island hope for a happier doom; unless she call forth all her virtue, and exert all her spirit, to deserve and to obtain it? Flushed with the false glories of her unnatural conquest, will the power of England spare her passive sister-kingdom, when she has crushed the active and just exertions of her sons? This unhappy country will then feel, and will lament too late, the mischiefs of her voluntary folly, in abetting the tyranny of the parent-state over her dependencies. For, what better name than tyranny can be given to a system of arbitrary exaction, supported by the sword? What other principles can actuate our rulers to the prosecution of such a war? What is its object? Not taxation. That, the Ministers have publickly disclaimed in parliament: and General Burgoyne in his letter to Lee expressly abandons it. "If, says he, relief from the uncommercial taxes (tea, etc.) be the object of the quarrel, the war is at an end." Why then was not that relief afforded them, in order to end the war? Because the Ministers pretended it would not have

---

[9]Hugh Boyd, *Letters Addressed to the Electors of the County of Antrim by a Freeholder* (Dublin: M. Mills, 1776), x–xviii.

satisfied America. . . . But shall the random or malicious guesses of ignorant men, for such they have been proved, be admitted as conclusive evidence against the peace and happiness of the empire? Certainly not: even if no answer were given to them. For to accuse is not to condemn; and administration are not yet participant of the infallibility of their new ally of Rome; so as to command implicit assent to their assertions, because they are theirs. . . . My inference is, that the avowal of the ministry is a pretence to cover the blackest designs. . . . Taxation is not the object of the war. The ministers disclaim it. To check the independent views of America, was not the motive, for no such views were entertained, and therefore no such motive could exist. But liberty existed, flourished, in that great continent; and that is a crime of the deepest dye in the ethicks of modern polity. . . . Precisely the same principle of arbitrary dominion over the property and liberty of America, unlimited and unconditional, which some of the publick bodies of this kingdom have applauded, will operate against the liberty and property of Ireland.

V. The Breaking Point (1775–1776)

In April 1775, open warfare began when Massachusetts militia ambushed a force of British soldiers at Lexington and Concord. Fighting raged during the year that followed. American troops under George Washington invested Boston and forced the British garrison to withdraw. The Americans then went on the offensive, mounting an invasion to conquer Canada (which failed) and even a raid on the Bahamas. Fighting on a smaller scale spread across the Thirteen Colonies, even the South. But this open warfare was not accompanied by a formal rupture. Even while pursuing the war effort, the Continental Congress still hoped to find a way to reconcile with Great Britain. Independence was not inevitable; rather, it was part of a political process that unfolded during the first year of the war, from mid-1775 through mid-1776.

10. DECLARATION OF THE CAUSES AND NECESSITY OF TAKING UP ARMS (JUNE 1775)[10]

In 1775, the Continental Congress issued a full-throated justification of its military opposition to Great Britain—while at the same time avoiding a declaration of independence and expressing the desire to restore imperial unity.

If it was possible for men, who exercise their reason to believe, that the divine Author of our existence intended a part of the human race to hold an absolute

---

[10]"A Declaration by the Representatives of the United Colonies of North-America, Now Met in Congress at Philadelphia, Setting Forth the Causes and Necessity of Their Taking Up Arms." The Avalon Project: Documents in Law, History and Diplomacy, http://avalon.law.yale.edu/18th_century/arms.asp

property in, and an unbounded power over others, marked out by his infinite goodness and wisdom, as the objects of a legal domination never rightfully resist-ible, however severe and oppressive, the inhabitants of these colonies might at least require from the parliament of Great-Britain some evidence, that this dreadful authority over them, has been granted to that body. But a reverence for our Cre-ator, principles of humanity, and the dictates of common sense, must convince all those who reflect upon the subject, that government was instituted to promote the welfare of mankind, and ought to be administered for the attainment of that end. The legislature of Great-Britain, however, stimulated by an inordinate passion for a power not only unjustifiable, but which they know to be peculiarly reprobated by the very constitution of that kingdom, and desperate of success in any mode of contest, where regard should be had to truth, law, or right, have at length, desert-ing those, attempting to effect their cruel and impolitic purpose of enslaving these colonies by violence, and have thereby rendered it necessary for us to close with their last appeal from reason to arms. Yet, however blinded that assembly may be, by their intemperate rage for unlimited domination, so to slight justice and the opinion of mankind, we esteem ourselves bound by obligations of respect to the rest of the world, to make known the justice of our cause.

Our forefathers, inhabitants of the islands of Great-Britain, left their native land, to seek on these shores a residence for civil and religious freedom. At the ex-pense of their blood, at the hazard of their fortunes, without the least charge to the country from which they removed, by unceasing labour, and an unconquerable spirit, they effected settlements in the distant and unhospitable wilds of Amer-ica, then filled with numerous and warlike barbarians. Societies or governments, vested with perfect legislatures, were formed under charters from the crown, and an harmonious intercourse was established between the colonies and the kingdom from which they derived their origin. The mutual benefits of this union became in a short time so extraordinary, as to excite astonishment. It is universally confessed, that the amazing increase of the wealth, strength, and navigation of the realm arose from this source; and the minister, who so wisely and successfully directed the measures of Great-Britain in the late war, publicly declared, that these colonies enabled her to triumph over her enemies.

Towards the conclusion of that war, it pleased our sovereign to make a change in his counsels. From that fatal movement, the affairs of the British empire began to fall into confusion, and gradually sliding from the summit of glorious prosper-ity, to which they had been advanced by the virtues and abilities of one man, are at length distracted by the convulsions, that now shake it to its deepest foundations. The new ministry finding the brave foes of Britain, though frequently defeated, yet still contending, took up the unfortunate idea of granting them a hasty peace, and then subduing her faithful friends.

These colonies were judged to be in such a state, as to present victories with-out bloodshed, and all the easy emoluments of statuteable plunder. The uninter-rupted tenor of their peaceable and respectable behaviour from the beginning of colonization, their dutiful, zealous, and useful services during the war, though so recently and amply acknowledged in the most honourable manner by his majesty, by the late king, and by parliament, could not save them from the meditated innovations. Parliament was influenced to adopt the pernicious project, and assuming a new power over them, have in the course of eleven years, given such decisive specimens of the spirit and consequences attending this power, as to leave no doubt concerning the effects of acquiescence under it. They have undertaken to give and grant our money without our consent, though we have ever exercised an exclusive right to dispose of our own property; statutes have been passed for extending the jurisdiction of courts of admiralty and vice-admiralty beyond their ancient limits; for depriving us of the accustomed and inestimable privilege of trial by jury, in cases affecting both life and property; for suspending the legislature of one of the colonies; for interdicting all commerce to the capital of another; and for altering fundamentally the form of government established by charter, and secured by acts of its own legislature solemnly confirmed by the crown; for exempting the "murderers" of colonists from legal trial, and in effect, from punishment; for erecting in a neighbouring province, acquiring by the joint arms of Great-Britain and America, a despotism dangerous to our very existence; and for quartering soldiers upon the colonists in time of profound peace. It has also been resolved in parliament that colonists charged with committing certain offences shall be transported to England to be tried.

But why should we enumerate our injuries in detail? By one statute it is declared, that parliament can "of right make laws to bind us in all cases whatsoever." What is to defend us against so enormous, so unlimited a power? Not a single man of those who assume it, is chosen by us or is subject to our control or influence; but, on the contrary, they are all of them exempt from the operation of such laws, and an American revenue, if not diverted from the ostensible purposes for which it is raised would actually lighten their own burdens in proportion, as they increase ours. We saw the misery to which such despotism would reduce us. We for ten years incessantly and ineffectively besieged the throne as supplicants; we reasoned, we remonstrated with parliament, in the most mild and decent language.

Administration sensible that we should regard these oppressive measures as freemen ought to do, sent over fleets and armies to enforce them. The indignation of the Americans was roused, it is true; but it was the indignation of a virtuous, loyal, and affectionate people. A Congress of delegates from the United Colonies was assembled at Philadelphia, on the fifth day of last September. We resolved again to offer an humble and dutiful petition to the King, and also addressed our fellow-subjects of Great-Britain. We have pursued every temperate, every respectable measure, we have even proceeded to break off our commercial intercourse with our fellow-subjects, as the last peaceable admonition, that our attachment to no nation upon earth should supplant our attachment to liberty. This, we flattered ourselves, was the ultimate step of the controversy: but subsequent events have shewn, how vain was this hope of finding moderation in our enemies.

Several threatening expressions against the colonies were inserted in his majesty's speech; our petition, tho' we were told it was a decent one, and that his majesty had been pleased to receive it graciously, and to promise laying it before his parliament, was huddled into both houses among a bundle of American papers, and there neglected. The lords and commons in their address, in the month of February, said, that "a rebellion at the time actually existed within the province of Massachusetts-Bay; and that those concerned with it, had been countenanced and encouraged by unlawful combinations and engagements, entered into by his majesty, that he would take the most effectual measures to inforce the obedience to the laws and authority of the supreme legislature." Soon after, the commercial intercourse of whole colonies, with foreign countries, and with each other, was cut off by an act of parliament; by another several of them were entirely prohibited from the fisheries in the seas near their coasts, on which they always depended for their sustenance; and large reinforcements of ships and troops were immediately sent over to general Gage.

Fruitless were all the entreaties, arguments, and eloquence of an illustrious band of the most distinguished peers, and commoners, who nobly and strenuously asserted the justice of our cause, to stay, or even to mitigate the heedless fury with which these accumulated and unexampled outrages were hurried on. Equally fruitless was the interference of the city of London, of Bristol, and many other respectable towns in our favor. Parliament adopted an insidious manoeuvre calculated to divide us, to establish a perpetual auction of taxations where colony should bid against colony, all of them uninformed what ransom would redeem their lives; and thus to extort from us, at the point of the bayonet, the unknown sums that should be sufficient to gratify, if possible to gratify ministerial rapacity, with the miserable indulgence left to us of raising, in our own mode, the prescribed tribute. What terms more rigid and humiliating could have been dictated by remorseless victories to conquered enemies? In our circumstances to accept them, would be to deserve them.

Soon after the intelligence of these proceedings arrived on this continent, general Gage, who in the course of the last year had taken possession of the town of Boston, in the province of Massachusetts-Bay, and still occupied it a garrison, on the 19th day of April, sent out from that place a large detachment of his army, who made an unprovoked assault on the inhabitants of the said province, at the town of Lexington, as appears by the affidavits of a great number of persons, some of whom were officers and soldiers of that detachment, murdered eight of the inhabitants, and wounded many others. From thence the troops proceeded in warlike array to the town of Concord, where they set upon another party of the inhabitants of the same province, killing several and wounding more, until compelled to retreat by the country people suddenly assembled to repel this cruel aggression. Hostilities, thus commenced by the British troops, have been since prosecuted by them without regard to faith or reputation. The inhabitants of Boston being confined within that town by the general their governor, and having, in order to procure their dismission, entered into a treaty with him, it was stipulated that the said inhabitants having deposited their arms with their own magistrate, should have liberty to depart, taking with them their other effects. They accordingly delivered up their arms, but in the open violation of honour, in defiance of the obligation of treaties, which even savage nations esteemed sacred, the governor ordered the arms deposited as aforesaid, that they might be preserved for their owners, to be seized by a body of soldiers; detained the greatest part of the inhabitants in the town, and compelled the few who were permitted to retire, to leave their most valuable effects behind.

By this perfidy wives are separated from their husbands, children from their parents, the aged and the sick from their relations and friends, who wish to attend and comfort them; and those who have been used to live in plenty and even elegance, are reduced to deplorable distress.

The general, further emulating his ministerial masters, by a proclamation bearing the date on the 12th day of June, after venting the grossest falsehoods and calumnies against the good people of these colonies, proceeds to "declare them all, either by name or description, to be rebels and traitors, to supercede the course of the common law, and instead thereof to publish and order the use and exercise of the law martial." His troops have butchered our countrymen, have wantonly burnt Charlestown, besides a considerable number of houses in other places; our ships and vessels are seized; the necessary supplies of provisions are intercepted, and he is exerting his utmost power to spread destruction and devastation around him.

We have received certain intelligence, that General Carleton, the governor of Canada, is instigating the people of that province and the Indians to fall upon us; and we have but too much reason to apprehend, that schemes have been formed to excite domestic enemies against us. In brief, a part of these colonies now feel, and all of them are sure of feeling, as far as the vengeance of administration can inflict on them, the complicated calamities of fire, sword and famine. We are reduced to the alternative of chusing an unconditional submission to the tyranny of irritated ministers, or resistance by force. The latter is our choice. We have counted the cost of this contest, and find nothing so dreadful as voluntary slavery. Honour, justice, and humanity, forbid us tamely to surrender that freedom which we received from our gallant ancestors, and which our innocent posterity have a right to receive from us. We cannot endure the infamy and guilt of resigning succeeding generation to that wretchedness which inevitably awaits them, if we basely entail hereditary bondage upon them.

Our cause is just. Our union is perfect. Our internal resources are great, and, if necessary, foreign assistance is undoubtedly attainable. We gratefully acknowledge, as signal instances of the Divine favour towards us, that his Providence would not permit us to be called into this severe controversy, until we were grown up to our present strength, had been previously exercised in warlike operation, and possessed of the means of defending ourselves. With hearts fortified with these animating reflections, we most solemnly, before God and the world, declare, that, exerting the utmost energy of those powers, which our beneficent Creator hath graciously bestowed upon us, the arms we have been compelled by our enemies to assume, we will, in defiance of every hazard, with unabating firmness and perseverance, employ for the preservation of our liberties; being with one mind resolved to die freemen rather than to live slaves.

Lest this declaration should disquiet the minds of our friends and fellow-subjects in any part of the empire, we assure them that we mean not to dissolve that union which has so long and so happily subsisted between us, and which we sincerely wish to see restored. Necessity has not yet driven us into that desperate measure, or induced us to excite any other nation to war against them. We have not raised armies with ambitious designs of separating from Great-Britain, and establishing independent states. We fight not for our glory or for conquest. We exhibit to mankind the remarkable spectacle of a people attacked by unprovoked enemies, without any imputation or even suspicion of offence. They boast of their privileges and civilization, and yet proffer no milder conditions than servitude or death.

In our own native land, in defence of our freedom that is our birthright, and which we ever enjoyed till the late violation of it, for the protection of our property, acquired solely by the honest industry of our fore-fathers and ourselves, against violence actually offered, we have taken up arms. We shall lay them down when hostilities shall cease on the part of the aggressors, and all danger of their being renewed shall be removed, and not before.

With an humble confidence in the mercies of the supreme and impartial Judge and Ruler of the Universe, we most devoutly implore his divine goodness to protect us happily through this great conflict, to dispose our adversaries to reconciliation on reasonable terms, and thereby to relieve the empire from the calamities of civil war.

11. THOMAS PAINE, *COMMON SENSE* (1776)[11]

Thomas Paine was an English political writer who immigrated to America in 1774. He published Common Sense *in January 1776 to convince Americans that they were fooling themselves by thinking that they could fight Britain while remaining loyal to the monarchy. To accomplish this, he made a strong argument for American independence and republicanism—accompanied by personal attacks on King George III who had hitherto before been spared the venom of patriot pamphleteers.* Common Sense *was a publishing success, with 500,000 copies printed during the Revolutionary Wars. It is often credited with pushing America to declare independence. Paine's revolutionary career did not end with the American Revolution. Thrilled by the French Revolution, he moved to France where he was elected to the revolutionary legislature. His impact on French revolutionary politics, however, was limited, for he barely understood the language.*

Some writers have so confounded society with government, as to leave little or no distinction between them; whereas they are not only different, but have different origins. Society is produced by our wants, and government by our wickedness;

---

[11]Thomas Paine, *Common Sense* (Philadelphia, PA: W. and T. Bradford, 1776), 7–80.

the former promotes our happiness positively by uniting our affections, the latter negatively by restraining our vices. The one encourages intercourse, the other creates distinctions. The first is a patron, the last a punisher.

Society in every state is a blessing, but government even in its best state is but a necessary evil, in its worst state an intolerable one; for when we suffer, or are exposed to the same miseries by a government, which we might expect in a country without government, our calamities are heightened by reflecting that we furnish the means by which we suffer! Government, like dress, is the badge of lost innocence; the palaces of kings are built on the ruins of the bowers of paradise. For were the impulses of conscience clear, uniform, and irresistibly obeyed, man would need no other lawgiver; but that not being the case, he finds it necessary to surrender up a part of his property to furnish means for the protection of the rest; and this he is induced to do by the same prudence which in every other case advises him out of two evils to choose the least. Wherefore, security being the true design and end of government, it unanswerably follows that whatever form thereof appears most likely to ensure it to us, with the least expense and greatest benefit, is preferable to all others. . . .

I have heard it asserted by some, that as America hath flourished under her former connection with Great Britain, that the same connection is necessary towards her future happiness, and will always have the same effect. Nothing can be more fallacious than this kind of argument. We may as well assert, that because a child has thrived upon milk, that it is never to have meat; or that the first twenty years of our lives is to become a precedent for the next twenty. But even this is admitting more than is true, for I answer roundly, that America would have flourished as much, and probably much more, had no European power had any thing to do with her. The commerce by which she hath enriched herself are the necessaries of life, and will always have a market while eating is the custom of Europe.

But she has protected us, say some. That she hath engrossed us is true, and defended the continent at our expense as well as her own is admitted, and she would have defended Turkey from the same motive, viz. the sake of trade and dominion.

Alas, we have been long led away by ancient prejudices and made large sacrifices to superstition. We have boasted the protection of Great Britain, without considering, that her motive was interest not attachment; that she did not protect us from enemies on our account, but from her enemies on her own account, from those who had no quarrel with us on any other account, and who will always be our enemies on the same account. Let Britain wave her pretensions to the continent, or the continent throw off the dependence, and we should be at peace with France and Spain were they at war with Britain. The miseries of Hanover last war ought to warn us against connections.

It hath lately been asserted in parliament, that the colonies have no relation to each other but through the parent country, i.e. that Pennsylvania and the Jerseys, and so on for the rest, are sister colonies by the way of England; this is certainly a very round-about way of proving enemyship, if I may so call it. France and Spain never were, nor perhaps ever will be our enemies as Americans, but as our being subjects of Great Britain.

But Britain is the parent country, say some. Then the more shame upon her conduct. Even brutes do not devour their young; nor savages make war upon their families; wherefore the assertion, if true, turns to her reproach; but it happens not to be true, or only partly so, and the phrase Parent or mother country hath been jesuitically adopted by the king and his parasites, with a low papistical design of gaining an unfair bias on the credulous weakness of our minds. Europe, and not England, is the parent country of America. This new world hath been the asylum for the persecuted lovers off civil and religious liberty from every Part of Europe. Hither have they fled, not from the tender embraces of the mother, but from the cruelty of the monster; and it is so far true of England, that the same tyranny which drove the first emigrants from home pursues their descendants still.

In this extensive quarter of the globe, we forget the narrow limits of three hundred and sixty miles (the extent of England) and carry our friendship on a larger scale; we claim brotherhood with every European Christian, and triumph in the generosity of the sentiment.

It is a pleasure to observe by what regular gradations we surmount the force of local prejudice, as we enlarge our acquaintance with the world. A man born in any town in England divided into parishes, will naturally associate most with his fellow parishioners (because their interests in many cases will be common) and distinguish him by the name of neighbor; if he meet him but a few miles from home, he drops the narrow idea of a street, and salutes him by the name of townsman; if he travels out of county, and meet him in any other, he forgets the minor divisions of street and town, and calls him countryman; i.e. countyman; but if in their foreign excursions they should associate in France or any other part of Europe, their local remembrance would be enlarged into that of Englishmen. And by a just parity of reasoning, all Europeans meeting in America, or any other quarter of the globe, are countrymen; for England, Holland, Germany, or Sweden, when compared with the whole, stand in the same places on the larger scale, which the divisions of street, town, and county do on smaller ones; distinctions too limited for continental minds. Not one third of the inhabitants, even of this province, are of English descent. Therefore I reprobate the phrase of parent or mother country applied to England only, as being false, selfish, narrow and ungenerous. . . .

I challenge the warmest advocate for reconciliation to shew a single advantage that this continent can reap by being connected with Great Britain. I repeat the challenge, not a single advantage is derived. Our corn will fetch its price in any market in Europe, and our imported goods must be paid for buy them where we will.

But the injuries and disadvantages we sustain by that connection, are without number; and our duty to mankind at large, as well as to ourselves, is to renounce the alliance. Because, any submission to, or dependence on, Great Britain tends directly to involve this continent in European wars and quarrels and sets us at variance with nations who would otherwise seek our friendship, and against whom we have neither anger nor complaint. As Europe is our market for trade, we ought to form no partial connection with any part of it. It is the true interest of America to steer clear of European contentions, which she can never do, while by her dependence on Britain, she is made the make-weight on the scale of British politics.

Europe is too thickly planted with kingdoms to be long at peace, and whenever a war breaks out between England and any foreign power, the trade of America goes to ruin, because of her connection with Britain. The next war may not turn out like the Past, and should it not, the advocates for reconciliation now will be wishing for separation then, because, neutrality in that case, would be safer convoy than a man of war. Every thing that is right or natural pleads for separation. The blood of the slain, the weeping voice of nature cries, 'TIS TIME TO PART. Even the distance at which the Almighty hath placed England and America, is a strong and natural proof, that the authority of the one, over the other, was never the design of Heaven. The time likewise at which the continent was discovered, adds weight to the argument, and the manner in which it was peopled increases the force of it. The reformation was preceded by the discovery of America, as if the Almighty graciously meant to open sanctuary to the persecuted in future years, when home should afford neither friendship nor safety.

The authority of Great Britain over this continent, is a form of government, which sooner or later must have an end. And a serious mind can draw no true pleasure by looking forward, under the painful and positive conviction, that what he calls the present constitution is merely temporary. As parents, we can have no joy knowing that this government is not sufficiently lasting to ensure any thing which we may bequeath to posterity. And by a plain method of argument, as we are running the next generation into debt, we ought to do the work of it, otherwise we use them meanly and pitifully. In order to discover the line of duty rightly, we should take our children in our hand, and fix our station a few years farther into life; that eminence will present a prospect, which a few present fears and prejudices conceal from our sight.

Though I would carefully avoid giving unnecessary offence, yet I am inclined to believe, that all those who espouse the doctrine of reconciliation, may be included within the following descriptions. Interested men, who are not to be trusted; weak men who cannot see; prejudiced men who will not see; and a certain set of moderate men, who think better of the European world than it deserves; and this last class by an ill-judged deliberation, will be the cause of more calamities to this continent than all the other three. . . .

The object contended for ought to bear some just proportion to the expense. The removal of North, or the whole detestable junto, is a matter unworthy the millions we have expended. A temporary stoppage of trade, was an inconvenience which we could have sufficiently balanced the repeal of all the acts complained of, had such repeals been obtained; but if the whole continent must take up arms, if every man must be a soldier, it is scarcely worth our while to fight against a contemptible ministry only. Dearly, dearly, do we pay for the repeal of the acts, if that is all we fight for; for in a just estimation, it is as great a folly to pay a Bunker Hill price for law, as for land. As I have always considered the independency of this continent as an event which sooner or later must arrive, so from the late rapid progress of the continent to maturity, the event could not be far off. Wherefore, on the breaking out of hostilities, it was not worth the while to have disputed a matter which time would have finally redressed, unless we meant to be in earnest; otherwise, it is like wasting an estate of a suit at law to regulate the trespasses of a tenant whose leasing is just expiring. No man was a warmer wisher of reconciliation than myself, before the fatal nineteenth of April 1775 (Massacre at Lexington), but the moment the event of that day was made known, I rejected the hardened, sullen tempered Pharaoh of England for ever, and disdain the wretch, that with the pretended title of FATHER OF HIS PEOPLE can unfeelingly hear of their slaughter, and composedly sleep with their blood upon his soul.

But admitting that matter were now made up, what would be the event? I answer, the ruin of the continent. And that for several reasons.

First, the power of governing still remaining in the hands of the king, he will have a negative over the whole legislation of this continent. And as he hath shown himself such an inveterate enemy to liberty and discovered such a thirst for arbitrary power, is he, or is he not, a proper man to say these colonies, "You shall make no laws but what I please." And is there any inhabitant in America so ignorant as not to know that according to what is called the present constitution, that this continent can make no laws but what the king gives leave to; and is there any man so unwise as not to see that (considering what has happened) he will suffer no Law to be made here, but such as suit his purpose. We may be as effectually enslaved by the want of laws in America as by submitting to laws made for us in England. After matters are made up (as it is called) can there be any doubt but the whole power of the crown will be exerted, to keep this continent as low and humble as possible? Instead of going forward we shall go backward, or be perpetually quarrelling or ridiculously petitioning. We are already greater than the king wishes us to be, and will he not hereafter endeavor to make us less? To bring the matter to one point. Is the power who is jealous of our prosperity a proper power to govern us? Whoever says No to this question is an independent, for independency means no more than whether we shall make our own laws, or whether the king, the greatest enemy this continent hath, or can have, shall tell us "there shall be no laws but such as I like." . . .

Secondly, that as even the best terms which we can expect to obtain can amount to no more than a temporary expedient or a kind of government by guardianship, which can last no longer than till the colonies come of age, so the general face and state of things, in the interim, will be unsettled and unpromising. Emigrants of property will not choose to come to a country whose form of government hangs but by a thread, and who is every day tottering on the brink of commotion and disturbance; and numbers of the present inhabitants would lay hold of the interval to dispose of their effects and quit the continent.

But the most powerful of all arguments is that nothing but independence, i.e. a continental form of government, can keep the peace of the continent and preserve it inviolate from civil wars. I dread the event of a reconciliation with Britain now, as it is more than probable that it will be followed by a revolt somewhere or other, the consequences of which may be far more fatal than all the malice of Britain. . . .

But where says some is the King of America? I'll tell you Friend, he reigns above and doth not make havoc of mankind like the Royal of Britain. Yet that we may not appear to be defective even in earthly honors, let a day be solemnly set apart for proclaiming the charter; let it be brought forth placed on the divine law, the word of God; let a crown be placed thereon, by which the world may know that so far as we approve of monarchy, that in America THE LAW IS KING. For as in absolute governments the King is law, so in free countries the law ought to be King; and there ought to be no other. But lest any ill use should afterwards arise, let the crown at the conclusion of the ceremony be demolished, and scattered among the people whose right it is. . . .

Should an independency be brought about . . . we have every opportunity and every encouragement before us to form the noblest, purest constitution on the face of the earth. We have it in our power to begin the world over again. A situation, similar to the present, hath not happened since the days of Noah until now. The birthday of a new world is at hand and a race of men perhaps as numerous as all Europe contains are to receive their portion of freedom from the event of a few months. The Reflection is awful and in this point of view how trifling, how ridiculous, do the little, paltry cavellings, of a few weak or interested men appear, when weighed against the business of a world. . . .

On these grounds I rest the matter. And as no offer hath yet been made to refute the doctrine contained in the former editions of this pamphlet, it is a negative proof that either the doctrine cannot be refuted or that the party in favor of it are too numerous to be opposed. WHEREFORE, instead of gazing at each other with suspicious or doubtful curiosity, let each of us hold out to his neighbor the hearty hand of friendship and unite in drawing a line which, like an act of oblivion, shall bury in forgetfulness every former dissention. Let the names of Whig and Tory be extinct and let none other be heard among us than those of a good citizen, an open and resolute friend, and a virtuous supporter of the RIGHTS of MANKIND and of the FREE AND INDEPENDENT STATES OF AMERICA.

12. CHARLES INGLIS, *THE TRUE INTEREST OF AMERICA IMPARTIALLY STATED* (1776)[12]

An Anglican minister of Irish origin who immigrated to America, Inglis wrote this pamphlet to refute Paine's argument for independence. An active loyalist during the war, he fled to Canada after the British defeat.

---

[12]Charles Inglis, *The True Interest of America Impartially Stated*, 2nd ed. (Philadelphia, PA: James Humphreys, 1776), 47–53, 61–63.

I think it no difficult matter to point out many advantages which will certainly attend our reconciliation and connection with Great-Britain, on a firm, constitutional plan. I shall select a few of these; and that their importance may be more clearly discerned, I shall afterwards point out some of the evils which inevitably must attend our separating from Britain, and declaring for independency. . . .

1. By a reconciliation with Britain, a period would be put to the present calamitous war, by which so many lives have been lost, and so many more must be lost, if it continues. This alone is an advantage devoutly to be wished for. This *author* says—*"The blood of the slain, the weeping voice of nature cries, 'Tis time to part."* I think that they cry just the reverse. The blood of the slain, the weeping voice of nature cries "It is time to be reconciled; it is time to lay aside those animosities which have been pushed on Britons to shed the blood of Britons; it is high time that those who are connected by the endearing ties of religion, kindred and country, should resume their former friendship, and be united in the bond of mutual affection, as their interests are inseparably united."

2. By a reconciliation with Great-Britain, Peace—that fairest offspring and gift of Heaven—will be restored. In one respect Peace is like health; we do not sufficiently know its value but by its absence. What uneasiness and anxiety, what evils, has this short interruption of peace with the parent-state, brought on the whole British empire! Let every man only consult his feelings—I except my antagonist—and it will require no great force of rhetoric to convince him, that a removal of those evils, and a restoration of peace, would be a singular advantage and blessing.

3. Agriculture, commerce, and industry would resume their wonted vigor. At present, they languish and droop, both here and in Britain; and must continue to do so, while this unhappy contest remains unsettled.

4. By a connection with Great-Britain, our trade would still have the protection of the greatest naval power in the world. . . . To suppose, with our author, that we should have no war, were we to revolt from England, is too absurd to deserve a confutation. . . .

5. The protection of our trade, while connected with Britain, will not cost a fiftieth part of what it must cost, were we ourselves to raise a naval force sufficient for this purpose.

6. Whilst connected with Great-Britain, we have a bounty on almost every article of exportation; and we may be better supplied with goods by her, than we could elsewhere. What our author says is true, *"that our imported goods must be paid for, buy them where we will"*; but we may buy them dearer, and of worse quality, in one place than another. . . .

7. When a Reconciliation is effected, and things return into the old channel, a few years of peace will restore everything to its pristine state. Emigrants will flow in as usual from the different parts of Europe. Population will advance with the same rapid progress as formerly and our lands will rise in value. . . .

Let us now, if you please, take a view of the other side of the question. Suppose we were to revolt from Great-Britain, declare ourselves Independent, and set up a Republic of our own—what would be the consequence? I stand aghast at the prospect. My blood runs chill when I think of the calamities, the complicated evils that must ensue, and may be clearly foreseen. It is impossible for any man to foresee them all. . . .

1. All our property throughout the continent would be unhinged; the greatest confusion, and most violent convulsion would take place. It would not be here, as it was in England at the Revolution in 1688. That revolution was not brought about by a defiance or disannulling of the right of succession. James II, by abdicating the throne, left it vacant for the next in succession; accordingly his eldest daughter and her husband stept in. Every other matter went on in the usual, regular way; and the constitution, instead of being dissolved, was strengthened. But in case of our revolt, the old constitution would be totally subverted. The common bond that tied us together, and by which our property was secured, would be snapt asunder. . . .

2. What a horrid situation would thousands be reduced to who have taken the oath of allegiance to the King: yet contrary to their oath, as well as inclination, must be compelled to renounce that allegiance, or abandon all their property in America! How many thousands more would be reduced to similar situation; who, although they took not that oath, yet would think it inconsistent with their duty and a good conscience to renounce their Sovereign; I dare say these will appear trifling difficulties to our author; but whatever he may think, there are thousands and thousands who would sooner loser all they had in the world, nay life itself, than thus wound their conscience. A Declaration of Independency would infallibly disunite and divide the colonists.

3. By a Declaration for Independency, every avenue to an accommodation with Great-Britain would be closed; the sword only could then decide the quarrel; and the sword would not be sheathed till one had conquered the other. . . .

4. Devastation and ruin must mark the progress of this war along the sea coast of America. Hitherto, Britain has not exerted her power. Her number of troops and ships of war here at present, is very little more than she judged expedient in time of peace—the former does not amount to 12,000 men—nor the latter to 40 ships, including frigates. Both she and the colonies hoped for and expected an accommodation; neither of them has lost sight of that desirable object. The seas have been open to our ships; and although some skirmishes have unfortunately happened, yet a ray of hope still cheered both sides that, peace was not distant. But as soon as we declare for independency, every prospect of this kind must vanish. Ruthless war, with all its aggravated horrors, will ravage our once happy land; our seacoasts and ports will be ruined, and our ships taken. Torrents of blood will be split, and thousands reduced to beggary and wretchedness. . . .

5. But supposing once more that we were able to cut off every regiment that Britain can spare or hire, and to destroy every ship she can send; that we could beat off any other European power that would presume to intrude upon this continent. Yet, a republican form of government would neither suit the genius of the people, nor the extent of America.

6. In nothing is the wisdom of a legislator more conspicuous than in adapting his government to the genius, manner, disposition and other circumstances of the people with whom he is concerned. If this important point is overlooked, confusion will ensue; his system will sink into neglect and ruin. Whatever check or barriers may be interposed, nature will always surmount them, and finally prevail. It was chiefly by attention to this circumstance, that Lycurgus and Solon were so much celebrated; and that their respective republics rose afterwards to such eminence, and acquired such stability.

The Americans are properly Britons. They have the manners, habits, and ideas of Britons and have been accustomed to a similar form of government. But Britons never could bear the extremes, either of monarchy or republicanism. Some of their Kings have aimed at despotism, but always failed. Repeated efforts have been made towards democracy, and they equally failed. Once indeed republicanism triumphed over the constitution, the despotism of one person ensued. Both were finally expelled. The inhabitants of Great-Britain were quite anxious for the restoration of royalty in 1660, as they were for its expulsion in 1642 and for some succeeding years. If we may judge of future events by past transactions, in similar circumstances, this would most probably be the case if America were a republican form of government adopted in our present ferment. After much blood was shed, those confusions would terminate in the despotism of some one successful adventurer; and should the Americans be so fortunate as to emancipate themselves from that thralldom, perhaps the whole would end in a limited monarchy, after shedding as much more blood. Limited monarchy is the form of government which is most favourable to liberty, which is best adapted to the genius and temper of Britons; although here and there among us a crack-brained zealot for democracy or absolute monarchy may be sometimes found.

Besides the unsuitableness of the republican form to the genius of the people, America is too extensive for it. That form may do well enough for a single city or small territory, but would be utterly improper for such a continent as this. America is too unwieldy for the feeble, dilatory administration of democracy. . . .

But here it may be said that all the evils . . . specified, are more tolerable than slavery. With this sentiment I sincerely agree; any hardships, however great, are preferable to slavery. But then I ask, is there no other alternative in the present case? Is there no choice left us but slavery or those evils? I am confident there is and that both may be equally avoided. Let us only shew a disposition to treat or negociate in earnest; let us fall upon some method to set a treaty or negociation with Great-Britain on foot and, if once properly begun, there is moral certainty that this unhappy dispute will be settled to the mutual satisfaction and interest of both countries. . . .

But a Declaration for Independency on the part of America, would preclude treaty entirely and could answer no good purpose. . . . We should instantly lose all assistance from our friends in England. It would stop their mouths, for were they to say any thing in our favour, they would be deemed rebels and treated accordingly. . . .

America is far from being yet in a desperate situation. I am confident she may obtain honourable and advantageous terms from Great-Britain. A few years of peace will soon retrieve all her losses. She will rapidly advance to a state of maturity, whereby she may not only repay the parent state amply for all past benefits, but also lay under the greatest obligations. . . .

However distant humanity may wish the period, yet, in the rotation of human affairs, a period may arrive, when (both countries being prepared for it) some terrible disaster, some dreadful convulsion in Great-Britain, may transfer the seat of empire to this western hemisphere—where the British constitution, like the Phoenix from its parent's ashes, shall rise with youthful vigour and shine with redoubled splendor.

13. DECLARATION OF INDEPENDENCE (JULY 4, 1776)[13]

In July 1776, the Continental Congress formally declared independence. The famous Declaration was drafted largely by Thomas Jefferson. Initially, he had sought to include language condemning the slave trade (blaming British kings, not planters, for it), but that language was expunged from the definitive version.

When in the Course of human events, it becomes necessary for one people to dissolve the political bands which have connected them with another, and to assume among the Powers of the earth, the separate and equal station to which the Laws of Nature and of Nature's God entitle them, a decent respect to the opinions of mankind requires that they should declare the causes of which impel them to the separation. We hold these truths to be self-evident, that all men are created equal, that they are endowed by their Creator with certain unalienable Rights, that among these are Life, Liberty and the pursuit of Happiness. That to secure these rights, Governments are instituted among Men, deriving their just powers from the consent of the governed, That whenever any Form of Government becomes destructive of these ends, it is the Right of the People to alter or to abolish it,

---

[13] *The Declaration of Independence of the United States of America, 1776* (Boston, MA: A. W. Williams & Co., 1862), 5–13.

and to institute new Government, laying its foundation on such principles and organizing its powers in such form, as to them shall seem most likely to effect their Safety and Happiness. Prudence, indeed, will dictate that Governments long established should not be changed for light and transient causes; and accordingly all experience hath shown, that mankind are more disposed to suffer, while evils are sufferable, than to right themselves by abolishing the forms to which they are accustomed. But when a long train of abuses and usurpations, pursuing invariably the same Object evinces a design to reduce them under absolute Despotism, it is their right, it is their duty, to throw off such Government, and to provide new Guards for their future security. Such has been the patient sufferance of these Colonies; and such is now the necessity which constrains them to alter their former Systems of Government. The history of the present King of Great Britain is a history of repeated injuries and usurpations, all having in direct object the establishment of an absolute Tyranny over these States. To prove this, let Facts be submitted to a candid world.

He has forbidden his Governors to pass Laws of immediate and pressing importance, unless suspended in their operation till his Assent should be obtained; and when so suspended, he has utterly neglected to attend to them.

He has refused to pass other Laws for the accommodation of larger districts of people, unless those people would relinquish the right of Representation in the Legislature, a right inestimable to them and formidable to tyrants only.

He has called together legislative bodies at places unusual, uncomfortable, and distant from the depository or their public Records, for the sole purpose of fatiguing them into compliance with his measures.

He has dissolved Representative Houses repeatedly, for opposing with manly firmness his invasions on the rights of the people.

He has refused for a long time, after such dissolutions, to cause others to be elected; whereby the Legislative powers, incapable of Annihilation, have returned to the People at large for their exercise; the State remaining in the mean time exposed to all the dangers of invasion from without, and convulsions within.

He has endeavoured to prevent the population of these States; for that purpose obstructing the Laws for Naturalization of Foreigners; refusing to pass others to encourage their migration hither, and raising the conditions of new Appropriations of Lands.

He has obstructed the Administration of Justice, by refusing his Assent to Laws for establishing Judiciary powers.

He has made Judges dependent on his Will alone, for the tenure of their offices, and the amount and payment of their salaries.

He has erected a multitude of New Offices, and sent hither swarms of Officers to harass our people, and eat out their substance.

He has kept among us, in times of peace, Standing Armies, without the Consent of our legislatures.

He has affected to render the Military independent of and superior to the Civil power.

He has combined with others to subject us to a jurisdiction foreign to our constitution, and unacknowledged by our laws; giving his Assent to their Acts of pretended Legislation:

For quartering large bodies of armed troops among us:

For protecting them, by a mock Trial, from Punishment for any Murders which they should commit on the Inhabitants of these States:

For cutting off our Trade with all parts of the world:

For imposing Taxes on us without our Consent:

For depriving us in many cases, of the benefits of Trial by Jury:

For transporting us beyond Seas to be tried for pretended offenses:

For abolishing the free System of English Laws in a neighboring Province, establishing therein an Arbitrary government, and enlarging its Boundaries so as to render it at once an example and fit instrument for introducing the same absolute rule into these Colonies:

For taking away our Charters, abolishing our most valuable Laws, and altering fundamentally the Forms of our Governments:

For suspending our own Legislatures, and declaring themselves invested with power to legislate for us in all cases whatsoever.

He has abdicated Government here, by declaring us out of his Protection and waging War against us.

He has plundered our seas, ravaged our Coasts, burnt our towns, and destroyed the lives of our people.

He is at this time transporting large Armies of foreign Mercenaries to compleat the works of death, desolation and tyranny, already begun with circumstances of Cruelty & perfidy scarcely paralleled in the most barbarous age, and totally unworthy the Head of a civilized nation.

He has constrained our fellow Citizens taken Captive on the high Seas to bear Arms against their Country, to become the executioners of their friends and Brethren, or to fall themselves by their Hands.

He has excited domestic insurrections amongst us, and has endeavored to bring on the inhabitants of our frontiers, the merciless Indian Savages, whose known rule of warfare, is an undistinguished destruction of all ages, sexes and conditions.

In every state of these Oppressions We have Petitioned for Redress in the most humble terms: Our repeated Petitions have been answered only by every act which may define a Tyrant, is unfit to be the ruler of a free people.

Nor have We been wanting in attentions to our British brethren. We have warned them from time to time of attempts by their legislature to extend an unwarrantable jurisdiction over us. We have reminded them of the circumstances of our emigration and settlement here. We have conjured them by the ties of our common kindred to disavow these usurpations, which, would inevitably interrupt our connections and correspondence. They too have been deaf to the voice of justice and of consanguinity. We must, therefore, acquiesce in the necessity, which denounces our Separation, and hold them, as we hold the rest of mankind, Enemies in War, in Peace Friends.

We, therefore, the representatives of the United States of America, in General Congress, assembled, appealing to the Supreme Judge of the World for the rectitude of our intentions, do, in the name, and by authority of the good people of these colonies, solemnly publish and declare, That these United Colonies are, and of right ought to be, Free and Independent States; that they are Absolved from all Allegiance to the British Crown, and that all political connection between them and the State of Great Britain, is, and ought to be totally dissolved; and that, as Free and Independent States, they have full Power to levy War, conclude Peace, contract Alliances, establish Commerce, and to do all other Acts and Things which Independent States may of right do. And for the support of this Declaration, with a firm reliance on the protection of Divine Providence, we mutually pledge to each our lives, our fortunes, and our sacred honor.

14. LOYALIST DECLARATION OF DEPENDENCE (1781)[14]

In 1781, a loyalist newspaper in New York published a counterdeclaration parodying the Declaration of Independence.

When in the course of human events it becomes necessary for men, in order to preserve their lives, liberties and properties, and to secure themselves, and to their posterity, that peace, liberty and safety, to which by the laws of nature and of nature's God they are entitled, to throw off and renounce all allegiance to a government, which under the insidious pretences of securing those inestimable blessings to them, has wholly deprived them of any security of either life, liberty, property, peace, or safety; a decent respect to the opinions of mankind, requires that they should declare, the injuries and oppressions, the arbitrary and dangerous proceedings, which impel them to transfer their allegiance from such their oppressors, to those who have offered to become their protectors.

We hold these truths to be self evident, that all men are created equal; that they are endowed by their Creator with certain rights, that among these, are life, liberty, and the pursuit of happiness;

It is not indeed prudent to change for light and transient causes, and experience hath ever shewn, that men are disposed to suffer much before they can bring themselves to make a change of government; but when a long train of the most licentious and despotic abuses, pursuing invariably the same objects, evinces a design to reduce them under anarchy, and the distractions of democracy, and

---

[14]*The Royal Gazette* (New York Gazette, November 17, 1781).

finally to force them to submit to absolute despotism, it is their right, it becomes their duty, to disclaim and renounce all allegiance to such government, and to provide new guards for their future security.

Such have been our patient sufferings, and such is now the necessity which constrains us to renounce all allegiance to Congress, or to the governments lately established by their direction.

The history of Congress, is a history of continued weakness, inconsistency, violation of the most sacred obligations of all public faith and honour, and of usurpations, all having in direct object the producing of anarchy, civil feuds, and violent injustice, which have rendered us miserable, and must soon establish tyranny over us, and our country.

To prove this let facts be submitted to the candid world.

They have recommended and caused laws to be passed, the most destructive of the public good, and ruinous to individuals.

Availing themselves of our zeal and unanimity to oppose the claims of the British Parliament, and our unsuspecting confidence in their solemn professions and declarations, they have forbidden us to listen to, or to accept any terms of peace, until their assent should be obtained.

They have refused to accept of, or even to receive proposals and terms of accommodation and peace, though they know the terms offered exceeded what the Colonies in America had unanimously declared would be satisfactory, unless the Crown would relinquish a right inestimable to it and to the whole empire, and formidable to Congress only.

They have excited and directed the people to alter or annul their ancient constitutions, under which, they and their ancestors, had been happy for many ages, for the sole purpose of promoting their measures.

They have by their misconduct, reduced us to all the dangers and distress of actual invasion from without, and to all the horrors of a cruel war within.

They have not only prevented the increase of the population of these states, but by the fines, imprisoning, and banishments, with the losses by war, they have caused a rapid depopulation.

They have corrupted all the sources of justice and equity by their Tender Law, by which they destroyed the legal force of all civil contracts, wronged the honest creditor, and deserving salary man of his just dues, stripped the helpless orphan of his patrimony, and the disconsolate widow of her dower.

They have erected a multitude of new offices, and have filled them with men from their own body, or with their creatures and dependants, to eat out the substance of the people; they have made their officers dependent on their will for the tenure of their offices, and the payment of their salaries.

They have raised a standing army and sent it into the field, without any act of the legislature, and have actually rendered it independent of the civil power, by making it solely dependant on them.

They have combined with France, the natural and hereditary enemy of our civil constitution, and religious faith, to render us dependant on and subservient to the views, of that foreign, ambitious, and despotic monarchy.

They have suffered their troops to live repeatedly on free quarters on the inhabitants, and to strip them by force of the necessaries of life, and have protected them from either trial or punishment under the plea of necessity, which necessity if real, was caused by their treacherous views, or unpardonable negligence.

They have ruined our trade, and destroyed our credit with all parts of the world.

They have forced us to receive their paper, for goods, merchandise, and for money due to us, equal to silver and gold, and then by a breach of public faith in not redeeming the same, and by the most infamous bankruptcy, have left it on our hands, to the total ruin of multitudes, and to the injury of all.

They have driven many of our people beyond the sea, into exile, and have confiscated their estates, and the estates of others who were beyond sea before the war, for the existence of Congress, on pretence of offences, and under the sanction of a mock trial, to which the person condemned was neither cited or present.

They have abolished the true system of the English constitution and laws, in thirteen of the American Provinces, and established therein a weak and factitious democracy, and have attempted to use them as introducing the same misrule and disorder into all the Colonies in the continent.

They have recommended the annihilating of our charters, abolishing many of our most valuable laws. And the altering fundamentally the form of our government.

They have destroyed all good order and government, by plunging us into the factions of democracy, and the ravages of civil war.

They have left our seas unprotected, suffered our coasts to be ravaged, our towns to be burnt, some of them by their own troops, and the lives of our people to be destroyed.

They have without the consent or knowledge of the legislatures, invited over an army of foreign mercenaries to support them and their faction, and to prevent the dreadful scenes of death and desolations from being closed by an honorable peace and accommodation with our ancient friend and parent.

They have fined, imprisoned, banished, and put to death some of our fellow citizens, for no other cause but their attachment to the English laws and constitution.

They have countenanced domestic tumults and disorders in our capital cities, and have suffered the murder of a number of our fellow citizens perpetrated under their eyes in Philadelphia, to pass unnoticed.

They first attempted to gain the savage and merciless Indians to their side, but failing in making them the presents promised and expected, have occasioned an undistinguished destruction to ages, sexes, and conditions on our frontiers.

They have involved us in an immense debt, foreign as well as internal, and did put the best port and island on our continent, into the hands of foreigners, who are their creditors.

They have wantonly violated our public faith and honor, and destroyed all grounds for private confidence, of the security of private property, have not blushed to act in direct contradiction to their most solemn declaration, and to render the people under their government, a reproach and a bye word among the nations.

In every stage of these proceedings, they have not been wanting to throw out before us, specious excuses for their conduct, as being the result of necessity and tending to the public good.

In every stage since their public conduct began to contradict their public declarations, our minds have been overwhelmed with apprehensions; and as our sufferings have increased, our tears have flown in secret.

It has been dangerous and even criminal to lament our situation in public.

The unsuspecting confidence which we with out fellow citizens reposed in the Congress of 1774, the unanimous applause, with which their patriotism and firmness were crowned, for having stood forth, as the champions of our rights, founded on the English constitution; at the same time that it gave to Congress the unanimous support of the whole continent, inspired their successors with very different ideas, and emboldened them by degrees to pursue measures, directly the reverse of those before adopted, and were recommended, as the only just, constitutional and safe.

Congress in 1774 reprobated every idea of a separation from Great-Britain, and declared that they looked on such an event as the greatest of evils.

They declared that a repeal of certain acts complained of would restore our ancient peace, and harmony.

That they *asked but for peace, liberty, and safety. That they wished not for a diminution of the royal prerogative, not did they solicit the grant of any new right.*

And they pledged themselves in the presence of Almighty God, that they *will ever carefully and zealously endeavor to support and maintain the royal authority of Great-Britain over us, and our connection with Great-Britain. . . .*

The acts complained of have been repealed, yet how have Congress given the lie, to these their solemn professions!

In 1774, they declared themselves concerned for the honour of Almighty God, whose pure and holy religion, our enemies were undermining.

They point out those enemies, and the danger in which our holy religion was by their complaints of the establishment of the Roman Catholic religion in Canada; they say it t is a religion which has deluged the Islands of Great Britain with blood, and dispersed impiety, persecution, murder, and rebellion through every part of the world.

We find the present Congress not only claiming a new right, and hazarding every thing valuable in life, to the present and future generations in support of it,

but we also find them, leagued with the eldest son of this bloody, impious, big-
oted, and persecuting church, to ruin the nation from whose loins we sprung, and
which has ever been the principal bulwark in Europe, against encroachments and
tyranny of that church, and of the kingdoms devoted to her.

We think it not too severe to say, that we find them as intoxicated with ambition of Independent sovereignty, as execrable Roman Daughter, who drove the
wheels of her chariot over the mangled body of her murdered father, in her way
to the capitol.

We find that all their fears and apprehensions from the Roman Catholic religion in Canada, have vanished, or sunk to nothing, when put in competition with
their political views, and that they have attempted to seduce the Canadian to their
side, by promises of still greater religious establishments; and to shew that they
were in earnest, have countenanced this impious religion by attending its ceremo-
nies and worship in a body.

We find them at one time boasting of their patriotic and religious ancestors,
who braved every danger of unknown seas, and coasts, to preserve civil and religious freedom, and who chose rather to become exiles, and suffer every misery
that must await them, on a savage and unexplored coast, than submit to civil, but
above all religious innovations. At another time we find them destroying the British
Constitution, the pride of their ancestors, and encouraging a religion which they
held in abhorrence, as idolatrous and tyrannical.

We find them contending for liberty of speech, and at the same time controlling the press, by means of a mob, and persecuting every one who ventures to hint
his disapprobation of their proceedings.

We find them declaring in September 1779, that to pay off their paper money,
at less than its nominal value, would be an unpardonable sin, an execrable deed.
"That a faithless bankrupt Republic would be a novelty in the political world, and
appear like a common prostitute among chaste and reputable matrons," would be
"a reproach and a bye-word among the nations, &c."

We find the same Congress in March following, liquidating their paper debt at
21/2 per cent. or 6d. in the pound.

We should fill volumes, were we to recite at large their inconsistency, usurpations, weaknesses and violations of the most sacred obligations. We content ourselves with the . . . brief recital of facts known to the world and attested by their
own records.

We have sufficiently shewn that a government thus marked and distinguished
from every other, either despotic or democratic, by the enormity of its excesses,
injustice and infamy, is unfit to rule a free people.

We therefore, Natives and Citizens of America, appealing to the impartial world
to judge of the justice of our cause, but above all to the supreme Judge of the World
for the rectitude of our intentions, do renounce and disclaim all allegiance, duty, or
submission to the United Colonies or States, so called, neither are, nor of right ought
to be independent of the crown of Great-Britain, or unconnected with that empire.

But that we do firmly believe and maintain "That the Royal Authority of the Crown of Great-Britain over us, and our connections with that kingdom ought to be preserved and maintained, and that we will zealously endeavor to support and maintain the same;" and in the support of this declaration, with a firm reliance on the protection of Divine Providence, we mutually pledge to each other, and to the crown and empire of Great-Britain, our lives, our fortunes, and our sacred honor.

CHAPTER 4

Winning American Independence

When war broke out in 1775, it seemed that the odds were heavily in Great Britain's favor. In addition to its larger population and economy, financial strength, professional army, and the world's preeminent navy, Britain was a globally recognized sovereign state, whereas the thirteen colonies were but rebel provinces with no international standing. But Britain threw away its advantage in the first years of the war. Lack of clear direction from London and mediocre, uncoordinated generalship in America gave the Continental Army, under its capable commander George Washington, the breathing room it needed to survive and gain confidence. When an entire British army was forced to surrender at the Battle of Saratoga in 1777, the war entered a new phase. Ever since its humiliating defeat in 1763, France had been preparing for revenge; the American victory gave it the opportunity it had been waiting for. Although a French expeditionary force would fight alongside the Continental Army, the real significance of French intervention lay elsewhere. French (and later Spanish) entry into the war forced Great Britain to divert military and financial resources from North America to the Caribbean (to defend its sugar islands) and the home islands themselves (to defend them from direct French invasion). From the moment of French intervention in 1778, Great Britain was unable to send significant reinforcements to North America. Its troops there continued to soldier on. Despairing of further aid, they adopted a strategy based on the assumption of strong loyalist support in the South. This strategy ultimately led to the surrender of a second British army at the Battle of Yorktown in 1781. With that, fighting ended, peace negotiations began, and in 1783 Great Britain recognized the independence of the United States. But as the Americans would soon learn, winning the peace posed challenges of its own.

I. Race, Slavery, and the War

Colonial America was a slave society. Enslaved people of African and, to a lesser extent, Indian descent constituted a segment of every colony's population—from less than 1% in some of the New England colonies to around 50% in South Carolina. Slavery became an important factor in the military calculations of both sides. At different times during the war, some American leaders proposed bolstering the Continental Army by offering slaves freedom for military service. Although the Continental Congress never adopted these plans, individual Northern states implemented emancipation-for-service schemes. Perhaps 20% of the Continental Army was composed of African Americans, most serving in integrated units. More generally, the Revolution created a climate in some states that was hostile to the continuation of slavery. During the war, Vermont, Pennsylvania, and Massachusetts all abolished slavery. Most of the other New England and Middle Atlantic States followed within ten years of independence. At least in the North, the revolutionary wars helped undermine slavery. The British too factored slavery into their military plans—not just as a source of recruitment, but as an offensive weapon as well.

1. LORD DUNMORE'S PROCLAMATION
(NOVEMBER 7, 1775)[1]

The British governor of Virginia, Lord Dunmore, saw slavery as the colony's Achilles heel. By offering emancipation to all slaves (and indentured servants) who left their masters and enrolled with the British forces, he could accomplish several goals at once: (1) augment his own troops, (2) damage the Virginian plantation economy, and (3) possibly spread so much disruption and fear that Virginian elites would submit to royal authority. The British government, however, rejected such a drastic measure. But had it been implemented throughout the colonies, Dunmore's policy could have destroyed slavery in the thirteen colonies and might have dealt a deadly blow to American Independence.

As I have ever entertained Hopes, that an Accommodation might have taken Place between Great-Britain and this Colony, without being compelled by my Duty to this most disagreeable but now absolutely necessary Step, rendered so by a Body of armed Men unlawfully assembled, firing on His Majesty's Tenders, and the formation of an Army, and that Army now on their March to attack his Majesty's Troops and destroy the well-disposed subjects of the Colony. To defeat such treasonable Purposes, and that all such Traitors, and their Abettors, may be brought to Justice, and that the Peace, and good Order of this Colony may be again restored,

---

[1]"Dunmore's Proclamation," www.nationalarchives.gov.uk/pathways/blackhistory/work_community/docs/dunmore_proclamation.htm

which the ordinary Course of the Civil Law is unable to effect; I have thought fit to issue this my Proclamation, hereby declaring, that until the aforesaid good Purpose can be obtained, I do in Virtue of the Power and Authority to ME given, by His Majesty, determine to execute Martial Law, and cause the same to be executed throughout this Colony: and so the Peace and good Order may the sooner be restored, I do require every Person capable of bearing Arms, to resort to His Majesty's STANDARD, or be looked upon as Traitors to His Majesty's Crown and Government, and thereby become liable to the Penalty the Law inflicts upon such Offenses; such as forfeiture of Life, confiscation of Lands, &c., &c. And I do hereby further declare all indented Servants, Negroes, or others (appertaining to Rebels) free that are able and willing to bear Arms, they joining His Majesty's Troops as soon as may be, for the more speedily reducing this Colony to a proper Sense of their Duty, to His Majesty's Crown and Dignity. I do further order, and require, all His Majesty's Liege Subjects, to retain their Quitrents, or any other Taxes due or that may become due, in their own Custody, till such a Time as Peace may be again restored to this at present most unhappy County, or demanded of them for their former salutary Purposes, by Officers properly to receive the same.

2. JOHN LAURENS RECOMMENDS RECRUITING SLAVES[2]

John Laurens was a young officer in Washington's army and son of a powerful South Carolina planter who represented his state in the Continental Congress. He believed that the emancipation and arming of slaves was the key to victory and repeatedly urged this policy. The following documents are letters to his father in which he describes his plans.

John Laurens to his father, Henry Laurens
(Valley Forge, January 14, 1778)
I barely hinted to you my dearest Father my desire to augment the Continental Forces from an untried Source. Had I any foundation to ask for an extraordinary addition to those favors which I have already received from you, I would solicit you to cede me a number of your able bodied men Slaves, instead of leaving me a fortune. I would bring about a twofold good, first I would advance those who are unjustly deprived of the Rights of Mankind to a State which would be a proper Gradation between abject Slavery and perfect Liberty, and besides I would reinforce the Defenders of Liberty with a number of gallant Soldiers. Men who have the habit of Subordination almost indelibly impress'd on them, would have one

[2]*The Papers of Henry Laurens*, vol. 1: Nov. 1, 1777-March 15, 1778; David R. Chesnutt, Editor; C. James Taylor, Editor; Peggy J. Clark, Assistant Editor; David Fischer, Assistant Editor; Published for the South Carolina Historical Society by the University of South Carolina Press, Columbia, 1990, 390–392. Reprinted with permission.

very essential qualification of Soldiers. I am persuaded that if I could obtain authority for the purpose I would have a Corps of such men trained, uniformly clad, equip'd and ready in every respect to act at the opening of the next Campaign. The Ridicule that may be thrown on the Colour I despise, because I am sure of rendering essential Service to my Country. I am tired of the Languor with which so sacred a War as this, is carried on. . . .

John Laurens to his father (Valley Forge, February 2, 1778)

The more I reflect upon the difficulties and delays which are likely to attend the completing our Continental Regiments, the more anxiously is my mind bent upon the Scheme which I lately communicated to you. The obstacles to the execution of it had presented themselves to me, but by no means appeared insurmountable. I was aware of having that monster popular Prejudice open-mouthed against me, of undertaking to transform beings almost irrational into well-disciplined Soldiers, of being obliged to combat the arguments and perhaps the intrigues of interested persons. But zeal for the public Service and an ardent desire to assert the rights of humanity determined me to engage in this arduous business, with the sanction of your Consent. My own perseverance aided by the Countenance of a few virtuous men will I hope enable me to accomplish it.

You seem to think my dear Father, that men reconciled by long habit to the miseries of their Condition, would prefer their ignominious bonds to the untasted Sweets of Liberty, especially when offer'd upon the terms which I propose. I confess indeed that the minds of this unhappy species must be debased by a Servitude from which they can hope for no Relief but Death and that every motive to action but Fear, must be also nearly extinguished in them. But do you think they are so perfectly moulded to their State as to be insensible that a better exists? Will the galling comparison between themselves and their masters leave them unenlighten'd in this respect? Can their Self-Love be so totally annihilated as not frequently to induce ardent wishes for a change?

You will accuse me perhaps my dearest friend of consulting my own feelings too much, but I am tempted to believe that this trampled people have so much human left in them, as to be capable of aspiring to the rights of men by nice exertions, if some friend to mankind would point the Road, and give them a prospect of Success. If I am mistaken in this, I would avail myself even of their weakness, and conquering one ear by another, produce equal good to the Public. You will ask in this view how do you consult the benefit of the Slaves? I answer that like other men, they are the Creature of habit, their Cowardly Ideas will be gradually effaced, and they will be modified anew. Their being rescued from a State of perpetual humiliation and being advanced as it were in the Scale of being will compensate the dangers incident to their new State. The hope that will spring in each man's mind respecting his own escape will prevent his being miserable. Those who fall in battle will not lose much; those who survive will obtain their Reward.

Habits of Subordination, Patience under fatigues, Sufferings and Privations of every kind are soldierly qualifications which these men possess in an eminent degree.

Upon the whole my dearest friend and father, I hope that my plan for serving my Country and the oppressed Negro-race will not appear to you the Chimara of a young mind deceived by a false appearance of moral beauty, but a laudable sacrifice of private Interest to Justice and the Public good. . . .

I have long deplored the wretched State of these men and considered in their history, the bloody wars excited in Africa to furnish America with Slaves, the Groans of despairing multitudes toiling for the Luxuries of Merciless Tyrants. I have had the pleasure of conversing with you sometimes upon the means of restoring them to their rights. When can it be better done, than when their enfranchisement may be made conducive to the Public Good, and be so modified as not to overpower their weak minds?

3. ALEXANDER HAMILTON'S RESPONSE TO THE IDEA[3]

Alexander Hamilton reacted favorably to Laurens's plan.

Alexander Hamilton to John Jay (Middlebrook, New Jersey, March 14, 1779)

Col Laurens, who will have the honor of delivering you this letter, is on his way to South Carolina, on a project which I think, in the present situation of affairs there, is a very good one and deserves every kind of support and encouragement. This is to raise two three or four batalions of Negroes with the assistance of the government of the state; by contributions from the owners in proportion to the number they possess. If you should think proper to enter upon the subject with him, he will give you a detail of his plan. He wishes to have it recommended by Congress to the state; and as an inducement, that they would engage to take those battalions into Continental pay.

It appears to me that an expedient of this kind, in the present state of Southern affairs, is the most rational, that can be adopted and promises very important advantages. Indeed, I hardly see how a sufficient force can be collected in that quarter without it; and the enemy's operations there are growing infinitely serious and formidable. I have not the least doubt that the Negroes will make very excellent soldiers, with proper management; and I will venture to pronounce that they cannot be put in better hands than those of Mr. Laurens. He has all the zeal, intelligence, enterprise, and every other qualification requisite to succeed in such an undertaking. It is a maxim with some great military judges that with sensible officers soldiers can hardly be too stupid; and on this principle it is thought that the Russians would make the best troops in the world, if they were under other officers than their own. The King of Prussia is among the number who maintain

---

[3]Alexander Hamilton to John Jay (Middlebrook, New Jersey, March 14, 1779). Founders Online, National Archives, http://founders.archives.gov/documents/Hamilton/01-02-02-0051.

this doctrine and has a very emphatical saying on the occasion, which I do not exactly recollect. I mention this because I frequently hear it objected to the scheme of embodying Negroes that they are too stupid to make soldiers. This is so far from appearing to me a valid objection that I think their want of cultivation (for their natural faculties are probably as good as ours) joined to that habit of subordination which they acquire from a life of servitude will make them sooner became soldiers than our White inhabitants. Let officers be men of sense and sentiment, and the nearer the soldiers approach the machines perhaps the better.

I foresee that this project will have to combat much opposition from prejudice and self-interest. The contempt we have been taught to entertain for the blacks makes us fancy many things that are founded neither in reason nor experience; and an unwillingness to part with property of so valuable a kind will furnish a thousand arguments to show the impracticability or pernicious tendency of a scheme which requires such a sacrifice. But it should be considered that if we do not make use of them in this way, the enemy probably will; and that the best way to counteract the temptations they will hold out will be to offer them ourselves. An essential part of the plan is to give them their freedom with their muskets. This will secure their fidelity, animate their courage, and I believe will have a good influence upon those who remain, by opening a door to their emancipation. This circumstance, I confess, has no small weight in inducing me to wish the success of the project; for the dictates of humanity and true policy equally interest me in favour of this unfortunate class of men.

4. GEORGE WASHINGTON'S REACTION[4]

Washington, himself a large slaveholding planter, was much more skeptical about Laurens's plan. Throughout the war, he never made the recruitment of slaves the official policy of the Continental Army, although he did accept state regiments with large contingents of African Americans.

George Washington to Henry Laurens (Middlebrook, New Jersey, March 20, 1779)

The policy of our arming Slaves is, in my opinion, a moot point, unless the enemy set the example; for should we begin to form Battalions of them, I have not the smallest doubt (if the War is to be prosecuted) of their following us in it, and justifying the measure upon our own ground. The upshot then must be, who can arm fastest, and where are our Arms? Besides, I am not clear that a discrimination will not render Slavery more irksome to those who remain in it; most of the good and evil things of this life are judged of by comparison, and I fear a comparison in

---

[4]John C. Fitzpatrick, ed., *The Writings of George Washington from the Original Manuscript Sources* (Washington, DC: United States Government Printing Office, 1931), vol. 14, 266–267.

this case will be productive of much discontent in those who are held in servitude. But as this is a subject that has never employed much of my thoughts, these are no more that the first crude Ideas that have struck me upon the occasion.

5. SLAVE PETITION FOR FREEDOM TO THE MASSACHUSETTS LEGISLATURE (JANUARY 13, 1777)[5]

Although the Continental Congress never adopted a general policy of emancipation in exchange for military service, individual states did—particularly in the North. Moreover, the political climate of the revolutionary years was hostile to slavery. The pervasive talk of liberty and frequent characterization of American subjection to Britain as a form of slavery could not help but undermine the actual institution. Accordingly, many enslaved people profited from the favorable circumstances of the Revolution to seek emancipation.

The petition of A Great Number of Blacks detained in a State of slavery in the Bowels of a free & Christian Country Humbly shuwith that your Petitioners apprehend that they have in Common with all other men a Natural and Unaliable Right to that freedom which the Grat Parent of the Unavers hath Bestowed equally on all menkind and which they have Never forfuted by any Compact or agreement whatever—but thay wher Unjustly Dragged by the hand of cruel Power from their Derest friends and sum of them Even torn from the Embraces of their tender Parents—from A popolous Pleasant and plentiful contry and in violation of Laws and Nature and off Nations and in defiance of all the tender feelings of humanity Brough hear Either to Be sold Like Beast of Burthen & Like the Condemnd to Slavery for Life—Among A People Profesing the mild Religion of Jesus A people Not Insensible of the Secrets of Rational Being Nor without spirit to Resent the unjust endeavours of others to Reduce them to a state of Bondage and Subjection your honoured Need not to be informed that A Life of Slavery Like that of your petioners Deprived of Every social privilege of Every thing Requisit to Render Life Tolerable is far worse then Nonexistence.

[In Imitat]ion of the Lawdable Example of the Good People of these States your petitioners have Long and Patiently waited the Evnt of petition after petition By them presented to the Legislative Body of this state and cannot but with Grief Reflect that their Success hath ben but too similar they Cannot but express their Astonishment that It has Never Bin Considered that Every Principle from which Amarica has Acted in the Cours of their unhappy Dificultes with Great Briton Pleads Stronger that A thousand arguments in favowrs of your petioners

---

[5]Massachusetts Archives Collection, 186: 134–136a, Petition of John Cuffe and other Free Blacks from Dartmouth to the Massachusetts Legislature, 10 February 1780. SC1/series 45X. Massachusetts Archives. Boston, Massachusetts. Reprinted with permission.

they therfor humble Beseech your honours to give this petition its due weights & consideration & cause an act of the Legislatur to be past Wherby they may be Restored to the Enjoyments of that which is the Naturel Right of all men—and their Children who wher Born in this Land of Liberty may not be heald as Slaves after they arrive at the age of twenty one years so may the Inhabitance of this Stats No longer chargeable with the inconsistancey of acting themselves the part which they condem and oppose in others Be prospered in their present Glorious struggle for Liberty and have those Blessing to them, &c.

6. PENNSYLVANIA ABOLISHES SLAVERY (1781)[6]

During the revolutionary years, some states went beyond granting manumission on a case-by-case basis and passed laws abolishing slavery within their borders. One of these was Quaker-influenced Pennsylvania.

When we contemplate our abhorrence of that condition, to which the arms and tyranny of Great Britain were exerted to reduce us; when we look back on the variety of dangers to which we have been exposed, and how miraculously our wants in many instances have been supplied, and our deliverances wrought, when even hope and human fortitude have become unequal to the conflict; we are un-avoidably led to a serious and grateful sense of the manifold blessings which we have undeservedly received from the hand of the Being from whom every good and perfect gift cometh. Impressed with these ideas, we conceive that it is our duty, and we rejoice that it is in our power to extend a portion of that freedom to others, which hath been extended to us and a release from that state of thralldom to which we ourselves were tyrannically doomed, and from which we have now every prospect of being delivered. It is not for us to enquire why, in the creation of mankind, the inhabitants of the several parts of the earth were distinguished by a difference in feature or complexion. It is sufficient to know that all are the work of an Almighty Hand. We find in the distribution of the human species, that the most fertile as well as the most barren parts of the earth are inhabited by men of complexions different from ours, and from each other; from whence we may reasonably, as well as religiously, infer, that he who placed them in their various situations, hath extended equally his care and protection to all, and that it beco-meth not us to counteract his mercies. We esteem it a peculiar blessing granted to us, that we are enabled this day to add one more step to universal civilization, by removing as much as possible the sorrows of those who have lived in undeserved bondage, and from which, by the assumed authority of the kings of Great Britain no effectual, legal, relief could be obtained. Weaned by a long course of experience from those narrow prejudices and partialities we had imbibed, we find our hearts

---

[6] *An Act for the Gradual Abolition of Slavery* (Philadelphia, 1781).

enlarged with kindness and benevolence towards men of all conditions and nations; and we conceive ourselves at this particular period extraordinarily called upon, by the blessings which we have received, to manifest the sincerity of our profession, and to give a substantial proof of our gratitude.

AND WHEREAS the condition of those persons who have heretofore been nominated negroe and mulatto slaves, has been attended with circumstances which not only deprived them of the common blessings that they were by nature entitled to, but has cast them into the deepest afflictions by an unnatural separation and sale of husband and wife from each other and from their children; an injury, the greatness of which can only be conceived by supposing that we were in the same unhappy case. In justice, therefore, to persons so unhappily circumstanced, and who, having no prospect before them whereon they may rest their sorrows and their hopes, have no reasonable inducement to render their service to society, which they otherwise might; and also in grateful commemoration of our own happy deliverance from that state of unconditional submission to which we were doomed by the tyranny of Britain.

Be it enacted, and it is hereby enacted, by the representatives of the freemen of the common wealth of Pennsylvania, in general assembly met, and by the authority of the same, That all persons, as well negroes and mulattoes and others, who shall be born within this state from and after the passing of this act, shall not be deemed and considered as servants for life, or slaves; and that all servitude for life, or slavery of children, in consequence of the slavery of their mothers, in the case of all children born within this state, from and after the passing of this act as aforesaid, shall be, and hereby is utterly taken away; extinguished and forever abolished.

II. Native Americans and the American Revolution

At the outbreak of fighting in 1775, Native Americans found themselves in a familiar position. During the colonial wars between the British and French for control of North America, each tribe had had to navigate between the belligerent powers and determine whether its own interests would be best served by joining Britain, France, or remaining neutral. They faced a similar choice in 1775. For their part, the thirteen colonies and Great Britain had to decide whether to seek active military engagement from the different tribes or whether their interests would be better served by neutrality. In general, the United States (with its vulnerable frontier population) pursued neutrality. In contrast, Great Britain (with its network of western forts, trading posts, and Indian agents) sought to obtain direct military commitment. But these are generalizations—the revolutionary history of each tribe is unique and, in many cases, tribes themselves split over what to do. In all cases, however, they were primarily concerned with assessing their own interests and choosing the course of action most likely to achieve them.

7. ONEIDA DECLARATION OF NEUTRALITY (1775)[7]

The Oneida were perhaps the weakest tribe in the six-nation Iroquois Confederacy. Aware of their vulnerability, they sought to remain neutral in the coming struggle.

These may certify all whom it may concern. That we the Chiefs, head men, councilors warriors, & youngmen of the Onoida nation, this day assembled together considng of affairs of importance, we say that these may certify all whom it may concern that we are altogether for Peace, and not only we of the Onoida nation. But other nations with whom we ar connected. Our desire is to be nutrail in these critical times—in these times of great confusion: we desire not to meddle with any disputers that are now in agitation. Let our English Brethren be assured of this truth that if we were called to assist them against any other Power that would not find us Backward in the Least. But we would Evidence to the world our regards for the English nation by fighting for their defence as in time past altho at the expence of our own lives, and Let all our new England Brethren be fully assured by these lines and the token of friendship we send with these lines, that no one shall prevail with us, or persuade to take up arms against you our English Brethren. we will not give you the least disturbance—and we will exert our uttmost Endeavours to keep our Brethren the Six nations and others further Back from disturbing you in the Present difficult times. So Let all be easy in their minds we are for Peace; ye are Brethren that are at varience and this is the reason we desire to be nutrails. we are in sincerity your very dear and true—friends Indian of the Onoida nation and we hope that peace may be restored soon between Great Britain and her colony.

8. CONTINENTAL CONGRESS SEEKS IROQUOIS NEUTRALITY (JULY 13, 1775)[8]

The Iroquois Confederacy was a powerful Native American polity. It had traditionally sided with Great Britain in its colonial wars against France. Although it had received assurances of Oneida neutrality, the Continental Congress was afraid that the other tribes in the Confederacy would mobilize their powerful forces on Britain's behalf. In this document, the Congress appeals to the Iroquois Confederacy to remain neutral.

---

[7]Samuel Kirkland Collection, Hamilton College Library Digital Collections. http://contentdm6 .hamilton.edu/cdm/compoundobject/collection/arc-kir/id/733/rec/1.
[8]The Continental Congress: Address to the Six Nations (July 13, 1775), in *Journals of the Continental Congress, 1774–1789*, Vol II, ed. Worthington C. Ford (Washington, DC: United States Government Printing Office, 1905), 178–183.

Brothers, Sachems, and Warriors

We, the Delegates from the Twelve United Provinces . . . Now sitting in general Congress at Philadelphia send this talk to you our brothers. We are sixty-five in number, chosen and appointed by the people throughout all these provinces and colonies, to meet and sit together in one great council, to consult together for the common good of the land, and speak and act for them.

Brothers, in our consultation we have judged it proper and necessary to send you this talk, as we are upon the same island, that you may be informed of the reasons of this great council, the situation of our civil constitution, and our disposition towards you our Indian brothers of the Six Nations and their allies.

Brothers and Friends, Now Attend

When our fathers crossed the great water and came over to this land, the king of England gave them a talk: assuring them, that they and their children should be his children, and that if they would leave their native country and make settlements, and live here, and buy, and sell, and trade with their brethren beyond the water, they should still keep hold of the same covenant chain and enjoy peace. And it was covenanted, that the fields, houses, goods and possessions which our fathers should acquire, should remain to them as their own, and be their children's forever, and at their sole disposal.

Trusting that this covenant should never be broken, our fathers came a great distance beyond the great water, laid out their money here, built houses, cleared fields, raised crops, and through their own labour and industry grew tall and strong.

They have bought, sold and traded with England according to agreement. . . .

The king of England and his people kept the way open for more than one hundred years, and by our trade became richer, and by a union with us, greater and stronger than the other kings and people who live beyond the water.

All this time they lived in great friendship with us, and we with them; for we are brothers—one blood.

Whenever they were struck, we instantly felt as though the blow had been given to us—their enemies were our enemies.

Whenever they went to war, we sent our men to stand by their side and fight for them and our money to help them and make them strong.

They thanked us for our love, and sent us good talks, and renewed their promise to be one people forever.

Brothers and Friends, Open a Kind Ear!

We will now tell you of the quarrel betwixt the counsellors of King George and the inhabitants and colonies of America.

Many of his counsellors are proud and wicked men. They persuade the king to break the covenant chain, and not to send us any more good talks. A considerable number have prevailed upon him to enter into a new covenant against us and have torn asunder and cast behind their backs the good old covenant which their ancestors and ours entered into and took strong hold of.

They now tell us they will slip their hand into our pocket without asking, as though it were their own; and at their pleasure they will take from us our charters or written civil constitution, which we love as our lives; also our plantations, our houses and goods whenever they please, without asking our leave; that our vessels may go to this island in the sea, but to this or that particular island we shall not trade any more; and in case of our non-compliance with these new orders, they shut up our harbours.

Brothers, this is our present situation, thus have many of the king's counsellors and servants dealt with us. If we submit, or comply with their demands, you can easily perceive to what state we will be reduced. If our people labour on the field, they will not know who shall enjoy the crop. If they hunt in the woods, it will be incertain who shall taste of the meat or have the skins. If they build houses, they will not know whether they may sit round the fire, with their wives and children. They cannot be sure whether they shall be permitted to eat, drink, and wear the fruits of their own labour and industry.

Brothers and Friends of the Six Nations, Attend

We upon this island have often spoke and intreated the king and his servants the counsellors, that peace and harmony might still continue between us. . . .

We told them again that we judged we were exceedingly injured, that they might as well kill us, as take away our property and the necessaries of life. We have asked why they treat us thus? What has become of our repeated addresses and supplications to them? Who hath shut the ears of the king to the cries of his children in America? No soft answer, no pleasant voice from beyond the water has yet sounded in our ears.

Brothers, thus stands the matter betwixt old England and America . . .

Brothers, Listen!

Notwithstanding all our intreaties, we have but little hope the king will send us any more good talks, by reason of his evil counsellors. They have persuaded him to send an army of soldiers and many ships of war to rob and destroy us. They have shut up many of our harbours, seized and taken into possession many of our vessels. The soldiers have struck the blow, killed some of our people. The blood now runs of American children. They have also burned our houses and towns, and taken much of our goods.

Brothers! We are now necessitated to rise and forced to fight or give up our civil constitution, run away, and leave our farms and houses behind us. This must not be. Since the king's wicked counsellors will not open their ears, and consider our just complaints and the cause of our weeping, and hath given the blow, we are determined to drive away the king's soldiers, and to kill and destroy all those wicked men we find in arms against the peace of the twelve United Colonies upon this island. We think our cause is just; therefore hope God will be on our side We do not take up the hatchet and struggle for honor and conquest, but to maintain our civil constitution and religious privileges, the very same for which our forefathers left their native land and came to this country.

Brothers and Friends!

We desire you will hear and receive what we have now told you and that you will open a good ear and listen to what we are now going to say. This is a family quarrel between us and Old England. You Indians are not concerned in it. We don't wish you to take up the hatchet against the king's troops. We desire you to remain at home and not join on either side, but keep the hatchet buried deep. In the name and in behalf of all our people, we ask and desire you to love peace and maintain it, and to love and sympathise with us in our troubles; that the path may be kept open with all our people and yours to pass and repass without molestation.

Brothers! We live upon the same ground with you. The same island is our common birth-place. We desire to sit down under the same tree of peace with you: let us water its roots and cherish its growth, till the large leaves and flourishing branches shall extend to the setting sun and reach the skies.

Brothers, Observe Well!

What is it we have asked of you? Nothing but peace, notwithstanding our present disturbed situation—and if application should be made to you by any of the king's unwise and wicked ministers to join on their side, we only advise you to deliberate with great caution and in your wisdom look forward to the consequences of a compliance. For, if the king's troops take away our property and destroy us who are of the same blood with themselves, what can you, who are Indians expect from them afterwards? . . .

Brothers!

We have said we wish you Indians may continue in peace with one another and with us the white people. Let us both be cautious in our behaviour towards each other at this critical state of affairs. This island now trembles, the wind whistles from almost every quarter. Let us fortify our minds and shut our ears against false rumors. Let us be cautious what we receive for truth, unless spoken by wise and good men. If any thing disagreeable should ever fall out between us, the twelve United Colonies and you, the Six Nations, to wound our peace, let us immediately seek measures for healing the breach.

III. Loyalists

Not everyone in the thirteen colonies supported independence. Historians now estimate that perhaps 20% of the population were committed loyalists. Because of these divisions, the American Revolution was not merely a revolution or an anticolonial struggle: it was also a civil war. In certain parts of the country, notably the New York–New Jersey area and the Carolina backcountry, loyalists felt confident enough to take up arms against prorevolutionary militias. The resulting fighting was cruel and bloody, as civil war usually is. After the war, as many as 80,000 loyalists fled the United States to settle in Canada, Jamaica, and other British dominions. Among them were thousands of African Americans, most of whom were enslaved, but others of whom had won their freedom fighting for the British. Many of these were resettled in Freetown (Sierra Leone), a new British colony established specifically as a home for freed slaves.

9. LAFAYETTE DESCRIBES THE AMERICAN REVOLUTION AS A CIVIL WAR[9]

The marquis de Lafayette was a wealthy, young aristocrat from France who served with Washington's army as a volunteer. He clearly perceived the fratricidal nature of the conflict.

Despite the independence of the new state, everything bore the mark of a civil war. The names "Whig" and "Tory" distinguished the republicans from the royalists; the English army was still called "the regular troops"; in saying "the King," one meant the British sovereign. Partisan fury divided provinces, cities, families; there were brothers who, serving as officers in the opposing armies, grabbed for their weapons to fight each other when they encountered each other in their father's house. While the English, in their prideful rage, indulged in all the horrors of licence and cruelty, while blind discipline brought in their wake those mercenary Germans who knew only how to kill, pillage, and burn houses, there were in the same army regiments of Americans who crushed their brothers underfoot and enslaved their devastated country. Each canton contained an even larger number whose sole object was to harm the friends of liberty and warn the supporters of despotism. In addition to these inveterate Tories, there were all those whom fear, self-interest, or religion distanced from the war. While the Presbyterians, children of Cromwell and Fairfax, all hated royalty, the Anglicans were more divided. The Quakers hated the carnage, but served as guides for the royal troops. Insurrections were frequent; near enemy posts, farmers shot at each other and even thieves were encouraged. When they travelled across the country, the rebel leaders ran great risks; they said that they were going to spend the night in one house, but actually lodged themselves in another where they barricaded themselves and went to sleep surrounded by weapons. . . .

10. LOYALIST SONG: "THE REBELS"[10]

The following is one of many loyalist songs written during the war. Like many of them, it mocks the patriots as uncouth, country bumpkins—thereby implying that

---

[9]Stanley J. Idzerda, ed., *Lafayette in the Age of the American Revolution: Selected Letters and Papers, 1776–1790*, vol. 1 (Ithaca, NY: Cornell University Press, 1977), 397.
[10]Frank Moore, *Songs and Ballads of the American Revolution* (New York: D. Appleton, 1856), 196–199.

the loyalists came from a better class of people. Historians still debate whether the loyalist/patriot divide reflected class distinctions.

Ye brave, honest subjects, who dare to be loyal
And have stood the brunt of every trial
 Of hunting-shirts and rifle-guns:
Come listen awhile, and I'll sing you a song;
I'll show you those Yankees are all in the wrong,
Who, with blustering look and most awkward gait,
'Gainst their lawful sovereign dare for to prate,
 With their hunting-shirts and rifle-guns.

The arch-rebels, barefooted tatterdemalions,
In baseness exceed all other rebellions,
 With their hunting-shirts and rifle-guns.
To rend the empire, the most infamous lies
Their mock-patriot Congress do always devise;
Independence, like the first of rebels, they claim,
But their plots will be damned in the annals of fame,
 With their hunting-shirts and rifle-guns.

Forgetting the mercies of Great Britain's king,
Who saved their forefathers' necks from the string;
 With their hunting-shirts and rifle-guns.
They renounce allegiance and take up their arms,
Assemble together like hornets in swarms.
So dirty their backs and so wretched their show
That carrion-crow follows wherever they go,
 With their hunting-shirts and rifle-guns.

With loud peals of laughter, your sides, sirs, would crack
To see General Convict and Colonel Shoe-black
 With their hunting-shirts and rifle-guns.
See cobblers and quacks, rebel priests and the like,
Pettifoggers and barbers, with sword and with pike,
All strutting, the standard of Satan beside,
And honest names using, their black deeds to hide.
 With their hunting-shirts and rifle-guns.

The perjured banditti now ruin this land,
And o'er its poor people claim lawless command,
 With their hunting-shirts and rifle-guns.
Their pasteboard dollars prove a common curse;
They don't chink like silver and gold in our purse.
With nothing their leaders have paid their debts off;

Their honor's dishonor, and justice they scoff,
  With their hunting-shirts and rifle-guns.

For the lawful ruler, many tyrants we've got,
Who force young and old to their wars, to be shot,
  With their hunting-shirts and rifle-guns.
Our good king, God speed him! never used men so;
We then could speak, act, and like freemen could go;
But committees enslave us, our Liberty's gone,
Our trade and church murdered, our country's undone,
  By hunting-shirts and rifle-guns.

Come take up your glasses, each true loyal heart,
And may every rebel meet his due desert,
  With his hunting-shirt and rifle-gun.
May Congress, Conventions, those damn'd inquisitions,
Be fed with hot sulphur, from Lucifer's kitchens,
May commerce and peace again be restored,
And Americans own their true sovereign lord!
  Then oblivion to shirts and rifle-guns.
    God save the King!

11. SHOW THE LOYALISTS NO MERCY (1779)[11]

The patriot press attacked loyalism without mercy. The following document offers a striking example. The context in which it was written—shortly after the British withdrawal from Philadelphia, which they had occupied for a year (to the great joy of local loyalists)—may help account for its particularly unforgiving tones.

Among the many errors America has been guilty of during her contest with Great-Britain, few have been greater, or attended with more fatal consequences to these States than her lenity to the Tories. At first it might have been right, or perhaps political; but is it not surprising that, after repeated proofs of the evils resulting therefrom, it should still be continued? We are all crying out against the depreciation of our money, and entering into measures to restore it to it's original value, while the Tories, who are one principal cause of the depreciation, are taken no notice of, but suffered to live quietly among us. I can no longer be silent on this subject and see the independence of my country, after standing every shock from without, endangered by internal enemies. Rouse, America! your danger is great—great from a quarter where you least expect it. The Tories, the Tories will yet be the ruin of you. 'Tis high time they were separated from among you. They are now

---

[11]"A Whig": To the Public; *Pennsylvania Packet*, August 5, 1779.

busily engaged in undermining your liberties. They have a thousand ways of doing it, and they make use of them all. Who were the occasion of this war? the Tories. Who persuaded the tyrant of Britain to prosecute it in a manner before unknown to civilized nations and shocking even to barbarians? the Tories. Who advised, and who assisted in burning your towns, ravaging your country, and violating the chastity of your women? the Tories. Who are the occasion that thousands of you now mourn the loss of your dearest connections? the Tories. Who have always counteracted the endeavours of Congress to secure the liberty of this country? the Tories. Who refused their money when as good as specie, though stamped with the image of *his most sacred Majesty*? the Tories. Who continue to refuse it? the Tories. Who do all in their power to depreciate it? the Tories. Who propagate lies among us to discourage the Whigs? the Tories. Who corrupt the minds of the good people of these States by every species of insidious counsel? the Tories. Who hold a traitorous correspondence with the enemy? the Tories. Who daily send them intelligence? the Tories. Who take the oaths of allegiance to the States one day, and break them the next? the Tories. Who prevent your battalions from being filled? the Tories. Who dissuade men from entering the army? the Tories. Who persuade those who have enlisted to desert? the Tories. Who harbour those who do desert? the Tories. In short, who wish to see us conquered, to see us slaves, to see us hewers of wood and drawers of water? the Tories And is it possible, my countrymen, that you should suffer men who have been guilty of all these and a thousand other calamities which this country has experienced to live among you! To live among you did I say? Nay, do they not mix in your Assemblies? Do they not insult you with their impudence? Do they not hold traitorous Assemblies of their own? Do they not walk in the streets at noon-day and taste the air of Liberty? In short do they not enjoy every privilege of the brave soldier who has spilt his blood, or the honest patriot who has sacrificed his all in your righteous cause? Yes, to your eternal shame be spoken they do. Those very men, who wish to entail slavery on your country, are caressed and harboured among you. Posterity will not believe it; if they do, they will curse the memory of their fore-fathers for their shameful lenity. Do you ever expect any grateful return for your humanity, if it deserves that name? Believe me, not a spark of that or any other virtue is to be found in a Tory's breast. For what principle can that wretch have who would sell his soul to subject his country to the will of the greatest tyrant the world at present produces? 'Tis time, my countrymen, to rid ourselves of these bosom-vipers. An immediate separation is necessary. I dread to think of the evils every moment is big with, while a single Tory remains among us. May we not soon expect to hear of plots, assassinations, and every other species of wickedness their malice and rancour can suggest? For what can restrain those who have already imbrued their hands in their country's blood? . . . For my own part, whenever I meet one in the street or at the Coffee-house, my blood boils within me. Their guilt is equaled only by their impudence. They strut and seem to bid defiance to every one. In every place and in every company they spread their damnable doctrines and then laugh at the pusillanimity of those who let them go unpunished. I flatter myself, however, with the hopes of soon seeing a period to their reign and a total end to their existence in America. Awake, Americans, to a sense of your danger. No time is to be lost—Instantly banish every Tory from among you. Let these walls, let America be sacred alone to freemen. Drive far from you every baneful wretch who wishes to see you fettered with the chains of tyranny. Send them where they may enjoy their beloved slavery in perfection. Send them to the island of Britain, there let them drink the cup of slavery and eat the bread of bitterness all the days of their existence. There let them drag out a painful life, despised and accursed by those very men whose cause they have had the wickedness to espouse. Never let them return to this happy land. Never let them taste the sweets of that independence which they strove to prevent. Banishment, perpetual banishment, should be their lot. . . .

IV. A Government for Independent America

No sooner had independence been formally declared than American political leaders found themselves obliged to set up a government for their new polity. I use the vague word "polity" deliberately, for it was not clear whether they were creating a unified state or a confederacy of sovereign states or something in between. The result was the Articles of Confederation (1777), effectively the first constitution of the United States.

12. JOHN ADAMS, *THOUGHTS ON GOVERNMENT* (APRIL 1776)[12]

Even before the formal declaration of independence, members of the Continental Congress had begun to contemplate what an independent American government might look like. They turned to one of their own, John Adams, for advice. In April 1776, he published his thoughts in pamphlet form. They were an important influence on American political thinking (although more on the Constitution of 1787 than the Articles of Confederation).

We ought to consider what is the end of government, before we determine which is the best form. Upon this point all speculative politicians will agree, that the happiness of society is the end of government, as all divines and moral philosophers will agree that the happiness of the individual is the end of man. From this principle it will follow, that the form of government which communicates ease, comfort, security, or, in one word, happiness, to the greatest number of persons, and in the greatest degree, is the best.

[12]John Adams, *Thoughts on Government* (1776), in *The Works of John Adams*, ed. Charles F. Adams (Boston, MA: Little, Brown, 1851), vol.4, 193–201.

All sober inquirers after truth, ancient and modern, pagan and Christian, have declared that the happiness of man, as well as his dignity, consists in virtue. Confucius, Zoroaster, Socrates, Mahomet, not to mention authorities really sacred, have agreed in this.

If there is a form of government, then, whose principle and foundation is virtue, will not every sober man acknowledge it better calculated to promote the general happiness than any other form?

Fear is the foundation of most governments; but is so sordid and brutal a passion, and renders men in whose breasts it predominates so stupid and miserable, that Americans will not be likely to approve of any political institution which is founded on it.

Honor is truly sacred, but holds a lower rank in the scale of moral excellence than virtue. Indeed, the former is but a part of the latter, and consequently has not equal pretensions to support a frame of government productive of human happiness.

The foundation of government is some principle or passion in the minds of the people. The noblest principles and most generous affections in our nature, then, have the fairest chance to support the noblest and most generous model of government. . . .

There is no good government but what is republican. That the only valuable part of the British constitution is so; because the very definition of a republic is "an empire of laws, and not of men." That, as a republican is the best of governments, so that particular arrangement of the powers of society, or, in other words, that form of government which is best contrived to secure an impartial and exact execution of the laws, is the best of republics.

Of republics there is an inexhaustible variety, because the possible combinations of the powers of society are capable of innumerable variations.

As good government is an empire of laws, how shall your laws be made? In a large society, inhabiting an extensive country, it is impossible that the whole should assemble to make laws. The first necessary step, then, is to depute power from the many to a few of the most wise and good. But by what rules shall you choose your representatives? Agree upon the number and qualifications of persons who shall have the benefit of choosing, or annexing this privilege to the inhabitants of a certain extent of ground.

The principal difficulty lies, and the greatest care should be employed, in constituting this representative assembly. It should be in miniature an exact portrait of the people at large. It should think, feel, reason, and act like them. That it may be the interest of this assembly to do strict justice at all times, it should be an equal representation, or, in other words, equal interests in it. Great care should be taken to effect this, and to prevent unfair, partial and corrupt elections. Such regulations, however, may be better made in times of greater tranquility than the present; and they will spring up themselves naturally, when all the powers of government come to be in the hands in all established modes, to which the people have been familiarized by habit.

A representation of the people in one assembly being obtained, a question arises, whether all the powers of government, legislative, executive, and judicial, shall be left in this body? I think a people cannot be long free, nor ever happy, whose government is in one assembly. My reasons for this opinion are as follow:

1. A single assembly is liable to all the vices, follies, and frailties of an individual; subject to fits of humor, starts of passion, flights of enthusiasm, partialities, or prejudice, and consequently productive of hasty results and absurd judgements. And all these errors ought to be corrected and defects supplied by some controlling power.

2. A single assembly is apt to be avaricious, and in time will not scruple to exempt itself from burdens, which it will lay without compunction, on its constituents.

3. A single assembly is apt to grow ambitious, and after a time will not hesitate to vote itself perpetual. . . .

4. A representative assembly, although extremely well qualified, and absolutely necessary, as a branch of the legislative, is unfit to exercise the executive power, for want of two essential properties, secrecy and despatch.

5. A representative assembly is still less qualified for the judicial power, because it is too numerous, too slow, and too little skilled in the laws.

6. Because a single assembly, possessed of all the powers of government, would make arbitrary laws for their own interest, and adjudge all controversies in their own favor.

But shall the whole power of legislation rest in one assembly? Most of the foregoing reasons apply equally to prove that the legislative power ought to be more complex; to which we may add, that if the legislative power is wholly in one assembly, and the executive power in another, or in a single person, these two powers will oppose and encroach upon each other, until the contest shall end in war, and the whole power, legislative and executive, be usurped by the strongest.

The judicial power, in such case, could not mediate, or hold the balance between two contending powers, because the legislative would undermine it. And this shows the necessity, too, of giving the executive power a negative upon the legislative, otherwise this will be continually encroaching upon that.

To avoid these dangers, let a distinct assembly be constituted, as a mediator between the two extreme branches of the legislature, that which represents the people, and that which is vested with the executive power.

Let the representative assembly then elect by ballot, from among themselves or their constituents, or both, a distinct assembly, which, for the sake of perspicuity, we will call a council. It may consist of any number you please, say twenty or thirty, and should have a free and independent exercise of its judgement, and consequently a negative voice in the legislature.

These two bodies, thus constituted, and made integral parts of the legislature, let them unite, and by joint ballot choose a governor, who, after being stripped of most of those badges of domination, called prerogatives, should have a free and independent exercise of his judgement, and be made also an integral part of the legislature. This, I know, is liable to objections; and, if you please, you may make him only president of the council, as in Connecticut. But as the governor is to be invested with the executive power, with consent of council, I think he ought to have a negative upon the legislative. If he is annually elective, as he ought to be, he will always have so much reverence and affection for the people, their representatives and counsellors, that, although you give him an independent exercise of his judgement, he will seldom use it in opposition to the two houses, except in cases the public utility of which would be conspicuous. . . .

The governor, lieutenant-governor, secretary, treasurer, commissary, attorney-general, should be chosen by joint ballot of both houses. And these and all other elections, especially of representatives and counsellors, should be annual, there not being in the whole circle of the sciences a maxim more infallible than this, "where annual elections end, there slavery begins." . . .

This mode of constituting the great offices of state will answer very well for the present; but if by experiment it should be found inconvenient, the legislature may, at its leisure, devise other methods of creating them, by elections of the people at large, as in Connecticut, or it may enlarge the term for which they shall be chosen to seven years, or three years, or for life, or make any other alterations which the society shall find productive of its ease, its safety, its freedom, or, in one word, its happiness. . . .

The dignity and stability of government in all its branches, the morals of the people, and every blessing of society depend so much upon an upright and skillful administration of justice, that the judicial power ought to be distinct from both the legislative and executive, and independent upon both, that so it may be a check upon both, as both should be checks upon that. The judges, therefore, should be always men of learning and experience in the laws, of exemplary morals, great patience, calmness, coolness, and attention. Their minds should not be distracted with jarring interests; they should not be dependent upon any man, or body of men. To these ends, they should hold estates for life in their offices; or, in other words, their commissions should be during good behavior, and their salaries ascertained and established by law. For misbehavior, the grand inquest of the colony, the house of representatives, should impeach them before the governor and council. . . .

A militia law, requiring all men, or with very few exceptions besides cases of conscience, to be provided with arms and ammunition, to be trained at certain seasons . . . is always a wise institution, and, in the present circumstances of our country, indispensable.

Laws for the liberal education of youth, especially of the lower class of people, are so extremely wise and useful, that, to a humane and generous mind, no expense for this purpose would be thought extravagant.

The very mention of sumptuary laws will excite a smile. Whether our countrymen have wisdom and virtue enough to submit to them, I know not; but the happiness of the people might be greatly promoted by them, and a revenue saved sufficient to carry on this war forever. Frugality is a great revenue, besides curing us of vanities, levities, and fopperies, which are real antidotes to all great, manly, and warlike virtues. . . .

A constitution founded on these principles introduces knowledge among the people, and inspires them with a conscious dignity becoming freemen; a general emulation takes places, which causes good humor, sociability, good manners, and good morals to be general. That elevation of sentiment inspired by such a government, makes the common people brave and enterprising. That ambition which is inspired by it makes them sober, industrious, and frugal. You will find among them some elegance, perhaps, but more solidarity; a little pleasure, but a great deal of business; some politeness, but more civility. If you compare such a country with the regions of domination, whether monarchical or aristocratical, you will fancy yourself in Arcadia or Elysium.

If the colonies should assume governments separately, they should be left entirely to their own choice of forms; and if a continental constitution should be formed, it should be a congress, containing a fair and adequate representation of the colonies, and its authority should sacredly be confined to these cases, namely, war, trade, disputes between colony and colony, the post office, and the unappropriated lands of the crown, as they used to be called.

These colonies, under such forms of government, and in such a union, would be unconquerable by all the monarchies of Europe.

13. ARTICLES OF CONFEDERATION (1777)[13]

Drafted mainly by John Dickinson, the Articles of Confederation were adopted on November 15, 1777, as the first permanent framework of independent American government. They left much power to the individual states and gave the central government only limited authority to raise revenue, enforce national laws, mediate conflicts between states, and so forth. Once they went into effect, after ratification in 1781, these drawbacks became apparent. But the Articles should not be dismissed as an unmitigated failure, for it was under them that the United States negotiated a very advantageous peace treaty with Britain (1783) and established a successful mechanism for admitting new states into the Union (the Northwest Ordinances of 1785 and 1787).

I. The stile of this confederacy shall be "The United States of America."

II. Each State retains its sovereignty, freedom and independence, and every power, jurisdiction and right, which is not by this confederation expressly delegated to the United States, in Congress assembled.

---

[13]"Articles of Confederation: March 1, 1781," The Avalon Project, http://avalon.law.yale.edu/18th_century/artconf.asp.

III. The said States hereby severally enter into a firm league of friendship with each other, for their common defence, the security of their liberties, and their mutual and general welfare, binding themselves to assist each other, against all force offered to, or attacks made upon them, or any of them, on account of religion, sovereignty, trade, or any other pretence whatever.

IV. The better to secure and perpetuate mutual friendship and intercourse among the people of the different States in this Union, the free inhabitants of each of these States, paupers, vagabonds and fugitives from justice excepted, shall be entitled to all privileges and immunities of free citizens in the several States; and the people of each State shall have free ingress and regress to and from any other State, and shall enjoy there all the privileges of trade and commerce, subject to the same duties, impositions and restrictions. . . .

If any Person guilty of, or charged with treason, felony, or other high misdemeanor in any State, shall flee from justice, and be found in any of the United States, he shall upon demand of the Governor or Executive power, of the State from which he fled, be delivered up and removed to the State having jurisdiction of his offence.

Full faith and credit shall be given in each of these States to the records, acts and judicial proceedings of the courts and magistrates of every other State.

V. For the more convenient management of the general interest of the United States, delegates shall be annually appointed in such manner as the legislature of each State shall direct, to meet in Congress on the first Monday in November, in every year, with a power reserved in each State, to recall its delegates, or any of them, at any time within the year, and to send others in their stead, for the remainder of the year.

No State shall be represented in Congress by less than two, nor by more than seven members; and no person shall be capable of holding any office under the United States, for which he, or another for his benefit receives any salary, fees of emolument of any kind. . . .

In determining questions in the United States, in Congress assembled, each State shall have one vote.

Freedom of speech and debate in Congress shall not be impeached or questioned in any court, or place out of Congress, and the members of Congress shall be protected in their persons from arrests and imprisonments, during the time of their going to and from, and attendance on congress, except for treason, felony, or breach of the peace.

VI. No state without the consent of the United States in Congress assembled, shall send any embassy to, or receive any embassy from, or enter into any conference, agreement, alliance or treaty with any king, prince or state; nor shall any person holding any office of profit or trust under the United States, or any of them, accept any present, emolument, office or title of any kind whatever from any king, prince or foreign state; nor shall the United States in Congress assembled, or any of them, grant any title of nobility.

No two or more States shall enter in to any treaty, confederation or alliance whatever between them, without the consent of the United States in Congress assembled, specifying accurately the purposes for which the same is to be entered into, and how long it shall continue.

No State shall lay any imposts or duties, which may interfere with any stipulations in treaties, entered into by the United States in Congress assembled, with any king, prince or state, in pursuance of any treaties already proposed by Congress, to the courts of France and Spain.

No vessels of war shall be kept up in time of peace by any State, except such number only, as shall be deemed necessary by the United States in Congress assembled, for the defence of such State, or its trade; nor shall any body of forces be kept up by any State, in time of peace, except such number only, as in the judgement of the United States, in Congress assembled, shall be deemed requisite to garrison the forts necessary for the defence of such State; but every State shall always keep up a well-regulated and disciplined militia, sufficiently armed and accoutered, and shall provide and constantly have ready for use, in public stores, a due number of field pieces and tents, and a proper quantity of arms, ammunition and camp equipage.

No State shall engage in any war without the consent of the United States in Congress assembled, unless such State be actually invaded by enemies, or shall have received certain advice of a resolution being formed by some nation of Indians to invade such State, and the danger is so imminent as not to admit of a delay, till the United States on Congress assembled can be consulted; nor shall any State grant commissions to any ships or vessels of war, nor letters of marque or reprisal, except it be after a declaration of war by the United States in Congress assembled, and then only against the kingdom or state and the subjects thereof, against which war has been so declared, and under such regulations as shall be established by the United States in Congress assembled, unless such State be infested by pirates, in which case vessels of war may be fitted out for that occasion, and kept so long as the danger shall continue, or until the United States in Congress assembled shall determine otherwise.

VII. When land forces are raised by any State for the common defence, all officers of or under the rank of colonel, shall be appointed by the Legislature of each State respectively by whom such forces shall be raised, or in such manner as such State shall direct, and all vacancies shall be filled up by the State which first made the appointment.

VIII. All charges of war, and all other expenses that shall be incurred for the common defence or general welfare, and allowed by the United States in Congress assembled, shall be defrayed out of a common treasury, which shall be supplied by the several States, in proportion to the value of all land within each State, granted to or surveyed for any person, as such land and the buildings and improvements thereon shall be estimated according to such mode as the United States in Congress assembled, shall from time to time direct and appoint.

IX. The United States in Congress assembled, shall have the sole and exclusive right and power of determining on peace and war, except in the cases mentioned in the sixth article—of sending and receiving ambassadors—entering into treaties and alliances, provided that no treaty of commerce shall be made whereby the legislative power of the respective State shall be restrained from imposing such imposts and duties on foreigners, as their own people are subjected to, or from prohibiting the exportation or importation of any species of goods, or commodities whatsoever—of establishing rules for deciding in all cases, what captures on land or water shall be legal, and in what manner prizes taken by land or naval forces in the service of the United States shall be divided or appropriated—of granting letters of marque and reprisal in times of peace—appointing courts for the trial of piracies and felonies committed on the high seas and establishing courts for receiving and determining finally appeals in all cases of captures, provided that no member of Congress shall be appointed a judge of any of the said courts.

The United States in Congress assembled shall also be the last resort on appeal in all disputes and differences now subsisting or that hereafter may arise between two or more States concerning boundary, jurisdiction, or any other cause whatever; which authority shall always be exercised in the manner following. Whenever the legislative or executive authority or lawful agent of any State in controversy with another shall present a petition to Congress, stating the matter in question and praying for a hearing, notice thereof shall be given by order of Congress to the legislative or executive authority of the other State in controversy, and a day assigned for the appearance of the parties by their lawful agents, who shall then be directed to appoint by joint consent, commissioners or judges to constitute a court for hearing and determining the matter in question: but if they cannot agree, Congress shall name three persons out of each of the United States, and from the list of such persons each party shall alternately strike out one, the petitioners beginning, until the number shall be reduced to thirteen; and from that number not less than seven, nor more than nine names as Congress shall direct, shall in the presence of Congress be drawn out by lot, and the persons whose names shall be so drawn or any five of them, shall be commissioners or judges, to hear and finally determine the controversy, so always as a major part of the judges who shall hear the cause shall agree in the determination: and if either part shall neglect to attend at the day appointed, without showing reasons, which Congress shall judge sufficient, or being present shall refuse to strike, the Congress shall proceed to nominate three persons out of each State, and the Secretary of Congress shall strike in behalf of such party absent or refusing; and the judgement and sentence of the court to be appointed, in the manner before prescribed, shall be final and conclusive; and if any of the parties shall refuse to submit to the authority of such court, or to appear or defend their claim or cause, the court shall nevertheless proceed to pronounce the sentence, or judgement, which shall in like manner be final and decisive. . . .

All controversies concerning the private right of soil claimed under different grants of two or more States . . . shall on the petition of either party to the Congress of the United States, be finally determined as near as may be in the same manner as is before prescribed for deciding disputes respecting territorial jurisdiction between different States.

The United States in Congress assembled shall also have the sole and exclusive right and power of regulating the alloy and value of coin struck by their own authority, or by that of the respective States—fixing the standard of weights and measures throughout the United States—regulating the trade and managing all affairs with the Indians, not members of any of the States, provided that the legislative right of any State within its own limits be not infringed or violated—establishing and regulating post-offices from one State to another, throughout all the United States, and exacting such postage on the papers passing thro' the same as may be requisite to defray the expenses of the said office—appointing all officers of the land forces, in the service of the United States, excepting regimental officers—appointing all the officers of the naval forces, and commissioning all officers whatever in the service of the United States—making rules for the government and regulation of the said land and naval forces, and directing their operations.

The United States in Congress assembled shall have authority to appoint a committee, to sit in the recess of Congress, to be denominated "a Committee of the States," and to consist of one delegate from each State; and to appoint such other committees and civil officers as may be necessary for managing the general affairs of the United States under their direction—to appoint one of their number to preside, provided that no more than one year in term of three years; to ascertain the necessary sums of money to be raised for the service of the United States, and to appropriate and apply the same for defraying the public expenses—to borrow money, or emit bills on the credit of the United States, transmitting every half year to the respective States an account of the sums of money so borrowed or emitted,—to build and equip a navy—to agree upon the number of land forces, and to make requisitions from each State for its quota, in proportion to the number of white inhabitants in such State; which requisition shall be binding, and thereupon the Legislature of each State shall appoint the regimental officers, raise the men and cloath, arm and equip them in a soldier like manner, at the expense of the United States; and the officers and men so cloathed, armed and equipped, shall march to the place appointed, and within the time agreed on by the United States in Congress assembled.

The United States in Congress assembled shall never engage in a war, nor grant letters of marque and reprisal in time of peace, nor regulate the value thereof, nor ascertain the sums and expenses necessary for the defence and welfare of the United States, or any of them, nor emit bills, nor borrow money on the credit of the United States, nor appropriate money, nor agree upon the number of vessels of war, to be built or purchased, or the number of land or sea forces to be raised, nor appoint a commander in chief of the army or navy, unless nine States assent to the same: nor shall a question on any other point, except for adjourning from day to day be determined, unless by the votes of a majority of the United States in Congress assembled.

The Congress of the United States shall have power to adjourn to any time within the year, and to any place within the United States, so that no period of adjournment be for a longer duration than the space of six months, and shall publish the journal of their proceedings monthly, except such parts thereof relating to the treaties, alliances or military operations, as in their judgement require secrecy; and the yeas and nays of the delegates of each State on any question shall be entered in the journal, when it is desired by any delegate; and the delegates of each State, or any of them, at his or their request shall be furnished with a transcript of the said journal, except such parts as are . . . excepted, to lay before the Legislatures of the several States.

X. The committee of the States, or any nine of them, shall be authorized to exercise, in the recess of Congress, such of the powers of Congress as the United States in Congress assembled, by the consent of nine States, shall from time to time think expedient to vest them with. . . .

XI. Canada acceding to this confederation, and joining in the measures of the United States, shall be admitted into, and entitled to all the advantages of this Union: but no other colony shall be admitted into the same, unless such admission be agreed to by nine States.

XII. All bills of credit emitted, monies borrowed and debts contracted by, or under the authority of Congress, before the assembling of the United States, in pursuance of the present confederation, shall be deemed and considered as a charge against the said United States, and the public faith are hereby solemnly pledged.

XIII. Every State shall abide by the determinations of the United States in Congress assembled, on all questions which by this confederation are submitted to them. And the articles of this confederation shall be inviolably observed by every State, and the Union shall be perpetual; nor shall any alteration at any time hereafter be made in any of them; unless such alteration be agreed to in a Congress of the United States, and be afterwards confirmed by the Legislatures of every State. . . .

V. The Constitution of 1787

The shortcomings of the Articles of Confederation soon became clear. With little reliable revenue, the central government could only maintain a nominal army (only 80 men in 1784!) and thus do nothing to extend effective control over the vast western territories Britain had ceded in the peace treaty of 1783. Nor was there a mechanism for compelling the states to observe national regulations on foreign trade. This led states into bidding wars with each other as they sought to lure foreign commerce to their shores. Worse, there was no mechanism for resolving disputes between states who at times risked going to war with each other over their many grievances (over land claims, trade policy, etc.) One state (New Hampshire) even considered leaving the Union and joining British Canada! In 1786, leading American political figures had come to the conclusion that the Articles of Confederation must be revised or replaced. To that end, a constitutional convention was summoned. Presided over by George Washington, it met in Philadelphia from July to September 1787. The result was the Constitution.

14. JAMES MADISON, *VICES OF THE POLITICAL SYSTEM OF THE UNITED STATES* (APRIL 1787)[14]

Regarded by many as the father of the Constitution because he authored so much of it, James Madison began to exert influence over the constitutional convention even before it met. He wrote this pamphlet shortly before the convention. Its trenchant critique of the weaknesses of the Articles of Confederation implies what a sounder form of government would entail.

1. *Failure of the States to Comply with the Constitutional Requisitions.* This evil has been so fully experienced both during the war and since the peace, results so naturally from the number and independent authority of the States, and has been so uniformly exemplified in every similar Confederacy, that it may be considered as not less radically and permanently inherent in it than it is fatal to the object of the present system.

2. *Encroachments by the States on the Federal Authority.* Examples of this are numerous and repetitions may be foreseen in almost every case where any favorite object of a State shall present a temptation. Among these examples are the wars and treaties of Georgia with the Indians, the unlicensed compacts between Virginia and Maryland, and between Pena. & N. Jersey, the troops raised and to be kept up by Massts.

3. *Violations of the Law of Nations and of Treaties.* From the number of Legislatures, the sphere of life from which most of their members are taken, and the circumstances under which their Legislative business is carried on, irregularities of this kind must frequently happen. Accordingly not a year has passed without instances of them in some one or other of the States. . . .

As yet foreign powers have not been rigorous in animadverting on us. This moderation, however, cannot be mistaken for a permanent partiality to our faults, or a permanent security agst. those disputes with other nations, which being among the greatest of public calamities, it ought to be least in the power of any part of the community to bring on the whole.

4. *Trespasses of the States on the Rights of Each Other.* These are alarming symptoms, and may be daily apprehended as we are admonished by daily experience. See the law of Virginia restricting foreign vessels to certain ports, of Maryland in favor of vessels belonging to her *own citizens,* of N. York in favor of the same.

Paper money, instalments of debts, occlusions of Courts, making property a legal tender, may likewise be deemed aggressions on the rights of other States. As the Citizens of every State aggressively taken stand more or less in relation of Creditors or debtors, to the Citizens of every other State, Acts of the debtor State in favor of debtors, affect the Creditor State, in the same manner as they do its own

---

[14]James Madison, "Vices of the Political System of the United States" (April 1787), in *The Writings of James Madison*, ed. Gaillard Hunt (New York: G. P. Putnam's Sons, 1901), vol. 2, 361–369.

citizens who are relatively creditors towards other citizens. This remark may be extended to foreign nations. . . .

The practice of many States in restricting the commercial intercourse with other States, and putting their productions and manufactures on the same footing with those of foreign nations, though not contrary to the federal articles, is certainly adverse to the spirit of the Union, and tends to beget retaliating regulations, not less expensive and vexatious in themselves than they are destructive of the general harmony.

5. *Want of Concert in Matters Where Common Interest Requires It.* This defect is strongly illustrated in the state of our commercial affairs. How much has the national dignity, interest, and revenue, suffered from this cause? Instances of inferior moment are the want of uniformity in the laws concerning naturalization & literary property; of provision for national seminaries, for grants of incorporation for national purposes, for canals and other works of general utility, wch may at present be defeated by the perverseness of particular States whose concurrence is necessary.

6. *Wants of Guaranty to the States of their Constitutions & Laws against Internal Violence.* The confederation is silent on this point and therefore by the second article the hands of the federal authority are tied. According to Republican Theory, Right and power being both vested in the majority, are held to be synonymous. According to fact and experience a minority may in an appeal to force, be an overmatch for the majority. 1. if the minority happen to include all such as possess the skill and habits of military life, & such as possess the great pecuniary resources, one-third only may conquer the remaining two-thirds. 2. one-third of those who participate in the choice of the rulers may be rendered a majority by the accession of those whose poverty excludes them from a right of suffrage, and who for obvious reasons will be more likely to join the standard of sedition than that of the established Government. 3. where slavery exists the republican Theory becomes still more fallacious.

7. *Wants of Sanction to the Laws and of Coercion in the Government of the Confederacy.* A sanction is essential to the idea of law, as coercion is to that of Government. The federal system being destitute of both, wants the great vital principles of a Political Constitution. Under the form of such a constitution, it is in fact nothing more than a treaty of amity and commerce and of alliance, between independent and Sovereign States. . . . A unanimous and punctual obedience of 13 independent bodies, to the acts of the federal Government ought not to be calculated on. Even during the war, when external danger supplied in some degree the defect of legal & coercive sanctions, how imperfectly did the States fulfill their obligations to the Union? In time of peace, we see already what is to be expected. How indeed could it be otherwise? In the first place, Every general act of the Union must necessarily bear unequally hard on some particular member or members of it, secondly the partiality of the members to their own interests and rights, a partiality which will be fostered by the courtiers of popularity, will naturally exaggerate the inequality where it exists, and even suspect it where it has no existence, thirdly a distrust of the voluntary compliance of each other may prevent the compliance of any. . . .

8. *Want of Ratification by the People of the Articles of Confederation.* In some of the States the Confederation is recognized by, and forms a part of the Constitution. In others however it has received no other sanction than that of the legislative authority. From this defect two evils result: 1. Whenever a law of a State happens to be repugnant to an act of Congress, particularly when the latter [former] is of posterior date to the former, [latter] it will be at least questionable whether the latter [former] must not prevail; and as the question must be decided by the Tribunals of the State, they will be most likely to lean on the side of the State. 2. As far as the union of the States is to be regarded as a league of sovereign powers, and not as a political Constitution by virtue of which they are become one sovereign power, so far it seems to follow from the doctrine of compacts, that a breach of any of the articles of the Confederation by any of the parties to it, absolves the other parties from their respective Obligations, and gives them a right if they chuse to exert it, of dissolving the Union altogether.

9. *Multiplicity of Laws in the Several States.* In developing the evils which viciate the political systems of the U S., it is proper to include those which are found within the States individually, as well as those which directly affect the States collectively, since the former class have an indirect influence on the general malady and must not be overlooked in forming a compleat remedy. . . .

10. *Mutability of the Laws of the States.* This evil is intimately connected with the former yet deserves a distinct notice, as it emphatically denotes a vicious legislation. We daily see laws repealed or superseded, before any trial can have been made of their merits, and even before a knowledge of them can have reached the remoter districts within which they were to operate. In the regulations of trade this instability becomes a snare not only to our citizens, but to foreigners also.

11. *Injustice of the Laws of the States.* If the multiplicity and mutability of laws prove a want of wisdom, their injustice betrays a defect still more alarming. . . . To what causes is this evil to be ascribed?[15]

15. THE PROBLEM OF SLAVERY AND REPRESENTATION[16]

The main question the delegates had to answer was whether representation should be based on population or whether states should be represented as entities. The former system favored the larger, more populous states, whereas the latter favored the smaller, less populous ones. The convention split along these lines. Ultimately, it compromised by creating an upper house (the Senate) in which states would enjoy

---

[15]He goes on to answer this question in terms so similar to those he would use several years later in *Federalist Number 10* (reading 17 in this chapter) that they have been omitted here to avoid repetition.

[16]"How to Count Slaves," in *The Records of the Federal Convention of 1787*, ed. Max Farrand (New Haven, CT: Yale University Press, 1911), vol. 1, 578–581, 586–588; and vol. 2, 369–375 and 449–453.

equal representation and a lower house (the House of Representatives) in which rep-
resentation would reflect population. But this raised a new question: in determining
a state's population, how (if at all) would slaves be counted? After much debate, the
delegates again compromised, deciding that slaves would be counted as three-fifths
of a person for the purpose of representation. Another compromise on the issue of
slavery was to continue to allow the import of new slaves until 1808. The following is
an excerpt from the debate over slavery and representation.

Mr. [Edmund] Randolph's motion requiring the Legislre. to take a periodical census for the purpose of redressing inequalities in the Representation was resumed. . . .

MR. [GEORGE] MASON: The greater the difficulty we find in fixing a proper rule of Representation, the more unwilling ought we to be, to throw the task from ourselves, on the Genl. Legislre. He did not object to the conjectural ratio which was to prevail in the outset; but considered a Revision from time to time according to some permanent & precise standard as essential to ye. fair representation required in the 1st. branch. According to the present population of America, the Northn. part of it had a right to preponderate, and he could not deny it. But he wished it not to preponderate hereafter when the reason no longer continued. From the nature of man we may be sure, that those who have power in their hands will not give it up while they can rather increase it. If the S. States therefore should have 3/4 of the people of America within their limits, the Northern will hold fast the majority of Representatives. 1/4 will govern the 3/4. The S. States will complain: but they may complain from generation to generation without redress. Unless some principle therefore which will do justice to them hereafter shall be inserted in the Constitution, disagreeable as the declaration was to him, he must declare he could neither vote for the system here nor support it, in his State. Strong objections had been drawn from the danger to the Atlantic interests from new Western States. Ought we to sacrifice what we know to be right in itself, lest it should prove favorable to States which are not yet in existence. If the Western States are to be admitted into the Union as they arise, they must, he wd. repeat, be treated as equals, and subjected to no degrading discriminations. They will have the same pride & other passions which we have, and will either not unite with or will speedily revolt from the Union, if they are not in all respects placed on an equal footing with their brethren. It has been said they will be poor, and unable to make equal contributions to the general Treasury. He did not know but that in time they would be both more numerous & more wealthy that their Atlantic brethren. The extent & fertility of their soil, made this probable; and though Spain might for a time deprive them of the natural outlet for their demands. He urged that numbers of inhabitants; though not always a precise standard of wealth was sufficiently so for every substantial purpose.

Mr. [Hugh] Williamson was for making it the duty of the Legislature to do what was right & not leave it at liberty to do or not to do it. He moved that Mr. Randolph's proposition be postponed. in order to consider the following "that in order to ascertain the alterations that may happen in the population & wealth of the several States, a census shall be taken of the free white inhabitants and the 3/5ths of those of other descriptions on the 1st year (after this Government shall have been adopted) and every year thereafter; and that the Representation be regulated accordingly." . . .

Mr. [Pierce] Butler & Genl. [C.C.] Pinkney insisted that blacks be included in the rule of Representation, *equally* with the Whites, and for that purpose moved that the words "three fifths" be struck out.

Mr. [Elbridge] Gerry thought that 3/5 of them was to say the least the full proportion that could be admitted.

> MR. [NATHANIAL] GHORUM: This ratio was fixed by Congs. as a rule of taxation. Then it was urged by the Delegates representing the States having slaves that the blacks were still more inferior to freemen. At present when the ratio of representation is to be established, we are assured that they are equal to freemen. The arguments on ye. former occasion had convinced him that 3/5 was pretty near the just proportion and he should vote according to the same opinion now.

Mr. Butler insisted that the labour of a slave in S. Carola. was as productive & valuable as that of a freeman in Massts., that as wealth was the great means of defence and utility to the Nation they are equally valuable to it with freemen; and that consequently an equal representation ought to be allowed for them, in a Government which was instituted principally for the protection of property, and was itself to be supported by property.

Mr. Mason could not agree to the motion, notwithstanding it was favorable to Virga. because he thought it unjust. It was certain that the slaves were valuable, as they raised the value of land, increased the exports & imports, and of course the revenue, would supply the means of feeding & supporting an army, and might in cases of emergency become themselves soldiers. As in these important respects they were useful to the community at large, they ought not to be excluded from the estimate of Representation. He could not however regard them as equal to freemen. . . .

Mr. Williamson reminded Mr. Ghorum that if the Southn. States contended for the inferiority of blacks to whites when taxation was in view, the Eastern States on the same occasion contended for their equality. He did not however either then or now, concur in either extreme, but approved of the ratio 3/5.

[The motion to consider blacks as equal to whites for the purpose of determining a state's population was defeated by a large majority.]

[On the question] . . . as to 3/5 of the negroes considered

Mr. [Rufus] King being much opposed to fixing numbers as the rule of representation, was particularly so on account of the blacks. He thought the admission of them along with Whites at all, would excite great discontents among the States having no slaves. He had never said as to any particular point that he would in no event acquiesce in & support it; but he wd. say that if in any case such a declaration was to be made by him, it would be in this. He remarked that in the temporary allotment of Representatives made by the Committee, the Southern States had received more than the number of their white & three fifths of their black inhabitants entitled them to.

> MR. [ROGER] SHERMAN: S. Carola. had not more beyond her proportion than N. York & N. Hampshire, nor either of them more than necessary in order to avoid factions or reducing them below their proportion. Georgia had more; but the rapid growth of that State seemed to justify it. In general the allotment might not be just, but considering all circumstances, he was satisfied with it. . . .

Mr. [James] Wilson did not well see on what principle the admission of blacks in the proportion of three fifths could be explained. Are they admitted as Citizens? . . . then why is it not other property admitted into the computation? These were difficulties however which he thought must be overruled by the necessity of compromise. He had some apprehensions also from the tendency of the blending of the blacks with the whites, to give disgust to the people of Pena. . . .

Mr. Gov[erno]r Morris was compelled to declare himself reduced to the dilemma of doing injustice to the Southern States or to human nature, and he must therefore do it to the former. For he could never agree to give such encouragement to the slave trade as would be given by allowing them a representation for their negroes, and he did not believe those States would ever confederate on terms that would deprive them of that trade.

[This motion passed, although the Convention's vote was sharply divided.]

16. THE CONSTITUTION (1787)[17]

The convention approved the constitution in September 1787. It attempted to balance the powers of the central government and those of the states, and it also attempted to establish a system of "checks and balances" between the three branches (executive, legislative, judiciary) that composed the central government itself.

---

[17]"The Constitution of the United States: 1787." The Heritage Foundation, www.heritage.org/ initiatives/first-principles/primary-sources/the-constitution-of-the-us.

Preamble

We the People of the United States, in Order to form a more perfect Union, establish Justice, insure domestic Tranquility, provide for the common defence, promote the general Welfare, and secure the Blessings of Liberty to ourselves and our Posterity, do ordain and establish this Constitution for the United States of America.

Article I

Section 1. All legislative Powers herein granted shall be vested in a Congress of the United States, which shall consist of a Senate and a House of Representatives.

Section 2. The House of Representatives shall be composed of Members chosen every second Year by the People of the several States, and the Electors in each State shall have the Qualifications requisite for Electors of the most numerous Branch of the State Legislature.

No Person shall be a Representative who shall not have attained to the age of twenty five Years, and been seven Years a Citizen of the United States, and who shall not, when elected, be an Inhabitant of that State in which he shall be chosen.

Representatives and direct Taxes shall be apportioned among the several States which may be included within this Union, according to their respective Numbers, which shall be determined by adding to the whole Number of free Persons, including those bound to Service for a Term of Years, and excluding Indians not taxed, three fifths of all other Persons. The actual Enumeration shall be made within three Years after the first Meeting of the Congress of the United States, and within every subsequent Term of ten Years, in such Manner as they shall by Law direct. The Number of Representatives shall not exceed one for every thirty Thousand, but each State shall have at Least one Representative. . . .

When vacancies happen in the Representation from any State, the Executive Authority thereof shall issue Writs of Election to fill such Vacancies.

The House of Representatives shall choose their Speaker and other Officers; and shall have the sole Power of Impeachment.

Section 3. The Senate of the United States shall be composed of two Senators from each State, chosen by the Legislature thereof, for six Years; and each Senator shall have one Vote.

Immediately after they shall be assembled in Consequence of the first Election, they shall be divided as equally as may be into three Classes. The seats of the Senators of the first Class shall be vacated at the Expiration of the second Year, of the second Class at the Expiration of the fourth Year, and of the third Class at the Expiration of the sixth Year, so that one third may be chosen every second Year; and if Vacancies happen by Resignation, or otherwise, during the Recess of the Legislature of any State, the Executive thereof may make temporary Appointments until the next Meeting of the Legislature, which shall then fill such Vacancies.

No Person shall be a Senator who shall not have attained to the Age of thirty Years, and been nine Years a Citizen of the United States, and who shall not, when elected, be an Inhabitant of the State for which he shall be chosen.

The Vice President of the United States shall be President of the Senate, but shall have no Vote, unless they be equally divided.

The Senate shall choose their other Officers, and also a President pro tempore, in the Absence of the Vice President, or when he shall exercise the Office of President of the United States.

The Senate shall have the sole Power to try all Impeachments. When sitting for that Purpose, they shall be on Oath or Affirmation. When the President of the United States is tried the Chief Justice will preside: And no Person shall be convicted without the Concurrence of two thirds of the Members present.

Judgement in Cases of Impeachment shall not extend further than to removal from Office, and disqualification to hold and enjoy any Office of honor, Trust or Profit under the United States: but the Part convicted shall nevertheless be liable and subject to Indictment, Trial, Judgement and Punishment, according to Law.

Section 4. The Times, Places and Manner of holding Elections for Senators and Representatives, shall be prescribed in each State by the Legislature thereof; but the Congress may at any time by Law make or alter such Regulations, except as to the Places of choosing Senators.

The Congress shall assemble at least once in every Year, and such Meeting shall be on the first Monday in December, unless they shall by Law appoint a different Day.

Section 5. Each House shall be the Judge of the Elections, Returns and Qualifications of its own Members, and a Majority of each shall constitute a Quorum to do Business; but a smaller Number may adjourn from day to day, and may be authorized to compel the Attendance of absent Members, in such Manner, and under such Penalties as each House may provide.

Each House may determine the Rules of its Proceedings, and from time to time publish the same, excepting such Parts as may in their Judgement require Secrecy; and the Yeas and Nays of the Members of either House on any question shall, at the Desire of one fifth of those Present, be entered on the Journal.

Neither House, during the Session of Congress, shall, without the Consent of the other, adjourn for more than three days, nor to any other Place than that in which the two Houses shall be sitting.

Section 6. The Senators and Representatives shall receive a Compensation for their Service, to be ascertained by Law, and paid out of the Treasury of the United States. They shall in all Cases, except Treason, Felony and Breach of the Peace, be privileged from Arrest during their Attendance at the Session of their respective Houses, and in going to and returning from the same; and for any Speech or Debate in either House, they shall not be questioned in any other Place.

No Senator or Representative shall, during the Time for which he was elected, be appointed to any civil Office under the Authority of the United States, which shall have been created, or the Emoluments whereof shall have been increased during such time; and no Person holding any Office under the United States, shall be a Member of either House during his Continuance in Office.

Section 7. All Bills for raising Revenue shall originate in the House of Representatives; but the Senate may propose or concur with amendments as to other Bills.

Every Bill which shall have passed the House of Representatives and the Senate, shall, before it become a Law, be presented to the President of the United States; If he approve he shall sign it, but if not he shall return it, with his Objections to that House in which it shall have originated, who shall enter the Objections at large on their Journal, and proceed to reconsider it. If after such Reconsideration two thirds of that House shall agree to pass the Bill, it shall be sent, together with the Objections, to the other House, by which it shall likewise be reconsidered, and if approved by two thirds of that House, it shall become a Law. But in all such Cases the Votes of both Houses shall be determined by yeas and nays, and the Names of the Persons voting for and against the Bill shall be entered on the Journal of each House respectively. If any Bill shall not be returned by the President within ten Days (Sunday excepted) after it shall have been presented to him, the Same shall be a Law, in like Manner as if he had signed it, unless the Congress by their Adjournment prevent its Return, in which Case it shall not be a Law.

Every Order, Resolution, or Vote to which the Concurrence of the Senate and the House of Representatives may be necessary (except on a question of Adjournment) shall be presented to the President of the United States; and before the Same shall take Effect, shall be approved by two thirds of the Senate and House of Representatives, according to the Rules and Limitations prescribed in the Case of a Bill.

Section 8. The Congress shall have Power To lay and collect Taxes, Duties, Imposts and Excises, to pay the Debts and provide for the common defence and general Welfare of the United States; but all Duties, Imposts and Excises shall be uniform throughout the United States;

To borrow Money on the credit of the United States;

To regulate Commerce with foreign Nations, and among several States, and with the Indian Tribes;

To establish a uniform Rule of Naturalization, and uniform Laws on the subject of Bankruptcies throughout the United States;

To coin Money, regulate the Value thereof, and of foreign Coin, and fix the Standard of Weights and Measures;

To provide for the Punishment of counterfeiting the Securities and current Coin of the United States;

To establish Post Offices and post Roads;

To promote the Progress of Science and useful Arts, by securing for limited Times to Authors and Inventors the exclusive Right to their respective Writings and Discoveries;

To constitute Tribunals inferior to the Supreme Court;

To define and punish Piracies and Felonies committed on the high Seas, and Offences against the Law of Nations;

To declare War, grant Letters of Marque and Reprisal, and make Rules concerning Captures on Land and Water;

To raise and support Armies, but no Appropriation of Money to that Use shall be for a longer Term than two Years;

To provide and maintain a Navy;

To make Rules for the Government and Regulation of the land and naval Forces;

To provide for calling forth the Militia to execute the Laws of the Union, suppress Insurrections and repel Invasions;

To provide for organizing, arming, and disciplining the Militia, and for governing such Part of them as may be employed in the Service of the United States, reserving to the States respectively, the Appointment of the Officers, and the Authority of training the Militia according to the discipline prescribed by Congress;

To exercise exclusive Legislation in all Cases whatsoever, over such District (not exceeding ten Miles square) as may, by Cession of Particular States, and the Acceptance of Congress, become the Seat of the Government of the United States, and to exercise like Authority over all Places purchased by the Consent of the Legislature of the State in which the Same shall be, for the Erection of Forts, Magazines, Arsenals, dock-Yards, and other needful Buildings—And

To make all Laws which shall be necessary and proper for carrying into Execution the foregoing Powers, and all other Powers vested by this Constitution in the Government of the United States, or in any Department or Officers thereof.

Section 9. The Migration or Importations of such Persons as any of the States now existing shall think proper to admit, shall not be prohibited by the Congress prior to the Year one thousand eight hundred and eight, but a Tax or duty may be imposed on such Importation, not exceeding ten dollars for each Person.

The Privelege of the Writ of Habeas Corpus shall not be suspended, unless when in Cases of Rebellion or Invasion the public Safety may require it.

No Bill of Attainder or ex post facto Law shall be passed.

No capitation, or other direct, Tax shall be laid, unless in Proportion to the Census of Enumeration herein before directed to be taken.

No Tax or Duty shall be laid on Articles exported from any State.

No Preference shall be given by any Regulation of Commerce or Revenue to the Ports of one State over those of another; nor shall Vessels bound to, or from, one State, be obliged to enter, clear or pay Duties in another.

No Money shall be drawn from the Treasury, but in Consequence of Appropriations made by Law; and a regular Statement and Account of the Receipts and Expenditures of all public Money shall be published from time to time.

No Title of Nobility shall be granted by the United States: And no Person holding any Office of Profit or Trust under them, shall, without the Consent of the

Congress, accept of any present, Emolument, Office, or Title, of any kind whatever, from any King, Prince or foreign State.

Section 10. No State shall enter into any Treaty, Alliance, or Confederation; grant Letters of Marque and Reprisal; coin Money; emit Bills of Credit; make any Thing but gold and silver Coin a Tender in Payment of Debts; pass any Bill of Attainder, ex post facto Law, or Law impairing the Obligation of Contracts, or grant any Title of Nobility.

No State shall, without the Consent of Congress, lay any Imposts or Duties on Imports or Exports, except what may be absolutely necessary for executing its inspection Laws: and the net Produce of all Duties and Imposts, laid by any State on Imports or Exports, shall be for the Use of the Treasury of the United States; and all such Laws shall be subject to the Revision and Control of the Congress.

No State shall, without the Consent of Congress, lay any Duty of Tonnage, keep Troops, or Ships of War in time of Peace, enter into any Agreement or Compact with another State, or with a foreign Power, or engage in War, unless actually invaded, or in such imminent Danger as will not admit of delay.

Article II
Section 1. The executive Power shall be vested in a President of the United States of America. He shall hold his Office during the Term of four Years, and, together with the Vice President, chosen for the same Term, be elected, as follows:

Each State shall appoint, in such Manner as the Legislature thereof may direct, a Number of Electors, equal to the whole Number of Senators and Representatives to which the State may be entitled in the Congress: but no Senator or Representative, or Person holding an Office of Trust or Profit under the United States, shall be appointed an Elector.

The Electors shall meet in their respective States, and vote by Ballot for two Persons, of whom one at least shall not be an Inhabitant of the same State with themselves. And they shall make a List of all the Persons voted for, and of the Number of Votes for each; which List they shall sign and certify, and transmit sealed to the Seat of the Government of the United States, directed to the President of the Senate. The President of the Senate shall, in the Presence of the Senate and House of Representatives, open all the Certificates, and the Votes shall then be counted. The Person having the greatest Number of Votes shall be the President, if such Number be a Majority of the whole Number of Electors appointed; and if there be more than one who have such Majority, and have an equal Number of Votes, then the House of Representatives shall immediately choose by Ballot one of them for President; and if no Person have a Majority, then from the five highest on the list the said House shall in like Manner choose the President. But in choosing the President, the Votes shall be taken by States, the Representation from each State having one Vote; a quorum for this Purpose shall consist of a Member or Members from two thirds of the States, and a Majority of all the States shall be necessary to a Choice. In every Case, after the Choice of the President, the Person having the greatest Number of Votes of the Electors shall be the Vice President.

But if there should remain two or more who have equal Votes, the Senate shall choose from them by Ballot the Vice President.

The Congress may determine the Time of choosing the Electors, and the Day on which they shall give their Votes; which Day shall be the same throughout the United States.

No Person except a natural born Citizen, or a Citizen of the United States, at the time of the Adoption of this Constitution, shall be eligible to the Office of President; neither shall any Person be eligible to that Office who shall not have attained to the Age of thirty five Years, and been fourteen Years a Resident within the United States.

In Case of the Removal of the President from Office, or of his Death, Resignation, or Inability to discharge the Powers and Duties of the said Office, the Same shall devolve on the Vice President, and the Congress may by Law provide for the Case of Removal, Death, Resignation or Inability, both of the President and Vice President, declaring what Officer shall then act as President, and such Officer shall act accordingly, until the Disability be removed, or a President shall be elected.

The President shall, at stated Times, receive for his Services, a Compensation, which shall neither be increased nor diminished during the Period for which he shall have been elected, and he shall not receive within that Period any other Emolument from the United States, or any of them.

Before he enter on the Execution of his Office, he shall take the following Oath or Affirmation;—"I do solemnly swear (or affirm) that I will faithfully execute the Office of President of the United States, and will to the best of my Ability, preserve, protect, and defend the Constitution of the United States."

Section 2. The President shall be Commander in Chief of the Army and Navy of the United States, and of the Militia of the Several States, when called into the actual Service of the United States; he may require the Opinion, in writing, of the principal Officer in each of the executive Departments, upon any Subject relating to the Duties of their respective Offices, and he shall have Power to grant Reprieves and Pardons for Offenses against the United States, except in Cases of Impeachment.

He shall have Power, by and with the Advice and Consent of the Senate, to make Treaties, provided two thirds of the Senators present concur; and he shall nominate, and by and with the Advice and Consent of the Senate, shall appoint Ambassadors, other public Ministers and Consuls, Judges of the Supreme Court, and all other Officers of the United States, whose Appointments are not herein otherwise provided for, and which shall be established by Law: but the Congress may by Law vest the Appointment of such inferior Officers, as they think proper, in the President alone, in the Courts of Law, or in the Heads of Departments.

The President shall have Power to fill up all Vacancies that may happen during the Recess of the Senate, by granting Commissions which shall expire at the End of their next Session.

Section 3. He shall from time to time give to the Congress Information on the State of the Union, and recommend to their Consideration such Measures as he shall judge necessary and expedient; he may, on extraordinary Occasions, convene both Houses, or either of them and in Case of Disagreement between them, with Respect to the Time of Adjournment, he may adjourn them to such Time as he shall think proper; he shall receive Ambassadors and other public Ministers; he shall take Care that the Laws be faithfully executed, and shall Commission all the Officers of the United States.

Section 4. The President, Vice President and all Civil Officers of the United States, shall be removed from office on Impeachment for, and Conviction of, Treason, Bribery, or other high Crimes and Misdemeanors.

Article III

Section 1. The Judicial Power of the United States shall be vested in one Supreme Court, and in such inferior Courts as the Congress may from time to time ordain and establish. The Judges, both of the supreme and inferior Courts, shall hold their Offices during good Behaviour, and shall at stated Times, receive for their Services, a Compensation, which shall not be diminished during their Continuance in Office.

Section 2. The judicial Power shall extend to all Cases, in Law and Equity, arising under this Constitution, the Laws of the United States, and Treaties made, or which shall be made, under their Authority; to all Cases affecting Ambassadors, other public Ministers and Consuls; to all Cases of admiralty and maritime Jurisdiction; to Controversies to which the United States shall be a Party; to Controversies between two or more States; between a State and Citizens of another State; between Citizens of different States; between Citizens of the same State claiming Lands under Grants of different States, and between a State, or the Citizens thereof, and foreign States, Citizens or Subjects.

In all Cases affecting Ambassadors, other public Ministers and Consuls, and those in which a State shall be Party, the Supreme Court shall have original Jurisdiction. In all the other Cases before mentioned, the Supreme Court shall have appellate Jurisdiction, both as to Law and Fact, with such Exceptions, and under such Regulations as the Congress shall make.

The Trial of all Crimes, except in cases of Impeachment, shall be by Jury; and such Trial shall be held in the State where the said Crimes shall have been committed but when not committed within any State, the Trial shall be at such Place or Places as the Congress may by Law have directed.

Section 3. Treason against the United States shall consist only in levying War against them, or in adhering to their Enemies, giving them Aid and Comfort. No Person shall be convicted of Treason unless on the Testimony of two Witnesses to the same overt Act, or on Confession in open Court. The Congress shall have Power to declare the Punishment of Treason, but no Attainder of Treason shall work Corruption of Blood, or Forfeiture except during the Life of the Person attained.

Article IV

Section 1. Full Faith and Credit shall be given in each State to the public Acts, Records, and judicial Proceedings of all other States. And the Congress may by general Laws prescribe the Manner in which such Acts, Records and Proceedings shall be proved, and the Effect thereof.

Section 2. The Citizens of each State shall be entitled to all Privileges and Immunities of Citizens in the several States.

A Person charged in any State with Treason, Felony, or other Crime, who shall flee from Justice, and be found in another State, shall on Demand of the executive Authority of the State from which he fled, be delivered up, to be removed to the State having Jurisdiction of the Crime.

No Person held to Service or Labour in one State, under the Laws thereof, escaping into another, shall, in Consequence of any Law or Regulation therein, be discharged from such Service or Labour, but shall be delivered up on Claim of the Party to whom such Service or Labour may be due.

Section 3. New States may be admitted by the Congress into this Union; but no new State shall be formed or erected within the Jurisdiction of any other State; nor any State be formed by the Junction of two or more States, or Parts of States, without the Consent of the Legislatures of the States concerned as well as of the Congress.

The Congress shall have Power to dispose of and make all needful Rules and Regulations respecting the Territory or other Property belonging to the United States; and nothing in this Constitution shall be so construed as to Prejudice any Claims of the United States, or of any particular State.

Section 4. The United States shall guarantee to every State in this Union a Republican Form of Government, and shall protect each of them against Invasion; and on Application of the Legislature, or of the Executive (when the Legislature cannot be convened) against domestic Violence.

Article V

The Congress, whenever two thirds of both Houses shall deem it necessary, shall propose Amendments to this Constitution, or, on the Application of the Legislatures of two thirds of the several States, shall call a Convention for proposing Amendments, which, in either Case, shall be valid to all Intents and Purposes, as Part of this Constitution, when ratified by the Legislatures of three fourths of the several States, or by Conventions in three fourths of the several States, or by Conventions in three fourths thereof, as the one or the other Mode of Ratification may be proposed by the Congress; Provided that no Amendment which may be made prior to the Year One thousand eight hundred and eight shall in any Manner affect the first and fourth Clauses in the Ninth Section of the first Article; and that no State, without its Consent, shall be deprived its equal Suffrage in the Senate.

Article VI

All Debts contracted and Engagements entered into, before the Adoption of this Constitution, shall be as valid against the United States under this Constitution, as under the Confederation.

This Constitution, and the Laws of the United States which shall be made in Pursuance thereof; and all Treaties made, or which shall be made, under the Authority of the United States, shall be supreme Law of the Land; and the Judges in every State shall be bound thereby, any Thing in the Constitution or Laws or any State to the Contrary notwithstanding.

The Senators and Representatives before mentioned, and the Members of the several State Legislatures, and all executive and judicial Officers, both of the United States and of the several States, shall be bound by Oath or Affirmation, to support this Constitution; but no religious Test shall ever be required as a Qualification to any Office or public Trust under the United States.

Article VII

The Ratification of the Conventions of nine States, shall be sufficient for the Establishment of this Constitution between the States so ratifying the Same.

VI. Ratifying the Constitution

Before becoming operative, the new Constitution had to be ratified by three-quarters of the states. It was thus submitted to conventions in each individual state. The three-quarters mark was reached in mid-1788, but it was not until two years later that the last state (Rhode Island) ratified it. During this entire period, the United States saw an intense political debate between supporters of the new constitution and its critics. This debate between federalists (who supported the constitution) and antifederalists (who had objections to it) produced some of the most significant political thinking in United States history.

17. JAMES MADISON, *FEDERALIST NUMBER 10*[18]

Three of the most influential delegates to the constitutional convention, Alexander Hamilton, John Jay, and James Madison, left the meeting determined to leave nothing to chance. Together they published a series of articles intended to convince the public of the merits of the new constitution. They are known collectively as the Federalist Papers, and, arguably, constitute the most important body of political thinking ever produced in the United States. One of the most important was James Madison's essay

---

[18]James Madison, "The Utility of the Union as a Safeguard Against Domestic Faction and Insurrection (continued)," *Daily Advertiser*, Thursday, November 22, 1787.

on the dangers that can beset a republic when majorities use their power to oppress minorities. It is known as "Federalist Number 10" and is still influential today.

Among the numerous advantages promised by a well constructed Union, none deserves to be more accurately developed than its tendency to break and control the violence of faction. The friend of popular governments never finds himself so much alarmed for their character and fate, as when he contemplates their propensity to this dangerous vice. He will not fail, therefore, to set a due value on any plan which, without violating the principles to which he is attached, provides a proper cure for it. . . . Complaints are everywhere heard from our most considerate and virtuous citizens, equally the friends of public and private faith, and of public and personal liberty, that our governments are too unstable, that the public good is disregarded in the conflicts of rival parties, and that measures are too often decided, not according to the rules of justice and the rights of the minor party, but by the superior forces of an interested and overbearing majority.

However anxiously we may wish that these complaints had no foundation, the evidence, of known facts will not permit us to deny that they are in some degree true. It will be found, indeed, on a candid review of our situation, that some of the distresses under which we labor have been erroneously charged on the operation of our governments; but it will be found, at the same time, that other causes will not alone account for many of our heaviest misfortunes; and, particularly, for that prevailing and increasing distrust of public engagements, and alarm for private rights, which are echoed from one end of the continent to the other. These must be chiefly, if not wholly, effects of the unsteadiness and injustice with which a factious spirit has tainted our public administrations.

By a faction, I understand a number of citizens, whether amounting to a majority or a minority of the whole, who are united and actuated by some common impulse of passion, or of interest, adverse to the rights of other citizens, or to the permanent and aggregate interests of the community.

There are two methods of curing the mischiefs of faction: the one, by removing its causes; the other, by controlling its effects.

There are again two methods of removing the causes of faction: the one, by destroying the liberty which is essential to its existence; the other, by giving to every citizen the same opinions, the same passions, and the same interests.

It could never be more truly said than that of the first remedy, that it was worse than the disease. Liberty is to faction what air is to fire, an ailment without which it instantly expires. But it could not be less folly to abolish liberty, which is essential to political life, because it nourishes faction, than it would be to wish the annihilation of air, which is essential to animal life, because it imparts to fire its destructive agency.

The second expedient as impracticable as the first would be unwise. As long as the reason of man continues fallible, and he is at liberty to exercise it, different opinions will be formed. As long as the connection subsists between his reason and his self-love, his opinion and his passions will have a reciprocal influence on each other; and the former will be objects to which the latter will attach themselves. The diversity in the faculties of men, from which the rights of property originate, is not less an insuperable obstacle to a uniformity of interests. The protection of these faculties is the first object of government. From the protection of different and unequal faculties of acquiring property, the possession of different degrees and kinds of property immediately results; and from the influence of these on the sentiments and views of the respective proprietors, ensues a division of the society into different interests and parties.

The latent causes of faction are thus sown in the nature of man; and we see them everywhere brought into different degrees of activity, according to the different circumstances of civil society. A zeal for different opinions concerning religion, concerning government, and many other points, as well of speculation as of practice; an attachment to different leaders ambitiously contending for pre-eminence and power; or to persons of other descriptions whose fortunes have been interesting to the human passions, have, in turn, divided mankind into parties, inflamed them with mutual animosity, and rendered them much more disposed to vex and oppress each other than to cooperate for their common good. So strong is this propensity of mankind to fall into mutual animosities, that where no substantial occasion presents itself, the most frivolous and fanciful distinctions have been sufficient to kindle their unfriendly passions and excite their most violent conflicts. But the most common and durable source of factions has been the various and unequal distribution of property. Those who hold and those who are without property have ever formed distinct interests in society. Those who are creditors, and those who are debtors, fall under a like discrimination. A landed interest, a manufacturing interest, a mercantile interest, a moneyed interest, with many lesser interests, grow up of necessity in civilized nations, and divides them into different classes, actuated by different sentiments and views. The regulation of these various and interfering interests forms the principal task of modern legislation, and involves the spirit of party and faction in the necessary and ordinary operations of the government.

No man is allowed to be a judge in his own cause, because his interest would certainly bias his judgement, and, not improbably, corrupt his integrity. With equal, nay with greater reason, a body of men are unfit to be both judges and parties at the same time; yet what are many of the most important acts of legislation, but so many judicial determinations, not indeed concerning the rights of single persons, but concerning the rights of large bodies of citizens? And what are the different classes of legislators but advocates and parties to the causes which they determine? Is a law proposed concerning private debts? It is a question to which the creditors are parties on one side and the debtors on the other. Justice ought to hold the balance between them. Yet the parties are, and must be, themselves the judges; and the most numerous party, or, in other words, the most powerful faction must be expected to prevail. Shall domestic manufacturers be encouraged, and in what degree, by restrictions on foreign manufactures? are questions which would be differently decided by the landed and the manufacturing classes, and probably by neither with a sole regard to justice and the public good. The appointment of taxes on the various descriptions of property is an act which seems to require the most exact impartiality; yet there is, perhaps, no legislative act in which greater opportunity and temptation are given to a predominant party to trample on the rules of justice. Every shilling with which they overburden the inferior number, is a shilling saved to their own pockets.

It is in vain to say that enlightened statesmen will be able to adjust these clashing interests, and render them all subservient to the public good. Enlightened statesmen will not always be at the helm. Nor, in many cases, can such an adjustment be made at all without taking into view indirect and remote considerations, which will rarely prevail over the immediate interest which one party may find in disregarding the rights of another or the good of the whole.

The inference to which we are brought is, that the *causes* of faction cannot be removed, and that relief is only to be sought in the means of controlling its *effects*.

If a faction consists of less than a majority, relief is supplied by the republican principle, which enables the majority to defeat its sinister views by regular vote. It may clog the administration, it may convulse the society; but it will be unable to execute and mask its violence under the forms of the Constitution. When a majority is included in a faction, the form of popular government, on the other hand, enables it to sacrifice to its ruling passion or interest both the public good and the rights of other citizens. To secure the public good and private rights against the danger of such a faction, and at the same time to preserve the spirit and the form of popular government, is then the great object to which our inquiries are directed. Let me add that it is the great desideratum by which this form of government can be rescued from the opprobrium under which it has been so long labored, and be recommended to the esteem and adoption of mankind.

By what means is this object attainable? Evidently by one of two only. Either the existence of the same passion or interest in a majority at the same time must be prevented, or the majority, having such coexistent passion or interest, must be rendered, by their number and local situation, unable to concert and carry into effect schemes of oppression. If the impulse and the opportunity be suffered to coincide, we well know that neither moral nor religious motives can be relied on as an adequate control. They are not found to be such on the injustice and violence of individuals, and lose their efficacy in proportion to the number combined together, that is, in proportion as their efficacy becomes needful.

From this view of the subject it may be concluded that a pure democracy, by which I mean a society consisting of a small number of citizens, who assemble and administer the government in person, can admit of no cure for the mischiefs of faction. A common passion or interest will, in almost every case, be felt by a majority of the whole; a communication and concert result from the form of government itself; and there is nothing to check the inducements to sacrifice the weaker party or an obnoxious individual. Hence it is that such democracies have ever been spectacles of turbulence and contention; have ever been found incompatible with personal security or the rights of property; and have in general been as short in their lives as they have been violent in their deaths. Theoretic politicians, who have patronized this species of government, have erroneously supposed that by reducing mankind to a perfect equality in their political rights, they would, at the same time, be perfectly equalized and assimilated in their possessions, their opinions, and their passions.

A republic, by which I mean a government in which the scheme of representation takes place, opens a different prospect, and promises the cure for which we are seeking. Let us examine the points in which it varies from pure democracy, and we shall comprehend both the nature of the cure and the efficacy which it must derive from the Union.

The two great points of difference between a democracy and a republic are: first, the delegation of the government, in the latter, to a small number of citizens elected by the rest; secondly, the greater number of citizens, and greater sphere of country, over which the latter may be extended.

The effect of the first difference is, on the one hand, to refine and enlarge the public views, by passing them through the medium of a chosen body of citizens, whose wisdom may best discern the true interest of their country and whose patriotism and love of justice will be least likely to sacrifice it to temporary or partial considerations. Under such a regulation, it may well happen that the public voice, pronounced by the representatives of the people, will be more consonant to the public good than if pronounced by the people themselves, convened for the purpose. On the other hand, the effect may be inverted. Men of factious tempers, of local prejudices, or of sinister designs, may, by intrigue, by corruption, or by other means, first obtain the suffrages, and then betray the interests, of the people. The question resulting is, whether small or extensive republics are more favorable to the election of proper guardians of the public weal; and it is clearly decided in favor of the latter by two obvious considerations:

In the first place, it is to be remarked that, however small the republic may be, the representatives must be raised to a certain number, in order to guard against the cabals of a few; and that, however large it may be, they must be limited to a certain number, in order to guard against the confusion of a multitude. Hence, the number of representatives in the two cases not being in proportion to that of the two constituents, and being proportionally greater in the small republic, it follows that, if the proportion of fit characters be not less in the large than in the small republic, the former will present a greater opinion, and consequently a greater probability of a fit choice.

In the next place, as each representative will be chosen by a greater number of citizens in the large than in the small republic, it will be more difficult for unworthy candidates to practice with success the vicious arts by which elections are too often carried; and the suffrages of the people being more free, will be more likely to centre in men who possess the most attractive merit and the most diffusive and established characters.

It must be confessed that in this, as in most other cases, there is a mean, on both sides of which inconveniences will be found to lie. By enlarging too much the number of electors, you render the representatives too little acquainted with all their local circumstances and lesser interests; as by reducing it too much, you render him unduly attached to these, and too little fit to comprehend and pursue great and national objects. The federal Constitution forms a happy combination in this respect; the great and aggregate interests being referred to the national, the local and particular to the State legislatures.

The other point of difference is, the greater number of citizens and extent of territory which may be brought within the compass of republican than of democratic government; and it is this circumstance principally which renders factious combinations less to be dreaded in the former than in the latter. The smaller the society, the fewer the distinct parties and interest, the more frequently will a majority be found of the same party; and the smaller the number of individuals composing a majority, and smaller the compass within which they are placed, the more easily will they concert and execute their plans of oppression. Extend the sphere, and you take in a greater variety of parties and interests; you make it less probable that a majority of the whole will have a common motive to invade the rights of other citizens; or if such a common motive exists, it will be more difficult for all who feel it to discover their own strength, and to act in unison with each other. Besides other impediments, it may be remarked that, where there is a consciousness of unjust or dishonorable purposes, communication is always checked by distrust in proportion to the number whose concurrence is necessary.

Hence, it clearly appears, that the same advantage which a republic has over a democracy, in controlling the effects of faction, is enjoyed by a large and a small republic, is enjoyed by the Union over the States composing it. Does the advantage consist in the substitution of representatives whose enlightened views and virtuous sentiments render them superior to local prejudices and schemes of injustice? It will not be denied that the representation of the Union will be most likely to possess these requisite endowments. Does it consist in the greater security afforded by a greater variety of parties, against the event of any one party being able to outnumber and oppress the rest? In an equal degree does the increased variety of parties comprised within the Union, increase this security? Does it, in fine, consist in the greater obstacles opposed to the concert and accomplishment of the secret wishes of an unjust and interested majority? Here, again, the extent of the Union gives it the most palpable advantage.

The influence of factious leaders may kindle a flame within their particular States, but will be unable to spread a general conflagration through the other States. A religious sect may degenerate into a political faction in a part of the Confederacy; but the variety of sects dispersed over the entire face of it must secure the national councils against any danger from that source. A rage for paper money, for an abolition of debts, for an equal division of property, or for any other improper or wicked project, will be less apt to pervade the whole body of the Union than a particular member of it; in the same proportion as such a malady is more likely to taint a particular county or district, than an entire State.

In the extent and proper structure of the Union, therefore, we behold a republican remedy for the diseases most incident to republican government. And according to the degree of pleasure and pride we feel in being republicans, ought to be our zeal in cherishing the spirit and supporting the character of Federalists.

18.   *ANTIFEDERALIST NUMBER 17*[19]

Those who opposed the new constitution were known as antifederalists. They took pen to paper to rebut the arguments of Madison and others of his ilk. Their principal concern with the new constitution was that it threatened states' rights and liberty. Like the Federalist Papers, the writings of the antifederalists still have resonance today (note the Internet source of this document).

This government is to possess absolute and uncontrollable powers, legislative, executive and judicial, with respect to every object to which it extends, for by the last clause of section eight, article first, it is declared, that the Congress shall have power "to make all laws which shall be necessary and proper for carrying into execution the foregoing powers, and all other powers vested by this Constitution in the government of the United States, or in any department or office thereof." And by sixth article, it is declared, "that this Constitution, and the laws of the United States, which shall be made in pursuance thereof, and the treaties made, or which shall be made, under the authority of the United States, shall be supreme law of the land; and the judges in every State shall be bound thereby, any thing in the Constitution or law of any State to the contrary notwithstanding." It appears from these articles, that there is no need of any intervention of the State governments, between the Congress and the people, to execute any one power vested in the general government, and that the Constitution and laws of every State are nullified and declared void, so far as they are or shall be inconsistent with this Constitution or the laws made in pursuance of it, or with treaties made under the authority of the United States. The Government, then, so far as it extends, is a complete one, and not a confederation. It is as much one complete government as that of New York or Massachusetts; has absolute and perfect powers to make and execute all laws, to appoint officers, institute courts, declare offenses, and annex penalties, with respect to every object to which it extends, as any other in the world. So far, therefore, as its powers reach, all ideas of confederation are given up and lost. It is true this government is limited to certain objects, or to

---

[19]http://firearmsandliberty.com/AntiFederalist/TheAntiFederalistPapers.pdf. With permission from Firearms and Liberty.

speak more properly, some small degree of power is still left to the States; but a little attention to the powers vested in the general government, will convince every candid man, that if it is capable of being executed, all that is reserved for the individual States must very soon be annihilated, except so far as they are barely necessary to the organization of the general government. The powers of the general legislature extend to every case that is of the least importance—there is nothing valuable to human nature, nothing dear to freemen, but what is within its power. It has the authority to make laws which will affect the lives, the liberty, and property of every man in the United States; nor can the Constitution or laws of any State, in any way prevent or impede the full and complete execution of every power given. The legislative power is competent to lay taxes, duties, imposts, and excises; there is no limitation to this power, unless it be said that the clause which directs the use to which those taxes and duties shall be applied, may be said to be a limitation. But this is no restriction of the power at all, for by this clause they are to be applied to pay the debts and provide for the common defense and general welfare of the United States; but the legislature have authority to contract debts at their discretion; they are the sole judges of what is necessary to provide for the common defense, and they only are to determine what is for the general welfare. This power, therefore, is neither more nor less than a power to lay and collect taxes, imposts, and excises, at their pleasure; not only the power to lay taxes unlimited as to the amount they may require, but it is perfect and absolute to raise them in any mode they please. No State legislature, or any power in the State governments, have any more to do in carrying this into effect than the authority of one State has to do with that of another. In the business, therefore, of laying and collecting taxes, the idea of confederation is totally lost, and that of one entire republic is embraced. It is proper here to remark, that the authority to lay and collect taxes is the most important of any power that can be granted; it connects with it almost all the powers, or at least will in process of time draw all others after it; it is the great mean of protection, security, and defense, in a good government, and the great engine of oppression and tyranny in a bad one. This cannot fail of being the case, if we consider the contracted limits which are set by this Constitution, to the State governments, on this article of raising money. No State can emit paper money, lay any duties or imposts, on imports, or exports, but by consent of the Congress; and then the net produce shall be for the benefit of the United States. . . .

It might be here shown, that the power in the federal legislature, to raise and support armies at pleasure, as well in peace as in war, and their control over the militia, tend not only to a consolidation of the government, but the destruction of liberty. I shall not, however, dwell upon these, as a few observations upon the judicial power of the government, in addition to the preceding, will fully evince the truth of the position.

The judicial power of the United States is to be vested in a supreme court, and in such inferior courts as Congress may, from time to time, ordain and establish. The powers of these courts are very extensive; their jurisdiction comprehends all civil causes, except such as arise between citizens of the same State; and it extends to all causes in law and equity arising under the Constitution. One inferior court must be established, I presume, in each State, at least, with the necessary executive officers appendant thereto. It is easy to see, that in the common course of things, these courts will eclipse the dignity, and take away from the respectability, of the State courts. These courts will be, in themselves, totally independent of the States, deriving their authority from the United States, and receiving from them fixed salaries; and in the course of human events it is to be expected that they will swallow up all the powers of the courts in the respective States.

How far the clause on the eighth section of the first article may operate to do away with all idea of confederated States, and to effect an entire consolidation of the whole into one general government, it is impossible to say. The powers given by this article are very general and comprehensive, and it may receive a construction to justify the passing almost any law. A power to make all laws, which shall be necessary and proper, for carrying into execution all powers vested by the Constitution in the government of the United States, or any department or officer thereof, is a power very comprehensive and definite, and may, for aught I know, be exercised in such manner as entirely to abolish the State legislatures. Suppose the legislature of a State should pass a law to raise money to support their government and pay the State debt; may the Congress repeal this law, because it may prevent the collection of a tax which they may think proper and necessary to lay, to provide for the general welfare of the United States? . . .

It is not meant, by stating this case, to insinuate that the Constitution would warrant a law of this kind! Or unnecessarily to alarm the fears of the people, by suggesting that the Federal legislature would be more likely to pass the limits assigned them by the Constitution, than that of an individual State, further than they are less responsible to the people. But what is meant is, that the legislature of the United States are vested with the great and uncontrollable powers of laying and collecting taxes, duties, imposts, and excises; of regulating trade, raising and supporting armies, organizing, arming, and disciplining the militia, instituting courts, and other general powers; and are by this clause invested with the power of making all laws, proper and necessary, for carrying all these into execution; and they may so exercise this power as entirely to annihilate all the State governments, and reduce this country to one single government. And if they may do it, it is pretty certain they will; for it will be found that the power retained by individual States, small as it is, will be a clog upon the wheels of the government of the United States; the latter, therefore, will be naturally inclined to remove it out of the way. Besides, it is a truth confirmed by the unerring experience of ages, that every man, and every body of men, invested with power, are ever disposed to increase it, and to acquire a superiority over everything that stands in their way. This disposition, which is implanted in human nature, will operate in the Federal legislature to lessen and ultimately to subvert the State authority. . . .

19. VIRGINIA DECLARATION OF RIGHTS (1776)[20]

One source of opposition to the new constitution was that it did not adequately guarantee individual liberty. This was an understandable concern, given that the central government framed by the constitution would be more powerful than that established by the Articles. To allay these fears, a bill of rights was appended to the Constitution. It was inspired by similar declarations of rights that had already been adopted by individual states. Here is Virginia's, the one which most directly inspired what would become the United States Bill of Rights.

1. That all men are by nature equally free and independent, and have certain inherent rights, of which, when they enter into a state of society, they cannot, by any compact, deprive or divest their posterity; namely, the enjoyment of life and liberty, with the means of acquiring and possessing property, and pursuing and obtaining happiness and safety.

2. That all power is vested in, and consequently derived from, the people; that magistrates are their trustees and servants, and at all times amenable to them.

3. That government is, or ought to be, instituted for the common benefit, protection, and security of the people, nation or community; of all the various modes and forms of government that is best, which is capable of producing the greatest degree of happiness and safety and is most effectually secured against the danger of maladministration; and that, whenever any government shall be found inadequate or contrary to these purposes, a majority of the community hath an indubitable, unalienable, and indefeasible right to reform, alter or abolish it, in such manner as shall be judged most conducive to the public weal.

4. That no man, or set of men, are entitled to exclusive or separate emoluments or privileges from the community, but in consideration of public services; which, not being descendible, neither ought the offices of magistrate, legislator, or judge be hereditary.

5. That the legislative and executive powers of the state should be separate and distinct from the judicative; and, that the members of the two first may be restrained from oppression by feeling and participating the burthens of the people, they should, at fixed periods, be reduced to a private station, return into that body from which they were originally taken, and the vacancies be supplied by frequent, certain, and regular elections in which all, or any part of the former members, to be again eligible, or ineligible, as the laws shall direct.

6. The elections of members to serve as representatives of the people in assembly ought to be free; and that all men, having sufficient evidence of

[20]Francis N. Thorpe, ed., *The Federal and State Constitutions* (Washington, DC: United States Government Printing Office, 1909), vol. 1, 3812–3814.

permanent common interest with, and attachment to, the community have the right of suffrage and cannot be taxed or deprived of their property for public uses without their own consent or that of their representatives so elected, nor bound by any law to which they have not, in like manner, assented, for the public good.

7. That all power of suspending laws, or the execution of laws, by any authority without consent of the representatives of the people is injurious to their rights and ought not to be exercised.

8. That in all capital or criminal prosecutions a man hath a right to demand the cause and nature of his accusation, to be confronted with the accusers and witnesses, to call for evidence in his favor, and to a speedy trial by an impartial jury of his vicinage, without whose unanimous consent he cannot be found guilty, nor can he be compelled to give evidence against himself; that no man be deprived of his liberty except by the law of the land or the judgment of his peers.

9. That excessive bail ought not to be required, nor excessive fine imposed; nor cruel and unusual punishments inflicted.

10. That general warrants, whereby any officer or messenger may be commanded to search suspected places without evidence of a fact committed, or to seize any person or persons not named, or whose offense is not particularly described and supported by evidence, are grievous and oppressive and ought not to be granted.

11. That in controversies respecting property in suits between man and man, the ancient trial by jury is preferable to any other and ought to be held sacred.

12. That the freedom of the press is one of the greatest bulwarks of liberty and can never be restrained but by despotic governments.

13. That a well regulated militia, composed of the body of the people, trained to arms, is the proper, natural, and safe defense of a free state; that standing armies, in time of peace, should be avoided as dangerous to liberty; and that, in all cases, the military should be under strict subordination to, and be governed by, civil power.

14. That the people have a right to uniform government; and therefore, that no government separate from, or independent of, the government of Virginia, ought to be erected or established within the limits thereof.

15. That no free government, or the blessings of liberty, can be preserved to any people but by a firm adherence to justice, moderation, temperance, frugality, and virtue and by frequent recurrence to fundamental principles.

16. That religion, or the duty which we owe to our Creator and the manner of discharging it, can be directed only by reason and conviction, not by force or violence; and therefore, all men are equally entitled to the free exercise of religion, according to the dictates of conscience; and that it is the mutual duty of all to practice Christian forbearance, love, and charity towards each other.

20. BILL OF RIGHTS[21]

Here is the Bill of Rights itself. Like the Constitution, it had to be ratified by the individual states (for it took the form of a collection of ten constitutional amendments). Ratification was complete by the end of 1791, and it went into effect the following March.

1. Congress shall make no law respecting an establishment of religion, or prohibiting the free exercise thereof; or abridging the freedom of speech, or of the press; or the right of the people peaceably to assemble, and to petition the Government for a redress of grievances.

2. A well regulated Militia, being necessary to the security of a free State, the right of the people to keep and bear Arms, shall not be infringed.

3. No Soldier shall, in time of peace be quartered in any house, without the consent of the Owner, nor in time of war, but in a manner to be prescribed by law.

4. The right of the people to be secure in their persons, houses, papers, and effects, against unreasonable searches and seizures, shall not be violated, and no Warrants shall issue, but upon probable cause, supported by Oath or affirmation, and particularly describing the place to be searched, and the persons or things to be seized.

5. No person shall be held to answer for a capital, or otherwise infamous, crime, unless on a presentment or indictment of a Grand Jury, except in cases arising in the land or naval forces, or in the Militia, when in actual service in the time of War or public danger, nor shall any person be subject for the same offence to be twice put in jeopardy of life or limb; nor shall be compelled in any criminal case to be a witness against himself, nor be deprived of life, liberty, or property, without due process of law; nor shall private property be taken for public use, without just compensation.

6. In all criminal prosecutions, the accused shall enjoy the right to a speedy and public trial, by an impartial jury of the State and district wherein the crime shall have been committed, which district shall have been previously ascertained by law, and to be informed of the nature and cause of the accusation; to be confronted with the witnesses against him; to have compulsory process for obtaining witnesses in his favor, and to have the Assistance of Counsel for his defence.

7. In suits at common law, where the value in controversy shall exceed twenty dollars, the right of trial by jury shall be preserved, and no fact tried by jury, shall

---

[21]National Archives, "America's Founding Documents www.archives.gov/exhibits/charters/bill-of-rights_transcript.html

be otherwise re-examined in any Court of the United States, than according to the rules of the common law.

8. Excessive bail shall not be required, nor excessive fines imposed, nor cruel and unusual punishments inflicted.

9. The enumeration in the Constitution, of certain rights, shall not be construed to deny or disparage others retained by the people.

10. The powers not delegated to the United States by the Constitution, nor prohibited by it to the States, are reserved to the States respectively, or to the people.

21. GEORGE WASHINGTON'S FAREWELL ADDRESS (1796)[22]

George Washington was elected to be the first president of the United States. In 1796, he decided not to run for a third term. Shortly before leaving office, he delivered a speech that has become known as the Farewell Address. At the time, Europe was embroiled in the wars of the French Revolution. Washington feared that the United States might be drawn into the conflict. He was even more concerned about how the ideological divisions inflamed by the French Revolution were poisoning American domestic politics. The Farewell Address gives a sense of the fragility of the new republic.

The period for a new election of a citizen to administer the executive government of the United States being not far distant, and the time actually arrived when your thoughts must be employed in designating the person who is to be clothed with the important trust, it appears to me proper, especially as it may conduce to a more distinct expression of the public voice, that I should now apprise you of the resolution I have formed to decline being considered among the number of those out of whom a choice is to be made. . . .

The acceptance of and continuance hitherto in the office to which your suffrages have twice called me have been a uniform sacrifice of inclination to the opinion of duty and to a deference for what appeared to be your desire. I constantly hoped that it would have been much earlier in my power, consistently with motives which I was not at liberty to disregard, to return to that retirement from which I had been reluctantly drawn. . . .

I rejoice that the state of your concerns, external as well as internal, no longer renders the pursuit of inclination incompatible with the sentiment of duty or propriety; and am persuaded, whatever partiality may be retained for my services, that, in the present circumstances of our country, you will not disapprove my determination to retire. . . .

---

[22]"Washington's Farewell Address 1796," The Avalon Project, http://avalon.law.yale.edu/18th _century/washing.asp.

Here, perhaps, I ought to stop. But a solicitude for your welfare, which cannot end but with my life, and the apprehension of danger natural to that solicitude, urge me, on an occasion like the present, to offer to your solemn contemplation, and to recommend to your frequent review, some sentiments which are the result of much reflection, of no inconsiderable observation, and which appear to me all-important to the permanency of your felicity as a people. . . .

The unity of government which constitutes you one people is also now dear to you. It is justly so, for it is a main pillar in the edifice of your real independence; the support of your tranquility at home, your peace abroad; of your safety; of your prosperity in every shape; of that very liberty which you so highly prize. But as it is easy to foresee that, from different causes and from different quarters, much pains will be taken, many artifices employed to weaken in your minds the conviction of this truth; as this is the point in your political fortress against which the batteries of internal and external enemies will be most constantly and actively (though often covertly and insidiously) directed, it is of infinite moment that you should cherish a cordial, habitual, and immovable attachment to it, accustoming yourselves to think and speak of it as of the palladium of your political safety and prosperity, watching for its preservation with jealous anxiety, discountenancing whatever may suggest even a suspicion that it can in any event be abandoned, and indignantly frowning upon the first drawing of every attempt to alienate any portion of our country from the rest of it to enfeeble the sacred ties which now link together the various parts.

For this you have every inducement of sympathy and interest. Citizens by birth or choice of a common country, that country has a right to concentrate your affection. The name of American, which belongs to you, in your national capacity, must always exalt the just pride of patriotism more than any appellation derived from local discriminations. With slight shades of difference, you have the same religion, manners, habits, and political principles. You have in a common cause fought and triumphed together. The independence and liberty you possess are the work of joint councils and joint efforts, of common dangers, sufferings, and successes.

But these considerations, however powerfully they address themselves to your sensibility, are greatly outweighed by those which apply more immediately to your interest. Here every portion of our country finds the most commanding motives for carefully guarding and preserving the Union of the whole.

The North, in an unrestrained intercourse with the South, protected by the equal laws of a common government, finds in the productions of the latter great additional resources of maritime and commercial enterprise and precious materials of manufacturing industry. The South, in the same intercourse, benefiting by the agency of the North, sees its agriculture grow and its commerce expand. Turning partly into its own channels the seamen of the North, it finds its particular navigation invigorated; and while it contributes, in different ways, to nourish and increase the general mass of the national navigation, it looks forward to the protection of a maritime strength, to which itself is unequally adapted.

The East, in a like intercourse with the West, already finds, and in the progressive improvement of interior communications by land and water will more and more find, a valuable vent for the commodities which it brings from abroad or manufactures at home. The West derives from the East supplies requisite to its growth and comfort, and, what is perhaps of still greater consequence, it must of necessity owe the secure enjoyment of indispensable outlets for its own productions to the weight, influence, and the future maritime strength of the Atlantic side of the Union, directed by any indissoluble community of interest, as one nation. Any other tenure by which the West can hold this essential advantage, whether derived from its own separate strength or from an apostate and unnatural connection with any foreign power, must be intrinsically precarious.

While then every part of our country thus feels an immediate and particular interest in Union, all the parts combined in the united mass of means and efforts cannot fail to find greater strength, greater resource, proportionably greater security from external danger, a less frequent interruption of their peace by foreign nations; and—what is of inestimable value!—they must derive from Union an exemption from those broils and wars between themselves which so frequently afflict neighboring countries not tied together by the same government, which their own rival ships alone would be sufficient to produce but which opposite foreign alliances, attachments, and intrigues would stimulate and embitter. Hence, likewise, they will avoid the necessity of those overgrown military establishments which under any form of government are inauspicious to liberty and which are to be regarded as particularly hostile to republican liberty. In this sense it is that your Union ought to be considered as a main prop of your liberty and that the love of the one ought to endear to you the preservation of the other. . . .

In contemplating the causes which may disturb our Union, it occurs as [a] matter of serious concern that any ground should have been furnished for characterizing parties by geographical discriminations: Northern and Southern; Atlantic and Western; whence designing men may endeavor to excite a belief that there is a real difference of local interests and views. One of the expedients of a party to acquire influence, within particular districts, is to misrepresent the opinions and aims of other districts. You cannot shield yourselves too much against the jealousies and heartburnings which spring from these misrepresentations; they tend to render alien to each other those who ought to be bound together by fraternal affection. . . .

To the efficacy and permanency of your Union, a government for the whole is indispensable. No alliances, however strict between the parts, can be an adequate substitute. They must inevitably experience the infractions and interruptions which all alliances in all times have experienced. Sensible of this momentous truth, you have improved upon your first essay by the adoption of a Constitution of government better calculated than your former for an intimate Union and for the efficacious management of your common concerns. . . .

Observe good faith and justice toward all nations. Cultivate peace and harmony with all. Religion and morality enjoin this conduct; and can it be that good policy does not equally enjoin it? It will be worthy of a free, enlightened, and, at no distant period, a great nation to give to mankind so magnanimous and novel an example of a people always guided by an exalted justice and benevolence. Who can doubt that in the course of time and things the fruits of such a plan would richly repay any temporary advantages which might be lost by a steady adherence to it? Can it be that Providence has not connected the permanent felicity of a nation with its virtue? The experiment, at least, is recommended by every sentiment which ennobles human nature. Alas! is it rendered impossible by its vices?

In the execution of such a plan nothing is more essential than those permanent, inveterate antipathies against particular nations and passionate attachments for others should be excluded and that in place of them just and amicable feelings toward all should be cultivated. The nation which indulges toward another an habitual hatred or an habitual fondness is in some degree a slave. It is a slave to its animosity or to its affection, either of which is sufficient to lead it astray from its duty and its interest. . . .

Hence, frequent collisions, obstinate, envenomed, and blood contests. The nation prompted by ill-will and resentment sometimes impels to war the government, contrary to the best calculations of policy. The government sometimes participates in the national prosperity, and adopts, through passion, what reason would reject; at other times, it makes the animosity of the nation subservient to projects of hostility instigated by pride, ambition, and other sinister and pernicious motives. The peace often, sometimes perhaps for liberty, of nations has been the victim.

So, likewise, a passionate attachment of one nation for another produces a variety of evils. Sympathy for the favorite nation, facilitating the illusion of an imaginary common interest in cases where no real common interest exists, and infusing into one the enmities of the other, betrays the former into a participation in the quarrels and wars of the latter without adequate inducement or justification. It leads also to concessions to the favorite nation of privileges denied to others, which is apt doubly to injure the nation making the concessions, by unnecessarily parting with what ought to have been retained, and by exciting jealousy, ill will, and a disposition to retaliate in the parties from whom equal privileges are withheld.

And it gives to ambitious, corrupted, or deluded citizens (who devote themselves to the favorite nation) facility to betray or sacrifice the interests of their own country, without odium, sometimes even with popularity, gilding with the appearances of a virtuous sense of obligation, a commendable deference for public opinion, or a laudable zeal for public good, the base or foolish compliances of ambition, corruption, or infatuation. As avenues to foreign influence in innumerable ways, such attachments are particularly alarming to the truly enlightened and independent patriot. How many opportunities do they afford to tamper with domestic factions, to practise the arts of seduction, to mislead public opinion, to influence or awe the public councils! Such an attachment of a small or weak toward a great and powerful nation dooms the former to be the satellite of the latter.

Against the insidious wiles of foreign influence, I conjure you to believe me, fellow citizens, the jealousy of a free people ought to be constantly awake, since history and experience prove that foreign influence is one of the most baneful foes of republican government. But that jealousy, to be useful, must be impartial, else it becomes the instrument of the very influence to be avoided instead of a defense against it. Excessive partiality for one foreign nation and excessive dislike of another cause those whom they actuate to see danger only on one side and serve to veil and even second the arts of influence on the other. Real patriots, who may resist the intrigues of the favorite, are liable to become suspected and odious, while its tools and dupes usurp the applause and confidence of the people to surrender their interests.

The great rule of conduct for us, in regard to foreign nations, is in extending our commercial relations to have with them as little political connection as possible. So far as we have already formed engagements, let them be fulfilled with perfect good faith. Here let us stop.

Europe has a set of primary interests which to us have none, or a very remote relation. Hence she must be engaged in frequent controversies, the causes of which are essentially foreign to our concerns. Hence, therefore, it must be unwise in us to implicate ourselves, by artificial ties, in the ordinary vicissitudes of her politics or the ordinary combinations and collisions of her friendships or enmities.

Our detached and distant situation invites and enables us to pursue a different course. If we remain one people, under an efficient government, the period is not far off when we may defy material injury from external annoyance; when we may take such an attitude as will cause the neutrality we may at any time resolve upon to be scrupulously respected. . . .

It is our true policy to steer clear of permanent alliances with any portion of the foreign world. So far, I mean as we are now at liberty to do it, for let me not be understood as capable of patronizing infidelity to existing engagements (I hold the maxim no less applicable to public than to private affairs that honesty is always the best policy). I repeat it, therefore: let those engagements be observed in their genuine sense. But, in my opinion, it is unnecessary and would be unwise to extend them.

CHAPTER 5

Origins of the French Revolution

Like the British Empire, France experienced a fiscal crisis after the Seven Years' War, which led to a constitutional crisis, and ultimately, a revolution. But unlike the British constitutional crisis that led to the revolt of its thirteen North American colonies and the creation of the independent United States, the French crisis took place primarily in France itself (although it had global ramifications, notably in the French Caribbean colony of Saint-Domingue). Unlike Great Britain, which managed to fund its mid-century wars through efficient borrowing and tariffs (thus avoiding an increase in the domestic land tax), France relied primarily on property taxes to pay for its military efforts. A continental power with vast landed wealth, which dwarfed that produced by all other sectors of its economy (colonial, manufacturing, etc.), France needed to tap this wealth to fund its army, navy, and global colonial presence. For France, the cost of eighteenth-century-imperial warfare could not be borne solely by trade and the colonies.

But taxing land was complicated in France. Many privileged social categories—notably the First Estate (the Church) and Second Estate (the nobility), but also particular provinces, cities, and professional groups—enjoyed fiscal autonomy, immunity, and privilege. Although the landed wealth of France was immense, much of it was thus beyond the reach of taxation. To tap this wealth, the government tried to impose new taxes, which ignored social distinction and fiscal privilege. These were bitterly opposed by the privileged—and especially by the highest courts in the land, the noble-dominated *parlements* (high courts). Their resistance prompted the royal government to employ heavy-handed methods to force through the new taxes. This, in turn, prompted the parlements and their allies to voice increasingly radical critiques of what they came to see as "despotism" and, drawing on materials furnished by various Enlightenment writers, to articulate constitutional theories at odds with absolutist, royal government. Thus did the strains of empire provoke a constitutional crisis that eventually metastasized into the French Revolution.

I. Resistance of the Parlements

Far from leading to the easing of wartime taxes, the end of the Seven Years' War in 1763 saw the royal government of France prolong existing impositions and even impose new ones. In large part it was driven to do so by the need to repay emergency loans taken out during the war, as well as to service more long-term debt incurred during that conflict and the previous ones. This unexpected increase in taxation *after* the war had ended provoked disbelief, frustration, and opposition.

Leading the resistance were the parlements. The highest courts in the land, they were staffed almost exclusively by rich noble magistrates who had purchased their positions and passed them down as property to their sons. Of these, the Parlement of Paris was preeminent.

Backed by lesser provincial courts, the Parlement of Paris deployed novel political arguments against royal power. It asserted that royal laws only became operative once they had been registered by the sovereign courts. It claimed that, in the absence of France's ancient national assembly (the Estates-General), the sovereign courts were responsible for representing the nation. It also claimed that the parlements formed a single body—a doctrine of unity that the royal government found particularly threatening.

In response, the royal government resorted to heavy-handed measures. These included forced registrations of royal laws, "royal sessions" in which the King in person ordered the magistrates to register the laws and the exile of recalcitrant magistrates. The Parlement countered by increasingly uncompromising reiterations of its antiabsolutist doctrines, striking, and refusing to administer justice.

The stand-off came to a head in 1771 when the royal government dissolved the Parlement (an event called the Maupeou coup after the minister who engineered it) and sought to impose new taxes without parlementary registration. Although the coup ultimately failed and parlement was recalled in 1775, the episode had dramatic consequences. On the one hand it revealed the weakness of the Parlement by showing that, for all its talk, it was unable to resist royal power effectively. On the other hand, it discredited the monarchy and led the emasculated Parlement that returned in 1775 to abandon its earlier claims to represent the nation and instead demand the outright return of the Estates-General. The decades-long conflict between the Parlement and royal government thus contributed to setting the stage for the Revolution: by weakening the Parlement, casting royal government as "despotism," and placing the issue of national sovereignty on the public agenda.

1. REMONSTRATION OF THE PARLEMENT OF PARIS AGAINST THE ACTS OF VIOLENCE COMMITTED AGAINST THE DIFFERENT PARLEMENTS (DECEMBER 26, 1763)[1]

This is one of the Parlement's first postwar remonstrations. It shows how the court's resistance to royal fiscal demands began to set the stage for a constitutional show-down immediately after the end of the Seven Years' War.

The unprecedented acts of violence committed against the magistracy, the efforts to silence its voice, the universal disorder caused in the Kingdom's administration (a perpetual subject of alarm for the whole nation), forces your parlement to have recourse to the justice, the goodness of Your Majesty.

The more your parlement, Sire, felt obliged to lend itself to the temporary needs of the State's exhausted finances, whose total ruin would have been a public catastrophe, whose recovery can reasonably be expected from the immense resources of France, the more it has the right to lay before Your Majesty its just complaints about the shocking violation of the laws of the Monarchy, about the overthrow of traditional forms, about the exactions of absolute despotism, about an administration which, for almost a year, has attempted to remedy public misfortunes with acts both fatal to the State's credit and certain to hasten its ruin.

This has evoked general protest from the entire Kingdom, Sire, and attempts have been made to defeat this protest by violence and assaults when only gentleness, wisdom, and compromise can uphold and repair the State; the damage caused by this kind of administration demands the influence of Your Majesty's wisdom and goodness. . . .

Posterity will never believe that attempts were made under Your Majesty's reign to reduce your subjects to the humiliating condition of a subjugated people by trying to establish taxes over them by force of arms, nor that an unexampled project was conceived and executed to hold the magistrates in captivity like hostages, nor yet that some of the nation's soldiers gloried in its oppression, that cities inhabited by their compatriots became victims of their blind obedience, the parlements the object of their enterprises, and military honors the reward of exploits so unworthy of generous souls.

France, shocked and groaning under a form of government so contrary to that which has made it happy for thirteen centuries, turns toward the throne of Your Majesty . . .

---

[1]Jules Flammermont and Maurice Tourneux, eds., *Remontrances du Parlement de Paris au XVIIIe siècle* (Paris: Imprimerie Nationale, 1895), vol. 2, 415–425.

No less than Your successors, Your Majesty knows and upholds this maxim of State, *that in France nothing can be considered a law until his parlement has ordered its publication.*

The need to verify all laws in the Parlement, Sire, is an immemorial tradition, recognized from age to age by all our sovereigns. . . .

In matters of taxation, Sire, the infringement of the sacred right of verification simultaneously violates both the rights of the Nation and those of legislation; it follows from this that the collection of a non-verified tax is an assault upon the constitution of the French government. . . . Thus, Sire, your parlement has always opposed the force of laws to the imposition of taxes levied without verification.

A law, Sire, upon which a free deliberation of Parlement has not imprinted the seal of the necessary authorization is obviously a non-verified law; in vain will authority arm itself with the most absolute power; it can have a law registered, it can have it read in the presence of the peoples, it can have it executed by force and constraint, but it will never be within its power to make a law upon which parlement has not deliberated into a verified law; it will always be the case that the most sustained efforts of absolute authority can only execute non-verified laws, but whose invalidity will always be ineffaceable and will always cry out against their execution.

All forced transcriptions, Sire, of edicts . . . upon the registers of the different parlements can only be viewed as illegitimate and deceptively placed upon the registers of Your Majesty's tribunals of sovereign justice, sacred repositories of laws, not of illegal acts. Such transcriptions are violations of the law, violations of which the magistrates themselves would be guilty if they allowed themselves to tolerate them.

Infused by the most profound respect for Your Majesty and all that bears the mark of your will, your parlement, Sire, is not afraid to compromise its respect and submission, nor to displease Your Majesty, by observing *that the ordinances of the Kingdom are the true commands of Your Majesty to which your parlement has sworn unshakeable loyalty, that although Your Majesty possesses the fullness of supreme power, that power is not above the laws of your state* . . .

If ignorant or self-interested people contradict these words, they are nonetheless worthy of the high sentiments of Your Majesty and the loyalty owed to You by your parlement, because they are the faithful expression of the fundamental law of the French constitution, the most solid guarantee of the stability of the Throne, and the preservation of the legitimate rights of all the orders of the State.

The invalidation of any act which attacks the fundamental law of the necessity of verifying laws in parlement is an immediate and inevitable consequence of these incontestable maxims; the illegitimacy of the collection of taxes established by simple transcriptions made by violence upon the registers of Parlement is but the application of these very maxims of State. . . .

One would look in vain, Sire, in the history of past centuries for examples of attacks comparable to those which the ambitious spirit of the devotees of absolute power have successively carried out from circumstance to circumstance; a parlement under arrest, another exiled from the city of its residence, guards surrounding the sanctuary of justice, soldiers holding lists permitting or refusing magistrates to enter the court. . . .

It behooves the wisdom and justice of Your Majesty, the good of your service, the preservation of your authority, and the glory of your reign that you deign, Sire, to eliminate all trace of these disorders by the most powerful and prompt measures.

It is important to Your Majesty that your subjects be free men and not slaves. The quality of King of the French is nothing but command over men of heart and not over convicts who obey because they are forced to, who fear the hand of the overseer and curse each day the authority they respect. The Prince should be afraid of being feared, and subjects who love their prince should fear for him, but never fear him.

2. THE ROYAL SESSION KNOWN AS THE "SESSION OF FLAGELLATION" (MARCH 3, 1766)[2]

The so-called Session of Flagellation saw the King himself chastise the court for its disobedience and lecture it on its proper place in the monarchical order.

I would not have made any response to the many remonstrations which have been made, had not their concertation, indecent style, temerity, mistaken principles, and novel expressions not revealed the pernicious consequences of the system of unity which I have already prohibited, but which you want to establish as a principle. . . .

I will not tolerate in my kingdom the formation of an association which would twist the natural bonds of common duties and obligations into a confederation of resistance, nor that an imaginary corps be introduced into the monarchy and disturb its harmony. The magistracy does not form a single body, nor an order distinct from the three orders of the Kingdom. The magistrates are my officers charged with carrying out the truly royal duty of rendering justice to my subjects, a function which attaches them to my person and will always make them worthy in my eyes. I know the importance of their services. It is thus an illusion, which can only upset public confidence by spreading false alarm, to imagine a project designed to annihilate the magistracy and to imagine that it has enemies around

---

[2]Flammermont and Tourneux, *Remontrances du Parlement*, vol. 2, 554–560.

the Throne. Its only true enemies are those who, in its own ranks, speak a language opposed to its principles; who make it say that all the parlements are nothing but a single, united corps; that this necessarily indivisible corps is essential to the Monarchy and serves as its base, that it is the seat, the tribunal, the voice of the Nation, that it is the protector and depository of its liberty, interests, and rights; that it is responsible for this deposit and would commit a crime against [the nation] if ever it abandoned it, that it is accountable for all parts of the public good not only to the King, but also to the Nation, that it is the judge between the King and his people, that, as guardian of both, it maintains the equilibrium of government by repressing excesses of liberty and abuses of power, that the parlements cooperate with the sovereign power in making laws, that they can nullify a registered law on their own authority and regard it as non-existent, that they must raise an insurmountable barrier to decisions they attribute to arbitrary authority and call illegal acts, as well as to orders they claim have been obtained by deception, and that, if a conflict of authority arises, it is their duty to abandon their functions and resign their offices. . . . To seek to elevate such pernicious innovations to the level of principles is to insult the magistracy, pervert its purpose, betray its interests, and misunderstand the fundamental laws of the State; as if it were permitted to forget that it is in my person alone that sovereign power resides, power whose distinctive characteristic is the spirit of council, justice, and reason, that it is to me alone that the courts owe their existence and authority, that the fullness of that authority, which they exercise only in my name, still remains in me and that its use can never be turned against me, that legislative power belongs to me alone without dependence or division, that it is by my authority alone that the officers of my courts participate not in the formation but in the registration, publication, execution of the law, and that they are permitted to remonstrate, which is the duty of good and useful councilors, that the entire public order emanates from me and that the rights and interests of the Nation, which you dare to consider a body distinct from the Monarch, are necessarily united to mine and lie in my hands alone. . . .

Remonstrations will always be received favorably if they are marked by the moderation that characterizes the magistrate and truth, if they maintain decency and usefulness by being issued discretely, if this wise mechanism is not twisted into a means of libel or presents submission to my will as a crime and the carrying out of the duties I order as a subject of opprobrium, if it does not assume that the whole Nation groans to see its rights, liberty, and security on the point of perishing at the hands of a terrible power, and if it does not proclaim that the bonds of obedience are on the point of giving way. But, if I persist in my desires after careful examination of a remonstration, my courts persevere in their refusal to submit, . . . if they try to repeal formally enregistered laws on their own authority, if they continue to oppose my authority after it has been deployed in its majesty, . . . confusion and anarchy will take the place of legitimate order, and the scandalous spectacle of a rival against my sovereign power will sadly force me to use all the power that I have received from God to save my peoples from the fatal consequences of these enterprises.

3. REMONSTRATIONS LEADING TO THE MAUPEOU COUP (DECEMBER 1770–JANUARY 1771)[3]

This series of documents traces the escalating tension between the royal government and the Parlement, leading up to the dissolution of Parlement in the Maupeou coup.

Royal Speech to Parlement, Read by the Chancellor (December 1770)

His Majesty wanted to believe that you would receive with respect and submission a law which contains true principles, principles recognized and upheld by our forefathers and enshrined in the monuments of our history.

Do you refuse to register this law because of your attachment to new ideas? Shall a temporary disturbance leave such deep traces upon your hearts?

Go back to the creation of the parlements; follow them in their progress; you will see that they owe their existence and power to the kings alone, that the fullness of that power remains in the hand that granted it.

They are neither an emanation of nor a part of each other; the authority which created them circumscribed their boundaries, assigned them limits, and fixed the competence and extent of their jurisdiction.

Entrusted with the application of laws, you have not been given the power to either extend or restrict their dispositions.

Only the power that established them can clear up their obscurities with new laws.

The most sacred oaths bind you to the administration of justice, and you can neither suspend nor abandon your functions without violating both the agreement you have made with the King and the obligations you have contracted with the people.

When the legislator wants to express his will, you are his organ, and out of his goodness he permits you to give him counsel; he invites you to enlighten him with your knowledge and orders you to show him the truth.

That is your entire ministry.

The King weighs your observations wisely; he balances them against the reasons which motivate him and with a surveying gaze that encompasses the whole Monarchy, he judges the advantages and inconveniences of the law.

If he then commands, you owe him perfect obedience.

If your rights went further than this, if your resistance had no end, you would no longer be his officers, but his masters. His will would be subject to yours. The majesty of the Throne would no longer inhabit your assemblies and, stripped of the most essential rights of the Crown, dependent in making laws, dependent in their execution, the King would conserve only the name and shadow of Sovereignty.

---

[3]Flammermont and Tourneux, *Remontrances du Parlement*, vol. 3, 162–184.

Parlement's Response (December 13, 1770)

SIRE,

Your Parlement can do nothing more than perish along with the laws, since the fate of the magistrates necessarily follows that of the State; but before that fatal moment, it must still warn Your Majesty that your edict may destroy the very laws on which the stability of the Throne depends. . . .

These laws, Sire, are, among others, the immutability of monarchical government, the inalienability of the Crown's rights, the succession to the Throne. . . . Unfortunately our history furnishes examples of attacks upon these sacred laws. . . .

May God never allow such things to occur again under the reign of the most just prince; but, Sire, what happened in distant times could happen again in times to come; and article 3 of the edict, if ever executed, would enchain the deliberations of your parlement by silencing it and strip it of the means it has used before to save the State.

No, Sire, an edict whose truly extreme consequences would be so damaging cannot be the true wish of Your Majesty. If such a dangerous law had been established by your predecessor kings, the wisdom of Your Majesty would have led you to revoke it. . . .

Sire, allow your parlement to conclude by addressing you the words that First President de Harlay addressed to King Henri IV on June 19, 1604: "If it is disobedience to serve well, the Parlement routinely makes this error, and whenever it finds a conflict between the absolute power of the King and the good of his service, it judges in favor of the latter not out of disobedience, but rather out of duty, in following its conscience."

[In response to the Parlement's continued resistance, the King issued royal letters on December 20, 1770, ordering it to comply. But in an unprecedented act of defiance, the Parlement refused to do so. The King issued new royal letters (January 4, 1771); but, undaunted, Parlement issued new remonstrations and declared that it was going on strike. Further royal letters elicited from Parlement the following remonstration.]

Parlement's Remonstration (January 17, 1771)

Your parlement, Sire, has always and will always consider it an inviolable maxim that Your Majesty holds power from God alone, that all authority in the political order emanates from that power, that the magistrates are but your officers, that the authority they exercise is but the authority of Your Majesty himself, and, finally, that the right of making laws belongs to you alone, without dependence or division.

But, Sire, you will not consider it an attack upon these unshakeable principles to represent to you that the august kings who preceded you always recognized that it was necessary, to uphold the rights of Royalty and the good of the State, that laws should be verified in the parlement and that the need for this verification stems from the constitution of the State, which can be neither changed nor altered. These maxims, Sire, are consecrated in authentic monuments [of history] which your parlement has already had the honor to place before your eyes. . . .

Sire, there are inviolable laws, and these laws cannot be changed. . . . When it comes to these essential laws, it is not enough to say that the magistrates must vigilantly maintain them. It is also their duty to be ready to sacrifice what they hold most dear, even their life, to ensure their execution. . . .

The preservation of the fundamental laws and safety of the State might sometimes require, Sire, that your parlement do things that the edict seeks to forbid. . . .

Your parlement, Sire, must also point out that the magistrates have always been exemplars of obedience, even when they believed it necessary to protest with the greatest force against laws registered by absolute authority; but the kings did not believe, in such cases, that they could require the magistrates to oversee the execution of laws of this type, because such is the spirit of the French Government that the legitimate liberty of the subjects must not be violated and that, above all, it must be maintained full and complete in the case of magistrates exercising their functions. The result of this wise conduct on the part of our kings has been to the inestimable advantage of both the Sovereign and his subjects that laws . . . contrary to the most essential interest of the Monarch and the peoples have remained without effect.

Concerning correspondence between the different parlements, we cannot imagine, Sire, what could have been the reason for the edict's prohibition of it. . . .

The importance of all these considerations, Sire, gives your parlement complete confidence that Your Majesty will deign to revoke an edict so contrary to the honor of the Magistracy and which would so endanger the essential laws of the Kingdom, the most sacred rights of the citizens, the security of the Throne, and the salvation of the State.

[The next day, the King responded to the Parlement's continued resistance with new orders to comply and a warning that if they did not, punishment would be forthcoming. The Parlement vowed to continue its resistance. On the night of January 20th to 21st, soldiers were dispatched to the houses of the magistrates. Those who refused to comply were stripped of their offices and banished to the provinces. The Parlement was dissolved. Although it would be restored in 1775, its attempt to carve out a preeminent constitutional role for itself had been decisively defeated.]

4. REMONSTRATION OF THE *COUR DES AIDES* (MAY 6, 1775)[4]

Despite the emasculation of the Paris Parlement, other courts continued to protest against royal fiscal measures—and ultimately against the arbitrary nature of the royal administration itself. The most sweeping denunciation was issued by the Cour des Aides (Fiscal Court) of Paris. This document shows an important shift in the constitutional content of the magistrates' critique of the royal government.

---

[4]Chrétien-Guillaume de Lamoignon de Malesherbes, *Mémoires pour Servir à L'histoire du Droit Public de la France en Matieres D'Impôts* (Brussels, 1775).

The distribution of direct taxes is essentially tied to the constitution of the Monarchy. The evils of this distribution are part of a general system of administration which was introduced into your Kingdom long ago. The remedy can only be found in the reform that Your Majesty may be pleased to bring to the general administration.

We will thus examine the administration of each direct tax, and Your Majesty will see how this fatal system took root; but we must first go back to its origin. We must inform Your Majesty of its essential principles and consequences; and perhaps you will be surprised, Sire, to see the extent to which the pretext of your authority has been abusively turned against that authority itself.

Permit us, Sire, to use the term *despotism*, odious though it may be; excuse us for eschewing awkward euphemisms when we have important truths to reveal.

The despotism we are denouncing is exercised behind your back by emissaries of the administration who are absolutely unknown to Your Majesty. No, Sire, we are not seeking to offer you useless and possibly dangerous dissertations on the limits of your sovereign power. To the contrary, we invoke for all Citizens the right to appeal to your power and mean by *despotism* only that type of administration which deprives your Subjects of that cherished right and hides from your Justice the People's oppressors.

Notions of despotism or absolute power have not been the same at different times and among different Peoples.

We often speak of a type of government called *oriental despotism* in which the Sovereign not only exercises absolute and unlimited authority, but in which each of his officials has boundless power. The inevitable result is tyranny; for there is an infinite difference between the power of a Master, whose true interest is that of the People, and that of a Subject who, puffed up with another's power, takes pleasure in increasing its weight on his equals. Transmitted hierarchically to Ministers of different ranks, this kind of despotism affects even the lowest Citizen, so that none in a vast Empire can escape it.

The vice of this type of government is in both its constitution and culture.

It is in the constitution because the Peoples subject to it have neither courts, laws, nor representatives. Since there are no courts, authority is wielded by a single man. Since there are no fixed and positive laws, he who holds authority rules according to his own lights, which is to say, according to his whims. Since there are no representatives of the People, a province's despot can oppress with impunity, both against the will and without the knowledge of the Sovereign.

Culture also contributes to this impunity because the Peoples subject to this sort of despotism are always prey to ignorance. No one reads, no one is connected to anyone else; the cries of the oppressed are not heard beyond the land he inhabits. Thus the innocent man cannot appeal to public opinion, which is such a powerful check on the tyranny of subalterns.

Such is the sad situation of these Peoples that even the most just Sovereign can only extend his justice to those closest to him or over the few matters he knows of directly.

All he can do for his Subjects is to choose the least bad people he can to exercise authority on his behalf and to urge them to choose the best people they can to serve as their subordinates. But whatever he does, the lowest order of Citizen always suffers under the authority of the lowest rank of despot. . . .

It would seem that this form of government cannot exist among Nations who have Laws, culture, and enlightenment; thus, in civilized countries, even when the Prince wields absolute power, the condition of his Peoples must be quite different.

However absolute the government may be, Justice can still be rendered by the deliberation of courts restrained by clear Laws.

If the Judges depart from these Laws, one can have recourse to superior courts and, ultimately, to the sovereign authority itself. . . .

Thus, in a civilized country, even one subject to an absolute power, there should not be any interest, whether general or particular, that is not defended. All those entrusted with sovereign power must be subject to three kinds of restraint: Laws, appeals to the superior authority, and public opinion.

This distinction between the different kinds of absolute power is not new . . . but we must restate it because a great truth emerges from it. We must make it known to Your Majesty that the government which some would like to establish in France is the true despotism of uncivilized countries. . . .

Like the rest of Europe, France was once governed by feudal law, but each Kingdom has undergone different changes since that type of government was destroyed.

Some Nations have been allowed to negotiate their rights with their Sovereign. . . .

In others, absolute authority prevailed so quickly that none of the nation's rights were examined. From this, at least one advantage resulted for those countries: that there was never a pretext for destroying the intermediate bodies and infringing the natural liberty of men to deliberate in common on their common interests and to appeal to the supreme power against the abuses of subaltern authorities. In France, the Nation has always had a profound sense of its rights and its liberty. Our maxims have repeatedly been recognized by our Kings; they have even gloried in being Sovereigns of a free People. However, the articles of this freedom have never been written out and real power, the power of arms, which was in the hands of the great lords under feudal government, has been totally joined to royal power.

Thus, when great abuses of authority have occurred, the Nation's representatives have not just complained of bad administration; they have felt obliged to demand national rights. They have spoken not only of justice, but of liberty; and the result has been that Ministers, always eager to find ways of sheltering their administration from investigation, have artfully neutralized both the claimant bodies and the claims themselves.

Appeals to the King against his Ministers have been seen as attacks on his authority. The grievances of the Estates, the Remonstrances of the Magistrates have been twisted into dangerous enterprises against which the government must preserve itself. The most powerful Kings of the earth have been made to fear the very tears of a submissive People; and on this pretext has been introduced into France a much more harmful government than despotism, one worthy of oriental barbarism. This is the clandestine administration by which, under the eyes of a just Sovereign and in the midst of an enlightened Nation, injustice can manifest itself. . . .

It is the despotism of the Administrators and, above all, this system of secrecy that we must denounce to Your Majesty; for we will not have the temerity to discuss the other sacred rights of the Throne. . . .

But we do not violate our *just subordination* by placing before your eyes a series of infractions against national liberty, the natural liberty of all men, which today make it impossible for you to hear your Subjects and see the conduct of your Administrators.

1. An attempt has been made to annihilate the true representatives of the Nation.
2. The protests of those representatives who have not yet been destroyed have been rendered illusory.
3. There is even a desire to make them impossible. Secrecy was introduced in order to achieve this. It comes in two types: one which seeks to hide the administration's doings from the Nation, and even from Your Majesty; the other, which hides from the Public the identity of the Administrators.

This, Sire, is the outline of the system which we denounce to Your Majesty and upon which we will elaborate.

We state as the first intention of this despotism the destruction of all the representatives of the Nation. . . .

The general assemblies of the Nation have not been convoked for one hundred and sixty years and, long before that, had become very rare and, we daresay, nearly useless because what most necessitated their presence, the establishment of taxes, was being done without them. . . .

At least each Corps, each Community of Citizens, retained the right of administering its own affairs, a right which we do not consider part of the original constitution of the Kingdom since it goes back much further. It is natural right, the right of reason. Yet, even it has been taken from your Subjects. . . .

Such, Sire, are the means which have been employed in France to extinguish, if possible, the last vestige of civic spirit; the whole Nation has been suspended, so to speak, and placed in guardianship.

The annihilation of the protesting Corps was the first step toward destroying the right to protest itself. We have not gone so far as to expressly prohibit all appeals to the Prince . . . but Your Majesty is not unaware that all petitions articulating the interests of a Province or the Nation as a whole are regarded as criminal temerity. . . . It was, however, necessary to give the Nation ostensible satisfaction when the Estates ceased to be convoked; to this end, the Kings announced that the Courts of Justice would take the place of the Estates, that the Magistrates would be the representatives of the People.

But after having given them this title, to console the Nation for the loss of its ancient and authentic representatives, the functions of the Judges were restricted to lawsuits and only within their own jurisdictions, and the same limits were placed on the right of representation. . . .

The combined interests of the Ministers and powerful individuals almost always overwhelm that of the King and his People.

This we have already shown on the subject of the *vingtième* and the *capitation*.[5] These two impositions, with which the Ministers and their subordinates have arrogated the right to tax your Subjects, . . . give rise to a despotism odious to France and shameful for a free Nation; a despotism opposed to the true interests of Your Majesty and even the interest of the fisc, which despots always sacrifice to their personal considerations; but a despotism which is most useful to the great and powerful, because they are always treated favorably by Ministers, Intendants, and other despots of their ilk.

This is also the case with excessive spending. Proposals are always made to restrain it, and everyone approves in principle; but when it comes to carrying them out, all the Ministers, all who disburse money, refuse to do so, and they are supported by all the powers of the Court and even the Capital, because it is always the powerful who reap the bounty of Ministers. . . .

On all these points, Sire, there must necessarily be two parties in a Kingdom; on one side, those with access to the Sovereign; on the other, the rest of the Nation. A King who wants to be just must thus draw his sentiments from his own heart and his knowledge from that of the entire Nation.

But how can a relationship be established between the King and the nation, one which will not be intercepted by those who surround the King? We must not conceal from you, Sire, that the simplest, most natural, and most constitutional means would be to hear the assembled Nation itself, or at least to permit assemblies of each Province. No one should be so cowardly as to tell you otherwise. No one should leave you unaware that the unanimous vow of the Nation is to obtain either the Estates-General, or at least Provincial Estates.

II. Alternative Pathways to Reform

The courts were not the only voices calling for change. After the Seven Years' War, France was seething with discussion of different ways to reform the socio-political order, to make it both more equitable and more efficient. Although they varied wildly in the means of improvement they proposed, they all sought to give the French people a greater role in their own government. As one would expect, traditional social elites loudly clamored for a greater role in public affairs. More surprisingly, members of the royal government were no less interested (although

---

[5]Recent inventions. Both struck all individuals, even nobles, regardless of their privileged status.

for somewhat different reasons) in finding ways of giving the people a stake in their own administration.

5. MARQUIS DE MIRABEAU, *MEMOIR ON PROVINCIAL ESTATES*[6]

The Marquis de Mirabeau was a noble political writer. Like the Parlement, he was concerned about limiting the oppressive power of the state. Inspired by his reading of Montesquieu and his own experience with the local assembly of his home province (the estates of Provence), Mirabeau articulated a different solution to the problem: a form of administrative decentralization capable of shielding the nation from the heavy hand of government and shoring up France's traditional social order. To this end, he called for the formation of local representative assemblies in all the provinces of France. Representation in these bodies would be assigned to distinct social categories (clergy, nobility, etc.) rather than individuals. Mirabeau hoped that these groups would moderate each other's pretentions. The idea of provincial autonomy rooted in traditional social structures proved popular with elites—for example, the noble-dominated Cour des Aides adopted it (see preceding document)—who felt that it would ensure them the leading public role they felt they deserved.

There are few Provinces in France which did not once have Estates; but almost all withered in the anarchy of the times of trouble and have not grown back since. There now remain only vestiges. . . .

Men have a natural love for liberty, but, like all other desires, if literally followed, it would drive them to excesses and produce the opposite result from what they were seeking. . . . This liberty is naturally destined to have fixed and invariable limits. . . . In a word, man is made to believe himself free but to be enchained, but voluntarily and by bonds whose necessity he feels. . . .

People think they enjoy freedom when they are allowed to take part in the administration of their province, when they only have to pay taxes they judge necessary to impose upon themselves, when they are not exposed to arbitrary taxation, and when they feel safe from the investigations of avid and self-interested tax collectors.

This is what makes the inhabitants of provinces with estates so jealous of this privilege, which they regard as liberty, even though it only has the appearance of it. In effect, what inestimable advantage for the tranquil citizen, for the farmer occupied solely with the details of his fields, not to have to ensure each year, by journeys and bribes, that his taxes not be increased. . . .

---

[6]First published in 1750. Marquis de Mirabeau, *Memoire sur les États Provinciaux*, excerpt from the 1787 edition, 54–63, 119.

By oppressing everything, tyranny makes everything equal.... To the contrary, legitimate authority organizes itself so that, like electricity, the impulse of sovereign power communicates itself strongly and rapidly from the highest to the lowest, always passing through each class.

Whether the power is granting benefits, whether it is asking for things, everyone has a right to receive, everyone has a duty to contribute, each according to his status and capabilities. Social regulation and justice are nothing but the establishing of the rights of each one.... This is the definition of the first duty of Sovereignty; but who better to entrust with the details of fulfilling it than the elites of each province?

Two things attract respect among men, birth and positions. One might add wealth, but only in times of anarchy. In all well-regulated States, wealth's only advantages will be tranquil possession, ease, and the comforts of life, but never social consideration....

It is said that some Princes have thought that all their subjects were equal before them. I can hardly imagine that a well-regulated State could have been governed by a Sovereign so blind and pusillanimous. It is true that all the orders of subjects owe equal respect and obedience to the Sovereign as such and as the bearer of sacred power according to divine and human laws; but the father of a family, the master, the lord also have rights founded on nature and divine law. It is the purpose of sovereign authority to maintain all those rights. If the Prince treats a father as a son, the master as a valet, the lord as a vassal, ... if all are equal in prerogative and authority in relation to him, he will become a source of anarchy rather than the upholder of good order.

Princes thus know that distinctions are necessary in their State. They naturally love and respect that of birth because, since they are almost all hereditary and proud of their blood, the advantages of this type enjoyed by others reinforce the preeminence of their own. It is completely different in Republics, where nobility is either destroyed or forced to maintain itself by tyrannical precautions. The nobility thus has an interest in maintaining the [Prince's] authority.

The relations of interest and inclination between the nobility and the Prince are about the same as those between the people and the nobility. Just as the memory of the services and loyalty of the fathers inclines the children to imitate them, so too does the memory of the [nobility's] luster and preeminence with the respect and affection of the people for their posterity. In every age and in every nation, when authority is given to lowly people, it is much more likely to excite opposition and murmuring than when given to those who have the advantages of a name to which long habit has attached sentiments of respect and deference....

In provinces with estates the nobility does not exercise all power; it only participates in its exercise. The clergy, who holds all it possesses from the King, who looks to him for everything, whose profession is to give daily counsel and to teach obedience, holds the first rank. The Third-Estate, destined to bear the brunt of taxes, enlightened by necessity, held back by mediocrity, has just as much right as the two other Corps. What equality of harmony! There is no arrangement more capable of freeing the Sovereign from the burden of exercising distributive justice, both in giving and taking. By the simplicity of its composition, it offers a distinct picture of the interior state of a province, which helps authority maintain its rights. . . .

Without doubt, in the establishment of the Monarchy, the first two orders were equal and they still are, even though respect and recognition have given precedence to the Clergy. They subsequently admitted the Third-Estate to the assemblies, doubtless out of a sense of justice. . . .

It is according to this scheme that I would like to arrange all the details, whether in the general assembly of Estates, the intermediate administration, or in the government of the different cantons of the provinces.

The Mayors, Consuls, or Deputies of the principal cities compose the Third Estate. To give more distinction to the municipality, . . . the highest administrative position (whatever it is called) must be given to a noble, fief-holder, or retired officer . . . in preference to the . . . city bourgeois. The sentiments inspired by birth, ease, superior education, all these things give a sort of elevation which reflects upon the position. . . .

The most stable, most secure Monarchy is that in which four orders are considered constitutive: 1) the Ecclesiastical order or Clergy which binds together society, corrects it, instructs it, encourages it to do good, warns it from evil; 2) the Military order or Nobility, which defends society, guides it, imprints it with and lends it its free and dominant genius; 3) the Civil order, which maintains good order; 4) the municipal order, which gives activity. These last two orders are composed of chosen people, drawn from the first two, as well as of leading members of the people.

All the different levels of administration and sub administration descend upon these four distinctive and separate orders from the summits of Sovereignty. . . .

These four orders depend only upon the Master . . . and are subordinate to one another for the matters that concern each one. If the Clergy has a lawsuit, it is resolved by the judgments of the Civil order; the Civil order, in turn, is included in the taxes assessed by the municipal order. It is the same with the Nobility. In this way, everyone is subordinate, but all are subject to the single and unique Master.

It is thus that, in a true Monarchy, sovereignty, sole key to the State, finds a way of associating its existence with the universality of its subjects and of forming and ensuring forever the political edifice. . . .

6. ANNE-ROBERT-JACQUES TURGOT, *MEMOIR ON MUNICIPALITIES*[7]

The idea of devolving state functions to local, representative assemblies also interested the royal government. To read only the criticisms of the Parlement, one would think that the royal government was authoritarian, despotic, and determined to

[7]Anne-Robert-Jacques Turgot, *Memoir on Municipalities*, in *Oeuvres posthumes de M. Turgot* (Lausanne, Switzerland: 1787), 6–98.

increase its power by crushing society. But key members of the royal administration saw themselves as progressive modernizers doing battle with the hidebound traditionalism of the parlements, nobility, and other privileged bodies. They articulated a rationalizing pathway to reform that drew on some of the same ideas advocated by their opponents. It might be said that, in the decades after 1763, the royal government was trying to revolutionize itself—and French society as a whole—to save itself from fiscal collapse.

The most influential plan to do so was proposed by the royal minister Turgot to the King in the 1770s. Although the institutional framework of municipal, provincial, and national assemblies it outlined resembled Mirabeau's schema, it was fundamentally different. Whereas Mirabeau's assemblies were based on traditional social categories, Turgot's adopted an entirely different rationale of representation that was self-consciously rational and would have corroded the traditional social order.

The rights of men joined in society are not based on their history, but on their nature; there is no reason to perpetuate things established without reason. The kings who preceded Your Majesty have pronounced the laws they judged appropriate in the circumstances in which they found themselves. They sometimes made mistakes, often because of the ignorance of their times and more often because they were hindered in their views by very powerful interests. . . . There is nothing in all that which can restrain you from changing the ordinances they handed down or the institutions they made, once you have recognized that such changes are just, useful, and possible. Those of your subjects, who are most accustomed to protesting, would not dare deny, when reforming abuses, that Your Majesty possesses a legislative power every bit as extensive as that of the Princes who came before you. . . . Your Majesty can thus regard yourself as an absolute legislator and count upon his good nation to execute his orders. . . .

The cause of the disorders, Sire, comes from the fact that your nation does not have a constitution. It is a society composed of different, disunited orders, of a people whose members are bound by very few social ties, [a society], consequently, in which almost everybody is concerned only with his exclusive, particular interest, where almost nobody bothers to fulfil his duties or to understand his relations with others. In this endless war of pretentions and enterprises, Your Majesty must decide everything by himself or by mandatories. [Your people] only contribute to the public good and respect the rights of others on your specific order. . . . You are forced to issue rulings on everything . . . whereas you would be able to govern like God, by general laws, if the component parts of your empire had a regular organization and established relations between them.

Your kingdom is composed of provinces. These provinces are composed of cantons or districts. . . . These are formed of a certain number of towns and villages. These towns and villages are inhabited by families. These families have lands which produce what the inhabitants need to live, furnish the revenues to pay salaries to the landless, and provide the taxes destined for public expenses. Finally, the families are composed of individuals who have many duties to fulfill toward one another and toward society; duties founded on the benefits they have received from it and which they continue to receive each day.

But individuals are poorly informed of their familial duties and utterly ignorant of those which bind them to the state. Families themselves barely know that they are part of the state. . . . They view the orders of authority for the payment of the taxes which will serve to maintain public order as the law of the strongest, with which there is no reason to comply but the impossibility of resistance and which they elude whenever they can. Thus, everybody tries to fool authority and pass on social burdens to ones neighbors. Revenue is hidden and can only be very imperfectly discovered by a sort of inquisition by which one might say that Your Majesty is at war with your people; and in this war . . . no one has any interest in favoring the Government. . . . There is no public spirit because there is no visible and clearly understood common interest. . . .

To dispel the spirit of disunion which hinders the work of your servitors and of Your Majesty, and which necessarily and prodigiously diminishes your power; to replace it with a spirit of order and union which will make the forces and capabilities of your nation work together for the common good, bring them together in your hand, and make them easy to lead, we must imagine a plan that links them by an order they cannot refuse, by obvious common interest, by the necessity of understanding that interest, of deliberating upon it, of conforming to it; which links, I say, individuals to their families, families to the village or town to which they belong, the towns and villages to the district where they are situated, the districts to the provinces of which they are part, and finally the provinces to the State.

. . .

[Turgot then proposed setting up a hierarchy of assemblies (municipal or village, provincial, and national), each with different powers and responsibilities, such as public works, poor relief, and, above all, the distribution of taxation.]

On what principles should the municipal village administration be based, and who should take part in it? . . . Should all the villagers have an equal influence? . . . At first glance, it would seem that all heads of families living in a village should have a vote. . . . But independently of the fact that such numerous assemblies are subject to many drawbacks, upheavals, and quarrels, and that it is difficult for reason to make itself heard within them and that the poverty of the voters would make them easy to corrupt, . . . we see, if we look closely, that the only people who really belong to a village or parish are those who possess real estate. The rest are just day laborers who are only temporary residents. They go off to mow hay in one canton, harvest grain in another, pick grapes in a third. Workers from the Limousin go to Paris to build houses; men from Auvergne sweep chimneys in Spain. Across the whole kingdom, the class of landless peasants who provide domestic servants, a large part of the armies, and petty craftsmen who carry their talent with them to the place where they find the most profitable employment, often outside of the kingdom. These people live in one place today, another tomorrow. . . .

It is not the same with the owners of the soil; they are bound to the land by their property. They must take interest in the canton in which it is located. They can sell it, it is true, but in that case it is only because they have ceased being property owners that they have stopped being interested in local matters, and their interest passes on to their purchaser. By indelibly linking the possessor to the state, ownership of land constitutes the veritable right of citizenship.

It thus seems, Sire, that you can legitimately grant use of this right, or a voice in the parish assemblies, to those who possess landed property.

This point having been made, a new question of the utmost importance arises, which is to determine if all the owners of real estate should have the same degree of voice.

I think that Your Majesty will be able to settle this question after several considerations.

The natural division of properties ensures that one which would hardly suffice for a single family will be divided between five or six children. . . .

These children and their family no longer subdivide the land. They rent, as best they can, this tiny property, which is quite insufficient for their most essential needs, entering the arts, crafts, commerce, and domesticity. It is by their labor that these new heads of family . . . manage to survive; they belong principally to the salaried class. . . . It is not natural that such men have the same say as the owner of 50,000 pounds of landed rent. It is not natural that one can acquire the right of suffrage or, in other words, the complete and supreme right of citizenship, simply by buying a small plot on which a citizen cannot subsist. We have already noted the grave inconvenience of giving the right of suffrage to people without fortune. . . .

I thus think that the man who does not have enough land to support his family is not a property-owning head of family, and should not have a vote in this capacity. But if he possesses some portion of land, however insufficient to support his household, this man has an interest in the good distribution of taxes and in the good administration of public services and works. . . . We cannot give him a full vote, but we cannot entirely refuse him voice. He is a not a whole citizen, but a larger or smaller fraction of a citizen. . . .

I thus propose to Your Majesty to give a full citizen's vote to every 600 pounds of revenue. Thus, in the parish assemblies, one who enjoys this revenue will speak for himself, but those with less revenue will have to join together to exercise their right. For example, two people with 300 pounds or four with 150 pounds, or six with 100 pounds, or twelve with 50 pounds will jointly choose a deputy who will vote for the others. . . . He alone will be able to participate in the parish assembly and will cast a single citizen's vote, both in his own name and in those of his associates. . . . Each fractionary citizen will thus join with the others who suit him best to form, of a common accord, their citizen's vote. . . .

If Your Majesty permits fractionary citizens to join together to have the vote attributed to a certain sum of revenue, . . . it would be equally equitable and, above all, useful to permit those whose revenues are sufficient to support many families . . . to have as many votes as they could muster through their possessions;

so that the man with 1200 pounds of revenue deriving from land in a parish would have two votes in the assembly. . . .

This arrangement is fair since he who has four times more landed revenue in a parish has four times more to lose if the affairs of the parish go badly and four times more to gain if everything prospers. . . .

This arrangement is also useful since, by usually placing the majority of votes in the hands of the better-educated, it will make the assemblies more reasonable than if poorly-schooled and uncultured people were to predominate. . . .

But the greatest advantages in distributing the votes of the citizens according to their wealth are, 1) to make the vanity and ambition of those who want to be leaders work against the greed of those who want to evade taxes, and 2) to spread, by the very form in which the votes will be distributed, the burden of taxation in the best and least contentious way.

Since votes will be attributed to a certain sum of revenue, one's demand for multiple votes, a single vote, or a fraction of a vote will serve as the avowal and declaration of one's revenue. The proportions of wealth thus being revealed, the distribution of taxes will be done automatically by the distribution of the inhabitants' votes themselves. . . .

The greatest, perhaps only, drawback of the simple operations entrusted to the municipal parish assemblies might come from the different nature of taxes. . . . The nobility is exempt from the *taille*.[8] . . . In addition to this same exemption, the clergy is also exempt from the *capitation* and the *vingtièmes*. . . . It results from this that the total sum of taxes, which would not be heavy if it were borne equally by all the revenues of the State, appears insupportable to a great number of taxpayers because it is only paid by a portion of these revenues. . . .

Without adding to the burden currently borne by the nobility and clergy (or even diminishing it a bit), but above all lessening it greatly for the people, it would be easy to introduce a less burdensome and less destructive form of taxation. . . . This will perhaps be a goal you would like to achieve, to make your kingdom sufficiently opulent and your treasury sufficiently rich to be able to free your peoples from the special taxes to which they are currently subject, so that there remains nothing more for the superior orders than honorable distinctions, but not monetary exemptions. From the perspective of both reason and patriotism, they are degrading to those who claim them and, from the perspective of pride and vanity, degrading to those who are excluded from them. . . .

It is not as a distinct order in the State, but as citizens with landed income, that nobles and ecclesiastics would be part of the municipal assembly of their parish. . . . It would not be reasonable . . . to introduce into assemblies designed to be peaceful and to concern themselves only with simple objects related to their very-obvious common interest, divisions and separations which would soon dispel public spirit under the cloud of the pretentions of corps or orders.

---

[8]Basic land tax, from which nobles, clergy, and certain privileged categories of Third Estate were exempt.

As Your Majesty wants to treat Your subjects like his children, one cannot strive too hard to encourage them to see each other as brothers. . . .

Allowing neither place nor expression to what is harmful in the divisions of orders, leaving only what is honorific for illustrious families and respectable positions, and classifying the citizens according to the real usefulness they can have for the State and of the place they occupy indelibly on the soil of their properties, they will lead the nation to regard itself as a single body, perfectly motivated by a single object—the preservation of the rights of everyone and the public good.

They will accustom the nobility and clergy to the replacement of the taxes from which they are not presently exempt and will thus provide solid rules of distribution through the clarity and equity they will bring. In general, they will make taxation less onerous to the people, even though [the State] will raise more revenue. . . .

It may thus become possible to achieve what has until now appeared chimerical: to align the State in a perfect and visible community of interest with all property owners. . . . All particular affairs, those of the parishes, those of the districts, even those of entire provinces will be decided by the most educated people who, ruling in their own cause, will never have any reason for complaint. The kingdom will thus be perfectly known. . . .

Finally, after several years, Your Majesty will have a new people, the best of peoples. Instead of the corruption, cowardice, intriguing, and greed one finds everywhere, there will be virtue, public-spiritedness, honor, zeal. [These qualities] will be shared by all men of goodwill. Your kingdom, united in all of its parts, which will mutually support one another, will unleash its vastly increased forces. . . . It will grow more beautiful each day, like a fertile garden. Europe will look at You with admiration and respect, and at your loving people with heartfelt admiration.

7. JACQUES NECKER, *ACCOUNT GIVEN TO THE KING* (1781)[9]

In 1777, as French intervention in the War of American Independence became likely, King Louis XVI appointed the Genevan banker, Jacques Necker, to take charge of state finances. An unorthodox choice (Necker was not only a foreigner, but a non-Catholic as well), the new minister was expected to mobilize his extensive financial connections to secure war loans for France. Necker succeeded in doing so and thus managed to finance the military effort with minimal tax increases. In 1781, he issued a glowing public accounting of finances, the first ever in French history. Boasting of the sound financial footing on which he had placed the kingdom, he urged that the state's financial operations be conducted with transparency to secure public confidence—key to lower interest rates. In fact, Necker's report concealed the true cost of his wartime borrowing, a cost that would lead to the collapse of the government several years later. Nonetheless, his concern for winning over public opinion and involving the people in the

[9]M. Jacques Necker, *Compte rendu au roi* (Paris: Imprimerie Royale, 1781), 1–4, 14–18.

administration of government (one of his initiatives had been to create experimental assemblies in several provinces) typified the reformist spirit of the time.

It is precious to me to be able to deliver a public account of the success of my labors and of the actual state of Your finances. . . .

However, I would have renounced this satisfaction . . . had I not thought that the publicity of such an account, and its authenticity, would be infinitely useful to the affairs of Your Majesty. I even think that, if this institution were made permanent, it would bring the greatest advantages. The obligation of bringing to light his entire Administration would influence the first steps that a Minister of Finances would take in the path he would follow. Shadows and obscurity encourage nonchalance; in contrast, publicity can only become an honor and reward if one has understood the importance of one's duties and striven to fulfil them. . . .

At the same time, the prospect of this publicity would neutralize those obscure Writings, which attempt to trouble the repose of an Administrator, and whose Authors, confident that a man with an elevated soul would not descend into the arena to respond to them, profit from his silence to sway opinion by their lies.

Finally, and this is a consideration worthy of the most serious examination, such an institution could have the greatest influence on public confidence.

In effect, if we focus on the immense credit enjoyed by England and which is today its principal strength in war, we cannot attribute it entirely to the nature of its government. . . .

There can be no doubt that another cause of England's great credit is the public notoriety to which the state of its Finances is subject. Each year it is presented to the Parliament and is then printed; and all those who lend to the government thus regularly know the proportion being kept between revenues and expenses; they are not troubled by chimerical suspicions and fears, the inseparable companions of obscurity.

In France, the state of Finances is constantly wrapped in mystery. If spoken of, it is only in the preambles of Edicts and always when new loans are being sought; but these words, too often the same to be true, have necessarily lost their authority, and men of experience no longer believe in them. . . . It is important to put public confidence on a more solid basis. I admit that we have sometimes been able to profit from the obscurity which covers the financial situation to obtain, in the midst of disorder, mediocre credit that was not deserved; but this fleeting advantage, by maintaining a misleading illusion and encouraging the indifference of the administration, has always been followed by unfortunate operations, whose impression persists and is very long in healing. It is thus only at the initial moment when a great State falls into disorder that light cast upon the situation of its Finances becomes inconvenient; but if this very publicity had headed off the disorder, what a service it would have rendered!

It is thus a far-sighted act of Administration on the part of Your Majesty to have permitted a public account of the state of His Finances; and I hope, for the happiness and power of the kingdom, that this happy institution will not be temporary. . . .

An exact balance between revenues and expenditures is all that is needed by a kingdom which is enjoying the good fortune of peace; it does not need loans since its revenues suffice for its needs. . . . But when war makes it seek out extraordinary resources, it must find capital to meet its requirements; and since circumstances are pressing, if credit is lacking, then troubles arise, an initial, forced operation requires further ones, momentary needs struggle against the Sovereign's justice, the Administration is disturbed, and the effects of discredit can sometimes temporarily resemble the entire disorder and subversion of the Finances.

But if the maintenance of credit interests the creditors of the State, if it is important for the power of the Sovereign, it is equally precious to the taxpayers, since it is credit that preserves them from the overwhelming taxes dictated by necessity and imposed when the People most need help, since war itself is a sort of tax because it leads to the stagnation of Commerce and the sale of national products.

Your Majesty's Kingdom doubtless contains more resources for supporting these extraordinary, temporary taxes than any other in Europe, but despite this superiority, this is only a feeble resource compared with credit and confidence. . . .

I would even note that when the state of Finances is cloaked in deep darkness and that 150 millions of extraordinary expenses must be met, I think it is not well regarded to establish twenty or thirty millions in temporary taxes which, expiring with the end of the war, cannot be used to pay the interest on loans. These fleeting levies do not counterbalance the damage they inflict upon credit. The Public, lacking knowledge of the situation of affairs, perceives these taxes as a sign of distress. . . . The mystery and obscurity of the state of Finances forces the Government to constantly manipulate the public imagination and to place part of its force in appearances. In contrast, clarity and frankness only need to speak in the voice of reason and give the public confidence a most dependable and solid basis.

It is for having followed these maxims that England can still borrow as much as 300 million per year and that it can deploy a sum of effort and power completely out of proportion with its actual riches and population.

Never before have we been able to see in so striking a manner the importance of public credit; the introduction of this means of force is not very old and it would perhaps have been better for the good of humanity had it never been discovered. It is through credit that the efforts of multiple generations have been able to be mobilized in an instant, and it is thus that . . . we have carried Armies to the ends of the world. . . .

This new kind of rivalry, this new means of domination having been introduced, it is essential to the power of a Sovereign to obtain and nurture it, just as He must maintain large, disciplined armies. . . .

Having thus sensed the importance of Credit in France, it was my duty to give it the greatest attention. I had to recognize that, since the last peace, everything possible had been done to destroy public confidence, whereas, in that long stretch of tranquility, it would have been so easy to erase the memories of the harmful operations of the last war and establish an order and regularity in the Finances that would have provided Your Majesty with means of extraordinary power. But this favorable opportunity was lost and, expenses having constantly exceeded revenues, it was necessary to have recourse to Loans. . . . whose weight finally led to the suspension of interest payments and all the forced reductions in interest rates which happened in 1771. Credit was so weakened that when I entered into the Ministry, [the Government had to borrow at excessively high rates of interest] . . . at the same time as we were preparing for war.

What a difference between this state of Credit and the price of government bonds at the beginning of the previous war! At that time, lenders could hardly find placements at four and a half percent. . . . However, in 1759, just three years after the outbreak of war, the payment of government notes was suspended, interest payments to venal office-holders suspended, and individuals were being urged to bring their silverware to the Mint, to convert it into coin.

I am thus able to present to Your Majesty, as a merit or a blessing, that, after having begun in a position very different from that of 1756 and after four years of war, the Credit has not suffered any damage, even though Your Majesty has made much use of it; one might even say in truth that, to the contrary, this Credit has gained strength, and we can see that clearly in the price of government bonds.

III. The Pre-Revolution (1787–1788)

The optimism produced by Necker's *Account* was short-lived. In May 1781, he was forced to resign. By 1786, it had become clear that a major financial crisis was imminent. The immediate cause was the short-term (ten-year), high-interest loans that Necker had contracted to fund French involvement in the American War. The first of these would come due for repayment in 1787, with others following year after year through 1793. There was no money to meet these obligations. Rejecting the idea of bankruptcy, the new minister, Calonne, opted for a comprehensive reform program. Its key features were the replacement of the existing patchwork of exemption-riddled taxes with a single, uniform land tax (the territorial subvention) and the creation of local assemblies to oversee its distribution. Afraid that the Parlement might block these measures, Calonne instead submitted them to a hand-picked Assembly of Notables, composed of 144 of the richest, most powerful people in France. The Notables gathered from February 22 through May 25, 1787, at Versailles. He expected them to rubber-stamp his reforms, but that is not what happened. Instead, Calonne's maneuver provoked the constitutional crisis that ultimately led to the French Revolution.

8. THE ASSEMBLY OF NOTABLES (1787)[10]

The gathering of 144 hand-picked elites—including princes of the blood, dukes, archbishops, field marshals, and wealthy representatives of the kingdom's major provinces and cities—was expected to be a rubber stamp for royal reforms. Instead, the grandees proved less pliable than anticipated.

---

[10]*Procès-verbal de l'Assemblée de notables* (Paris: Imprimerie royale, 1788), 101–118.

Proposal to Establish Provincial Assemblies

Informed of and moved by the evils that attend inequality, lack of proportion, and arbitrariness in the distribution of public charges, the King saw as his primary concern and the first of the comforts which he owes to his People, to spare them from [these ills].

To have the taxpayers participate in the distribution of their own taxes seemed to him the best means of making them easier to bear and fairer, to lighten their burden both in public opinion and in reality, to prevent complaints and, finally, to inspire national interest which, by unifying the subjects to each other and the people to their Sovereign, ensures enlightened authority of voluntary obedience. . . .

His Majesty has thus judged it proper to establish in all the Provinces of his Kingdom, in which He does not convoke Estates, elective Assemblies which will renew themselves every three years. . . . They will represent the universality of all the estates indistinctly. . . .

These Assemblies will have their primary level in the country parishes and in the cities; the second in districts formed of a certain number of these parishes and cities; . . . the third in the gathering of the representatives of the entire Province.

There will thus be three kinds of Assembly.

Parish and municipal Assemblies composed of property-owners whose interest can never be separated from that of the place where their properties are situated, and who alone know their reciprocal faculties and the needs of their community.

District Assemblies formed by the deputies of the cities and local rural parishes.

Finally, Provincial Assemblies with deputies chosen by the different districts. . . .

The gradation of these three kinds of elementary Assemblies, which will each be able to understand its own interests and to enlighten the one above it, will express the common wish of the urban and rural population relative to the distribution of public charges to the representatives of each Provinces' property-owners and, thence, to the Sovereign. . . .

The parish Assemblies will supervise the distribution of the local tax burden, public works useful to the parish, and charity to the poor in the community.

The city Assemblies will be composed of municipal officers and notables. . . . Like the parish Assemblies, they will each send a Deputy charged with their instructions to the district Assembly. . . .

These Assemblies will oversee the distribution of royal taxes and local charges between the towns and parishes of their district. . . .

They will name a deputy to carry [their wishes] to the provincial Assembly.

They will choose this Deputy either from their own members or from among the ecclesiastical, Noble, or Third-Estate property owners with at least 1000 pounds of landed revenue in the province. . . .

The rank of the Deputies in the provincial Assembly will be based on the amount of the taxes paid by the districts they represent. . . .

The provincial Assemblies will be responsible for the distribution of public contributions and charges. They will determine what each district must pay toward the total amount of provincial taxes determined by the Council of His Majesty.

They will classify lands for the distribution of the Territorial Subvention. . . .

Thus, by useful and mutual relations, the parish and district Assemblies will form and enlighten the provincial Assemblies; and the provincial Assemblies will direct the district and parish Assemblies.

As a result of this constitution, the King's desires will always be explained to his Subjects by representatives they themselves have chosen. Administration will always be enlightened and never hindered in its operations, but always seconded by the national will and never contradicted by murmurs, always benevolent, and never forced to use rigorous measures. A common interest, a veritable public spirit, will unite in all hearts love of the fatherland to love of the Sovereign; and the King, father of a sensitive and generous people will have nothing but benefits to distribute and benedictions to receive.

Proposal for a Territorial Imposition

The sovereign must protect his subjects' properties. The subjects owe the price of that protection to the Sovereign. This is the principle and first law of taxation.

When the Crown's vassals served the State and King in person, they acquitted their portion of the general contribution by their service.

Later, when it was deemed more useful to replace feudal service with subsidies, the tax consented to by the Nation . . . took the place of the duty of vassality. . . .

To claim freedom from taxation and to demand particular exemptions is to break the link that binds Citizens to the State.

The only reasonable desire, the wish of all, must be limited to seeking just moderation in taxation and that complete equality be observed in its distribution.

To achieve this goal, the King proposes to substitute for the current *Vingtièmes* a Territorial Subvention. . . .

The idea of a territorial tax is the first to occur to a reasonable mind [for] it is the type most perfectly compatible with justice.

It is the land which produces; its productions are protected and guaranteed by the Sovereign; land must thus pay taxes.

It owes part of its fruits to the property-owner who purchased the soil, part to the one who cultivates it, and part to the Prince who protects the soil, the property-owner, and the cultivator. . . .

The collection of this subvention will itself form the Kingdom's cadaster, which we have always desired but never dared to undertake. We will at last know the precise force of each province, distribute taxes equally, and know the full resources of public power. . . .

But to be useful, this imposition must be general. It is incompatible with privileges and exemptions, both personal and local. . . . Thus, it is the King's intention to subject to the territorial Subvention his own domain, that of the Princes his brothers, that of the princely lands, and all the lands of his Kingdom without distinction. . . .

Since they have an equal need for the Sovereign's protection, all members of a State have equal duties to fulfill. Contributing to the common charges of the State is the common debt of all. Preference for one is an injustice for the other. Finally, the right to be exempt from public charges would be the right to not be protected by public authority, the right to not be subject to it, to not be a Citizen.

These truths are unshakeable since they are based on reason, justice, and national interest.

[Calonne's proposals were submitted to the Notables, who broke into bureaus (each headed by a royal prince) to consider them. Unexpectedly, the bureaus protested against the proposed measures, with one speaking of the "recognized impossibility of establishing a territorial imposition in kind" and another denouncing the provincial assemblies as "unconstitutional." Following is the published summary of the 5th Bureau's protest.]

The Bureau believes that provincial Assemblies could be useful, but that the plan proposed . . . is at odds with the French Constitution because, by mixing the three Orders, it destroys the hierarchy necessary to uphold the authority of the Monarch and the existence of the Monarchy. The Bureau thus proposes to give these Assemblies a form more analogous to the constitution of the Kingdom. . . .

The Bureau believes that taxation in kind cannot be allowed, as it is necessarily indefinite, disproportionate, unequal, and costly; that taxation in silver should be distributed across all the lands of the Kingdom without exception, in proportion to their revenues [but only as a temporary emergency measure and only if the King produces documents proving that the fiscal crisis is real].

9. PARLEMENT'S REMONSTRATION AGAINST THE STAMP TAX (JULY 26, 1787)[11]

Although the Notables reluctantly approved the proposal to create local assemblies, they rejected the territorial subvention. Desperate for revenue, the government tried to get the Parlement to approve a stopgap extension of existing taxes. In addition, it created a new stamp tax, which it asked the Parlement to approve. Encouraged by the opposition of the Notables, the Parlement refused. Its remonstration against the

---

[11]Flammermont and Tourneux, *Remontrances du Parlement*, vol. 3, 674–675.

stamp tax shows how what had begun as a fiscal crisis had evolved into a debate over national sovereignty.

Alarmed by a deficit that seems to be growing enormously and by the disorders that produced and perpetuate it, [the Parlement] wishes to see the Nation assembled prior to any new tax. Informed of the true state of Finances, it alone can extirpate great abuses and offer great resources.

Only Your Majesty can restore the national assemblies that constituted the grandeur of Charlemagne's reign. . . . If ever the Nation had the right to nourish this hope, it is surely at this celebrated moment when authority has recognized that mystery is only suited to misdeeds and weakness; that the more force it has, the more confidence it should feel. . . .

The Notables have prepared the Nation for the return of this great and noble censure that it has so often exercised over itself, for those incredible sacrifices which seem to cost nothing when requested by a sensitive monarch at a time of real need.

Your Parlement believes that the moment has come to present to Your Majesty a wish dictated by the purest zeal. Yes, Sire, the monarch of France can never be grander than amidst his subjects. . . . All is to be gained from that union. . . .

IV. Radicalization and the Shifting Alignment of Political Conflict

The Parlement's opposition provoked a sharp government response. It exiled the magistrates in 1787 and, the following year, suppressed the court outright. But, as with the Maupeou coup, financial weakness eventually forced the government to back down. Its heavy-handed tactics dried up credit, and the disruption of the justice system made it difficult to enforce the payment of taxes. With his treasury empty, the King surrendered. On September 23, 1788, the royal government issued a declaration recalling the Parlement and convoking the Estates-General, the ancient representative body that had not met since 1614. The Parlement registered the declaration but added language to the effect that the Estates-General would be restored with the same social composition and voting procedures as during its last meeting 175 years earlier. At that time, it had been dominated by the clergy and nobility, and voting had taken place separately by social order, with each estate having a single vote and an absolute veto over any proposed laws.

Members of the Third-Estate reacted sharply. Many saw the Parlement's call for the "forms of 1614" as a maneuver to ensure that the privileged classes would dominate the Estates-General. In response, the Third Estate demanded greater representation for itself and voting by head. Far from calming the waters, therefore, the summoning of the Estates-General unleashed a struggle for political power between the privileged and nonprivileged orders. The Third-Estate's demands were discretely encouraged by the royal government, which hoped to regain control of events by winning the support of the people. After all, royal ministers thought, the cash-strapped government and the suffering people shared a common goal: to make the privileged pay their fair share of taxes.

But riding the tiger of popular discontent was a risky strategy, especially for a monarchy whose own credibility had suffered from years of Parlementary charges of "despotism." Ultimately, the people of France would formulate a new synthesis. Opting neither for the Crown nor the aristocracy, they would turn on both and claim sovereignty for themselves.

10. DELIBERATION TO BE TAKEN BY THE THIRD ESTATE IN ALL THE MUNICIPALITIES OF THE FRENCH KINGDOM (1788)[12]

This is one of the more influential pamphlets directed against Parlementary and aristocratic pretention. Note how it interweaves monarchical and popular strands.

While many Corps are uncertain about the nature and extent of their obligations to the Monarch, the Third-Estate, whose loyalty has never and will never undergo the slightest alteration, should display it again in the present circumstances.

Upon which, the Assembly applauding enthusiastically, unanimously decrees and recognizes:

1. That in France there is only one legitimate authority: the King.
2. That he alone is the Supreme Chief and sovereign Legislator of the Nation in all its foreign and domestic relations.
3. That sovereign power is indivisible and inalienable by nature, even independently of the will of the Monarch, who can only grant the partial use of it.
4. That there is no Corps, no individual, in the Nation whose authority the King cannot take back. . . .
5. That as sovereign Legislator, the King has supreme jurisdiction over the Kingdom; that he can reform or suppress the existing Tribunals at will, create new ones, limit or increase their powers, abolish and create laws on the administration of Justice, the manner of possessing and disposing of property, etc.
6. That consent or opposition to these laws by the Tribunals is alien to the will of the People, who are not represented by the Courts of Justice. . . .
7. That representations or remonstrance only exist because of the goodness

[12]*Délibération à prendre par le Tiers-Etat, dans toutes les Municipalités du Royaume de France* (1788).

and wisdom of the Kings [who may want] to know the observations of their Officers. . . .

9. That any suspension or modification [of the laws], whether before or after registration, is a maneuver against royal authority.

10. That any ruling against the manifest will of the King . . . is an attack on the sovereign Power.

11. That the violation of the profound respect owed to the King, depository of this Power, is a crime of high treason.

12. That anyone who charges that . . . the King of France is a despot, is perfidious or deceitful. A despot, who scorns the use of laws, governs only with acts of his own will which strike individuals and not the Nation. In contrast, the King of France, a true Monarch, governs only by laws which are considered to be emanations of the general will, which he represents, and which bear only upon the Nation, never individuals. . . .

14. That nevertheless there are fundamental laws which the Monarch cannot violate, such as those on the order of succession, the guarantee of property promised and owed by the Sovereign, the voluntary or presumed consent of property-owners to new taxes which necessarily diminish their properties, etc. etc.; but these properties do not include charges and offices which are but emanations of Power and thus revocable at will. . . .

11. PARLEMENT'S DENUNCIATION OF THE *DELIBERATION TO BE TAKEN* (DECEMBER 16, 1788)[13]

The Parlement took the Deliberation to be Taken *so seriously that it formally condemned it.*

[In this writing], can one fail to recognize a systematic spirit that is quietly preparing a revolution in the principles of Government? . . . We see this pamphlet as the first effect of an anarchy that is on the point of bursting forth, and if the guardian of the constitution does not hasten to preempt the effect of this sedition, it will become the source of the disorders that the system of equality seeks to introduce into ranks and conditions.

A cursory glance reveals vices and illusion; it entirely misunderstands the laws, denatures the truest principles, overthrows the most ancient corps, and even reduces the Estates-General to absolute powerlessness. In a word, it totally destroys the Constitution of the French Government, a constitution which has existed for so many centuries. . . .

---

[13]Flammermont and Tourneux, *Remontrances du Parlement*, vol. 3, 782–784.

One no longer hesitates to cast doubt on the earliest times of the Monarchy, the limits of sovereignty, the real separation of orders, the extent of privileges, in a word, on the rights of the assembled Nation. All these questions, which were previously problematic, are resolved according to the whim and character of writers. Wise institutions, which are the foundations of the Monarchy, are abolished. Laws requested by the Nation, granted by the Sovereign, and executed for entire centuries are no longer anything than empty illusions, spawned by ignorance and weakness. Our very principles, the separation of the three orders of the State, . . . are now viewed as the fruit of the errors of infancy or as the product of injustice made into law by force. . . .

Can one be so blind as to assert that the people alone constitutes the entire Nation, that only its interest must be consulted, that its consent alone suffices? Can we cast into oblivion the ancient form of our general assemblies? The distinction of the three orders, their right to deliberate separately, the equality of their respective suffrages? To destroy their respective independence, shatter this wise equilibrium, and give preponderance to the majority is to banish from society the spirit of concord which should suffuse all hearts. The power of the King, the rights of the Nation, public order are but a single thing called by different names; they have the same origin, strive for the same goal, and are all upheld by the observation of law. General happiness is the result of their reunion.

We cannot move too swiftly to proscribe a work, distributed in the shadows, whose principles, if adopted, will infallibly produce civil dissention and spark fatal troubles . . . which will be difficult to stop once the unconstitutional system of the predominance of the Third Estate has divided all the orders. . . . [It is imperative] . . . to discover the authors of a writing equally opposed to: royal power, whose holiness and character it denatures, to the Clergy and Nobility, whose prerogatives it effaces, to the interests of the Magistracy, whose offices it declares revocable at will, and, above all, to the interests of the People itself, who would be become the strongest support for an entirely new kind of despotism. . . .

12. ABBÉ SIEYES, *WHAT IS THE THIRD ESTATE?* (JANUARY 1789)[14]

The most influential intervention in the pamphlet war preceding the convocation of the Estates-General was What is the Third Estate? Written by a Catholic clergyman, the Abbé Sieyes, it redrew the parameters of the debate. Previously, the debate had pitted the King and nation against the aristocracy. Now Sieyes claimed power for the nation against both. He would soon go on to greater fame as a leading member of the revolutionary National Assembly.

---

[14]Abbé Sieyes, *Qu'est-ce que le Tiers État?* (n.p., 1789), 3–14, 28–32, 61, 104–142.

The plan of this writing is fairly simple. We have three questions:

1. What is the Third-Estate? EVERYTHING.
2. Until now, what has it been in the political order? NOTHING.
3. What does it want? To become SOMETHING.

Chapter One, "The Third-Estate is a complete nation"

What does a Nation need to subsist and prosper? Private works and public functions.

There are four types of private works [agriculture, industry, sales and distribution, and the scientific and liberal professions]. . . . Such are the works which uphold Society. Who does them? The Third-Estate.

Public functions can also be broken into four well-known classes: the word, the robe, the church, and the administration. It would be superfluous to examine them in detail to see that the Third-Estate performs nineteen-twentieths of them, with this one difference: that is does everything truly difficult, everything the privileged order refuses to do. The privileged only occupy lucrative and honorific positions. . . .

It has dared to lay an interdiction on the order of the Third. It has told it: "Whatever your services, whatever your talents, you will go only so far, but no farther. It is not right that you be honored. . . . "

If this exclusion is a social crime against the Third-Estate, is it at least useful to the public? . . . The supposed usefulness of a privileged order for the public service is but a chimera. Without it, everything difficult is carried out by the Third; without it, the superior places would be filled infinitely better. They should naturally be the reward of recognized talents and services. If the Privileged have succeeded in usurping all lucrative and honorific posts, it is both an odious injustice toward the generality of Citizens and treason against the public good.

Who would dare say that the Third-Estate does not contain within itself everything necessary to form a complete Nation? It is like a strong and robust man with one arm bound. If we remove the privileged order, the Nation would not be less, but rather more. What, then, is the Third? Everything—but an everything which is enchained and oppressed. What would it be without the privileged order? Everything, but an everything which would be free and flourishing. Nothing can work without it, everything would go infinitely better without the others.

It is not enough to have shown that the Privileged, far from being useful to the Nation, only weaken and harm it; we must also prove that the noble order is not even part of the social organization. . . .

What is a Nation? A body of Associates living under a common law and represented by the same legislature.

Is it not obvious that the noble Order has privileges, dispensations, even rights separate from the great body of Citizens? Because of this, it departs from the common order, the common law. Its civil rights thus make it a distinct People apart from the great Nation. It is truly a state within the state.

With regard to its political rights, it also exercises them apart. It has its own representatives who are in no way entrusted with the procuration of the People. Its deputies sit as a separate body; and even when it gathers in the same hall with the deputies of the simple Citizens, its representation is essentially distinct and separate. It is foreign to the Nation by its very essence, since its mandate does not come from the People, and by its purpose, which consists of defending not the general interest, but rather its particular interest.

The Third thus embraces everything that belongs to the Nation; and everything that is not the Third cannot claim to be the Nation. What is the Third? EVERYTHING. . . .

Chapter Three, "What does the Third-Estate want? To become something"

It wants to have true representatives at the Estates-General, which is to say, deputies drawn from its own Order who can interpret its wishes and defend its interests. What would be the point of attending the Estates-General if an interest contrary to its own predominated there? Its presence would only legitimize its oppression. It is thus clear that it can only participate in the Estates-General if its influence is at least equal to that of the Privileged and has a number of Representatives equal to those of the two other orders combined. But this equality of representation would be perfectly illusory if each chamber had a separate vote. The Third thus demands that votes be taken by head, not by Order. . . .

The Third-Estate's real intention is to have at the Estates-General an influence equal to that of the Privileged. Can it demand less? And is it not clear that if its influence is less than equal, it will have no hope of casting off its political nullity and becoming something?

But what is truly unfortunate is that the three articles which constitute the demand of the Third are insufficient to give it that indispensable equality of influence. Vainly it would obtain an equal number of Representatives drawn from its Order; the influence of the Privileged would install itself in and dominate the very sanctuary of the Third. Where are the posts, the employments, the benefices to give? On whose side is the need for protection; on which side lays the power to protect? . . .

It is impossible not to fear that the qualities necessary for the defense of the national interest will be prostituted. . . . The most intrepid defenders of the aristocracy will be in the Order of the Third-Estate and among men who, born with great intelligence but shallow souls, are more avid for wealth, power, and flattery than they are capable of understanding the value of liberty.

In addition to the power of the aristocracy, which controls everything in France, and feudal superstition, which still abases most souls, there is the influence of property. This is natural, and I don't condemn it; but we must agree that it is entirely to the advantage of the Privileged. . . . In the countryside and everywhere, is there a lord with even a slightly down-to-earth manner who does not have at his orders . . . an indistinct crowd of men of the People? . . .

Can the three Orders, as presently constituted, come together to vote by head? This is the crux of the matter. No. According to true principles, they cannot vote in common, either by head or by Order. Whatever proportion you adopt, it cannot meet our goal, which is to bind the totality of Representatives by a common will. . . .

Chapter 5, "What ought to have been done. Principles in this regard"

In all free Nations—and all Nations ought to be free—there is only one way of settling all disagreements over the constitution. Recourse must be had not to Notables, but to the Nation itself. . . .

The Nation exists before all else. It is the origin of everything. Its will is always legal; it is the Law itself. Before and above it, there is only natural law. If we want a correct idea of the series of positive laws that can emanate from its will alone, we first see constitutional laws, which are divided into two parts. The first regulate the organization and functions of the legislative body, the others determine the organization and functions of the different active bodies. These laws are called fundamental, not in the sense that they can become independent of the national will, but because the bodies which exist and act through them cannot touch them. In all of its parts, the constitution is not the product of constituted power, but rather of constituting power. No delegated power can change the conditions by which it was delegated. It is in this sense that constitutional laws are fundamental. The first, those which establish the legislature, are created by the national will before any constitution; they form the first degree. The second ones must be established by a special representative will. Thus, in the final analysis, all parts of the government respond to and depend upon the Nation. . . .

A Nation neither can nor should restrict itself to constitutional forms because, at the first disagreement that arises between the parts of that constitution, what would become of a Nation which could act only according to the disputed constitution itself? . . . It is essential in the civil order that Citizens find in a branch of the active power an authority to settle their lawsuits promptly. Similarly, the diverse branches of the active power should, among a free People, invoke the decision of the legislature in all unforeseen difficulties. But if your legislature itself, if the different parts of that first constitution, do not agree among themselves, who will be the supreme judge? For there must always be one, or anarchy will take the place of order.

How can one imagine that a constituted body could rule upon its own constitution? One or several integral parts of a moral body are nothing separately. Power belongs only to the totality. When one part is in disagreement, that totality exists no longer; and if it exists no longer, how can it judge? Thus, we must understand that there would no longer be a constitution in a country, at the slightest dispute among its parts, if the Nation did not exist independently of all constitutional rules and forms.

In the light of these clarifications, we can answer our question. It is clear that the parts of what you believe to be the French constitution are not in agreement.

It is thus up to whom to decide? The Nation, independently, as it always necessarily is, of all positive form. Even if the Nation had its regular Estates-General, this constituted Body could not rule on a dispute touching upon its constitution. . . .

It is time to return to the title of this Chapter, "What ought to have been done" in the midst of the troubles and disputes over the upcoming Estates-General. Appeal to the Notables? No. Let the Nation and its affairs languish? No. Maneuver among the interested parties to get them each to give up something? No. We have recourse to that grand means of extraordinary representation. It is that Nation that must be consulted.

Where can we find the Nation? Where it is: in the forty thousand parishes which embrace the entire territory, all its inhabitants, and all the tributaries of the republic. Doubtless the Nation is there. . . .

But, you will say, . . . what will become of the distinction of the three Orders? What will become of privileges? What they should be. The principles I have just laid out are clear. We must recognize them or renounce all social order. The Nation is always free to reform its constitution. Above all, it must give itself a clear one, when it is contested. Everyone agrees on this today. . . . A Corps subject to constituted forms can only decide things according to its constitution. It cannot give itself another one. It ceases to exist the moment it moves, speaks, and acts other than according to the forms that have been imposed on it. Even if assembled, the Estates-General would thus be incompetent to decide on the constitution. This right belongs to the Nation alone, free, as we have constantly repeated, of all forms and conditions.

As we see, the Privileged have good reasons to spread confusion. Today they brazenly argue the opposite of what they did six months ago. At that time, there was but one cry in France: "we don't have a constitution and we must form one." Today, we not only have a constitution, but, to believe the Privileged, it contains two excellent and unassailable dispositions. The first is the division of Citizens by Order; the second is equality of influence for each Order in the formation of the national will. We have already proven that even if all these things did form our constitution, the Nation would still be free to change them. It remains to examine more closely the nature of that equality of influence over the national will attributed to each Order. We will see that there is no Nation which can place anything like this in its constitution.

A political Society is nothing but a combination of Associates. A Nation cannot decide that it will not be the Nation. . . . Similarly, a Nation cannot decree that its common will cease being the common will. . . . Thus, a Nation can never decree that the right to the common will, which is to say, to the plurality, will be transferred to the minority. The common will cannot destroy itself. It cannot change the nature of things and make the opinion of the minority the opinion of the plurality. Clearly such a decree, rather than being a legal or moral act, would be an act of insanity.

Thus, if it is claimed that the French constitution has the power to give two-thirds of the common will to two or three hundred thousand individuals out of [a total of] twenty million Citizens, how can we respond except by arguing that two and two make five?

Individual wills are the only elements of the common will. One can neither deprive the majority of the right to participate in it nor decide that ten wills are only worth one against ten others which are worth thirty. These are contradictions in terms, veritable absurdities.

If we abandon, for the moment, the obvious principle that the common will is the opinion of the plurality, not the minority, it is useless to speak reason. We may just as well decide that the will of one will be called the plurality and there will no longer be a need for the Estates-General or the national will. For if one will can be worth ten, why should it not be worth one hundred, a million, twenty-six million? . . .

It is clear that, in the national representation, whether ordinary or extraordinary, influence can only be a function of the number of individuals who have the right to be represented. . . . Let us conclude . . . 1) that an extraordinary representation can alone modify the constitution or give us one, and 2) that this constituting representation should be formed without regard to the distinction of orders. . . .

Thus, no difficulty on the question, "what should have been done?" The Nation should have been convoked, so that it could send to the capital extraordinary representatives authorized to decide upon the constitution of the ordinary national assembly.

Chapter Six, "What Remains to be done. Development of some principles"

The time has passed when the three Orders, seeking only to protect themselves from ministerial despotism, were ready to join together against the common enemy. . . .

The Third-Estate would wait in vain for the other classes to restore its full political and civil rights. The fear of seeing abuses reformed inspires in the first two Orders more alarm than they desire liberty. Between it [liberty] and a few odious privileges, they have chosen the latter. Their soul has identified itself with the favors of servitude. Today they fear the Estates-General which they previously called for so loudly. Everything is now fine for them; they no longer complain of anything except the spirit of innovation. They lack nothing; fear has given them a constitution.

The Third-Estate must see . . . that its only hope lies in its own insight and courage. Reason and justice are on its side . . . No, it is no longer the moment to reconcile the different parties. What kind of agreement could one hope for, given the energy of the oppressed and the rage of the oppressors? They have spoken the word "scission." They have threatened the King and the People. Well! Good God, it would be wonderful for the Nation if this scission were permanent. How easy it would be to dispense with the Privileged! How difficult it would be to induce them to become Citizens! . . .

Given this, what remains for the Third to do if it wants to recover its political rights in a manner useful to the Nation? . . . The Third must assemble separately. It will not cooperate with the Nobility and Clergy. It will vote with them neither by order nor by head. I beg you to note the enormous difference between the Assembly of the Third-Estate and those of the two other Orders. The first represents twenty-five million men and deliberates on the interests of the Nation. Even joined together, the two others would only bear the mandate of two hundred thousand individuals and think only of their own privileges. By itself, you will say, the Third cannot form the Estates-General. Well, so much the better! It will form a National Assembly. . . .

13. MEMOIR OF THE PRINCES (DECEMBER 12, 1788)[15]

Alarmed by the growing radicalism of the Third-Estate, the royal princes (including two of the King's own brothers) warned of the danger facing the monarchy. Their dire predictions foreshadowed the content of the emerging ideology of counter-revolution.

Sire, the State is in peril; . . . a revolution in the principles of government is afoot. . . . Sacred institutions, through which the Monarchy has prospered for centuries, are now questioned or even decried as injustices. . . .

Everything presages a systematic plan of insubordination. . . . Mere writers set themselves up as Legislators; eloquence or literary skill . . . now seem sufficient titles to regulate the constitution of Empires. Whoever advances a daring proposition, whoever proposes changing the laws, is sure to have readers and followers.

This upheaval is spreading so fast that opinions that would have seemed most reprehensible only a short time ago today seem reasonable and just. . . . The rights of the Throne have been called into question. The rights of the two Orders of the State divides opinion. Soon the right of property will be attacked. Inequalities of wealth will be presented as a matter for reform. Already the suppression of feudal dues is proposed as the abolition of a system of oppression, the vestige of barbarous times. . . .

[The undersigned Princes] cannot hide the horror with which they view the success of the pretentions of the Third-Estate and the fatal consequences of the revolution it proposes for the constitution of the Estates [General]. . . .

Let the Third-Estate stop attacking the rights of the first two Orders, rights which are as old as the Monarchy and should be as unchangeable as its constitution. Let them be satisfied with asking for a reduction in taxes, with which they might be overburdened. Then the first two Orders, recognizing in the third

---

[15]M. J. Mavidal and M. E. Laurent, eds., *Archives Parlementaires de 1787 à 1860* [henceforth *AP*] (Paris: Société d'Imprimerie et Librairie Administrative P. Dupont, 1867–1879), série 1, vol. 1, 487–489.

Citizens who are dear to them, will be able, thanks to their feelings of generosity, to renounce their pecuniary prerogatives and consent to supporting the public charges with the most perfect equality. . . .

Let the Third-Estate understand what will ultimately result from the infraction of the rights of the Clergy and Nobility and the confusion of Orders. . . . The French Monarchy will degenerate into despotism or become a democracy. . . .

14. RESULT OF THE COUNCIL ON THE COMPOSITION OF THE ESTATES-GENERAL (DECEMBER 27, 1788)[16]

At the end of 1788, the government finally issued its long-awaited ruling on the upcoming Estates-General. It was profoundly ambiguous. Although it mandated that the deputies of the Third-Estate would be equal in number to those of the first two orders combined, it did not say whether voting would take place by head (in which case a single defection from the clergy or nobility would have given the majority to the Third-Estate) or separately by order (which would allow the two privileged orders to block reform). Rather than settling the ongoing contest for political power, the royal council had done little more than leave it to the Estates-General to decide on its own voting procedures.

Report Delivered to the King

Should the number of Third-Estate deputies be equal to that of the two other Orders combined? Or should that number form simply one-third of the total?

This important question, the most important of all, now divides the kingdom. . . .

The Third-Estate is being accused of wanting to encroach upon the first two Orders, but it is only asking for as many representatives . . . as the limited number of citizens who enjoy privileges or favorable exemptions.

The first two Orders would still have the ascendancy that comes from their superior social status and the various favors they can distribute, either by their own means or by the credit they have at Court and in the Ministries. . . .

Since the ancient [method of] deliberation by Order can only be changed by the three Orders together, . . . the number of Third-Estate deputies is, until then, only a means of bringing together knowledge useful to the State. One cannot deny that this knowledge belongs, above all, to the Third-Estate because there are a multitude of public affairs that it alone understands, such as the transactions of foreign and domestic commerce, the state of manufacturing, the best way to encourage it, public credit, interest, and the circulation of money, abuses in tax collection and privileges, and many other areas in which it alone has experience.

---

[16]*Rapport fait au Roi dans son conseil, par le ministre de ses finances* (Versailles, December 27, 1788) and *Résultat du Conseil d'Etat du Roi* (Versailles, December 27, 1788).

Public opinion will always support the cause of the Third-Estate. . . .

Even if there is no longer any inequality in the distribution of taxes, it would still be right to give the Third-Estate a numerous representations because the wisdom of the deliberations of the Estates-General, the goodness and justice of the Sovereign, should be announced and explained across the Kingdom . . . to enlighten and reinforce the confidence of 24 million men.

We place here a reflection: the disapproval of the first two Orders can easily bring down a minister. The discontent of the Third, however, does not have that power, but it sometimes undermines public love for the person of the Sovereign.

Finally, the will of the Third-Estate, when unanimous and in conformity with the general principles of equity, will always carry with it the national will. Time will consecrate it, the judgment of Europe will encourage it, and the just and wise Sovereign can only ordain . . . what circumstance and opinion will themselves bring about.

Result of the Council

1. The deputies to the forthcoming Estates-General will number at least 1,000.
2. This number will be formed, to the greatest extent possible, in proportion to the population and tax burden of each bailiwick.
3. The number of Third-Estate deputies will be equal to that of the two other Orders combined. . . .

V. The Nation Speaks

In the spring of 1789, the French began to prepare for the meeting of the Estates-General, scheduled to open in May at Versailles. Royal instructions directed the inhabitants of each bailiwick to assemble separately by social estate to elect representatives and write *cahiers de doléances* (lists of grievances) to guide their deliberations. The result was an unprecedented expression of the nation's complaints, hopes, and fears. The following documents are all cahiers from the bailiwick of Rouen, in Normandy.

15. CAHIER OF THE CLERGY OF ROUEN[17]

Every male member of the nonmonastic clergy was invited to attend his order's bailiwick assembly, participate in drafting its cahier, and vote for its representatives to the Estates-General. The voting regulation was remarkably democratic, with all participants, from lowly village priests to eminent prelates, entitled to one vote each. The monastic orders, including female ones, were represented collectively by proxy.

---

[17]Mavidal and Laurent, *AP*, vol. 4, 590–594.

Assembled by order of a sovereign who cherishes the love of his people, . . . we are called upon to treat the greatest interests of the nation. The constitutional status of the monarchy unknown or shaken, the criminal code stained with blood, . . . civil legislation obscure, contradictory, awkward, frustratingly slow, and ruinous by its cost; wounds which afflict the Church; abuses which dishonor it; enemies who insult it [by] . . . the ruses of sophism and all the impostures of calumny; the debts of the State accumulated without limit by a flawed administration . . . ; onerous taxes, infinitely varied, attached to all basic needs, arbitrarily distributed, imperiously demanded, . . . which devour all the resources of agriculture and weigh cruelly on that indigent part of the nation to whom Providence has given only labor to subsist; . . .

Such is the bare sketch of some of the abuses the King wants to have reformed. . . .

In consequence, the clergy of the bailiwick of Rouen gives its deputies the power to represent it at the Estates-General, while expressly directing them to exercise this inviolable power only according the clauses and in the spirit of the articles [following]:

1. The deputies will demand that the Catholic, Apostolic, and Roman religion continue to be the kingdom's only one, and that public worship not be permitted for non-Catholics.

2. The clergy of the bailiwick of Rouen does not protest against the legal and civil status accorded to non-Catholics by the recent edict; but its deputies will forcefully insist on the prohibition of mixed marriages. . . .

3. It has always been a law in the kingdom that Protestants baptize their children in [Catholic] parish churches. The deputies will insist on the re-establishment of that law.

4. To prevent the infinitely dangerous consequences of liberty of the press, the deputies will demand, in case that liberty is accorded despite the wish of the clergy, that all printers be obliged to place their names on the works produced by their press and that they be held responsible for false, defamatory, or scandalous facts in them, and that all authors, booksellers, or peddlers convicted of having composed or distributed works against religion or morality be condemned to severe penalties.

5. The deputies will demand that police officers enforce the ordinances on the observation of Sundays and holidays, as well as those rendered against cabarets and gambling, and that violators of those laws be prosecuted and punished. . . .

7. To maintain ecclesiastical discipline and order, the Church had wisely established the periodic assembly of provincial councils and assemblies of synods in the dioceses. The deputies will demand their re-establishment.

8. They will also demand the observation of the ancient and respectable laws that require benefice-holders to reside [in the place of their benefice], and also those . . . against the holding of multiple benefices. . . .

13. The deputies will demand the retention of the municipalities and that in the absence of the lord, they be presided over by the priest.

14. The deputies will expose the insufficiency of the pensions accorded to priests . . . [and demand] an augmentation. . . .

15. The deputies will also demand an augmentation in vicars' pensions. . . .

16. The deputies . . . will seek guaranteed retirement [pensions] for all urban and rural ecclesiastics who are infirm or who have grown old exercising the noble and respectable profession of religion and humanity.

18. The shackles that chain the liberty of the citizen, handing him over to the vexations and tyranny of the fisc, should be banished from a free State. It is thus most important that the deputies claim in favor of the clergy: 1) emancipation from the onerous taxes on the sale of ecclesiastical property; 2) freedom to issue leases privately, like all other subjects of the State; . . . 4) exemption for religious houses from all taxes on the dowries of girls who [become nuns]. . . .

25. The clergy of the bailiwick of Rouen, as penetrated by patriotic feeling as any other order of the State, consents that all of its properties be subject to pay to the State a sum equal to that paid by the equivalent properties of the other orders.

But determined to keep its ancient and respectable form of [autonomous fiscal] administration, . . . it neither wants nor intends to depart in any manner from it.

To reconcile this just pretention with its desire to contribute to the needs of the State like all the other orders, it expressly directs its deputies to demand:

1. That all the clergy's properties be evaluated conjointly by the three orders in the same manner . . . as the properties of all other subjects of the kingdom. This will prove the sincere willingness of the clergy to bear, in a perfectly equal proportion with the other citizens, the burden of the State. . . .

2. That after this evaluation has precisely determined the sum that the clergy should contribute as its proportional share of the needs of the kingdom, the distribution and imposition of this sum on the different members who compose the clergy will be left to the clergy itself . . . in the spirit of the ancient form.

26. The debts of the clergy, having been contracted for the needs of the State, should be folded into the national debt. It is only on this condition that the clergy of the bailiwick of Rouen consents to proportionally equal taxation.

27. The deputies will oppose any proposition to sell Church property to pay the debts of the Clergy.

28. The clergy of the bailiwick of Rouen declares that it wants to keep all personal and honorific rights it enjoys, and it directs its deputies to protest against anything that might harm the dignity of its order, divide it, or restrain it.

29. Since the Estates-General cannot gain a better understanding of the affairs of the clergy than through the knowledge of its agents, the deputies will demand that those agents be admitted to the Estates. . . .

30. The deputies will declare that the clergy intends to keep its assemblies, as the only barrier capable of stopping the excessive liberty of writing and morality, of opposing the progress of a deadly philosophy that daily multiplies its attacks against religion and the Church, and as necessary to maintaining its administration.

31. The bishops will have the right to attend the assemblies of the clergy, but the deputies will demand that representatives of the [lesser clergy] be elected to attend it, according to the form adopted for the Estates-General. . . .

33. The deputies will demand that the clergy's taxes be paid directly into the treasury of the provincial Estates. . . .

35. The deputies will seek the suppression of ruinous taxes, such as the salt tax. . . .

36. The deputies will propose to unify under a single denomination all taxes on land. . . . They will also consider the best way to establish a tax . . . on non-landed wealth and the properties of capitalists.

37. Since one of the principal objects of taxation should be paying off the national debt, the deputies will attentively discuss the nature of that debt, the causes and abuses that created and sustain it. They will measure the immense deficit [and] . . . determine the means of covering and guaranteeing the solidity of the debt.

38. The deputies will make all efforts to reestablish financial order and economy; suppress all useless expenses, charges, commissions, and superfluous positions; restrain pensions and bonuses; annul exchanges that have been ruinous to the Crown endowment; reduce interest to the legal rate; annihilate speculation . . . ; establish an administrative regime that will forever prevent the return of profiteering and finally . . . avoid creating new taxes that the people, already exhausted, are utterly incapable of bearing.

39. The deputies will examine the many loans in which the French ministry has imprudently placed its confidence. Instead of having healed the wounds of the State, they have been a failed palliative which has disguised the progress of the disease and made it almost incurable. To prevent future royal ministers from arbitrarily and excessively employing these ruinous methods and to secure public confidence, the deputies will declare that all loans judged necessary can only be taken out with the consent of the nation.

40. The deputies are specially charged with demanding the confirmation of the charter of the Duchy of Normandy . . . given by Louis X in 1315. . . .

41. The obscurity of civil legislation, its contradictions, the difficulty and slowness of its forms, the harshness of the criminal code, necessarily demand a reform. The deputies will ask for it; they will also emphasize the abuses of venality of office.

42. The deputies will demand that justices of the peace be established in each parish to judge minor contestations gratis. . . .

47. The heartbreaking plight into which the people have been cast by the high price and shortage of grain makes it absolutely necessary to adopt the wisest and quickest remedy. The deputies will demand that the export of grain be permitted only after the provincial Estates have verified that there is great abundance. . . .

49. The army is the glory and defense of the kingdom; it is the duty of the fatherland to improve its lot.

50. Agriculture is one of the State's most precious sources of wealth. Everything should be done to favor it; everything must remove the evils which halt its progress or diminish its fruits. The deputies will ask for the exact and severe execution of the wise regulations concerning hunting and pigeon-breeding rights.

51. Public instruction especially deserves the attention of the nation; the universities, high schools, and seminaries which form and perfect the talents which will one day honor and serve the State and religion are worthy of exciting the greatest interest. The deputies will ask the Estates to establish them in places where they seem necessary [and] consolidate them where they already exist; to improve their regime; to correct their abuses; to perfect their instruction and attend seriously to the morality and capacity of the teachers, and the progress of the students.

52. One's first instruction is acquired in primary schools. By multiplying them, we will spread their benefits to a greater number of individuals. The deputies will demand that they be established in all parishes where they are deemed necessary, with the approval and under the inspection of the priests.

53. The begging which fills the cities with vagabonds and the countryside with thieves and arsonists deserves the attention of the assembled nation. . . . The deputies will forcefully recommend [a remedy] . . . which can lead to the desired success; but they will recall that mendicants are men and that if justice requires that their disorders be repressed, humanity makes it a duty to provide for their needs.

54. Charity always pleads in favor of the unfortunate in the heart of the ministers of religion. . . . The prisons, frightful places where misery and infection reign, have often caught their attention. . . . Inspired by sentiments of Christian charity, the deputies will demand . . . that [the prisoners'] wants be eased and that their misfortunes be at least softened by the aid due to humanity.

55. Regarding the constitutional manner of voting in the national assembly, a question which will probably be discussed at the opening of the Estates-General, the deputies will ask to keep the ancient and constitutional custom of vote by order and not by head. . . .

These are the powers and instructions that the order of the clergy of the bailiwick of Rouen gives its deputies. . . . To guard against the insidious artifice in which perfidious courtiers too-often cover themselves in order to fool righteousness and betray good faith, the clergy believes it necessary to direct its deputies to consent to no tax until they have obtained the reestablishment of the Estates of Normandy . . . [and until] they have inviolably fixed a time for the second meeting of the Estates-General. . . .

16. CAHIER OF THE NOBILITY OF ROUEN[18]

As with the clergy, every adult male noble was allowed to participate personally in the bailiwick assembly of his order, according to the principle of one man, one vote. In addition, nonresident male nobles with fiefs in the bailiwick were allowed to participate by proxy, as were female nobles with local fiefs.

---

[18]Mavidal and Laurent, *AP*, vol. 4, 594–597.

The Estates General seemed to have been lost in the mists of time, never more to figure in the annals of the monarchy, . . . when a revolution prepared from afar by causes which we still ignore revived these constitutional assemblies which will soon regenerate the French nation. . . .

Its monarch will appear in their midst, less with the brilliance which surrounds him than in the guise of paternal goodness, which makes him reign over our hearts. . . .

These sentiments, which we share with all the orders of the kingdom, will be brought confidently before him by the nobility of the bailiwick of Rouen: they will be laid at the foot of the throne, in the presence of the assembled nation, in their *cahier* of demands. . . .

Before all else, the assembly charges its deputies with having the following articles recognized in the most authentic form:

French Constitution

1. That the French monarchy is essentially composed of the sovereign, in whose person resides undivided executive power, and the nation, whose free consent, expressed through the Estates-General and joined to the will of the prince, forms the legislative power.

2. That the crown is hereditary from male to male, in rank of age, among the princes of the reigning household.

3. That the nation is divided into three, mutually free orders [which are] so distinct and independent that one cannot be bound by the deliberations of the other two; thus, their deliberations can only take place by order and not in any other way.

4. That an explicit declaration assure the nation of the periodic return of the Estates-General. . . .

5. That no tax can be extended or collected . . . more than six months beyond the term fixed by the Estates-General for their periodic return, and that no loan can be contracted without their consent. . . .

7. That individual liberty, the first of all properties, be inviolably guaranteed.

8. That the reciprocal rights of the monarch and the nation be consigned in a constitutional and national charter . . .

Norman Constitution

9. That, to maintain the national constitution of the Duchy of Normandy, all rights, privileges, capitulations, treaties, and charters—and notably that given by Louis X in 1315—be confirmed anew. . . .

10. That all laws specific to the Duchy . . . can be promulgated only after the examination and free consent of the [provincial] estates. . . .

General Administration

12. The order specially charges its deputies to demand that no more [arbitrary royal arrest warrants] be issued against any citizen. . . .

13. That the motives for detaining people in castles and prisons be verified.

14. That anyone arrested be sent before his natural judges within 24 hours and, unless charged with a felony, be released on bail.

15. That the right of property be inviolable. . . .

16. That the secrecy of letters sent through the postal service be respected and that those convicted of an abuse in this domain be specially prosecuted.

17. That freedom of the press be granted. . . .

19. That the consent of the Estates-General be required for the reminting and alteration of metal coinage. . . .

20. That the rural police be expanded and placed under the authority of the provincial estates. . . .

22. That the Estates-General determine how to use the Crown endowment, and that the administration of its forests . . . be entrusted to the provincial estates. . . .

25. That all general laws proposed by the King and approved by the Estates-General, or proposed by the Estates-General and approved by the King, be sent to the provincial estates. . . .

30. The deputies will notably beg the King, Duke of Normandy, to convoke . . . a large assembly representative of the province. [This] will propose by order, and in no other manner, . . . the form of convoking its unjustly suspended estates, their composition, and the exercise of their powers, because the estates of the Duchy have the imprescriptible right to distribute the burden of taxation. . . .

Taxes

Before deliberating on taxes, the deputies will demand

31. That they be provided with exact and detailed accounts of revenues and expenditures and the size of the public debt . . . in order to determine the true financial situation.

32. After having acquired this preliminary information and adopted all possible means of cost-cutting, . . . the deputies are authorized to recognize and consolidate the national debt.

33. They will then consider the changes which should be made to the existing taxation system, will demand the abolition of the immoral game of the lottery, will solicit the suppression of the disastrous salt tax, will determine the taxes which can be kept, and do everything they can to make the capitalists and merchants pay their just share.

34. Taxation should be organized so that it not only establishes equilibrium between revenue and expenses, but also guarantees the exact payment of interest on the public debt and gradually reimburses its capital.

35. If, to fulfil this object and replace the taxes which are deemed disastrous, it becomes necessary . . . to consent to new taxes, the deputies will declare that the nobility does not have to give up any of its rights or prerogatives. . . .

36. Once the amount of taxation is determined, the deputies will demand that its distribution and collection be entrusted to the estates of each province. . . .

37. That the national debt be shared between the different provinces of the kingdom. . . .

40. That the Estates-General will, in their wisdom, decide upon the means of guaranteeing prompt and necessary aid in case of war or public calamity.

41. That all pensions be reduced; . . . that the list of them be published, with an explanation of the reasons why each recipient deserves the benefit he is enjoying. . . .

43. That the ministers be accountable and responsible to the Estates-General. . . .

Nobility

44. The deputies will demand that the units of the former Royal Household troops be reestablished as an economical way to give the nobility new occasions to show its inviolable love for the sacred person of the King and its ardent zeal for the service of the fatherland.

45. That a corps of gentlemen cadets particular to each province be created.

46. That noble religious and educational houses be established in favor of the nobility of both sexes of this province.

47. The repeal of the most recent military regulation, which reserves certain positions for a class of gentlemen designated "premier nobility," as that expression tends to divide an order which is essentially indivisible and whose members are all equal.

48. That the laws on the bearing of arms be strictly maintained and observed, and that non-military nobles can never carry swords, whatever their profession.

49. That the King be asked to suppress ennoblement [by venal office holding], or at least reduce it to personal nobility and, in future, to grant nobility only to a long series of services rendered to the State and recognized as sufficient by the provincial estates, or to striking actions judged as such by army and navy commanders.

50. The observation of the ordinances on the usurpation of titles and qualities.

51. May the tax on non-noble fief-holders be maintained.

52. The deputies will employ all means possible to have the Estates-General confirm the edict of 1680 which permits the nobility to engage in large-scale commerce. . . .

Instructions

53. The deputies will propose that [internal] customs barriers be pushed back to the frontiers.

54. That the strictest precautions be taken against the excessive price of grain.

55. That efficacious steps be taken immediately to help the inhabitants of the countryside, exposed without resources to sickness and the horrible depopulation it causes, and even more at the mercy of all the horrors of misery, both because of the exorbitant price of subsistence commodities and because of the loss of the principal means of their subsistence because of the commercial treaty with England.

56. That attention be paid to the militia, and its abuses be remedied. . . .

58. That the lot of the soldier be improved, and that he no longer be exposed to the humiliating punishment of blows with the flat of a saber.

59. That the troops be employed at road and canal building. . . .

62. That the Estates-General be asked to rule in the most positive manner on the status of non-Catholics. . . .

64. That in the future and under any pretext whatsoever, no exclusive privilege may be granted, nor any company be formed, harmful to commerce and the progress of the liberal and mechanical arts. . . .

Additional Cahier

1. That the King be asked not to grant multiple military positions to a single gentleman.
2. That the Cross of Saint-Louis be awarded to all officers without distinction after 24 years of service.
3. That, since there should be no differences within the order of nobility, military positions be awarded to seniority and not favoritism. . . .
4. That all pensions of 2,000 pounds and less granted to soldiers for grave wounds not be reduced. . . .
5. That the time that a gentleman has served as a common soldier be counted toward [that required to obtain] the Cross of Saint-Louis. . . .

17. CAHIER OF THE THIRD-ESTATE OF ROUEN[19]

The Third-Estate was deemed too numerous to participate personally in a single bailiwick assembly. Instead, villages and urban trade guilds met in preliminary assemblies to draw up cahiers and elect representatives to the bailiwick assembly. This second-stage assembly drew up the general cahier for the Third Estate and elected deputies to the Estates-General. The preliminary assemblies had a very large franchise, essentially all adult males. Some women even participated in these assemblies. But the representatives to the second-stage, bailiwick assembly tended to be drawn from the ranks of the wealthier and more educated, as were the deputies they sent to the Estates-General.

[19]Mavidal and Laurent, *AP*, vol. 4, 597–602.

National Constitution

Convinced that the principal source of the errors and abuses of the administration is the lack of a fundamental law that determines in a precise and authentic manner the effects of the national constitution and the respective limits of the different powers, the assembly desires that it be solemnly decreed at the upcoming Estates:

1. That France is a hereditary monarchy, from male to male in order of primogeniture; that the power to govern according to the laws resides exclusively in the King, as chief of the nation, and that legislative power belongs to the nation assembled in the Estates-General conjointly with the King.

2. That personal liberty is inviolable; that no citizen can be deprived of it except according to the law and by the judgment of the ordinary tribunals.

3. Since the liberty of communicating one's thought is an integral part of personal liberty, all citizens are allowed to print without censorship or hindrance, under the reservations and modifications which may be established by the Estates-General.

4. Since the liberty of letter-writing is also an integral part of personal liberty, the confidentiality of letters entrusted to the postal service is inviolable. . . .

5. That the property of each citizen is inviolable and that no one can be deprived of it except for the public interest, and then only with preliminary compensation. . . .

6. That the right of granting or extending taxes, authorizing loans, and creating offices with emoluments paid for by the public belongs exclusively to the nation assembled in the Estates-General.

7. That taxation . . . be equally supported by all, without distinction of rank or status, in proportion to one's properties and capacities.

8. That coinage can only be changed . . . with the consent of the Estates-General.

9. That the ministers are responsible to the nation. . . .

10. That the periodic return of the Estates-General is the right of the nation and should, in future, be the permanent administrative regime of the kingdom.

11. Each session of the Estates-General will treat all matters relative to the amount, nature, and collection of taxes, and to the legislation and administration of the kingdom. . . .

13. Provincial estates will be established in each province; their form and power will be determined by the Estates-General. . . .

14. That the judicial power, safeguard of liberty and property, be maintained in all of its activity . . . and that no act of arbitrary power either suspend or divert [its course]. . . .

15. In order to unshakably establish the national constitution on these essential foundations, the Estates-General will demand that the preceding articles be sanctioned by a law . . . before they take up any further object of deliberation.

Constitution of the Estates-General . . .

16. That the upcoming Estates-General declare that they alone can determine the form of future convocations, their composition, and their internal discipline.

17. They will then proclaim that, because the nation is now assembled in the Estates, it is thus reintegrated in the exercise of its rights. Their first act . . . will be to revoke all current taxes which have been established or extended without the consent or grant of the nation, and at the same instant consent to their continuation for the duration of their session only and until they have taken steps to ensure their replacement. . . .

19. That the Estates-General will determine the date of their future and successive assemblies. . . .

20. That they will determine the form of future convocations . . . for the citizens of all classes, so that no act or regulation of the executive power can interfere with national liberty.

21. That they will determine the future composition of the Estates-General, the proportion of the deputies between the orders, the form of discussion, the counting of votes, and the making of rulings. The desire of the present assembly, however, is for the vote by head, not order. . . .

Provincial Estates

The assembly considers the establishment of particular estates for each province as the necessary complement of the national constitution, and it is convinced that it is preferable that all the provinces join together to obtain them . . . through the wish and participation of the Estates-General, of which they will become a direct emanation, rather than to owe them merely to particular concessions that would unite them neither to one another by a common bond, nor to the national regime by a constitutional principle.

For this reason, the assembly desires:

23. That the Estates-General will decree that provincial estates be created or reestablished in the whole kingdom, and that their composition and powers be fixed in a uniform manner, except for modifications required by local circumstances.

24. That the provincial estates be composed of members freely elected in the provinces, charged with distributing taxes, collecting them, and depositing them directly into the royal treasury. . . .

25. That the provincial estates cannot contravene any ruling of the Estates-General. . . .

26. That the deputies of this bailiwick specially assert in all their force the particular rights of Normandy to have its estates reestablished, rights based on its original constitution, its charters, and the recent promises of His Majesty. . . .

Legislation . . .

30. That the deputies will demand, at the upcoming Estates-General, the confirmation of the Norman charter and the maintenance of the privileges it assures to the province.

31. That it be decreed that the laws prompted or approved by the nation in the Estates-General require only the national will and royal authority to be valid and obligatory throughout the kingdom.

32. That the laws sent . . . to the parlements and sovereign courts . . . be registered purely and simply, without modification or restriction. . . .

35. That civil law and judicial forms be reformed, in order to simplify procedures. . . .

36. That the penal code and criminal procedure also be reformed, so that trials are public, that the accused can be defended; . . . and that the penalty of property confiscation and those cruel tortures that do nothing but add useless and morally-revolting torment to the death penalty be abolished.

37. That penal laws apply equally to all guilty parties, without distinction of rank or birth. . . .

38. That the Estates find means of suppressing venality of magisterial office, so that future sovereign courts will be composed only of subjects elected and presented to the King by the provincial estates, in the same proportion between the three orders as that established for the formation of the Estates-General. . . .

Finances . . .

46. That [the deputies] will grant taxes only after the law on the constitution has been determined, accorded, and sanctioned. . . .

48. That the verification of expenses and the public debt will be conducted through the detailed examination of each type of expense and debt, in order to know the source of abuses. . . .

49. That all taxes . . . originate in the free concession of the Estates. . . .

50. That, in regards to all taxes without exception, it be expressly announced that they are only granted for the duration of the interval between sessions of the Estates . . . after which they will automatically stop. . . .

51. That no tax be retained or newly granted if it cannot be levied and distributed equally among all citizens, without distinction of order, rank, and status. . . .

56. That the account of public revenue and expenditure, and that of graces and pensions, with indication of the reasons which led them to be granted, be printed and made public each year.

Commerce, Manufacture, and Agriculture

57. That the King will be asked not to conclude any commercial treaty with foreign powers without having first consulted the chambers of commerce of the kingdom. . . .

58. That all remedies within the power of the administration . . . be sought to the actual disadvantages of the treaty of commerce concluded with England. . . .

65. That the collection of import and export duties be pushed back to the frontiers of the kingdom and that the tariff be so clear and the method of collection so simple that merchants can know exactly what they will need to pay. . . .

67. That the Estates-General determine the most efficacious methods of establishing uniformity of weights and measures across the kingdom. . . .

72. That in all artisanal and craft guilds, widowers and widows, as well as the sons of masters, be allowed to continue the profession, without being required to pay anything. . . .

75. That the vexatious and abusive militia regime, which diminishes the rural population and thus weakens the principal nerve of agriculture, be abolished.

76. That it be left up to the provincial estates to determine for each province . . . the period in which the exportation of grain may be permitted or prohibited.

77. That severe regulations address the damage caused by flocks of pigeons, above all at harvest and planting time, . . . and also the devastation caused by wild beasts.

78. That the impolitic and inhuman regime which prohibits the inhabitants of the countryside from having firearms to defend their houses and livestock be revoked. . . .

80. That the disorders caused by wandering beggars and the fear they cause, being one of the great plagues of the countryside, be dealt with [by measures] to suppress begging, and that . . . a portion of ecclesiastical property be used for its original purpose [of charity]. . . .

Objects Relative to the Nobility

85. That, in future, no venal charge confer hereditary nobility or even personal privileges. . . .

86. That, in future, ennoblement only be granted by the prince, for long and useful service to the State, as recognized . . . by the vote of the provincial estates. . . .

87. That the Estates-General decree that no obstacle prevent the citizens of the Third-Estate from occupying all charges and places whatsoever in all cases where constitutional equilibrium is not to be observed between the orders; and, reciprocally, that no employment or profession be incompatible with noble status.

Objects Relative to the Clergy

88. That the clergy be subjected to the same taxes and same method of collection as the two other orders, there being no reason to distinguish it from the others in everything concerning the advantages and charges of citizenship.

89. That bishops, abbots, and priors be required to reside in their diocese or place of their benefice, . . . and not be allowed to have a residence and maintain a household in any other city.

90. That the holding of multiple benefices be prohibited. . . .

94. That the collection of [the tithe] be fixed by a clear and precise regulation, in order to ease the burden it places on agriculture, . . . [and that] all priests be provided with revenue proportionate to the dignity, utility, and expenses of their profession.

18. CAHIER OF THE BARREL-MAKERS OF ROUEN[20]

This is the cahier from the barrel-makers' guild of the town of Rouen. It was typical of the guild cahiers forwarded to the bailiwick assembly.

Given the intentions of His Majesty, and to fulfill his benevolent intentions both for the good of his finances and the good of his people,

1. Salt should be an object of free commerce. . . .

2. The taxes on beverages being an even more burdensome object to the people . . . it would be more advantageous to the State and people to pay a single and unique duty. . . .

3. Let the order of nobility and the clergy be required to pay the same taxes . . . as the order of the Third Estate.

4. Suppression of the treaty of commerce with England, as being fatal to all manufacturing in the interior of the kingdom . . . and also the suppression of mechanical devices for the spinning of cotton and wool, which eliminate a number of occupations that many individuals once held [and who are now] reduced to begging.

5. The pushing back of customs barriers to the frontiers . . . in order to permit the free circulation of merchandise in the interior of the kingdom. . . .

6. Establishment of provincial estates which will report to His Majesty on the government and finances of their provinces.

7. May the tribunals render justice with more speed and integrity . . .

8. Encouragements for commerce, agriculture, and industry.

9. May masterships be made hereditary; . . . may widows occupy them for the duration of their widowhood; and may the sons of the master enjoy their fathers' privileges. . . .

10. Suppression of the fees masters have to pay guild inspectors . . . [which are sometimes] heavier than the main royal taxes.

19. CAHIER OF LE VAL DE LA HAYE[21]

This is the cahier from the primary assembly of Le Val de la Haye, a village inhabited by 140 families.

1. No exemptions for the clergy and nobility from any taxes whatsoever. . . . And in future, lords will no longer be able to levy [feudal dues on sales of land in their fiefs].

---

[20]Marc Bouloiseau, *Cahiers de Doléances du Tiers-Etats du bailliage de Rouen* (Paris: Presses universitaires de France, n.d.), vol. 1, 206–208.
[21]Bouloiseau, *Cahiers de Doléances*, vol. 2, 116–117.

2. Suppression of the salt tax and duties on beverages. . . .

3. Suppression of taxes for the repair and straightening of roads. . . .

4. Suppression of pigeon-houses . . . which do considerable harm to the sowing and harvesting of all grains and plants; may property-owners to whom they cause damage be allowed to destroy them.

5. Suppression of the water and forest courts. . . .

6. May all newly-created seigneurial jurisdictions be suppressed. . . . It is of the greatest necessity to reform the criminal code, so that the accused is free to choose a lawyer-councilor for himself. . . .

7. Suppression of the Custom of Caux. [22]

8. Suppression of cotton spinning machines because they do considerable harm to the cotton-spinning girls who are put out of work and reduced to begging.

9. It is absolutely necessary to make the large farmers furnish grain to the markets. May commissioners be appointed to force them to do it, [because] its exorbitant price . . . makes it impossible for the poor to survive.

10. That rural bakers be required to mark their bread, note its weight, and follow the [bread] regulations of Rouen. . . .

11. May all the taxes known by the names of *taille*, *capitation* and accessories, *vingtièmes*, and others be combined into a single article.

12. May all who live on the edge of the forest be allowed to pasture their livestock there. . . .

---

[22]A local inheritance regime which, in contrast to that in the rest of Normandy, mandated primogeniture.

CHAPTER 6

The French Revolution

The political crisis triggered in 1787 by the collapse of the French state's finances possessed a dynamic of seemingly inexorable radicalization. Dire circumstances—not just the fiscal chaos, but other issues ranging from climactic conditions to domestic and foreign opposition—helped drive this dynamic. But it also drew energy, perhaps most of its energy, from the radicalism of revolutionary principles themselves: liberty, equality, and fraternity. These aspirational ideals had—and still have—a capacious, expansive quality that opened the realm of political and social inclusion to marginalized groups such as religious minorities, the poor, people of color, and (to a lesser extent) women. The idea of universal natural rights challenged the older notion of socially differentiated rights rooted in history and custom. The bitter opposition of those attached to these traditional rights fed the Revolution's sense of embattlement and undermined attempts to consolidate its gains on a peaceful, stable footing. Only when an ambitious general, Napoleon Bonaparte, seized power in 1799 did France begin to emerge from the bloody dialog between revolution and counterrevolution, albeit at the cost of political liberty. Yet not all was lost. Legal equality was preserved under Napoleon. And political liberty started a slow comeback after his downfall. Although the Revolution itself last only ten years, it planted hardy seeds that would ultimately flourish.

I. From Estates-General to the National Assembly

The Estates-General opened in May 1789. There was an almost millennial sense of optimism among the deputies who gathered at Versailles and the country at large. All believed that France would be "regenerated" by the unified efforts of the three estates. These expectations were soon dashed. The royal council had left it up to the Estates themselves to decide on their method of voting—jointly or separately by order—but there was no consensus. The Third-Estate insisted on a vote by head in a single assembly, while the two privileged orders withdrew into separate chambers and refused to join the Third. Far from regenerating France, the Estates-General found itself paralyzed, locked in a poisonous stand-off. In the course of the stalemate, the Third-Estate declared itself to be the National Assembly and claimed sovereignty for the nation (which it claimed to represent). Matters were only settled in mid-July 1789, when the city of Paris rose to defend both itself and the National Assembly from a suspected royal military coup. From that point on, the three orders would meet together as the National Assembly to abolish old abuses and design a new regime for France.

1. ARTHUR YOUNG, *TRAVELS IN FRANCE* (1789)[1]

The political crisis that unfolded as the Estates-General painfully transformed itself into the National Assembly fascinated French and foreign observers. The best account is that of Arthur Young, a British agronomist who was travelling in France at that time and actually attended several of the key meetings of the Estates in Versailles.

June 8 [1789]. Paris is at present in such a ferment about the States General. . . . Not a word of any thing else talked of. Every thing is considered, and justly so, as important in such a crisis of the fate of four-and-twenty millions of people. It is now a serious contention whether the representatives are to be called the Commons or the Tiers Etat; they call themselves steadily the former, while the court and the great lords reject the term with a species of apprehension, as if it involved a meaning not easily to be fathomed. But this point is of little consequence, compared with another, that has kept the states for sometime in inactivity, the verification of their power separately or in common. The nobility and the clergy demand the former, but the Commons steadily refuse it; the reason why a circumstance, apparently of no great consequence, is thus tenaciously regarded, is that it may decide their sitting for the future in separate houses or in one. Those who are warm for the interest of the people declare that it will be impossible to reform some of the grossest abuses in the state, if the nobility, by sitting in a separate chamber, shall have a negative on the wishes of the people: and that to give such a veto to the clergy would be still more preposterous; if therefore, by the verification of their powers in one chamber, they shall once come together, the popular party hope that there will remain, no power afterwards to separate. The nobility and clergy foresee the same result, and will not therefore agree to it. . . . The king, court, nobility, clergy, army, and parliament, are nearly in the same situation. All these consider, with equal dread, the ideas of liberty, now afloat; except the first, who, for reasons obvious to those who know his character, troubles himself little, even with

---

[1]Arthur Young, *Travels, During the Years 1787, 1788, and 1789* (Bury St. Edmunds, England: J. Rackham, 1792), 102–140.

circumstances that concern his power the most intimately. Among the rest, the feeling of danger is common, and they would unite, were there a head to render it easy, in order to do without the states at all. That the commons themselves look for some such hostile union as more than probable, appears from an idea which gains ground, that they will find it necessary should the other two orders continue to unite with them in one chamber, to declare themselves boldly the representatives of the kingdom at large, calling on the nobility and clergy to take their places— and to enter upon deliberations of business without them, should they refuse it. All conversation at present is on this topic, but opinions are more divided than I should have expected. There seem to be many who hate the clergy so cordially, that rather than permit them to form a distinct chamber would venture on a new system, dangerous as it might prove.

June 9. The business going forward at present in the pamphlet shops of Paris is incredible. I went to the Palais Royal to see what new things were published, and to procure a catalogue of all. Every hour produces something new. Thirteen came out to-day, sixteen yesterday, and ninety-two last week. . . . This spirit of reading political tracts, they say, spreads into the provinces, so that all the presses of France are equally employed. Nineteen-twentieths of these productions are in favour of liberty, and commonly violent against the clergy and nobility. . . . Is it not wonderful, that while the press teems with the most levelling and even sedi-tious principles, that if put in execution would overturn the monarchy, nothing in reply appears, and not the least step is taken by the court to restrain this extreme licentiousness of publication. It is easy to conceive the spirit that must thus be raised among the people. But the coffee-houses in the Palais Royal present yet more singular and astonishing spectacles; they are not only crowded within, but other expectant crowds are at the doors and windows, listening [rapt] to certain orators, who from chairs or tables harangue each of his little audience: the eager-ness with which they are heard, and the thunder of applause they receive for every sentiment of more than common hardiness or violence against the present govern-ment, cannot easily be imagined. I am all amazement at the ministry permitting such nests and hotbeds of sedition and revolt. . . .

June 11. There seem to be no settled ideas of the best means of forming a new constitution. Yesterday the Abbé Sieyes made a motion in the house of commons, to declare boldly to the privileged orders, that if they will not join the commons, the latter will proceed in the national business without them; and the house de-creed it, with a small amendment. This causes much conversation on what will be the consequence of such a proceeding; and on the contrary, on what may flow from the nobility and clergy continuing steadily to refuse to join the commons, and should they so proceed, to protest against all they decree, and appeal to the King to dissolve the states, and recall them in such a form as may be practicable for business. In these most interesting discussions, I find a general ignorance of the principles of government; a strange and unaccountable appeal, on one side, to ideal and visionary rights of nature; and, on the other, no settled plan that shall give security to the people for being in future in a much better situation than hitherto;

a security absolutely necessary. But the nobility, with the principles of great lords that I converse with, are most disgustingly tenacious of all old rights, however hard they may bear on the people; they will not hear of giving way in the least to the spirit of liberty, beyond the point of paying equal land-taxes, which they hold to be all that can with reason be demanded. The popular party, on the other hand, seem to consider all liberty as depending on the privileged classes being lost, and out-voted in the order of the commons, at least for making the new constitution. . . .

June 13. This morning in the states three curés of Poitou have joined them-selves to the commons, for the verification of their powers, and were received with a kind of madness of applause; and this evening at Paris nothing else is talked of. . . .

June 15. This has been a rich day, and such an one as ten years ago none could believe would ever arrive in France; a very important debate being expected on what, in our house of commons, would be termed the state of the nation. My friend, Mons. Lazowski and myself were at Versailles by eight in the morning. We went immediately to the hall of the states to secure good seats in the gallery; we found some deputies already there, and a pretty numerous audience collected. The room is too large; none but stentorian lungs, or the finest clearest voices can be heard; however the very size of the apartment, which admits 2000 people, gave a dignity to the scene. It was indeed an interesting one. The spectacle of the rep-resentatives of twenty-five millions of people, just emerging from the evils of 200 years of arbitrary power, and rising to the blessings of a freer constitution, assem-bled with open doors under the eye of the public, was framed to call into animated feelings every latent spark, every emotion of a liberal bosom. To banish whatever ideas might intrude of their being a people too often hostile to my own country—and to dwell with pleasure on the glorious idea of happiness to a great nation—of felicity to millions yet unborn. Mons. l'Abbé Sieyes opened the debate. He is one of the most zealous sticklers for the popular cause; carries his ideas not to a regula-tion of the present government, which he thinks too bad to be regulated at all, but wishes to see it absolutely overturned; being in fact a violent republican. . . . His motion, or rather string of motions, was to declare themselves the representatives known and verified of the French nation. . . .

In regard to their general method of proceeding, there are two circumstances in which they are very deficient: the spectators in the galleries are allowed to in-terfere in the debates by clapping their hands, and other noisy expressions of ap-probation: this is grossly indecent; it is also dangerous; for, if they are permitted to express approbation, they are, by parity of reason, allowed expressions of dissent; and they may hiss as well as clap; which, it is said, they have sometimes done:—this would be to over-rule the debate, and influence the deliberations. Another circumstance is the want of order among themselves; more than once to-day there were an hundred members on their legs at a time. . . .

June 18. Yesterday, the commons decreed themselves, in consequence of the Abbé Sieyes's amended motion, the title of Assemblée Nationale; and also, consid-ering themselves then in activity, the illegality of all taxes; but granted them during the session, declaring that they would, without delay, deliberate on the consolidating of the debt; and on the relief of the misery of the people. These steps give great spirits to the violent partizans of a new constitution, but amongst more sober minds, I see evidently an apprehension, that it will prove a precipitate measure. It is a violent step, which may be taken hold of by the court, and converted very much to the peoples' disadvantage. . . .

June 20. News! News! Every one stares at what every one might have expected. A message from the King to the presidents of the three orders, that he should meet them on Monday; and, under pretence of preparing the hall for the séance royale, the French guards were placed with bayonets to prevent any of the deputies entering the room. The circumstances of doing this ill-judged act of violence have been as ill-advised as the act itself. . . . The resolution taken on the spot was a noble and firm one; it was to assemble instantly at the Jeu de Paume, and there the whole assembly took a solemn oath never to be dissolved but by their own consent, and consider themselves, and act as the national assembly, let them be wherever violence or fortune might drive them. . . .

June 21st. The present moment is, of all others, perhaps that which is most pregnant with the future destiny of France. The step the commons have taken of declaring themselves the national assembly, independent of the other orders, and of the King himself, precluding a dissolution, is in fact an assumption of all the authority in the kingdom. They have at one stroke converted themselves into the long parliament of Charles I. It needs not the assistance of much penetration to see that if such a pretension and declaration are not done away, King, lords, and clergy are deprived of their shares in the legislature of France. . . . If it is not opposed, all other powers will lie in ruins around that of the common. . . .

June 23. The important day is over: in the morning Versailles seemed filled with troops. . . . This military preparation was ill judged, for it seemed admitting the impropriety and unpopularity of the intended measure, and the expectation, perhaps fear of popular commotions. They pronounced, before the King left the chateau, that his plan was adverse to the people, from the military parade with which it was ushered in. The contrary, however, proved to be the fact. . . . The plan was a good one; much was granted to the people in great and essential points. . . . I apprehend the deputies will accept them conditionally: the use of soldiers, and some imprudencies in the manner of forcing the King's system, relative to the interior constitution, and assembling of the deputies, . . . prevented the commons from receiving the King with any expressions of applause; the clergy, and some of the nobility, cried Vive le Roi! But treble the number of mouths being silent, took off all effect. It seems they had previously determined to submit to no violence: when the King was gone, and the clergy and nobility retired, the Marquis de Brézé waiting a moment to see if they meant to obey the King's express orders, to retire also to another chamber prepared for them, and perceiving that no one moved, addressed them—["Messieurs, you have heard the King's intentions']. A dead silence ensued; and then it was that superior talents bore the sway, that overpowers in critical moments all other considerations. The eyes of the whole assembly were turned on the count de Mirabeau, who instantly replied to the Marquis de Brézé—["Yes, Monsieur, we have heard the intentions that have been suggested to the King, and you, who are but his spokesman to the Estates-General, you who have neither place nor vote nor right to speak, you who have no right to recall to us his discourse. . . . I declare to you that if you have been directed to make us leave, you should go ask for orders to employ force, because we will only leave our places if forced to by the power of the bayonet"] . . . They then immediately passed a confirmation of their preceding [resolutions]; and, on the motion of the count de Mirabeau, a declaration that their persons, individually and collectively, were sacred; and that all who made any attempts against them should be deemed infamous traitors to their country.

June 24. The ferment at Paris is beyond conception; 10,000 people have been all this day in the Palais Royal; a full detail of yesterday's proceedings was brought this morning, and read by many apparent leaders of little parties, with comments, to the people. To my surprise, the King's propositions are received with universal disgust. He said nothing explicit on the periodical meeting of the states; he declared all the old feudal rights to be retained as property. These . . . give the greatest offence. . . . The people seem, with a sort of phrenzy, to reject all idea of compromise, and to insist on the necessity of the orders uniting, that full power may consequently reside in the commons, to effect what they call the regeneration of the kingdom, a favourite term, to which they affix no precise idea, but add the indefinite explanation of the general reform of all abuses. . . . It is plain to me, from many conversations and harangues I have been witness to, that the constant meetings at the Palais Royal, which are carried to a degree of licentiousness and fury of liberty, that is scarcely credible, united with the innumerable inflammatory publications that have been hourly appearing since the assembly of the states, have so heated the peoples' expectations, and given them the idea of such total changes, that nothing the King or court could do, would now satisfy them. . . .

June 25. Yesterday at Versailles, the mob was violent. They insulted, and even attacked all the clergy and nobility that are known to be strenuous for preserving the separation of orders. The Bishop of Beauvais had a stone on his head, that almost struck him down. The archbishop of Paris had all his windows broken, and forced to move his lodgings; and the cardinal de la Rochefoucauld hissed and hooted. The confusion is so great that the court have only the troops to depend on; and it is now said confidently, that if an order is given to the French Guards to fire on the people, they will refuse obedience. . . .

June 26. Every hour that passes seems to give the people fresh spirit: the meetings at the Palais Royal are more numerous, more violent, and more assured; and in the assembly of electors, at Paris, for sending a deputation to the National Assembly, the language that was talked, by all ranks of people, was nothing less than a revolution in the government, and the establishment of a free constitution: what they mean by a free constitution, is easily understood—a *republic*; for the doctrine of the times runs every day more and more to that point; yet they profess that the kingdom ought to be a monarchy too; or, at least, that there ought to be a king. . . . The supineness, and even stupidity of the court, is without example: the moment demands the greatest decision—and yesterday . . . the king went a hunting! . . . It is now understood by every body, that the King's offers, in the séance royale, are out of the question. The moment the commons found a relaxation, even in the trifling point of assembling in the great hall, they disregarded all the rest, and considered the whole as null. . . . They lay it down for a maxim, that they have a right to a great deal more than what the King touched on, but that they will accept of nothing as the concession of power; they will assume and secure all to themselves, as matters of right. . . . If the commons are to assume every thing as their right, what power is there in the state, short of arms, to prevent them from assuming what is not their right? . . .

June 27. The whole business now seems over, and the revolution complete. The King has been frightened by the mobs into overturning his own act of the séance royale, by writing to the presidents of the orders of the nobility and clergy, requiring them to join the commons. . . . The joy this step occasioned was infinite; the assembly, uniting with the people, all hurried to the chateau. Vive le Roi might have been heard at Marly: the King and Queen appeared in the balcony, and were received with the loudest shouts of applause. . . . I have to-day had conversation with many persons on this business; and, to my amazement, there is an idea, and even among many of the nobility, that this union of the orders is only for the verification of their powers, and for *making the constitution*, which is a new term they have adopted. . . . In vain I have asked, Where is the power that can separate them hereafter, if the commons insist on remaining together, which may be supposed, as such an arrangement will leave all the power in their own hands? . . . All real power will be henceforward in the commons, having so much inflamed the people in the exercise of it, they will find themselves unable to use it temperately; the court cannot sit to have their hands tied behind them; the clergy, nobility, parliaments, and army will, when they find themselves all in danger of annihilation, unite in their mutual defence; but as such an union will demand time, they will find the people armed, and a bloody civil war must be the result. . . . The tide now runs so strongly in favour of the people, and the conduct of the court seems to be so weak, divided, and blind, that little can happen that will not clearly date from the present moment. . . .

II. Dismantling the Old Regime

Although the uprising of Paris in July 1789 secured the victory of the Third Estate and completed the transformation of the Estates-General into the National Assembly, the structure of what was beginning to be called "the Old Regime" was still intact. It was not at all clear if the deputies were yet considering demolishing it. In the two weeks following the taking of the Bastille, they focused on discussing the abstract principles on which to base a constitution. But the showdown between the Third-Estate and the privileged orders had alarmed the countryside. In the second half of July, rural communities began to stir, arming themselves against "brigands" (supposedly sent by their lords to oppress them), destroying feudal property titles, and even burning down chateaux. The disorder in the country-side spread like wildfire across most of France, eventually acquiring the name "the Great Fear" and spurring the Assembly to action.

2. A WIGMAKER RECOUNTS THE GREAT FEAR AT CREMIEU (1789)[2]

Although the Great Fear affected most of rural France, one of its epicenters was the southeastern province of Dauphiné, at the foothills of the Alps. An inhabitant of the small Dauphinois town of Cremieu, Jean-François Ollivet, a wigmaker by trade, lived through it and recorded what he observed in his diary.

Monday, July 27, 1789 at 9 PM, there was the most terrible alarm at Cremieu. In a dark and rainy night, Monsieur Laloge, vicar of Vessilieux, arrived at a gallop, saying that 10,000 Savoyards had entered France; that La Tour du Pin and Bour-goin had been fired and put to the sword. At the same instant, all the church bells of Cremieu began to ring; all the citizens believed they were doomed; the entire city armed itself with rifles, pitchforks, halberds, tridents—in a word, everything they could find to defend themselves. The gates of the city were shut and all the citizens passed the cruelest night that one could ever imagine. No one slept.

At 10:30 PM, Monsieur Perrin, the royal notary of St. Marcel, sent a servant with a letter . . . saying that this Savoyard troop had pillaged and burned from Pont de Beauvoisin to Bourgoin. I was present when the letter was read.

This doubled the panic at Cremieu. After having run hither and thither all night long, day finally arrived.

At dawn, a quantity of stones were hauled on top of the city gates, so that they could be thrown down at the enemies when they arrived at Cremieu. During that terrible night, all the women and children cried for mercy.

The city of Bourgoin was alerted at 9 PM by the business agent of Madame de Valin, who said that the Savoyards were burning and killing everything. The bells were rung; many men from the parishes where the bells were ringing gathered at Bourgoin (8,000), armed with rifles, pitchforks, and tridents. They spent the night at Bourgoin. The officers gave them food and drink. The next day, seeing that the enemy wasn't coming, they dispersed, troop by troop. After having burned on the town square all the papers and feudal land records they could find in the chateaux of Bourgoin and in the offices of the local notaries, these unfortunates concluded

---

[2]Archives départementales de l'Isère, 1 J 372, Jean-François Ollivet, "Chronique des évenements qui se sont produits à Cremieu au début de la Révolution."

that the lords and nobles were the reason why they had come to Bourgoin and that their chateaux should be burned down.

They began to burn the chateau of Monsieur de Vaux at Vaulx; from there, they went on to pillage and loot Monsieur de Vaulx's at La Verpillière. Note: these unfortunates forcibly seized Monsieur de Rival, lieutenant of the rural police, at Bourgoin. A pistol at his throat, they led him to the chateau of Vaulx, which they set on fire.

The same day, the 28th, they came to Monsieur de Loran at Chamagnieu. They did not burn the chateau, but damaged, stole, and pillaged. In a word, they didn't leave anything, not even a nail. The chateau of Monsieur de Vayre at Bonne underwent the same carnage. They even tried to burn it three times, but it would not catch. Some of the local people put the fire out.

During the night of the 28th to 29th they set fire to that of Madame de Poisieur at Sammeyriat, at 10 PM to that of Monsieur de Pusignan at Pusignan; from there to Monsieur the Abbot de Josse; from there to that of Jonage, but the fire would not catch. Some people put it out.

During the day of the 29th, they set fire to that of Monsieur de Meydieu at Villette; then to that of Monsieur de Combes at Anthon. These two chateaux were reduced to ashes. Nothing remained but the outside walls. Then these unfortunates went to the Carmelite Brothers at Chavanoy. They took 25 pounds worth of wine, but they did not set [the monastery] on fire. The same day, Wednesday the 29th, they went to Vernay, to Monsieur Le Baron; after having stolen and pillaged, they set his chateau on fire. The fire was set at 7 PM.

The same day about forty of these brigands went to Monsieur Montlevoux's chateau, Bienassis. They broke windows and some dishes and bottles. They stole and pillaged.

At about the same moment, a similar troop went to Monsieur Bovet at La Tour de Moras, to Monsieur de Veyssillieux in his chateau, to Lozan to Monsieur de Peret's, to St. Marcel at Monsieur de Loran's. They did not set fire, but they broke, damaged, and stole all the furniture, as well as the wine cellar. . . . The same day, the 29th, the chateau of the Marquis de la Poepe at Hière was set on fire; it was reduced to ashes, except for the outside walls which were as black as a chimney. The fire was set at 10 PM. That same night, they set fire to the chateau of Monsieur de Rachais, at Amblerieu, near La Balme.

The next day, the 30th, they went to the Chartreuses of Salette. They wanted to set it on fire, but in exchange for 1,000 ecus,[3] they agreed not to.

The same day, around 10 AM, three companies of the urban guard of Lyon arrived. After a drink, they set off with two dragoons of the Regiment of Monsieur. They went as far as Salette. There, they killed several brigands. . . . With the aid of the militia of Cremieu, these gentlemen arrested 60 men and 5 women. They were imprisoned at Cremieu. Most were tied together with ropes; the others were tied to

[3]3,000 French pounds.

the wagons, all wounded, some by gunshots, others by blows from rocks or sabers. It was horrifying.

The same day, at 11 PM, a wagon arrived from Salette, full of these unfortunates; it was covered with blood.

Friday the 31st, these unfortunates, numbering 59 men and 5 women, were taken to Loyette . . . and from there to the prison at Lyon. One, who had received a saber blow to the throat, had to stay at the Cremieu hospital. He died several days later.

All these unfortunates came from Cremieu and surrounding villages; some were fathers who left behind wives and children.

From Provence to Dauphiné, alarm bells were tolling everywhere. We could not understand from whence the alarm had come. All night long, the local peasants . . . hid in the woods with their wives and children. Bells tolled near Cremieu. We had three alerts that week. Alarm bells even tolled in broad daylight. One would have thought that the enemy was on the point of burning Cremieu. . . .

The gates of the city remained closed from July 27th through August 5th, when we began to reopen them. . . . All strangers who arrived were led by the rifleman of the guard to the room of M. de Chapponay (now deceased). There, a permanent committee was established which asked where they were going and where they came from.

3. THE MARQUIS D'AGOULT DESCRIBES THE NIGHT OF AUGUST 4TH[4]

When the National Assembly learned of the violence in the countryside, its initial reaction was to respond with tough law-and-order measures. But a group of more radical deputies seized the opportunity of the Great Fear to engineer a dramatic abolition of the feudal order. At the nighttime session of August 4th, two of them, the Viscount de Noailles and the Duke d'Aiguillon, voluntarily renounced their feudal rents. This prompted other deputies, from all three orders, to renounce privileges of their own—venal office, exclusive noble access to prestigious professions, court pensions, provincial privilege, the ecclesiastical tithe, and much more. By the time the session came to an end at 2 AM, the Old Regime was no more.

Yesterday, at 8 AM, we gathered at the Archbishop's. There, we read news of the disorders in the province. After some discussion, everyone was convinced that a law from the Assembly was needed to give force to the magistrates, as well as an order to the troops and urban militias to do all within their power to help them. This was proposed, but the hatred of the parlements, as well as the faction that we

---

[4]Archives départementales de l'Isère, 1 MI 461/2, Letter from the Marquis d'Agoult to the Marquis de Viennois (Versailles, 4 August 1789).

have in our assembly, united to that of Paris, opposed it with all their forces because, if the troubles were to cease, they would lose their influence. You will see by the end of this letter that, without the terror they inspire in the wealthy of the first two orders, they would perhaps not have obtained the sacrifices that were made yesterday evening. . . .

At 7 PM yesterday there was an extraordinary assembly to make a new declaration. Everyone was sad because we could see that this would not amount to much. The Viscount de Noailles and Duke d'Aiguillon made a motion to consent to the reimbursement of their [feudal] rents. This caused much pleasure and was received with applause. Another came and [offered to sacrifice] personal rights and forced labor service which would be reimbursed according to their value. More applause and emotion burst forth. A deputy proposed abolishing pigeon houses and hunting privileges (like the preceding ones, a motion made by nobles). Still more applause and great joy. Another proposed abolishing seigneurial justice; the priests renounced their fees. At this point, everybody lost their heads. The bishops proposed replacing the tithe by a reimbursable contribution in silver; the members of the parlements proposed making justice free and abolishing venality of office. Embarrassed and wanting to do something agreeable to the Assembly, we renewed the abandonment of the particular privileges of the province and declared that we wanted to bear equally both the charges and advantages of the French. . . . the Bretons did the same, [as did] Languedoc, Bourg, Franche-Comté, Loraine, Alsace, Artois, Normandy, the city of Bordeaux, Marseille, Paris, Dombres, Orange. Everyone consented to the equality of charges and advantages. So, my dear compatriots, we went crazy with joy. We exceeded our binding mandates, as you can see. We thought only of the salvation and well-being of France. We gave the king the title, Restorer of the French Empire, and voted for a medal to eternally commemorate this happy day. . . .

4. DECREE OF AUGUST 10, 1789[5]

In the week that followed the Night of August 4th, the Assembly debated and codified the renunciations. Although there was some contention, particularly over the tithe, the proceedings were remarkably consensual, especially given the magnitude of what had been sacrificed. On August 10th, the Assembly approved a decree formalizing the renunciations of the 4th. This decree effectively dismantled the Old Regime.

1. The National Assembly hereby completely abolishes the feudal system. It decrees that, among the existing rights and dues, both feudal and censual,[6] all

[5]J. H. Robinson, *Readings in European History* (Boston, MA: Ginn and Company, 1906), vol. 2, 405–409.
[6]Dues paid by tenants to their lords.

those originating in or representing real or personal serfdom shall be abolished without indemnification. All other dues are declared redeemable, the terms and mode of redemption to be fixed by the National Assembly. Those of the said dues which are not extinguished by this decree shall continue to be collected until indemnification.

2. The exclusive right to maintain pigeon houses and dovecotes is abolished. . . . Every one shall have the right to kill them upon his own land.

3. The exclusive right to hunt and to maintain unenclosed warrens is likewise abolished, and every landowner shall have the right to kill, or to have destroyed on his own land, all kinds of game. . . .

4. All seigneurial courts are hereby suppressed without indemnification. But the magistrates of these courts shall continue to perform their functions until such time as the National Assembly shall provide for the establishment of a new judicial system.

5. Tithes of every description, as well as the dues which have been substituted for them . . . are abolished, on condition, however, that some other method be devised to provide for the expenses of divine worship, the support of the officiating clergy, for the assistance of the poor, for repairs and rebuilding of churches and parsonages, and for the maintenance of all institutions, seminaries, schools, academies, asylums, and organizations to which the present funds are devoted. Until such provision shall be made . . . the said tithes shall continue to be collected according to law and in the customary manner. . . .

6. All perpetual ground rents . . . shall be redeemable at a rate fixed by the Assembly. No due shall in the future be created which is not redeemable.

7. The sale of judicial and municipal offices shall be abolished forthwith. Justice shall be dispensed gratis. Nevertheless the magistrates at present holding such offices shall continue to exercise their functions and to receive their emoluments until the Assembly shall have made provision for indemnifying them.

8. The fees of the country priests are abolished, and shall be discontinued so soon as provision shall be made for increasing the minimum salary of the parish priests. . . .

9. Pecuniary privileges, personal or real, in the payment of taxes are abolished forever. Taxes shall be collected from all the citizens, and from all property, in the same manner and in the same form. . . .

10. Inasmuch as a national constitution and public liberty are of more advantage to the provinces than the privileges which some of these enjoy, and inasmuch as the surrender of such privileges is essential to the intimate union of all parts of the realm, it is decreed that all the peculiar privileges, pecuniary or otherwise, of the provinces, principalities, districts, cantons, cities, and communes are once for all abolished and are absorbed into the law common to all Frenchmen.

11. All citizens, without distinction of birth, are eligible to any office or dignity, whether ecclesiastical, civil, or military; and no profession shall imply any derogation.

12. Hereafter no remittances shall be made . . . to the court of Rome. . . .

13. [This article abolishes various ecclesiastical dues.]

14. Pluralities shall not be permitted hereafter in cases where the revenue from the benefice or benefices held shall exceed the sum of three thousand pounds. . . .

15. The National Assembly shall consider, in conjunction with the king, the report which is to be submitted to it relating to pensions, favors, and salaries, with a view to suppressing all such as are not deserved and reducing those which shall prove excessive. . . .

16. The National Assembly decrees that a medal shall be struck in memory of the recent grave and important deliberations for the welfare of France, and that a prayer of thanksgiving shall be chanted in gratitude in all the parishes and churches of France.

17. The National Assembly solemnly proclaims the king, Louis XVI, the Restorer of French Liberty. . . .

III. The New Regime . . . and Its Limits

Having signed the death warrant of the Old Regime on August 10, 1789, the Assembly now had to lay the foundations for what was to replace it. The keystone of the new order was the Declaration of the Rights of Man and Citizen. Passed into law on August 26, 1789, it outlined a society based on human rights. It remains the most important constitutional document in France and still serves as an inspiration for aspiring democracies around the world. But the new order had certain limitations—notably the exclusion of women, the poor, people of color, and others from political rights. These exclusions were opposed at the time; and over the course of the French and Haitian Revolutions, some were lifted. The French Revolution had not only defined a new order of citizenship and human rights; it had also unleashed an expansive dynamic of inclusion that remains powerful today.

5. DECLARATION OF THE RIGHTS OF MAN AND THE CITIZEN (AUGUST 26, 1789)[7]

During the second half of August, the National Assembly debated both whether to issue a statement of rights and what those rights would be. Many deputies were concerned that a blanket declaration of civic and universal rights would lead to social insubordination and unrest. To guard against this, they proposed accompanying the declaration of rights with a declaration of duties. They were defeated, but the Declaration itself nonetheless contained a number of limitations and ambiguities.

---

[7]http://www.conseil-constitutionnel.fr/conseil-constitutionnel/francais/la-constitution/la-constitution-du-4-octobre-1958/declaration-des-droits-de-l-homme-et-du-citoyen-de-1789.5076.html

The representatives of the French People, formed into a National Assembly, considering ignorance, forgetfulness, or contempt of the rights of man to be the only cause of public misfortunes and the corruption of Governments, have resolved to set forth, in a solemn Declaration, the natural, unalienable, and sacred rights of man, to the end that this Declaration, constantly present to all members of the body politic, may remind them unceasingly of their rights and their duties; to the end that the acts of the legislative power and those of the executive power, since they be continually compared with the aim of every political institution, may thereby be the more respected; to the end that the demands of the citizens, founded henceforth on simple and incontestable principles, may always be directed toward the maintenance of the Constitution and the happiness of all.

In consequence whereof, the National Assembly recognizes and declares, in the presence and under the auspices of the Supreme Being, the following Rights of Man and of the Citizen.

1. Men are born and remain free and equal in rights. Social distinctions may be based only on considerations of the common good.

2. The aim of every political association is the preservation of the natural and imprescriptible rights of Man. These rights are Liberty, Property, Security, and Resistance to Oppression.

3. The principle of Sovereignty lies primarily in the Nation. No corporate body, no individual may exercise any authority that does not expressly emanate from it.

4. Liberty consists in being able to do anything that does not harm others; thus, the exercise of the natural rights of every man has no bounds other than those that ensure to the other members of society the enjoyment of these same rights. These bounds may be determined only by Law.

5. The Law has the right to forbid only those actions that are injurious to society. Nothing that is not forbidden by Law may be hindered, and no one may be compelled to do what the Law does not ordain.

6. The Law is the expression of the general will. All citizens have the right to take part, personally or through their representatives, in its making. It must be the same for all, whether it protects or punishes. All citizens, being equal in its eyes, shall be equally eligible to all high offices, public positions, and employments, according to their ability, and without other distinction than that of their virtues and talents.

7. No man may be accused or detained except in the cases determined by the Law, and following the procedures that it has prescribed. Those who solicit, expedite, carry out, or cause to be carried out arbitrary orders must be punished; but any citizen summoned or apprehended by virtue of the Law, must give instant obedience; resistance makes him guilty.

8. The Law must prescribe only the punishments that are strictly and evidently necessary; and no one may be punished except by virtue of a Law drawn up and promulgated before the offence is committed, and legally applied.

9. As every man is presumed innocent until he has been declared guilty, if it should be considered necessary to arrest him, any undue harshness that is not required to secure his person must be severely curbed by Law.

10. No one may be disturbed on account of his opinions, even religious ones, as long as the manifestation of such opinions does not interfere with the established Law and Order.

11. The free communication of ideas and opinions is one of the most precious rights of man. Any citizen may therefore speak, write, and publish freely, except what is tantamount to the abuse of this liberty in the cases determined by Law.

12. To guarantee the Rights of Man and of the Citizen, a public force is necessary; this force is therefore established for the benefit of all, and not for the particular use of those to whom it is entrusted.

13. For the maintenance of the public force, and for administrative expenses, a general tax is indispensable; it must be equally distributed among all citizens, in proportion to their ability to pay.

14. All citizens have the right to ascertain, by themselves, or through their representatives, the need for a public tax, to consent to it freely, to watch over its use, and to determine its proportion, basis, collection, and duration.

15. Society has the right to ask a public official for an accounting of his administration.

16. Any society in which no provision is made for guaranteeing rights or for the separation of powers has no Constitution.

17. Since the right to Property is inviolable and sacred, no one may be deprived thereof, unless public necessity, legally ascertained, obviously requires it, and just and prior indemnity has been paid.

6. OLYMPE DE GOUGES, *THE RIGHTS OF WOMEN* (SEPTEMBER 1791)[8]

Notably absent from the Declaration of the Rights of Man and Citizen were women. Although the Assembly intended that they enjoy the protection of the law, they explicitly denied women political rights. Their exclusion provoked protest, the most famous of which was the actress/writer, Olympe de Gouges in her The Rights of Women. *In addition to offering a long discussion of women's equality and capacity for political rights, Gouges's pamphlet featured a formal declaration of the rights of women, modelled upon the Assembly's.*

Man, are you capable of being just? A woman asks: you will not strip me of this right? Who gave you the sovereign power of oppressing my sex? . . .

---

[8]Olympe de Gouges, *Les droits de la femme, à la Reine* (n.p.), 5–11. Available on the Bibliothèque nationale de France web site: http://gallica.bnf.fr/ark:/12148/bpt6k64848397.

As representatives of the nation, mothers, daughters, and sisters demand that they be constituted as a national assembly. Considering that ignorance, neglect, or disdain for the rights of woman are the sole causes of public misfortune and government corruption, they have resolved to set out in a solemn declaration the natural, inalienable, and sacred rights of woman; so that by being ever present to all the members of the social body, this declaration constantly remind them of their rights and duties; so that the acts of power of women and men may be compared at each moment to the goals of all political institutions and thus be more fully respected; and so that, by being founded henceforth on simple and incontestable principles, the demands of the female citizens always tend toward upholding the constitution, good morals, and the wellbeing of all.

In consequence, the sex that is superior in beauty and courage, in maternal suffering, recognizes and declares, in presence and under the auspices of the Supreme Being, the following Rights of Woman and the Female Citizen.

1. Woman is born free and remains equal to man in rights. Social distinctions can only be based on common utility.

2. The goal of all political association is the preservation of the natural and imprescriptible rights of Woman and Man. These rights are liberty, property, security, and, above all, resistance to oppression.

3. The principle of all sovereignty resides essentially in the Nation, which is but the joining together of Woman and Man; no body or individual can exercise authority which does not emanate expressly from it.

4. Liberty and justice consist in giving back all that belongs to another; thus, the exercise of woman's natural rights has no other limit than what man's perpetual tyranny imposes on it; this limit must be reformed according to the laws of nature and reason.

5. The laws of nature and reason prohibit all actions harmful to society; everything not prohibited by these wise and divine laws is permitted, and no one can be forced to do what those laws do not ordain.

6. The law should be the expression of the general will; all female and male citizens should take part in its formation either personally or through their representatives; it must be the same for all; being equal in its eyes, all female and male citizens should be equally admissible to all public dignities, places, and employments according to their capacity and with no other distinctions than their virtues and talents.

7. No woman is exempted; she is accused, arrested, and detained in the cases determined by Law. Women obey this rigorous Law just as men.

8. The law should only establish those punishments which are strictly and obviously necessary, and no one can be punished except by virtue of a Law established and promulgated before the crime and legally applied to women.

9. Any woman declared guilty [will be subject to] the full rigor of the Law.

10. No one should be troubled for his opinions, even fundamental ones; since the woman has the right to mount the scaffold [to be executed], she should also have the right to mount the rostrum, provided that these manifestations do not trouble public order as established by Law.

11. The free communication of thought and opinion is one of the woman's most precious rights, because this liberty guarantees the legitimacy of fathers toward their children. Every female citizen can thus say freely, I am the mother of your child, without a barbarous prejudice forcing her to hide the truth. . . .

13. For the maintenance of public force and administration, taxation of woman and man should be equal. She participates in all public labor, all difficult tasks, and should thus have the same share of places, employments, offices, dignities, and industry.

14. The female and male citizens have the right of verifying personally or through their representatives the necessity of taxes. Female citizens can accept them only if there is an equal division of wealth and public administration, and also in the determination of the amount, distribution, collection, and duration of taxes.

15. The mass of women, allied to the men in the payment of taxes, has the right to demand an account from any public agent of his administration.

16. Any society in which the guarantee of rights is not assured and the separation of powers not determined does not have a constitution. The constitution is null if the majority of individuals composing the Nation have not participated in drafting it.

17. Properties belong to all the sexes, whether united or separate; each [sex] has an inviolable and sacred right. Since property is a true patrimony of nature, no one can be deprived of it unless legally determined public necessity obviously demands it, and only on the condition of a just and preliminary compensation.

7. MAXIMILIAN ROBESPIERRE, SPEECH AGAINST PROPERTY QUALIFICATIONS TO EXERCISE THE FULL RIGHTS OF CITIZENSHIP (APRIL 1791)[9]

Many members of the National Assembly believed that only those with a certain amount of wealth should be allowed full participation in the political process. Although they believed that everyone (including foreigners) possessed natural rights, they also felt that only those with a material stake in society should be allowed to vote and hold public office. Consequently, they proposed establishing two degrees of citizenship. Active citizens (those who annually paid taxes equivalent to what a worker earned in three days) would be allowed to vote, while passive citizens would enjoy only the protection of the law. Moreover, only very substantial property owners would be eligible for election to public office. The majority of the National Assembly

[9]*Pour le Bonheur et pour la liberté: discours* (Paris: La Fabrique, 2000), 72–80.

THE FRENCH REVOLUTION   267

approved these conditions, but some protested. The most influential was the Third-Estate deputy, Maximillian Robespierre.

I hesitated for a moment whether I should propose my ideas on the project that you want to adopt. But I realized that I had to speak, in order to defend the cause of the nation and that of liberty. . . .

Why are we gathered in this temple of laws? In order to restore to the French nation the exercise of the imprescriptible rights that belong to all men. This is the purpose of all political constitutions. A constitution is free and just if it fulfills this goal. It is an attack upon humanity if it hinders it. You yourselves have recognized this truth when . . . you solemnly declared that . . . "all men are born and remain free and equal in rights. Sovereignty resides essentially in the nation. The law is the expression of the general will. All citizens have the right to participate in its formation, whether directly or through their freely elected representatives. All citizens are admissible to all public positions, without any other distinction than their virtue and talents." These are the principles you consecrated. It will be easy now to understand the dispositions that I am going to combat. All we need to do is harmonize them with the invariable rules of human society.

1. Is the law the expression of the general will when the majority of those for whom it is made cannot participate in any way in its formation? No. However, to bar all those who do not pay taxes equivalent to the wages a worker earns in three days from choosing the electors destined to name the members of the legislative assembly, is that not to exclude the majority of the French from the formation of the law? In its essence, this disposition is anti-constitutional and anti-social.

2. Are men equal in rights when some are exclusively eligible to be elected to the legislature or other public places? . . . No. But such are the monstrous differences established by the decree which makes a citizen active or passive . . . according to the different degrees of wealth. . . . All these distinctions are essentially anti-constitutional, anti-social.

3. Are men admissible to all public positions without any other distinction than virtues and talents when their inability to pay a certain level of taxes excludes them from those same positions, regardless of their virtues and talents? No. All these dispositions are thus essentially anti-constitutional and anti-social.

4. Finally, is the Nation sovereign when most of the individuals who compose it are stripped of the political rights that constitute sovereignty? No. Yet you want to take them away from a large part of the French. What would become of your Declaration of rights if this was allowed to stand? Empty words. What would become of the Nation? A Slave, because liberty consists in obeying laws we have given to ourselves, while servitude means being forced to submit to a foreign will. What would become of your Constitution? A true aristocracy, for aristocracy is when some citizens are sovereign and the rest are subjects. And what kind of aristocracy would it become? The most unbearable of all: an aristocracy of wealth.

8. ABBÉ GRÉGOIRE, *MOTION IN FAVOR OF THE JEWS* (DECEMBER 23, 1789)[10]

At the end of 1789, the National Assembly addressed whether non-Catholics could enjoy the right of citizenship. Since the late seventeenth century, Protestant worship had been illegal in France, and Protestants had been persecuted. Although attitudes toward them had softened, and the state had granted them limited tolerance in 1787, they still faced legal disabilities. The situation of French Jews was no more enviable. Although several Jewish communities, counting a total of 40,000 individuals, were tolerated in Eastern and Southern France, Jews were subject to official discrimination, such as exclusion from land ownership, membership in most trades and professions, and access to educational institutions. When it took up the issue of religious minorities in December 1789, the National Assembly unanimously granted citizenship to Protestants. But it was divided over the question of the Jews. A deputy of the Catholic clergy, the Abbé Henri Grégoire, spoke powerfully on behalf of full Jewish emancipation. For Grégoire, this would be but the first of his many revolutionary calls to extend citizenship to excluded groups.

You have consecrated the rights of man and citizen; please permit a Catholic priest to raise his voice in favor of the 50,000 Jews scattered across the kingdom who, as men, demand the rights of citizens. . . .

For seventeen centuries, the Jews have struggled and maintained themselves in the face of persecution and carnage. The nations have all vainly joined together to wipe them out. . . . The Assyrians, Persians, Medes, Greeks, and Romans are no more, but the Jews . . . survive with their laws. . . .

Europe has produced 400 regulations to raise a wall of separation between Christian and Jew. Rather than bridge the gap which separates them, we have enlarged it by closing to them all the paths of honor. . . .

It is the conduct of other nations towards the Jews that forces them to become perverse. The only thing that should surprise us is that they have not become worse. What among others would be seen as virtue is heroism among them. Our ancestors subordinated justice to their hatred. When will we pay off their debt and ours? Is it by making the misfortunes of the Jews eternal that we will acquire rights to posterity's blessings? When will we return their humanity to this people, insulted, persecuted, hatefully regarded as something between man and beast, without rank in society, seeing scorn all around him, and dragging his tear-soaked chains wherever he goes?

To the shame of our century, the name "Jew" is still dishonoring. . . . In this century which calls itself the century of enlightenment, which boasts of giving

[10]Abbé Grégoire, "Motion in Favor of the Jews," in *Archives parlementaires de 1787 à 1860* [henceforth *AP*], eds. M. J. Mavidal and M. E. Laurent (Paris: Société d'Imprimerie et Librairie Administrative P. Dupont, 1867–1879), série 1, vol. 10, 766–775.

back to man his rights and original dignity, it is, in my opinion, immoral of those who speak most of tolerance to make a striking exception against the Jews. . . .

But how, you will say, can we grant citizenship to a horde so bastardized that it has no hope of regeneration, a sect who is intolerant out of principle, whose habits are incompatible with those of the peoples to whom it has vowed a venomous hatred? . . .

I have heard it said (and I can hardly get over my surprise) that it is impossible to place on the same level of citizenship people who never want to united themselves in marriage to other peoples. Here is a rebuttal which, for all its humor, is still good: "Christians or Jews, your distancing from one another is reciprocal; with this fine argument I will prove to you that the French can never be citizens because they will not marry Jewish girls." . . .

As for their habits, which we supposed to be incompatible because they refuse to share a Christian's table, nothing is more false, as daily experience shows. And, anyway, how does this dietetic difference matter to public order? Some provinces of Poland and Russia offer a bizarre mélange: next to the Protestant who eats his chicken on Friday there is a Catholic who eats only eggs; both drink wine and work on Friday next to a Turk who abstains from wine and does not work that day. This diversity does not endanger civil harmony. . . .

But, you will reply, the Jew is the born enemy of everything that is not himself. I respond that this hatred is condemned by Mosaic Law, which imposes the obligation of universal philanthropy. Do you find this supposed hatred in those sacred books which so formally and so frequently mandate that the stranger be welcomed. . . . If, however, the Jew, shamed, insulted and proscribed everywhere, has sometimes detested his tyrants; if the Jew, harassed by continual hostilities . . . has sometimes opposed force with force or opposed fury with hatred, this conduct is entirely natural. . . . Will you take these momentary outbursts of vengeance for the habitual and necessary state of his soul? . . .

You reproach them for not being patriots; no, when they are not treated like the sons of the motherland. . . . You demand that he love a motherland; well, give him one. . . . Once on the same level as the other members of the nation, attached to the State by pleasure, security, liberty, and ease, he will not be tempted to take his wealth elsewhere. His lands will keep him in the country where he acquired them, and then he will cherish his mother, which is to say, the motherland, whose interest will be the same as his own. . . .

Everything proves that it is as unjust as it is impolitic to let the Jews vegetate in their current degradation; while we accuse the taste for luxury of drawing laborers away from the countryside, we have among us a nation to whom we forbid agriculture. . . .

When speaking of the Jews, we must speak of usury; these two notions have gone together for a long time. In the Middle Ages, their calculating genius invented letters of exchange, useful to protect commerce and make it flourish across the globe. But this benefit was counterbalanced by the evils their rapacity caused, for we must admit, this vice has infected the Hebrew people for a long time.

However, if the Jews have become the brokers of all the nations and have often sacrificed probity to greed, governments must blame themselves for these excesses. By taking from them all other means of subsistence, they forced this people under the yoke of the harshest oppression; by loading them down with taxes, by forbidding them to exercise the arts, they limited their work, tied their hands, and forced them to become merchants. . . .

Since today's Jews are limited to small-scale peddling, necessity almost forces them to supplement the modest profits of subaltern commerce with duplicity or speculation. For, if you are hungry and thirsty, have no resources, and hear the touching cries of a large family begging for help, you must steal or perish. . . . It is the height of injustice to blame the Jews for crimes we force them to commit. . . . Direct the character of this people toward another object than commerce, . . . and show them that fortune lies along the path of honor. In truth, such a reform will not be the work of a moment, because you cannot change the character of a people like the uniform of a military unit. The progress of reason is only felt after a considerable lapse of time; but once the Jew has our education, our legislation, our discoveries (in which he will share) before his eyes, their combination will give a universal impulse, shake up all individuals, even carry along those who are recalcitrant; and soon reason will recover its rights among this people, its character will receive a new shape, and its morality will be reformed. . . .

Almost everywhere, Jews are assigned to live in neighborhoods. . . . In some cities, they are shut up every night in the *ghetto*. To isolate the Jews in this manner is to encourage Christians' hatred of them, by distinguishing its object in the most precise manner. . . . There, the Jews are always a people apart, a State in the State. . . .

The consequence of this is that we must allow the Jews to live anywhere in the kingdom. Give them permanent relations with all the citizens, and soon a sweet sensibility will attach them to those around them. . . .

You will doubtlessly ask if we should also make them farmers; I would like that. There has never been a people more concerned with agronomy than the Israelites in Palestine. . . . The possibility of restoring to them their original taste is proven by facts. Without leaving Europe, we find in Lithuania Jews engaged in farming. Thus, let rustic labors summon the Hebrew into our fields, which were once drenched in the blood of his ancestors, but will henceforth be watered by his sweat. . . .

A consequence of this is permission to acquire, for land is never better cultivated than by its owner. . . . The right to buy land will attach the Jew to his locale, to the motherland, and the price of real estate will be driven up by the multiplication of buyers.

The Jews . . . ask for the right to attend our colleges and universities. . . . Why should we close the door of our lycées, our literary societies? Is not the Academy of Sciences honored by having a Negro among its correspondents? Let us not hope too much from the grown man, for his character is already formed; he will escape us. Let us take hold of the generation just being born and that which is approaching puberty. May these youth partake of our education, may wise teachers love their Christian and Jewish students impartially and establish between them that cordiality which will prevent explosions of hatred. . . .

Should we let the Jews keep their right of autonomy? . . . The problem for the Jews is that their religion encompasses all branches of legislation, even the slightest details of conduct. . . . To resolve this question, let us distinguish within their law that which concerns religious practice from that which is only the object of civil and criminal jurisprudence; these things are very separable. Let us grant the Jews complete liberty on the first article and on everything that does not concern the property and honor of citizens; but for all the rest, let them be subject to national law. . . .

Too often we see cold-hearted men who profane the word "goodness." They cherish humans at 2,000 years' or 2,000 leagues' distance. Their hearts open up in favor of Helots or negroes, while the unfortunate they actually encounter elicits from them barely a glance of compassion; here is at our door the suffering remains of an ancient people . . . As long as they are slaves to our prejudices and victims of our hatred, let us not brag of our sensitivity. . . .

A new century is dawning. . . . The Jews are members of that universal family that brotherhood must establish between the peoples. The revolution spreads its majestic robe over them as over you. Children of the same father, . . . may the Jew, in returning the tenderness of the Christian, embrace me as his fellow-citizen and friend.

IV. The Church's Place in the New Regime

What role would the Catholic Church play in the New Regime? This question occupied much of the deputies' time and ultimately caused deep division among the French. In 1789, Catholicism was France's official religion, and the population was 99% Catholic. The Catholic Church formed a distinct, autonomous body within the state. Its power came not only from its religious and moral authority but also from its vast, tax-exempt wealth and the key public functions (the performance of baptisms, marriages, and burials, as well as public record-keeping and education) it monopolized. Despite its power, the Church faced serious threats in 1789. One of these came from the powerful anticlerical current of the Enlightenment which condemned the stultifying hold of what it viewed as "religious superstition." Another was the feeling among some influential deputies that the Church's continued existence as a state within the state was an intolerable threat to national unity. Finally, the lands and properties of the Church struck many as an ideal resource for paying off the national debt and solving the fiscal crisis that had provoked the collapse of the government in the first place. These causes coalesced to form a perfect storm that burst forth in the Assembly in October 1789, when a deputy (the Bishop of Autun!) proposed that the nation confiscate the Church's property, end its independent corporate existence, and transform the clergy into salaried public officials.

9. THE CONSTITUTIONALITY OF CORPS: LE CHAPELLIER (OCTOBER 31, 1789)[11]

Although the debate over Church lands pitted the need to safeguard religion and morality against that of paying off the national debt, it also had constitutional implications. The Third-Estate deputy, Le Chapellier, was instrumental in turning the debate over Church property into a discussion of the compatibility of distinct corporate bodies with unified, national sovereignty.

I am surprised to see some of our colleagues join together, make common cause, and defend themselves like a distinct group. . . . It is extremely important to finally destroy the ideas of corps and order which are constantly being reborn.

Can the nation declare corps incapable of possessing property? That is the question.

We have often wandered in the discussion. I respond by two propositions.

First, in relation to the nation, corps never had property.

All establishments, from the most revered to the least respectable, received their existence from the nation for the good of the State. They were charged with a mission, received means of execution, and administered these means, but did not become their owners. The clergy is one of these establishments.

The clergy has thus never been a property-owner, but only an administrator.

I cannot recognize property in the holder of usufruct. . . . He is only an administrator. Even had the clergy been a property-owner, would it still be one? This corporation, this order, has it not ceased to exist? I no longer perceive it except among the superb debris of an immense revolution. It has become the patrimony of history. . . .

You have sought to destroy the orders because their destruction was necessary to save the State. If the clergy keeps its properties, the order of the clergy is not destroyed. You leave it the power to assemble, consecrate its independence, and disorganize the political body which you are charged with organizing. . . . Henceforth, let the individuals who compose the clergy be but citizens.

10. THE CLERICAL POSITION: ARCHBISHOP BOISGELIN (OCTOBER 31, 1789)[12]

Attacked on the grounds of unified national sovereignty, the Church responded by mobilizing another constitutional principle—the sanctity of property—to defend its holdings.

---

[11]Mavidal and Laurent, *AP*, vol. 9, 639.
[12]Mavidal and Laurent, *AP*, vol. 9, 615–620.

The properties of the Church belong to their donors. . . . By natural law, they had the liberty to donate. . . . This same liberty, guaranteed by the law, formed a part of their property. The property of the churches belongs to those citizens who endowed them. The same law which protected the free use of their possessions during their lifetime . . . protects the use they made of those same properties to favor churches. We cannot violate the law that maintains the gift without violating the law that maintains the power to give. . . .

[Thus] you must annul contracts which emanate from all classes of citizens if you wish to invade the property of the churches.

You either have to recognize these contracts or contest them.

Can you contest their existence? You would have to overturn all the monuments of the history of France and Europe to cast doubt upon them.

Can you deny that these contracts were sanctioned by the law?

Can you deny that they have been recognized as valid, perpetual, and irrevocable for many centuries?

You cannot destroy them without destroying all the laws which have sanctioned them. . . .

The Church even has possessions acquired before the foundation of the monarchy. Metropoles and dioceses were organized in part of France under the Roman Empire. . . .

It has been argued that ecclesiastical property is not true property.

First, because it cannot be alienated freely, but is limited to simple use and usufruct.

Second, because the Church is a moral body, incapable of owning.

Entailments do not allow the liberty to alienate, but they are properties. You can outlaw entailments in the future, but you cannot take the property of those to whom it is entailed. . . . Apply these principles to ecclesiastical property. . . .

Today, the churches of France are not free to alienate. But they were free to alienate in the past, at the time of their donations and acquisitions. . . . It was to conserve them that a protective law stripped their beneficiaries of the right to alienate them. To destroy ecclesiastical possessions, you cannot invoke a law intended to conserve them. . . .

We respect usufruct as a [component of] property. . . . It would cast doubt upon all property not to regard the usufruct of each generation as a property. The usufruct of the current beneficiary is actually the title of perpetual property of each church. The usufruct is in the hands of the beneficiary, the property in the hands of each church. It is thus unreasonable to say that a church does not have true property because the titularies of benefices only have usufruct.

It remains to be seen if the Church, or each church, which is and can only be a moral corps, is capable of ownership. . . .

Why can't each church possess, like a hospital, college, or a public establishment like the communities, provinces, and even the nation? The nation itself is nothing but a moral body. If it is true that a moral body cannot have property, then the nation itself cannot own. If it is true that it cannot own, then it cannot dispose of the properties of the churches [because] it cannot exert a right of property over the churches if it itself does not have one. . . .

This is the true principle. It is not the nation which gave the churches their properties, but it is from the nation that each church holds its power to own. . . . It is by virtue of laws that [the king and the citizens] gave this right to the churches; it is the authority of the laws, the authority of the nation, which confirms all the powers and rights of the churches and which protects them from all attacks. Yes, we possess under the most respectable title, that of the national will, ever since the establishment of the monarchy. Our possessions lack nothing of what can legitimate true property. Hereditary private possessions are founded on the same titles as our own, because it is impossible to separate any property from the law which protects it. . . .

The nation gave the Church the power to own.

It can take it away. . . .

It can prohibit the Church from acquiring new possessions. . . .

But it cannot make this ban retroactive. It cannot today declare that it had not granted the power to possess to the churches. Such a declaration would be contradicted by the actual state of ecclesiastical possessions, as well as by all historical evidence.

If the churches were allowed to possess in virtue of national law, their possessions are legitimate. They are under the protection of justice and public faith, and no human force can legitimize any infraction of justice and public faith. . . .

We have not only defended the rights of the churches. We have been pleading the very cause of the laws. And we cannot imagine that it would be in the interest of the nation to overthrow the principles which give laws their force.

It is certain that that State cannot take over the properties of the churches without betraying the intentions of the original donors, without destroying rights which have been acquired and recognized at all times, [without destroying] properties which predate the monarchy, and without annulling all laws on donations and acquisitions, [and] the very law of prescription, without which there is no property. . . .

Do you think you can distinguish the properties of the Church from those of the citizens? The same laws protect both. The same laws—and we are violating them. And what does it matter that they are violated in one area rather than another? The infraction is the same. The law was general; it ceases to be so. It can multiply its exceptions if even just one is admitted.

It has been said that the properties of the churches are similar to the ancient fiefs charged with [military] service and given in the name of the nation. . . . It will be said that the nation can take them back, just like the lands given to the Church. . . .

If ever the propertyless come to dominate the National Assembly, what rights of landowners will not be violated?

These are your rights, they are the same as other citizens'. We want no others. We have happily abjured the privileges which tend to separate us from the nation. . . . Read our *cahiers.* . . . There is no mandate expressed more strongly than the one concerning equality of taxation. . . . We never thought that you would take our properties when we agreed to have them taxed. Rather than confirming the principle of equality of taxation, . . . you have reduced us to giving the first example of the infraction of the law of property. . . .

One might say that you want to separate our generation from all those which have come before, like a nation from all other nations. We are overturning all established rights. We no longer recognize ancient possessions. We seem to be severing the fleeting moment of our feeble and passing existence from all connection with times that are no more. The past no longer has any link to the present. The present no longer influences the future. What we do, what we do not do, will be of no concern to those who come after us. They will follow our examples, but not our laws. They will deplore our decrees, which are the rights that we can acquire over posterity, just like you are deploring the rights of the churches, rights acquired and recognized from time immemorial.

11. THE CIVIL CONSTITUTION OF THE CLERGY (JULY 12, 1790)[13]

On November 2, 1789, the National Assembly voted to "place the properties of the Church at the disposition of the state." In mid-1790, they began to be auctioned to the public. By abolishing the tithe (on the night of August 4th) and stripping the Church of its land, the Assembly transformed the clergy into salaried public servants. A decree reorganizing the new, publicly funded Church was not long in coming. This was the Civil Constitution of the Clergy. In some ways, it met the demands the clergy had expressed in its cahiers; but in other ways, it imposed unwanted changes on the Church. Even more traumatic was the loyalty oath the Assembly imposed. It required priests to recognize the supremacy of the National Assembly in spiritual and secular matters. About half of the parish priests and nearly all of the bishops refused to take the oath. This split the Church and the population. Hostility to the Revolution's religious policy became the main source of counter-revolution. It was only after a decade of horrendous violence that Napoleon's Concordat (1802) began the process of reconciling with Rome and healing the schism dividing the French nation.

Title I
Article I.   Each department shall form a single diocese, and each diocese shall have the same extent and limits as the department. . . .

IV.   No church or parish of France, nor any French citizen, may acknowledge upon any occasion, or upon any pretext whatsoever, the authority of a bishop or archbishop whose see shall be under the supremacy of a foreign power. . . .

---

[13]Robinson, *Readings*, vol. 2, 423–427.

VI. A new arrangement and division of all the parishes of the kingdom shall be undertaken immediately in concert with the bishop and the district administration. . . .

XX. All titles and offices other than those mentioned in the present constitution, dignities, canonries, prebends, half prebends, chapels, chaplainships, both in cathedral and collegiate churches, all regular and secular chapters for either sex, abbacies and priorships, both regular and in commendam, for either sex, as well as all other benefices and prestimonies in general, of whatever kind or denomination, are from the day of this decree extinguished and abolished and shall never be reestablished in any form.

Title II

Article I. There shall be but one mode of choosing bishops and parish priests, election.

II. All elections shall be by ballot and shall be decided by the absolute majority of votes.

III. The election of bishops shall take place according to the forms and by the electoral body designated . . . for the election of members of the departmental assembly. . . .

VII. In order to be eligible for a bishopric, one must have fulfilled for fifteen years at least the duties of the church ministry in the diocese, as a parish priest, officiating minister, or curate, or as superior, or as directing vicar of the seminary. . . .

XIX. The new bishop may not apply to the pope for any form of confirmation. . . .

XXI. Before the ceremony of consecration begins, the bishop elect shall take a solemn oath, in the presence of the municipal officers, of the people, and of the clergy, to guard with care the faithful of his diocese who are confided to him, to be loyal to the nation, the law, and the king, and to support with all his power the constitution decreed by the National Assembly. . . .

XXV. The election of parish priests shall take place according to the forms and by the electors designated . . . for the election of members of the administrative assemblies of the district. . . .

XL. Bishoprics and cures shall be looked upon as vacant until those elected to fill them shall have taken the oath . . . mentioned.

Title III

Article I. The ministers of religion, performing as they do the first and most important functions of society and forced to live continuously in the place where they discharge the offices to which they have been called by the confidence of the people, shall be supported by the nation.

II. Every bishop, priest, and officiating clergyman . . . shall be furnished with a suitable dwelling. . . . Salaries shall be assigned to each, as indicated. . . .

XII. In view of the salary which is assured to them by the present constitution, the bishops, parish priests, and curates shall perform the episcopal and priestly functions gratis.

Title IV

Article I. The law requiring the residence of ecclesiastics in the districts under their charge shall be strictly observed. . . .

II. No bishop shall absent himself from his diocese more than two weeks consecutively during the year, except in case of real necessity and with the consent of the directory of the department in which his see is situated.

III. In the same manner, the parish priests and the curates may not absent themselves from the place of their duties beyond the term fixed . . . , except for weighty reasons, and even in such cases the priests must obtain the permission both of their bishop and of the directory of their district. . . .

VI. Bishops, parish priests, and curates may as active citizens, be present at the primary and electoral assemblies; they may be chosen electors or as deputies to the legislative body, or as members of the general council of the communes or of the administrative councils of their districts or departments.

V. Reaction to the Revolution

Observers from across the Atlantic world noted the rapid course of events with astonishment. All agreed that the Revolution was an entirely novel phenomenon that was breaking radically with the old order—and even history itself. But that is where agreement ended. Some saw the revolutionaries' attempts to cast off the chains of the past and build a new world as a horrendous monstrosity. Others, however, looked on this effort with admiration and optimism. The contrast between the two positions would provide fuel for the growing split between revolutionaries and counter-revolutionaries and powerfully inform later distinctions between progressives and conservatives.

12. EDMUND BURKE, *REFLECTIONS ON THE REVOLUTION IN FRANCE* (1790)[14]

The first conservative critique of the French Revolution's attempt to break with existing traditions, laws, and institutions was Edmund Burke's. In contrast to his sympathetic view of the American Revolution, Burke viewed the National Assembly with extreme alarm and criticized all of its reforms. Burke's revulsion was rooted in a particular understanding of sovereignty and individual rights. In this excerpt from his influential 1790 denunciation of the French Revolution, Burke laid out what he considered to be the true nature of these principles and explained how the French were violating them. Burke's Reflections on the Revolution *in France may be considered the first written expression of modern political conservatism. It is still influential today.*

---

[14]*Reflections on the Revolution in France* (London: Dodsley, 1791), 46–51.

In the famous law of the 3rd of Charles I, called the Petition of Right, the parliament says to the king, "Your subjects have *inherited* this freedom," claiming their franchises not as abstract principles . . . but as a patrimony derived from their forefathers. . . . [The authors of the petition] preferred this positive, recorded *hereditary* title to all which can be dear to the man and the citizen, to that vague speculative right, which exposed their sure inheritance to be scrambled for and torn to pieces by every wild litigious spirit.

The same policy pervades all the laws which have since been made for the preservation of our liberties. . . .

It has been the uniform policy of our constitution to claim and assert our liberties, as an *entailed inheritance* derived to us from our forefathers, and to be transmitted to our posterity; as an estate specially belonging to the people of this kingdom without any reference whatever to any other more general or prior right. By this means our constitution preserves a unity in so great a diversity of its parts. We have an inheritable crown; an inheritable peerage; and a House of Commons and a people inheriting privileges, franchises, and liberties from a long line of ancestors.

This policy appears to me to be the result of profound reflection; or rather the happy effect of following nature, which is wisdom without reflection, and above it. A spirit of innovation is generally the result of a selfish temper and confined views. People will not look forward to posterity, who never look backward to their ancestors. Besides, the people of England well know, that the idea of inheritances furnishes a sure principle of conservation, and a sure principle of transmission; without at all excluding a principle of improvement. It leaves acquisition free; but it secures what it acquires. Whatever advantages are obtained by a state proceeding on these maxims are locked fast as in a sort of family settlement; grasped as in a kind of mortmain for ever. By a constitutional policy, working after the pattern of nature, we receive, we hold, we transmit our government and our privileges, in the same manner in which we enjoy and transmit our property and our lives. . . .

In this choice of inheritance, we have given to our frame of polity the image of a relation in blood; binding up the constitution of our country with our dearest domestic ties; adopting our fundamental laws into the bosom of our family affections; keeping inseparable, and cherishing with the warmth of all their combined and mutually reflected charities, our state, our hearths, our sepulchres, and our altars. . . .

You [the French people] might, if you pleased, have profited of our example and have given to your recovered freedom a correspondent dignity. Your privileges, though discontinued, were not lost to memory. Your constitution, it is true, whilst you were out of possession, suffered waste and dilapidation; but you possessed in some parts the walls, and in all the foundations of a noble and venerable castle. You might have repaired those walls; you might have built on those old foundations. Your constitution was suspended before it was perfected; but you had the elements of a constitution very nearly as good as could be wished. In your old States you possessed that variety of parts corresponding with the various descriptions of which your community was happily composed; you had all that combination, and all that opposition of interests, you had that action and counteraction which, in the natural and in the political world, from the reciprocal struggle of discordant powers, draws out the harmony of the universe. These opposed and conflicting interests, which you considered as so great a blemish in your old and in our present constitution, interpose a salutary check to all precipitate resolutions. They render deliberation not a matter of choice, but of necessity; they make all change a subject of *compromise*, which naturally begets moderation; they produce *temperaments*, preventing the sore evil of harsh, crude, unqualified, reformations; and rendering all the headlong exertions of arbitrary power, in the few or in the many, for ever impracticable. Through that diversity of members and interests, general liberty had as many securities as there were separate views in the several orders; whilst by pressing down the whole by the weight of a real monarchy, the separate parts would have been prevented from warping and starting from their allotted places.

You had all these advantages in your ancient States; but you chose to act as if you had never been moulded into civil society, and had everything to begin anew.

13. THOMAS PAINE, *RIGHTS OF MAN* (1791)[15]

One of those who read Burke's denunciation of the French Revolution was Thomas Paine, the British writer whose pamphlets The American Crisis *and* Common Sense *had helped push the Thirteen Colonies toward independence. A committed republican, Paine rejoiced at the outbreak of revolution in France, applauded its radicalism, and was appalled at Burke's attacks. His* Rights of Man *was a direct rebuttal to Burke's* Reflections. *In this excerpt from it, Paine criticizes Burke's notion of rights.*

We have seen, says Mr. Burke, "the French rebel against a mild and lawful monarch, with more fury, outrage, and insult, than any people has been known to rise against the most illegal usurper, or the most sanguinary tyrant." This is one among a thousand of other instances in which Mr. Burke shows that he is ignorant of the springs and principles of the French Revolution.

It was not against Louis XVI, but against the despotic principles of the government, that the nation revolted. These principles had not their origin in him, but in the original establishment, many centuries back; and they were become too deeply rooted to be removed, and the Augean stable of parasites and plunderers too abominably filthy to be cleansed by anything short of a complete and universal revolution. . . .

The King was known to be the friend of the nation, and this circumstance was favorable to the enterprise. Perhaps no man bred up in the style of an absolute

---

[15]Thomas Paine, *The Rights of Man* (London: J. S. Jordan, 1791), 19–21, 74–75, 134–137.

king, ever possessed a heart so little disposed to the exercise of that species of power as the present King of France.

But the principles of the government itself still remained the same. The monarch and the monarchy were distinct and separate things, and it was against the established despotism of the latter, and not against the person or principles of the former, that the revolt commenced, and the Revolution has been carried. . . .

The natural moderation of Louis XVI contributed nothing to alter the hereditary despotism of the monarchy. All the tyrannies of the former reigns, acted under that hereditary despotism, were still liable to be revived in the hands of a successor. . . .

Every office and department has its despotism, founded upon custom and usage. . . . The original hereditary despotism, resident in the person of the king, divides and subdivides itself into a thousand shapes and forms, till at last the whole of it is acted by deputation.

This was the case in France; and against this species of despotism, proceeding on through an endless labyrinth of office till the source of it is scarcely perceptible, there is no mode of redress. . . .

What Mr. Burke considers as a reproach to the French Revolution (that of bringing it forward under a reign more mild than the preceding ones), is one of its highest honors. The revolutions that have taken place in other European countries, have been excited by personal hatred. The rage was against the man, and he became the victim. But, in the instance of France, we see a revolution generated in the rational contemplation of the rights of man, and distinguishing from the beginning between persons and principles. . . .

The idea of hereditary legislators is as inconsistent as that of hereditary judges, or hereditary juries; and as absurd as an hereditary mathematician, or an hereditary wise man; and as ridiculous as an hereditary poet. . . .

To arrange this matter in a clearer view . . . it will be necessary to state the distinct heads under which (what is called) an hereditary crown, or, more properly speaking, an hereditary succession to the government of a nation, can be considered; which are,

First, the right of a particular family to establish itself.

Secondly, the right of a nation to establish a particular family.

With respect to the first of these heads, that of a family establishing itself with hereditary powers on its own authority, and independent of the consent of a nation, all men will concur in calling it despotism; and it would be trespassing on their understanding to attempt to prove it.

But the second head, that of a nation establishing a particular family with *hereditary powers*, does not present itself as despotism on the first reflection; but if men will permit a second reflection to take place, and carry that reflection forward but one remove out of their own persons to that of their offspring, they will then see that hereditary succession becomes in its consequences the same despotism to others, which they reprobated for themselves. It operates to preclude the consent of the succeeding generations; and the preclusion of consent is despotism.

When the person who at any time shall be in possession of a government, or those who stand in succession to him, shall say to a nation, I hold this power in "contempt" of you, it signifies not on what authority he pretends to say it. It is no relief, but an aggravation to a person in slavery, to reflect that he was sold by his parent; and as that which heightens the criminality of an act cannot be produced to prove the legality of it, hereditary succession cannot be established as a legal thing.

In order to arrive to a more perfect decision on this head, it will be proper to consider the generation which undertakes to establish a family with *hereditary powers*, apart and separate from the generations which are to follow; and also to consider the character in which the *first* generation acts with respect to succeeding generations.

The generation which first selects a person, and puts him at the head of its government, either with the title of king, or any other distinction, acts its *own choice*, be it wise or foolish, as a free agent for itself. The person so set up is not hereditary, but selected and appointed; and the generation who sets him up, does not live under an hereditary government, but under a government of its own choice and establishment. Were the generation who sets him up, and the person so set up, to live forever, it never could become hereditary succession; and of consequence, hereditary succession can only follow on the death of the first parties.

As therefore hereditary succession is out of the question with respect to the *first* generation, we have not to consider the character in which that generation acts with respect to the commencing generation, and to all succeeding ones.

It assumes a character, to which it has neither right nor title. It changes itself from a *Legislator* to a *Testator*, and affects to make its will, which is to have operation after the demise of the makers, to bequeath the government; and it not only attempts to bequeath, but to establish on the succeeding generation, a new and different form of government under which itself lived.

Itself, as is already observed, lived not under an hereditary government, but under a government of its own choice and establishment; and it now attempts, by virtue of a will and testament (which it has not authority to make), to take from the commencing generation, and all future ones, the rights and free agency by which itself acted.

But exclusive of the right which any generation has to act collectively as a testator, the objects to which it applies itself in this case, are not within the compass of any law, or of any will or testament.

The rights of men in society are neither devisable, nor transferable, nor annihilable, but are descendible only; and it is not in the power of any generation to intercept finally and cut off the descent. If the present generation, or any other, are disposed to be slaves, it does not lessen the right of the succeeding generation to be free: wrongs cannot have a legal descent. . . .

In whatever light hereditary succession, as growing out of the will and testament of some former generation, presents itself, it is an absurdity. A cannot make a will to take from B the property of B, and give it to C; yet this is the manner in which (what is called) hereditary succession by law operates.

VI. Revolution and Counter-revolution

The National Assembly's divisive religious policy was the principle source of opposition to the Revolution; but it was only one of many. Nearly all of the Assembly's reforms hurt particular interests and offended certain sensibilities. Counter-revolutionaries mobilized by forming armies of émigrés on France's borders, inviting foreign military intervention, playing on popular Catholic sentiment to whip up hostility to the Revolution, and skewering the Assembly's policies in pamphlets and the press. Revolutionaries responded vigorously, not only through the organ of the Assembly itself, but also by grass roots activism. During the course of 1790 and 1791, tensions reached a crisis point.

14. THE JACOBIN CRUSADE[16]

The most important manifestation of grass-roots revolutionary activism was the network of political clubs that sprung up and proliferated from 1789 on. At the heart of the movement was the Jacobin Club of Paris. Meeting in the building that had formerly housed a Jacobin monastery, the Paris club lent its name to a nationwide movement. With encouragement from the center, local clubs were formed in all provincial towns and cities and, ultimately, in thousands of rural villages as well. The Jacobins saw themselves as the vigilant vanguard of the nation, ever ready to preach love of nation and combat the insidious efforts of the counter-revolutionaries. The following document is a 1792 appeal from the Paris club to its provincial affiliates, urging them to spread the movement to the countryside.

Brothers and Friends,

The Fatherland is demanding of your civic zeal the most important of services. We have already asked for it in calmer times. Your efforts have produced some good effects; several new Popular Societies have been formed, and we have affiliated them. But today, when the circumstances are pressing, when civil war looms, we need a general measure. . . .

You know, brothers and friends, that perverse men who seem to desire only the constitution have attacked the Patriotic Societies and tried to dissolve them and take from the French the precious right of free men to assemble peacefully and without arms. . . . Well then, let us employ our zeal and efforts to multiply the Patriotic Societies and spread them all across France. . . .

It is all too true that a fatal division of opinion reigns among the French, and we must say, with sighs and bitter tears, that this contagion has not spared patriots.

---

[16]Alphonse Aulard, ed., *La société des Jacobins: recueil de documents* (Paris: Jouast, 1892), vol. 3, 413–417.

This disease, one of the worst ever sprung from Pandora's Box, is causing ravages everywhere; it will infect, weaken, and destroy France if the true friends of the constitution do not halt its spread.

Division of opinions produces hatred, disdain, factions, and discussions which lead to civil war.

This war causes anarchy and the violation of laws; and anarchy will soon bring the return of despotism.

Such is the bloody circle through which the French have so often cycled ever since the establishment of their empire in Gaul. . . . Civil war always favored the executive power. It was also quite useful to the two insolent and perverse classes of former privileged persons, who separated themselves from the nation during times of barbarism and ignorance and who now want to make war on us because the constitution made them return to the great body of the people and took away their power to humiliate and oppress us. In a word, the Court, the clergy, and the nobility will never stop plotting, maneuvering, and conspiring in order to cause trouble and feed upon the carcass of the people. . . .

It is a constant, generally-recognized fact that the diverse enemies of the people of which we have spoken seem to be acting together to spark a civil war. . . . But another fact, a new phenomenon which has never before been seen in France during the centuries and revolutions that preceded our own, is that there now exists Societies of free men, who will never surrender the rights of liberty and equality and who have sworn to defend them or die. The usefulness of the Patriotic Societies is an incontestable truth. . . .

But despite their ever-active vigilance, the enemies of equality, far from halting their infernal maneuvers, become grimmer with the obstacles they encounter. They have made new efforts, employed new methods, and have succeeded in giving credence to the idea of an imminent counter revolution. . . .

Brothers and friends, the more they try to ignite a civil war, the more we must resist their efforts.

To make that resistance real, solid, and victorious, it must exist in public opinion. That is where the unique and so-envied sway of the Jacobins lies. But opinion does not enlighten all French soil equally. It exists in the cities, but has barely penetrated the countryside. . . . If we bring the sacred fire to the 6,000 rural cantons, we will bring unity of principles and feelings to the entire political body and quench the flames of civil war.

How was Christianity established? By the missions of the apostles of the Church.

How can we solidly establish the Constitution? By the missions of the apostles of liberty and equality.

In the name of our cherished fatherland, of the august liberty we have conquered and must never lose, and of the holy, sweet equality which so enrages our enemies, . . . in their name we thus invite you, brothers and friends, . . . to undertake this honorable mission as soon as possible. . . . Each Society can take responsibility for the rural cantons of its district. . . .

It will be enough to send them a patriot with knowledge and zeal, with a regulation adapted to each locality, the declaration of rights, the constitution, the *Almanac of Father Gérard*, a good pamphlet against fanaticism (such as the *Letter* of M. Creuzé la Touche), a good newspaper, and a good model of a pike.

These writings will be read on the mornings and evenings of holidays. We think that, since most country folk have been deprived of the advantages of education, . . . we must restrict ourselves to readings and lessons, and to avoid, at least in the beginning, discussions which might embitter people and lead to the formation of party spirit. . . . Soon, the country folk, instructed and touched by these fraternal institutions, will look with horror upon those evildoing beings who are fanning the flames of civil war. They will feel the need to pay their taxes scrupulously. They will acquire great energy, and we will see the genius of liberty, armed with bonnet and pike, march proudly in the smallest hamlets of France and menace enemies both foreign and domestic.

These missionaries . . . will be the precursors of the teachers that the National Assembly will one day send to spread the new public education. They will prepare the indolent minds of our farmers for greater knowledge. They will open their good and generous hearts to the sweet, sublime sentiment of love of fatherland.

15. THE KING'S FLIGHT (JUNE 21–22, 1791)[17]

Louis XVI witnessed the radicalization of the Revolution with dismay. The hapless monarch had been carried along by events, suffering various indignities at the hands of the Paris people and reluctantly accepting a host of radical reforms. By mid-1791, his patience had run out. On the night of June 21, 1791, he fled from Paris with his queen, Marie-Antoinette, with the intention of escaping to friendly military forces (and possibly to a foreign country, where military aid might be obtained). The following morning, however, he was caught at Varennes, in eastern France, and brought back to Paris, a virtual prisoner. Before fleeing, he had left behind a written statement explaining his opposition to the Revolution.

As long as the king hoped to see the order and wellbeing of the kingdom restored by the National Assembly, and by his residence near that Assembly in the capital of the kingdom, he did not baulk at any personal sacrifice; he would have even overlooked the nullity with which his absolute lack of liberty had stained everything he had done since October 1789 if that hope had been fulfilled. But, today, now that his only recompense for so many sacrifices is seeing the destruction of the kingdom, disregard for all powers, properties violated, the safety of persons everywhere placed in danger, crimes gone unpunished, and total anarchy establishing itself above the laws, without the appearance of authority given him by the

---

[17]Mavidal and Laurent, *AP*, vol. 27, 378–383.

new Constitution being sufficient to repair a single one of the evils that afflict the kingdom, the King, after having solemnly protested against all of his acts during his captivity, believes himself obliged to place before the eyes of the French and the entire universe the portrait of his conduct and that of the Government which has established itself in the kingdom. . . .

The convocation of the Estates-General, the doubling of the deputies of the Third-Estate, . . . all the reductions the King made in his personal expenditures, . . . and, finally, the reunion of the Orders, carried out at the King's wish (a measure that His Majesty then deemed indispensable to energize the Estates-General), all his cares, pains, generosity, devotion for his people, everything was ignored and denatured.

Once the Estates-General, having named itself the National Assembly, began to work on the Constitution of the kingdom, let us recall the petitions that the factious skillfully had sent from several provinces, as well as the upheavals of Paris, to make the deputies violate one of the principal clauses in all their cahiers—that the confection of laws would be done together with the King. In violation of this clause, the Assembly placed the King entirely outside of the Constitution by refusing him the right to grant or refuse his sanction on constitutional articles . . . and, on purely legislative ones, by limiting the royal prerogative to a right of suspension until the third legislature, a purely illusory right, as so many examples prove.

What was left for the King but a vain shadow of royalty? He was given 25 million for his Civil List; but the splendor of his Household . . . must absorb it all. He was given the use of a few Crown domains, with many restrictions on their enjoyment. These domains are only a small part of those that the kings had possessed since ancient times, or the patrimony of His Majesty's ancestors which they united to the Crown. . . .

Something which hurt the King gravely was the attention paid to separating . . . services rendered personally to the King from those rendered to the State, as if these objects were not truly inseparable, and that services rendered to the King were not being rendered to the State.

Let us now examine the different parts of the government.

JUSTICE. The King cannot participate in any way in the making of laws. He only has the right to suspend, until the third legislature, objects which he does not consider to be constitutional and also the right to ask the Assembly to take up this or that matter without actually having the right to make a formal proposal. Justice is rendered in the King's name . . . but this is pure form. . . . One of the Assembly's most recent decrees has just deprived the King of one of the finest prerogatives attached everywhere to Royalty: that of granting pardons and commuting sentences. . . . This disposition greatly diminishes Royal Majesty in the eyes of the people, since they have long been accustomed to appealing to the King in their needs and suffering and in seeing him as the common father who can soothe their afflictions!

INTERIOR ADMINISTRATION. It is entirely in the hands of the departments, districts, and municipalities. . . . All these bodies are elected by the people and do not depend upon the government. . . . These bodies have gained little force and respect, and the Societies of the Friends of the Constitution . . . are often stronger than they are, thus nullifying their action. . . . However much they may want to maintain good order, they have not dared to use the means given them by the law, for fear of the people. . . .

According to the decrees, the disposition of the military forces is in the King's hands. He was declared supreme chief of the Army and Navy. But all the work on the formation of these two branches was done by the Assembly's committees without the participation of the King. Everything, down to the most minor disciplinary regulation, was done by them. And if the King still retains the right to appoint officers to a third or a quarter of posts, . . . this right has been rendered almost illusory by the multiple obstacles and opposition that everybody throws in the way. He was even obliged to redo his choice of the entire body of general officers because the appointments he proposed displeased the Clubs. . . . The Clubs and administrative bodies meddle in all the inner details of the army. . . . The Clubs are responsible for the spirit of revolt against the officers and military discipline that has spread through many regiments and which, if it is not dealt with promptly, will be the destruction of the Army. What is an army without leaders or discipline? . . .

FINANCES. . . . There is still no exact account of income and expenditure and of the resources that could help fill the deficit. [The Assembly] has settled for hypothetical calculations. The Assembly has rapidly destroyed several taxes whose weight, in truth heavily burdened the people, but which offered guaranteed resources. . . . Ordinary tax collection is in great arrears, and the extraordinary resources of the first 1.2 billion in *assignats* has already been spent. . . .

Finally, some decrees have declared the King to be supreme chief of the kingdom's administration, but subsequent ones regulated the organization of the ministry in such a manner as to prevent the King . . . from doing anything without a decision from the Assembly. The system of the heads of the dominant party . . . has cast such mistrust over all the agents of government that it has now become almost impossible to fill places in the administration. . . .

This form of government, so inherently flawed, is made worse by two causes.

1st. Through its committees, the Assembly constantly exceeds the limits it has placed on itself. . . . It even exercises, through its Committee of Investigations, a veritable despotism more barbarous and unbearable than anything in history.

2nd. In almost all the cities and even in several burgs and villages of the Kingdom, associations known as Friends of the Constitution have been established . . . which form an immense corporation much more dangerous than those which existed previously. . . . They deliberate on all aspects of government, correspond with each other on these objects, issue and receive denunciations, make rulings, and have gained such a preponderance that the administrative and judicial bodies, and even the National Assembly itself, almost always obey its orders. . . . The spirit of the Clubs dominates and infects everything. The thousands of slanderous and incendiary newspapers and pamphlets which appear each day are but their echoes. . . . [Their ultimate goal is] to destroy the vestiges of the royalty maintained by the first decrees and establish a metaphysical, philosophical government. . . .

People of France, is this what you wanted when you sent your representatives to the National Assembly? Do you want anarchy and the despotism of the Clubs to replace the monarchical government under which the nation has prospered for fourteen centuries?

VII. War

After the King's Flight, the war of words between revolutionaries and counter-revolutionaries flared into armed conflict, as European monarchs sympathetic to the captive monarch threatened dire consequences if he were harmed. On April 20, 1792, the Assembly declared war on the house of Austria. Radicals looked forward to war as a way to unmask hidden counter-revolutionaries, forge national unity, and replace the monarchy with a republic. Counter-revolutionaries hoped that war would lead to the speedy defeat of France's disorganized, mutinous armies and a restoration of the Old Regime. By 1793, the war had become an ideological struggle pitting nearly all of the monarchical powers of Europe against revolutionary France.

16. THE DECLARATION OF WAR (APRIL 20, 1792)[18]

Although it was the National Assembly that formally declared war, it justified its action as both a defensive struggle and a crusade to liberate the people of Europe from superstition, monarchy, and feudalism. It consequently invited the subjects of the other European powers to join France in throwing off the yoke of tyranny and reclaiming their rightful liberty.

The National Assembly, deliberating upon the formal proposition of the king, in view of the fact that the court of Vienna, in contempt of treaties, has not ceased to extend open protection to French rebels;

That it has instigated and formed a concert with several of the powers of Europe directed against the independence and safety of the French nation;

That Francis I, the king of Hungary and Bohemia, has, by his diplomatic notes of the 18th of March and the 7th of April last, refused to renounce this concert;

That, in spite of the proposition made to him by the note of March 11, 1792, to reduce to a peace basis the troops upon the frontiers, he has continued, and hastened, hostile preparations;

[18]Robinson, *Readings*, vol. 2, 440–441.

That he has formally attacked the sovereignty of the French nation by declaring his intention of maintaining the claims of the German princes who hold territory in France, whom the French nation has repeatedly offered to indemnify;

· That he has endeavored to divide the citizens of France and arm them against one another by holding out to the malcontents the hope of assistance from a concert of the powers;

And that, finally, by his refusal to reply to the last dispatches of the king of France, he leaves no hope of obtaining, by way of friendly negotiation, the redress of these several grievances—which is equivalent to a declaration of war—the Assembly decrees that immediate action is urgent.

The National Assembly proclaims that the French nation, faithful to the principles consecrated by its constitution, "not to undertake any war with a view to conquest nor ever to employ its forces against the liberty of any people," only takes up arms for the maintenance of its liberty and independence;

That the war which it is forced to prosecute is not a war of nation against nation, but the just defense of a free people against the unjust aggression of a king;

That the French nation never confuses its brethren with its real enemies;

That it will neglect nothing which may reduce the curse of war, spare and preserve property, and cause all the unhappiness inseparable from war to fall alone upon those who have conspired against its liberty;

That it adopts in advance all foreigners who, abjuring the cause of its enemies, shall range themselves under its banners and consecrate their efforts to the defense of liberty; and that it will promote by all means in its power their settling in France.

Deliberating upon the formal proposition of the king and after having decreed the matter one of urgent importance, the Assembly decrees war against the king of Hungary and of Bohemia.

17. THE BRUNSWICK MANIFESTO (JULY 25, 1792)[19]

The war went badly for France. In September 1792, it was invaded by Austrian and Prussian troops. Their commander, the Duke of Brunswick, issued a manifesto to the French people. In it, he cast the invasion as a campaign to restore common-sense law and order and the authority of the King. He promised not to punish those who submitted peacefully, but threatened the city of Paris with collective punishment if the royal family were molested in any way.

Their majesties the emperor and the king of Prussia having intrusted to me the command of the united armies which they have collected on the frontiers of France, I desire to announce to the inhabitants of that kingdom the motives which

---

[19]Robinson, *Readings*, vol. 2, 443–445.

have determined the policy of the two sovereigns and the purposes which they have in view.

After arbitrarily violating the rights of the German princes in Alsace and Lorraine, disturbing and overthrowing good order and legitimate government in the interior of the realm, committing against the sacred person of the king and his august family outrages and brutalities which continue to be renewed daily, those who have usurped the reins of government have at last completed their work by declaring an unjust war on his Majesty the emperor and attacking his provinces situated in the Low Countries. Some of the territories of the Germanic empire have been affected by this oppression, and others have only escaped the same fate by yielding to the threats of the dominant party and its emissaries.

His Majesty the king of Prussia, united with his Imperial Majesty by the bonds of a strict defensive alliance and himself a preponderant member of the Germanic body, would have felt it inexcusable to refuse to march to the help of his ally and fellow-member of the empire. . . .

To these important interests should be added another aim equally important and very close to the hearts of the two sovereigns—namely, to put an end to the anarchy in the interior of France, to check the attacks upon the throne and the altar, to reestablish the legal power, to restore to the king the security and the liberty of which he is now deprived and to place him in a position to exercise once more his legitimate authority.

Convinced that the sane portion of the French nation abhors the excesses of the faction which dominates it, and that the majority of the people look forward with impatience to the time when they may declare themselves openly against the odious enterprises of their oppressors, his Majesty the emperor and his Majesty the king of Prussia call upon them and invite them to return without delay to the path of reason, justice, order, and peace. In accordance with these views, I, the undersigned, the commander in chief of the two armies, declare:

1. That, drawn into this war by irresistible circumstances, the two allied courts entertain no other aims than the welfare of France, and have no intention of enriching themselves by conquests.

2. That they do not propose to meddle in the internal government of France, and that they merely wish to deliver the king, the queen, and the royal family from their captivity. . . .

3. That the allied armies will protect the towns and villages, and the persons and goods of those who shall submit to the king and who shall cooperate in the immediate reestablishment of order and the police power throughout France.

4. . . . That, on the contrary, the members of the National Guard who shall fight against the troops of the two allied courts, and who shall be taken with arms in their hands, shall be treated as enemies and punished as rebels to their king. . . .

7. That the inhabitants of the towns and villages who dare to defend themselves against the troops of their Imperial and Royal Majesties and fire on

them . . . shall be punished immediately according to the most stringent laws of war, and their houses shall be burned or destroyed. . . .

8. The city of Paris and all its inhabitants without distinction shall be required to submit at once and without delay to the king, to place that prince in full and complete liberty, and to assure to him, as well as to the other royal personages, the inviolability and respect which the law of nature and of nations demands of subjects toward sovereigns. . . .

Their said Majesties declare, on their word of honor as emperor and king, that if the chateau of the Tuileries is entered by force or attacked, if the least violence be offered to their Majesties the king, queen, and royal family, and if their safety and their liberty be not immediately assured, they will inflict an ever memorable vengeance by delivering over the city of Paris to military execution and complete destruction, and the rebels guilty of the said outrages to the punishment they merit. . . .

18. THE *MARSEILLAISE* (1792)[20]

In response to the crisis, the National Assembly called on the National Guards (a citizen's militia that began to be formed in the summer of 1789) to defend the homeland. By the end of 1792, perhaps 200,000 had armed themselves, formed battalions, and rushed to the frontier. A particularly patriotic group of volunteers from the southern city of Marseille adopted as their marching song a defiant chant written by an artillery officer, Rouget de L'Isle. It came to be known as the Marseillaise after their hometown. On their way to the front, the Marseillaise volunteers passed through Paris where they played a key role in attacking the royal palace (the Tuileries) on August 10th and overthrowing the monarchy. A Republic was formally declared the following month and elections were held for a National Convention to draft a republican constitution. But before it did so, the Convention put Louis XVI on trial for treason and found him guilty. He was executed in January 1793. The Marseillaise is still the national anthem of the French Republic.

Forward children of the fatherland
The day of Glory has arrived
Against us stands tyranny
The bloody flag is raised
The bloody flag is raised
Can you hear in the countryside
The howls of these savage soldiers
They come right up to us
To cut the throats of your wives and children

---

[20]http://legacy.fordham.edu/Halsall/mod/MARSEILL.asp

To arms, citizens!
Form up your battalions
Forward march, Forward march!
Let their impure blood
Water our fields

Sacred love of the fatherland
Guide and support our vengeful arms
Liberty, beloved liberty
Fight with your defenders
Fight with your defenders
Under our flags, so that victory
Will rally around your manly strains;
Let your dying enemies
Behold your triumph and our glory

19. DECREE FOR THE LEVY EN MASSE (AUGUST 23, 1793)[21]

The Austro-Prussian invasion of France was stemmed at the Battle of Valmy (September 20, 1792), and the invaders retired across the Rhine into Germany. But French armies were in disarray. It was obvious that the invasion would be renewed with even more force the following spring, when the weather became suitable for military campaigning. To prepare for the onslaught, the National Convention declared the general mobilization of the population. Known as the levy en masse, this marked the beginning of modern, total war.

1. From this moment, until the enemy has been driven from the soil of the Republic, all Frenchmen are in permanent requisition for the service of the armies. Young men shall go to battle; married men shall forge arms and transport provisions; women shall make tents and clothing and shall serve in the hospitals; children shall turn old linen into lint; the aged shall go to public places in order to arouse the courage of the warriors and preach hatred of kings and the unity of the Republic.

2. National buildings shall be converted into barracks, public places into arms' workshops, the soil of the cellars shall be washed in order to extract saltpeter.

3. Arms of regulation caliber shall be reserved exclusively for those who march against the enemy; [military] service in the interior shall be performed with hunting pieces and side arms.

---

[21]Frank Maloy Anderson, ed., *The Constitutions and Other Select Documents Illustrative of the History of France, 1789–1907*, 2nd ed. (Minneapolis, MN: H. W. Wilson, 1908), 184–185.

4. Saddle horses are requisitioned in order to fill out the cavalry units; draft horses, other than those employed in agriculture, shall convey artillery and provisions.

5. The Committee of Public Safety is charged with taking all measures to establish without delay an extraordinary manufacture of arms of every sort, which correspond to the ardor and energy of the French people. It is thus authorized to form all the establishments, factories, workshops, and mills deemed necessary for the execution of these works, as well as to requisition, throughout the entire extent of the Republic, the skilled craftsmen and workers who can contribute to their success.

6. The representatives of the people dispatched for the execution of the present law . . . are vested with unlimited powers. . . .

7. Nobody can get himself replaced in the service for which he has been requisitioned. Public functionaries shall remain at their posts.

VIII. The Republican Revolution

When the National Convention convened in September 1792, the nascent republic faced multiple existential threats. Economic hardship, inflation, foreign invasion, seething internal counter-revolution that erupted into armed conflict (notably in the western region known as the Vendée), popular militancy, and murderous factional infighting complicated the Convention's task: to give France a republican constitution. Nonetheless, while they confronted these existential challenges, the deputies of the Convention found the time and energy to undertake the task for which they had been elected. They not only recast laws and institutions along republican lines but also implemented a pervasive republican pedagogy to transform the French into virtuous citizens. They outlined new systems of schooling to republicanize the youth, remade the calendar to efface Catholic worship, and replaced it with festivals, such as the Festival of Reason, celebrating natural law and human rights. Although these efforts were short-lived, ending with the overthrow of Robespierre and his supporters on the 9th of Thermidor (July 27, 1794), they were the high-water mark of the revolutionary tide.

20. SAINT-JUST, *REPUBLICAN INSTITUTIONS* (1794)[22]

One of the most fervent proponents of republican regeneration was Louis-Antoine de Saint-Just. The youngest deputy in the Convention, he was a close associate of Robespierre and would share his fate. His dream of an egalitarian, agricultural, and military society drew on classical models.

---

[22]Robinson, *Readings*, vol. 2, 452–454.

I challenge you to establish liberty so long as it remains possible to arouse the unfortunate classes against the new order of things, and I defy you to do away with poverty altogether unless each one has his own land. . . . Where you find large landowners you find many poor people. Nothing can be done in a country where agriculture is carried on a large scale. Man was not made for the workshop, the hospital, or the poorhouse. All that is horrible. Men must live in independence, each with his own wife and his robust and healthy children. We must have neither rich nor poor.

The poor man is superior to government and the powers of the world; he should address them as a master. We must have a system which puts all these principles in practice and assures comfort to the entire people. Opulence is a crime. . . .

Children shall belong to their mother, provided she has suckled them herself, until they are five years old; after that they shall belong to the republic until death. The mother who does not suckle her children ceases to be a mother in the eyes of the country. Child and citizen belong to the country, and a common instruction is essential. Children shall be brought up in the love of silence and scorn for fine talkers. They shall be trained in laconic speech. Games shall be prohibited in which they declaim, and they shall be habituated to simple truth.

The boys shall be educated, from the age of five to sixteen, by the country; from five to ten they shall learn to read, write, and swim. No one shall strike or caress a child. They shall be taught what is good and left to nature. He who strikes a child shall be banished. The children shall eat together and shall live on roots, fruit, vegetables, milk, cheese, bread, and water. The teachers of children from five to ten years old shall not be less than sixty years of age. . . . The education of children from ten to sixteen shall be military and agricultural.

Every man twenty-one years of age shall publicly state in the temples who are his friends. This declaration shall be renewed each year during the month Ventôse.[23] If a man deserts his friend, he is bound to explain his motives before the people in the temples; if he refuses, he shall be banished. Friends shall not put their contracts into writing, nor shall they oppose one another at law. If a man commits a crime, his friends shall be banished. Friends shall dig the grave of a deceased friend and prepare for obsequies, and with the children of the deceased they shall scatter flowers on the grave. He who says that he does not believe in friendship, or who has not friends, shall be banished. A man convicted of ingratitude shall be banished.

The French people recognize the existence of the Supreme Being and the immortality of the soul. The first day of every month is consecrated to the Eternal. Incense shall burn day and night in the temples and shall be tended in turn for twenty-four hours by the men who have reached the age of sixty. The temples shall never be closed. The French people devote their fortunes and their children to the Eternal. The immortal souls of all those who have died for the fatherland, who

---

[23]Late February through late March.

have been good citizens, who have cherished their father and mother and never abandoned them, are in the bosom of the Eternal.

The first day of the month Germinal,[24] the republic shall celebrate the festival of the Divinity of Nature and of the People; the first day of the month Floréal,[25] the festival of the Divinity of love, and of husband and wife, etc.

Every year on the first day of Floréal the people of each commune shall select from among the inhabitants of the commune, and in the temple, a young man rich and virtuous without deformity, at least twenty-one years of age and not over thirty, who shall in turn select and marry a poor maiden, in everlasting memory of human equality.

21. MAXIMILLIAN ROBESPIERRE, *THE PRINCIPLES OF POLITICAL MORALITY* (1794)[26]

As committed republicans like Saint-Just understood, the creation and diffusion of republican civic virtue would be the work of many years of educational efforts, both formal and informal. But attacked on all sides and facing growing disillusionment and apathy from a public weary of war and economic hardship, the Convention did not have time to spare. In this influential speech, Maximillian Robespierre argued that even if most of the French had not yet become selfless republicans in their hearts, they could be made to act like good republican citizens by terror. This speech is associated with the inauguration of the Reign of Terror, the year-long period beginning in the summer of 1793 during which the Convention enforced its authority and morality by coercion, notably the guillotine.

What is the goal of our revolution? The tranquil enjoyment of liberty and equality; the reign of that eternal justice, the laws of which are graven not on marble or stone, but on the hearts of men, even in the heart of the slave who has forgotten them, and in that of the tyrant who disowns them.

We want an order of things where all low and cruel passions are enchained, all beneficent and generous passions awakened by the laws; where ambition consists of the desire to deserve glory and serve the country; where distinctions grow from the system of equality, where the citizen submits to the magistrate's authority, the magistrate obeys the people, and the people are governed by love of justice; where the country secures each individual's comfort, and where each individual prides himself on the prosperity and glory of his country; where every soul expands by a free communication of republican sentiments, and by the necessity of deserving the esteem of a great people; where the arts serve to embellish that liberty which

---

[24]Late March through late April.
[25]Late April through early May.
[26]*Report upon the Principles of Political Morality* (Philadelphia, PA: Benjamin Franklin Bache, 1794).

gives them value and support, and commerce is a source of public wealth and not merely of immense riches to a few individuals.

We wish in our country that morality replace egotism, probity for false honor, principles for usages, duties for good manners, the empire of reason for the tyranny of fashion, a contempt of vice for a contempt of misfortune, pride for insolence, magnanimity for vanity, the love of glory for the love of money, good people for good company, merit for intrigue, genius for wit, truth for tinsel show, the attractions of happiness for the ennui of sensuality, the grandeur of man for the littleness of the great, a people magnanimous, powerful, happy, for a people amiable, frivolous, and miserable; in a word, all the virtues and miracles of a Republic instead of all the vices and absurdities of a Monarchy.

We wish, in a word, to fulfill the intentions of nature and the destiny of man, realize the promise of philosophy and acquit providence of a long reign of crime and tyranny. That France, once illustrious among enslaved nations, may, by eclipsing the glory of all free countries that ever existed, become a model to nations, a terror to oppressors, a consolation to the oppressed, an ornament of the universe and that, by sealing the work with our blood, we may at least witness the dawn of the bright day of universal happiness. This is our ambition, this is the end of our efforts. . . .

Since virtue and equality are the soul of the republic, and that your aim is to found, to consolidate the republic, it follows that the first rule of your political conduct should be to let all your measures tend to maintain equality and encourage virtue, for the first care of the legislator should be to strengthen the principles on which the government rests. Hence all that tends to excite a love of country, to purify manners, to exalt the mind, to direct the passions of the human heart towards the public good, you should adopt and establish. All that tends to warp them into selfish egotism, to awaken an infatuation for littleness, and a disregard for greatness, you should reject or repress. In the system of the French revolution, that which is immoral is impolitic, and what tends to corrupt is counter-revolutionary. Weaknesses, vices, prejudices are the road to monarchy. Carried away, too often perhaps, by the force of ancient habits, as well as by the innate imperfection of human nature, to false ideas and pusillanimous sentiments, we have more to fear from the excesses of weakness than from excesses of energy. The warmth of zeal is not perhaps the most dangerous rock that we have to avoid; but rather that languor which ease produces and a distrust of our own courage. Therefore continually wind up the sacred spring of republican government, instead of letting it run down. . . .

It is not necessary to detail the natural consequences of the principle of democracy, it is the principle itself, simple yet copious, which deserves to be developed.

Republican virtue may be considered as it respects the people and as it respects the government. It is necessary in both. When however, the government alone want it, there exists a resource in that of the people; but when the people themselves are corrupted, liberty is already lost.

Happily virtue is natural in the people [despite] aristocratical prejudices. A nation is truly corrupt when, after having by degrees lost is character and liberty, it slides from democracy into aristocracy or monarchy; this is the death of the political body. . . .

But, when by prodigious effects of courage and of reason, a whole people breaks asunder the feters of despotism to make of the fragments trophies to liberty; when, by their innate vigor, they rise in a manner from the arms of death to resume all the strength of youth; when, in turns forgiving and inexorable, intrepid and docile, they can neither be checked by impregnable ramparts nor by innumerable armies of tyrants leagued against them, and yet of themselves stop at the voice of the law; if then they do not reach the heights of their destiny, it can only be the fault of those who govern.

Again, it may be said, that to love justice and equality, the people need no great effort of virtue; it is sufficient that they love themselves. . . .

If virtue be the spring of a popular government in times of peace, the spring of that government during a revolution is virtue combined with terror; virtue, without which terror is destructive; terror, without which virtue is impotent. Terror is only justice prompt, severe, and inflexible; it is then an emanation of virtue; it is less a distinct principle than a natural consequence of the general principle of democracy, applied to the most pressing wants of the country.

It has been said that terror is the spring of despotic government. Does yours then resemble despotism? Yes, as the steel that glistens in the hands of the heroes of liberty resembles the sword with which the satellites of tyranny are armed. Let the despot govern by terror his debased subjects; he is right as a despot: conquer by terror the enemies of liberty and you will be right as founders of the republic. The government in a revolution is the despotism of liberty against tyranny. Is force only intended to protect crime? Is not the lightning of heaven made to blast vice exalted?

The law of self-preservation, with every being whether physical or moral, is the first law of nature. Crime butchers innocence to secure a throne, and innocence struggles with all its might against the attempts of crime. If tyranny reigned one single day, not a patriot would survive it. How long yet will the madness of despots be called justice and the justice of the people barbarity or rebellion? How tenderly oppressors and how severely the oppressed are treated! Nothing more natural; whoever does not abhor crime cannot love virtue. Yet one or the other must be crushed. Let mercy be shown the royalists, exclaim some men. Pardon the villains! No, be merciful to innocence, pardon the unfortunate, show compassion for human weakness.

The protection of government is only due to peaceable citizens; and all citizens in the republic are republicans. The royalists, the conspirators, are strangers, or rather enemies. Is not this dreadful contest, which liberty maintains against tyranny, indivisible? Are not the internal enemies the allies of those in the exterior? The assassins who lay waste the interior; the intriguers who purchase the consciences of the delegates of the people: the traitors who sell them; the mercenary libellists paid to dishonor the cause of the people, to smother public virtue, to fan the flame of civil discord, and bring about a political counter-revolution by means of a moral one; all these men, are they less culpable or less dangerous than the tyrants they serve? . . .

To punish the oppressors of humanity is clemency; to forgive them is cruelty. The severity of tyrants has barbarity for its principle; that of a republican government is founded on beneficence. Therefore, let him beware who should dare to influence the people by that terror which is made only for their enemies! Let him beware who, regarding the inevitable errors of civism in the same light, with the premeditated crimes of perfidiousness, or the attempts of conspirators, suffers the dangerous intriguer to escape and pursues the peaceable citizen! Death to the villain who dares abuse the sacred name of liberty or the powerful arms intended for her defence, to carry mourning or death to the patriotic heart. . . .

22. DECLARATION OF THE RIGHTS OF MAN AND CITIZEN (1793)[27]

In June 1793, the Convention fulfilled its original remit, the drafting of a republican constitution for France. Although it was approved in a national referendum, it was never implemented. The Constitution of 1793 was accompanied by a new, more democratic declaration of rights that was widely circulated. The new declaration captured the essence of the nonimplemented republican constitution.

The French people, convinced that forgetfulness and contempt of the natural rights of man are the sole causes of the miseries of the world, have resolved to set forth a solemn declaration of these sacred and inalienable rights, in order that all citizens, being able to compare unceasingly the acts of the government with the aim of every social institution, may never allow themselves to be oppressed and debased by tyranny; and in order that the people may always have before their eyes the foundations of their liberty and welfare, the magistrate the rule of his duties, the legislator the purpose of his commission.

In consequence, it proclaims in the presence of the Supreme Being the following declaration of the rights of man and citizen.

1. The aim of society is the common welfare. Government is instituted in order to guarantee to man the enjoyment of his natural and imprescriptible rights.
2. These rights are equality, liberty, security, and property.
3. All men are equal by nature and before the law.
4. Law is the free and solemn expression of the general will; it is the same for all, whether it protects or punishes; it can command only what is just and useful to society; it can forbid only what is injurious to it.

[27]Anderson, *The Constitutions*, 170–174.

5. All citizens are equally eligible to public employments. Free peoples know no other grounds for preference in their elections than virtue and talent.

6. Liberty is the power that belongs to man to do whatever is not injurious to the rights of others; it has nature for its principle, justice for its rule, law for its defence; its moral limit is this maxim: Do not do to another that which you do not wish should be done to you.

7. The right to express one's thoughts and opinions by means of the press or in any other manner, the right to assemble peaceably, the free pursuit of religion, cannot be forbidden. . . .

8. Security consists in the protection afforded by society to each of its members for the preservation of his person, his rights, and his property.

9. The law ought to protect public and personal liberty against the oppression of those who govern.

10. No one ought to be accused, arrested, or detained except in the cases determined by law and according to the forms that it has prescribed. . . .

11. Any act done against man outside of the cases and without the forms that the law determines is arbitrary and tyrannical; the one against whom it may be intended to be executed by violence has the right to repel it by force.

12. Those who may incite, expedite, subscribe to, execute, or cause to be executed arbitrary legal instruments are guilty and ought to be punished.

13. Every man being presumed innocent until he has been pronounced guilty, if it is thought indispensable to arrest him, all severity that may not be necessary to secure his person ought to be strictly repressed by law.

14. No one ought to be tried and punished except after having been heard or legally summoned, and except in virtue of a law promulgated prior to the offence. . . .

15. The law ought to impose only penalties that are strictly and obviously necessary; the punishments ought to be proportionate to the offence and useful to society.

16. The right of property is that which belongs to every citizen to enjoy, and to dispose at his pleasure, of his goods, income, and of the fruits of his labor and skill.

17. No kind of labor, tillage, or commerce can be forbidden to the skill of the citizens.

18. Every man can contract his services and his time, but he cannot sell himself nor be sold; his person is not an alienable property. The law knows of no such thing as the status of servant; there can exist only a contract for services and compensation between the man who works and the one who employs him.

19. No one can be deprived of the least portion of his property without his consent, unless a legally established public necessity requires it, and upon condition of a just and prior compensation.

20. No tax can be imposed except for the general advantage. All citizens have the right to participate in the establishment of taxes, to watch over their employment, and to cause an account of them to be rendered.
21. Public relief is a sacred debt. Society owes subsistence to unfortunate citizens, either by giving them work or by providing subsistence to those unable to work.
22. Education is needed by all. Society ought to favor with all its power the advancement of public reason and to put education at the door of every citizen.
23. The social guarantee consists in the action of all to secure to each the enjoyment and the maintenance of his rights; this guarantee rests upon national sovereignty.
24. It cannot exist if the limits of public functions are not clearly determined by law and if the responsibility of all the functionaries is not secured.
25. Sovereignty resides in the people; it is one and indivisible, imprescriptible, and inalienable.
26. No portion of the people can exercise the power of the entire people, but each section of the sovereign, in assembly, ought to enjoy the right to express its will with entire freedom.
27. Let any person who may usurp sovereignty be instantly put to death by free men.
28. A people always has the right to review, reform, and alter its constitution. One generation cannot subject future generations to its law.
29. Each citizen has an equal right to participate in the formation of the law and in the selection of his mandatories or agents.
30. Public functions are necessarily temporary; they cannot be considered as distinctions or rewards, but as duties.
31. The offences of the representatives of the people and of its agents ought never to go unpunished. No one has the right to claim for himself more inviolability than other citizens.
32. The right to present petitions to the depositories of the public authority cannot in any case be forbidden, suspended, or limited.
33. Resistance to oppression is the consequence of the other rights of man.
34. There is oppression against the social body when a single one of its members is oppressed; there is oppression against each member when the social body is oppressed.
35. When the government violates the rights of the people, insurrection is for the people and for each portion of the people, the most sacred of rights and the most indispensable of duties.

IX. The Directory

The overthrow of the reign of Terror in July 1794 ushered in a period of political retrenchment. The Constitution of 1793 was definitively abandoned. The remaining deputies in the Convention (known as Thermidorians) began to work on a new constitution for what they hoped would be a stable, moderate, republican regime. The result was the Constitution of 1795 that instituted a new government known as the Directory after its five-member executive body. Although the Directory lasted for four years, making it the longest lived of all the revolutionary governments, it could not end the Revolution. Caught between counter-revolutionaries hoping for a royalist, Catholic restoration and radical revolutionaries who wanted to revive the full-throated republicanism of 1793–1794 or adopt an even more radical system, the Directory never found its footing. Indeed, its electoral tampering, tendency to impose local military rule, and the coups it dealt alternately to the left and right may have made the situation worse.

23. DRAFTING THE DIRECTORIAL CONSTITUTION (1795)[28]

The political divisions that would destabilize the Directorial regime were already apparent in the work of the commission charged with drafting the Constitution of 1795. This is not surprising, for these fractures were themselves the product of more than five years of divisive revolutionary history. The following account by a left-leaning member of the drafting commission gives a sense of how these divisions were reflected in the drafting process and the Constitution itself.

There was a monarchical party in the [Constitutional] Commission, composed of Lesage d'Eure-et-Loire, Boisy d'Anglas, and Lanjuinais. . . . The other members were republicans in good faith.

The commission unanimously decided to shelve the Constitution of 1793. . . . Discussion was friendly and deliberations calm. We sought a middle way between monarchy and demagogy. My intention here is not to recount the Commission's daily work. . . . I will only recall several principal articles which illustrate our opinions and views. . . .

Declaration of Rights: Lesage d'Eure-et-Loire and Creuzé-Latouche did not want one, because it would give rise to false interpretations and would be a source of anarchic troubles and agitations. These arguments did not prevail. We felt we could remedy these drawbacks by a sort of commentary or antidote, under the name *Declaration of Duties*.

In order not to place before the primary assemblies [which were to vote on the constitution] the question of the form of government, the republic, we adopted this phrase, *The French Republic is one and indivisible*, instead of this one, which was proposed, *The French people constitute themselves as a republic*. . . .

[28]A. C. Thibaudeau, *Mémoires sur la Convention et le Directoire* (Paris: Baudouin Frères, 1824), vol. 1, 179–182.

Division of the Territory: . . . We kept the departments, but substituted grand municipalities or municipal administrations for the districts, almost solely for the reason given by Boisy, that the departmental administrations had always been for maintaining the established order, while the district administrations had been opposed [to it]. . . . He added that the district administrators had been agents of the Terror. . . .

Exercise of Political Rights: Some, such as Lesage and Lanjuinais, wanted to make it dependent upon the payment of taxes; Baudin upon the ability to read and write; the others, to give the greatest scope to equality. This opinion prevailed.

Legislature: By rejecting the establishment of two chambers, the Constituent Assembly had undertaken an innovation contrary to the doctrines of the greatest thinkers, consecrated by the example of England and the more recent one of the United States. This experiment had been a failure, because it was clear that it contributed to hasten the overthrow of the monarchy. The Commission did not think itself wiser than the founders of the American republic. . . . The system of two chambers was thus adopted almost unanimously. . . . We called them Senate and Chamber of Representatives. But since the word Senate had an aristocratic sound, the Convention called the chambers *Council of 500*, after the number of its members, and *Council of Elders*, because of the age required to enter it. All conditions of property or taxpaying were rejected; there was no other distinction than age, which we saw as a sufficient guarantee of maturity and wisdom. . . .

Executive Power: Baudin and Daunou wanted two supreme magistrates or biennial consuls, one of whom would govern during the first year and the other during the second. Lesage, Lanjuinais, and Durand-Maillane [wanted] one annual president; the others a council of at least three members. We ultimately adopted one of five. Each of us preferred this or that number, in proportion to our fear of anything hinting of royalty. The method of nomination to the executive power was the object of the most serious reflection. There were basically two choices: the immediate and mediate vote of the people or that of the legislature. The last choice won out. Louvet was afraid that, otherwise, the primary assemblies or their elected delegates would one day name a Bourbon. The majority was swayed by fear that the executive power would be too powerful if it derived from popular election. . . .

Location of the Legislature: To ensure its independence, it was proposed to establish it outside of Paris. This was my opinion. Experience made us fear the influence of the capital; against this, it was argued that the movements which had agitated it belonged to a time of revolution and that a constitutional government would surely prevent them; that Paris would be destroyed, its population would diminish, the arts would suffer, that to abandon the city would be a sign of weakness, that counterrevolutionaries would take control of it, etc. These reasons did not seem very convincing to me. I responded that, under a constitutional regime, the police would have even less force than under revolutionary government; . . . that, in addition to the inherent instability of republics, France would long be exposed to the struggle of the factions that the Revolution had created, . . . that if it were deprived of the presence of a Spartan government, the capital would not lose much; that it had prospered under the royal government, which was not located there; that if we placed the legislature at Versailles, but left the executive power at Paris, that would be enough so that the national representation would not be taken by surprise, invaded, and dissolved, as had happened several times to the Convention; finally, that once this arrangement put an end to the ever-growing aggrandizement of the capital, . . . I would see nothing but a happy result for the rest of France. The question remained undecided. . . .

24. INAUGURAL MESSAGE OF THE DIRECTORY TO THE FRENCH PEOPLE (NOVEMBER 5, 1795)[29]

The Constitution of 1795 went into effect late in the year. In one of its first acts, the Executive Directory issued a proclamation to the French people announcing its aim of bringing stability while defending core republican values. Acknowledging the difficulty of the task, the proclamation called on the French to have patience.

Frenchmen, the Directory has just been installed.

Resolved to maintain liberty or to perish, it is determined to consolidate the Republic and give the Constitution full energy and force.

Republicans, rely on it; its fate will never be separated from yours; inflexible justice and the strictest observation of the laws will be its guiding rule. To wage an active war against royalism, revive patriotism, repress all factions vigorously, extinguish partisan politics, destroy all desire for vengeance, establish concord, restore peace, regenerate morality, reopen the sources of reproduction, revive industry and commerce, stifle speculation, revive the arts and sciences, reestablish abundance and public credit, replace the chaos inseparable from revolutions with social order, and finally to achieve long-awaited happiness and glory for the French Republic: such is the task of your legislators and that of the Executive Directory. . . .

Wise laws, promptly and energetically executed, will soon lead us to forget our long sufferings.

But so many ills cannot be remedied, and so much work accomplished in a day. The French people are just and loyal: they will sense that in the confusion in which the State finds itself, at the moment when its government is entrusted to us, we need time, calm, and patience, and a confidence proportional to the efforts we have to make. This confidence will not be misplaced if the people no longer allows itself to be misled by the perfidious suggestions of royalists, who are reviving their plots; by fanatics who constantly inflame the people's imaginations; and by public leeches who always found their hopes on our miseries.

This confidence will not be misplaced if the people do not attribute to the new authorities the disorders brought about by six years of revolution, which can

---

[29]*Gazette nationale ou le Moniteur universel*, no. 49, 19 brumaire IV, 386. Translation by Stephen Clay.

only be repaired with time; it will not be misplaced if the people recall that for more than three years, every time the enemies of the Republic, profiting from our troubles, have agitated public opinion and caused unrest; under the pretext of diminishing the burden of these problems, these agitations have no other effect but to increase discredit, and to diminish reproduction and abundance that can only be the fruit of order and public tranquility.

Frenchmen, you will not hinder the nascent government; you will not require of it at its inception what it will be able to do once it has acquired its full vigor; rather you will calmly support the ever-active efforts and imperturbable progress of the Directory towards the prompt establishment of public happiness, and soon, you will be lastingly assured of having, with the glorious title of republicans, peace and national prosperity.

25. DOCTRINE OF GRACCHUS BABEUF[30]

Although the greatest threats the Directory faced came from domestic counter-revolution, foreign invasion, and general apathy, it also faced threats from its left. Of these, the most famous was the plot hatched by Gracchus Babeuf, a former feudal agent. Like many of the Directory's left-wing opponents, Babeuf wanted to implement the Constitution of 1793. But he went further. His belief that true equality required the systematic redistribution of wealth presaged the doctrines of nineteenth-century communists. He and his co-conspirators were tried in a widely publicized hearing and put to death.

1. Nature has bestowed upon each and every individual an adequate right to the enjoyment of property.
2. The purpose of society is to defend such equality, often assailed by the strong and the wicked in the state of nature, and to augment the general welfare through the co-operation of all.
3. Nature has imposed on each and every individual the obligation to work; anyone who evades his share of labor is a criminal.
4. Both work and benefits must be common to all.
5. There is oppression when one person is exhausted by labor and is destitute of everything, while another lives in luxury without doing any work at all.
6. Anyone who appropriates exclusively to himself the products of the earth or of manufacture is a criminal.
7. In a real society there ought to be neither rich nor poor.
8. The rich who are not willing to renounce their surplus in favor of the poor are enemies of the people.
9. No one, by accumulating to himself all power, may deprive another of the instruction necessary for his welfare. Education ought to be common to all.

[30]http://web.archive.org/web/19981202134533/http:/pluto.clinch.edu/history/wciv2/civ2ref/babeuf.htm

10. The aim of the French Revolution is to destroy inequality and to re-establish the general welfare.
11. The Revolution is not complete, because the rich monopolize all the property and govern exclusively, while the poor toil like slaves, languish in misery, and count for nothing in the State.
12. The Constitution of 1793[31] is the real law of Frenchmen, because the people have solemnly accepted it; because the Convention had no right to change it; because, in order to supersede it, the Convention has caused people to be shot for demanding that it be put into effect; because it has pursued and slaughtered deputies who were performing their duty by defending it; because terror against the people, and the influence of émigrés have presided over the fabrication and the alleged acceptance of the Constitution of 1795, despite the fact that it is not supported by a quarter of the votes obtained by that of 1793; because the Constitution of 1793 has sanctioned the inalienable right of every citizen to consent to the laws, to enjoy political rights, to meet in assembly, to demand what he deems useful, to receive education, and not to die of hunger; rights which the counter-revolutionary Act of 1795 openly and totally violated. . . .

X. The Brumaire Coup and Consulate

In the month of Brumaire (November) 1799, a group of plotters overthrew the Directory, jettisoned the Constitution of 1795, and established a new government with a stronger executive. The plotters included prominent legislators, including the perennial Abbé Sieyes, as well as the Revolution's most successful general, Napoleon Bonaparte. Bonaparte quickly took over the movement and imposed himself as First Consul, the head of what became known as the Consular government. The aim of Bonaparte and his associates was virtually identical to that of the Thermidorians—to end the Revolution and stabilize France while preserving fundamental revolutionary principles. Within a few years, Bonaparte had succeeded where the Directory before him had failed.

26. CONSULAR ADDRESS TO THE FRENCH PEOPLE (NOVEMBER 19, 1799)[32]

Like the Directory, the Brumarians issued a proclamation to the French people immediately upon taking power. The reasons it advanced to justify the seizure of power were largely the same as those put forward in 1795.

---

[31]The Constitution of 1793 was approved in a national referendum but never implemented. Although it is not included in this document collection, its principles are reflected in the 1793 Declaration of Rights.

[32]*Projet de resolution portant qu'il sera fait une addresse au peuple français, présenté au nom d'une commission par Cabanis, deputé de la Seine, séance du 19 brumaire an 8.*

People of France! Your liberty, tattered and bleeding from the excesses of revolutionary government, had just found shelter in a constitution [of 1795] that promised repose. . . . Your military glory overshadowed the greatest memories of antiquity; in astonished admiration, the peoples of Europe trembled before it and secretly prayed for your success. Your enemies begged for peace; in a word, everything seemed to be coming together to ensure the tranquil enjoyment of liberty and well-being. . . .

But seditious men unrelentingly assaulted . . . your constitution's weaknesses. . . . Soon the constitutional regime was a storm of revolutions, manipulated by the different parties; even those who sincerely wanted to uphold the constitution had to violate it constantly in order to prevent its demise. This state of governmental instability produced even greater legislative instability; and the most sacred social rights were at the mercy of the whims of factions and events.

It is time to end these storms; it is time to ensure civic liberty, popular sovereignty, the independence of constitutional powers, and the republic, whose name has served all too often to justify the violation of all principles; it is time that the great nation had a government worthy of it, a firm and wise government which can give you a prompt and durable peace and bring you true well-being.

People of France! These are the considerations that motivated the vigorous determinations of the Legislative Body.

A provisional government has been instituted to speed the definitive and complete reorganization of all parts of the public establishment; it has sufficient force to see that laws are respected, to protect peaceful citizens, to crush plotters and evildoers.

Royalism will no longer rear its head; the hideous traces of revolutionary government are effaced; republic and liberty will no longer be empty words: a new era is beginning.

27. THE CONCORDAT (1802)[33]

Although he pursued the same basic aim as the Directory, political and social stability, Bonaparte displayed considerably more understanding of how this could be done. He realized that the principal cause of popular dissatisfaction with the Revolution was its hostility to the Catholic Church. To heal the breach with Rome and reconcile French Catholics to his rule, Bonaparte reached out to the Pope. After some months of negotiation, the result was the Concordat (1802), a formal agreement with the Papacy restoring (and regulating) Catholic practice in France. Although it confirmed the seizure of Church property, did not make Catholicism the official state religion, and maintained toleration for other faiths, it satisfied the Pope and most French Catholics. Religiously based opposition to the Consulate

---

[33]*Rapport fait au nom d'une commission spéciale par le citoyen Siméon, sur le projet de loi relatif au Concordat (17 Germinal X).*

declined immediately. The Concordat remained the basic framework of church–state relations in France until 1905. What follows is an excerpt from a speech unveiling the Concordat.

Horrified by the scale and excesses of our revolution, [other nations] feared for the two essential social bonds: civil authority and religion. It appeared that we had simultaneously thrown off the authority that restrains even the freest peoples and the regulator, more potent and universal than law itself, . . . which not only forbids evil but commands good; which animates and fortifies morality, lends to its precepts hope and fear of life to come, and adds heaven's dictates to the often-feeble voice of conscience. . . .

Since we had to strengthen anarchy-weakened government, give it simpler and more energetic forms, surround it with the power and brilliance suitable for the supreme magistracy of a great people, bring it closer to the customs of other nations without losing what is essential to republican liberty, we also had to return to this other point, common to all civilized nations: religion. . . .

The Constituent Assembly . . . was careful not to extend religious tolerance to the point of indifference. It recognized that, as one of the most ancient and powerful means of governance, religion had to be placed more firmly in the government's hands. . . .

The Constituent Assembly made only one mistake . . . Its failure to coordinate with the head of the Church. This . . . produced schism instead of reform. This schism planted the seeds of civil war, some brought to fruition by revolutionary excesses.

It is in our divided families and towns, in the devastated fields of the Vendée, that we must respond to those troubled that the government is concerning itself with religion.

What does France want? . . . Liberty of conscience and public worship, to be spared derision because one is Christian, to avoid persecution because one prefers the old church . . . to the new and abstract cult of human reason.

With arms in hand, what did the Vendéens demand? Priests and altars. It is true that evildoers, rebels, and foreigners . . . placed the throne next to the altar. But the Vendée was pacified as soon as we promised to redress their primary grievance. . . .

We must not applaud a treaty which, domestically, restores to morality the powerful sanction it had lost; which calms, consoles, and satisfies the spirit; which, abroad, gives nations a guarantee . . . which no longer separates us from other peoples by indifference and disdain for a common bond. . . .

[The Concordat will provide:]

Public worship to occupy and attach individuals without enslaving them, and unite those who want to follow it without compelling those who do not.

A church subject to all the regulations that circumstances require.

Nothing exclusive; the Protestant as free and protected in his faith as the Catholic.

The name of the republic and its leaders take the place they deserve in temples and public prayer. . . .

The ministers of all denominations subject to the influence of the government. . . .

The renunciation of the Church's rich and ancient endowment. . . .

No more worry for purchasers of national property, no more concern that riches distract or corrupt the ministers of the Church; all powerful for the good we expect of them, they will be utterly powerless to do ill.

28. THE CIVIL CODE (1804)[34]

Social and familial structures had undergone profound changes in revolutionary France. Vast amounts of property (much of it confiscated from the Crown, Church, and counter-revolutionaries) had changed hands. Inflation had compromised individual and family fortunes. The family itself had been transformed by revolutionary laws permitting divorce and mandating equal inheritance. At the same time, aspects of the regional legal diversity that had characterized France before 1789—notably regarding women's property rights—had remained untouched. This combination of dramatic change on a nationwide scale and persistent regional disparities made the interwoven issues of property, inheritance, parental authority, and the balance of power between spouses uncertain. To remedy this, Bonaparte assembled a commission of distinguished jurists to draft a uniform code of civil law. It was approved on March 21, 1804. The most durable and far-reaching of Bonaparte's reforms, it remains the basis of civil law in France, a dozen other countries, and the state of Louisiana. In the document following, the jurist Etienne-Marie Portalis, one of the principal architects of the Code, explains its fundamental purpose.

All revolutions are conquests. If laws are made during the transition from the old government to the new, these laws, by the very force of things, are necessarily hostile, partial, and destructive. One is carried away by the need to break old habits, to weaken all bonds, to marginalize discontent. One no longer attends to the private relations of man-to-man; rather, one only perceives political and general objects; one seeks confederates rather than citizens. Everything becomes public law.

If one attends to civil laws at all, it is less to make them wiser or more just than to make them more favorable to those whose support is sought by the new regime. The power of fathers is overthrown because children are more inclined toward innovations. Marital authority is not respected because it is by giving greater liberty to women that new forms and a new tone can be introduced into the commerce of life. The whole system of inheritance must be turned upside down because it is expedient to prepare a new order of citizens through a new order

---

[34]*Discours préliminaire sur le projet de Code Civil, présenté le 1er Pluviôse an IX.*

of property-owning. At each instant, change is born from change, circumstances from circumstances. Institutions succeed one another rapidly without any one of them acquiring solidity. We call *revolutionary spirit* the exalted desire to sacrifice violently all rights to a political goal and no longer consider anything but a mysterious and variable interest of state.

It is not in such a moment that one can hope to regulate people and things with the wisdom that presides over durable establishments and according to the principles of that natural equity which human legislators must respectfully interpret.

Today France breathes again. . . .

Good civil laws are the greatest good that men can give and receive; they are the source of morality, the palladium of prosperity, and the guarantee of all public and private peace: although they do not establish the government, they maintain it; they moderate its power and help make it respected as if it were justice itself. They touch each individual, they intermingle with the principal acts of his life, they follow him everywhere; they are often the only morality of the people and are always a part of its liberty; finally, they console each citizen for the sacrifices that the political law dictates for the common good, by protecting him, when necessary, in his person and property, as if he alone was the entire collectivity. Thus, the drafting of the Civil Code was the principal care of the hero that the nation has established as its first magistrate. . . .

We have respected, in the civil laws published by our national assemblies, everything linked to the great changes which occurred in the political order, as well as everything that seemed to us obviously preferable to the [Old Regime's] worn out, defective institutions. You must change when the most fatal of all innovations would be, in a manner of speaking, not to innovate. We must not give in to blind prejudice. Everything that is old was once new. It is essential to imprint upon the new institutions that character of permanence and stability which can secure for them the right to become old. . . .

Marriage, the government of families, the status of children, the guardianship [of minors], the questions of domicile, the rights of absent [spouses], the different nature of properties, the diverse means of acquiring, keeping, or augmenting one's fortune; inheritance, contracts, these are the principal objects of a civil code. . . .

The civil laws must interpose their authority between spouses, between parents and children; they must regulate the government of the family. We have sought in nature the blueprint for this government. Marital authority is based on the need to give, in an association of two individuals, preponderance to one of the associates, as well as on the preeminence of the sex to which this advantage is attributed. The authority of parents is motivated by their tenderness, experience, mature reason, and weakness of their children. This authority is a magistracy to which it is important—above all, in free states—to give a certain scope. Yes, fathers must be true magistrates, wherever liberty demands that the magistrates be but fathers. . . .

[The father] administers and oversees everything . . . ; but the husband's administration should be wise, his surveillance moderate; his influence should consist more in protection than authority; the strongest must defend and uphold the weakest. Unlimited power over women, such as found in certain countries, would offend our national character and the moderation of our laws. We tolerate as grace in the fair sex indiscretions and frivolities; and, without encouraging actions which could disturb order and offend decency, we have rejected all measures incompatible with public liberty.

Children should submit to their father; but he should heed only nature's voice, milder and tenderer than all others. . . . His magistracy has been termed "paternal piety." . . .

Man and woman have obvious similarities and differences. What they have in common derives from the species; the differences come from their sex. They would be less likely to unite if they were more alike. Nature made them different in order to join them.

Difference in their being supposes difference in their respective rights and duties. Spouses work together in marriage for common goals, but not in the same way. They are equal in some things, but incomparable in others.

Force and audacity belong to man; timidity and modesty to woman.

Man and woman cannot share the same work, endure the same burdens, nor pursue the same occupations. Law, not nature, determines the destiny of the two sexes.

Woman needs protection because she is weaker; man is freer because he is stronger.

Man's preeminence is dictated by the very constitution of his being, which does not subject him to so many physical cares and gives him more freedom in the use of his time and exercise of his faculties. This preeminence is the source of the husband's protective power.

Husband and wife obviously must be faithful. . . . But woman's infidelity requires more corruption and has more dangerous effects than man's; moreover, man has always been judged less severely than woman. All nations, enlightened by experience and instinct, agree that, for the good of humanity, the fair sex should also be the most virtuous.

Women would misunderstand their true interest if they viewed the apparent severity against them as tyrannical rigor rather than an honorable and useful distinction. Destined by nature for the pleasure of one man, . . . they have received from heaven that sweet sensitivity which animates beauty and is so easily dulled by the heart's slightest missteps; this fine and delicate tact, which serves them as a sixth sense, is preserved and perfected only by the exercise of virtue. . . . It is not in our injustice, but in their natural vocation, that women will find the reason for the more austere duties imposed on them. . . .

In the Old Regime, the distinction between privileged and non-privileged persons, between nobles and commoners, resulted in a mass of property distinctions that have disappeared and must never be revived.

One might say that things were classified like persons. There were feudal properties and non-feudal ones, servile properties and free ones. All that is no more. . . .

In general, men should be able to contract freely on everything that concerns them. Their needs bring them together: their contracts multiply in proportion to their needs. There is no legislation in the world which can determine the number and define the type of the conventions to which human affairs are prone. A mass of contracts results. . . . Freedom of contract can be limited only by justice, morality, and public utility. . . .

One governs badly when one governs too much. A man who contracts with another man should be attentive and prudent; he should look out for his own interest, gather the necessary information, and attend to all that may be useful to him. The role of the law is to protect us against another's fraud, but it is not to excuse us from using our own reason. If it were otherwise, the life of men, under the tutelage of the laws, would be nothing but a long and shameful minority. Tutelage would itself degenerate into an inquisition. . . .

These are the principal bases from which we drafted the Civil Code. Our aim was to link morality to law and propagate the spirit of the family which is so favorable, whatever one may say, to public spirit. . . . Private virtues can alone ensure public virtues; and *it is through the little fatherland, which is the family, that we are attached to the great fatherland*; good fathers, husbands, and sons make good citizens. It is essential that civil institutions sanction and protect all the respectable affections of nature. . . .

XI. The Empire

By 1802, Bonaparte had achieved remarkable successes. He had restored order, forced France's remaining foreign enemies (Austria and Great Britain) to come to terms, and had built a lasting legal and institutional foundation for the country. Although he had dramatically curtailed press freedom and had all but abolished meaningful elections, the French people were genuinely appreciative. Flushed with domestic and foreign triumph, Bonaparte decided to found a dynasty. He would be a new kind of monarch, an emperor.

29. THE MOTION TO MAKE BONAPARTE
A HEREDITARY RULER (APRIL 30, 1804)[35]

An obscure legislator named Curée made the formal motion to make Bonaparte a hereditary ruler. The following is an excerpt of the speech he delivered to justify the measure.

The success and duration of any political system depends on government stability. . . . This principle is valid in all times and circumstances. But its application is even more urgent when, great changes in the State having created [a new order

---

[35]Mavidal and Laurent, *AP*, series 2, vol. 8, 269–271.

of things], one can convincingly show that the reestablishment of an authentic, hereditary course of succession in the Government associated with these changes and linked to them like roots to a tree would consecrate these political changes for centuries. . . .

The noble movement which animated the French people in 1789 was principally directed against feudal institutions. Yet we made the error of allowing supreme power to remain in the hands of an essentially feudal family. . . . Louis XVI never wanted to be King of the French. Born sovereign, he could not truly accept becoming a magistrate. Your constitution was violated as soon as it was proclaimed, and in the midst of a general war, anarchy followed the collapse of the throne.

While the Constituent Assembly made the mistake of not creating a new dynasty for the regime, I do not mean to blame it. The Revolution was just starting. No great reputation capable of inspiring confidence had yet emerged. . . .

Then General Bonaparte touched French shores. Since then we have enjoyed the fruits of wise, foresightful, and tireless administration. . . . Has not glorious peace been conquered? . . . Has not the Civil Code, the most complete and methodical system of law ever, risen majestically from the learned and laborious discussions of legal scholars and statesmen and spread knowledge of civil rights to the people? In a word, everything the people wanted in 1789 has been established. Equality has been maintained. Law, which alone can impose burdens on citizens for the good of the State, has been respected. The government has severely defeated all threats to the irrevocability of the sale of national properties. . . . Finally, the altar has been raised up and religion sanctified at the same time as liberty of conscience.

In this happy situation, where the French people have all the rights they sought in the Revolution of 1789, only uncertainty for the future still troubles the State. . . .

What guarantee can we offer? . . . Heredity of power in a family that the Revolution has made famous, that equality and liberty have consecrated; heredity in the family of a leader who was the Republic's first soldier before becoming its first magistrate; of a leader whose civil qualities alone would have eminently distinguished him had he not filled the entire world with the sound of his arms and brilliant victories. . . .

In this way, an eternal barrier will protect us from the return of the factions that divided us and the house we proscribed in 1792 because it had violated our rights. . . .

In voting for the heredity of a leader . . . we will prevent the return of a master.

30. NAPOLEON'S NEW NOBILITY (1807)[36]

It had long been a truism among political theorists that hereditary monarchies needed hereditary nobilities to endure. Napoleon (like other European monarchs, General Bonaparte chose to be known by his first name once he had been crowned)

---

[36]Archives Nationales, AF IV 1040.

also believed this to be the case. But at the same time, he was determined not to rec-
reate a privileged nobility, which would violate the core revolutionary principles of
equality and legal uniformity. His challenge was to create a hereditary nobility com-
patible with equality and meritocracy. In a speech he delivered in 1807, Napoleon
explained how he would do this.

For the stability of our throne and glory of our crown, for the benefit of our people,
we must grant titles to the most distinguished citizens to whom we owe a debt of
gratitude for the nation's prosperity. . . . A nation is not completely organized if
the means of reward are not proportionate to the services its citizens are asked
to render. Monetary rewards would be onerous to our people and would not correspond to the sentiments which stimulate good service and inspire great actions.
While wealth is honorable when it is the fruit of labor and a long and useful career,
it is shameful when it comes from fraud, monopoly, or corruption. It is thus necessary to distinguish and elevate honorably gained fortunes by titles. It is also consonant with the feelings of the human heart to permit the transmission of titles
which, by recommending the sons of those who have served well, will impose on
them the duty of sacrificing everything for their country's honor and the glory of
our throne. We have also considered that if these rewards were granted only to
military service, we would harm the civil services that prepare more quietly, but
with equal merit, the prosperity of the State and triumph of our armies. . . .

Titles that would confer hereditary rights to employment or which would
grant rights of jurisdiction and vassalage over our subjects would injure their dignity. Equal before the law, they are all under our jurisdiction. Whether they contribute to the prosperity of this vast Empire by professing the arts and sciences,
engaging in agriculture and commerce, serving the state in the courts, administrations, or armies, whether rich or poor, magistrates or simple citizens, they have an
equal right to our affection. . . .

We will let no other consideration govern our choice than personal service. . . .

31. WHY THE FRENCH SUBMITTED
TO NAPOLEON'S RULE[37]

Although Napoleon abolished many of the most important attributes of political lib-
erty (election, freedom of the press and assembly, etc.), he encountered little domestic
opposition. His empire was authoritarian, but not totalitarian. Its police spied on the
French people, and some were held as political prisoners, but the scale of Napoleonic
political repression was miniscule compared to that of modern dictatorial regimes.
The reason for this is simple: political resistance to his regime was never widespread,
nor did it ever pose a serious threat to its stability. By and large, the French accepted

---

[37]Robinson, *Readings*, vol. 2, 490–491.

Napoleonic rule. Contemporaries tried to understand why the French had given up their hard-won political freedoms so quickly and easily. The political theorist and historian, Alexis de Tocqueville, believed that they did so because they preferred social equality under an all-powerful ruler (the same laws for all, careers open to talent, etc.) to political liberty in the midst of civil division and anarchy. The chronicler Madame de Remusat proposed a somewhat different answer.

I can understand how it was that men worn out by the turmoil of the Revolution, and afraid of that liberty which had long been associated with death, looked for repose under the dominion of an able ruler on whom fortune was seemingly resolved to smile. I can conceive that they regarded his elevation as a decree of destiny and fondly believed that in the irrevocable they should find peace. I may confidently assert that those persons believed quite sincerely that Bonaparte, whether as consul or emperor, would exert his authority to oppose the intrigues of faction and would save us from the perils of anarchy.

None dared to utter the word "republic," so deeply had the Terror stained that name; and the government of the Directory had perished in the contempt with which its chiefs were regarded. The return of the Bourbons could only be brought about by the aid of a revolution; and the slightest disturbance terrified the French people, in whom enthusiasm of every kind seemed dead. Besides, the men in whom they had trusted had one after the other deceived them; and as, this time, they were yielding to force, they were at least certain that they were not deceiving themselves.

The belief, or rather the error, that only despotism could maintain order in France was very widespread. It became the mainstay of Bonaparte; and it is due to him to say that he also believed it. The factions played into his hands by imprudent attempts which he turned to his own advantage. He had some grounds for his belief that he was necessary; France believed it too; and he even succeeded in persuading foreign sovereigns that he constituted a barrier against republican influences, which, but for him, might spread widely. At the moment when Bonaparte placed the imperial crown upon his head there was not a king in Europe who did not believe that he wore his own crown more securely because of that event. Had the new emperor granted a liberal constitution, the peace of nations and of kings might really have been forever secured.

XII. The Restoration

Napoleon's fatal flaw was that he loved war and conquest. In 1814–1815, his Empire fell—victim of military overreach and domestic apathy in a country tired of seeing its sons and treasures consumed in endless conflict. The Emperor was exiled to a remote island and replaced by Louis XVIII, brother of Louis XVI. The restored monarch must have taken Madame Remusat's warnings to heart, for he put in place a representative (albeit elite) constitution that restored political liberties France had not enjoyed since the Revolution. In contrast, the states of continental Europe pursued a coordinated, antirevolutionary policy intended to stamp out sparks of political unrest wherever they flared up. Paradoxically, Napoleonic France's most determined foe, Great Britain, was the only other major European country to move in a liberal direction. By the 1830s, the liberal political cultures of the two former rivals, Britain and France, stood in sharp contrast to the reactionary regimes of continental Europe.

32. LOUIS XVIII'S CONSTITUTIONAL CHARTER (1814)[38]

The Restoration gave the French a degree of political liberty they had not enjoyed since the Revolution. Although Louis XVIII was criticized for his instance on "giving" the Charter to the French people, it laid the foundations of nineteenth-century French liberalism.

Public Rights of the French
Article 1. All Frenchmen are equal before the law, whatever their title or rank.
2. They contribute without distinction to taxes in proportion to their wealth.
3. They are all equally eligible to civil and military positions.
4. Their personal liberty is likewise guaranteed; no one can be prosecuted or arrested except in the cases and in the manner prescribed by law.
5. All may with equal liberty make profession of their religion and enjoy the same protection for their worship.
6. Nevertheless the Roman Catholic and apostolic religion is the religion of the state.
7. The ministers of the Roman Catholic and apostolic religion, and those of other Christian forms of worship only, shall receive subsidies from the royal treasury.
8. All Frenchmen have the right to publish and cause their opinions to be printed, if they conform to the laws destined to check the abuse of liberty.
9. All property is inviolable; that known as national property forms no exception, since the law recognizes no difference between that and other property.
10. The state may demand the surrender of property in the interest of the public when this is legally certified, but only with previous indemnification.
11. All investigation of opinions expressed or of votes cast previous to the Restoration is prohibited; oblivion of these is imposed upon the courts and upon citizens alike.
12. Conscription is abolished; the method of recruiting both for the army and the navy shall be determined by law.

---

[38]Robinson, *Readings*, vol. 2, 540–541.

33. REACTIONARY EUROPE (1820)[39]

In 1815, Austria, Prussia, and Russia established a "Holy Alliance" to stamp out revolution wherever it appeared in Europe. In 1820, revolutions in Naples, Spain, and Portugal forced their monarchs to accept liberal constitutions. In response, the Austrian foreign minister, Prince Metternich, issued a justification of armed, counter-revolutionary intervention. It would be put into practice in Naples (1821) and in Spain (1823).

The [revolutionary] events which have taken place . . . emphasized the necessity of uniting in order to determine in common the means of checking the misfortunes which threaten to envelop Europe. It was but natural that these sentiments should leave a deep impression upon those powers which had but lately stifled revolution and which now beheld it once more raise its head.

Nor was it less natural that these powers should have recourse to the same methods which they had employed with so much success in the memorable struggle which freed Europe from a yoke she had borne for twenty years. Everything encouraged the hope that the alliance, formed in the most critical circumstances, crowned with the most brilliant successes, and strengthened by the conventions of 1814, 1815, and 1818, as it had prepared the way for, established, and assured the peace of the world, and delivered the European continent from the military representatives of revolution, so it would be able to check a new form of oppression, not less tyrannical and fearful, namely that of revolt and crime.

Such were the motives and the aim of the meeting at Troppau. . . .

The powers are exercising an incontestable right in taking common measures in respect to those states in which the overthrow of the government through a revolt, even if it be considered simply as a dangerous example, may result in a hostile attitude toward all constitutions and legitimate governments. The exercise of this right becomes an urgent necessity when those who have placed themselves in this situation seek to extend to their neighbors the ills which they have brought upon themselves and to promote revolt and confusion around them. . . .

Hence the representatives of the powers . . . agreed at Troppau upon the plan of action to be followed in regard to those states in which the governments had been overturned by violence; and upon the pacific or coercive measures which might bring these states once more into the European alliance, in case the allies should succeed in exercising a salutary influence. . . .

The system pursued in concert by Prussia, Austria, and Russia is in no way new. It is based upon the same principles upon which the conventions rested which created the alliance of the European states. . . .

Moreover it is needless to prove that the resolutions taken by the powers are in no way to be attributed to the idea of conquest, or to any intention of interfering

---

[39]Robinson, *Readings*, vol. 2, 552–554.

with the independence of other governments in their internal administration, or, lastly, to the purpose of preventing wise improvements freely carried out and in harmony with the true interests of the people. Their only desire is to preserve and maintain peace, to deliver Europe from the scourge of revolution, and to obviate or lessen the ills which arise from the violation of the precepts of order and morality.

34. GREAT BRITAIN AND EUROPEAN REACTION[40]

Although Great Britain had led the long fight against France and emerged a global hegemon, it looked with dismay on the growing strength of reaction in continental Europe. In a memorandum drafted in response to Spain's 1820 revolution, it explained why it rejected the interventionist policy of the Holy Alliance.

The events which have occurred in Spain have, as might be expected, excited in proportion as they have developed themselves, the utmost anxiety throughout Europe. . . . There can be no doubt of the general danger which menaces more or less the stability of all existing governments from the principles which are afloat, and from the circumstances that so many states of Europe are now employed in the difficult task of casting anew their governments upon the representative principle: but the notion of revising, limiting, or regulating the course of such experiments, either by foreign council or by foreign force, would be as dangerous to avow as it would be impossible to execute; and the illusion, too prevalent on this subject, should not be encouraged in our intercourse with the allies.

That circumstances might arise out of such experiments in any country directly menacing to the safety of other states cannot be denied, and against such a danger well ascertained, the allies may justifiably and must in all prudence be on their guard, but such is not the present case [Spain]; fearful as the example which is furnished by Spain, of an army in revolt, and a monarch swearing to a constitution which contains in its frame hardly the semblance of a monarchy, there is no ground for apprehension that Europe is likely to be speedily endangered by Spanish arms. . . .

It remains to be considered what course can best be pursued by the allies in the present critical state of Europe, in order to preserve in the utmost cordiality and vigor, the bonds which at this day so happily unite the great European powers together, and to draw from their alliance, should the moment of danger and contest arise, the fullest extent of benefit, of which it is in its nature susceptible.

In this alliance, as in all other human arrangements, nothing is more likely to impair or even to destroy its real utility than any attempt to push its duties and its obligations beyond the sphere which its original conception and understood principles will warrant; it was an union for the re-conquest and liberation of a good

[40]British National Archives, Foreign Office 72, "Memorandum on the Events in Spain" (1820).

proportion of the continent of Europe from the military dominion of France, and having subdued the conqueror, it took the state of possession as established by the peace under the protection of the alliance; it never was however intended as an union for the government of the world, or for the superintendence of the internal affairs of other states. It provided specifically against an infraction on the part of France of the state of possession then created. It provided against the return of the Usurper or of any of his family to the throne. It further designated the revolutionary power, which had convulsed France and desolated Europe as an object of its constant solicitude, but it was the revolutionary power more particularly in its military character—actual and existent within France—against which it intended to take precautions, rather than against the democratic principles, then as now, but too generally spread throughout Europe.

CHAPTER 7

Toward the Haitian Revolution

On the eve of the French Revolution, France's Caribbean colony, Saint-Domingue, was flourishing. Its sugar production, which sweetened beverages across the globe, accounted for 40% of French exports. Because it was produced on plantations by slaves, imports of captives from Africa had increased apace, reaching nearly 50,000 annually by 1790. By that year, the island colony counted about 500,000 enslaved Africans. There were only about 30,000 whites in the colony. Many of the largest white plantation owners were absentee aristocrats who lived in Paris. Resident planters often split their time between their plantation and the booming capital, Le Cap. The center of trade and government, the city was home to merchants, sailors, artisans, officials, and soldiers—a group that, because it was less wealthy than the planters, was known collectively as the *petits-blancs* (little whites). Alongside the enslaved African and free white populations was a substantial group (about 25,000 in 1789) of people of mixed ancestry known as free people of color. They occupied a variety of social positions, ranging from plantation owner (albeit of comparatively small size) to militiaman to artisan. The diverse colony seemed stable in 1789 and poised to continue on its sharp upward trajectory of economic growth.

But all was not well. By calling into question traditional social norms, the distribution of political power, and the very concept of sovereignty, the French Revolution unleashed the conflicting aspirations and grievances of the colony's diverse inhabitants. As a whole, whites saw 1789 as an opportunity to throw off the yoke of royal government, lift the mercantilist trade regime (the *exclusif*), and assume a large measure of autonomy for themselves. But they soon split among themselves—along the lines of region, political faction, and, above all, class—over how exactly power would be allocated among them in the new order. By 1790, rivalries within the white elite had led to armed clashes. The free people of color were not passive bystanders. They realized that the devolution of local autonomy to Saint-Domingue would create a space for political participation and that the Revolution's language of liberty, equality, and rights gave them a means of demanding entry to that space. Their claim to citizenship was supported by powerful backers in the National Assembly.

The complex struggle over the future of Saint-Domingue and its place in the French Empire raged from 1789 through mid-1791. The enslaved population of the island must have been acutely aware of the fractures it was producing in the colonial power structure: rich white against poor, whites against people of color, planters (of whatever color) against nonplanters, the North against the South, patriots against royalists. In August 1791, they seized their chance. In a coordinated uprising on dozens of plantations across the northern plain (near Le Cap), thousands of slaves rose up to claim their freedom. They would never be put down.

I. Abolitionist Sentiment in Pre-Revolutionary France

The abolitionist movement came late to France. Although it had already taken root in parts of North America and Great Britain by the 1770s, France had no discernable abolitionist movement before 1788. In that year, a radical journalist who had been inspired by the British abolitionists, Jacques-Pierre Brissot, founded France's first abolitionist society, the Society of the Friends of the Blacks. Although its membership was small and restricted to social elites, its position was more uncompromising, more ambitious, than that of its American and British counterparts. Indeed, for Brissot, the abolition of colonial slavery was just one component of a greater dream: the general emancipation of humanity.

1. THE SOCIETY OF THE FRIENDS OF THE BLACKS[1]

The following is an excerpt of the pamphlet Jacques-Pierre Brissot wrote in 1788, calling for the creation of a French abolitionist society.

We do not appreciate the prodigious influence of liberty on the development of human reason and the establishment of universal peace. We do not understand that reason has never advanced, and will never reach its ultimate degree of perfection, without liberty; that universal peace will exist only when all Societies are free!

In a free Society, man is led by his self-interest to develop his faculties to the highest degree. A free Society is only governed by universal reason, and universal reason essentially forces us to desire peace and good for all men.

In contemplating this sweet idea, I must point out the error into which we fall when we seek to enlighten men who are in the grip of servitude, without destroying it. You hear the cry everywhere: "Enlighten men, and they will become better."

---

[1]Jacques-Pierre Brissot, "*Discours sur la nécessité d'établir à Paris une Société pour concourir, avec celle de Londres, à l'abolition de l'esclavage des Nègres*" (Paris, 1788), in *La Révolution Francaise et l'Abolition de l'Esclavage* (Paris: Éditions d'histoire sociale, 1968), vol. 6, 6–9.

But the experience of centuries has told us: "Make men free, and they will necessarily and rapidly become enlightened, and they will necessarily be better."

In effect, what good is enlightenment when the spirit is subordinated, when the mind is captive? Don't you see that captivity compromises the faculty of thought in almost all men? Don't you realize that those who resist cannot use their ideas, but must keep them to themselves, if they want to avoid persecution? Don't you see that, in this case, political truths are restricted to a small circle of men? Independently of the timidity or insufficiency of this small number of men, misery, the inseparable companion of despotism and ignorance, absorbs all the people's time, energy, and thought, and leaves it neither ability nor leisure to enlighten itself. General enlightenment, which tends toward public happiness, is thus doubly incompatible with the spirit of servitude. To propose spreading enlightenment, while keeping men in chains, is to try to open the eyes of men who have been deprived of eyes, to try to procreate by abortion.

If I insist on this idea, it is because it is a deadly error accredited by the partisans of despotism. They seek to justify it. They try to console men for their vexations by claiming that reason can develop in the midst of chains. I speak not of the agreeable arts or the art of arranging words; they can shine under despotism. But is this the case with the political or moral sciences? Sometimes a few sparks escape from the depths of despotism's shadows. Sometimes men of genius break their chains and rise up to preach the great truths. . . . But what do these flashes of reason really accomplish? . . . They never enlighten the entire mass of the Nation. To become enlightened requires attention, and attention requires time, faculties, and interest. But the mass of an enslaved people has neither time, nor faculties, nor interest. Only liberty brings these three things.

Thus, if we want to enlighten mankind seriously and improve his social and individual condition, we must not restrict ourselves to giving him books or academies. We must untie his hands. Make man free and he will enlighten himself and become good a thousand times more easily and promptly than by giving him the best books, while keeping him a Slave. In effect, how could he take these books seriously when he sees their authors violate the first of all truths: *all men are born free*. How could he not conclude that they were making a fool of him through the vilest hypocrisy? . . .

There is only one way to raise up mankind and augment the mass of public happiness—Liberty. By giving it to the Negroes, we shall stop fearing them. Having become our brothers, they will rapidly enlighten themselves, become good, and, what is perhaps more difficult, the Masters themselves will be forced to enlighten themselves and become good. For slavery is a fool-proof means of corrupting two men at the same time: the Master and the Slave.

II. The Beginning of the French Revolution

The planters greeted news of the Revolution with a mixture of hope and fear. On one hand, its rhetoric of popular sovereignty and national regeneration promised an end to absolutist rule over the colony, the institution of local self-government, and free trade. On the other, the Revolution's sweeping declarations of liberty, equality, and human rights threatened slavery and the racial hierarchies that underpinned the colonial order. To seize the opportunities and counter the threats the Revolution held out, the planters drew up grievance lists and sent representatives to the National Assembly. In addition, powerful planters resident in Paris formed a lobbying group, called the Massiac Club, to pressure the legislature. But white colonial political mobilization on both sides of the Atlantic (spurred by the prospect of home rule for Saint-Domingue) awakened internal rivalries that threatened to create an opening for excluded groups to claim their rights.

2. THE PLANTERS' FEARS OF REVOLUTIONARY RADICALISM[2]

The night of August 4th confirmed the planters' fears of revolutionary radicalism. Although a motion to end slavery had been defeated, the sweeping abolitions actually adopted on that night suggested that no existing institution was safe. It did not help that the calls to dismantle feudalism and abolish serfdom were explicitly described as freeing the French from slavery. Nor did the passage of the Declaration of the Rights of Man and Citizen a few weeks later do anything to allay their concerns. It was in this context that alarmed colonial deputies wrote to their friends and colleagues in Saint-Domingue, warning them to be vigilant and urging them to mobilize to defend colonial interests.

The colony faces a double danger. An external danger: WHAT DO THESE VESSELS WANT, that the newspapers inform us have left England? Interior danger; efforts are being made to get our Negroes to revolt. We consider both dangers as fearful; but the second truly causes us the most horrible disquiet. THEY ARE DRUNK WITH LIBERTY. A society of enthusiasts, who have taken the title *friends of the blacks* writes openly against us. It seeks a favorable moment to set off an explosion against slavery. Perhaps all it will take for them to demand the emancipation of our Negroes is if we utter the word [slavery]. Our fear of this reduces us to silence, in spite of ourselves. This is not a favorable moment for us to try to persuade the National Assembly to take steps to protect us from this danger. It is up to you, Messieurs, to determine the measures to be taken in this critical circumstance. . . . The peril is great, the danger is near. . . . *Let us not rouse the enemy,* but let us not be taken by surprise. . . . The National Assembly is too occupied with the interior of the kingdom to attend to us. We are warning all Americans to come to the defense of their fatherland. Most will probably embark [for the colonies]. . . . Take appropriate measures; carefully observe people and things. *Arrest suspect persons and seize writings which pronounce the word liberty.* Double the guard on your

---

[2]Letter from colonial deputation to colonies (Versailles, August 12, 1789), in Julien Raimond, *Correspondence de Julien Raimond avec ses freres de Saint-Domingue* (Paris: Cercle Social, year II of French Republic, 1794), 7–10.

plantations, hamlets, and villages. *Wherever you can, try to get the people of color on your side, but beware of those who arrive from Europe.* It is most unfortunate that we were not able to prevent the embarkation of people of color who were in France. We asked the minister to do it, but *the spirit of the day was in opposition to our desire.* To even try to prevent slaves from embarking would be seen as an act of violence and would be denounced to the nation. . . .

P.S. It is possible, even probable, that the alarming rumors that are the subject of this letter have no basis in fact. In that case, it would be unfortunate if this letter produces too much of a sensation in the colony. . . . It might even give rise to real dangers. So, it is up to you to act with circumspection and prudence. . . . A false sense of security must not prevent you from keeping watch for the dangerous effects that might be produced in the colonies by the fermentation of the kingdom. You should take every precaution to maintain order, peace, and subordination amongst you. It seems to us that the best means of keeping calm in the colony is *to win over to your cause the class of people of color.* They want nothing more than to blend their interests with yours and work for common security. All that is required is for you to be just toward them and treat them better. *We consider this species to be the true rampart of the colony's security.* You can assure them that your deputies, who are also their own, will work zealously in the National Assembly to ameliorate their condition and obtain for them the just consideration due to all citizens who comport themselves honorably.

3. PLANTER GRIEVANCES AND ASPIRATIONS[3]

The following is an excerpt from one of the planter cahiers de doléances, *perhaps drafted in response to the colonial deputies' letter of August 12th.*

If you compare the administration of Saint-Domingue with that of other places in France, you will see that the Colony is perhaps the province with the most-founded complaints to present.

Placed under two administrators who change every three years, who have incomparably great authority, who have (to say everything in one word) both legislative and executive power, it is no wonder that [the colony] is poorly governed and badly run.

[A place] 2,000 leagues distant from the metropole, Saint-Domingue—which differs in its climate, soil, habits, productions, and ideas about slavery—requires special study from those to whom its government is entrusted; four or five years are barely enough time for this study, but the administrators are withdrawn after

[3]"Cahier de Doléances and the Rectification of Wrongs, presented by the Western part of Saint-Domingue to the Estates-General" (November 1789), in *Cahiers de doléances présentés par la partie Ouest de Saint-Domingue aux Etats-Généraux de 1789,* ed. Blanche Maurel (Paris: Ernest Leroux, 1933), 299–302.

three years, which is to say, before they have been able to acquire the knowledge required to govern it.

All power is thus concentrated in the hands of two people without experience . . . who are not counterbalanced by any rival authority, for there is only a Superior Council without real force, which does not even have a veto and is forced to register not only the laws of the prince, but even the simple ordinances of the administrators. . . .

One source of disorder is the administrators' unlimited power to make laws and have them registered, a practice which has the double drawback of making . . . property dependent on the will of two men and of constantly changing the laws. . . .

Persuaded of the imperfection of the government, convinced that the best form of administration is always that in which a large number of persons participate, the Colony wants to administer itself and share all the advantages accorded to the other provinces of France by the establishment of provincial Estates.

At this moment, it could adopt the same rights as the provinces of France. . . . But since the Colony has been governed by a different system, by specific laws, it has particular grievances to present; it demands:

1. That the Colony of Saint-Domingue be recognized as an integral part of the State, as forming one body with the nation.
2. That the laws intended to govern it cease being entrusted to the Minister of the Navy and instead be placed in the hands of the Chancellor.
3. That the powers and functions of the general and intendant be reduced to those of provincial governors and intendants.
4. That they be prohibited from making laws and regulations of any sort, except at the request of the colonial Estates.
5. That colonial Estates be established upon the model of the provincial Estates of France. They will regulate the distribution of taxes and oversee their collection; occupy themselves with everything needed for the administration of the Colony; propose and approve all civil, criminal, regulatory, and administrative laws which may be useful for its amelioration; and finally, participate in all the advantages of liberty and regeneration like the other provinces.
6. That all military districts be suppressed and replaced with civil municipalities.
7. That the Colony be allowed to purchase Negroes from abroad, and also all types of provisions.
8. That it be assimilated to the other provinces of France in the freedom to conduct maritime ventures.
9. That all citizens be under the empire of the laws and that the administrators no longer have the power to deprive anyone of their liberty.
10. That, in the future, the Colony be established on a stable basis and constitution, and that all laws which would tend to place it at the mercy of arbitrary leaders and deprive it of its natural advantages be repealed and annulled.
11. That it continue to be free from all fiscal dues and manipulations.

4. A PLANTER PAMPHLET[4]

Like so many other interest groups during the early Revolution, the planters also employed pamphlets to express their wishes. This one addresses their four major concerns. Even though the Revolution was only a few months old when it was written, it shows that slavery was already beginning to overshadow all other issues.

The colonies want to remain united to France; but France would force them to change their mind if it does not respect their properties and rights. . . .

Their properties would be violated by freeing the Negroes the Colonists purchased. . . .

By suppressing the slave trade, they would be violated too, by making it impossible for most Colonists to cultivate their lands. . . . Almost all plantations need new recruits. And in any case, this would be just a step toward emancipation.

Our enemies dare not propose emancipation; but they are preparing for it, and they want to suppress the slave trade, shamelessly using sophisms to prove that we would gain from that suppression.

No one can know our interests better than we ourselves. It is certainly not the place of people who have spent their lives 2,000 leagues from us to tell us what our needs are.

If our lands could be cultivated by free hands; if we could maintain our labor force through natural population increase, we would not spend such enormous sums purchasing the necessary labor.

It is easy to lie about how we treat our servants. Wherever a single man directs a large number of ignorant men and demands hard work from them, you need discipline. But we also understand the duties of humanity and beneficence. Even if we only listened to self-interest, it too would tell us to preserve our Negroes. Not only must they be healthy and live long lives, they must also be happy in order to serve us usefully.

The French Nation has recovered its rights. But the Colonies have their own. . . . Among the rights it demands is respect for their property. . . .

If [the Colonies] were no longer capable of supporting themselves [if slavery and the slave trade were abolished], they would have to make a new contract, just and solid, with some other Nation that would respect its rights.

We do not believe that we are yet at that point. . . .

Four things concern our constituents.

1. Ministerial despotism.
2. The despotism of exclusive trade.
3. The insinuations and fatal projects of the so-called friends of the Blacks.
4. The fear of the absolute and literal application of your Constitution, *in so much as it is founded on the declaration of rights*, to our Negroes.

---

[4]*Mémoire des députés de Saint-Domingue* (n.p., 1789), 3–17. http://catalogue.bnf.fr/ark:/12148/cb364011561.

1. United to the Nation in the august Assembly of Representatives, the Colony will no longer have to fear ministerial despotism; it has been destroyed in France, it soon will be in the Colony; but we must be reassured on the other points.

2. Merchants are always the same. They act only in self-interest. At the moment, the slave-trade is useful to them. They want the Nation's paternal attention to the Colonies to bear upon that object and bring protectionism to it.

On the first article, it is only out of attachment to the Nation that we want to receive Negroes from the French slave-trade.

Thanks to the luxury and ignorance of our Commerce, we must pay 2,500 pounds for its Negroes, despite Government subsidies, while at Jamaica, they cost the English 1,400 pounds. Our merchants know full well that if they cease to provide us with Negroes, we won't lack for them. No force, no surveillance can deprive us of them, unless all the Nations of Europe renounce this Trade—and that will not happen. . . .

As for the exclusive regime, it is absurd that [the merchants] of Bordeaux want to impose it fully against us, while, at the same time, they attack the exclusive regime of the Indies Company. . . . They admit themselves *that they could not sustain, in our Ports, competition with foreigners who enjoy a vast superiority through their low-priced, high-quality manufactured goods.*

This exclusive commerce has partly ruined the French mercantile economy. Sure to make us pay for their faults, they have not tried to acquire the perfection of the English. . . .

3. The Colonists will never feel safe among the Negroes as long as the writings of the so-called friends of the Blacks . . . encourage them to rise up and massacre their masters; above all, when an absolute and unlimited Declaration of liberty and equality for all men without distinction is placed at the head of the National Constitution. We dare say that one cannot expect either attachment or fidelity from those who are thus held in a continual state of terror for their lives and properties.

4. A Constitution made for France cannot be entirely that of the tropical Colonies; too many physical and moral differences mandate this incompatibility. . . .

According to reason, good policy, and justice, the Constitution of the Colonies should be drafted or at least proposed by them; this has already been implied by the decisions of the National Assembly which want each People to make the Laws which suit them best.

We must say here that our constituents, who had at first expressly charged us with proposing a colonial Constitution to the National Assembly, have, once they saw the Declaration of rights, now expressly forbid us from accepting one. The Colony does not want to reject liberty and equality for all Citizens, for it already exists at Saint-Domingue; but it is considering the Declaration of rights in relation to the slaves. . . .

You must thus authorize the Colonies to propose their own Constitution, after having decided upon it themselves. . . .

5. DIVISIONS AMONG WHITES[5]

Increasingly, petits-blancs *began to make their voices heard. It soon became clear that their interests were not identical to those of the planters. In the following document, a petty colonial legal official, Chachereau, criticizes the elitism of a planter plan for local governing institutions.*

As for the *formation of the tribunals*, nothing seems more flawed than the plan you have traced; you want the high Magistracy to be composed *exclusively* of *grand* proprietors, despite their *inexperience*.

This word, *grand proprietor* that you repeat so often . . . brings to mind the erroneous opinion of several people misled by pride and vanity, who think that dignities and charges are made to honor a particular class of men. But public instruction and the enlightenment of the century has finally established the principle that men must be made for public charges and that they must be worthy of filling them.

Profound erudition, purity of sentiments, even-handedness, and all the other qualities necessary in a Magistrate, are they attached to *grand* properties? Can they be measured by extent of land? A citizen who does not own a vast plantation, can he have none of the qualities required for the Magistracy? . . .

On the contrary, it seems that the grand proprietors are in fact the least suited to the Magistracy. First, their great wealth draws them to France. The education they receive is rarely that of the legal profession, but rather military. If their business calls them here [to Saint-Domingue], it is to oversee their properties. . . . They return frequently to France. When they are in the colony, they are occupied with great interests and cannot put them aside to come to town to study law. Thus, it is not the quality of grand proprietor that prepares one for the Magistracy, but rather sustained application, serious study, and long experience. . . . From this perspective, it is the small proprietor . . . who seems to be more particularly summoned to it.

But, I repeat, we should not determine access to public charges by the measure of fortune. Rather, it should be the degree of personal merit, the scope of one's knowledge, the purity of his morals—irrespective of his social class—where we should seek them. . . . By summoning all enlightened citizens to the Magistracy, we will banish the idea of privilege from this colony. We must not revive aristocracy here, when it has been uprooted in France and when that example might extirpate it across Europe as a whole.

6. THE ATLANTIC MERCHANTS WEIGH IN[6]

The merchants of France's great Atlantic port cities had always attended closely to colonial developments, for their fortunes depended on the strength of the plantation economy. They followed the public discussion of slavery and the divisions within

---

[5]Chachereau, *Examen rapide du cahier de doléances de la colonie* (Port-au-Prince, Chez Mozard, 1789), 18–19.

[6]Archives Municipales de Bordeaux, "Adresse à l'Assemblée nationale" (December 3, 1789).

the colonial elite with growing alarm. When word reached them in late 1789 that slaves in the French colony of Martinique had risen in revolt, they made their concerns known to the National Assembly. Although the revolt was crushed, it exposed the fragility of the slave system underpinning the French colonial economy.

Last September, the inhabitants of Martinique narrowly escaped from a horrifying danger. A revolt of their slaves . . . threatened the lives of all the whites . . . We are told that the slaves' plan was to exterminate all free men, but to spare the women, in order to reduce them to servitude and use them for their pleasure. Their example would have been followed in the neighboring islands. . . .

We are not trying to justify slavery to you, for you have won our respect and eternal gratitude by laying the foundations of our liberty. We are not trying to claim that this terrible slavery is free from abuses and negative consequences. Finally, we would not dare claim that these abuses and negative consequences are sufficiently compensated by the wealth that only the enslavement of colored people can generate for the state. No, Messieurs, it is not in this light that we will present our demands. We are careful not to attack the principles of universal liberty that immortal writers have established with such incontrovertible evidence; principles that you have consecrated in the declaration of the rights of man and citizen.

But we will confidently tell you that the sudden emancipation of the slaves who people our colonies offends all notions of justice, humanity, and good policy.

It offends justice in that these slaves are, for a large number of our fellow citizens, veritable property.

It is the entire nation which, by the laws which have governed it for a century and by the universal consent to these laws, has given ownership of slaves all the characteristics of property. Our kings, in their quality of representatives of the nation and administrators of the public weal, have constantly protected it. . . .

If we now conclude that it was a mistake to acquire colonies which could only be cultivated by slaves, . . . we still cannot deny that the nation and all of Europe shared—and continues to share—that error. . . .

It was under the guarantee of public faith that laborious and enterprising men risked their lives to bring their industry to an unhealthy clime and deadly land, which they made flourish by their sweat and hard work, with the aid of the slaves who became their property. . . .

How can the nation strip them of their property, without real compensation and without their express consent? . . .

Humanity is no less offended by the upheavals and calamities that the abolition of slavery would cause in our colonies and interior of the kingdom.

Reason demonstrates that if the slave regains his liberty in spite of his master and against his express wishes, both their lives will be endangered. The master will not pardon the slave for having freed himself from legitimate bondage. For his part, the slave will forever harbor a mortal hatred of a master who, unjust and cruel in his view, had refused to let him enjoy the benefits of liberty. No reconciliation is possible between such men.

Thus, among all the peoples who had slaves, there was only one remedy for uprisings: to punish their authors with the greatest tortures. No revolt, or even plan of revolt, has failed to spill torrents of blood. The masters are all the more severe, all the more rigorous, in that they have to punish simultaneously multiple crimes they see as unforgiveable: that of having endangered their lives and that of having wanted to take their properties, which are as dear to them as life itself. To them, no torment seems cruel enough to punish such attacks, frightening enough to deter new ones. Once the slaves have risen up, there will be a cruel war between them and their masters. Death of the enemy will be the only solution. . . .

Do not doubt that even in the unlikely case that the slaves of our colonies do not abuse their liberty, once free from bondage and feeling themselves incomparably stronger because of their greater number, they will regard their former masters as tyrants who deserve death. A terrible war will flare up, and the masters, seeing themselves reduced to the most extreme misery by the loss of their properties, will do anything rather than consent to what they see as an unjust expropriation. They would die a thousand times rather than permit it.

Thus, we foresee only disasters, blood, and carnage in a policy which, at first blush, seems to be dictated only by sentiments of humanity and charity.

But if justice and humanity both stand against the freeing of the slaves in our colonies, could wise policy permit it?

We will not insist, Messieurs, on the commercial advantages France derives from its colonies. No one doubts that, if, by some misfortune, we are deprived of them, our ports would be ruined, our factories would decay, a great number of farmers in the kingdom would be discouraged by the closing of a guaranteed market for their products.

Nor can we calculate the horrifying losses the ruin of the colonists would inflict on French commerce. The immense capital of our commercial barons is almost entirely in the hands of the colonies. They can only reimburse it through the product of their harvests. It is thus obvious that the loss of the colonies would provoke a mass of bankruptcies from one end of the kingdom to the other and plunge a host of citizens into the most frightful despair. Who can envisage without horror our ships rendered useless, a huge number of laborers without work or salary, universal stagnation halting the circulation of money and goods? Who would dare to deny that the economic blow that would result from the loss or abandonment of the colonies would not completely block the channels of the fisc and that, in our current financial crisis, the state would be unable to resist the violent shock.

Moreover, is it possible to confuse the independence the slaves want with holy liberty, the most beautiful attribute of man in society? Will we grant the rights of citizenship to those unaware of the duties it entails? Can we share it with men who have always lived under the yoke of slavery without compromising liberty?

Leaving aside the interest of the masters, to assimilate the slaves of our islands to their masters would actually worsen the lot of the slaves. How would they feed themselves? Most of them are irresponsible, having always lived in profound stupidity, and have no idea of what is needed for their own survival and well-being. How would they contribute to the good of society through work, given that, for them, rest is the supreme good. How would they use their liberty, if they have no real idea what it is? . . .

We want all men to be happy; doubtless, it is soothing to imagine the possibility of destroying slavery in the future; but . . . the means of doing this are necessarily very slow and very difficult. We will fail if we try to do it prematurely. . . .

7. THE COLONIAL ORDER RIPS ITSELF APART[7]

By 1790, the different classes of whites in the colony were struggling with each other for power. Although the resulting instability did not directly cause the massive slave uprising of August 1791, the fragmentation of the colonial power structure created an opening that they—and the free people of color before them—would perceive and exploit. The following is an account of the complex internal struggles that shattered the unity of the colonial order.

In a new regimen the proprietors looked to some aggrandizement either in property or consequence; the free people of colour anticipated a favourable change in their condition; and even the slaves viewed, through the political alterations that began to occupy the attention of those above them, something to excite their curiosity, and a vigilance to gratify it. Each motion of the French court became canvassed by every class throughout the island. When a spirit of deliberation upon subjects usually considered above the capacities of the vulgar begins to spread, it seldom ends precisely as it begun; whatever may be the event, it does not fail to call into notice circumstances and opinions not easily repressed, and characters in their support who might otherwise have preserved through life "the noiseless tenor of their way." It had its full effect in St. Domingo, already so ripe to receive it; and when the news arrived that the States-General of France were to be summoned (the last convulsive effort of expiring monarchy), all parties resolved on making their own interests a part of the general concern.

In opposition to the wishes of a judicious few . . . and even to the prohibitions of the government, the impetuous proprietors summoned provincial and parochial meetings, for the purpose of electing *themselves* to legislative functions; heated resolutions were passed; and eighteen deputies were elected, to represent the island in the meeting of the States-General, without any other authority than the noise of demagogues, and their own inclinations. Twelve were never recognized in France, and the other six were received with difficulty. The mulattoes, who could have no share in this self-created body, thought it naturally time to show an attention to themselves; and, accordingly, not only communicated with numbers of their brethren then resident in the mother-country, but augmented those powerful advocates in their behalf, with much more effect than was produced by the self-created body of colonial deputies. . . .

The states-general . . . declared themselves the National Assembly in May 1789, and on the 20th of August they made their *Declaration of Rights*. Between these two periods, the public mind had been heated against the white colonists. . . . The publication of the Declaration of Rights did not tend to remedy this unfavourable impression of the people against one of their own communities; for the article that "All men are born, and continue, free and equal as to their rights," implied an entire subversion of their establishments and created a complete ferment among the whole of the French proprietors. They conceived . . . that the effect of this declaration was to rouse the Negroes to an assertion of those rights it was supposed to give them. Apprehensive of disorders arising in the colony, the governor soon received orders from his new constituents, the National Assembly, to call together the inhabitants for the purpose of interior regulation. The measure had been anticipated by the ready disposition of the self-constituted legislators, and a provincial assembly for the northern district had already met at Cape Francois; an example which was soon followed by the western and southern provinces, the former of which met at Port-au-Prince, and the latter at Aux Cayes. For more immediate communication between the people, and to accommodate every description, parochial committees were also established. These committees were of the disposition which might be expected, and, by dividing among themselves upon every occasion, they served only to inform the negroes of their frivolity, and to excite them to take advantage of their want of unanimity and power; and the principal determination in their proceedings was that, of the necessity of a full and speedy colonial representation. The order of the king, however, which was received in January 1790, tended to supersede their deliberations, by convoking a general Colonial Assembly, which was appointed to meet in the central town of Leogane. The mode which it directed of electing the members did not satisfy the provincial assemblies, and they substituted a plan of their own, changing the town of Leogane to that of St. Mark. . . .

Such was the confused state of the colony, and every one seemed to be so bent upon harassing the metropolitan government, that it was, with great reason, apprehended in France, that the island was about to declare itself independent, or to submit to some foreign power. The alarm became general throughout those places which had any concern with St. Domingo, and the National Assembly on being earnestly implored to consider of the best means of saving so valuable a dependancy resolved after a serious discussion of the subject, "That it was not the intention of the Assembly to interfere with the interior government of the colonies, or to subject them to laws incompatible with their local establishments; they therefore authorized the inhabitants of each colony to signify their own plan of legislation and commercial arrangement, preserving only a conformity with the principles of the mother country, and a regard for the reciprocal interests of both." It superadded, that no innovation was intended in *any system of commerce in which the colonies were already concerned.* It will easily be conceived that this conciliating resolution, so necessary, as regarded the discontented white colonists, would be very differently received by the people of colour. It excited among them a general clamour. . . .

III. Free People of Color

It was in this context of inter-white power struggle that the free people of color began to claim full political rights. The category (which was used at the time) of "free people of color" covered great social diversity. All had mixed European and African heritage, none of them were slaves, they tended to live in the southern and western provinces of the island, and they were required to perform militia service. But there the generalities ended. Some owned small plantations (with no more than a couple dozen slaves) on which they grew coffee and indigo, rather than sugar. Others had been educated in France and worked as doctors and other professionals. Many practiced skilled trades. Despite their economic and military importance, they faced discrimination and legal restrictions. But the Revolution, with its fracturing of white unity and discourse of equality allowed them to claim citizenship as free, property-owning men.

8. THE FREE PEOPLE OF COLOR ENTER THE SCENE[8]

The issue of the rights of free people of color was first broached in the National Assembly on October 22, 1789. On that day, a white member of the Society of the Friends of the Blacks, Etienne-Louis-Hector de Joly, stood before the deputies and urged them to recognize the free people of color as citizens. His appeal had been coordinated several days earlier with leading free men of color (including Vincent Ogé and Julien Raimond) who had come to Paris to defend their group's interests.

Your Lordships, the free, property-owning citizens of color of the French islands and colonies have the honor to represent to you:

That there still exists, in one part of the empire, a type of man who is debased and degraded, a class of citizens which is condemned to disdain and all the humiliations of slavery. In a word, they are Frenchmen who are groaning under the yoke of oppression.

Such is the fate of the unfortunate American colonists known in the isles by the name of mulattoes, quarteroons, etc.

Although free-born citizens, they live like foreigners in their own land. Excluded from all positions, dignities, and professions, they are even forbidden from exercising some of the mechanical arts. Subject to the most demeaning distinctions, they live in slavery in the very home of liberty.

---

[8]*Archives parlementaires de 1787 à 1860* [henceforth AP], eds. M. J. Mavidal and M. E. Laurent (Paris: Société d'Imprimerie et Librairie Administrative P. Dupont, 1867–1879), série 1, vol. 9, 476–468.

The Estates-General were convoked.

Throughout France . . . citizens of all classes were summoned to the great task of public regeneration. Everybody took part in the formation of the *cahiers* and the nomination of the deputies charged with defending their rights and stipulating their interests.

The cry of liberty was heard in the other hemisphere.

It should have stifled even the memory of those outrageous distinctions between citizens of the same land. Instead it gave rise to new, even more hateful ones.

For the power-hungry aristocracy, liberty is but the right to exclusive domination over other men.

The white colonists acted on this principle. It is still today the constant motive of their conduct.

They arrogated to themselves the right to assemble and elect representatives for the colonies.

Excluded from these assemblies, the citizens of color were deprived of the faculty of tending to their personal interests, of deliberating on common affairs, and carrying their wishes, complaints, and demands to the National Assembly.

Under this strange system, the citizens of color find themselves represented by the deputies of the white colonists, even though it is a fact that they were not summoned to the electoral assemblies, that they gave no power to these deputies, and that their obvious opposition of interests would make such representation absurd and contradictory.

It is up to your Lordships to weigh these considerations. It is up to you to return to oppressed citizens the rights of which they have been unjustly deprived. It is up to you to finish your glorious work by guaranteeing liberty to French citizens in both hemispheres.

Instructed by the Declaration of the Rights of Man and the Citizen, the colonists of color have become aware of what they are. They have elevated themselves to the dignity that you have assigned to them. They have understood their rights and used them.

They have assembled. They have drafted a *cahier* containing all their requests. They have included in it demands based on the code that you have given to the universe. They have entrusted it to their deputies. At present, they are limiting themselves to requesting, in this august Assembly, the representation they need to assert their rights and, above all, to defend their interests against the tyrannical pretentions of the whites.

The citizens of color obviously have the same right to representation as the whites.

Like them, they are all free French citizens. The edict of the month of March 1685 gives them full rights and privileges. It mandates that "freed slaves (and, with all the more reason, their descendants) deserve the liberty they have acquired; that this liberty bestows upon them and their properties the same good effects as the liberty natural to all Frenchmen." Like them, they are property-owners and cultivators. Like them, they contribute to the support of the State by paying taxes and bearing the same charges as whites. Like them, they have already spilled (and are ready to spill again) their blood for the defense of the fatherland. Finally, like them (but with less encouragement and means), they have given multiple proofs of patriotism. . . .

The citizens of color have voted, and depose here by our hands, the solemn promise to contribute one-fourth of their revenues to help pay for the expenses of the State. They declare that this quarter comes to 6 million pounds. They have also offered two percent of their property to help guarantee the national debt. They beg you to accept this homage. . . .

However, banish from your minds all idea, all spirit of personal interest. The citizens of color are not making these offers to influence your judgment.

They beg your Lordships to forget the offers and consider only the rigor of principles.

They are asking for no favors.

They are demanding the rights of man and citizen, rights founded on nature and the social contract, rights that you have solemnly recognized and authentically consecrated when you established as the basis of the Constitution that "all men are born and remain free and equal in rights"

"That the law is the expression of the general will; that all citizens have the right to participate personally or by their representatives in its formation."

"That each citizen has the right, whether personally or through his representatives, to verify the necessity of public taxes and to freely consent to them."

Who would dare reject these fundamental maxims, under the pretext of the whites' and colonies' well-being? Could considerations of sordid self-interest lead one to silence the voice of nature?

Do you not see in this the language of ambition and greed that measures the prosperity of the State only in terms of personal pleasures?

But now is not the place to give ourselves over to serious discussions of the fundamental principles on which the rights of the citizens of color are founded.

Once you have admitted their preliminary demands, once they have descended into the arena to combat their adversaries, they will easily demonstrate that the legitimate interest of the whites themselves and the interest of the colonies requires that the status and liberty of the citizens of colors be guaranteed, because the happiness of a State consists in the peace and harmony of the members who compose it and that there can be no real peace and union between the force which oppresses and the weakness which gives in, between the master who commands and the slave who obeys.

Once again, Your Lordships, the citizens of color are only demanding a right of representation at this moment. They hold that right in virtue of both nature and the law. With full confidence, they hope your decision will confirm these inviolable titles.

9. THE ABBÉ GRÉGOIRE INTERVENES[9]

The appeal of the free people of color received powerful support from the Abbé Grégoire. Grégoire was introduced to their cause by Julien Raimond, one of their spokesmen, in 1789. Previously known as an advocate of Jewish emancipation, Grégoire now threw his moral authority and passionate rhetoric into the cause of racial equality.

Feudalism never penetrated our isles. . . . But they escaped that calamity only by experiencing another. Having force on their side, the Whites pronounced, against Justice, that brown skin would mean exclusion from the advantages of society. Drunken with pride in their skin tone, they raised a wall of separation between themselves and a class of free men whom they improperly call *people of color* or *mixed-bloods*. They condemned to shame and degradation several thousand estimable individuals, as if all were not children of the same mother. . . .

When will we stop saying that political convenience should counterbalance justice and weaken its rigor? It is ever true that the morality of nations is nothing but that of individuals. In this continual fracas, in this successive revolution of all human things, virtue is the only fixed point for States as well as men, and the stability, the happiness of Empires results from the felicitous agreement of political principles with those of justice.

A rigorous consequence of this is that the rejection of the people of color threatens the State with a crisis capable of shaking it to its foundations. If, however, you bridge the gap separating them from Whites, if you bring their minds together, you will cement the mutual attachment of these two classes. Their reunion will form a mass of force most effective in containing the slaves, whose sufferings you will undoubtedly want to lighten . . . until the best moment for emancipating them.

The people of color will value this act of justice toward them as a great gift. Their gratitude, so natural to their souls, will attach them firmly to the Metropole, which will have truly earned the name Mother Country. Many are property-owners. The secret charm that binds the free man to his field will increase their patriotism, a new enthusiasm will flower in their souls, making their talents flourish and favoring agriculture, commerce, and industry. With mixed marriages no longer subject to the anathema of prejudice, the Whites will renounce the illegitimate relations which have dishonored their youth. The almost-certain hope of an honorable establishment will encourage girls of color to conduct themselves well. These respectable relations will leave nothing but the detested memory of detestable concubinage. This new order of things offers the happy perspective of

---

[9]Abbé Henri Grégoire, *Mémoire en faveur des gens de couleur ou sang-melés de st. Domingue et des autres Isles francoises de l'Amerique, adressée à l'Assemblées Nationale* (Paris: Belin, 1789), 4, 37–47.

regenerated education, purified morals, population growth, and wealth that will nourish the State and console humanity.

With the people of color on par with the Whites, it will no longer be a question if they should be active in legislation and send deputies to the National Assembly. Subject to laws and taxes, citizens have the right to consent to both, failing which they can refuse obedience and payment. . . .

Against the demands of the people of color are arrayed the colonial deputies in all their force, claiming to be their only true representatives. *True*, that may be so, for the National Assembly ruled in their favor despite the complaints of many white Colonists. But *only* we deny, for they can only represent their constituents, the Whites. . . .

I propose to the Assembly the following decree:

"The people of color of Saint-Domingue and the other French Colonies, including the free negroes, are declared citizens in the full meaning of the term and be assimilated in everything to the Whites. Consequently, they can exercise all crafts and professions, leave the isles, attend public schools and aspire to all ecclesiastical, civil, and military positions."

"The militia companies of mixed-bloods and whites shall be merged. . . ."

"Masters will be allowed to free their slaves without paying anything. Slaves will be allowed to purchase their freedom by paying their masters alone [and no fees]. A register of emancipations will be kept. . . ."

"Concubinage will be punished. If a Negro woman gives birth to an illegitimate child of color, her child will be emancipated, and if the father is known, he will be condemned by law to paying 2,000 pounds of sugar to provide for his child. . . ."

"It will be forbidden to insult the origin of mixed-bloods. . . ."

"Priests will be urged to use all the influence of their ministry to efface prejudice and help execute the present decree."

"The people of color gathered in Paris will choose five deputies who . . . will be provisionally admitted to the National Assembly, just like the other Colonial Deputies, until there have been new elections in the Isles, carried out by regular assemblies of all free citizens, in conformity with the regulations of the National Assembly."

Feudalism, which was happily destroyed on the French continent, has reproduced itself in another form in our Colonies. But the persistence of abuses is yet one more reason to extirpate them. It is time that reason rises above the prideful pretentions of grandeur and opulence. Let us erase all the humiliating distinctions which nature condemns and religion outlaws. Vice and virtue should be the only measure of political consideration, equality the only measure of the rights of man. To live is nothing. To live free is everything. Should this liberty, which French soldiers helped plant in the fields of America, be foreign to our Isles? No! Forty-thousand individuals, free under the law but enslaved by derogatory decrees and prejudice, look to you for their happiness. For humanity, it will be yet another triumph, yet another title of glory.

IV. The Assembly Debates Equality for the Free People of Color

The demand of the free people of color for equality ran headlong into the colonial lobby's insistence on their exclusion from political rights. Caught between these opposing imperatives, the National Assembly formed a colonial committee in March 1790 to reconcile the two fundamentally irreconcilable positions. Its solution—granting elected colonial assemblies the power to make their own internal laws, while remaining vague about whether free people of color would be allowed to participate in those same assemblies—pleased no one. Rather than resolving the matter, the National Assembly's equivocation prolonged the controversy. The resulting back and forth over the political rights of the free people of color, which continued through mid-1791, produced the French Revolution's most significant debate over the relationship between race and citizenship.

10. THE COLONIAL COMMITTEE'S INITIAL APPROACH (MARCH 1790)[10]

On March 8, 1790, the colonial committee presented its recommendation. Its author, Antoine Barnave, tried to balance the concerns of the white colonial elite with those of the free people of color to defuse the crisis and maintain colonial stability. It failed to achieve these goals.

Barnave's Report Presenting the Committee's Draft Law

The French nation's interest in supporting its commerce, preserving its colonies, and favoring their prosperity by all means compatible with the metropole seems to us, from all points of view, to be an incontestable truth. . . .

The measures required to fulfill this object seem to us to be indicated clearly by principles and circumstances.

To reassure the colonists about their most critical interests, receive their views on the type of government required for their prosperity . . . , invite them to present their views, concurrently with French commerce, on their reciprocal relationship— these are the steps dictated by circumstances, justice, and reason. . . .

The colonies suffered from great oppression under the arbitrary and ministerial regime. For many years they have complained in vain. . . . This is incontestably the principal cause of the insurrections that have occurred. None of them have been directed against the nation or king, but rather against the arbitrary regime. In a word, these movements, which were transmitted from the metropole to the colonies, had the same stamp and bore the same character.

---

[10]Mavidal and Laurent, *AP*, vol. 12, 68–73.

There was another cause of discontent. . . . Whether through fatal negligence or as a consequence of the food shortage we have ourselves experienced, the colonies have recently lacked provisions. This has provoked renewed complaints against the extreme rigor of the exclusive regime of trade. . . .

Finally, the enemies of France's happiness have used different means of fomenting trouble and disquiet among the colonists. . . .

It is to these three causes that we can trace all the events that have taken place in the colonies. Thus, it is by remedying them that we can calm them down, that we can safeguard our own interests by safeguarding theirs, that we can satisfy those of French commerce, which are directly linked to the colonies' preservation and prosperity. . . .

There are three objects of consideration . . . 1. the necessity of constituting the colonies, 2. the reciprocal complaints of commerce and the colonies on the current state of the exclusive regime, 3. the alarm of both at the application of several of your decrees.

On the first point, your committee thinks that the various laws passed for the provinces of France are not applicable to our colonial regime. In the political order, the colonies contain a class of particular beings that cannot be confused or assimilated with the other social bodies. Whether we consider the colonies domestically or in their relation to the metropole, the rigorous and universal application of general principles is not suitable for them. . . . Different locale, habits, climate, and agricultural production all require different laws. . . . We do not believe that the colonies can be included in the constitution decreed for the kingdom.

In deciding that the colonies should have particular laws and a particular constitution, your committee thinks that it would be advantageous and fair to consult them. . . . Their wish should be decisive on a subject connected to their most precious rights. . . .

To formulate the wish of the colonies, assemblies must be formed. But your committee thinks that in those colonies where freely elected assemblies already exist, they should be allowed to express their colony's wish. The essential condition of representation is confidence. It seems better to deal with assemblies which already enjoy it than to send to far-off lands convocation regulations drawn up according to imperfect notions and likely to inflame rivalries, slow down operations, and increase or prolong a dangerous fermentation. . . .

On the second point, the complaints about the prohibitive regime . . . your committee feels that, before issuing a ruling, it is necessary to gather as much information as possible. Thus, it proposes that the colonial assemblies present their views on the changes they desire. . . .

Finally, the third object concerns the alarm that has been raised about the application of several decrees. You must not, you cannot, speak but one language, that of truth, which consists in disavowing the false extension which has been given to [the decrees in question]. You have not changed anything relative to the colonies, because your laws did not have the colonies for their object. You could not have changed anything, because public safety and even humanity raised insurmountable obstacles to what your hearts were inspiring you to do. Thus, let us say it now, at this moment, because doubts have been raised: you have made no innovation. This declaration should suffice. . . . But it is just to accompany it with a disposition aimed at reassuring the colonies against those who, by their culpable schemes, would try to trouble them, to stir up rebellion. . . .

Draft Law

Considering the colonies as part of the French empire and wanting them to enjoy the fruits of the happy regeneration that has occurred, [the National Assembly] never meant to include them in the constitution it has decreed for the kingdom and to subject them to laws which could be incompatible with their local and particular needs.

In consequence, it decrees what follows:

1. Each colony is authorized to express its wish for the constitution, legislation, and administration best suited to the prosperity and happiness of its inhabitants. . . .
2. In colonies which already have assemblies freely elected by the citizens and recognized by them, these assemblies will be allowed to express the wish of the colony; in those where there are no such assemblies, they will be formed. . . .
4. The plans prepared by the colonial assemblies will be submitted to the National Assembly to be examined and decreed by it. . . .
5. The National Assembly's decrees on the organization of municipalities and administrative assemblies will be sent to the colonial assemblies. They will be empowered to put into execution the parts of the aforesaid decrees that can be adapted to local needs and customs. . . .
6. The same colonial assemblies will express their views on the changes which could be made to the prohibitive regime of commerce. . . .

Moreover, the National Assembly declares that it did not mean to make any innovation in any branch of direct or indirect commerce between France and its colonies. It places the colonists and their properties under the special protection of the nation. It declares criminal against the nation anyone who would try to excite uprisings against them. . . .

11. ABBÉ GRÉGOIRE, *LETTER TO THE LOVERS OF HUMANITY* (OCTOBER 1790)[11]

Barnave's draft decree was approved by the Assembly and accompanied by an instruction (of March 28th) on its implementation. The wording of the instruction's fourth article was ambiguous. This obscured still further the question of the political

---

[11]Abbé Grégoire, *Lettre aux philantropes, sur les malheurs, les droits, et les reclamations des Gens de couleur de Saint-Domingue, et des autres iles françoises de l'Amérique* (Paris: Belin, 1790).

rights of free people of color. Worse, the decree's promise that colonial assemblies would be allowed to determine the laws they wanted for themselves increased the stakes in the struggle for citizenship. Now more than ever, the free people of color needed to participate, for the assemblies would determine the conditions of colonial political participation. Tension increased not only in Paris but in the colonies themselves. In Saint-Domingue, rival regional assemblies and their allied militias mobilized for conflict. Civil war seemed imminent. The National Assembly responded on October 12, 1790 with a new law intended to reassure the colonists. The law expressed the Assembly's "firm commitment to establishing as a constitutional article that laws on the status of persons in the colonies will only be decreed at the express and formal request of the colonial assemblies." The free people of color and their allies reacted with outrage and dismay. The most effective protest was the Abbé Grégoire's, Letter to the Lovers of Humanity.

October 12, 1790 will be forever remembered as a fatal day in the annals of history. On its anniversary, liberty, humanity, and justice will go into mourning. On that day, posterity . . . will remember that part of the French nation was sacrificed to the prejudices and greed of the other. . . .

Do not blame the National Assembly, but rather those who led it into error, for enslaving our brothers, which has now been consecrated in the most formal manner. It was decided (a thing unheard of among all nations!) that nothing would be changed about the status of persons in our isles except at the request of the colonists; in other words, that we will only get rid of abuses at the request of those who live off them and who solicit their prolongation! In other words, that the eternal rights of man will be subordinated to pride and avarice. In other words, that they will be the playthings of oppression until it suits their despots to ease their fate. . . .

I will prove that, by its decree of the 12th, the National Assembly, violated its, 1. promises, 2. principles, 3. justice, and 4. humanity. . . . I will then prove that the decree is impolitic. I address this issue for those who, compromising on the most inflexible principles, believe that interest is everything and justice nothing. . . .

1. By its decree of the 12th, the National Assembly broke its promise. On October 22, 1789, a deputation of mixed-bloods was admitted and read its address. We responded to them: "No part of the nation will demand its rights in vain from the assembly of the representatives of the nation, etc." Did we keep our word? . . .

2. The National Assembly contradicts its principles. By this I mean that celebrated declaration of rights which guarantees to all men the inalienable patrimony of liberty. . . . Would you dare to say that *only whites* are born and remain free and equal in rights? Would you geographically constrain this moral principle, which embraces all regions and all ages? . . .

Just a word about M. Barnave [the colonial committee spokesman who proposed the decrees of the March 8th and October 22nd]. After having said that it was the Assembly's intention to rule on the status of people only at the request of the colony, he stated that the National Assembly would make this a constitutional decree. The National Assembly does not have the right to do this, and I will prove it. The constitution is the distribution of political powers; but the status of persons, their equality, their liberty are outside of and prior to the constitution. The National Assembly can recognize these rights, declare them, and guarantee their exercise. But what we hold directly from God, what is part of the essential order of the laws of nature, cannot be the object of a decree. Men have the right to exercise their liberty just as much as they have the right to eat, sleep, etc. Thus, Barnave's proposition is an absurdity.

3. What we have just said clearly establishes the injustice of the decree. . . . Either the mixed-bloods are an integral part of the French empire, in which case they must be citizens, or they are a foreign people, in which case they are at war with their despots. But they can never be rebels. Have you not consecrated the principle that resistance to oppression is legitimate? Frenchmen, I ask you: with your sense of the dignity of man, with your knowledge of your rights, and with the certainty of your superiority, what would you do if you were in their shoes?

4. The decree of the 12th is opposed to humanity. If your heart is not closed off to pity, hear the sobbing of forty thousand unfortunates whose rights are inviolable, whose sufferings are incontestable. . . .

5. I add that the preamble of the decree is impolitic. . . .

The political world is taking on a new aspect. The volcano of liberty which erupted in France will soon produce a general explosion and change the destiny of the human race in both hemispheres. The interest of both metropole and colony, their internal and external security, demand that their forces be united. . . . It is always a detestable policy to abase part of the people, rather than interesting it in keeping order. . . .

The mixed-bloods see the [liberty] cockade worn everywhere—a cockade that will travel around the globe. They see the standard of revolution parade proudly. Do you really believe that the cry of liberty, which sounds constantly in their ears, will not awaken in their hearts the sentiment of their rights? . . .

Would you try to limit this population, whose future growth is guaranteed by the furious libertinage of a large number of whites? . . . Fearing a slave uprising, would you disarm all the militias of color and the rural mounted police? If so, they must be replaced . . . by repeated convoys of troops to serve in a burning climate which devours effeminate Europeans and oppressed Negroes.

Who can tell . . . if the mulattoes will make common cause with the Negroes? . . .

Moreover, are you not afraid of a coalition of the mixed-bloods and a party of whites seeking independence, together with others who, heavily indebted to the metropole, would seize the opportunity to liberate themselves without paying? Will not the bitterness and ambition of the ones, combined with the others' lack of integrity, foment troubles and cause a scission with incalculable results? Who knows if the rival powers will not profit from this interior shock to attack our colonies? . . .

I hope my prophecies are false. But if my fears are realized, at least I won't have to blame myself for not having called your attention to these important considerations. Is it not obvious that, if pride renounces its pretentions, the most numerous class of citizens [the mulattoes] would render the [threat of] the slaves less formidable? Brought together by the same interests and advantages, the unified mass of mixed-bloods and whites would assure the tranquility of the colonies more effectively. Take it as certain that, sooner or later, the repressed energy of the mulattoes will burst forth with irresistible violence. . . .

12. THE DEBATE OVER RACE AND CITIZENSHIP (1791)[12]

The decree of October 12, 1790 only exacerbated the crisis. Frustrated at the Assembly's pandering to the colonists, one of the original spokesmen for the free people of color, Vincent Ogé, sailed to Saint-Domingue where he led an armed uprising. Although he was captured and executed in February 1791, his insurrection prompted the Assembly to reopen the issue of citizenship. In May 1791, its colonial committee presented a new plan. It called for a general congress of representatives from all of France's Caribbean colonies to meet on the neutral island of Saint-Martin and present their wishes for the colonial constitution. This sparked an intense debate over the issues of race and citizenship. The document following is the committee's proposal of May 7, 1791, for a colonial congress.

Art. 1st. The National Assembly decrees as a constitutional principle that no law on the status of persons can be made for the colonies by the Legislature except upon the precise and formal request of the colonial assemblies.

Art. 2. Given that it is important for the general good that they express their position on the men of color and free Negroes in a common and uniform manner . . . and in accordance with the right of legislative initiative guaranteed to them by the preceding article, the National Assembly orders the formation of a general committee of the colonies. . . .

Art. 3. Each colonial assembly of America will appoint commissioners drawn from their ranks: Saint-Domingue, 12; Martinique, 5; Guadeloupe and its dependencies, 6; Sainte-Lucie, 2; Tobago, 2; and Cayenne, 2.

Art. 4. The sole mission of the commissioners, who will be chosen by majority vote, will be to pronounce, in the name of the colonies, on the men of color and free Negroes. . . .

Art. 5. The commissioners will assemble on the French part of the island of Saint-Martin. . . .

[12]Mavidal and Laurent, AP, vol. 25, 638, 640–642, 737–742, 747–750, 752–759; vol. 26, 4–5, 7–13, 15–17, 41–43, 47–49, 51–56, 58–60, 90, 95.

Art. 14. Once the Legislature has definitively ruled on the status of men of color and free Negroes, upon the proposition of the committee of Saint-Martin, the first article of the present decree will have been fully executed, and future legislatures will not be allowed to ask the colonies for a new proposition on the status of any persons whatsoever.

[Debate began immediately and lasted for a week. It finally ended on May 15, 1791, with a decree granting certain categories of free people of color political rights. The following documents are chronologically arranged excerpts from the speeches in that debate.]

GRÉGOIRE: In my view, this is an adroit means of constitutionally consecrating tyranny and oppression. . . .

MOREAU DE SAINT-MÉRY:[13] I am not surprised to hear the project described as horrible by those who constantly publish . . . incendiary writings. . . . All of the bad things that have happened to the colonies have come from their hands. . . .

Do you think that the Constitution you have given France is suited to the colonies? You have a choice: either renounce your riches and commerce or declare frankly that the declaration of rights is not applicable to the colonies.

The colonies don't resemble France. . . . They cannot have the same interior regime, nor the same organization. . . . Their commerce in no way resembles that of the other parts of the empire. . . . If you subject them to the same rules [as the rest of France], they will soon become useless, and you will lose your colonial commerce. And without their commerce, you will lose your splendor and political rank within Europe. . . .

PÉTION DE VILLENEUVE:[14] What is really being proposed here today? Free men are not asking for a favor. They are asking for rights they already have. They are only asking you not to sacrifice them. . . . When there are two classes of men who know their rights, one of whom is enslaved and the other is free to continue oppressing, tranquility cannot last long.

It is being proposed that you strip the free men of color of their political rights. . . . There are two classes of men with opposing interests, and you want to make one the judge of the other.

Are the colonies a separate state? If a department of the kingdom demanded the right to initiate legislation and limited you to the negligible right of confirming the laws it proposed, wouldn't such a demand lead to the dissolution of the empire. How is it possible that you can calmly listen to such a decree? You are being asked to assemble a congress of white colonists to determine the fate of the free men of color.

---

[13]Moreau de Saint-Méry was a former royal official in Saint-Domingue and a leading expert on colonial law.

[14]Pétion de Villeneuve was a political writer and second mayor of revolutionary Paris.

They are concealing the true purpose of the project by saying that you will have the right to confirm or not to confirm the laws that this general assembly of the colonies presents to you.

Have no illusions. . . . You are being told: "It will only be a wish." Messieurs, once all the colonies have been gathered together and have voiced a desire that we know in advance (since there will be only white colonists giving their opinion on the free men of color), I ask the National Assembly if it would then dare to rule against the formal wish of all the colonies. . . . If you don't grant their wish, you will set the colonies ablaze. . . .

MALOUET:[15] You have granted the colonies the power to initiate legislation. The English colonies have their own legislatures. Do the French colonists, represented here by only a few deputies, have less of a right to demand legislative initiative? Do you want to assimilate the colonies to the departments of the kingdom? Which department has interests different from the others? . . . The colonies will only be satisfied once you have guaranteed them legislative initiative. Only this will ensure the security of the colonists' properties. The slightest sign of doubt you express on this point will increase their mistrust. . . .

GRÉGOIRE: This decree would dishonor France and the National Assembly, and alienate the most precious class of colonist. It would strip France and the National Assembly of supremacy over the colonies. It would dishonor them by sacrificing a class of free men to the greed of a few individuals and by stripping that class of the inalienable right of man to obey only those laws to which he consented through his representatives. And finally, it will spark an eternal war within the colonies while separating them from the metropole. These would be the fatal consequences of the project if you adopt it. . . .

The cause of the troubles [in the colonies] was the incendiary letter written on August 12, 1789, by the colonial deputies. In it they insult our enthusiasm for liberty, foment panic, and raise imaginary fears about English vessels, emissaries, and thousands of rifles that they accuse the friends of the blacks of sending. . . .

This letter tries to pit the blacks against the people of color. . . .

This letter, tailored to cause trouble in the colonies, was followed by a host of others. This began the inquisitions, persecutions, and a sort of universal conspiracy against the men of color. . . .

You can feel all the injustice of the first article of the project, that you have been pressured into approving by the threat of losing your colonies. . . . What! Because you grant free men, property-owners, and taxpayers the same rights as whites, your colonies will be lost? Was France lost when you decreed that the people's rights were equal to those of the nobles and clergy? . . .

---

[15]Malouet was a former royal naval official with strong colonial ties.

Let me speak about the legislative initiative that is being proposed for the colonies. What will be its result? In two words, this: either you will only be able to issue laws that the colonial assemblies have presented, or you will issue none at all. . . .

Moreover, let me remind you once more that when the free people of color were admitted to speak to the National Assembly in November 1789, they were explicitly promised, in a phrase applauded by the Assembly, that *no group of French citizens would demand their rights in vain from the representatives of the nation.* Now is the time to keep your promise. . . . I demand that we reject the project your committee has presented and propose that you pass the following decree instead:

"The National Assembly decrees that the men of color and free Negroes who own property and pay taxes are included in article 4 of the decree of March 28th."

"Orders the commissioners charged with re-establishing order in the islands to use all means in their power to ensure that the men of color enjoy all the rights of active citizenship." . . .

GOUY D'ARCY:[16] Even after four of your committees have attentively examined a most delicate political question, even after the unanimous conclusion of their enlightened members and the colonial deputies summoned to testify before it that you consecrate what you had already formally declared, it is proposed that you pronounce against your opinion, your word, your security, our properties, our existence, and the most priceless interests of the nation, and thus start a horrible war in the midst of nine colonies that ask only for protection and repose.

In a word, it is being proposed today that you adopt the first of these three fatal propositions, that the abominable sect of the Friends of the Blacks has sworn to make you decree: the concession of political rights, the abolition of the slave trade, and the emancipation of the slaves.

Do not fool yourselves. These three propositions are inseparable. They flow from the same principle. The adoption of the first means the adoption of the two others by overthrowing the barrier between free man and slave that has been maintained for 150 years by a necessary prejudice.

The class of free people of color form that salutary barrier. . . . It will be one small step to accomplish such a fine work by solemnly decreeing the emancipation of the slaves. This will destroy the colony and the metropole, sacrifice 100,000 whites to the fury of 1,000,000 blacks. These same blacks will be immolated by their own fury and destroyed by anarchy. . . .

With the measure you seek to pass, the free people of color would be admitted to the same honors as whites. The free Negro would become the

---

[16]Gouy d'Arcy was a military officer elected to represent the nobility of Saint-Domingue.

colleague of his former master. His brother, his parents, his friends—all still slaves—would have difficulty understanding the equality of this black with a white, whose superiority over them would seem a painful problem.

Then, with the abolition of the slave trade that they have also sworn to decree, the plantation owner would be required to spread the tasks among a smaller number of slaves, because recruitment [of new ones] would be prohibited. Once the work load of each had increased, once they felt their health deteriorating and their energy evaporating, would they not be tempted to use their remaining force to throw off a yoke which had previously been light but had progressively become heavier and, ultimately, unbearable? Would they not be inclined, given their limited ability to reason, to blame the master for all the wrongs actually caused by an impolitic, national measure?

Finally, once universal emancipation had been decreed, but prudently suspended, these slaves would learn that they had been granted their liberty, but that they would only enjoy it in proportion to their intellectual advancement. Who among them would not feel instantly worthy of the benefit intended for them? . . . Who among them could stand to see their peers emancipated, but not themselves? Who among them would not want to be the first? Who among them would consent to leave liberty to their children without having savored it themselves?

All of them will want to be free, and all will be free the day they learn that they can be. I can and must say: one does not wait for liberty. This axiom of the Revolution does not need proof in this Assembly. But if I wanted proof, it would stand forth on its own.

If, on July 13, 1789, all the sovereigns of the earth had said to the inhabitants of Paris: "You are groaning under an odious yoke. Liberty will end your suffering. But you must be prepared for this new condition. . . . In four years, we will release you from your chains and give you liberty." Would the people of Paris have waited patiently? . . .

It would be the same in America. The slightest vibration on this delicate cord will echo in all hearts. Do not touch it when it is clear that frightful misfortunes, irreparable losses, and multiple massacres would drench your imprudent act in blood. . . .

The importance of the French colonies is obvious. Their existence depends on the preservation of the colonial regime.

The colonial regime is entirely based on the system of slavery.

The system of slavery is based on the slave trade and the ancient prejudice that sets up the people of color as a necessary barrier between blacks and whites.

These two safeguards of our property are threatened by the philanthropists.

These widespread threats have provoked universal alarm in all the colonies.

The general alarms were the cause or pretext of all the disturbances.

These troubles have provoked all sorts of crimes and misfortunes.

Now that we have traced the causes to their effects, let us consider . . . the desirable remedies.

Our misfortunes will end once calm is restored.

Calm will only return when confidence is restored. It will never be restored if the National Assembly, breaking its own promises, makes the slightest attack against the legislative initiative that it has granted to us over everything related to our Constitution—notably the status of persons.

DE TRACY:[17] When we had no Constitution, the colonies had none either . . . Now that we have one, the colonies need one too. The Constitution must be created. Before the creation of the world, there had to be a creator. You are that creator. It is up to you to arrange the elements of the thing you are creating. . . .

Well, Messieurs, these elements have all been arranged by your decrees. You have decreed that all individuals who are either property-owners or taxpayers have the right to participate in the primary electoral assemblies. You based this not on written laws, but on natural rights that are the same everywhere. Well, Messieurs, it should be exactly the same over there as it is here. . . . There is a single principle that arranges everything. . . .

I accept the decree of Monsieur l'Abbé Grégoire. . . .

MALOUET: This is not the place to examine if the institution of slavery is justified by law and principle. No sensible man with some degree of morality can profess this doctrine. But here we are trying to know if it is possible, without an accumulation of frightful crimes and misfortunes, to change the state of things in the colonies. . . .

I will try to prove morally and politically that the love of good and humanity that militates for such changes would be the bloodiest, most disastrous crusade one could undertake against the French. I will prove that the result would be not only the proscription of all the colonists, but also the ruin of some of your naval installations and most of your manufacturing establishments. It is impossible to apply integrally the declaration of rights in the colonies. . . .

Do you want to rule immediately on the status of the people of color and invest them with all the rights guaranteed by your declaration? If you do, you will subject your colonies to all the principles of your Constitution. But I think it is incompatible with their continued existence. . . .

PÉTION DE VILLENEUVE: It will be easy to show that the dispositions adopted by your committee are the cause of all the disorders. . . . We are constantly taking as given that the power to initiate legislation has already been granted. . . .

---

[17]De Tracy was a military officer and political writer.

I say that we have not granted or decided upon legislative initiative. And, above all, you have never granted [the colonies] legislative initiative on the status of persons. . . .

In the eyes of all men of good faith, article 4 formally decides the question in favor of the men of color. It says that "all persons" who own property, are resident, and pay taxes, will gather to form the parish assemblies.

Focusing on that general expression "all persons," I ask if free men of color are not persons. If they are persons, own property, are resident, and pay taxes, I see no reason to deny them the advantages attached to these qualities. . . .

To destroy such a formal decree, what was said in the preamble? The preamble states: "No law on the status of persons will be decreed for the colonies except upon the formal and precise request of their colonial assembly." But if a fact is asserted and that fact is either an error or a falsehood, what consequence can be drawn from it? Can it undo what has previously been done? Can we do so based upon an inexact preamble, on an insidious exposé?

Before your decrees, the free men of color had a positive law in their favor. You cannot strip them of that law's benefits without stating so precisely.

The free men of color can thus say, with your decrees in hand, that they have retained their existing rights.

You cannot destroy a decree with a preamble. Not only do humanity and justice speak in favor of the men of color, but so does good politics. Who are the free men of color? They are the boulevard of liberty in the colonies. They have always rushed to the defense of the colonies. They are the most interesting property-owners in the colonies. . . .

The men of color know and demand their rights. If you deprive them of those rights, they will become enemies of those who enjoy the spoils of that deprivation. The white colonists are only able to keep their slaves because of the active surveillance of the free men of color. The white colonists cannot deny that these men are the veritable troops of our isles. . . .

What is the origin of the troubles in our colonies? Despite what they say, they were not started by writings [of the Friends of the Blacks] which never actually reached the colonies, but rather by the letter of August 12, 1789 in which deputies of France insult our Revolution and say we are drunk with liberty . . .

The Assembly must explain itself positively. This is the only way of avoiding self-interested interpretations which pit two classes of men against each other. Their conflict will stop only when you have decreed what reason, justice, and liberty demand.

The [committee's] project will perpetuate disorder and dishonor the National Assembly.

What! You would decree as a constitutional article "that no law on the status of persons will be made for the colonies by the Legislative Body except upon the precise and formal demand of the colonial assemblies." By this, you place yourselves under the absolute dependence of the colonies. The article is injurious to the majesty of this assembly and violates all the nation's rights. Is this how colonies should be part of the Empire? If the colonies have the right to dictate the law, . . . they will be an independent State.

But you have already ruled on the status of persons. By article 4 of the instructions of March 28th, you said that all property-owning, resident, and taxpaying persons will gather to form the parish assemblies. You cannot go back on this decree. The article is formal and, as men of color are truly persons, I call for the rejection of the committee's project.

BARNAVE: Everybody knows that the colonies need reassurance on the Negro question. Prosperous colonies, those of England and Holland, all have the right to make their own laws on that issue. We did not want to give ours that particular right. To the contrary, we offered them a colonial constitution in which their rights will be safeguarded. . . .

You thus have one veritable point to discuss, one true question to resolve: do you want to have colonies or not? If the colonial constitution . . . does not promote humanity to the greatest extent possible without jeopardizing and annihilating our colonies, it is flawed. But if it does, then I return to my question: you must either adopt it or renounce the colonies. In that case, you must say: the existence of our commerce, our navy, our commercial advantages are not precious to us. Their preservation is less important to us than the consecration of principles. . . .

If you give in to the demand of the people of color, they will think that you have pronounced against the whites. The whites will think that you have pronounced against their wishes. And through a resolution intended to calm spirits and pacify the colonies, you will actually obtain only the continuation of party hatred. . .

If however, the wish of the assembly of Saint-Martin does not conform to justice, reason, and good policy, the Legislature will reform it. (Murmurs.)

Some of you seem to think that our project does not reserve this right to the Legislature. I formally declare that it does. . . .

I know that it is difficult to fight against principles. But I also know that we have obeyed imperious reasons of national interest.

LANJUINAIS:[18] What you are being asked to decide, supposedly as a provisional measure that prejudges nothing, tends to irrevocably deprive of their rights a portion of the free population of our colonies. . . .

The congress which is to be established will either decide in favor of justice and liberty, or it will decide against true principles.

In the first case, if it proposes to render justice to the citizens of color, . . . there is no drawback to declaring right now what you expect from the justice and enlightenment of the colonists.

---

[18]Lanjuinais was a jurist by profession.

But we must pause at the alternative. If the congress declares that it cannot allow citizens of color to exercise political rights—and given that we are told constantly not to decide this question ourselves—you will give the signal for carnage and all will be lost. Once this congress has spoken and pronounced the eternal separation of citizens of color from white citizens, what will you be able to do. With what arms could you combat it? If baseless fears are being inspired in the colonies now, what will happen when the colonists' pretentions are backed up by the influence of such a congress? Invested with all the colonies' powers, won't it have enough force to resist the authority of the nation?

ROBESPIERRE: First of all, it is important to establish the true state of the question. It is not to know if you will grant political rights to citizens of color, but rather if you will maintain them, because they already enjoyed them before your decrees.

I say that the men of color enjoyed rights that the whites are now claiming exclusively for themselves. . . . The Revolution gave back political rights to all citizens. Since before 1789 the men of color were equal in rights to the white men, it follows that they should have received the same rights, and that the Revolution raised them all . . . to the same rank as white men, which is to say, to political rights.

Have your previous decrees taken these away? No, because you will recall that you passed a law that gave the quality of active citizen to all property-owners in the colonies who paid taxes. . . . And since color was not mentioned, all these men of color who pay taxes are included in the decree and are recognized by it as active citizens.

You will note as well that the decree has not been revoked and that the preamble of the decree of October 12th does not say what some claim it does. Far from being favorable to their pretentions, it forecloses them. It says that you intended not to make any change in the status of persons except on the initiative of the colonies. This is to say the citizens of the colonies and, thus, the people of color who, as citizens according to the non-abrogated law . . . must participate in that initiative.

Your later decrees have not revoked your previous ones.

What could force you to violate your laws and decrees, as well as the principles of justice and humanity? You will lose your colonies, they say, if you do not deprive the free citizens of color of their rights. If those are not their exact words, it is their meaning. And why would you lose the colonies? Because some citizens, those called whites, want to enjoy exclusive rights of citizenship. And they are the same who dare tell you, through their deputies: ["]If you do not give political rights to us exclusively, we will be angry. Your decree will spread trouble throughout the colonies. It might have fatal results. You should fear the consequences of our discontent.["] Here we have a factious party who threatens you with destroying your colonies, of dissolving the links which unite them to the metropole, if you do not confirm its pretentions!

I ask the National Assembly if it is compatible with the dignity of leg-islators to make transactions of this sort with the self-interest, greed, and pride of a class of citizens. I ask if it is politically wise to let the threats of a party make you bargain away the rights of man, justice, and humanity! . . .

Let us examine the objections of this party of whites. On what grounds do they seek to take away the rights of their fellow-citizens? What is the reason for their extreme distaste for sharing political rights with their brothers? They say that if you give the quality of active citizen to free men of color, you will diminish the respect of the slaves for their masters. . . . An absurd objection. Did the rights exercised by free men of color before the Revolution have any influence on the obedience of the blacks? Did they diminish the empire of force that masters exercised over their slaves? . . .

Maintaining the political rights of the property-owning people of color will only strengthen the masters' power over the slaves. By giving the property-owning people of color and masters the same interest in keeping the blacks in a state of subordination, it is obvious that you will reinforce subordination in the colony. On the other hand, if you deprive the men of color of their rights, you will create a scission between them and the whites and naturally bring together all men of color. . . . You will bring them closer to the class of negroes and then, any insurrection . . . will be much more redoubtable because it would be supported by the free men of color. . . .

MOREAU DE SAINT-MÉRY: I must admit that I feel the greatest fear for the colonies when I see the Assembly raise doubts about the legislative initia-tive that it gave them on the status of persons. It is clear that the Assembly did not mean to include the colonies in the constitution it decreed. . . . The colonial deputies see it as a sacred duty to call for the preamble of October 12th. . . . It attests that the Assembly wanted nothing to be changed about the status of persons without the input of the colonies. Since then, you have constantly respected the principle that legislative initiative belongs to them. . . .

But, it is said, that initiative cannot be granted to them on the admis-sion of the people of color. To this I respond that it was granted . . . without any restriction. I also say that if it were compromised on a single point, it would be impossible to convince the colonies that it would not successively be compromised on all others. . . .

I hear much talk of natural rights from those who seek the perfect as-similation of men of color with the whites. I ask you: what chapter of the book of nature discusses the question of active citizenship. The quality of active citizen is obviously the result of a purely social compact. The proof of this is in the Constitution itself, for . . . there are inactive citizens. You have thus recognized some circumstances which prevent the enjoyment of citizenship. I find another example concerning the Jews of Alsace.

I maintain that the title of active citizen is the result of the Constitution you have made for the kingdom. But you have always declared, notably by your decree of March 8th, that you never intended to include the colonies in the Constitution decreed for the interior of the kingdom. How you could possibly want the colonies to be subject to your Constitution, given that you have said that it was not designed for them and that you were waiting to hear our wishes? . . .

England had immense colonies. Those colonies wanted legislative initiative. The Parlement refused. . . . You have seen the evils that ensued.

It all boils down to this: will the Assembly break its promise to leave the colonies initiative?. . . .

DÉMEUNIER:[19] In examining the project, I find two fundamental dispositions. The first is that the Legislature will not rule on the status of persons in the colonies except upon the formal, precise demand of the colonial assemblies. The second is that the colonial assemblies are supposed to express their wishes.

There is no doubt that the Legislature will feel obliged to rule in conformity with those wishes. You will thus compromise the rights of the men of color. Neither justice, nor humanity, nor political reasons can induce you to adopt such a measure. Messieurs, you must declare frankly in the decree itself that the Legislature will rule definitively on the status of the men of color whatever the wishes of the colonial assembly or committee of Saint-Martin. . . .

SIEYES: I want to ask a question. Could Monsieur Barnave clarify what seems to be the true heart of the question? The Assembly granted legislative initiative to the colonies to make their own constitution and even on the status of persons. It gave that initiative to people. The question is: to which men was that initiative granted? I believe that it was to all free men, not just a portion of free men. . . .

You can divide into three classes the inhabitants of the colony: the *grands blancs*, the *petits blancs*, and the free men of color. All are equally included in the National Assembly's decrees [of March 8 and 28]. The Assembly excluded none of these three groups from liberty and political rights. If you tell me that there is a difference between them in that some exercised the rights of active citizens while others did not, I answer that it is false: before the Revolution no one exercised rights of active citizenship. . . .

BARNAVE: I am being asked to answer a question. I will respond clearly. . . .

By its decree of March 8th—a decree which saved the colonies and whose repeal would destroy them—the National Assembly decided that each colony would express its wishes for its own constitution and legislation. In colonies where there were already elected colonial assemblies, they would be retained and declared capable of expressing these wishes. In colonies where none existed, they would be convoked to express their wishes, following the mode of convocation that would be addressed to them.

---

[19]Démeunier was a deputy of Paris and author of a number of political treatises.

On March 28th the National Assembly established a provisional mode of convocation. . . .

But there were already elected colonial assemblies formed in all the colonies, so that the provisional convocation of March 28th had no practical effect.

When drafting that provisional convocation, we said in the instructions that the colonial assemblies, whether pre-existing or newly formed, would express their wishes for the Constitution, on the qualifications for active citizenship and eligibility. It is thus truly legal that the currently existing colonial assemblies express their wishes on this point. This had already been decreed. They were legally authorized to express their opinion on the entire Constitution and notably on the qualifications for active citizenship. And even if it were true that, in the provisional mode of convocation designed to form colonial assemblies where none already existed, the free people of color would have been admitted, it is no less true that the existing colonial assemblies, which you declared valid and legally authorized to express their opinion on the Constitution and qualifications for active citizenship, are equally capable of withdrawing that status from them today. If you take away that right from them, you would be retracting a law you have passed and going back on a disposition you have formally decreed. . . .

SIEYES: Monsieur Barnave promised to respond to my observations. Although he has not done so now, he did so in advance. Here is what he said on March 28th, when the National Assembly issued its decree: "To know the wishes of the colonies, colonial assemblies must be formed where they do not already exist or where they do not enjoy the confidence of the citizens."

Based on this, I ask if the existing assemblies could possibly enjoy the citizens' confidence when a very large number of citizens were excluded from their formation. . . .

I think that the best thing the Assembly could do now is to table the committee's project.

PÉTION DE VILLENEUVE: It has been said that you gave legislative initiative on the constitution to your colonies. But it is essential to explain what is meant by legislative initiative. In effect, you have asked our colonies to send you their plans for a suitable colonial constitution. Some say that you also wanted to give them legislative initiative generally, on their interior regime. This point must be clarified. It is upon this that the retention of your colonies and interests of your commerce, truly depends. . . .

There are several types of initiatives. In this case, you have granted [the colonies] legislative initiative not so that you automatically rule in conformity with the wishes that will be presented to you, but to take them into consideration. Should that colonial imitative be necessary in all things concerning their interior regime? Is the Legislature henceforth forbidden from issuing decrees without that initiative?

Some want us to decide this question immediately, without any examination. But it is too important, for this legislative initiative risks placing your commerce under the most absolute dependence of the colonies.

It is possible that the colonies be granted the power to initiative legislation, but, at the same time, you should be able to make laws on your own initiative. You should ask the colonies to express their wishes; but you may not want to grant them.

It is also most essential to agree upon what is meant by "interior regime."

Yesterday, one of us said to the Assembly: "Let us positively explain that the Legislature can issue decrees it thinks appropriate, even if the colonies have legislative initiative." . . . [If it were otherwise,] the colonies would be able to dictate the law to us. . . .

Thus, . . . your committees must explain clearly the scope they intend to give to the legislative initiative [of the colonies].

Now, the article on legislative initiative mentions the status of persons. We must know if, by the term "status of persons," we are including the men of color. The article says in general: "no law on the status of persons." But the article does not say on which persons. This will always be a point of difficulty until the Assembly explains itself in a precise manner. To do this, we have to see what we have ruled previously; if we do, I maintain that the article cannot refer to men of color. . . .

Recall what happened with the instruction of March 28th. I spoke positively of all property-holding and taxpaying persons; and under the word "persons," you clearly included the men of color, because free men of color are persons. You also included them in the discussion which took place about it.

[Here followed a dispute about what exactly was said during the debate over the March 28th instruction.]

GRÉGOIRE: I will here invoke the testimony of many of our colleagues, who will surely remember.

In the session of March 28, 1790, I asked that the men of color be explicitly denominated in article 4 of the instructions. Many members, colonial deputies themselves, and particularly Monsieur Barnave, who is here, told me that they were included under the word "person" in eneral. . . .

MOREAU DE SAINT-MÉRY: The national interest is intimately linked to the calm and tranquility of the colonies because they are a principal source of public wealth and because they nourish our navy and commerce, without which France cannot survive. It is thus imperiously necessary to protect and guarantee explicitly the existence of the colonists. . . . In the current state of affairs, there is only one way [to do this]. . . . It is to declare solemnly that those who dare to inspire in the colonists the fear of losing their slaves, who perhaps even hope to tempt their fidelity, be declared guilty. . . .

[Moreau de Saint-Méry then presented amendments to articles 1 and 14.]

[New Article 1:] "The National Assembly decrees, as a constitutional article, that no law on the status of slaves in the colonies of America can be made by the Legislature without the formal and spontaneous request of their colonial assemblies." . . .

[New Article 14:] "Once the political status of men of color and free negroes has been definitively decided by the Legislative Body, upon the proposition of the congress assembled at Saint-Martin, there will be no changes without the formal and spontaneous request of the colonial assemblies." . . .

BOUCHOTTE:[20] We promised to protect the Americans' properties, among which are their slaves. But did we promise the white colonists that we would augment these properties with free black or mulatto colonists by making of them, if not exactly slaves, Helots? Would we make them work for a government, which was oppressing them? Would we make them spill their blood for a fatherland that was not their own? Would we make them pay taxes to which they have not consented? Would we have them bear all the burdens of liberty (to the profit of the whites) without letting them enjoy its advantages? Did they not fight for France against England? The blood they have mixed with that of the whites, is it not blood? . . .

MAURY:[21] The partisans of the men of color want to . . . proclaim in the new world the reign of liberty. . . . It is the emancipation of the slaves that inspires their vehement interest in the mulattoes.

In their turn, the opposing orators have imitated their tortuous march. At first, they were afraid to address the question of slavery directly. They wanted to have it prejudged implicitly in their favor not by a formal decree, but by preambles. . . . By expelling the men of color from the exercise of political rights, they thought that it would be an additional obstacle to prevent you from reaching the slaves and breaking their chains.

By such detours and provisional laws, by concealing their true means and ends, . . . both sides together have placed us in a perilous position. . . .

Let us first pose the fundamental principle that in all well-organized governments, both ancient and modern, the laws distinguish between slaves, freed-men, free men, and citizens. All these political gradations are strongly marked in legislation, and everywhere there are intermediate classes between slavery and citizenship. I thus maintain that citizenship is not a necessary consequence of liberty and that the men of color of our colonies should only be able to obtain it under conditions maturely and profoundly discussed by the National Assembly.

The men of color in our colonies are free and property-owning thanks to the generosity of our fellow-citizens—colonists to whom they owe, for

[20]A military officer before the Revolution, Bouchotte served as minister of war in 1793–1794.
[21]Maury was a right-wing cleric who was one of the most effective legislative critics of the Revolution.

two or three generations, their liberty and properties. Today they ask us for a law admitting them to the exercise of political rights. . . .

Let me first observe that, to me, free Negroes are more worthy than mulattoes or free men of color. A free Negro is a man who has personally merited . . . his emancipation. On the contrary, the men of color are all, or almost all, the shameful result of the libertinage of their masters. I demand that, in ruling on their pretentions, we consider only the very small group of mulattoes who can legally prove their emancipation and who were born from a legitimate marriage between free parents. . . .

After having posed this fundamental, preliminary principle, I confidently maintain that it is indecent to call into question what you decreed on March 18th and October 12th. You declared that your Constitution is inapplicable in your colonies; that you were granting them legislative initiative and that you would never pass a law on the status of persons in the colonies without the formal request of the colonial assemblies. . . . Messieurs, I appeal to the Assembly's honor. When one makes a promise, when that promise is in writing, when it is expressed in legal form, when it has become a law, one neither debates, interprets, nor eludes it; one executes it.

Your committee is today demanding the literal execution of your promises. You must thus adopt its project without hesitation, but with several amendments so that you do not render vain and illusory your firm determination to summon successively, but with prudence, all Frenchmen to their constitutional rights. . . .

[But] you must place the national interest between yourselves and the people of color. . . . Abstract principles cannot be applied here, especially not with absolute rigor. We are not legal theorists, we are not defending a dissertation, we are not debating in a schoolroom, we are not arguing a point of law in court. We are discussing an important national interest! Our first concern should thus be to pose the sacred principle, the principle which preserves all societies, that, even in the freest governments, the right of liberty is absolutely separate from the right of citizenship. The right of liberty is an emanation of natural law. In contrast, the right of citizenship is a simple delegation from the social body. . . .

What policy has been followed by a new nation which, in rousing itself from its former political torpor, seems to have awakened liberty in the entire human race? In America, and especially in Carolina and Virginia, there are a very large number of property-owning cultivators who are also free men of color. The rights of humanity have just been examined with the most scrupulous rigor in these states. . . .

Well, in those happy countries, where all the prejudices have fallen, have the men of color been admitted to the rank of active citizen by these same Americans who have just conquered their Independence so gloriously? No, Messieurs, no men of color were admitted to this great national prerogative. . . .

Let the men of color become active citizens in our colonies, but only after a certain time, a certain number of generations. Let them acquire this national privilege, but only upon wisely determined conditions, with limitations and reservations based on their legitimacy, on the status of their parents, on their level of taxation, on their proportion in the overall population, so that their influence can never dominate the colonial assemblies. . . .

But if this political emancipation is the sudden benefit of a new and unlimited law; if men who have only just broken the chains of slavery are indistinctly granted, in just one day, the full political power of citizenship over their fellow citizens, over their former masters, over 50,000 Frenchmen that they could exterminate at any moment by placing themselves at the head of an army of 600,000 negroes who are their true fellow-citizens— then this is not a measure French legislators can ever adopt.

LOUIS MONNERON:[22] My constituents are French people carried 4,000 leagues from their homeland by hope for a better life. They are the same distance from the equator as Saint-Domingue. They have 50,000 slaves. Their neighbors, the inhabitants of the Ile Bourbon, who are not yet represented [in the Assembly], have more than 70,000. The Ile de France is peopled by freed-persons, mulattoes, and, above all, a large number of people of color. . . .

My constituents seem to have foreseen our present debate when they directed me to uphold the interest of the free-born men of color. . . . I have been expressly charged with placing before your eyes the proof of their moderation, of putting forth all the reasons for you to look kindly on them, and of begging you to rule on their status in the most favorable manner possible.

After such a solemn declaration, I cannot remain silent on the committee's project. It formally contradicts your most beneficent principles and, consequently, violates the Constitution. The project invites you to strike a numerous class of citizens with civil death. It creates a tribunal . . . of 29 self-interest judges who will necessarily rule that 100,000 free citizens will have no other place in the community than to pay taxes. . . .

ROBESPIERRE: I have a simple observation on the amendment. The crux of this debate is to design a decree which does not attack the Assembly's principles and honor in too revolting a manner. Once you speak the word *slaves*, you will have proclaimed both your own dishonor and the overthrow of your Constitution. . . .

It is important to keep the colonies. . . . But the supreme interest of the nation and colonies themselves is that you preserve your liberty. . . . Let the colonies perish if we must pay that price to keep them. (Murmurs and applause). If we have to choose between losing the colonies and sacrificing happiness, glory, and liberty, I repeat: let them perish. . . .

---

[22]Louis Monneron was an arms dealer, elected to represent the East Indies in the Estates-General.

[On May 15, 1791, the Alsatian deputy Rewbell (paradoxically, an outspoken opponent of Jewish emancipation) proposed a new measure that confirmed the citizenship of free-born (as opposed to manumitted) people of color. It was approved by the Assembly after only a few more speeches.]

REGNAUD (DE SAINT-JEAN-D'ANGÉLY):[23] As we are sadly forced . . . to compromise a principle that, for my part, I would prefer to uphold in its entirety, we must compromise absolutely. . . . It is in that spirit that I second Rewbell's decree. . . .

ROBESPIERRE: It is impossible to sacrifice . . . the most sacred rights of humanity, the most precious principles of our Constitution. I am far from supporting the amendment of Monsieur Rewbell. On the contrary, I cannot adopt it. I believe that I am here to defend the rights of the free men of color of America to their fullest extent. I feel that I am not allowed to . . . sacrifice them. . . .

All free men have the same rights, whoever their parents. We must adopt this principle in its entirety. I believe that each member of this Assembly recognizes that he has already gone too far by constitutionally consecrating colonial slavery. . . .

Decree of May 15, 1791

The National Assembly decrees that the Legislature will never deliberate on the political status of people of color not born of free parents, except upon the free and spontaneous wish of the colonies; that the actually existing colonial assemblies will continue, but that people of color born of free parents will be admitted into future parish and colonial assemblies if they meet the required conditions. . . .

V. The Slave Revolt (August 1791)

Saint-Domingue had experienced political violence since the outbreak of the Revolution, as opposing white factions fought each other and free people of color militated for citizenship. But the enslaved population, ten times larger than the entire free population, had not budged. That changed dramatically on August 22, 1791, when a vast, coordinated slave uprising took place in the Northern Province. Within days, dozens of the colony's richest plantations were smoking ruins, many whites were dead, and the survivors had fled to Le Cap. Although the rebels' attempts to capture the city failed, they remained in control of the northern plain. Over the next weeks and months, the rebellion spread. It would never be put down. There are no eyewitness accounts of the revolt written by the rebels, but a number of white survivors described horrific acts of violence. Rather than dwell on these accounts—often lurid and written long after events to discredit the Republic of Haiti and disparage Blacks generally—this section focuses on how the slave revolt was appropriated for political purposes both in Revolutionary France and foreign plantation colonies in the Caribbean.

---

[23]Regnaud (de Saint-Jean-d'Angély) was a lawyer by profession who would become one of Napoleon's most trusted advisors.

13. THE JAMAICANS REACT (NOVEMBER 1, 1791)[24]

One of Saint-Domingue's closest island neighbors, Jamaica, was Great Britain's largest and richest sugar colony. News of the slave revolt reached it long before it reached Europe. Fearful that their own slaves would follow the example of Saint-Domingue, they called for military reinforcements.

We, your Majesty's dutiful and loyal subjects, the Assembly of Jamaica, called upon by the impending danger of our situation, look up to your most excellent Majesty as the august and impartial father for all your people, to whom we are to represent the apprehensions and terrors which now surround us, and on whose paternal care for our safety and preservation we solely depend for that efficient protection which will ensure our security.

The dreadful effects of those wild and enthusiastic doctrines, prevalent among certain mistaken and ill-informed persons in Europe, respecting the slave trade and the nature of our property in the West Indies (against which your Majesty's subjects in these islands have had of late to contend) are at length severely felt by the French inhabitants of St. Domingo; and, whatever temporary advantage our staples may derive from their calamities, the tenure both of our properties and lives is precarious, while our slaves have such a precedent of the triumph of savage anarchy over all order and government. This island, every class and colour of whose inhabitants (so far as their state of civilization will admit) possess the blessings of a mild and equitable government under which the several rights of person and property are secured by laws framed for the general welfare and protection, would then become one general scene of horror and confusion; murder, robbery, rape, conflagration, would then prove inadequate terms to depict our calamities, as, in that event, the blackest crimes, as if receiving a deeper dye from the complexion of the cruel and merciless enemy, would be perpetrated in the most savage and shocking manner.

Suffer us, gracious Sire, to lay this, the faint representation of our alarms, at the foot of the Throne, and humbly to beseech that your most gracious Majesty would be pleased to encrease the military force on this station. . . .

14. THE FRENCH REACTION: THE POLITICAL RIGHT[25]

In late 1791, French political opinion was sharply divided between the monarchist right and republican left. When news of the revolt reached the National Assembly in late November, it became a political hot potato, with each side using it to discredit the other. The following excerpt of a speech by the deputy Thomas Millet, a former slave trader, expresses the position of the colonial lobby and the political right.

---

[24]British National Archives, Colonial Office, series 140, Box 77.
[25]Mavidal and Laurent, *AP*, vol. 35, 464–467.

A society was formed in the bosom of France and from afar prepared the divisions and convulsions afflicting us. At first obscure and modest, it spoke only of improving the lot of the slaves. . . .

But soon this society called for suppression of the slave trade; which is to say, that the profits of French commerce be abandoned to foreigners. For its sentimental philosophy will never persuade all the powers of Europe that it is their duty to abandon the cultivation of the colonies and leave the inhabitants of Africa at the mercy of their tyrants' barbarity, rather than employing them, under the most humane masters, to exploit a land which would remain uncultivated without them and whose rich productions are a fertile source of industry and prosperity for the nation that possesses them.

Then, meddling in the Revolution of France, this society linked its exaggerated, thoughtless system to the nation's plan for freeing itself. Profiting from the universal enthusiasm of the French for liberty, it made them interested in its project for destroying the slavery of the Negroes by drawing a parallel with their own former servitude. In its blind enthusiasm, or perversity, this society forgot that these crude men are incapable of knowing liberty and enjoying it wisely, and that the imprudent law which would destroy their prejudices would be a death warrant for both them and us.

From that moment, this society (or at least some of its members) knew no limits. All means seemed good to them, if they could help achieve their goal. Blending deception and audacity, they used direct attacks, carefully laid schemes, the lowest and most disgusting calumnies to achieve their design. At one point, this society flattered us by inviting us to throw off the yoke of the French merchants and assuring us of its support if we would join them in seeking to obtain free trade. At another, it turned the merchants against us, by telling them that we were considering declaring a dishonorable bankruptcy, a chimerical independence, and that, in our pride, we wanted to raise ourselves up as a power alongside France. Thus, after having tried to set the merchants and colonists against each other, . . . it seized hold of the Declaration of the rights of man, a work immortal and salutary for enlightened men, but inapplicable and even dangerous in our regime. It spread it profusely throughout the colonies. The newspapers that it bankrolls or hoodwinks trumpet this declaration amongst our plantations. The writings of the friends of the blacks openly announce that the liberty of the Negroes is proclaimed by the Declaration of rights.

It seemed as if the decree of March 8th would halt these brazen plots; but the friends of the blacks recognize no law except . . . their vow to bring fire and murder to our homes. If a law seems to lead to this, they adopt it. . . . But if the law goes against them, they ignore, disavow, and shamelessly insult it, and try to discredit the authority from which it emanates.

The colonists, merchants, and men who are sufficiently enlightened not to be manipulated by their lies are all equally the object of their insults. It is not enough for them to have made themselves the arbiters of our properties and peace; they also claim the right to defame us. We are not allowed to defend ourselves . . .

without being showered with their cowardly insults. Thus, by corrupting public opinion and stripping us of all means of defense, they undermine the ground on which our possessions rest. . . . Our ruin is becoming inevitable.

Once they understood that the National Assembly was not going to pronounce the emancipation of the slaves, they sought to spread disorder among us by convincing it to take up the question of men of color. We had asked to be allowed to make our own laws on this point, which required many precautions and great prudence. We had promised that these laws would be humane and just.

But such a benefit granted by the white colonists, which would have forever tightened the bonds of affection and goodwill which existed between these two classes of men, was presented by the friends of the blacks as a pretention of vanity and a means of eluding the just demands [of the men of color.]

They sought to achieve their goal through other measures. They assembled some men of color at Paris, riled them up, and urged them to link their cause to the Negroes'. Then, in the state of delirium into which they had been plunged, they returned to Saint-Domingue and communicated to the slaves the false hopes they had been given. They brought with them libels and books which encouraged men of color and slaves to launch a general insurrection and massacre the whites.

Ogé was the first victim of this fatal error. . . .

It was in this turmoil, in this general intoxication, while the whites were roiled by mistrust and terror, while the Negroes were indulging themselves in thousands of harmful dreams, that you discussed the decree of May 15th. A mass of writings which preceded and followed it were distributed, even on the plantations. In them . . . were these terrible words, which signaled carnage and fire: "Let the colonies perish!" . . .

Attacked by so much seduction, worked over by so many maneuvers, agitated by these libels written in characters of blood (which they read at night in their huts in the midst of assemblies of their leaders, men who breathed only disorder and pillage), could the negroes long resist the vertigo overcoming them? The memory of their masters' benefits was lost; they no longer felt anything except the desire for a new condition, and they made themselves the pawns of some profoundly twisted men who found in the writings of the friends of the blacks . . . arms for their uprising. . . .

The baleful influence of the authors of all these disasters has been proven by the totality of their actions and condemnable writings? Can there be any doubt at this moment that they are responsible for our ruin? . . .

The influence of the friends of the blacks is destroying the colonies; whatever the sophisms with which they surround themselves, they will never annihilate the evidence of our misfortunes. No man of good faith can doubt that their works, declamations, writings, and infamous emissaries are the active and constant cause which has, for two years, prepared our ruin, which is now taking place.

15. THE FRENCH REACTION: THE POLITICAL LEFT[26]

None other than Brissot—founder of the Society of the Friends of the Blacks, outspoken abolitionist, and now leader of the republican left—rose to refute Millet's claims. The following excerpt from his long speech encapsulates the left's view of the slave revolt and shows how it sought to use it to accelerate the pace of political change in France itself.

It is high time that we pull back the veil on the conspiracy woven in Saint-Domingue to take that colony from France. It is not just a revolt of blacks that we have to punish, it is also a revolt of whites. The revolt of the blacks is only a means, an instrument, in the hands of those whites who want, by freeing themselves from dependence on France, to free themselves from laws that humiliate their vanity and debts that interfere with their taste for dissipation. . . .

There are four classes within the population of Saint-Domingue: white planters with large properties; *petits blancs* without properties who live from their industry; people of color with honorable properties or professions; and, finally, slaves.

The white planters are divided into two classes. . . . There are some with vast properties who owe little, because they keep their expenses in order. But a greater number are heavily indebted, because of the disorganization of their business affairs.

The first ones love France, are attached to it and respect its laws, because they understand that they need its protection to preserve their properties and public order. They love and support the men of color because they see them as the true defenders of the colony, as the men most suited to stopping the blacks' revolts. . . .

Crushed by debt, the dissipated planters love neither French laws, nor the men of color. This is why: they fully realize that a free State cannot subsist without good laws and respect for one's obligations. Thus, sooner or later they will be forced by those laws to pay their debts. . . .

At the same time, these prodigal, indebted planters do not like the citizens of color any more than the blacks, because they clearly foresee that these men of color, who are almost all free of debt and regular in their business affairs, will always be inclined to uphold the laws and that their courage, numbers, and zeal . . . can guarantee the execution of the laws, even without the aid of European troops. Another thing turns the dissipated planters against the men of color: shameful prejudice. . . . The [planters] treat love of equality as a crime and, even while railing against ministerial despotism, they want to consecrate . . . the despotism of white skin. . . .

Disorder, which needs injustice to survive, must ferociously defend the prejudices that are useful to it; this explains why we find in the heart of the same planter hatred against the man of color demanding his rights, against the merchant claiming repayment of his debts, and against the free government that wants to see justice done to all.

---

[26]Mavidal and Laurent, AP, vol. 35, 475–490.

We should thus regard the enemies of the men of color as the most violent enemies of our Constitution. They detest it because they see in it the annihilation of their pride and prejudices; they miss—and would bring back—the old order of things. . . .

The cause of the men of color is thus the cause of patriots, of the former Third Estate, of the people who have been oppressed for so long. Here I should make clear that when I describe these planters, who for the past three years have been scheming in the most criminal way to cut their ties to the mother country, to crush the men of color, I speak only of those who, indigent despite their immense properties, rich despite their indigence, prideful despite their profound ineptitude, audacious despite their cowardice, . . . stir up trouble and seek to transform the various colonial assemblies into an independent aristocracy. . . .

This type of man has the greatest influence over another class, no less dangerous, called "the *petits blancs*." It is composed of adventurers, men with neither principles nor morals. This class is the true plague of the colonies, because it is drawn exclusively from the dregs of Europe. This class is jealous of the men of color, whether they are craftsmen (because they are more skilled, charge less, and are thus more sought-after) or property-owners (because their wealth breeds envy and hurts their pride). This class wants turmoil, because they like to pillage; independence, because they hope to despoil the men of color once they have become masters of the colony. . . .

Who are these men of color, whose cries of suffering have echoed for so long in France? They are not (and it is important to repeat it constantly in order to combat the perfidious insinuations of the colonists) black slaves. They are men whose immediate or distant ancestry is composed of a mix of European and African blood. Do you not shudder, Messieurs, to think of the atrocity of a white who wants to abase a mulatto! In doing so, he insults his own blood. . . .

Note as well that the men of color who demand equality of political rights with their white brothers are almost all free, tax-paying property-owners; and what is more, they are the true foundation of the colony. They are its Third-Estate, laborious yet despised by such profoundly vicious, useless, and stupid beings. . . .

The last class is that of the slaves, a large class numbering more than 400,000, while the whites, mulattoes, and free Negroes together make up barely a sixth of the population.

I will not pause here to describe the fate of these unfortunates, wrenched away from their liberty and fatherland to water a foreign soil with their sweat and blood . . . under the whip of their barbarous masters. Despite the double torture of slavery and the sight of others' liberty, the slave of Saint-Domingue has, until the recent troubles, been tranquil, even in the midst of the violent commotions that have rocked our islands. Everywhere he heard the magical word "liberty," and his heart was moved, for the heart of a black beats for liberty too. Nonetheless, he kept quiet and continued to bear his chains for two-and-a-half years without dreaming of breaking them; and if he has thrown them off, it is because of the instigation of atrocious men. . . .

These are the different kinds of men who inhabit Saint-Domingue. From the sketch I have traced, you will easily be able to guess the sentiments which animated each class at the news of the French Revolution. The honest, good property-owning colonists were happy to get rid of ministerial despotism and replace it with a popular, colonial government; they loved the Revolution. The men of color found in it hope of annihilating the prejudice that dishonored them and recovering their rights; they loved the Revolution. The dissipated planters who, until then, had lurked in the antechambers of the intendants, governors, and ministers, savored the moment of their humiliation; to pay them back for their disdain and insolence, they preached liberty. . . . They threw the ministers down from their thrones because, like the nobles of France, they wanted to take their place.

The *petits blancs* who, until then, had been restrained by the administration . . . eagerly seized the occasion to rip apart and shatter these idols, before which they had been forced to prostrate themselves. Thus, the first cry, which was heard throughout the islands, was for liberty. For the dissipated planters and *petits blancs* the second cry was for personal despotism, but for the respectable colonists and men of color it was order, peace, and equality. . . . [This is] the source of the combats that have torn apart our islands. . . .

The colonists' system has undergone three variations on which we must comment. Each bears the mark of independence, toward which they have constantly aspired, despite their changes in tactics. First, they sought to throw off the yoke of the minister and run the risk of liberty with the Estates-General, without clearly foreseeing that [liberty] would also apply to them. Then, once they saw the Assembly stay faithful to the principles of equality and base the Constitution on them, they sensed that these principles would not suit their pretentions and aims. From then on, they secretly separated themselves from the Constitution; they imagined detaching the colonies from the National Assembly of France and making them a separate government ruled by a colonial assembly. . . .

Thirdly, once they saw the National Assembly resist this system, reject their puerile vanity in the cause of the men of color, and reject the Congress of Saint-Martin (which was nothing but a means of organizing the independence of the colonies), they formed a plan to separate themselves from the metropole. The revolt of the blacks was to have favored this last project; that is why it broke out.

Do not let yourselves be seduced by the word "independence." The colonists have often cited the example of the United States to justify themselves. But what a difference! The colonists do not want to establish liberty, but rather eternal slavery. They want to be independent only in order to be tyrants. The United States laid the foundations of the declaration of rights; the colonists abhor it. Therefore, when I make reference to their system of independence, I speak only of independent tyranny.

Let us follow the colonists' strategy in the National Assembly. It didn't take them long to realize that the spirt of liberty was going to win over the colonies. . . . "They are drunk with liberty," they wrote, trembling, to their constituents in the famous letter of August 12, 1789—the letter which started the fire now consuming the colonies. . . .

It was in a spirit of independence that they saw the National Assembly setting itself up as absolute legislator, as they wrote, to create a completely new Constitution based on "absolute equality and identical rights." . . .

A threat of secession was always in all their public writings and on their factious lips. They threatened to hand themselves over to England if their right to constitute themselves was opposed. Only the colonies, they said, should determine their interior regime, their particular laws, and fate of their inhabitants. They should only have relations with the King. . . . Wouldn't it be easy for the colonial assemblies, invested with a legislative power broader than and superior to that of the executive, to elude French commercial laws? France's sovereignty would be nothing more than a shadow. . . .

But [in May 1791] the colonists received a setback. Still pursuing their favorite fantasy of independence, they had imagined proposing to the National Assembly the formation of a congress of deputies from the different islands on Saint-Martin. This congress seemed to have no other purpose than expressing their wish on the question of men of color. But the colonists were aware that when men have assembled at a single point—above all, during a moment of crisis—they could easily take control. They thus hoped that this congress, like the famous American congress, would treat all colonial questions and become the center of the colonies' political relations. . . .

The superiority of France over its colonies and the supervision of the colonial committee would evaporate before this congress. The patriots sensed the trap . . . and avoided it. In its disappearance, the hope for this ridiculous congress carried with it the colonists' illusions of independence. . . .

The decree of May 15th was detested as strongly by the colonists as it was praised by the French people. No sooner had it been passed than, giving free rein to their fury, the colonists publicly swore to die rather than carry it out; to arm their slaves to kill the free men of color rather than see them enjoy their rights. They spoke only of daggers, gallows, and revolt. Cursing France, they turned to England and invoked its aid. Impatient with its slow, indirect policy, they wanted its warships to depart immediately and take over our islands. In their furious resentment, some of the colonists took ship for London. Others embarked for the islands, after having left in our ports proof of their insane determination to break with the metropole. No less irritated, but more circumspect, their deputies in the National Assembly limited themselves to declaring that they would boycott its sessions. That guilty declaration, which announced secession, was received with more disdain than anger. For we had become accustomed to seeing the colonists as children incapable of controlling their anger, as objects of pity rather than hatred. . . .

Conspirators do not write down their plans, but they can be found in both the opinions and deeds of their authors. I have exposed the opinions and deeds of those whom I accuse; they demonstrate beyond any doubt that they wanted to establish a system of independence. The facts that I am going to present will shed new light on it. . . .

The long-desired moment finally arrived. . . . On August 22nd, a conspiracy against the city of Le Cap was denounced. The date here is critical. They had just learned of the flight of the king. Was it mere chance that the flight . . . coincided with the design of the factious? It is more likely that the news of the flight accelerated their revolt. . . .

On the 23rd, it became known that Negroes on several plantations had risen up. Those who know the islands know that the standard response would be to strike at the heart of the blaze, to send troops to those plantations to put out the revolt. But if this precaution had been taken, the revolt would have been over too soon, and they would not have been able to send envoys to Jamaica and the United States on the 25th to ask for help.

I will linger upon this suspicion. . . . Why did General [Blancheland] amuse himself by sending a detachment off to camps, where they spent two days in total uselessness? Why didn't he split this large detachment, which would have prevented the revolting plantations from joining forces? Why did he waste his time forming imaginary regiments and making regulations for them instead of setting off to fight with the ones he had? . . .

Instead of going straight for the rebels, why did this brave general barricade and entrench himself in a city that was already fortified and had nothing to fear from undisciplined enemies without weapons, munitions, or knowledge of siege tactics? Didn't this give time and resources to the rebels, allowing them to expand their troop and ravage all the plantations on the plain? . . .

There is something obscure about this affair. Should we blame it on cowardice, ignorance of the local area, or treason? We don't know. But it is clear that whoever advised waiting for the enemy in Le Cap rather than seeking him out in the plain or on the plantations is the principal author of the horrible catastrophe that devastated Saint-Domingue. . . .

I ask again: rather than marching against the enemy, why was this general amusing himself with the colonial assembly and writing dispatches to the Spanish, English, and Americans? It is said that he needed help. But on the 24th, the day of his dispatch, he hadn't yet encountered the enemy. He still had no knowledge of the extent of the danger. All he knew was that a few plantations had been burned. What! To repulse several hundred brigands was it not extravagant to trust in distant and uncertain dispatches rather than the arms he had at hand? Was it not extravagant to fight a fire by fetching pumps 700 or 800 leagues away in Philadelphia? . . .

This dispatch to Philadelphia . . . was intended to cover the one sent to Jamaica. The [colonists] wanted to prove their impartiality by addressing three powers when they really wanted help from just one. Everything betrays their guilt. The colonial assembly wasn't satisfied with the governor's dispatch to Jamaica. It sent another one itself. If we believe information from Saint-Domingue, this one was actually preceded by another sent on August 16th. . . . What could the object of this special dispatch have been? Either it contained the same appeals as the governor's, in which case it was useless, or it had a special purpose, in which case it is suspicious. . . .

Why were the general and assembly so active in seeking aid from England? Why didn't they employ the means they had at hand? Why did the assembly not arm the men of color, who shared a common interest in stopping the rebellion? . . .

That is not all. Jamaica learned of the revolt of the blacks on the 27th, but it had still not been heard of at Léogane [in southwest Saint-Domingue] on the 28th? . . . This long silence of the general and colonial assembly vis-à-vis the West and South raises the most violent suspicion. It was known that these regions contained numerous troops and men of color who would have promptly dissipated the rebellion. But not only was aid not demanded from them, they were not even informed of the danger even as the alarm was being sent to Jamaica and Philadelphia! . . . The colonial assembly knew that patriotism predominated in these regions, which hated the idea of delivering the island to England. . . .

The colonial assembly did not just contemplate the possibility of independence; it executed it not only by asking for English help, but also by assuming the powers of an independent legislature. Taxing, administering, judging, imprisoning, it even had the audacity to impose duties on French merchandise. . . .

Slavery is and will always be a perpetual source of trouble. . . .

But slavery did not play a role in the troubles of Saint-Domingue except in the August revolt, and this singular fact corresponds to the violent satire which has targeted the blacks. [The colonial deputies] have cited atrocities to make you shudder and, by playing on your emotions, distract your attention from the misdeeds of the colonial assembly. . . .

You are horrified. . . . But who is the real assassin? Is it the black? No, it is the white who first . . . ripped a black from his mother's breast. . . . Let them list all the crimes committed by the black race. They evaporate before the ferocity of the monstrous whites, before the ferocity of the conquerors of Peru and even Saint-Domingue. A million Indians perished under their blades. With each step you crunch their bones which cry out for vengeance. And you condemn their avengers! . . .

Philosophy cringes before this picture. It is ashamed to belong to the human race and tries to moderate its ferocity. But it is calumnied and torn apart, even as it strives to help its detractors. What was the goal of Montesquieu, Rousseau, Raynal, Voltaire? Was it to spill men's blood? Are we tigers? No, but we tell you: brothers, your system is detestable and will be fatal to you. Servitude cannot exist eternally alongside liberty. Be good and you will avoid bloodshed. Be just and you will be loved. But is it just to condemn to the hell of eternal slavery a free-born man like you? Eternal slavery breeds crime because it is the greatest of all crimes. Prepare to give your slaves liberty—not suddenly but by preparing them for it and improving their condition. . . .

Is it still possible to hide from ourselves the causes and authors of the troubles of Saint Domingue? The most general cause is in the French Revolution. . . . It is in the overthrow of the old powers, in the struggle between those who wanted to raise themselves up upon their debris, in the relaxation of all the mechanisms that checked individual passions, in the destruction of the tribunals, in the absence of justice, in the distance of the governed from the country that governs them.

The next cause is in the system of independence affected by the white colonists at the outset of the Revolution, a system elaborated in their writings and pretentions, a system put into practice in their committees, provincial assemblies, and colonial assemblies.

The cause of the troubles lies in the audacity with which these factious took control of all powers—not to extend the reign of liberty and the Constitution, but to substitute aristocratic for ministerial tyranny. . . .

The cause of the troubles lies in the coordination between the factious colonists in both hemispheres; in the troubles that one group stirred up to support the libels of the others. . . .

The cause of the troubles lies in the weakness which encouraged the factious, in the corruption that ensured them impunity, in the ignorance which favored their odious schemes, in the moderation that protected them; and finally in the stubborn air of mystery with which they constantly cloaked colonial affairs.

The cause of the troubles lies in the equivocation of all our decrees and variations in those decrees; in the weakness of not wanting to name the people of color in article 4 of the decree of March 28th, even as we were declaring openly that this was everyone's intention and even as we were witnessing the factious independentists exploiting our silence to exclude the people of color.

The cause of the troubles lies in the partiality with which we treated the general assemblies of Saint-Marc and Le Cap in the decree of October 12th; in the punishment inflicted upon one and the rewards bestowed upon the other even though both were guilty of the same crime of independence. . . .

The cause of the troubles lies in the preamble of the decree of October 16th . . . which armed the whites against the people of color and gave the signal for civil war in the colonies.

The cause of the troubles lies in the persecution that the despotic whites felt authorized to exercise against the men of color, in virtue of these decrees or, rather, by perverting their meaning, . . . culminating in the cruel execution of Ogé.

The cause of the troubles lies in the non-execution of the decree of May 15th. . . .

Finally, the cause of the troubles lies in the absurdity and imprudence of having disarmed and enchained the men [of color] who would have been able to contain the 400,000 to 500,000 slaves in Saint-Domingue.

Who are the people guilty of these crimes? They are those who preached, practiced, and decreed these systems of independence.

They are those who flooded the country with libels against the National Assembly. . . .

They are those who said they would do everything in their power to oppose the decrees of the National Assembly.

They are those who, although they could have easily quelled the revolt, let it spread and who, although they had forces at hand, instead sought the help of foreigners. . . .

They are those who did not take the necessary measures . . . to have the laws executed.

They are those who, persecuting their brothers, their best guardians, violated the declaration of rights and who, disarming the people of color, stripped the island of its firmest support.

They are those who flew the colors of a foreign power, summoned its vessels, and corresponded with its agents and ministry.

They are those who, to hide their crimes, have just accused good people of having caused the troubles of which they themselves are guilty.

They are those who insult philosophy, liberty, the Declaration of rights in the very temple of philosophy, liberty, and rights. . . .

France owes the whites of the islands protection, but it also owes it to their victims. France owes the whites justice, but it also owes it to those who guarantee the tranquility of the islands, to the people of color. France also owes it to the whites' creditors and to commerce. France owes it to itself and surely such treason will not go unpunished.

CHAPTER 8

Emancipation and Independence

From August 1791, when the uprising of the Northern Province began, to February 1794, when the French government ratified the emancipation decrees that had been issued locally by its representatives in Saint-Domingue, the former slaves won their freedom by hard, determined fighting. The cost was heavy as they battled French soldiers and (after the local emancipation measures of 1793) the invading armies of Spain and Great Britain. By the end of 1796, they had expelled all foreign troops. But that was not the end of the fighting. In 1800, a civil war broke out between the northern and southern halves of the island. No sooner had that conflict ended than the new ruler of France, Napoleon Bonaparte, sent a huge expeditionary force of battle-hardened veterans to impose his authority. The invasion was defeated, but at a terrible cost. Hundreds of thousands perished in the years of warfare. The fruit of these sacrifices was independence, formally declared on January 1, 1804, when Saint-Domingue became the Republic of Haiti. But the years of warfare—and hostile treatment by the United States and Europe—left a bitter legacy. By their own efforts, the Haitians had conquered freedom from slavery and independence from France, but stability and prosperity remained frustratingly elusive.

I. Emancipation

The massive slave revolt that had erupted in August 1791 proved impossible to quash. The French government responded in April 1792 by a combination of conciliation (extending full citizenship to all free people of color) and repression (sending more troops). But it was too little too late. Moreover, when Spain and Great Britain went to war against Revolutionary France in early 1793, they invaded the colony. Sent from Jamaica to the south, British troops received the support of local planters, thankful for the arrival of a force capable of maintaining slavery. From Santo-Domingo, the Spanish invaded the north and enlisted the rebel slaves under their banner with the promise of military aid and freedom.

The French commissioners who had been sent to deal with the emergency, the deputies Leger-Félicité Sonthonax and Étienne Polverel, found themselves almost powerless to confront these multiple challenges. Out of desperation, but also in keeping with their own ideals, the commissioners issued emancipation decrees in 1793 to win over the rebels to France. The strategy worked. Soon proficient armies of emancipated slaves were fighting under the French flag. A leader soon emerged from their ranks: Toussaint Louverture.

1. SONTHONAX'S EMANCIPATION PROCLAMATION (AUGUST 29, 1793)[1]

The French commissioner in charge of the Northern Province, Sonthonax, issued his emancipation proclamation in late August 1793. At the time, he was facing not only continuing slave revolt and Spanish invasion but also a new threat: opposition from white colonists in Le Cap.

Men are born and remain free and equal in rights; this, citizens, is the gospel of France; it is high time to proclaim it in all the departments of the Republic.

Sent by the Nation to Saint-Domingue, as Civil Commissioners, our mission was to implement it in all its force, and, without sowing divisions or disturbances, to prepare gradually for the general emancipation of the slaves.

Upon our arrival, we found a horrible schism among the whites who, divided by interests and opinions, could agree on only one point—that of forever perpetuating the servitude of the negroes. . . . To foil the ill-intentioned and to reassure spirits, all on edge in fear of a sudden uprising, we declared that *slavery was necessary for agriculture.*

We speak the truth, Citizens. At that time slavery was as essential for the continuation of work as for the preservation of the colonists. Saint-Domingue was still in the power of a horde of ferocious tyrants who were publicly preaching that skin color should be the sign of power or reprobation; the judges of the unfortunate Ogé, the lackeys and members of those infamous military commissions which filled the towns with gallows and wheels to sacrifice Africans and Men of color to their atrocious pretensions—all these bloodthirsty men still populated the colony. If, by the greatest imprudence, we had then broken the ties that bound the slaves to their masters, there is no doubt that their first movement would have been to throw themselves on their tormentors and, in their most just anger, they would have easily confused the innocent with the guilty; moreover, our powers did not extend so far as determining the fate of the Africans, and we would have been perjurers and criminals if we had violated the law.

---

[1]H. Pauleus Sannon, *Histoire de Toussaint Louverture* (Port-au-Prince, Haiti: L'Imprimérie Aug. A. Heraux, 1938), vol. 1, 146–151.

Today, circumstances have changed greatly; the slave-traders and man-eaters are no more. Some have perished, victims of their impotent rage, and others have sought safety in flight and emigration. The remaining whites are friends of French law and principles. The majority of the population is formed of the men of April 4th, men to whom you owe your liberty, who were the first to give you the example of courage in defending the rights of nature and humanity; men who, proud of their independence, preferred the loss of their properties to the shame of putting on their former shackles. Never forget, citizens, that they gave you the arms that won for you your liberty; never forget that it is for the French Republic that you fought; that, of all the whites in the universe, the only ones who are your friends are the French of Europe.

The French Republic wants liberty and equality for all men without distinction of color; only kings are happy among slaves; it is they who, on the African coast, sold you to the whites; it is the tyrants of Europe who would like to perpetuate this infamous traffic. The Republic adopts you as its children; kings aspire only to cover you with chains or to annihilate you.

It is the representatives of that same Republic who, to come to your aid, have untied the hands of the Civil Commissioners by giving them the power to change provisionally *the regulation and discipline of the workshops*. That regulation and that discipline are going to be changed; a new order of things will arise and the old servitude will disappear.

But do not imagine that the liberty you are to enjoy is a state of laziness and leisure. In France, everyone is free, but everyone works; at Saint-Domingue, under the same laws, you will follow the same example. Return to your workshops or to your former owners; you will receive wages for your pains; you will no longer be subjected to the humiliating punishments which were formerly inflicted on you; you will no longer be the property of another; you will be masters of your own [property] and live happily.

Having become citizens by the will of the French Nation, you must also obey its decrees zealously; doubtless, you will defend the interests of the Republic against kings, less from a sense of your independence than out of gratitude for the benefits it has showered upon you. Liberty makes you pass from nothingness to existence. Show yourselves worthy of it. Forever abjure indolence and brigandage; have the courage to become a people and soon you will equal the European Nations.

Your slanderers and tyrants claim that the African, once free, will no longer work; prove them wrong; redouble your striving at the sight of the prize awaiting you; prove to France, through your activity, that by associating you with its interests, it has truly increased its resources and power.

And you, citizens misled by infamous royalists; you who, under flag and livery of the cowardly Spaniard, you are fighting blindly against your own interests, against the liberty of your women and children; open your eyes to the immense advantages the Republic is offering you. The kings promise you liberty; but do you actually see them giving it to their own subjects? Is the Spaniard freeing his slaves? Certainly not! On the contrary, he will surely load you with irons as soon as your services are no longer useful to him. Did he not hand Ogé over to his assassins? Unfortunates! If France ever again had a king, you would soon become the prey of the émigrés; one day they would flatter you, the next they would become your executioners. . . .

1. The Declaration of the Rights of Man and Citizen will be printed, published, and posted wherever necessary. . . .

2. All negroes and people of mixed blood who are currently enslaved are declared free in order to enjoy all the rights of French citizens; they will, however, be subjected to a regime whose details are contained in the following articles.

3. All former slaves must register in the municipality where they reside. . . .

9. Negroes currently attached to the plantations of their former masters must remain there; they will be employed in agriculture. . . .

11. Former field slaves will be hired for one year [contracts], during which time they can only move to another plantation with the permission of the local judge. . . .

12. The profit from each plantation will be divided into three equal parts. . . . One third belongs to the property of the land and, thus, to the property-owner. He will also take another third for the costs of land-improvement. The remaining third will be divided between the cultivators. . . .

27. Whipping is absolutely suppressed. . . .

33. Fifteen days from the promulgation of the present proclamation, all men without properties and who are neither in the army, attached to cultivation, or employed in domestic service, and who are discovered wandering about shall be arrested. . . .

36. Persons attached to agriculture and domestic service cannot, for any reason, leave the commune where they reside without the permission of the municipality; those who contravene this disposition will be punished. . . .

2. THE NATIONAL CONVENTION RATIFIES EMANCIPATION (FEBRUARY 4, 1794)[2]

In spring 1794, the National Convention was preoccupied with issues other than slavery. It was trying to defend France from foreign invasion of the Europeans, fight counter-revolutionary rebellion, manage a swollen and floundering wartime economy, direct the Terror, and make the Republic virtuous. But when the recently elected legislative deputation from Saint-Domingue arrived, the Convention quickly pivoted. The three new deputies, Jean-Baptiste Mills (a man of color), Jean-Baptiste Belley (a former slave who had been born in Africa), and Louis Dufay (a white) brought news of the commissioners' emancipation decrees. The Convention welcomed the "tricolor" by decreeing the abolition of slavery.

---

[2]*Réimpression de l'ancien Moniteur* (Paris: Bureau Central, 1841), vol. 19, 385–388.

CAMBOULAS:[3] "Since 1789 a great trial has been pending. The aristocracies of sword and church have been annihilated, but an aristocracy of skin color still ruled. It has just expired. Equality has been consecrated. A black, a yellow, and a white will sit among you to represent the free citizens of Saint-Domingue."

DANTON:[4] "Yes, equality has been consecrated, but we must end arbitrary authority. I move that the colonial committee make a report on the persecutions that blacks in France have suffered since 1787." Approved.

The three Saint-Domingue deputies enter, greeted by repeated applause.

LACROIX (DE L'EURE):[5] "This assembly has long wanted to have in it men of color who have been oppressed for so many years. Today it has two. I move that a fraternal kiss from the president honor their arrival." Applause.

The three deputies of Saint-Domingue approach the president and receive the fraternal kiss. Applause.

One of the new Saint-Domingue deputies delivers a brief report on events there. He analyzes the causes of the misfortunes . . . and detects the odious policy and intrigues of England and Spain who, wanting the Republic to lose this valuable colony, found a way to foment civil war in it. But the brave negroes, armed for the cause of France, foiled these perfidious projects and have asked, as a reward for their services, liberty, which was granted.

The speaker begged the Convention to confirm this promise and make the colonies enjoy the full benefits of liberty and equality. . . .

LEVASSEUR (DE LA SARTHE):[6] "I ask that the Convention not yield to momentary enthusiasm, but rather to the principles of justice and faith in the Declaration of the Rights of Man. Decree that slavery is henceforth abolished in all the territory of the Republic. Saint-Domingue is part of this territory, yet we still have slaves in Saint-Domingue. I thus demand that all men be free, without distinction of color."

LACROIX (DE L'EURE): "In working on the constitution of the French people, we did not look at the unfortunate men of color. Posterity will blame us for this. We must repair this wrong. Will it have been in vain that we declared that no feudal due be collected in the French Republic? You have just heard one of our colleagues say that there are still slaves in our colonies. It is time to rise to the level of the principles of liberty and equality. Although it is said that there are no slaves in France, is it not

---

[3]Camboulas was a merchant by profession; he held municipal office early in the Revolution before being elected to the Convention.

[4]Danton was a very prominent revolutionary and the first president of the Committee of Public Safety.

[5]Lacroix (de l'Eure) was a lawyer by profession and a member of the Committee of Public Safety.

[6]Levasseur (de la Sarthe) was a medical man by profession and a strong supporter of Robespierre.

true that men of color are slaves in our colonies? Let us proclaim the liberty of men of color. This act of justice will give a grand example to the men of color enslaved in the English and Spanish colonies. Like us, the men of color want to break their chains. We have broken ours. We have refused to bow under the yoke of any master. Let us grant them the same benefit. . . ."

The whole assembly rises in agreement. The president pronounces the abolition of slavery, amidst applause and thousands of repeated cries of Long Live the Republic! Long live the Convention! Long live the Mountain! The two deputies of color stand upon the podium and kiss each other. Lacroix escorts them to the president who gives them a fraternal kiss. They are embraced by all the deputies in turn. . . .

> DANTON: "Until now our decrees of liberty have been self-interested, for ourselves alone. But today we announce it to the universe. Future generations will glory in this decree. We are proclaiming universal liberty. . . . Let us launch liberty into the colonies. The English are now doomed. We are casting liberty into the New World where it will establish deep roots and bear much fruit. In vain will Pitt and his accomplices try to counter the effects of this good deed. They will sink into the void, and France will regain the rank and influence it deserves. . . ."
>
> DECREE: The National Convention declares that slavery of negroes is abolished in all the colonies. In consequence, it decrees that all men living in the colonies, without distinction of color, are French citizens and enjoy all the rights guaranteed by the Constitution.

II. Post-Emancipation

Sonthonax, Polverel, and the Convention supported emancipation not only because it seemed to be the only way to hold Saint-Domingue for France but also because they believed that slavery was an affront to the natural rights of humanity. However, they were also French nationalists. Accordingly, they felt that there was no reason to devote blood and treasure to Saint-Domingue if the colony was not contributing to the overall strength of France. Accordingly, the commissioners included in their emancipation decrees articles requiring the former slaves to continue working on their plantations. During the 1790s, they and their successors continued to refine their labor schemes, trying to find a way to reconcile emancipation with the sugar export economy. In subsequent decades, Saint-Domingue leaders of color—Toussaint, Dessalines, and others—would continue to grapple with this issue. Their solutions closely resembled those of the original French commissioners. Even after Haitian independence, freedom from slavery would not mean freedom from plantation labor.

3. POLVEREL'S LABOR REGULATIONS (1793–1794)[7]

The following document is Polverel's justification for the plantation labor regulation he instituted in the South and West.

The enemies of liberty predicted that one could never obtain labor from free Africans, that they would pillage, devastate, and burn everything, that they would slit the throats of all free men, both white and of color. It was even claimed in circular letters distributed in the various parishes that this was actually the plan and hope of the civil commissioners.

Well, the Africans have been declared free. For three months they have been left to themselves with neither coactive nor repressive laws. They have neither pillaged, nor devastated, nor burned, nor slit throats. Order was reestablished on the plantations, and it is being maintained. The insurgents, whom some called brigands, have all returned to work or have rallied to the flag of the Republic in order to fight for it.

If there have been some refusals to work, it is because the enemies of public peace gave the cultivators false ideas of liberty, because the plantation owners and managers continued to treat them like slaves, hid my proclamations, or applied them improperly. . . .

If there has been vagabondage, if there has been laziness in the work of some of those who have remained on the plantations, if cultivators have almost everywhere chosen to rest on Saturday as well as Sunday, it is because they were testing their liberty to make sure that it was not a dream and that it was really up to them to work or not, to come and go as they pleased.

We now know what to fear or hope for from the newly freed. In the first effervescence of new liberty, they committed faults, but not crimes. Their faults are the fruit of error, ignorance, and poorly understood self-interest. If we enlighten them, they will act like us, even better than us because they are less corrupt.

Saturday rest seems to be what they want most. Under slavery, they had Sunday free. They feel that they have hardly improved their condition if they don't get an extra day each week.

Africans, listen well. You can rest on Saturday, Monday, all the days of the week if you want. Nobody has the right to force you to work even a single day against your will. That is your liberty, in all its fullness.

But you must feed and clothe yourselves; you sometimes even want to feast with your friends. You want your women to be well-dressed. . . . You yourselves want to be properly clothed and accoutered. . . .

You can only get what you need to achieve these objects in the products of the land.

---

[7]"Documents aux origines de l'abolition de l'esclavage," *Revue d'Histoire des Colonies*, vol. 36, 1949, 3rd and 4th trimesters, no. 127 and 128, 391–397.

This land does not belong to you. It belongs to those who purchased or inherited it. . . .

Your only right to the products of this land comes from your agricultural labor; and I have warned you that your portion of its revenues will only be given to you as recompense for your work.

When I set that portion at a third of net revenue, I was assuming that you would work six days a week. You want to eliminate Saturday. I have already told you that you are free to do so, but this is what will result from it.

To eliminate one day of work each week is to diminish your total labor by one-sixth and, consequently, to diminish the revenue by one-sixth. . . .

The property-owner's liberty consists in the faculty of cultivating his land as he pleases, by whomever he wants, and under the conditions he desires.

He would begin by expelling from the plantation all who were lazy and would make his laborers cultivate the land for a daily wage.

He would no longer have to provide lodgings or a garden to the cultivators. It is clear that he would no longer owe anything to the Africans he dismissed, since, just like the portion of revenue, lodgings and a garden are given only to those attached to the plantation by assiduous and sustained labor. Nor would he owe anything to those working for a daily wage, because they would be seen as only temporary. . . .

Africans, you have now been informed. Consider if you will persist in preferring Saturday rest and inevitable misery to the good I have prepared for you.

I must warn you against other capital errors. . . .

You have been persuaded that, today, now that you are free and since we want to improve your lot, you should have larger gardens than when you were slaves. . . .

Then you had no share of plantation revenues; today each of you has your share of these revenues, in proportion to his work.

Thus, you have less need than ever for your little gardens. . . .

Moreover, the more land you are given for your own use, the more you will grow disgusted with cultivating the common lands of the plantation. . . .

By proclaiming your freedom, the Republic wanted to give you the means of living happily and comfortably, but only on condition that you contribute with all your force to the well-being of others. It wanted the happiness of each one of you to be inseparable from that of the property-owners. . . .

The tyrants of Europe only sought slaves because they needed labor for their mines or for clearing and cultivating the land. . . . They believed that they could only obtain labor from Africans by enchaining them, showering them with blows, and mutilating them.

They are all watching our experiment . . . to see if we obtain from you free labor, whose fruits you will share with the land-owners. If the land-owner's profits equal or surpass the revenue he obtained from the former mode of cultivation, all the tyrants of Europe will follow our example and soon there will be no more slaves anywhere. European ships will no longer go to the coast of Africa to purchase human beings. . . .

However, if you betray the hopes and desires of the Republic's delegates, if your conduct vindicates your former persecutors' idea of your indolence, if your refusal to work or your lack of effort destroys or diminishes agricultural output, no colony will be tempted to follow our example; the English, Dutch, Spanish, and Portuguese will tighten the chains of your brothers. Even the French Republic—which does not want a single slave on its territory, but which would have tried in vain to make you worthy of liberty—will abandon all of its colonies: your brothers of Martinique, Guadeloupe, Guyana, and other French possessions will be enslaved by the first kings who conquer them; the traffickers of human beings will continue to visit and depopulate the coasts of Africa. And what will happen to you? I do not suppose that you would be so cowardly as to consent to reenslavement after having tasted liberty. But without work, you will have only fallow lands and no means of subsistence. Without laws, you will have no means of restraining your passions and the disorders they produce. Driven by need, you will strip what is left of this uncultivated land, you will devastate it, you will have bloody wars with the whites and mulattoes who were your former masters. You will prevail because you are stronger. You will pillage and massacre your former masters. And once there is no longer a single white or mulatto to despoil or slaughter, you will fight among yourselves. And once you have become so disunified and weakened by your internecine divisions, the sea will vomit new brigands who will take your land and plunge you back into a state of slavery even worse than that from which we saved you.

Africans, this is the fate that awaits if you refuse to make some effort to preserve and defend your liberty. . . .

4. TOUSSAINT LOUVERTURE'S LABOR REGULATIONS (OCTOBER 12, 1800)[8]

Toussaint Louverture is generally considered to be the father of independent Haiti. Born a slave, he was freed as a young man and became an overseer and property owner in his own right. Although free, he took part in the uprising of August 1791 and became an officer in the rebel armies. After rallying to France in 1794, he rose rapidly to become the leading general in Saint-Domingue and an independent head of state in all but name. After defeating his rival, General Rigaud, in 1800 in a civil war (known as the War of the South), his authority was unchallenged across Saint-Domingue. As ruler of what was effectively an independent country, Toussaint faced the same problems of governance as the French commissioners had before him. Perhaps the most intractable was the problem of reconciling freedom with plantation labor. Realizing Saint-Domingue's needed revenue from sugar exports to purchase weapons and pay the army, Toussaint adopted a labor regime similar to that of the commissioners.

[8]From B. Ardouin, *Etudes sur l'histoire d'Haiti* (Paris: Dezobry and Magdaleine, 1853), vol. 4, 248–253. My thanks to Philippe Girard for providing me with this document.

You can easily understand, citizens, that agriculture is the foundation of government, because it provides commerce, ease, and abundance; gives birth to arts and industry; gives everyone work, since it is the mainspring of all professions; and when each citizen is industrious, public tranquility is the result, troubles disappear with the idleness that spawns them, and everyone peacefully enjoys the fruit of his work.

Military and civil authorities, this is the plan we must adopt. . . .

Considering that, to guarantee liberty . . . everyone must be usefully employed. . . .

Considering that the military has sacred duties to fulfill—since it is the sentinel of the people and is always active in executing the orders it receives from its leader, whether to maintain interior order or combat the exterior enemies of the Republic—it is essentially obedient to its leaders. It is equally important that managers, overseers, and cultivators, who also have leaders, conduct themselves like officers, non-commissioned officers and soldiers in everything connected with their duties;

Considering that when an officer, non-commissioned officer, or soldier neglects his duties, he is brought before a court martial, to be judged and punished according to the laws of the Republic. . . . Since the managers, overseers, and cultivators should be equally subordinated to their leaders and assiduously attached to their tasks, they will also be punished if they neglect their duties;

Considering that a soldier . . . cannot leave his company, battalion, or regiment . . . without the formal permission of his leaders, . . . cultivators are equally forbidden to leave their plantations . . . without legal permission. . . .

Considering that, since the revolution, both male and female cultivators who, because they were young at the time did not engage in cultivation, do not want to engage in it today because, they say, *they are free*, and pass their days running around and lazing about, setting a very bad example for the other cultivators, at the same time as the *generals, officers, non-commissioned officers, and soldiers* are on permanent alert every day to protect the sacred rights of all;

Finally, considering that my proclamation of 25 brumaire year 7 (15 November 1798) to the people of Saint-Domingue should have induced them to undertake active and assiduous work, since it announced to all citizens without distinction that, in order to achieve the restoration of Saint-Domingue, the cooperation of the agricultural worker, soldier, and civil authorities was indispensable;

Consequently, absolutely desiring that my proclamation be executed fully and that all the abuses which have taken root among the cultivators cease. . . .

I most positively command what follows:

1. *All managers, overseers, and cultivators* are required to carry out their duties with precision, submission, and obedience—*just like soldiers.*
2. *All managers, overseers, and cultivators* who do not carry out their duties with the assiduousness that agriculture requires, *will be arrested and punished with the same severity as soldiers who neglect their duties. . . .*

3. *All male and female cultivators* in a state of idleness, who have hidden themselves in cities, villages, or plantations other than their own, in order to evade agricultural work, . . . *are required to return immediately to their respective plantations.* . . .

4. *All individuals who are neither male nor female cultivators* must immediately prove that they practice a useful profession. . . . If they fail to do so, those found in violation will be immediately *arrested* and, if they are found guilty, *incorporated into an army regiment.* [If found innocent, they will be sent to a plantation where they will be forced to work.] This measure, which must be severely executed, will prevent vagrancy, because it *will force* everyone to work usefully. . . .

7. The managers and overseers of each plantation are required to report to the military commander of their district . . . on the conduct of the *male and female cultivators* under their orders. . . .

13. We order the generals commanding departments and the generals and superior officers commanding districts to oversee the execution of the present regulation, for which I make them personally responsible . . . *liberty* cannot exist without work.

5. TOUSSAINT'S CONSTITUTION (MAY 9, 1801)[9]

After securing his rule over the entire island, Toussaint issued a constitution. He did this on his own initiative, without any authorization from France (of which Saint-Domingue was still technically a colony). The following is the constitution's introductory text and some of its key articles.

The colony of Saint-Domingue has existed for years without positive laws; long governed by ambitious men, its annihilation was inevitable without the wise and active genius of the general in chief, Toussaint Louverture. By the finest combinations, the most carefully thought-out plans, and the most energetic actions, [he] was able to deliver it almost simultaneously from its exterior and interior enemies; to stifle all the seeds of discord; lay the groundwork for its recovery in the midst of anarchy; make abundance succeed misery and love of work and peace succeed civil war and vagrancy, security replace terror, and finally place it firmly under the French Empire. The Revolution had violently overthrown everything which constituted the former administrative regime of the island of Saint-Domingue. At different times, the various legislative assemblies of France had put in its place new laws, but the incoherence of these laws, which were repealed just as soon as they had been passed, their vices, and their inadequacy, which was immediately

[9]Louis-Joseph Janvier, *Les constitutions d'Haiti* (Paris: Marpon and Flammarion, 1886), 4–22.

recognized by their authors, the manner by which they were executed by the factious and men of party spirit, adept at interpreting laws according to their interests, helped to spread, rather than diminish, the disorder. The natural consequence of this was to make the laws, which should have been received with feelings of respect, seem like objects of alarm or, when they were powerless, like objects of disdain.

The wise men who made the French Constitution of the year VIII [1799] felt the need to adopt a new system for the distant colonies and, when creating laws to govern them, to consult the morals, customs, habits, and needs of the French inhabitants, and even the present circumstances in which they found themselves. Would it be easy to weigh all these factors through often-inaccurate reports, to appreciate at such great distance the changes which have taken place in the spirit of a people, to know its ills and offer appropriate and effective remedies to them, above all during a war? . . .

Article 91 of the French Constitution could have alone authorized the inhabitants of Saint-Domingue to present to the French government the laws to govern them, if past experience had not made it an imperious duty; and what better moment for this important work than when chaos is lifting, when the ruins of the ancient edifice are being cleared away, when prejudices are being healed and passions calmed. . . .

In addition to these fundamental considerations, which demonstrate the necessity for a Constitution for the island of Saint-Domingue . . . are equally pressing reasons: the just demands of the departments of the colony to bring the tribunals closer to the people, the necessity of bringing in new cultivators to increase agricultural production, the revival of commerce, and the reestablishment of manufacturing; the utility of cementing the union of the former Spanish with the old French part [of the island]; the metropole's inability to aid and feed this immense colony during war with the maritime powers; the need to establish a simple and uniform financial administration for the colony and to reform its abuses; the need to reassure absent property-owners about their properties; finally, the importance of consolidating and stabilizing the internal peace, of augmenting the prosperity the colony is beginning to enjoy after the storms that roiled it, of informing everyone of their rights and duties, and of quelling mistrust by presenting a Code of laws which will bind all affections and rally all interests.

These are the reasons that convinced the General in Chief to convoke a legislative Assembly charged with proposing to the French government the most suitable Constitution for the colony of Saint-Domingue. . . .

Title II, The Inhabitants
Art. 3. There can be no slaves on this territory; servitude is forever abolished there. All men born there live and die free and French.

Art. 4. All men, regardless of color, are eligible for all employments.

Art. 5. There is no other distinction than that of virtues and talents. . . . The law is the same for all, whether it is punishing or protecting.

Title III, Religion

Art. 6. The Catholic, apostolic, and Roman religion is the only one that can be professed in public. . . .

Art. 8. The governor of the colony will assign each minister of religion a specific territory, and these ministers cannot, under any pretext, form a corps in the colony.

Title IV, Morality

Art. 10. There will be no divorce in the colony. . . .

Title VI, Agriculture and Commerce

Art. 14. As it is essentially agricultural, the colony cannot tolerate any interruption in its agricultural work.

Art. 15. Each plantation is a factory which requires a collection of cultivators and workers; it is the tranquil haven of an active and constant family, whose owner (or his representative) is necessarily the father.

Art. 16. Each cultivator and worker is a member of the family and has a right to part of its revenues. Whenever the cultivators change their domicile, it leads to the ruin of agriculture. To repress a vice as fatal to the colony as it is contrary to public order, the governor will issue all necessary police regulations. . . .

Title VIII, The Government

Art. 27. The administration of the colony is entrusted to a governor who will correspond directly with the metropole. . . .

Art. 28. The Constitution names as governor, citizen Toussaint-Louverture, General in Chief of the army of Saint-Domingue, and, in consideration of the important services he rendered to the colony in the critical circumstances of the revolution, and according to the wish of the grateful inhabitants, the reins of government are entrusted to him for the rest of his glorious life. . . .

Art. 30. To consolidate the tranquility the colony owes to the firmness, activity, indefatigable zeal, and rare virtues of General Toussaint-Louverture, and as a sign of the unlimited confidence of the inhabitants of Saint-Domingue, the Constitution attributes exclusively to this general the right of choosing the citizen who, in the unfortunate event of his death, will immediately replace him. This choice will be secret; it will be kept in a sealed packet. . . .

Art. 34. The governor officializes and promulgates the laws; he appoints to all civil and military positions. He is commander-in-chief of the armed forces and charged with their organization. . . .

Art. 35. He exercises general police powers over the inhabitants and plantations, and ensures the obligations of property-owners . . . to the cultivators and workers, and the duties of the cultivators toward the property-owners. . . .

Art. 36. He proposes laws and Constitutional amendments to the central Assembly. . . .

Art. 37. He directs and oversees the collection, deposit, and use of the colony's finances. . . .

Art. 39. He oversees and censures . . . all writings printed in the island. He suppresses foreign ones which tend to compromise morality or trouble the colony. . . .

Art. 40. If the governor learns of a conspiracy against the colony's tranquility, he will immediately arrest the persons presumed to be its authors, agents, or accomplices. . . .

Title XIII, General Dispositions

Art. 67. There shall be no corporations or associations contrary to public order. No assembly of citizens can call itself a popular society. All seditious gatherings will be dispersed immediately by verbal command or, if necessary by armed force. . . .

Art. 77. General-in-Chief Toussaint-Louverture is and remains charged with presenting the Constitution for the sanction of the French government. Nonetheless, given the absence of laws, the urgency of ending this state of peril, the necessity of promptly reestablishing agriculture, and the unanimous, strongly pronounced wish of the inhabitants of Saint-Domingue, the General-in-Chief is invited, in the name of the public good, to execute it in the entire territory of the colony.

III. Napoleon's Expedition

When Napoleon learned that Toussaint had unilaterally issued a constitution for Saint-Domingue, setting himself up as ruler for life, he was furious. Not only did this rub his substantial ego the wrong way, it also interfered with Napoleon's plan to reestablish a French colonial empire in America. The keystone of this plan was the restoration of the plantation-based, sugar-export economy in the French Caribbean. The vast labor force required for this economic revival would be fed from the fertile agriculture of Louisiana (which had secretly been retroceded to France by Spain). Napoleon put the plan into execution. An expeditionary force of over 30,000 battle-hardened troops, the largest France had ever sent to the western hemisphere, was dispatched to Saint-Domingue under the command of Napoleon's brother-in-law, General Leclerc. It landed in early 1802. After initially encouraging results—most of the Saint-Domingue generals submitted to Leclerc's authority. Toussaint was seized and imprisoned in France, where he soon died— and things began to go wrong for the French. Fear spread that their ultimate goal was to reimpose slavery. When news arrived that the French had actually reimposed slavery in Guadeloupe, a full-blown uprising broke out. Cruel fighting raged across the island. So did yellow fever. Both took a terrible toll on the French troops. Of the 80,000 French soldiers and sailors ultimately sent to the island, only a tenth survived. Soon after their departure, Jean-Jacques Dessalines, the general who had taken command after Toussaint's abduction, declared Haitian independence.

6. THE FATE OF LOUISIANA[10]

One unexpected byproduct of the defeat of the French expedition was the sale of Louisiana to the United States. Realizing that Louisiana was of no use to him without Saint-Domingue, Napoleon sold it to the United States as soon as he decided to abandon the reconquest of Saint-Domingue. The following account by a French diplomat involved in negotiating the sale tells how the failure of the expedition led to the Louisiana Purchase.

[After the Treaty of Amiens in 1802], France found in peace all the advantages which she had long sought. . . . For her commerce and navigation she had the most justly founded expectations that the possession of Louisiana and the subjection of St. Domingo, enlarged by the whole part that had belonged to Spain, would enable her to resume her rank among the maritime powers and commercial states. . . .

Napoleon, who did not foresee the near return of war . . . thought that he ought to proceed without delay to the execution of the plan that he had formed. It consisted in first subjecting the revolted colony, by sending there such considerable force that he might be justified in regarding success as infallible. After the reduction of the rebels, a part of the army was to be conveyed to Louisiana.

The events, of which St. Domingo was then the bloody theatre, are closely connected with the history of the treaty of cession [of Louisiana]. We shall therefore anticipate the course of the principal narrative, and state summarily the issue of the expedition, which had for its object the re-establishment of the French sovereignty in that island.

At the end of the last century, and after the frightful catastrophes that resulted from a manumission imprudently proclaimed, order had begun to be re-established in that fine colony. But ambition soon induced a black man and a mulatto to take up arms, and the rivalry of these two men kindled anew a civil war, which the mother country had not excited, but which she probably witnessed without dissatisfaction.

The two factions and their chiefs were equally ardent in the profession of attachment to France, and it was difficult to refuse credence to their declarations; for they had both equally contributed to the expulsion of the English. But the character of their fidelity was affected by the difference of their castes. Rigaud, a free born mulatto, had wished, while he restored the colony to France, to maintain slavery, and to keep for his party the plantations conquered from the whites, who had emigrated or been allies of our enemies. He united with a remarkable capacity the advantage of an excellent education. He had become chief of all the people of colour, who were born free or had been manumitted before the revolution. These men, for the most part owners of blacks, refused to obey the laws of

[10]Barbé Marbois, *The History of Louisiana, Particularly of the Cession of that Colony to the United States of America* (Philadelphia: Carey & Lea, 1830), 177–200.

the Convention, which, by proclaiming the abolition of slavery, only left them land without value, for they did not conceive the possibility of its being cultivated in any other manner than by slaves. Liberty, moreover, appeared to them to be less precious, since the multitude were admitted to enjoy it in the same manner with themselves. This chief commanded, in the south of the island, an army composed of about six thousand mulattoes and blacks, and a few whites. This band was very much attached to him; but a feeling of hatred, which was sometimes open and declared, and at others secret and dissembled, divided the mulattoes and blacks, even though they followed, whilst under his orders, the same standard.

Toussaint-Louverture, a black, and formerly a slave, commanded at the Cape and in all the northern and central parts of the colony. He had recalled the former proprietors who had emigrated, had protected them and restored their lands, with the exception of a few plantations that had been seized on by his friends and himself. But he had only exhibited this generosity in tranquil times. He acted very differently in war, and being persuaded that it was necessary to carry it on without mercy, when the sword is once drawn, he pushed his success without giving his adversaries any intermission, and if he met with a reverse, he revenged it by fire and plunder. His enemies accused him of hypocrisy and dissimulation. He was, they said, coldly cruel and the extermination of the whites formed part of his plan for rendering the colony independent. His partisans made him a hero and a statesman.

Toussaint may be more impartially judged from a view of his life. Obliged in his infancy to obey as a slave, unexpected events suddenly made him the equal of the whites, and he filled his new place without embarrassment or arrogance. He entirely forgot what he had suffered in his first condition, and was generous even towards many of whom he had reason to complain. His activity and strength were prodigious, and he moved with extraordinary rapidity from one extremity of the colony to the other, according as circumstances required his presence. Vigilant, sober, and abstemious, he quitted the table and gave up every relaxation the moment that business demanded his attention. An upright judge, without learning or education, an able general from the very day that he ceased to be a private soldier, he was dear to his army, and the negroes obeyed with a sort of pride a man of colour, whom they considered the superior, or the equal, at least, of the most distinguished white man.

He was aware that a community, without labour or industry, soon falls into a state of barbarism, and he had revived agriculture with regulations which had been attended with the most happy results. The privileged productions, the precious aliment of a flourishing commerce, had become as abundant as formerly; but their destination was much changed. The plantations were sequestered, and the greatest part of the revenue was paid into the colonial treasury, instead of being sent to France. . . . He exacted labour, not in order to accumulate treasures, but to fulfil one of the conditions of the social state. "I know how," he frequently said, "to unite liberty and labour." To this end all his proceedings were directed, but as soon as he perceived that its attainment was questionable, he became, though he was not without elevation of soul, suspicious and implacable. He saw flow, without pity, the blood of every one who was convicted of having put in danger that liberty which was so dear to him, on his own account, as well as on that of all the people of his colour, and he no longer treated of business with the candour and good faith that smooth all difficulties. According to him, it was the safety of the blacks, his own safety that obliged him to oppose cunning to perfidy; and the secret intelligence which he kept up with the emissaries of the government of Jamaica was rendered necessary by the condition of St. Domingo, at the period that he was acknowledged as its master.

His army was composed, in 1800, of about twelve thousand blacks. War between men who are distinguished from one another by the colour of the skin is always terrible, because they at last believe themselves to be of two different species; thus when a black man and a mulatto met, each saw in the other an enemy. The slightest hostilities had then an exterminating character scarcely known among savages. Treason and secret violence destroyed in this colony more human beings than battles. Rigaud, too weak against adversaries infinitely superior in number, had thought proper to abandon an unequal contest, and had fled to France. Toussaint made a constitution for the colony; he sent it to the first consul, who was very much dissatisfied with it, and declared that it should never be put in force.

Such was the state of affairs when Bonaparte, on the faith of the preliminaries of London, and on the point of concluding the definitive peace, conceived the design of sending to the colony a fleet and army under the command of General Leclerc, his brother-in-law. Eighteen thousand troops were, at first, embarked on board of thirty ships of the line. . . .

Re-enforcements were, from time to time, sent both to the fleet and army. There were among the French officers an extraordinary emulation to be of this expedition. Accustomed to glory, . . . they had foreseen none of the dangers, which are incurred by all who are exposed to the sun or even the night air in tropical regions. It was considered a high favour to belong to the expedition, and the number of generals and officers, compared with that of soldiers, far surpassed the ordinary proportions. A part of these forces was composed of Spaniards and Germans; some Poles were also among them. These legions, which had been drawn from their country to contribute to the great events that changed the face of Europe, had become embarrassing to France in her new state of peace. The idea occurred of sending them to St. Domingo. Thus these soldiers, many of whom were scarcely manumitted from servitude, were destined to restore to the bonds of slavery, Africans, with whom they had no ground of quarrel. The French troops landed on the 3[r]d of February, 1802. On the arrival of these forces, the black general, Christophe, set fire to Cape Français, and this beautiful city was partially consumed. The blacks adopted it as their law to lay waste their own country, and to burn down the houses, in order to deprive the enemy of resources. This rage, and these conflagrations but too well announced the disasters which ensued. From the beginning, the success of the Europeans, who gained several battles from the blacks, was balanced by the losses that they sustained from the climate. There was no longer any question of rebellion, but the hostilities had assumed the character of a war between two independent nations.

A great change had followed the abolition of slavery. During a century and a half, an habitual terror had kept the blacks in the most abject subjection to their masters. They had then such an idea of the superiority of the whites, that, in the thickest and most solitary forest, the sight of a white man would have been sufficient to inspire twenty blacks with dread. This almost supernatural power, which had vanished at the proclamation of liberty, had been suddenly renewed, on the arrival of a numerous army of white troops, and, for some time, it only required a mere patrol to put to flight a battalion of blacks. Some, however, resisted with success, and then almost every engagement became a battle. These whites, so long dreaded as beings of a superior species, were but ordinary enemies, when the negroes discovered that it was so easy to make them prisoners, or put them to death. They daily recovered their courage, and soon had as their rallying words, wherever the French were found in small numbers, "Let us kill our oppressors." . . .

Louisiana had been destined to supply the colony with provisions, cattle, and wood; and as St. Domingo was lost to France, the importance of Louisiana was also diminished. . . . [Napoleon had] expected to make use of the one colony to preserve the other.

7. THE FATE OF THE FRENCH EXPEDITION[11]

Leclerc brought with him a private letter from Napoleon to Toussaint and a public proclamation to the people of Saint-Domingue. Both urged submission to Leclerc and loyalty to France. In classic Napoleonic fashion, promises of peace and prosperity were accompanied by threats of merciless retribution should resistance continue. In addition, Napoleon provided Leclerc with secret instructions, detailing the steps he was to take to reimpose French authority. These instructions differed from the private letter to Toussaint and the public proclamation to the people.

"Napoleon to Toussaint Louverture" (November 18, 1801)

Peace with England and all the powers of Europe has elevated the Republic to the highest degree of power and grandeur and makes it possible for the Government to attend to the colony of Saint-Domingue. We are sending General Leclerc, our brother-in-law, as Captain-General, to be the colony's chief magistrate. He comes with enough troops to enforce the sovereignty of the French people. Under these circumstances, we hope that you will prove to us, in particular, and all of France, the sincerity of the sentiments you have constantly expressed in the different letters you have written to us. We hold you in esteem, and hope to recognize and

---

[11]Paul Roussier, ed., *Lettres du General Leclerc* (Paris; Leroux, 1937), 263–274, 307–309.

proclaim the great services you have rendered to the French people. It is because of you and your brave blacks that the French flag still flies over Saint-Domingue. Called by your talents and by imperious circumstances to supreme command, you extinguished civil war, stopped the persecution exercised by ferocious men, and restored religion to a place of honor. . . . But your constitution, although it contains many good things, also has some which are contrary to the dignity and sovereignty of the France, of which Saint-Domingue is a part.

The difficult circumstances in which you found yourself—surrounded on all sides by enemies, with the Metropole unable to help or feed you—made these articles of your constitution legitimate. But today, when circumstances have changed, we expect that you will be the first to recognize the sovereignty of the Nation which counts you among its most illustrious citizens because of the services you have rendered and your natural talents and force of character. The contrary course of action could not be reconciled to our high idea of you. It would make you lose the many rights you have earned to the Republic's recognition and generosity and would dig under your feet a chasm which, in swallowing you up, would contribute to the misfortune of those brave blacks . . . whom we would have to punish for rebellion. . . .

Use your advice, influence, and talents to help the Captain-General. What do you desire? Liberty for the blacks? You know that wherever we went, we have given liberty to the people. Consideration, honors, wealth? Given the services you have rendered and shall render in this circumstance, together with the particular sentiments we have for you, you cannot doubt the consideration, honors, and wealth that await you.

Let the people of Saint-Domingue know that France's concern for their well-being has often been thwarted by the imperious circumstances of war; that the men who came from the Continent to spread division were the product of the factions that tore apart the homeland itself; that henceforth, peace and vigorous government will guarantee their prosperity and liberty. Tell them that liberty, their most prized possession, can only be enjoyed under the title of French citizen and that any act against the interests of the Fatherland, the obedience they owe to the Government and its delegate, the Captain-General, would be a crime against national sovereignty. . . .

And you, General, remember that, while you are the first of your color to have attained such great power . . . you are ultimately responsible for their conduct to God and ourselves. . . .

"Proclamation to the Inhabitants of Saint-Domingue" (November 18, 1801)

Whatever your origin or color, you are all French, you are all free and all equal before God and before the Republic.

Like Saint-Domingue, France was in the grip of factions, torn apart by civil strife and foreign war. But everything has changed. All the peoples have embraced the French and sworn peace and friendship to them. All the French have embraced each other too and have sworn to be friends and brothers. You too must come embrace the French and rejoice to see your friends and brothers from Europe once again.

The Government is sending you Captain-General Leclerc. He brings with him large forces to protect you against your enemies and against the enemies of the Republic. If you are told "these forces are destined to take away our liberty," answer "the Republic gave us liberty, the Republic will not allow it to be taken away."

Rally to the Captain General. He brings you peace and plenty. Everybody rally to him. Whoever dares to reject the Captain General will be a traitor to the Fatherland, and the anger of the Republic will consume him like fire consumes your dried sugar canes.

"Secret Instruction to Leclerc"

The Spanish, English, and Americans are all distressed by the existence of a Black Republic. The Admiral and Captain will write to the neighboring establishments to let them know the goal of the government, the common advantage Europeans will gain by destroying this rebellion of Blacks. . . .

Jefferson promised that once the French army arrives, all measures will be taken to starve out Toussaint. . . .

[But] the French nation will never enslave men it has recognized as free. Thus, all the blacks of Saint-Domingue will live like those in Guadeloupe today.

Your conduct will follow the three phases, outlined below.

In the first, you will disarm only blacks who are rebels.

In the third, you will disarm them all.

In the first phase, you will not be demanding. You will negotiate with Toussaint, you will promise him all he wants in order to control the fortresses and occupy the country.

Once this goal is achieved, you will become more demanding. You will order him to respond categorically to the proclamation and my letter. You will order him to Le Cap.

In your talks with Moyse, Dessalines, and Toussaint's other generals, treat them well.

Win over Christophe, Clairveaux, Maurepas, Félix, Romain, Jasmain, etc., and all the other blacks. . . . In the first phase, confirm their ranks and positions. In the third, send them all to France with their ranks if they served well during the second phase.

In phase one, Toussaint's principal agents, both whites and men of color, should be honored and confirmed in their ranks. In the last phase, they should be sent to France with their ranks if they behaved well in the second. If not, they should be deported.

During the first phase, all blacks in positions of authority should be flattered and well-treated, but, in general, you should try to diminish their popularity and power. You should treat Toussaint, Moyse, and Dessalines well during this phase, but send them to France in the final phase, either with their rank or under arrest, depending on their conduct. . . .

Toussaint will have submitted only if he has come to Le Cap or Port-au-Prince and sworn a loyalty oath. . . . On that day, you must embark him on a frigate . . . and send him to France. If you can, arrest Moyse and Dessalines at this moment or pursue them mercilessly. Send back to France all of Toussaint's white supporters and all blacks in positions of authority, whom you suspect of ill-will. Declare Moyse and Dessalines to be traitors to the Fatherland and enemies of the French people. Deploy the troops and do not rest until you have their heads and have dispersed and disarmed their partisans.

If, after the first 15 or 20 days, it is impossible to catch Toussaint, you must issue a proclamation declaring that if, after a certain period, he has not come to swear a loyalty oath to the Republic, he will be declared a traitor. When the delay expires, you will begin a merciless war. . . .

IV. Defining the Meaning of Independence

On January 1, 1804, General Dessalines summoned his principal lieutenants to a meeting at the town of Gonaïves. There he formally declared independence. He named the new country Haiti, an indigenous word used by the island's original inhabitants. At first Haiti was a republic, but Dessalines soon proclaimed himself emperor as Jacques I. His rule was short-lived. He was assassinated in 1806 by two of his generals, Henri Christophe and Alexandre Pétion.

8. DECLARATION OF INDEPENDENCE AND ABJURATION OF THE FRENCH NATION (1804)[12]

In preparation for the Gonaïves independence ceremony, Dessalines considered various drafts for a formal declaration of independence. After rejecting versions imbued with universalist, Enlightenment principles, he adopted one that spoke more directly to the recent experiences of colonization, slavery, and war. Accompanying the declaration itself was a formal abjuration of the French nation. The following are excerpts from both.

"Declaration of the Independence"
In the Name of the Black People and Men of Color of St. Domingo
The Independence of St. Domingo is proclaimed. Restored to our primitive dignity, we have asserted our rights; we swear never to yield them to any power on earth; the frightful veil of prejudice is torn to pieces, be it so for ever. Woe be to them who would dare to put together its bloody tatters.

Oh! Landholders of St. Domingo, wandering in foreign countries: by proclaiming our independence, we do not forbid you, indiscriminately, from

---

[12]Marcus Rainsford, *An Historical Account of the Black Empire of Hayti* (London: Albion Press, 1805), 439–446.

returning to your property; far be from us this unjust idea. We are not ignorant that there are some among you that have renounced their former errors, abjured the injustice of their exorbitant pretensions, and acknowledged the lawfulness of the cause for which we have been spilling our blood these twelve years. Toward those men who do us justice, we will act as brothers; let them rely for ever on our esteem and friendship; let them return among us. The God who protects us, the God of Freemen, bids us to stretch out toward them our conquering arms. But as for those who, intoxicated with foolish pride, interested slaves of a guilty preten-sion, are blinded so much as to believe themselves the essence of human nature, and assert that they are destined by heavens to be our masters and our tyrants, let them never come the land of St. Domingo: if they come hither, they will only meet with chains or deportation; then let them stay where they are; tormented by their well-deserved misery, and the frowns of the just men whom they have too long mocked, let them still continue to move, unpitied and unnoticed by all.

We have sworn not to listen with clemency towards all those who would dare to speak to us of slavery; we will be inexorable, perhaps even cruel, towards all troops who, themselves forgetting the object for which they have not ceased fight-ing since 1780, should come from Europe to bring among us death and servitude. Nothing is too dear, and all means are lawful, to men from whom it is wished to tear the first of all blessings. Were they to cause rivers and torrents of blood to run; were they, in order to maintain their liberty, to conflagrate seven eighths of the globe, they are innocent before the tribunal of Providence, that never created men to see them groaning under so harsh and shameful a servitude.

In the various commotions that took place, some inhabitants against whom we had not to complain have been victims by the cruelty of a few soldiers or cul-tivators, too much blinded by the remembrance of their past sufferings to be able to distinguish the good and humane land-owners from those that were unfeeling and cruel, we lament with all feeling souls so deplorable an end, and declare to the world, whatever may be said to the contrary by wicked people, that the murders were committed contrary to the wishes of our hearts. It was impossible, especially in the crisis in which the colony was, to be able to prevent or stop those horrors. They who are in the least acquainted with history, know that a people, when as-sailed by civil dissentions, though they may be the most polished on earth, give themselves up to every species of excess, and the authority of the chiefs, at that time not firmly supported, in a time of revolution cannot punish all that are guilty, without meeting new difficulties. But now a-days the Aurora of peace hails us, with the glimpse of a less stormy time; now that the calm of victory has succeeded to the trouble of a dreadful war, every thing in St. Domingo ought to assume a new face, and its government henceforward be that of justice.

"Abjuration of the French Nation"

Citizens, it is not enough to have expelled from your country the barbarians who have for ages stained it with blood—it is not enough to have curbed the factions which, succeeding each other by turns, sported with a phantom of liberty which

France exposed to their eyes. It is become necessary, by a last act of national authority, to ensure for ever the empire of liberty in the country which has given us birth. It is necessary to deprive an inhuman government, which has hitherto held our minds in a state of the most humiliating torpitude, of every hope of being enabled again to enslave us. Finally, it is necessary to live independent, or die. Independence or Death! Let these sacred words serve to rally us—let them be signals of battle, and of our re-union.

Citizens—Countrymen—I have assembled on this solemn day those courageous chiefs who, on the eve of receiving the last breath of expiring liberty, have lavished their blood to preserve it. These generals, who have conducted your struggles against tyranny, have not yet done. The French name still darkens our plains; every thing recalls the remembrance of the cruelties of that barbarous people. Our laws, our customs, our cities, every thing bears the characteristic of the French. Hearken to what I say! The French still have a footing in our island! And you believe yourselves free and independent of that republic, which has fought all nations, it is true, but never conquered those who would be free! What! Victims for fourteen years by credulity and forbearance! Conquered not by French armies, but by the canting eloquence of the proclamations of their agents! When shall we be wearied with breathing the same air with them? What have we in common with that bloody-minded people? Their cruelties compared to our moderation, their colour to ours, the extension of seas which separate us, our avenging climate—all plainly tell us they are not our brethren; that they will never become such; and, if they find an asylum among us, they will still be the instigators of our troubles and of our divisions. Citizens, men, women, young and old, cast round your eyes on every part of this island; seek there your wives, your husbands, your brothers, your sisters. What did I say? Seek your children. Your children at the breast, what is become of them? I shudder to say: the prey of vultures. Instead of these interesting victims, the affrighted eye see their assassins, tigers still covered with their blood, and whose terrifying presence reproaches you for your insensibility, and your guilty tardiness to avenge them. What do you wait for, to appease their manes? Remember that you have wished your remains to be laid by the side of your fathers. When you have driven out tyranny, will you descend into their tombs, without having avenged them? No: their bones would repulse yours. And ye, invaluable men, intrepid Generals, who, insensible to private sufferings, have given new life to liberty, by lavishing your blood; know, that you have done nothing if you do not give to the nations a terrible, though just example, of the vengeance that ought to be exercised by a people proud of having recovered its liberty, and zealous of maintaining it. Let us intimidate those, who might dare to attempt depriving us of it again: let us begin with the French; let them shudder at approaching our shores, if not on account of the cruelties they have committed, at least at the terrible resolution we are going to make: to devote to death whatsoever native of France should soil with his sacrilegious footstep, this territory of liberty.

We have dared to be free. Let us continue free by ourselves and for ourselves; let us imitate the growing child; his own strength breaks his leading-strings, which become useless and troublesome of him in his walk. What are the people who have fought us? What people would reap the fruits of our labours? And what a dishonourable absurdity, to conquer to be slaves!

Slaves—leave to the French this odious epithet; they have conquered to be no longer free. Let us walk in other footsteps; let us imitate other nations, who, carrying their solicitude into futurity, and dreading to leave posterity an example of cowardice, have preferred to be exterminated, rather than be erased from the list of free people. Let us, at the same time, take care, lest a spirit of proselytism should destroy the work. Let our neighbours breathe in peace. Let them live peaceably under the shield of those laws which they have framed for themselves; let us beware of becoming revolutionary fire-brands, of creating ourselves the legislators of the Antilles, of considering as a glory the disturbing the tranquility of the neighbouring islands. They have not been, like the one we inhabit, drenched with the innocent blood of the inhabitants. They have no vengeance to exercise against the authority that protects them; happy, never to have experienced the pestilence that has destroyed us, they must wish well to our posterity.

Peace with our neighbours, but accursed be the French name—eternal hatred to France: such are our principles.

9. A BLACK REPUBLIC (APRIL 1804)[13]

By the time Haitian independence was formally declared, there were very few whites left on the island. A huge wave had fled in 1793, many eventually settling in the United States. Others continued to leave in dribs and drabs during the 1790s. But several thousand still remained, mostly in the coastal cities, when Leclerc's ships arrived in 1802. Their hopes were dashed with the destruction of the expeditionary force. Most of them fled with the surviving troops in 1803, but a handful still remained. Even this small remnant was too much for Dessalines. In April 1804, he issued a proclamation making it illegal for whites to set foot in Haiti. He backed up his words by massacring most of those who remained. The following is an excerpt from Dessalines's proclamation and what was probably the first account of the massacres to reach the outside world.

"Dessaline's Proclamation of a Black Republic"

Crimes, the most atrocious, such as were hitherto unheard of, and would cause nature to shudder, have been perpetrated. The measure of their cruelty overflowed. At length the hour of vengeance has arrived, and the implacable enemies of the rights of man have suffered the punishment due to their crimes.

My arm, raised above their heads, has too long delayed to strike. At that signal, which the justice of God has urged, your hand, righteously armed, has brought the

---

[13]Rainsford, *Black Empire*, 447–452; and British National Archives, Admiralty, series 1, Box 254.

axe to bear upon the decrepit tree of slavery and prejudice. In vain had time, and more especially the infernal politics of Europeans, defended it with triple brass; you have stripped it of its armour; and have placed it upon your heart, that you may become (like your natural enemies) cruel and merciless. Like an overflowing and mighty torrent, that bears down all opposition, your vengeful fury has swept away, every obstacle to its impetuous course. Perish thus all tyrants over innocence, all oppressors of mankind!

What then? Bent for many ages under an iron yoke, the sport of the passions, or the injustice of men, and of the caprices of fortune; mutilated victims of the cupidity of white Frenchmen; after having fattened by our toils, these insatiate blood-suckers, with a patience and resignation unexampled, we should again have seen that sacrilegious horde attempt our destruction, without any distinction of sex or age; and we, whom they call, men without energy, of no virtue, of no delicate sensibility, should not we have plunged in their breast the dagger of desperation? Where is that Haytian so vile, Haytian so unworthy of his regeneration, who thinks he has not fulfilled the decrees of the Eternal, by exterminating these blood-thirsty tygers? If there be one, let him fly; indignant nature discards him from our bosom; let him hide his infamy far from hence; the air we breathe, is not suited to his gross organs; it is the air of liberty, pure, august, and triumphant.

Yes, we have rendered to these true cannibals, war for war, crime for crime, outrage for outrage; yes, I have saved my country; I have avenged America. The avowal I make in the face of earth and heaven, constitutes my pride and my glory. Of what consequence to me is the opinion which contemporary and future generations will pronounce upon my conduct? I have performed my duty; I enjoy my own approbation; for me that is sufficient. But, what am I saying? The preservation of my unfortunate brothers, and the testimony of my own conscience, are not my only recompence: I have seen two classes of men, born to cherish, assist, and succour one another—mixed in a world, and blended together—crying for vengeance, and disputing the honor of the first blow.

Blacks and Yellows, whom the refined duplicity of Europe for a long time endeavoured to divide; you, who are now consolidated, and make but one family; without doubt it was necessary that our perfect reconciliation should be sealed with the blood of your butchers. Similar calamities have hung over your proscribed heads; a similar ardor to strike your enemies has signalized you: the like fate is reserved for you, and the like interests must therefore render you for ever one, indivisible, and inseparable. Maintain that precious concord, that happy harmony, amongst yourselves; it is the pledge of your happiness, your salvation, and your success; it is the secret of being invincible.

It is necessary, in order to strengthen these ties, to recal to your remembrance the catalogue of atrocities committed against our species; the intended massacre of the entire population of this island, meditated in the silence and *sang-froid* of the cabinet; the execution of that abominable project to me was unblushingly proposed, when already begun by the French, with the calmness and serenity of a countenance accustomed to similar crimes. Guadeloupe pillaged and destroyed;

its ruins still reeking with the blood of the children, women, and old men put to the sword . . . and (dread harbinger of death) the frightful despotism exercised at Martinique? Unfortunate people of Martinique, could I but fly to your assistance, and break your fetters! Alas! An insurmountable barrier separates us; yet, perhaps a spark from the same fire which enflames us, will alight on your bosoms: perhaps, at the sound of this emotion, suddenly awakened from your lethargy, with arms in your hands, you will reclaim your sacred and indelible rights.

After the terrible example I have just given, sooner or later Divine Justice will unchain on earth some mighty minds, above the weakness of the vulgar, for the destruction and terror of the wicked. Tremble tyrants, usurpers, scourges of the new world! Our daggers are sharpened, your punishment is ready! Sixty thousand men, equipped, inured to war, obedient to my orders, burn to offer a new sacrifice to the manes of their assassinated brothers. Let that nation come who may be mad or daring enough to attack me. Already at its approach, the irritated Genius of Hayti, arising from the bosom of the ocean, appears; his menacing aspect throws the waves into commotion, excites tempests, and with his mighty hand disperses, or dashes fleets in pieces; to his formidable voice the laws of nature pay obedience; disease, plague, famine, conflagration, poison, are his constant attendants. But why calculate on the assistance of the climate and of the elements? Have I forgot that I command a people of no common cast, brought up in adversity, whose haughty daring, frowns at obstacles, and increases by dangers? Let them come, these homicidal cohorts! I wait for them with a firm and steady eye. I abandon to them freely the shore, and the places where cities have existed, but woe to those who may approach too near the mountains! It were better for them that the sea received them into its profound abyss, than to be devoured by the anger of the children of Hayti.

"War, even to Death, to Tyrants!" This is my motto. "Liberty! Independence!" This is our rallying cry.

Generals, Officers, Soldiers, somewhat unlike him who has preceded me, the Ex-General Toussaint L'Ouverture, I have been faithful to the promise I made to you, when I took up arms against tyranny, and whilst the last spark of life remains in me, I will keep my oath. "Never again shall a colonist, or an European, set his foot upon this territory with the title of master or proprietor." This resolution shall henceforward form the fundamental basis of our constitution.

Should other chiefs, after me, by pursuing a conduct diametrically opposite to mine, dig their own graves, and those of their own species, you will have to accuse only the law of destiny, which shall have taken me away from the happiness and welfare of my fellow-citizens. May my successors follow the path I shall have traced for them! It is the system best adapted for consolidating their power; it is the highest homage they can render to my memory.

As it is derogatory to my character, and my dignity, to punish the innocent for the crimes of the guilty, a handful of whites, commendable by the religion they have professed, and who have besides taken the oath to live with us in the woods, have experienced my clemency. I order that the sword respect them, and that they be unmolested.

I recommend anew, and order all Generals of Departments, &c. to grant succours, encouragement, and protection, to all neutral and friendly nations, who may wish to establish commercial relations in this island.

"Dispatch from Captain John Perkins, HMS Tartar, off Cape Nicholas Mole, Haiti, to Rear Admiral Duckworth, Commanding the West Indies Station" (April 8, 1804)

I was informed by a respectable English merchant at present residing in Port au Prince that on General Dessaline's return, he ordered all the white men then remaining in the town to be immediately put to death; this order was executed without the least ceremony, the black soldiers being at liberty to satisfy their inclinations in the most barbarous manner, they having a thirst for the blood of those unfortunate people. Some they shot, having tied them from 15 to 20 together. Some they pricked to death with their bayonets, and others they tortured in a manner too horrid to be described; in the space of 8 days no less than 800 were actually murdered by these assassins and their bodies thrown into the bogs and marshes to rot away. The white women are spared provided they consent to live with the black men as their wives, but should they refuse, they would instantly be put to death or sent to the mountains to work as slaves on the plantations. I have been informed of eleven that were murdered for not consenting to the embraces of the black brutes. One a beautiful young lady who, after being forced by Colonel Germaine (a negro) and 25 of his men to satisfy their brutish desires, was afterwards pricked to death with their bayonets. Even the mulatto women are in danger of their lives and particularly those who have lived with white men, being promised the same fate if they do not consent to live with the black officers.

It is supposed there is still remaining hid away in different places about 50 white men and although the negroes have been making diligent search after them, they have hitherto escaped their vigilance. The plunder Dessalines is supposed to have collected by the sacrifice of so many lives is calculated at no less a sum than one million of dollars.

On Monday the 25th March, Dessalines left Port au Prince for Cape Francois, there being at that place from 1800 to 2000 white people whom he is determined shall fall a sacrifice to his vengeance. In fact, he thinks nothing of being the executioner himself, for he ordered a man to be brought bound into his chamber and while in conversation stabbed him with his poinard to his heart. The immense treasure that has been collected at different places is deposited in the mountains where they cannot be surprised and where they are also erecting strong fortifications and magazines for the reception of ammunition which is plentifully [supplied] them of every description by the Americans. I am actually told that an American schooner lately arrived at one of their ports with gun powder which was sold for four dollars per pound.

10. FOREIGN REACTIONS TO HAITIAN INDEPENDENCE[14]

Foreign reactions to Haitian independence were varied. Unsurprisingly, countries whose economies relied on slavery (among them France, Great Britain, Spain, and the United States) regarded the new republic with hostility and, to varying degrees, imposed naval blockades and economic boycotts on it. Slave owners in neighboring colonies and the southern United States were especially hostile and fearful. They adopted measures to tighten the slave regime and prevent what they saw as the Haitian contagion from spreading. Others had a more mixed view, such as the author of the following article that appeared in an American magazine in late 1804.

When I first heard of the black chief of St. Domingo bestowing on himself the title of emperor of Hayti, I could not help smiling. I thought, at first, it was the device of some wag, who wanted to ridicule the ambition of Bonaparte, but it turned out to be a specimen of that miserable and childish spirit of imitation, which some think characteristic of the negro race.

The affairs of St. Domingo constitute an extraordinary picture. A sovereign and independent nation of blacks, endowed with the language and many of the arts, especially the military art, of the most refined nation of the earth, presents itself to our view, in an island separated by a wide ocean from their native or original country. A mob of slaves have contrived to expel their masters from the finest spot on the globe, and to form themselves into a political body, probably not less than twelve or fifteen times more numerous than any other community of their colour. In Africa, there are doubtless many millions of negroes, but the largest *community* of them probably does not exceed a few thousands; whereas, at the breaking out of the revolution, the negro population of St. Domingo somewhat exceeded 600,000: so that, if the denominations of empire or emperor are justified by comparative importance, Hayti and its chief are more entitled to these splendid titles, by their superiority to all other black nations, than France and its new emperor are, by their pre-eminence above other European nations.

What, says the inquisitive mind, is to be the future destiny of Hayti? Should it be, in future, left to itself, or should it be able to resist the external efforts made to subdue it? The blacks are wholly unacquainted with the arts of government. They are, by education and condition at least, a lawless and ferocious race, who will bow to nothing but a stern and sanguinary despotism. For a time, at least, we can expect nothing but a series of bloody revolutions, in which one military adventurer shall rise upon the ruins of another, till, at length, some breathing interval will occur long enough to furnish the hereditary principle room to operate, and to engage the affections and obedience of the people to some one fortunate family.

That the blacks of St. Domingo will be left to themselves is, however, by no means probable. They will, no doubt, remain unmolested till the conclusion of the

---

[14]"St. Domingo," *The Literary Magazine and American Register,* vol. II, no. 15, December 1804, 655–657.

present war in Europe; but *then*, it is easy to forsee, that the whole power of France will be bent to the recovery of this valuable colony. Revenge, pride, interest, every motive that usually governs individuals or nations, will combine to stimulate the efforts of the French towards this quarter. . . .

The interest of the European colonists is such, that we cannot expect that the French designs upon St. Domingo will meet with any interruption from their neighbours. Such, at least, will be the notions of the British government. A common politician would be inclined to suppose, that the British power in the West Indies would be more endangered by the re-establishment of their great rivals in St. Domingo, than by the independence of the Hayti empire. The wealth and population of all the British isles bear a slender proportion to those of St. Domingo, after a conquest and a peace of a few years, while the latter has over the former the important advantage which attends one compact realm over scattered and disjointed provinces. Against the French, even during peace, a great naval and military establishment must be maintained, which will, by no means, be necessary against the blacks.

Should Hayti continue independent, or should it regain independence at any future period, its history will be a curious chapter in *the book of great contingency*, and such as, I believe, has no parallel in the former history of mankind. A fertile island, in America, inhabited by a race of negroes, derived from a stock in the heart of Africa, who have been raised, by the very slavery of their ancestors, to a similitude in manners, religion, arts, and language with the most potent and refined of the christian or European nations, is the grand outline of this history.

What, indeed, will become of the posterity of the negroes now residing in North and South America? Their present servile condition cannot possibly continue for ever, but the race must necessarily continue, and they cannot fail to go on multiplying to an indefinite extent. They must gradually become personally free, but, no doubt, will, for ages to come, constitute the lowest class of that society to which they belong. They are so distributed throughout the two continents, that no separate community can possibly be generated by their separate interests. Their situation in the islands is somewhat different; and it is by no means impossible, that they may all, at some remote period, become, what St. Domingo has already become, sovereign nations or communities of negroes, by whom the whites shall be tolerated, at one time, as useful guests, and persecuted, at another, as detested enemies.

11. AFRICAN AMERICAN REACTIONS[15]

For African Americans (and people of African ancestry across the Atlantic world, whether enslaved or free), Haitian independence was a profound inspiration. This comes through forcefully in the following article, which appeared in 1827 in Freedom's Journal, *the first African American newspaper in the United States.*

---

[15] J., "Haytien Revolution," *Freedom's Journal*, vol. 1, no. 4 (April 6, 1827), eds. Samuel E. Cornish and John B. Russwurm, 2.

The last half century will ever be regarded as a period in which changes the most interesting, and occurrences the most remarkable, in the history of man have happened. And the revolution of St. Domingo, which developed the resources and aroused the energies of a people deemed but a step above the brute creation, is not the least remarkable and interesting.

Fifty years ago, when the flame of civil and religious liberty was first kindled in this country, and spread *too soon* across the Atlantic, who, of all the gifted souls that genius marshalled under its standard, would have predicted such an event? Did the mighty spirit of Burke, when he beheld in his "mind's eye" all the horrors that afterwards befell poor France, or could the "prophetic ken" of Fox foretell this anomaly of nature? The man who could think it possible that the degraded African slave would take up arms in defence of his birthright and spend his heart's blood for its possession, would have been regarded as a madman, and his reflections branded as the dreams of a visionary.

But times have changed. We have seen the establishment of an independent nation by men of our own colour; the world has seen it; and its success and durability are now placed beyond doubt. There is something in the firm establishment of a free government by those who but lately were in the bonds of slavery that strikes us as manifesting in a peculiar degree the interposition of Divine Providence.

The commencement of the revolution of St. Domingo was looked upon with horror by men in all parts of the world. It was thought so unnatural a crime, that slaves should rise against their masters, that their downfall was earnestly desired and frequently prayed for by every one. Other revolutions have happened; other governments have been formed, but under far different auspices. The American revolution which first led the way in asserting the great principles of liberty, was hailed with enthusiasm by the wise and the good. It found advocates even in England, against whose oppression they were contending. The French revolution too, ere it acted those deeds of terror and madness which will not soon be forgotten, had supporters and well-wishers in every heart, except those whose feelings were blunted in the service of a cold and chilling despotism. But the revolution in St. Domingo, which taught the world that the African, though trodden down in the dust by the foot of the oppressor, yet had not entirely lost the finer sensibilities of his nature, and still possessed the proper spirit and feelings of a man. No one wished it well. No fervent prayer was put up for its success. None bid it "God speed." In their glorious career, alone and unaided, save by the arms of HIM who is ever ready to protect the oppressed, the Haytiens withstood the power of the greatest monarch that ever sat upon a throne. So true is it, that "the race is not always to the swift, nor the battle to the strong."

When we reflect upon the condition of those men who bade defiance to the chosen troops of Napoleon, commanded by one of his bravest generals, we are struck with astonishment and admiration. Most of their leaders were of little education, of still less experience in military affairs, and more expert in the use of the hoe and the spade, than in wielding a sword or levelling a musket. But the *occasion* called forth their hidden powers. The cause for which they fought developed talents unknown before to the possessor. And soon as the standard was raised and the blow that was to unrivet their chains forever, was struck, thousands arose of young and old, bond and free, eager to expose their lives and property in defence of what to every man should be dearer than life itself. The struggle of liberty against slavery; of light against darkness, cannot last long. And tho' our brethren of St. Domingo had to contend against "fearful odds," (being opposed by the flower of the French army), yet such success attended their noble efforts, that in a short time there was scarcely a Frenchman left on the island. Of the fifteen thousand troops which Napoleon had deemd sufficient to rivet new fetters for "the *slaves*," very few returned to France to tell the news of their disaster. Disease, famine, and the sword destroyed one after another, till finally Leclerc himself fell in the land over which in the proud exultation of his heart, he had fondly hoped to rule. Thus perished the French army, and so perish every attempt against the liberties of a people.

V. Independent Haiti

For Haitians, however, the picture was not so rosy. Although they had won freedom and independence, the state of their nation remained grim. International hostility (including naval blockades, economic embargoes, and even threats of invasion) was one major cause of independent Haiti's troubles. But there were internal causes as well. Principal among these were intractable political instability, civil strife, and a legacy of militarization.

After Christophe and Pétion assassinated Dessalines in 1806, they split the country. A former slave, Christophe took over the north with black support and crowned himself King Henri I in 1811. Pétion, a mulatto popular with free people of color, ruled the south as a republic with himself as president. Tensions were high between the two rulers and fighting broke out sporadically—a reflection of the fraught relationship between the two ethnic groups they represented. In 1818, Pétion died and was replaced by his lieutenant, Jean Boyer, also a mulatto and also an army officer. When Christophe took his own life in 1820, Boyer united the country under his rule. He then invaded and annexed the Spanish portion of the island (present-day Dominican Republic). In 1825, Boyer secured French recognition of Haitian independence, but at the heavy price of a 150 million franc indemnity. To pay this colossal sum, Haiti had to borrow the money. It was not repaid until 1947.

12. HAITI IN 1807[16]

Because of the international quarantine imposed on Haiti, it was difficult for outside observers—including foreign governments—to learn what was going on inside the country. Having refused to recognize the new republic, they did not have diplomatic missions that could send back reliable information. Instead, they relied on periodic

[16]Historical Manuscripts Commission, *Report on the Manuscripts of Earl Bathurst Preserved at Cirencester Park* (London: H. M. Stationary Office, 1923), 58–62.

reports from the merchants who still traded with the island and occasional visits by naval forces. Like all texts, these reflected their authors' assumptions and prejudices. The following is a report from a British merchant to the British foreign minister, Viscount Castlereagh.

"J. Clarke to Viscount Castlereagh" (June 22, 1807)

... An immense island ruled by three different chiefs; the first and the least considerable is the French general Ferrand at Santo Domingo; the second and far the most powerful and who wishes to be on the terms of the closest amity with this country is Henry Christophe, styled President of the State of Haiti since Feb. 17 last, when the new constitution was published at Cape François. Henry Christophe was the first general in rank next to Dessalines, called the Emperor of Haiti, after whose murder, though he had no hand in it, he was unanimously called upon to place himself at the head of the government. The third is Petion, a man of colour, and one of Dessalines' generals who, seeing with a jealous eye that men of colour had little chance of ever having one of theirs at the head of the state in a country where their number to the blacks is not in the proportion of one to fifteen, thought that the death of Dessalines was a favourable opportunity to try whether the mental abilities of the people of his description (the people of colour are the natural children of the ancient white inhabitants and not deficient in learning) could not at least in some parts of St. Domingo, where they were to the blacks in a more equal ratio, counterbalance real and physical power; and that he effected at Port au Prince when deputies had met there from the different parts of St. Domingo and were going to declare Henry Christophe their president for life. The influence and affluence of his people at that place, where in proportion to the northern parts of the island they are numerous, served his ambitious projects. To betray at once his fondness for power would not have answered his purpose—he knew too well that almost all the hearts and votes of the deputies were for Henry Christophe. To contrive then to have a constitution framed in such a manner as to render unacceptable to Henry Christophe the place of the chief magistrate under that constitution was all that he for the moment wished, and that he brought about by bribery and threats. The presidentship of the state only to be exercised for the space of five years was invested with so little power to operate the good of the country and put a stop to the crimes daily committed that Christophe immediately refused to accept it; but adored by his soldiers and the people was in the northern districts proclaimed their lawful chief, and afterwards by their constitution of Feb. 17 last nominated president for life with the right to name his successor, and generalissimo of the land and sea forces of the state of Haiti.

Petion, when apprized of the refusal of Christophe, for which he was prepared, began to descant at great length upon Christophe's thirst for power, and, under the cloak of patriotism hiding his preconcerted projects, found but little trouble at Port au Prince and the south dependencies to be made a chief under the very same name of President of the State of Haiti assumed by Christophe.

It may be now asked how long will Petion be able to retain his power in direct opposition to Christophe?

The answer, I think, is, as long as Christophe, who to the military character adds notions of humanity, will be unwilling to sacrifice men, and no longer; for his troops, far more numerous than those of his antagonist, being all composed of blacks and commanded by blacks, coming in contact with those of Petion, whose officers are men of colour like himself, when his soldiers are almost all blacks, will certainly have all in their favour; but that measure Christophe told me, my Lord, he would only resort to if some others he was making use of should prove ineffectual.

The consequence naturally to be drawn from the different situations of those three chiefs appears to me to be that the French general Ferrand, shut up in Santo Domingo with the rest of the French army that escaped the sword of the blacks under Dessalines, will not retain his post the moment England has fixed his fate; some of our frigates ordered to blockade closely the city of Santo Domingo, and by that cutting off all supplies by sea when at the same time the troops of Christophe would besiege it by land, would soon oblige Ferrand to act the same part General Rochambeau did at Cape François, to surrender with all his troops to our naval force to avoid falling in the hands of their sable enemies.

Secondly, that Petion, independent of his being at the mercy of Christophe's forces, whenever the latter shall choose to do it, has no hope of seeing his power last long, for the very parts that constitute it now will not certainly be long, left even to themselves, to operate its annihilation; the natural antipathy that at all times I saw generally existing between blacks and men of colour, though [it] seemed for the present to be stifled at Port au Prince, will soon show itself, and the usurped authority of a few over a mass of people cease to exist.

Of those two chiefs, my Lord, England in the first sees her enemy, and in the second, if she does not consider him in that light, perceives at least only a man whose ephemeral power is built on sand, and with whom all political connexion is to be avoided.

It is not so now, my Lord, of Christophe's situation. He is a warrior, a politician, and fond of commerce. He is a black man, commands to[o] numerous a black army, and rule[s] over a black people. His dominions are the only ones where are to be found fortresses of the greatest strength. I have visited some of the strongest holds on the continent, but I must confess none are to be compared for natural strength to those built now in Christophe's possessions at St. Domingo. With the troops he has under his command, and leaving the plain to an invading army if not at first able to contend with [it], and retiring to the mountains where everything has been prepared against such event, he could bid defiance to his enemies and see without almost any risk on his side their number dwindle to nothing in a short time: the climate is dreadful to European soldiery.

On such a man as Christophe, if England wishes to extend her trade more and more, she will not look with indifference. Acknowledging him publicly as the President of the State of Haiti, which he most earnestly desires, would put England in possession of all the trade of that country on very advantageous terms. I conversed daily with General Christophe; he looks on England as the first nation in the world and the English as the most virtuous people. He would sometimes say to me—"What difference, Mr. Clarke, between your nation and the Americans! In the moment of danger these forsook us, when the brave Captain Walker (a captain in his Majesty's navy) provided me with gunpowder when we were almost conquered by the French, and so it is to a man of your nation we are really indebted for our becoming an independent and free people. Let not the English be afraid for their colonies. The blacks of Haiti, if required of England, would most willingly in case of a rebellion amongst the slaves in the British islands assist in quelling it, but would never, never favour it. We from our hearts and also by one article of our constitution confine to our state the enjoyment of the sweets of liberty. The only thing we wish for is to be acknowledged by England as a free and an independent state; that we may rest assured that in the event of a peace between England and France (which would to God may never exist) the French should not again be left at liberty to attempt to reduce us, but that on the contrary their planning anything against us should be looked [on] by England as a declaration of war. I would, continued Christophe, have sent an envoy to England, had I been assured he would be received, for I cannot help, Mr. C[larke], looking on your King's licence to come to Haiti but as a wish expressed by England to be on the best terms with us. Try when you are back to your country to ascertain the fact and in case an envoy from me was to be received I should be glad to have a British consul at Haiti." And many things would Christophe add concerning the way to increase the population at Haiti, where negroes from the coast of Africa might be imported on board British ships and purchased at a price that would insure a handsome benefit to the merchants, who would besides the profit have the satisfaction of having procured happiness to those men who at their landing on the territory of Haiti would become free and immediately [be] allowed a certain tract of land for their maintenance.

It is no wonder Christophe should be desirous of increasing the population of his state. The wars have too much contributed to diminish it, when I really think had they always been in a state of peace, its increase would not have been inconsiderable; as there are annually more births than natural deaths at St. Domingo. Formerly, in that part of St. Domingo that belonged to His Most Christian Majesty, the population amounted to 500,000 slaves, 45,000 men of colour, and 22,000 whites; and as the deaths far exceeded the births amongst the slaves, it required the annual importation of more than 80,000 Africans to keep up that number of 500,000 slaves necessary for the cultivation of the island. At this time, in that very same part of St. Domingo, in spite of the wars and without any recruiting from Africa, are still, however, to be found more than 350,000 blacks and 22,000 men of colour, a certain proof that at least in that country war was less destructive of the human species than slavery.

Women at Haiti are less numerous than men, but as, except bearing arms, they perform all other works like the men, that inferiority is no real injury to the state.

Under the constitution which, considering the people it has to deal with, very properly lodges an immense power in the hands of the chief magistrate, I am certain the natives will be happy; but should England come to a treaty with Haiti, it would be advisable to stipulate that in no case whatever should a British subject be tried for his life by the tribunals of the country, for the laws of Haiti and the powers of life and death exercised by the President can never easily be digested by a British subject.

The government of St. Domingo being almost military, the discipline amongst the soldiery is very strict; so that there are now none of those murders committed which of late were too common, everyone being more or less under the immediate power of the public force.

The produce of the place is sugar, coffee, and cotton, but the sugar estates necessitating not only a great number of hands, but also immense buildings, and these having been almost entirely destroyed, the sugar cane is little cultivated now, and will be so long as the blacks of St. Domingo will consider their state precarious; for always ready to abandon the plain to an enemy if ordered so to take shelter under the protection of their inexpugnable fortresses built at the summit of their mountains, they are very loth to cultivate estates the possession of which they are not assured to retain. It is not so with coffee plantations. Such estates requiring less labour, men, women, and children being alike able to gather the coffee berries, the cultivation of the coffee tree has always been attended to, so that there is a great deal of that produce to be had at St. Domingo, but it was not lately so cheap as it should be, owing to the government having fixed by a momentary measure its price at about 8*d* English money per pound, when without that law, it could have been had at 6½*d*, the only price the trade of England can afford to give. Cotton is the third article of the St. Domingo produce. There is a great quantity to be procured there at 54*s* the hundred French livres, being only 4 lbs less than the English hundredweight of 112 lbs. Coffee, sugar, and cotton are subject to a duty of 10 per cent on exportation, and goods imported pay a like duty, and in order that the government should never be defrauded by false invoices of the goods imported, or lesser prices than those that are really given for produce exported, every article of goods that may be imported has a determinate price at the custom-house to Haiti and pay[s] duty accordingly, and goods exported likewise. The duty on cotton is perceived as if that article was sold for 24 dollars per hundred pounds weight, which is English money 108*s*, and as if coffee was sold at 25 sous—8*d* sterling: so that buy the produce cheap or dear the duty to pay is the same.

St. Domingo has occasion for most of the articles of our manufactures, but the government is above all in want of many thousands of hoes of a certain description, clothing for soldiers, firearms, saltpetre, and brimstone for making gunpowder, for they manufacture it. I have in hands from that government an order to a great amount, but as it does not specify the profit that is to be granted I shall have, I am afraid, some difficulty to execute it, though I can attest I have proof of the good faith of that government. . . .

Besides the importation and exportation duty, the government has the fourth part of every estate, the produce of which is so divided: the government ¼, the owner ¼, the cultivators ¼, and the other ¼ goes towards paying the necessary tools and for the estate. By cultivators, I mean the negroes belonging to the land for though they are called free, no man of that description can be absent without leave. In that respect there exists a great similarity between the boyars in the Russian Empire and the cultivators of Haiti.

13. HAITI IN 1826[17]

The following is a report on Haiti from a British naval officer. Written a year after French recognition, it discusses how Haitians were responding to it—and to the heavy indemnity.

"Commander Elliot, HMS Harlequin, Port-au-Prince, Haiti, to Rear-Admiral Halstead, Commanding the West Indies Station" (December 16, 1826)

It is a fact that the publick press of the Republick of Haiti affords no means of judging of the situation of the country or the feelings of its population, and from intercourse alone with the various classes in the community is it at all in the power of a stranger to arrive at any conclusion upon these important matters of consideration.

With such a conviction, therefore, mixed in society with the Englishman, the foreigner or the native, either publick functionary or private individual, it has always been my desire in an easy and unconstrained manner to turn the conversation to these subjects and from amidst a mass of matter, much of it indeed both uninstructive and uninteresting, I shall attempt to extract as distinctly and as briefly as I can what I conceive may be acceptable to you to receive upon the following heads of enquiry.

Firstly, the apparent content or dissatisfaction of the people, in the first instance with the professed form of the Constitution and secondly with its actual practice. The general tone of the domestic and foreign policy of the administration and the attachment or dislike of the nation to the person and measures of their present rulers. Secondly, the state of the military establishments. Lastly, the finances of the Republick.

The Constitution, nominally republican, is essentially a Military Despotism. The President holding his office for life with the choice of his successor, in complete possession of the military influence and power—and in all cases of legislation (money bills excepted) with the initiative voice, is precisely what has always been the case either by the title of chief, emperor, king, or president—the sole and absolute ruler.

---

[17]British National Archives, Admiralty, series 1, box 278.

From the date of the declaration of the Independence of Haiti to this hour, however divided it may have been into different states and however varied the forms of the Constitutions, the practice of government has in all cases been the same. The military chiefs (whatever their denomination has been) have directed and ruled the people.

It might be supposed that this striking difference between a declared republican form and a really arbitrary character of government afforded reasonable ground for cause of discontent, but from such a cause feelings of that nature (so far as I have been able to learn or judge) exist only in a limited degree.

In allusion to the Senate and House of Assembly, I cannot refrain from remarking that the accounts which are given of the talent and character of the elected, and the condition of the electors, joined to the military power of the President, renders the fact of their complete insignificance as deliberative bodies of restrictive tendency very reconcilable to the apprehension and expectations of any understanding.

The domestic policy of the present government, till the late promulgation of the "Code Rural," has been mainly directed to the support and increase of an immense military establishment. The progress of education, the restoration or construction of publick works, improvement of any description in the civil establishments, appear to have been completely neglected.

The "Code Rural," strictly compulsory in its nature, and operating upon a very numerous class of the community, constitutionally indolent and for many years plunged into a state of idleness and inactivity, is an experiment, the success of which leaves the greatest room for doubt and distrust. This law (entrusted for its execution to the military commandants of the districts), loaded with penalties of the heaviest nature, to the infliction of which the disinclination of the cultivators to hard labor or labor of any description may too frequently expose them, affording no protection against the exercise of the most absolute and unreflecting authority, appears in every point of view calculated to prevent the possibility of concealing from these unfortunate people the indisputable and painful truth that, much worse taken case of and incomparably more rigidly treated, their situation is altered alone by having become the slaves of masters of another color, and there is too much reason to apprehend of a much less amiable character.

The natural consequence of such circumstances and feelings has rendered this law most obnoxious to the great mass of the population and has excited sentiments of disgust towards the person and government of the President, which have been very unequivocally, as well as generally, displayed on several late occasions.

That the foreign policy of His Excellency the President, as it regards his engagements with the Court of Versailles, should be most unpopular cannot in any degree cause surprise.

In illustration of what is to follow, it may be useful in this place to say a few words on the origin of a distinction of feeling which manifestly exists between the two great classes of the population, the mulatto (or the coloured people) and the negro.

The coloured people, in point of numerical strength, not nearly half equal to the unmixid black, consider themselves to be superior (and with respect to intelligence and information, they actually are so) to their darker brethren of the Republick. Almost every officer of consequence in the nation, the Presidency inclusive, is filled by a mulatto. By virtue of one of the original laws of the state, decreeing the inheritance of property to the nearest relations by blood of the white proprietors (it being of course wholly unnecessary as well as impossible to produce any proof of legitimate descent) a large portion of the individual wealth of the country is in the hands of these people.

The negroes, in addition to their numerical strength, are possessed of a natural but savage resolution, in which the mulattos are very commonly deficient. Envious, avaricious, and perfidious, they are objects of fear and dislike to the coloured people, and conscious and proud of their own superior exertions in the revolutionary struggle, these sentiments are returned by them with hatred and contempt.

It has been supposed, and with great appearance of probability, that feelings of such a character (mingled perhaps with some inclinations naturally leaning towards the country and blood of his fathers) may have induced the President to receive with so little hesitation the Royal Ordonance of His Most Christian Majesty, for with every reason to apprehend intestine commotion, the policy of conciliating a powerful friend is sufficiently obvious. But whatever refuge this act may secure to him in the event of revolution, it has certainly rendered his political existence in the state imminently critical. Putting the tone of the ordinance wholly out of view (not calculated indeed to sooth any feelings of national vanity), the unwillingness of the people and principally the negroes to contribute one shilling more to the payment of the 30 millions of indemnity, has been clearly manifested, and the continuance of the remission of the half duties in favor of the French, it is universally acknowledged, cannot be permitted with such a sacrifice of financial resource as the expense of the establishments of the Republick renders utterly impossible.

In cases of emergency, the only councillors of real influence are the military chiefs and on my arrival at this place, I found the general officers in command of districts assembled at Port-au-Prince by order of the President, and tho' the cause for their meeting or the result of their deliberations was not made publick, there is no reason to doubt that it was to receive from His Excellency a statement of the difficulties which presented themselves in the faithful performance of his engagements with France, and to consider, in such a case, what course it would be most expedient to pursue.

A few of the most influential of the generals agreed in thinking that enough had already been done. 2 millions and a half had been paid. The relaxed system of the half duties in favour of the French had been admitted for 18 months. They declared that they would pay no more, and at all events, be the consequences what they might, they were of opinion that the duties should be equalized and that any particular engagement in favour of France should immediately cease. The various reasons which were urged by the President and his advisors to conciliate or temporize were wholly without success.

The negro officers particularly never could admit the force of any argument which rested upon the claim of France to particular advantages, as being connected with them by blood and old associations. They could have no feelings of such a nature in common with the mulattos. It was asked "why they were not called together before these steps were taken?" In whatever manner the President may have decided upon acting (for the meeting is dissolved and the generals have returned to their commands), it is most certain that to the present moment, his whole conduct in the matter has rendered him very unpopular. . . .

I have taken such opportunities as have offered to make some observations on the appearance, equipment, and discipline of the troops. Upon one occasion, I have seen 5 or 6,000 men under arms at the same time for the purpose of being reviewed by the President, consisting perhaps of some of the finest troops in the service and if I may be allowed to offer an opinion, the attention which the government is said to have devoted to this subject is by no means satisfactorily evinced by the conditions of the soldiery.

Of the artillery practice, I have seen nothing but I have heard that it is very inefficient: this corps is principally composed of colored people and I have been told that it is part of the policy of the President to exclude the negros as much as possible from that service.

The soldiers have no rations and they are paid at the rate of about 3 dollars per month Haitien currency, equal to about 10 shillings sterling, payments which have never been very fairly made. They are now about 3 months in arrears. The result of the straightened state of the publick treasury in consequence of the state remittances to France.

The military defence of Port-au-Prince either towards the sea or by land deserves no consideration.

In a previous observation on the appearance etc. of the troops, I confine myself strictly to the apparent slightness of their pretentions to the character of a regularly organized and disciplined force, for I suppose they must be excellently adapted for the desultory mode of warfare to which it is natural to conclude they would resort in the event of foreign invasion, and which the impracticable nature of their country for regular military operations so admirably favors. But the nature of the climate is perhaps the most solid defence and that circumstance considered, it is not easy to account for the necessity of a military establishment so large and expensive, except indeed it be intended for the purpose of keeping the people in subjection.

The only marine force consists of 4 or 5 small schooners, but I believe that the government desire to encrease it and encourage its improvement. . . .

The taxes are raised by the military commandants of the districts.

I have lately visited one of the finest plantations in this neighborhood and in the days of St. Domingo's prosperity it was considered to be one of the finest in the island; it is now the property of the President's family.

Out of a tract of 1700 carreaus (each carreau being nearly equal to 3 acres English), which were in full cultivation at the commencement of the Revolution, there are now only 10 carreaus, and I have been told by experienced people that this calculation may be considered to be a fair average of the present state of agriculture over the whole face of the country.

The progress of the condition of society to an advanced degree of civilization or the gradual decline toward a state of ignorance and barbarity is a subject of reflection which affords much matter for melancholy apprehension.

Without entering into further detail, I will merely observe that from all I have been able to learn upon the subject, nothing can be more discouraging than the present prospect. The account I have received of the condition of the people in the interior is beyond conception wretched and degraded. I will only add that I am informed that the brutal superstition of "Obeah"[18] is very largely practiced and after much enquiry on the subject, I have not been able to discover that the government take the least interest in preventing its exercice.

I have now drawn this statement to a close and I willingly leave to more experienced judgments the task of forming an opinion on the probability of consistency in a state of affairs thus constituted—but here I permit myself to remark that, with much depending on the personal character of the head of the government, it is to be lamented that a more sanguine hope for the progress of improvement is not to be derived from such a source of reflection. . . .

14. COLONIAL FEARS OF HAITI[19]

Haiti was a beacon of hope for enslaved people around the world. To slave owners, however, it represented an existential threat. Fear of Haitian influence—and even Haitian agents—was endemic in the slave societies that ringed the Caribbean and Gulf of Mexico. All took steps to prevent a repetition in their own lands of what had occurred in Saint-Domingue. The following document gives a sense of the fear—and real influence in inspiring a planned revolt of free people of color (called the Aponte Rebellion, after its leader)—of the Haitian example in Cuba.

"Formation of a Junta of White Colonists to Protect the Existing Order" (1799)

The insurrection of the slaves of the French colonies was what most strongly influenced the creation of this junta. . . . [Its purpose was] to study the means of ensuring that our growing negro population would remain tranquil and obedient. . . . The mere independence of the negroes of St. Domingue entirely justifies our present fear and concern for, if the English help them to spread their diabolical

---

[18]A Haitian religious tradition with West African roots.

[19]Jose Luciano Franco, *La Conspiracion de Aponte, 1812* (La Habana, Cuba: Editorial Ciencias Sociales, 2006), 9–11, 34, and 133.

ideas, we will certainly see in our country an eruption of these barbarians. At the very least, it is urgent that we take precautions to avoid a catastrophe. . . .

"Royal Order Barring Haitians from Cuba" (September 14, 1806)
It having come to the King's notice that emissaries of Dessalines have left St. Domingue to organize a revolution of slaves in the American Establishments of the European Powers, His Majesty desires that all men of color who arrive in the Spanish Colonies from St. Domingue be immediately arrested, as well as all Colonists who have contact with the aforesaid emissaries.

"Interrogation of Melchor Chirinos, a Chino of Havana, arrested under suspicion of being part of Aponte's 1812 conspiracy" (March 30, 1812)
He was asked if he saw the image of Our Lady of Remedios . . . in the house of Mr. Aponte. He responded that he never saw it, nor any other Saint's picture in the house of the aforesaid Mr. Aponte. But that Mr. Aponte sometimes showed him a painting of a *Negro King of Haiti with other Generals: Lauvertu [Louverture], Juan Fransua [Jean Francois] and Tusen [Toussaint]*; that Aponte sometimes showed them to Ternero [a free negro and ladino who also frequented Aponte]; that on another occasion he saw at Mr. Aponte's house various visiting negroes who, according to him, were French mulatto officers. . . .

15. HAITI AS SANCTUARY[20]

Haiti did not actually dispatch emissaries to foment slave revolt. It was desperate for international recognition and reintegration into the circuits of world trade. It pursued these goals by a strict policy of nonintervention in the affairs of the surrounding slave societies. But it refused to return slaves who escaped to Haitian soil. Independent Haiti was thus more than a symbol; it was a real sanctuary for people seeking to flee bondage. The following documents describe the fruitless efforts of two British pilots, supported by an admiral, to secure the return of their slaves.

Memorial of Robert McKowen to Rear Admiral J. E. Douglas (n.d.)
James McKowen, about six weeks ago, departed from Port Royal in a pilot boat schooner called the Deep-Nine, his sole property, for the purpose of cruizing off the East end of [Jamaica] to furnish shipping bound to Ports on the South side, and took with him a number of slaves to be put on board such vessels as pilots, and also had on board the following slaves, vis. Five Negro men named Dublin, Kingston, James, Archy, and Quashie, and two Negro Boys named Robert and James, the property of the said James McKowen.

[20]British National Archives, Admiralty, series 1, Box 268.

That the Deep-Nine continued cruizing for some time, during which several Pilot Slaves were put on board different Vessels to carry them into Port so that there remained on board only the slaves . . . particularly named, and the Deep-Nine becoming in want of wood and water, the same James McKowen took her into Rocky Point in St. Thomas in the East to get supplied with those articles, and there she arrived about the thirteenth day of January last, and the said James McKowen having given orders to the said Slaves to proceed on shore to procure the wood and water, he himself landed. In a few hours after, it was reported to James McKowen that the wood and water had been shipped and he then directed the canoe to be brought that he might go on board the Deep-Nine and proceed to sea, but instead of complying with such directions, the people proceeded to sea and ran away with the Deep-Nine, leaving the said James McKowen on shore at Rocky Point.

And your Memorialist further sheweth that on the fifteenth day of January last your Memorialist then being at sea in his Pilot Boat happened to put into Rocky Point and there found the said James McKowen who came on board of your Memorialist's Vessel and they proceeded in search of the Deep-Nine and about the twentieth day of January found her at Jeremie in the Island of Santo Domingo and represented the case to the Commandant of that place who referred the said James McKowen and your Memorialist to the President Petion, and thereupon they proceeded to Port-au-Prince where they had a personal interview with Petion who at first seemed willing to direct that the vessel and people should be delivered up but afterwards declared that by their Constitution and Laws he had not the power to deliver up the people. And your Memorialist and the said James McKowen deeming it essentially necessary and proper that this subject and the proceedings relative thereto with the Government of Hayti should appear in writing, they joined in a letter adressed to Petion, a true copy whereof is herunto annexed numbered one, to which they received the answer in French, a true copy whereof is also hereunto annexed, numbered two.

Your Memorialist further sheweth that the said schooner Deep-Nine was delivered up to the said James McKowen but sundry articles which were on board of her at the time she was ran away with being missing and the said slaves not having been delivered up the said James McKowen addressed another letter to Petion, a true copy whereof is hereunto annexed number three, to which no answer was received previous to the departure of your Memorialist, it having been concluded between the said James McKowen and your Memorialist that it was advisable for your Memorialist immediately to return to Jamaica and report the circumstances to the Commander-in-Chief upon the Station whilst he remained for the purpose of using his endeavours to obtain the missing articles.

To the above facts, your Memorialist begs leave to add that he has been informed that a Brown Man, a native of Guadeloupe but whose name is unknown, got on board the Deep-Nine at Rocky Point and seduced the said slaves to run away with the Vessel and carry her to Hayti.

Your Memorialist, impressed with the conviction that great mischiefs will ensue to this Island in general and more especially to the commercial part of the

Community should offences of this nature escape with impunity and feeling more particularly the danger which persons carrying on the Pilotage business are exposed if a system of protection so contiguous can be established for the encouragement of slaves to run off with the shipping in which they are employed, he deems it a duty incumbent upon him to call your attention to the subject and to entreat your interference to put a stop to so great an evil, and if possible to obtain the restitution of the slaves beforementioned that they may be brought to justice.

No.1 James and Robert McKowen to President Pétion of Haiti (Port-au-Prince, January 28, 1817)

We have already had the honour by a personal communication of making known to Your Excellency the circumstances that have brought us here to claim from the justice of your Govt the restitution of property that has been piratically taken from us, and to which you have in part had the goodness to accede, tho you decline to deliver up the individuals (also our property) who assisted in the commission of the Act upon the ground that by the 44 clause of the constitution of Hayti, persons of their description having once obtained a footing within the Republick, they are entitled to its protection. We cannot procure to call in question the policy of such an enactment, tho we trust we may be permitted to observe that from the peculiar nature of your exterior relations, more particularly with the Govt of which we are subjects, the sanction of such acts or even the protection afforded the perpetration thereof must necessarily involve political questions of very great moment, the agitation of which upon reflection Your Excellency may see the expediency of avoiding.

We do not however by any means wish to rest our claim upon such grounds. We seek only the justice that every civilized state affords in similar cases. Piracy and barratry are crimes so heinous as well as destructive in their consequences to commercial states that it is the interest of all, not only to discourage but to punish the commission of them with the utmost severity. We therefore pray that the individuals in question be delivered up to us that we may have them tried by the laws of their country.

Any persons bringing a vessel into a British Port under similar circumstances would be immediately thrown into Prison and tried for the offense.

To confirm the piratical intention of these people, we beg leave to observe that at the first small harbour they put into called Trou-bon-bon, they sought to purchase arms and ammunition for which purpose we consider is sufficiently evident. This circumstance awakened the suspicion of the commandant there who very properly arrested the people and seized the vessel.

We are well aware that it is your desire to prevent by every means in your power any piratical system obtaining ground along your coast, but if the present attempt be not made a pointed example of the Negroes in every drogger or small plantation not belonging to Jamaica will be availing themselves of your numerous bays and creeks to take refuge in and become a nest of daring marauders and this would render necessary that your coast should be continually watched by His Majesty's cruizers, which would cause very serious interruption to your trade.

We further beg leave to urge in favour of our claims that as master pilot we are more especially to protection as the lives and property of so many would be exposed to considerable risk if Negroes we have instructed with much labour and care are encouraged to desert from us and leave us without the means of bringing in the numerous vessels continually flocking to the ports of Jamaica.

Permit us to state to Your Excellency that during the long war between Great Britain and the United States, in more instances than one our boats with our Negroes on board were captured by the enemy's cruizers and carried into America from whence they were sent back to us, when the nature of the property was known.

We therefore again most humbly submit to Your Excellency's consideration the propriety of delivering up not only the vessel but the Negroes that came in her, four of whom are Boys who have been forced away against their will.

We likewise beg to call to Your Excellency's attention the hardships of our case. The value of the property at stake is to us of considerable magnitude. Our occupation is labourious in the extreme and to be thus deprived of our hard earnings is what we are confident is far from Your Excellency's wish.

If however from reasons of state policy you still conceive it necessary to refuse our claim, we entreat that you will be pleased to signify your reasons.

No. 2, Alexander Pétion, President of Hayti, to Mr. James McKowen (Port-au-Prince, January 30, 1817, 14th Year of Independence)

Sir, I have received your letter of the 28 Instant claiming the English Schooner Deep-Nine, together with the individuals who brought her from Jamaica to Troubon-bon as your property. I have just given directions for restoring to you the vessel and everything appertaining to her. But as to the men, they are recognized to be Haytians by the 44th Article of the Constitution of the Republick from the moment they set foot on its territory, and it is out of my power to restore them to you agreeably to your demand. Every country has its Laws, as you must know, Sir, and fortunately for the cause of humanity, Hayti is not the only one where slavery is abolished. The allusions you make in your letter cannot be attended with any serious consequences, because nobody here has been guilty of suborning subjects belonging to other Powers. But such persons as arrive on this territory must be protected since the laws require it. If there be among the men you claim any who have committed crimes against the rights of men, they will (on your furnishing me with proofs of their crimes) be delivered over to the proper Tribunals established for the purpose of taking cognizance of them by the local laws of the country of which they are now citizens.

Rear Admiral J. E. Douglas to President Pétion (Port Royal Harbour, HMS Salisbury, March 12, 1817)

General and President, upon the return of Messrs James and Robert McKowen, master pilots, from Hayti to this port, I have been put in possession of copies of the letters they addressed to you and of your answers regarding the detention at Hayti of seven slaves, the property of Mr. James McKowen, who ran away with his

Pilot Vessel, called the Deep-Nine, and carried her into "Trou-bon-bon," one of the ports of Hayti.

The reason you allege for refusing to deliver up those Slaves not appearing to me to be founded upon principles of either Publick or Private justice, I deem it my imperious duty to protest against their detention. You say that every country has its laws, a point not to be disputed, but you must be well aware, Sir, that if any one of those Laws should operate to the prejudice of the political interests of other countries or go to affect the property of the subjects of those countries, that Law will not be recognized—and if the power that has framed it should refuse to amend the objectionable points, it will as a natural consequence draw down upon itself the armed resistance of all that feel its hurtful effects.

The law of the Haytian Republick (44th article of the Constitution) upon which you have grounded your refusal to deliver up the Slaves, the property of Mr. James McKowen, a British Subject, is just such an one as I have alluded to—it aims a deadly blow at the Colonial Interests, not only of Great Britain, but of all the powers of Europe—it is fraught with most mischevious consequences to the owners of vessels employed in the Coasting Trade of this Island, and, indeed is big with evil, both to the Colonies and to the Mother Country.

In your letter to Mr. James McKowen, dated the 30th of January last, you say "if there be among the men you claim any who have committed crimes against the rights of men, they will, on your being furnished with proofs of their crimes, be delivered over to the proper tribunal established for taking cognizance of them and be tried by the local laws of the Country of which they are now Citizens." I would fain ask Sir, how Mr. McKowen could possibly be benefitted by the trial or punishment of his Slaves in Hayti. Would that remunerate him for the loss of their services? Would it operate by the publicity of its example, as a check to other slaves of this Island from being guilty, in future, of a similar offence? The answer is obviously no—and it must be strikingly impressive upon the mind of every man that the refusing to give up slaves who have been guilty of the atrocious crime of sezing and running away with their master's vessel, is opening the door to mischiefs of a still more serious tendency.

President Pétion to Rear Admiral Douglas (Port-au-Prince, March 29, 1817, 14th Year of Independence)

I have received the letter which you have done me the honour to write me, under date of the twelfth of the present month. . . .

I have answered Messrs James and Robert McKowen, agreeably to the dictates of my duties as Chief of the Nation, which I represent—and of which I am charged to enforce the laws; they are absolute and result from the general will, expressed in the Constitutional Act of the Republick. As Chief of the Executive powers, I can neither modify nor discuss them; they belong to the Nation itself.

There is no doubt, Sir, that the removal of a subject from one Govt to another places him under the jurisdiction of that which has adopted him, and that, once under its protection, he is no longer amenable to the laws of the Govt which he has abandonned. England herself furnishes an example of it, in the right of affording an asylum, which she has so generously exercised during the Revolutionary Convulsion which has agitated the world. That if the people claimed by Messrs James and Robert McKowen could have effected a footing on British Territory, there, where there are no slaves, the claim of those gentlemen would certainly not be admitted.

The dangers, which, it appears from your observations, are apprehended to result, serve rather to affect the Colonial System than that of your Government, the consideration which has ever animated us towards it, the justice and protection which we have never ceased to afford to the subjects of His Britannick Majesty, and to the Commerce of Great Britain; our Political Situation, in a word, which has maintained us in the peculiar exercise of our rights, without making any stir to the disturbance of those who are our neighbours, is an evident proof in favour of our Institutions.

You will do me the justice, I think Sir, to believe, that my conduct is influenced by no other motives than the discharge of the duty I owe to myself and to my fellow citizens; that no allotment has been held out by us, in the case in point, of the escape of the persons whom you claim and I have not the power to give up— and if any serious consequence should result, which is very far from my thought, I shall not have to reproach myself with having aggravated it. . . .

I have given directions to the Commandant of the Department of Grand Anse to deliver up to Messrs McKowen the articles which were taken out of the schooner Deep-Nine (which sloop has already been restored). If those articles should not be forthcoming, I will cause them to be paid for.

CHAPTER 9

The Struggles for Latin American Independence

From 1808 to 1826, Spanish and Portuguese America was rocked by struggles for independence. Along with the American and Haitian revolutions, these were the first wars of decolonization. When fighting ended, the two largest and oldest European empires in America were no more. In their place were more than a dozen republics. With the exception of Brazil, which adopted an imperial form of government, and several small European colonies, the western hemisphere had become republican.

There were many distinct independence movements with only tenuous connections between them. All of them were simultaneously civil wars and revolutions. They were civil wars because they pitted members of the worldwide Spanish polity (including in Spain itself) against each other. The causes of division were many. In addition to the fundamental split between loyalists (known as royalists) and those seeking independence, there were bitter ideological differences (between liberals and conservatives, republicans and monarchists, progressives and traditionalists), regional rivalries, and social conflicts. Many of these divisions persisted after independence—in Portugal and Spain as well as the new American states.

The struggles for Latin American independence were also revolutions. Although they were generally led by wealthy creoles who did not want to overturn the social order, most of them were liberals, imbued with Enlightenment culture, who wanted to build republican polities based on the principle of equality. They adopted a moderate approach to social change. They abolished formal racial classifications between Indians, people of mixed race, and those of European descent; but they maintained distinctions of wealth, education, gender, and class. They abolished slavery, but only gradually, and required freed slaves to serve post-emancipation "apprenticeships." In practice, however, the upheaval of war accelerated this gradualist, top-down approach to social change—notably through the recruitment (and emancipation) of slaves by both insurgent and royalist armies.

I. Forerunners of Independence

As seen in chapter 2, Spanish Americans had a number of grievances, many of which were related to the Bourbon Reforms. At the same time, Enlightenment ideas, as well as the examples of the American and French Revolutions, promoted hope for change among Spanish American liberals. Most only wanted to ameliorate their condition within the Spanish empire. But some dreamed of independence. In the 1790s, they began to act. The first attempts to achieve independence took the form of secret discussions with the British, French, and American governments; the publication of tracts calling for independence; and actual plots (never involving more than a handful of creole elites). Although these first stirrings of independence found little popular support, they created an ideology and a "useable past" that the later, successful independence movements tapped into.

1. COUNT DE ARANDA'S SECRET REPORT TO KING CARLOS III[1]

The Count de Aranda (1718–1798) was a Spanish soldier, diplomat, and states-man with a fondness for Enlightenment ideas. Like most aristocrats, he entered the military profession as a young man and rose rapidly to a high rank. After the Seven Years' War, he entered the diplomatic service, eventually serving as Spain's ambassador to Portugal, Poland, and France. After American independence, Aranda became concerned about the threat the United States posed to Spain's American possessions. His report to Carlos III discussed this threat and proposed an original remedy.

The independence of the English colonies is a source of fear and pain for me. France has few American possessions, but Spain, her close ally, has many which, from now on, will be exposed to great danger. . . . This is not the place to examine the opinion of some statesmen, both national and foreign, . . . on the difficulty of retaining our dominions in America. It has never been possible to hold such vast and distant possessions for so long. To this general consideration must be added several others specific to the Spanish possessions: the difficulty in sending aid; conflict between some governors and the inhabitants; the distance separating them from the supreme [judicial] authority . . .; the difficulty of getting accurate information at such a great distance. . . . The conjunction of these circumstances must add to the discontent of the inhabitants of America and ultimately induce them to seek independence once the time is right.

Therefore, without discussing these considerations in detail, we must accept that we face a serious threat from the new power [the United States] we have

---

[1]Juan Nido y Segalerva, ed., *Antologia de las Cortes de 1879 y 1881* (Madrid, Spain: Prudencio P. de Velascon, 1912), 12–17. Translation by Daniel Arenas.

just recognized in a part of the world where no other power exists to limit its ambition. The federal republic was born a pigmy. It needed help from two powerful nations, France and Spain, to gain independence. But a day shall come when it will grow gigantic and fearsome. It will forget our help and think only of expansion. Freedom of religion, the ease of settling new populations in its vast territories, its advantages as a young country, all this shall attract farmers and craftsmen from all nations. In a few years, we shall see this tyrannical colossus arise. Once it has grown sufficiently, its first move will be to establish itself in the Floridas in order to dominate the Gulf of Mexico, thus threatening communications with New Spain. It will try to conquer our vast Empire, which we will be unable to defend against such a powerful neighbor. . . . How can we ensure that the North Americans respect the Kingdom of New Spain when they can seize that rich and beautiful country? . . . I firmly believe that there is no other way to avoid these great losses than the desperate measure that I will now present to Your Majesty.

Your Majesty should abandon all his American possessions except for Cuba and Puerto Rico and whatever is indispensable [south of the equator]. These shall be a base or entrepot for Spanish commerce.

To do this in the manner best suited to Spanish interests, you should install three princes in America: one as King of Mexico, another as King of Peru, and the third as King of Costa Firme. Your Majesty will take the title of Emperor. . . . The three new kings and their successors will recognize Your Majesty and Your successors as supreme chiefs of the family. . . . These sovereigns and their children must marry Spanish princesses, and Spanish princes shall likewise marry the princesses of these new, overseas kingdoms. This will create an intimate bond between these four crowns. . . . Commerce will be strictly reciprocal, and each of the four nations will be united by the strongest offensive and defensive alliances. . . . As our industry is not strong enough to provide America with all the manufactured goods it needs, it will be necessary for France, our ally, to supply them with whatever we cannot provide, to the absolute exclusion of England. . . .

This plan will produce the following benefits: the contributions of the three New World Kingdoms will be much more profitable for Spain than the woeful amount of money America now sends; the Spanish population will grow, because the constant emigration to our [American] possessions will end; and once the three kings of America are firmly united by the measures I have suggested, no power in Europe could possibly equal them, not even Spain or France. At the same time, there will now be a power capable of opposing the American colonies or any other power seeking to establish itself in that part of the world. With the union of the kingdoms and Spain, Spanish commerce will trade national goods for the colonial merchandise our consumers need. We will expand our merchant marine and, consequently, the navy will be respected on all seas. The islands I have cited . . . will suffice for our commerce, without the need for other possessions. We will enjoy all the advantages our American possessions give us without any of their inconveniences.

2. JUAN PABLO VISCARDO Y GUZMAN, *LETTER TO THE SPANISH AMERICANS* (1810)[2]

The Peruvian Juan Pablo Viscardo (1748–1798) was originally a Jesuit priest. With the suppression of his order in 1767, he was expelled from the Spanish dominions and settled in London. Inspired by the French Revolution, he wrote his Letter to the Spanish Americans *in 1791. It is the most comprehensive statement of Spanish American grievances and a powerful argument for independence. It was disseminated widely in Spanish America and was translated into English and French.*

The New World is our country; its history is ours; and it is in the latter, that duty and interest oblige us to examine our present situation with its causes, in order to determine us, after mature deliberation, to espouse with courage, the part dictated by the most indispensable of duties towards ourselves and our successors.

Although our history for three centuries, as it relates to causes and effects the most worthy of our attention, be so uniform and plain, that one might abridge it into these four words—*ingratitude, injustice, slavery, and desolation. . . .*

All that we have lavished upon Spain has been snatched from ourselves and from our children, whilst our folly has been forging chains for us, which, if we do not break in time, no other resource remains to us than to bear patiently this ignominious slavery. . . .

An immense empire by us acquired, with treasures which surpass all imagination; a glory and a power superior to all that was known to antiquity: these are our titles to the gratitude of Spain and of her government, and to their most distinguished protection. Yet our recompense has been such that the most rigid justice would have hardly inflicted it as a punishment. . . . She exiles us from the whole of the Old World, and cuts us off from the society to which we are connected by every tie; adding to this unprecedented usurpation of our personal liberty, a second usurpation, no less important, that of our properties. . . .

We have been cut off, as in a besieged town, from every channel through which we might have been able to obtain from other nations, at moderate prices and by fair exchanges, the commodities which we wanted. The imposts of government, the fees of officers, the avarice of the merchants empowered to exercise conjointly the most unbridled monopoly—all bearing the same way, scarcity no longer left a choice to the purchaser; and as this mercantile tyranny might force us to have recourse to our industry to supply our wants, the government took care to enchain it. . . .

To fill the measure of our humiliating slavery, indigence, covetousness, and ambition have always furnished to Spain a host of adventurers ready to hurry to America; they arrive there determined to repay themselves amply with our

[2]William Walton, *The Present State of the Spanish Colonies* (London: Longman, Hurst, Rees, Orme, and Brown, 1810), vol. 2, 327–348.

substance, for that which they have advanced to obtain their employments; they indemnify themselves for the abandoning of their native country, for their hardships and dangers, by bringing with them all possible calamities. . . .

Thus it is that, after having thriven in robbery covered with the name of commerce, in exactions of the government in return for its liberal benefits, and in rich places for the innumerable crowd of foreigners who, under different denominations . . . gorge themselves to satiety on our properties; the remaining part is the continual object of the snares of those proud tyrants; whose rapacity knows no other bounds than those of insolence and the certainty of impunity.

Thus, whilst at court, in the armies, and in the tribunals of the monarchy, they lavish riches and honours upon foreigners of all nations, we alone are declared unworthy of them; we are declared ineligible of filling, even in our own country, places which, in the strictest right, belong to us exclusively. Thus the hard-earned glory of our ancestors is converted for us into an inheritance of infamy; and with our immense treasures we have purchased only misery and bondage. . . .

Let us consult our annals for three centuries; they discover to us the ingratitude and injustice of the Court of Spain, and its treachery in not fulfilling the engagements contracted at first with Columbus, and afterwards with the other conquerors, who gave to it the empire of the New World, on conditions solemnly stipulated. . . .

Three whole centuries, during which this government has without interruption held the same conduct with regard to us, afford complete proof of a meditated plan to sacrifice us entirely to the interests and convenience of Spain. . . . Notwithstanding the multiplied efforts of a false and iniquitous policy, our establishments have acquired such consistence that Montesquieu, that sublime genius, has said, "The Indies and Spain are two powers under one master, but the Indies are the principal; Spain is only the accessory. . . . "Reasons for tyrannizing over us are every day increasing; like a perverse guardian who is accustomed to live in pride and opulence at the expence of his ward, the Court of Spain sees with the greatest fear the moment approach, which nature, reason, and justice have prescribed, for emancipating us. . . .

The void and confusion which the annihilation of this prodigal administration of our wealth will produce, are not the only motives which engage the Court of Spain, in perpetuating our minority, to increase the weight of our chains: the despotism which, with our treasures, she exercises over the ruins of Spanish liberty, would receive a mortal blow from our independence. . . .

The claim of the Court of Spain to a passive obedience to its arbitrary laws is founded principally on the ignorance which she has taken care to keep up and encourage, especially with regard to the indefeasible rights of man, and the indispensable duties of every government; she succeeded in persuading the common people that it is a crime to reason on subjects which concern vitally every individual, and consequently, that it is a duty to extinguish the precious torch which the Creator has put into our hand to enlighten and conduct us. . . .

The treasures of the Indies gave to the crown of Spain an unforeseen preponderance which became so powerful, that in a very little time, it overthrew all the barriers raised by the prudence of our forefathers, for assuring the liberty of their posterity: the royal authority, like the sea overflowing its boundaries, inundated the whole monarchy, and the will of the king and his ministers became the general law.

Despotic power once so solidly established, even the shadow of the ancient Cortes existed no more; there remained to the natural, civil, and religious rights of the Spaniards no other safeguard than the will and pleasure of the ministers. . . . *Where kings will, the law gives way. . . .*

The government of Spain has . . . constantly consider[ed] you as a people distinct from the European Spaniards, and this distinction imposes on you the most ignominious slavery. Let us agree on our part to be a different people; . . . let us renounce a government whose excessive distance prevents us from procuring, even in part, the advantages which every man ought to expect from the society to which he is attached; this government, which in place of performing its indispensable duty, in protecting the liberty and safety of our persons and properties, has shewn the greatest eagerness to destroy them; and which, in place of endeavouring to render us happy, continues to overwhelm us with all kinds of calamity. Since the rights and duties of government and of the subjects are reciprocal, Spain has been first in transgressing all her duties towards us; she also has first broken those feeble bonds which would have been able to attach and retain us.

Nature has separated us from Spain by immense seas; a son who should find himself at a similar distance from his father, would without doubt be a fool, if in the conduct of his least concerns, he always waited the decision of his father. The son is set free by natural right: and ought a numerous people, who do not depend for any thing on another people, of whom they have no need, to be subjected to them like the vilest slaves?

The local distance which proclaims our natural independence is still less than that of interests. We have essential need of a government which would be in the midst of us, for the distribution of benefits—the object of the social union. To depend on a government removed two or three thousand leagues is equal to our renouncing those benefits; and this is the interest of the Court of Spain, which aspires to give us laws, to domineer over our commerce, our industry, our wealth, and our persons, only to sacrifice them to its ambition, its pride, and its avarice.

In fine, under whatever aspect our dependence on Spain may be viewed, we shall see that all our duties oblige us to put an end to it. We owe it in gratitude to our ancestors, who were far from lavishing their blood and sweat, in order that the theatre of their glory and of their labours should become that of our miserable slavery. We owe it to ourselves, by the indispensable obligation of preserving the natural rights received from our Creator, those precious rights which we have not the power to alienate, and which cannot, under any pretext, be ravished from us without crime. Can man renounce his reason, or can it now be torn from him by force? Personal liberty belongs to him, not less essentially than reason. The free enjoyment of those same rights is the inestimable inheritance which we ought to transmit to our posterity. . . .

The many regions in Europe, which the crown of Spain has been obliged to renounce, such as the kingdom of Portugal, . . . tell us that a continent infinitely larger than Spain, richer, more powerful, and more populous, ought not to depend on that kingdom, when it finds itself at such a distance; and still less when it is reduced to the hardest slavery.

The valour with which the English colonies of America have fought for the liberty, which they gloriously enjoy, covers our indolence with shame; we have yielded to them the palm with which they have been the first to crown the New World by their sovereign independence. Add the eagerness of the Courts of Spain and of France to assist the cause of the English Americans; it accuses us of insensibility; let at least the feelings of honour be roused—by outrages which have endured for three hundred years.

We have no longer any pretext to cover our resignation; and if we longer bear the oppressions which overwhelm us, it will be said with reason that our cowardice has merited them; our descendants will load us with imprecations, when, biting in vain the curb of slavery—of a slavery which they shall have inherited—they will remember the moment in which to be free, we had only to will it.

That moment is arrived, let us seize it with all the feelings of pious gratitude; and if our efforts be ever so faint, well-ordered liberty, that precious gift of heaven, accompanied by every virtue, and followed by prosperity, will commence her reign in the New World, and tyranny will be speedily exterminated.

3. FRANCISCO DE MIRANDA, DRAFT CONSTITUTION FOR SPANISH AMERICA (LATE 1790S)[3]

Francisco de Miranda (1750–1816) was a career revolutionary. Born in Caracas, Venezuela, Miranda served in the Spanish navy during the War of American Independence. Inspired by the example of the United States, Miranda left the navy and embarked on a journey that took him all over Europe and the Mediterranean world. Enthused by the French Revolution, Miranda volunteered for the French army and became a general. In 1793, he fled to England to save himself from revolutionary factionalism. But he remained committed to the revolutionary cause. His London home became a rallying point for discontented Spanish Americans. In 1807, he mounted an expedition to liberate Venezuela from royalist rule. Although it failed, Miranda was undaunted and tried again in 1811. This time he succeeded, but the independent Venezuelan republic he founded faced fierce royalist military opposition and was undermined by a terrible earthquake. Although he was given dictatorial powers to save the republic, Miranda was defeated. In 1812, the republic fell, and Miranda was captured. He died in prison four years later. The following document is a constitution for an independent America that he drafted during his London exile.

---

[3]Francisco Miranda, *America Espera*, ed. J. L. Salcedo-Bastardo (Caracas, Venezuela: Biblioteca Ayacucho, 1982), 208–210.

Territory: The state to be created from the Spanish American colonies will have the following boundaries: to the north, the Mississippi River from its mouth to its headwaters; to the west, the Pacific Ocean to Cape Horn, including islands up to ten degrees off the coast; to the east, the Atlantic Ocean from Cape Horn to the Gulf of Mexico and extending from there to the mouth of the Mississippi. Brazil and Guyana are not included. . . . Cuba will be included, because the port of Havana is the key to the Gulf of Mexico.

Form of Government: It should be mixed, like that of Great Britain. It will have an executive Power represented by an Inca, as Emperor. He will be hereditary.

Upper Chamber: It will be composed of senators or Caciques designated by the Inca. They will hold their offices for life, but will not be hereditary. They will only be able to be removed by the Censors. . . . They will be recruited exclusively among citizens who have been entrusted with the most important functions of the Empire, such as General, Admiral, Grand Judge in the Supreme Courts, Censor, Edile, or Questor. . . .

Chamber of the Commons: Will be elected by all the citizens of the Empire. . . . While they are serving, they will be inviolable, except in case of capital crime. Each legislature will sit for five years.

Judicial Power: Its members will be named by the Inca, chosen from among the citizens of the highest distinction within the Judicial Body. They will hold their offices for life and only be removable for corruption. . . . The high courts of England will be the model.

Censors: There will be two Censors, elected by the people and confirmed by the Inca. They will serve for five years and be re-eligible. Their function is to oversee the good conduct of the Senators. . . . They will also supervise the morality of the youth. . . .

Ediles: They will be elected for five-year terms by the Senate and be confirmed by the Inca. They will be in charge of all major highways in the Empire, ports, canals, public monuments, national holidays, etc. . . .

Questors: They will be nominated by the Chamber of Commons for five-year terms, be confirmed by the Inca, and be re-eligible. Their function is to oversee the conduct of the Treasury officials, public forest officers, customs agents, etc. . . . In a word, they will look out for the public interest in matters of state finance.

The Making of Laws: As in England, it will require the sanction of the three powers. . . .

II. The Napoleonic Wars and Latin American Independence

By the early 1800s, Spanish America had accumulated many grievances. They were potentially combustible but required a spark to burst into flame. Napoleon's aggression toward Spain provided that spark. In 1807, French troops crossed into the country to enforce the Continental Blockade. The following year, Napoleon forced both the Spanish king (Carlos IV) and his son Prince Fernando (the future Fernando VII) to cede him their rights to the throne. Napoleon then imprisoned them in France and gave his brother Joseph the Spanish crown. Most Spaniards refused to accept Joseph as their ruler and took up arms. They formed local governing committees (juntas) and a supreme junta to rule in the name of Fernando VII. Similar juntas were formed in parts of Spanish America. Exercising all the powers of government with little or no input from the homeland, these juntas were effectively independent. In 1810, the supreme junta had to flee to Cadiz, where it summoned a Cortes (an assembly of elected representatives from all Spanish dominions) to write a constitution.

4. PROCLAMATION OF KING JOSEPH TO THE SPANISH AMERICANS (OCTOBER 2, 1809)[4]

Napoleon and Joseph were keenly aware of the value of the Spanish American colonies, especially in the context of the ongoing war with Great Britain. To try to win them over, Joseph issued a proclamation summoning the Spanish Americans to recognize his authority. It failed miserably. By 1810, the French had recognized that they would never be able to assert control over Spanish America and changed their strategy. Now they would promote independence and did in fact send secret agents to foment rebellion. Their impact is unclear. The following is an excerpt from Joseph's proclamation.

Spaniards of my American possessions! Your Legitimate Sovereign summons you to submit, unless you prefer the penalty reserved for rebellious subjects. Those inhabitants of the Metropole whose blindness induced them to rebel have been punished for their crimes. Those who obeyed and heeded the voice of reason now enjoy peace, happiness, and tranquility. Would you be so blind as to reject what will improve your condition? Would you prefer the misleading suggestions of perverse men to the voice of a tender father who only wants your happiness? No, you cannot convince me that such a shameful thing could ever happen.

If, despite my wishes, you persist in error, I will punish you as I would a rebel son. The punishment will be so severe . . . that even the bravest will tremble. But if you calmly submit to the cause of justice and reason, I will reward you according to your merits. It is useless to uphold the rights of a phantom king who no longer has any, since he voluntarily ceded them to my august brother, the Emperor of the French. Am I not your legitimate king, since he transferred those same rights to me? . . . Yes, I am your king, and, with my entire being, I want to make you happy. . . . Disobedience will bring ruin.

My dear subjects, it is by your union with and confidence in me that the hydra of fanaticism can be destroyed. . . . From the degraded state in which you were kept

⁴www.banrepcultural.org/sites/default/files/proclama-de-don-josef-rey-de-las-espanas.pdf.   My thanks to Peter Hicks for providing this document. Translation by Daniel Arenas.

by a vicious and ignorant administration, you shall attain the greatest glory and prosperity. Do not heed the sly suggestions of hypocritical monks who want you to suffer in order to rule over you. Rather, listen to the words of peace of the learned pastors who guide you toward happiness and salvation. They will clarify the principles of religion, not deceive you or make you sin. It is time that the Spaniards of both hemispheres resume their former dignity among civilized nations. . . .

Do not imagine that Ferdinand, in whose name the European Spaniards have revolted approves of them. No. . . . Listen instead to how indignantly he speaks. . . . "Spaniards, your rebellion against your legitimate king fills my heart with pity. What do you intend? Do you wish to be exterminated? In the name of God, spare yourselves. My cession [of the Crown] was voluntary. It was meant to make you happy. In cahoots with the fanaticism that used to dominate Spain, the English . . . are fomenting civil discord to make us destroy one another and hold back our growth. Together with the Great Napoleon, we have taken this step to foil their evil projects. . . . Distrust anything that may be said to the contrary, since it will be false. You have enough sense to know that we seek only to lead the nation of Spain to the height of prosperity. So then, my dear Spaniards, regenerate yourselves under the standard of the virtuous king who governs you today. If you want to please me and achieve your own happiness, ignore the suggestions of the Junta that has led you astray, as well as the malicious promises of the English, a most Machiavellian nation. . . . They pretend to be philanthropists. But far from deserving this title, they are furious enemies of mankind! . . . They have inflicted years of war on Europe through their insidious insinuations. . . ."

"Under the decrees of the Great Napoleon, the pawns of this proscribed nation will be destroyed. Spaniards, remember the state of infamy in which you had been sunk . . . before I ceded my crown to the Great Napoleon. It is because I love you that I made that great sacrifice so that that extraordinary man could make you happy. Do not let the English deceive you with false promises. Think about the kings and nations they have betrayed; they plan the same fate for you. Exclude from your commerce those cruel enemies of the human race. . . . The Great Napoleon shall generously reward those who distinguish themselves by their attachment and loyalty. Traitors who persist in rebellion shall be punished with the greatest rigor and condemned to perpetual infamy. Trust in the measures the Great Napoleon had adopted to make you happy. Everything has been arranged for your security and happiness. . . . "

5. FRANCISCO MARTINEZ MARINA,
THEORY OF THE CORTES (1813)[5]

Francisco Martinez Marina (1754–1833) was a Spanish ecclesiastic, historian, and legal theorist. His Theory of the Cortes *wove together the Enlightenment idea of popular sovereignty with traditional Spanish ideas about the relationship between*

---

[5]Francisco Martinez Marina, *Teoria de las Cortes o Grandes Nacionales* (Madrid: Fermin Villalpando, 1813), vol. 2, 69–71, 96, 199–201, 380–382, 428–436.

the nation and its king. A powerful argument for the subordination of the mon-archy to national sovereignty, the work was banned by Fernando VII in 1817 as subversive.

Chapter 8, "The National Representative Body, not the Monarchy, has the Right to Interpret, Modify, and, for a Just cause, Change the Laws Relative to the Succession of the Kingdom"

The constitution of any state is the form and fundamental regulation, or system of government, adopted by societies. As the foundation of public tranquility and guarantee of the preservation, protection, perfection, and happiness of nations, as well as the bulwark of the citizens' liberty and security, it must be respected by all the members of the body politic—princes, magistrates and other public persons no less than private individuals. No one may violate, vary, or alter the constitution, except for society itself, for whose safety and prosperity it has been established. . . . Who can doubt that the nation can change what it has instituted by common consent and adopt something more beneficial? . . .

From this, it naturally follows that the nation is obliged to maintain . . . the laws relative to the succession. . . . Without a doubt, the prince designated to succeed and his descendants have a real right to the royal dignity. . . .

But it is incontestable and indubitable that this right is subordinate to that of the nation and the prosperity of the state. Consequently, if the established method [of succession] were destructive of public order and harmful to society, or if changing it would be beneficial, in that case the body politic could interpret, alter, or modify it. . . .

We must reject the ancient opinion, born in barbaric times when the most basic notions of philosophy and public law were entirely unknown, that allowed the prince to dispose of his kingdom at will, just like his own property, or of instituting as heir whomever he wanted. . . . In this view, the prince is a great property-owner and the kingdom his hereditary property just like a private individual with his field and flocks. With what speed did this doctrine spread to all the states of Europe and with what obstination have learned men upheld this maxim, so injurious to humanity and so antithetical to reason and good policy! . . . No one can revoke, alter, or modify the laws relative to the order of succession but the nation itself, source of government and sovereignty. . . .

This is even more the case in Spain than in other countries, because, as we have already demonstrated, its government was originally elective. . . .

We have said, and it is necessary to repeat it a thousand and one times, that sovereignty resides naturally and essentially in the nations who, for reasons of convenience and public utility . . . lent its exercise to a single person and his descendants. . . .

Chapter 17, "On Sovereign Authority; and, Firstly, Legislative Power"

The founders of the Spanish monarchy who, for reasons of convenience and public utility, deposited in a sole person the exercise of sovereign authority, . . . did not think it advantageous to society to give him legislative power and grant him absolute power to make new laws, or to change, modify, suspend, or annul existing ones. Understanding that the concentration of those powers in a single person would be destructive of national liberty and fatal to the security of the citizen, they reserved part of that power for themselves, to oppose the despotism of kings and repress abuses of executive power with the sacred check of the law. What is more just and sacred than that those subject to the [law] participate in its formation? And given that there is no law greater than the happiness of all, who is more capable than society itself of knowing the laws that can make it happy?

I am not claiming that the Spanish reserved for themselves legislative power in such a manner as to absolutely exclude their kings from intervening in the formation of the law. . . . Rather, from the origin of the monarchy until the time of Austrian domination, all laws were made in great assemblies of the kingdom . . . or by the king with the agreement, consent, and council of the nation. . . .

Chapter 18, "Continuation of the Previous Chapter"
For the laws to be valid, they must be made in the general Cortes, or by the members of the Great Council, or proposed with the agreement and council of the representatives of the nation. . . .

Chapter 30, "On the Power of Taxation and the Right to Demand Imposts and Subsidies. Do Princes have an Absolute and Unlimited Authority to Impose Taxes and Contributions?"
In civil society, everything should lead toward the good, the security, and the prosperity of the people. . . . All members of society must cooperate and contribute, according to their means, to this important object. The security of persons and the protection of individual property, which is the goal and benefit of the general association and the most sacred of all rights, demand many sacrifices and require that individuals relinquish part of their liberty and property in order to provide for the needs of the state, the upkeep of the head of the state, of the magistrates, and of the armed forces. . . .

However, since natural law does not permit anyone to infringe the property or dispose of the holdings of the body politic . . . except for the nation itself, it alone can deprive individuals of part of their property to form the national treasury. . . .

It follows from this incontestable and luminous principle that kings have neither the right nor legitimate authority to impose taxes unless the nation has directly or implicitly given them that power. . . .

But the prince who finds himself invested with such a great power must not regard the revenues raised from the people as his own property, nor lose sight of the purpose for which they were granted. . . .

Many other nations, wiser and more prudent, have not found it convenient or safe to entrust their princes with an authority so easy to abuse. . . .

Chapter 36, "Does the Political Existence of Kings Depend upon Fulfilling Their Duties? Is the Right of the Sworn and Acclaimed Monarch to his Crown Irrevocable?"

The essential rights of nations, rights inscribed by the hand of God on the hearts of man, cannot be annihilated by twenty centuries of tyranny and oppression. And if despotism and arbitrary government—backed by superstition and protected by an army of fanatics who, astutely taking advantage of the ignorance and credulity of the people, propagate error and superstition in the guise of religion—managed for a time to obfuscate and obscure the truth, manipulate the vulgar masses, . . . and overcome the most sacrosanct laws of society, still no one can ever destroy rights based on the unchanging foundation of reason and nature. . . .

It has always been and will always be an incontestable principle that men only joined together in society, formed a body politic, and subjected themselves to its laws for their own convenience and happiness. The social body, the source and location of sovereign authority, not being able to exercise it itself, entrusts its exercise to a body of chosen persons or to a single man . . . a luminous principle from which naturally derives the following maxims: that political authority is established only for the common good of all citizens, that it does not change its nature because it has passed from the body of the nation into the hands of a prince or monarch; that all supreme magistrates must understand that they have been granted power only to provide for the security of the state and the happiness of the people; that consequently, they may not abuse that authority nor seek in its exercise their own satisfaction or particular interests. Far from it, they are required to direct all their intentions, views, undertakings, actions, and operations toward the greater good, glory, and honor of the state and the people. . . .

But if a prince, disdaining the most sacred conditions and pacts, transgresses the limits prescribed by the nation, tramples all rules, brazenly violates the fundamental laws, shamelessly attacks the constitution of the state, the rights of the people, and liberties of the nation, and if, finally, having lost all notions of justice and sentiments of humanity, he uses his power to ruin of the republic, who can doubt that he has forfeited his dignity, titles, and rights? . . . [In such a case], the people recovers its liberty and independence, takes back sovereign authority, can resist the prince's unjust orders, defend itself against him as a public enemy, judge him, free itself from his domination, and depose him! . . . Such is the privilege and right of political societies, a right that the Spanish nation has used on different occasions [in the past]. . . .

6. COLONIAL REPRESENTATION IN THE CORTES (1810)[6]

In September 1810, the Cortes began to meet in Cadiz. It included representatives from Spanish America and the Philippines, as well as Spain itself. Its liberal majority was committed to establishing electoral, representative government. The constitution

---

[6]*Diario de Sesiones de las Cortes Generales y Extraordinarias*, 5–7, 17–18, 21, 35–38, 43–44. Biblioteca Virtual Miguel de Cervantes, http://www.cervantesvirtual.com/obra/diario-de-sesiones-de-las-cortes-generales-y-extraordinarias--5/

it decreed in 1812 (generally called the Constitution of Cadiz) was one of the most liberal documents of the age. By enshrining the principle of equality and giving Spanish Americans a proportionate voice in government, it could have addressed their grievances and preserved the political unity of the Spanish Atlantic. But the European deputies feared that the more populous American provinces would be too powerful if the criteria of citizenship and representation were too broad. To limit colonial representation, they denied automatic citizenship to people of mixed racial ancestry (although not Indians) and entirely excluded slaves. Many colonial deputies (who were all wealthy creoles) opposed these attempts to restrict American representation. Some, however, were more concerned to preserve racial hierarchies than to secure greater representation. The following excerpts from the Cortes' debates over American representation give a sense of the conflict over this issue.

Session of September 25, 1810

The commission of the American deputies . . . wanted to issue a declaration to the American dominions to complement the recent decrees [installing the Cortes]. Some said that it was necessary to reassure the Americans that their rights would be equal to those of European Spaniards, that they would be given national representation as an integral part of the Monarchy, and that an amnesty or pardon would be granted for misdeeds related to the recent divisions in parts of America. The [American] deputy José Mejia Lequerica asked that this proposal should be discussed in secret session. Nevertheless, the subject was discussed. The American deputies emphasized the necessity, justice, and usefulness of accompanying the decrees with a declaration, while many of the European deputies argued that this would be ill-timed at the present moment. . . .

Finally, the majority decided that the American deputies' proposal could not be voted on at the present moment . . . and postponed further discussion. . . .

Session of October 1, 1810

Mr. Mejia renewed the proposition the American deputies had made on September 25th, that the Americas be considered an integral part of Spain and that amnesty that should be granted for the many errors that had occurred in certain American provinces. . . .

[After some debate, the majority again voted a postponement. In the course of these proceedings, Mejia reportedly warned that "without an army, America will not submit; without money, there will be no army; and without America, there will be no money."]

Session of October 3, 1810

The American deputies renewed their motion. One of the deputies of Buenos Aires distilled it down to the following points:

1. That the Cortes expressly decrees . . . that the overseas territories are an integral part of the Spanish Monarchy.

2. That the government not severely punish those Americans who indulged in turbulence and unrest; but that the Cortes investigate the disorders and inform itself of what the [royal] government has done to address it.

[The majority again voted to postpone consideration of the matter.]

Secret Nighttime Session of October 10, 1810

This session was devoted exclusively to discussing the concerns of the American deputies.

This issue was discussed at length, rehashing what had already been said on other occasions. The majority of the American deputies argued that the declaration they sought in favor of the Americas was just, politic, and appropriate. But the majority of the European deputies felt that there was not enough time to decide on such important points, which would require gathering much information and, moreover, the presence of the propertied deputies of America. In the wide-ranging and lively debate that ensued, there was a particular focus on the declarations that had already been made in favor of the Americans by the Central Junta and the Regency. The American deputies also emphasized how imperative it was for the Cortes to ratify those declarations, which established the legal principle that the overseas territories were an integral part of the Monarchy and that they enjoyed equal rights with the Motherland. For these reasons, the American deputies insisted that America be given greater representation in the Cortes. Some American deputies even insisted that America's commercial interests be taken into account. Finally, they asked for a general pardon for the troubles that had occurred in several parts of America, so long as the legitimate government were recognized. Although convinced of their perfect brotherhood with the Americans, many European deputies insisted that a declaration was not a pressing matter at present. Seeking to demonstrate the grave inconveniences which would result for Spain and even the overseas dominions, they also spoke against admitting into the national representation the different castes and people of color of America. This discussion of castes degenerated into heated arguments for and against. . . . Mr. Perez de Castro presented a compromise bill recognizing overseas dominions as an integral part of the Monarchy, but making no mention of commerce or representation. This bill was added to the others which had already been presented. . . .

It was decided that there would be another closed session the following night to deliberate on these important points.

Secret Nighttime Session of October 11, 1810

This session was held to vote on the proposition of the American deputies. . . . Three proposals or draft decrees were read. That of Mr. Perez de Castro received the most votes. He rose to speak and, among other things, stated that nothing in the decree touched upon the issue of free trade because of the lack of data about it and also to avoid the inconveniences that it might occasion. He also stated that the question of representation should not be raised until the form of the constitution had been settled. In his speech, he explained the grave inconveniences that would attend any contrary resolution.

Opposing these ideas, Mr. Mejia insisted upon the claims of the American deputies and urged that the Cortes adopt the decree presented by them.

And Mr. Vincente Morales, deputy of Peru, proposed expunging from the decree all words tending to give equality to the colored castes, because of the grave dangers that such equality would produce, especially in Peru. . . .

Mr. Arguello proposed closing the session and postponing a decision until another day; this was approved by Mr. Rodrigo and other deputies.

Mr. Mejia insisted that the Cortes proceed to a vote. . . .

Since it was so late at night and since the majority felt that the matter could not be decided in this session, it was asked:

"Should this matter, which had been sufficiently discussed, be postponed to another day or not?"

The vote was to defer it to another day.

Session of October 14, 1810

The session being opened, Mr. Toledo asked the Cortes to treat the much-discussed American business.

Mr. Power, deputy of Puerto-Rico, presented a bill, taken from that of Mr. Perez de Castro, and it was read three times to see if it would be approved.

Mr. Morales, deputy of Peru, presented another bill, that varied slightly. It was also read three times.

As opinion was quite divided on the two bills, . . . it was asked:

"Should we vote on the first or the second?"

It was decided to vote on the first bill, Mr. Power's.

The deputies proceeded to vote. New debates broke out, which interfered with the voting process, and the decree was altered slightly, as follows:

"The General and Extraordinary Cortes confirm and sanction the incontrovertible principle that the Spanish dominions of both hemispheres form a same and single Nation, one sole family, and that the natural born subjects originating from the said dominions, whether European or American, are equal in rights. The Cortes must treat with particular interest everything that can contribute to the happiness of the overseas territories. It is also charged with determining the number and form required to ensure the national representation of both hemispheres. The Cortes likewise decree that, once the overseas territories which have been the scene of troubles have recognized the legitimate authority that has been established in the Motherland, there be a general pardon. . . ."

The proposed decree was read three times and, after observations and corrections had been made, the Cortes proceeded to a vote, asking:

"Is the present bill approved in these terms or not?"

The bill was approved in these terms.

7. MANIFESTO TO THE MEXICAN PEOPLE FROM THEIR REPRESENTATIVES TO THE CORTES (NOVEMBER 6, 1813)[7]

The following document is an excerpt from a protest written by the Mexican deputies to the Cortes expressing colonial frustration with the policies of that body.

Fellow citizens! Until the year 1810 foreign domination trampled our rights; and the evils of arbitrary power, exercised with fury by the cruelest conquerors, did not even permit us to ask if liberty was a real benefit or only a bauble to captivate the frivolity of the people. Sunk in ignorance and servitude, we were unaware of the social contract, happiness was banished from our hearts, and the habit of obedience inherited from our forefathers reigned supreme. The royal court seemed to us a palace of infallibility, from whence the oracle was occasionally heard, terrorizing us with the majesty of its voice. We adored, as did the Athenians, an unknown God, and so did not suspect that there were other principles of government than the political fanaticism that blinded our reason. The passage of time had so ingrained the habit of tyranny that the viceroys, councilors, captains-general, and other subaltern ministers totally controlled our lives and goods. . . . The shield of law covered all their crimes, and the complaints of the oppressed were either not heard or were cut short by the approbation with which the king honored their iniquitous proceedings. . . .

This unhappy situation, under which the nation has long suffered, would still endure if the chaos of the throne and the extinction of the reigning dynasty had not created a new relationship with the peninsula. Its sudden insurrection gave hope to America that it would be considered as a free nation by the new government and equal to the metropole in rights, just as it had been equal in loyalty and love for the sovereign. The world can attest to our heroic zeal for the cause of Spain, and the generous sacrifices we make for its defense. While they promised us that we would participate in the new system of government that was being introduced in the metropole in the first period of revolution, they did not fulfill any of our hopes. We kept watch for the happy moment, so many times announced, when the bonds of three centuries of slavery would be forever torn asunder—such was the language of the new government, such were the hopes they dangled in their misleading manifestos and hallucinatory proclamations. The name of Ferdinand VII, under which were established the Juntas in Spain, served only to prevent us from imitating their example and to deprive us of the advantages that the reform of our domestic institutions would produce. . . . The Central Junta intended only

---

[7]*Colección de Documentos para la Historia de la Guerra de Independencia de Mexico de 1808 a 1821*, ed. Juan E. Hernandez y Davalos, vol. 5, ed. Virginia Guedea and Alfredo Avila (Universidad Nacional Autonoma de Mexico, 2007), 1–6. Proyecto Independencia de Mexico. Universidad Nacional Autonoma de Mexico. http://www.pim.unam.mx/catalogos/hyd/HYDV/HYDV092.pdf. Translation by Daniel Arenas.

to perpetuate in America the despotism and ancient order of things introduced in the time of kings. . . .

From the creation of the first regency, we found ourselves elevated to the dignity of free men and were summoned to the Cortes of Cadiz to seek the happiness of the two worlds. But this step, that should have promised so much to oppressed America, instead consecrated its slavery and decreed its inferiority to the metropole. . . . There the Peninsula's need for our help, nor the growing belief that only independence could free us from the havoc of despotism, were enough to earn us our rightful place in the Cortes. . . . Before any other province rose up against these injustices, Caracas claimed its rights and armed itself to defend them. It created a junta, a paragon of moderation and wisdom. And when insurrection, like a seedling in fertile soil began to produce the fruits of life and liberty in that part of America, . . . our immense continent prepared to imitate the example of Venezuela. . . .

III. Declaring Independence

Although the Napoleonic invasion of Spain and imprisonment of its monarch had severed the connection between the metropole and the colonies (thus making Spanish America independent in practice), there was no rush to declare formal independence. Like those in Spain, the juntas that took power across Spanish America claimed only to be ruling in the name of their legitimate king, Fernando VII. They based their claims on the traditional Spanish political doctrine that, in the absence of the king, power reverted to the people until his return. Explicit declarations of independence came only gradually, their timing determined by specific local circumstances. The first was issued in 1811 by Venezuela and the last in 1830 by Ecuador.

8. VENEZUELAN DECLARATION OF INDEPENDENCE (JULY 5, 1811)[8]

In April 1810, the Captain-General of Venezuela was deposed and replaced by a Supreme Junta in Caracas. Cities across Venezuela and New Granada (modern-day Columbia) followed suit, creating juntas of their own. To establish a unified governmental framework, the Caracas junta invited the provinces of Venezuela to send delegates to a congress. Seven of ten Venezuelan provinces agreed. Their deputies met in Caracas in July 1811. Although they had not been planning on declaring independence, radical deputies led by Bolivar and Miranda convinced them to adopt a declaration of independence and establish the first Venezuelan Republic. This was the first formal declaration of Latin American independence.

---

[8]British National Archives, Foreign Office, Series 72, Box 125.

We, the representatives of the federal provinces of Caracas, Cumana, Barinas, Margarita, Barcelona, Merida, and Truxillo, constituting the confederation of Venezuela, on the southern continent of America, in congress assembled; considering that we have been in the full and entire possession of our natural rights since the 19th of April 1810, which we resumed in consequence of the transactions at Bayonne, the abdication of the Spanish throne, by the conquest of Spain, and the accession of a new dynasty, established without our consent. While we avail ourselves of the rights of men, which have been withheld from us by force for more than three centuries, and to which we are restored by the political revolutions in human affairs, we think it becoming to state to the world the reasons by which we are called to the free exercise of the sovereign authority.

We deem it unnecessary to insist upon the unquestionable right which every conquered country holds to restore itself to liberty and independence; we pass over in a generous silence the long series of afflictions, oppressions, and privations, in which the fatal law of conquest has indiscriminately involved the discoverers, conquerors, and settlers of these countries, whose condition had been made wretched by the very means which should have promoted their felicity, throwing a veil over three centuries of Spanish dominion in America, we can confine ourselves to the narration of recent and well-known facts, which prove how much we have been afflicted; and that we should not be involved in the commotions, disorders, and conquests which have divided Spain.

The disorders in Europe had increased the evils under which we before suffered; by obstructing complaints and frustrating the means of redress; by authorising the governors placed over us by Spain to insult and oppress us with impunity, leaving us without the protection or support of the laws.

It is contrary to the order of nature, impracticable in relation to the government of Spain, and has been most afflicting to America that territories so much more extensive and a population incomparably more numerous should be subjected and dependent on a peninsular corner of the European continent.

The cession and abdication made at Bayonne . . . authorized the exercise of these rights, which till that period the Americans had sacrificed to the preservation and integrity of the Spanish nation.

The people of Venezuela were the first who generally acknowledged and who preferred that integrity, never forsaking the interests of their European brethren, while there remained the least prospect of salvation.

America had acquired a new existence; she was able and was bound to take charge of her own safety and prosperity; she was at liberty to acknowledge or to reject the authority of a king who was so little deserving of that power as to regard his personal safety more than that of the nation over which he had been placed.

All the Bourbons who concurred in the futile stipulations of Bayonne, having withdrawn from the Spanish territory contrary to the will of the people, abrogated, dishonored, and trampled upon all the sacred obligations which they had contracted with the Spaniards of both worlds who, with their blood and treasures, had placed them on the throne, in opposition to the efforts of the house of Austria;

such conduct has rendered them unfit to rule over a free people, whom they disposed of like a gang of slaves.

The intrusive governments which have arrogated to themselves the authority which belongs only the national representation, treacherously availed themselves of the known good faith, the distance, and effects which ignorance and oppression had produced among the Americans to direct their passions against the new dynasty which had been imposed upon Spain, and in opposition to their own principles, kept up the illusion amongst us in favor of Ferdinand, but only in order to baffle our national hope, and to make us with greater impunity their prey; they held forth to us promises of liberty, equality, and fraternity, in pompous discourses, the more effectually to conceal the snare which they were insidiously laying for us by an inefficient and degrading show of representation.

As soon as the various forms of the Spanish government were overthrown, and others had been successfully substituted and imperious necessity had taught Venezuela to look to her own safety in order to support the king, and afford an asylum to their European brethren against the calamity by which they were menaced, all their former services were disregarded; new measures were adopted against us; and the very steps taken for the preservation of the Spanish government were branded with the titles of insurrection, perfidy, and ingratitude, but only because the door was closed against a monopoly of power which they had expected to perpetuate in the name of a king whose dominion was imaginary.

Notwithstanding our moderation, our generosity, and the purity of our intentions, and in opposition to the wishes of our brethren in Europe, we were declared to the world in a state of blockade, hostilities were commenced against us; agents sent among us to excite revolt and arm us against each other; whilst our national character was traduced and foreign nations excited to make war upon us.

Deaf to our remonstrances, without submitting our reasons to the impartial judgment of mankind, an deprived of every other arbitration but that of our enemies, we were prohibited from all intercourse with our brethren; and adding contempt to calumny, they undertook to appoint delegates for us and without our consent, who were to attend their Cortes, the more effectually to dispose of our persons and property and render us subject to the power of our enemies.

In order to defeat the wholesome measures of national representation, when obliged to recognize it, they undertook to seduce the ratio of our population, submitting the forms of election to servile committees, acting at the disposal of arbitrary rulers; thus insulting our inexperience and good faith, and utterly regardless of our political importance, or our welfare.

The Spanish government, ever deaf to the demands of justice, undertook to frustrate all our legitimate rights by condemning as criminal and devoting to the infamy of the gibbet, or to confiscation and banishment, those Americans who at different periods had employed their talents and services for the happiness of their country. This treatment we experienced when of late we were compelled to look to our own security and to avert those disorders and horrible calamities which we could perceive were otherwise inevitable and from which we shall ever keep aloof;

by their fell policy they have rendered our brethren insensible to our misfortunes, and have armed them against us; they have effaced from their hearts the tender impressions of love and consanguinity, and converted into enemies many members of our great family.

When, faithful to our promises, we were sacrificing our peace and dignity to support the cause of Ferdinand of Bourbon, we saw that to the bonds of power by which he united his fate to that of the Emperor of the French, he added those of kindred and friendship, and that on this account the existing Spanish rulers themselves have already resolved to acknowledge him only conditionally. In this painful state of perplexity, three years have elapsed in political irresolution, so dangerous, so fraught with evil, that this alone would have authorized the determination which the faith we had pledged and other fraternal attachments had caused us to defer till imperious necessity compels us to proceed further than we had first contemplated; but pressed by the hostile and unnatural conduct of the Spanish rulers, we are at length absolved from the condition which we had taken and not take upon us the august sovereignty which we are called here to exercise.

But as our glory consists in establishing principles consistent with human happiness and not erecting a partial felicity on the misfortunes of our fellow mortals, we hereby proclaim and declare that we shall regard as friends and companions in our destiny, and participators in our happiness, all those who, united by the relations of blood, language, and religion, have suffered oppression under the ancient establishments and who shall assert their independence thereon, and on any foreign power whatsoever, engaging that all who shall co-operate with us shall partake in life, fortune, and opinion, declaring and recognizing not only these, but those of every nation, in war enemies, in peace friends, brethren, and fellow citizens.

In consideration, therefore, of these solid public and incontestable motives, which force upon us the necessity of re-assuming our natural rights, thus restored to us by the revolution of human affairs and in virtue of the imprescriptible rights of every people to dissolve every agreement, convention, or social compact which does not establish the purposes for which alone all governments are instituted, we are convinced that we cannot and ought not any longer to endure the chains by which we were connected with the government of Spain; and we do declare, like every other independent people, that we are free and determined to hold no dependence on any potentate, power, or government than we ourselves establish; and that we now take among the sovereign nations of the earth the rank which the Supreme Being and nature have assigned to us, and to which we have been called by the succession of human events, and by a regard for our own happiness.

Although we foresee the difficulties which may attend our new situation, and the obligations which we contract by the rank which we are about to occupy in the political order of the world; and above all, the powerful influence of ancient forms and habits, by which (to our regret) we have been hitherto affected; yet we also know that a shameful submission to them, when it is in our power to shake them off, would prove more ignominious to ourselves and more fatal to posterity than our long and painful servitude. It therefore becomes our indispensable duty to provide for our security, liberty, and happiness, by an entire and essential subversion and reform of our ancient establishments.

Wherefore, believing, for all these reasons, that we have complied with the respect which we owe to the opinions of mankind, and to the dignity of other nations, with whom we are about to rank, and of whose friendly intercourse we assure ourselves.

We the representatives of the Confederated Provinces of Venezuela, invoking the Most High to witness the justice of our cause and the rectitude of our intentions, imploring his divine assistance to ratify, at the epoch of our political birth, the dignity to which his providence has restored us, the ardent desire to live and die free, and in the belief and the defence of the Holy Catholic and Apostolic Religion of Jesus Christ, as the first of our duties;

We therefore, in the name, by the will, and under the authority which we hold for the virtuous people of Venezuela, do solemnly declare to the world that these united provinces are and ought to be, from this day forth, in fact and of right, free, sovereign, and independent states; that they are absolved from all allegiance and dependence on the Crown of Spain and of those who now call or may hereafter call themselves its representatives or agents; and that, as free, sovereign, and independent states, we hold full power to adopt whatever form of government may be deemed suitable to the general will of its inhabitants; to declare war, make peace, form alliance, establish commercial treaties, define boundaries, and regulate navigation; and to propose and execute all other acts, usually made and executed by free and independent nations; and for the due fulfilment, validity, and stability of this, our solemn declaration, we mutually and reciprocally pledge and bind the provinces to each other, our lives, fortunes, and the honor of the nation.

9. ARGENTINIAN INDEPENDENCE IMPLIED (1811)[9]

Unlike Venezuela, which proclaimed its independence early and openly, Argentina (which at the time called itself the United Provinces of South America) exercised de facto independence long before it made an open break with Spain. The victories of the Buenos Aires civic militia (including free people of color and armed slaves) over British invasion attempts in 1806 and 1807 revealed Spanish impotence and Argentinian self-reliance. In 1810, the Spanish viceroy was deposed and replaced by a junta in Buenos Aires. From 1810 through 1815, it tried to exert its authority over the outlying provinces while at the same time trying to invade royalist-held Montevideo and Peru. In 1814, its armies finally entered Montevideo, but its three attempted invasions of Peru were disastrous failures. Despite the state of open warfare, Argentina

[9]"Governing Junta of the Provinces of the Rio de la Plata to James Madison, President of the United States" (Buenos Aires, February 11, 1811), in *Diplomatic Correspondence of the United States Concerning the Independence of the Latin-American Nations*, ed. William R. Manning (New York: Oxford University Press, 1925), vol. 1, 319–320.

still refrained from declaring formal independence. That only came in 1816, at the Congress of Tucuman, after Fernando VII returned to power, repudiated the Constitution of Cadiz, and restored absolutism. Nonetheless, from 1810 through 1816, the junta of Buenos Aires acted like an independent government, going so far as to seek international recognition.

The marked proofs which your Excellency has given of your Beneficence and magnanimity towards the Province of Caracas are irrefragable testimonies of the lively Interest which your Excy takes in the Rights of Humanity. In truth, none are more likely to respect them in others than those who have had the misfortune to see them outraged towards themselves. The perfect conformity of our Political Situation, and of the causes of it, with that of the Noble Caraquans, gives us an equal Right to hope that it will be agreeable to your Excellency, that the United States should tighten with the Provinces on the Rio de la Plata the common chain of Nations, by a Cordiality more firm and expressive.

The Inhabitants of these Provinces, for a long time past, altho' much oppressed under the yoke of an arbitrary authority, fulfilled their Duties with all the fidelity of subjects and all the Honor of Citizens. They were persuaded that the Reunion of the whole Spanish Monarchy was the only thing that could save it from Ruin. To secure this Union there could have been no Sacrifice that could have appeared too great for a People, who had at the price of their Blood succeeded in redeeming these Dominions. In effect, to save the Kingdom from this assassinating [h]orde which now crams itself with the carcass of Europe, every thing was put in contribution, and so long as our Hopes lasted, we considered it our Duty not to think of ourselves. The Theatre changed its scene—almost the whole of the Peninsula fell under the Dominion of the common oppressor and that Body of Ambitious Egotists, of which was composed the Central Junta, was dissolved and dispersed. This was precisely the case in which the same Principles of Loyalty which had until then retained us in Union with Spain authorised our separation. Our Security being threatened, there was no obligation to prostitute ourselves to the ephemeral authorities which had lost the Character of Dignity & Independence.

Moreover, a Club of proud oligarchists composing this "audiencia," over whom presided a Vice-Roy as avaricious as ambitious, in place of softening the evils of the Country and of gaining our Confidence, endeavor'd to keep us in a torpid State, and thro' our negligence to confirm their Tyranny. Their re-iterated attempts to subvert the State, and their suspicious measures obliged us to depose them.

Such are the Reasons which have induced the Capital of the kingdom of La Plata to install the governing Junta, which happily rules over these Provinces. The towns in the Interior, now freed from their ancient Tyrants, do not cease to bless the moment in which they saw re-established the imprescriptible Rights with which nature endowed them. . . .

10. MEXICAN DECLARATION OF INDEPENDENCE (NOVEMBER 6, 1813)[10]

The struggle for Mexican independence began in 1810. It was only three years later, however, that a formal declaration of independence was issued. The following document is an excerpt from that declaration. Catholicism played a large role (on both sides) in the Wars of Mexican Independence; the 1813 declaration of independence is no exception.

The Congress of Anahuac, legitimately installed in the city of Chilpancingo, Mexico: Solemnly declares in the presence of the Lord God, the moderating arbiter of empires and the author of society, who gives and takes away according to the inscrutable designs of his providence, that due to the present circumstances of Europe, Mexico has reclaimed the exercise of its usurped sovereignty; that its former dependence on the Spanish throne is forever broken and dissolved; that it is free to establish the laws best suited to its own interior happiness, to make war and peace and establish alliances with the monarchs and republics of the old continent, and, not least of all, to conclude concordats with the High Roman Pontiff for the organization of the Apostolic and Roman Catholic Church, and to maintain embassies and consulates; that it does not profess or recognize any other religion than Catholicism, nor does it permit or tolerate the public or private practice of any other religion; that it will protect it with all its power and ensure the purity of the faith and its dogmas, as well as the preservation of the monastic orders. The Congress hereby declares guilty of high treason all who oppose independence either directly or indirectly, who defend its Europeans oppressors by word or deed, or who refuse to contribute to the costs, subsidies, and pensions necessary to pursue the war until [Mexico's] independence is recognized by foreign nations.

IV. Mexican Independence (1810–1815)

The struggle for Mexican independence began on September 16, 1810. On that day, the priest of Dolores, Miguel Hidalgo y Costilla, issued his famous call to arms, the "Grito de Dolores." Thousands of peasants—mostly Indians and people of mixed ancestry—answered his call. Looting and killing their way across Mexico, Hidalgo's following grew until it numbered about 50,000 and threatened to take Mexico City itself. Inexplicably, Hidalgo did not attack the capital but turned north. This gave the royal authorities time to organize military forces to combat the insurrection. They were supported by creole elites who, terrified by the prospect of a massive social uprising, flocked to the royalist armies. In 1811, they caught up with

---

[10]*Documentos de la Guerra de Independencia* (Biblioteca Enciclopedica popular, Mexico, 1945), 59–60. Translation by Daniel Arenas.

Hidalgo, defeated his forces, and executed him. After this, all that remained of the Mexican independence movement was a much smaller, disorganized, and often demoralized insurgency under the leadership of another priest, José Maria Morelos. Like Hidalgo, Morelos was committed to racial and social equality. Because of this, the creole elites (unlike in most of Spanish America) remained firmly within the royalist camp. With their support, the Spanish authorities defeated Morelos and executed him in 1815. Guerilla warfare simmered, but the creole-staffed royalist army had ended any real threat to Spanish control.

11. EXCOMMUNICATION OF HIDALGO (SEPTEMBER 24, 1810)[11]

The Catholic hierarchy in Mexico responded swiftly and sternly to Hidalgo's revolt. Within days, it excommunicated Hidalgo in an attempt to undermine his legitimacy and popular appeal. The following document is an excerpt from the sentence of excommunication pronounced by the Bishop of Michoacán.

Every kingdom divided into factions will be destroyed and ruined, says our dear lord Jesus Christ. . . . Yes, beloved faithful, the history of all ages, people, and nations; what has occurred before our eyes in the French Revolution; what is now happening in the Peninsula, in our beloved and unfortunate homeland, all this confirms the infallible truth of this divine oracle. But the example most analogous to our situation is Saint-Domingue, whose proprietors were the richest, most comfortable, and happiest men on earth. The population was composed almost like ours, of Europeans, creoles, indigenous Indians, blacks, mulattoes, and people of mixed ancestry. . . . Anarchy and division was introduced by the French Revolution, and absolutely destroyed everything. The anarchy in France caused the death of two million Frenchmen . . . ruined their trade and navy, and hindered industry and agriculture. But the anarchy in Santo Domingo slaughtered all white French and creoles without exception and killed four-fifths of all the other inhabitants, leaving the Negroes and mulattoes locked in an endless war to the death in which they will utterly destroy themselves. It devastated the entire country, destroying and burning all cities, villages, and plantations. . . . What was once the most populated and cultivated land in the Americas is now a desert, the lair of tigers and lions. Such is the horrible, but true, picture of the ravages of anarchy in Santo Domingo.

New Spain, which has astonished Europe with the most shining example of loyalty and patriotism toward the homeland, supporting and sustaining it with its treasures, opinions, and writing, . . . is today threatened by discord and anarchy. . . .

---

[11]Juan Hernandez y Davalos, ed., *Coleccion de documentos para la historia de la Guerra de Independencia de Mexico* (Mexico City, Mexico: Universidad Nacional Autonoma de Mexico, 2007), vol. 2, no. 44, ed. Virginia Guedea and Alfredo Avila, http://www.pim.unam.mx/catalogos/hyd/HYDII/HYDII044.pdf. Translated by Daniel Arenas.

A minister of the God of Peace, a priest of Jesus Christ, a pastor of souls (though I wish not to say it), the priest of Dolores, Don Miguel Hidalgo . . . raised the standard of rebellion, lit the torch of discord and anarchy, and misled some innocent peasants into taking up arms. On the 16th of the current month, they descended at dawn on the village of Dolores, surprised and seized the Europeans, sacked and stole their goods. At seven o'clock they moved on to the village of San Miguel and proceeded in the same fashion, taking over authority and government. On Friday the 21st, they occupied Celaya in the same way, and it seems that they have extended their control as far as Salamanca and Irapuato. They take with them the Europeans they have detained, including the sacristan of Dolores, the priest of Chamacuero, and some Carmelite friars from Celaya. They threaten all towns in their path with destruction if they try to resist. Insulting our religion and sovereign, Ferdinand VII, they painted on their standard the image of our august patron, Our Lady of Guadalupe and added the following inscription: *Long Live Religion, Long Live Our Holy Mother of Guadalupe, Long Live Ferdinand VII, Long Live America, Death to Bad Government*. Since our religion condemns rebellion, murder, and the oppression of the innocent, and as the mother of God cannot protect crime, it is clear that the priest of Dolores, by painting on his seditious standard the image of Our Lady and referencing her in the inscription, committed two grave acts of sacrilege: insulting Religion and Our Lady. He also insulted our sovereign by deprecating and attacking the government that represents him, oppressing his innocent subjects, disturbing public order, and violating his oath of fealty. . . . Confusing religion with crime and obedience with rebellion, he has nonetheless succeeded in leading astray the innocent people.

As your bishop, pastor, and father, I must go forth to meet this enemy . . . using reason and truth against deception and the terrible lightning bolt of excommunication against impertinence and arrogance. . . .

Yes, my dear and faithful friends. . . . I am of European origin, but American by choice. I have lived here for more than thirty-one years. No one is more concerned than I about your happiness. . . . Nobody has worked like I to promote the public good, peace, and concord among all the inhabitants of America, and to prevent the anarchy I have feared so much ever since my return from Europe. . . . Using my episcopal authority, . . . I declare that Don Miguel Hidalgo . . . is a disturber of public order, rabble-rouser, sacrilegious, a perjurer, and has incurred the greatest Canonic excommunication . . . for having attacked the sacristan of Dolores, the priest of Chamacuero, and monks of the Convent of Carmen de Celaya. . . .

I exhort and require that the people who have been misled by the title of soldier and brother-in-arms return home and forsake [Hidalgo] within three days of receiving this communication, under the same penalty of excommunication. [I also] declare all those who voluntarily enlist beneath his banners, or provide any manner of aid, to be complicit. . . .

I declare Hidalgo and his henchmen to be demagogues and slanderers of the Europeans. Yes my dear friends, he is a notorious slanderer. The Europeans do not have, and cannot have, any other interest than the same interests as the people, the natural interests of the country; that is to say, to help the homeland in any way possible, to defend its dominions from foreign invasion on behalf of the king—the sovereign to whom we have sworn fealty and the government representing him (or any descendant of the same dynasty) in the manner decreed by the Cortes, which represents the nation and is now meeting in Cadiz . . . with interim deputies from America until proper ones arrive.

12. HIDALGO'S MANIFESTO AGAINST HIS EXCOMMUNICATION[12]

Hidalgo did not accept excommunication meekly. His response proclaimed the stead-fastness of his Catholic faith and called into question that of his enemies.

I unfortunately see the need to satisfy my countrymen about something I never thought they could suspect about me. I am speaking of the most important, sacred, and, for me, joyous thing: the Holy Religion of the supernatural faith which I received in baptism.

My beloved countrymen, I swear that I have never questioned a single bit of my belief in the Holy Catholic Church. I have never doubted any of her truths; I have always been deeply convinced of its dogmas, and am ready to shed my blood in defense of each and every one of them. . . .

They claim that I have denied the authenticity of the sacred books. They accuse me of following the perverse dogmas of Lucifer. . . .

Any crimes I may have committed originated from my desire for your happiness. If I had not had to take up arms, I would have enjoyed a sweet, calm, and comfortable life. I would die a true Catholic—which I am and which I profess to be. No one would have dared to brand me with the infamous title of heretic.

But the European Spaniards who oppress us will use any means against us. Their yoke was too heavy. Long dormant, the nation was suddenly roused from its slumber by the sweet voice of liberty. The people rushed to take up arms and will do everything in their power to defend her [the nation].

Our oppressors have neither weapons nor men to force us back into the horrific slavery to which they have condemned us. What means do they have to fight us? They use all kinds of unjust means, anything to sustain their despotism and the oppression of America. They have abandoned their last shred of honesty and uprightness. The most honorable authorities have prostituted themselves and have fulminated excommunications. No one knows better than they do themselves that they have no real strength. So, they try to scare the unwary and terrorize the ignorant by hurling anathemas, when there is no real need for fear. . . .

Open your eyes, Americans! Don't let our enemies fool you. They are not Catholics. Money is their God, and their summations are only intended to oppress

---

[12]Hernandez y Davalos, *Coleccion de documentos*, vol. 1, no. 54.

you. Do you think that one must accept submission to Spanish despotism to be a good Catholic? Where does this new dogma, this new article of faith, come from? Open your eyes, I say again! Reflect upon your own interests. For what is at stake at this critical juncture is the happiness or unhappiness of your children and numerous posterity. My beloved compatriots, you are courting disaster if you do not seize this fortunate opportunity that Divine Providence has placed in your hands. Do not listen to the false words or our enemies, who are trying to use religion to make you the victims of their insatiable greed. . . .

My fellow Americans, let us break the ties of ignominy which have bound us for so long. All we need is to be united. If we do not fight against ourselves, the war is won, and our rights are saved. Let all who were born on this blessed soil join together. All who are not Americans are foreigners and enemies of our rights.

We will establish a congress composed of representatives of all the cities, villages, and places of this kingdom. Its primary objective will be to maintain our holy religion, craft mild laws, with benefits and accommodations for the specific circumstances of each village. It will govern with the sweetness of parents, treat us as brothers, banish poverty, and heal the devastation of the kingdom. It will tax us, but use the revenue to foster the arts, encourage industry. After a few years, we will freely use the delicious products of our fertile lands and appreciate all the delights that the sovereign author of nature has bestowed upon this vast continent.

13. JOSÉ MORELOS, *SENTIMENTS OF THE NATION* (SEPTEMBER 14, 1813)[13]

After Hidalgo's defeat and execution, most of his following melted away. But the insurrection continued on a smaller scale under another priest, Jose Maria Morelos. In 1813, he summoned a congress in Chilpancingo to proclaim Mexican independence and design a constitution for the new country. Document 10 is a translation of the declaration of independence. The following document is an excerpt from Morelos' Sentiments of the Nation, *a short work he published in which he laid out the features he thought the new constitution should have.*

1. America is free and independent from Spain and any other nation, government, or monarchy. . . .
2. The Catholic faith shall be the only one, with none other to be tolerated.
3. The Church's ministers shall support themselves solely from tithes. . . .
4. The existing Church hierarchy shall be maintained. . . .

[13]Ernesto de la Torre Villar, Monses Gonzalez Navarro, and Stanley Ross, eds., *Historia Documental de Mexico* (Mexico City, Mexico: Universidad Nacional Autonoma de Mexico, 1964), vol. 2, 111–112. Translation by Daniel Arenas.

5. Sovereignty emanates directly from the People, which wishes to delegate that Sovereignty to its representatives, divided into Legislative, Executive, and Judicial branches, at the provincial and national level.

6. [No article six was included in the original]

7. These representatives shall serve for four years, with a revolving membership whereby the oldest serving members shall be replaced by younger electees.

8. The representatives' salary shall be sufficient, but not excessive, and shall not exceed eight thousand pesos.

9. All [public] positions shall be reserved for Americans.

10. Foreigners shall not be allowed to immigrate, with the sole exception of irreproachable artisans capable of sharing their knowledge.

11. The Nation shall not be free until the Government is reformed, tyranny replaced by liberty, and the Spanish enemy, who has declared himself against this nation, expelled from our soil. . . .

12. [The laws] dictated by our Congress must promote constancy and patriotism, reduce opulence and poverty, raise the wages of the poor, improve their lives, eliminate ignorance, and punish theft and lawlessness.

13. The general laws will apply to all, with no exception for privileged bodies.

14. All laws must be debated in Congress and approved by a plurality of votes.

15. Slavery shall be abolished for eternity, as well as all distinction of castes. . . . The only distinction that may remain between one American and another is that of vice and virtue.

16. Our ports shall be open to friendly foreign nations, but . . . with a 10% tariff [except in government-designated free ports].

17. The sanctity of the citizens' property shall be respected. Those who infringe this right shall be punished.

18. Torture is henceforth abolished.

19. By a constitutional law, December 12th shall be instituted as a holiday, dedicated to the patron of our liberty, Our Most Holy Lady of Guadalupe.

20. Troops of foreign nations shall not be admitted onto our soil except those who come to aid us. In this case, they shall remain in quarters designated by the Supreme Junta.

21. We renounce offensive military operations, except for those intended to spread the benefits of liberty to our brethren on the American continent.

22. All existing taxes and impositions are abolished. Henceforth, each individual shall pay five percent of his earnings, as well as light sales taxes, state monopolies, tribute, and others. With this small contribution and the efficient administration of properties confiscated from our enemy, the wartime burden shall be lifted.

23. September 16th shall be celebrated every year as the day when the fight for our independence and holy liberty began, the day when the nation cried out to recover its rights. It shall commemorate for all eternity the merit of the great heroes Miguel Hidalgo y Costilla and his companion Don Ignacio Allende.

V. The Rise, Fall, and Rebirth of Latin American Independence

The year 1815 marked the end of the first phase of the struggles for Latin American independence. In Mexico, the creole-staffed royalist army had defeated Morelos and eliminated all but isolated sparks of rebellion. In southern South America, a third Argentine invasion of royalist Peru had been routed. Although Buenos Aires itself was not threatened with royalist reconquest, it was beset by internal factionalism and centrifugal, federalist tensions. In northern South America, the end of the Napoleonic wars made it possible for Fernando VII (who had been restored to the throne) to send an army to reimpose Spanish authority. Commanded by the able general Pablo Morillo and numbering over 10,000 battle-hardened veterans, it easily reconquered Venezuela and New Granada. With the fall of the last independent bastion, Cartagena, it seemed that the independence movement in the Costa Firme had been extinguished. By the end of 1815, the prospects of Latin American independence seemed bleak.

But during the next five years, a dramatic reversal would take place. Whereas the end of the Napoleonic Wars in 1815 made possible the Morillo expedition, it also released a flood of arms onto the world market, many of which found their way into insurgent hands. They were accompanied by thousands of military volunteers who would serve with distinction in Bolivar's and San Martin's armies, as well as a swarm of privateers eager to find glory and gold in the cause of liberation. Foreign arms and volunteers would play a significant role in turning the tide. Equally important was Fernando VII's decision to reestablish absolutism and tear up the liberal Constitution of Cadiz. This ended the possibility that Spanish America might find an acceptable place within a liberal imperial framework. This injected a new sense of determination into the independence movements. From 1815 on, the only alternative to independence would be to return as colonial subjects under the most reactionary of absolutisms.

In 1817, Bolivar returned to the continent. After hard fighting, his army liberated New Granada at the Battle of Boyaca (1819) and then Venezuela at the Battle of Carabobo (1821). In September of that year, he proclaimed the formation of the Republic of Grand Columbia (comprising modern day Venezuela, Columbia, Ecuador, and Panama) and was proclaimed its president. He then turned south, liberating Quito in 1822 and moving to converge on royalist Peru with San Martin's troops, which were advancing from the south. For his part, the Argentinian commander, San Martin, liberated Chile in 1817–1818; and, in an amphibious campaign that covered more than a thousand miles of Pacific coastline, moved on Lima, the capital of the royalist stronghold of Peru. He captured it in 1821 and declared Peruvian independence. The noose was tightening around the remaining royalist forces in the Andean highlands. They were finally cornered and defeated in 1824. With the exception of the fortified coastal bastions of San Juan de Ulloa (Mexico), Porto Cabello (Venezuela), Callao (Peru), and Chiloe (Chile), Spanish America was free from Spanish troops and authorities.

14. BOLIVAR'S PROCLAMATION OF WAR
TO THE DEATH (JUNE 15, 1813)[14]

By 1813, the Venezuelan independence movement was fighting for survival. The first Venezuelan republic had collapsed, and war was raging with local royalist forces. It was in this context that one of the patriot leaders, Simon Bolivar, issued a declaration of "war to the death." It attempted to radicalize his compatriots by drawing a stark line between Americans and Europeans, painting the conflict (which was really a civil war) as a foreign invasion, and forcing them to choose sides.

Venezuelans! An army of your brothers, sent by the Sovereign Congress of New Granada, has come to liberate you. Having expelled the oppressors from the provinces of Merida and Trujillo, it is now among you.

We are sent to destroy the Spaniards, to protect the Americans, and to reestablish the republican governments that once formed the Confederation of Venezuela. The states defended by our arms are again governed by their former constitutions and tribunals, in full enjoyment of their liberty and independence, for our mission is designed only to break the chains of servitude which still shackle some of our towns, and not to impose laws or exercise acts of dominion to which the rules of war might entitle us.

Moved by your misfortunes, we have been unable to observe with indifference the afflictions you were forced to experience by the barbarous Spaniards, who have ravished you, plundered you, and brought you death and destruction. They have violated the sacred rights of nations. They have broken the most solemn agreements and treaties. In fact, they have committed every manner of crime, reducing the Republic of Venezuela to the most frightful desolation. Justice therefore demands vengeance, and necessity compels us to exact it. Let the monsters who infest Colombian soil, who have drenched it in blood, be cast out forever; may their punishment be equal to the enormity of their perfidy, so that we may eradicate the stain of our ignominy and demonstrate to the nations of the world that the sons of America cannot be offended with impunity.

Despite our just resentment toward the iniquitous Spaniards, our magnanimous heart still commands us to open to them for the last time a path to reconciliation and friendship; they are invited to live peacefully among us, if they will abjure their crimes, honestly change their ways, and cooperate with us in destroying the intruding Spanish government and in the reestablishment of the Republic of Venezuela.

Any Spaniard who does not, by every active and effective means, work against tyranny in behalf of this just cause, will be considered an enemy and punished; as a traitor to the nation, he will inevitably be shot by a firing squad. On the other hand, a general and absolute amnesty is granted to those who come over to our

[14]Simon Bolivar, "Proclamation to the People of Venezuela" (Trujillo, June 15, 1813), in *Selected Writings of Bolivar*, ed. Harold A. Bierck (New York: Colonial Press, 1951), vol. 1, 31–32.

army with or without their arms, as well as to those who render aid to the good citizens who are endeavoring to throw off the yoke of tyranny. Army officers and civil magistrates who proclaim the government of Venezuela and join with us shall retain their posts and positions; in a word, those Spaniards who render outstanding service to the State shall be regarded and treated as Americans.

And you Americans who, by error or treachery, have been lured from the paths of justice, are informed that your brothers, deeply regretting the error of your ways, have pardoned you as we are profoundly convinced that you cannot be truly to blame, for only the blindness and ignorance in which you have been kept up to now by those responsible for your crimes could have induced you to commit them. Fear not the sword that comes to avenge you and to sever the ignoble ties with which your executioners have bound you to their own fate. You are hereby assured, with absolute impunity, of your honor, lives, and property. The single title, "Americans," shall be your safeguard and guarantee. Our arms have come to protect you, and they shall never be raised against a single one of you, our brothers.

This amnesty is extended even to the very traitors who most recently have committed felonious acts, and it shall be so religiously applied that no reason, cause, or pretext will be sufficient to oblige us to violate our offer, however extraordinary and extreme the occasion you may give to provoke our wrath.

Spaniards and Canary Islanders, you will die, though you be neutral, unless you actively espouse the cause of America's liberation. Americans, you will live, even if you have trespassed.

15. BOLIVAR'S JAMAICA LETTER (SEPTEMBER 6, 1815)[15]

In 1813, Simon Bolivar achieved military success in what has come to be known as the "admirable campaign." He liberated Caracas and proclaimed the Second Venezuelan Republic. He then moved into New Granada and liberated its capital, Bogota, in 1814. Bolivar seemed to be well on his way toward achieving his dream of unifying Venezuela and New Granada under a single government. However, he suffered serious military reverses later in 1814; and the independence movement began to be torn apart by disputes between rival towns, provinces, and factions. Bolivar found himself persona non grata and was forced to flee. He went to Jamaica to seek direct British aid. Although he failed to obtain this, he did sketch out his inspiring, overall vision of Latin American independence while there—the "Jamaica Letter."

Success will crown our efforts, because the destiny of America has been irrevocably decided; the tie that bound her to Spain has been severed. Only a concept maintained that tie and kept the parts of that immense monarchy together. That

[15]Simon Bolivar, "Reply of a South American to a Gentleman of this Island [Jamaica]: Kingston, Jamaica, September 6, 1815," in *Selected Writings of Bolivar*, ed. Harold A. Bierck (New York: Colonial Press, 1951), vol. 1, 104–122.

which formerly bound them now divides them. The hatred that the Peninsula has inspired in us is greater than the ocean between us. It would be easier to have the two continents meet than to reconcile the spirits of the two countries. The habit of obedience; a community of interest, of understanding, of religion; mutual goodwill; a tender regard for the birthplace and good name of our forefathers; in short, all that gave rise to our hopes, came to us from Spain. As a result there was born a principle of affinity that seemed eternal, notwithstanding the misbehavior of our rulers which weakened that sympathy, or rather, that bond enforced by the domination of their rule. At present the contrary attitude persists: we are threatened with the fear of death, dishonor, and every harm; there is nothing we have not suffered at the hands of that unnatural step-mother, Spain. The veil has been torn asunder. We have already seen the light, and it is not our desire to be thrust back into darkness. The chains have been broken; we have been freed, and now our enemies seek to enslave us anew. For this reason America fights desperately, and seldom has desperation failed to achieve victory.

Because successes have been partial and spasmodic, we must not lose faith. In some regions the Independents triumph, while in others the tyrants have the advantage. What is the end result? . . . We have but to look around us on this hemisphere to witness a simultaneous struggle at every point.

The war-like state of the La Plata River provinces has purged that territory and led their victorious armies to Upper Perú, arousing Arequipa and worrying the royalists in Lima. Nearly one million inhabitants there now enjoy liberty.

The territory of Chile, populated by 800,000 souls, is fighting the enemy who is seeking her subjugation; but to no avail, because those who long ago put an end to the conquests of this enemy, the free and indomitable Araucanians, are their neighbors and compatriots. Their sublime example is proof to those fighting in Chile that a people who love independence will eventually achieve it.

The viceroyalty of Peru, whose population approaches a million and a half inhabitants, without doubt suffers the greatest subjection and is obliged to make the most sacrifices for the royal cause; and, although the thought of cooperating with that part of America may be vain, the fact remains that it is not tranquil, nor is it capable of restraining the torrent that threatens most of its provinces.

New Granada, which is, so to speak, the heart of America, obeys a general government, save for the territory of Quito, which is held only with the greatest difficulty by its enemies, as it is strongly devoted to the country's cause; and the provinces of Panamá and Santa Marta endure, not without suffering, the tyranny of their masters. Two and half million people inhabit New Granada and are actually defending that territory against the Spanish army under General Morillo, who will probably suffer defeat at the impregnable fortress of Cartagena. But should he take that city, it will be at the price of heavy casualties, and he will then lack sufficient forces to subdue the unrestrained and brave inhabitants of the interior.

With respect to heroic and hapless Venezuela, events there have moved so rapidly and the devastation has been such that it is reduced to frightful desolation and almost absolute indigence, although it was once among the fairest regions that are the pride of America. Its tyrants govern a desert, and they oppress only those unfortunate survivors who, having escaped death, lead a precarious existence. . . .

According to Baron von Humboldt, New Spain, including Guatemala, had 7,800,000 inhabitants in 1808. Since that time, the insurrection, which has shaken virtually all of her provinces, has appreciably reduced that apparently correct figure. . . . There the struggle continues by dint of human and every other type of sacrifice, for the Spaniards spare nothing that might enable them to subdue those who have had the misfortune of being born on this soil, which appears to be destined to flow with the blood of its offspring. In spite of everything, the Mexicans will be free. . . . The time has come at last to repay the Spaniards torture for torture and to drown that race of annihilators in its own blood or in the sea. . . .

This picture represents a military map, an area of 2,000 longitudinal and 900 latitudinal leagues at its greatest point, wherein 16,000,000 Americans either defend their rights or suffer repression at the hands of Spain, which, although once the world's greatest empire, is now too weak, with what little is left her, to rule the new hemisphere or even to maintain herself in the old. And shall Europe, the civilized, the merchant, the lover of liberty, allow an aged serpent, bent only on satisfying its venomous rage, devour the fairest part of our globe? What! Is Europe deaf to the clamor of her own interests? Has she no eyes to see justice? Has she grown so hardened as to become insensible? The more I ponder these questions, the more I am confused. I am led to think that America's disappearance is desired; but this is impossible because all Europe is not Spain. What madness for our enemy to hope to reconquer America when she has no navy, no funds, and almost no soldiers! Those troops which she has are scarcely adequate to keep her own people in a state of forced obedience and to defend herself from her neighbors. On the other hand, can that nation carry on the exclusive commerce of one-half the world when it lacks manufactures, agricultural products, crafts and sciences, and even a policy? Assume that this mad venture were successful, and further assume that pacification ensued, would not the sons of the Americans of today, together with the sons of the European reconquistadores twenty years hence, conceive the same patriotic designs that are now being fought for?

Europe could do Spain a service by dissuading her from her rash obstinacy, thereby at least sparing her the costs she is incurring and the blood she is expending. And if she will fix her attention on her own precincts, she can build her prosperity and power upon more solid foundations than doubtful conquests, precarious commerce, and forceful exactions from remote and powerful peoples. Europe herself, as a matter of common sense policy, should have prepared and executed the project of American independence, not alone because the world balance of power so necessitated, but also because this is the legitimate and certain means through which Europe can acquire overseas commercial establishments. A Europe which is not moved by the violent passion of vengeance, ambition, and greed, as is Spain, would seem to be entitled, by all the rules of equity, to make clear to Spain where her best interests lie. . . .

Not only the Europeans but even our brothers of the North have been apathetic bystanders in this struggle. . . .

It is ... difficult to foresee the future fate of the New World, to set down its political principles, or to prophesy what manner of government it will adopt. Every
conjecture relative to America's future is, I feel, pure speculation. When mankind
was in its infancy, steeped in uncertainty, ignorance, and error, was it possible to
foresee what system it would adopt for its preservation? Who could venture to
say that a certain nation would be a republic or a monarchy; this nation great,
that nation small? To my way of thinking, such is our own situation. We are a
young people. We inhabit a world apart, separated by broad seas. We are young
in the ways of almost all the arts and sciences, although, in a certain manner, we
are old in the ways of civilized society. I look upon the present state of America
as similar to that of Rome after its fall. Each part of Rome adopted a political
system conforming to its interests and situation or was led by the individual am-
bitions of certain chiefs, dynasties, or associations. But this important difference
exists: those dispersed parts later reestablished their ancient nations, subject to
the changes imposed by circumstances or events. But we scarcely retain a vestige
of what once was; we are, moreover, neither Indians nor Europeans, but a species
midway between the legitimate proprietors of this country and the Spanish usurpers. In short, though Americans by birth, we derive our rights from Europe, and
we have to assert these rights against the rights of the natives, and at the same time
we must defend ourselves against the invaders. This places us in a most extraordinary and involved situation. Notwithstanding that it is a type of divination to
predict the result of the political course which America is pursuing, I shall venture
some conjectures which, of course, are colored by my enthusiasm and dictated by
rational desires rather than by reasoned calculations.

The role of the inhabitants of the American hemisphere has for centuries been
purely passive. Politically they were nonexistent. We are still in a position lower
than slavery, and therefore it is more difficult for us to rise to the enjoyment of
freedom. . . .

Americans today, and perhaps to a greater extent than ever before, who live
within the Spanish system occupy a position in society no better than that of serfs
destined for labor, or at best they have no more status than that of mere consumers. Yet even this status is surrounded with galling restrictions, such as being
forbidden to grow European crops . . . or to establish factories. . . . To this add the
exclusive trading privileges, even in articles of prime necessity, and the barriers
between American provinces, designed to prevent all exchange of trade, traffic,
and understanding. In short, do you wish to know what our future held? Simply
the cultivation of the fields of indigo, grain, coffee, sugar cane, cacao, and cotton;
cattle raising on the broad plains; hunting wild game in the jungles; digging in the
earth to mine its gold. But even these limitations could never satisfy the greed of
Spain. . . . Is it not an outrage and a violation of human rights to expect a land so
splendidly endowed, so vast, rich, and populous, to remain merely passive? . . .

We were cut off and, as it were, removed from the world in relation to the science of government and administration of the state. We were never viceroys or governors, save in the rarest of instances; seldom archbishops and bishops; diplomats

never; as military men, only subordinates; as nobles, without royal privileges. In brief, we were neither magistrates nor financiers and seldom merchants—all in flagrant contradiction to our institutions. . . .

There are explicit laws respecting employment in civil, ecclesiastical, and tax-raising establishments. These laws favor, almost exclusively, the natives of the country who are of Spanish extraction. Thus, by an outright violation of the laws and existing agreements, those born in America have been despoiled of their constitutional rights. . . .

From what I have said it is easy to deduce that America was not prepared to secede from the mother country; this secession was suddenly brought about by the effect of the illegal concessions of Bayonne. . . .

The Americans have risen rapidly without previous knowledge of, and what is more regrettable, without previous experience in public affairs, to enact upon the world state, the eminent roles of legislator, magistrate, minister of the treasury, diplomats, generals, and every position of authority, supreme or subordinate, that comprises the hierarchy of a fully organized state.

When the French invasion . . . routed the fragile government of the peninsula, we were left orphans. Prior to that invasion, we had been left to the mercy of a foreign usurper. Thereafter, the justice due us was dangled before our eyes, raising hopes that only came to naught. Finally, uncertain of our destiny, and facing anarchy for want of a legitimate, just, and liberal government, we threw ourselves headlong into the chaos of revolution . . . thus we were able to found a constitutional government worthy of our century and adequate to our situation.

The first steps of all the new governments are marked by the establishment of *juntas* of the people. These *juntas* speedily draft rules for the calling of congresses, which produce great changes. Venezuela erected a democratic and federal government, after declaring for the rights of man. A system of checks and balances was established, and general laws were passed granting civil liberties, such as freedom of the press and others. In short, an independent government was created. New Granada uniformly followed the political institutions and reforms introduced by Venezuela. . . . I understand that Buenos Aires and Chile have followed this same line of procedure, but, as the distance is so great and documents are so few and the news reports so unreliable, I shall not attempt even briefly to sketch their progress.

Events in Mexico have been too varied, confused, swift, and unhappy to follow clearly the course of that revolution. We lack, moreover, the necessary documentary information to enable us to form a judgment. The Independents of Mexico, according to our information, began their insurrection in September 1810, and a year later they erected a central government in Zitacuaro, where a national *junta* was installed under the auspices of Ferdinand VII, in whose name the government was carried on. The events of the war caused this *junta* to move from place to place; and, having undergone such modifications as events have determined, it may still be in existence. . . .

Events in Costa Firme have proved that institutions which are wholly representative are not suited to our character, customs, and present knowledge. In

Caracas party spirit arose in the societies, assemblies, and popular elections; these parties led us back into slavery. Thus, while Venezuela has been the American republic with the most advanced political institutions, she has also been the clearest example of the inefficiency of the democratic and federal system for our new-born states. In New Granada, the large number of excess powers held by the provincial governments and the lack of centralization in the general government have reduced that fair country to her present state. For this reason her foes, though weak, have been able to hold out against all odds. As long as our countrymen do not acquire the abilities and political virtues that distinguish our brothers of the north, wholly popular systems, far from working to our advantage, will, I greatly fear, bring about our downfall. . . . It is harder, Montesquieu has written, to release a nation from servitude than to enslave a free nation. . . .

I cannot persuade myself that the New World can, at the moment, be organized as a great republic. Since it is impossible, I dare not desire it; yet much less do I desire to have all America a monarchy because this plan is not only impracticable but also impossible. Wrongs now existing could not be righted, and our emancipation would be fruitless. . . .

The party spirit that today keeps our states in constant agitation would assume still greater proportions were a central power established, for that power—the only force capable of checking this agitation—would be elsewhere. Furthermore, the chief figures of the capitals would not tolerate the preponderance of leaders at the metropolis, for they would regard these leaders as so many tyrants. Their resentments would attain such heights that they would compare the latter to the hated Spaniards. Any such monarchy would be a misshapen colossus that would collapse of its own weight at the slightest disturbance.

[One recent writer] has wisely divided America into fifteen or seventeen mutually independent states, governed by as many monarchs. I am in agreement on the first suggestion, as America can well tolerate seventeen nations; as to the second, though it could easily be achieved, it would serve no purpose. Consequently, I do not favor American monarchies. My reasons are these: The well-understood interest of a republic is limited to the matter of its preservation, prosperity, and glory. Republicans, because they do not desire powers which represent a directly contrary viewpoint, have no reason for expanding the boundaries of their nations to the detriment of their neighbors, solely for the purpose of having their neighbors share a liberal constitution. They would not acquire rights or secure any advantage by conquering their neighbors. . . .

The policy of a king is very different. His constant desire is to increase his possessions, wealth, and authority; and with justification, for his power grows with every acquisition, both with respect to his neighbors and his own vassals, who fear him because his power is as formidable as his empire, which he maintains by war and conquest. For these reasons, I think that the Americans, being anxious for peace, science, art, commerce, and agriculture, would prefer republics to kingdoms. . . .

From the foregoing, we can draw these conclusions: The American provinces are fighting for their freedom, and they will ultimately succeed. Some provinces as a matter of course will form federal and some central republics; the larger areas will inevitably establish monarchies, some of which will fare so badly that they will disintegrate in either present or future revolutions. To consolidate a great monarchy will be no easy task, but it will be utterly impossible to consolidate a great republic.

It is a grandiose idea to think of consolidating the New World into a single nation, united by pacts into a single bond. It is reasoned that, as these parts have a common origin, language, customs, and religion, they ought to have a single government to permit the newly formed states to unite in a confederation. But this is not possible. Actually, America is separated by climactic differences, geographic diversity, conflicting interests, and dissimilar characteristics. How beautiful it would be if the Isthmus of Panama could be for us what the Isthmus of Corinth was for the Greeks! Would to God that someday we may have the good fortune to convene there an august assembly of republics, kingdoms, and empires to deliberate upon the high interests of peace and war with the nations of the other three-quarters of the globe. . . .

Among the popular and representative systems, I do not favor the federal system. It is over-perfect, and it demands political virtues and talents far superior to our own. For the same reason I reject a monarchy that is part aristocracy and part democracy, although with such a government England has achieved much fortune and splendor. Since it is not possible for us to select the most perfect and complete form of government, let us avoid falling into demagogic anarchy or monocratic tyranny. These opposite extremes would only wreck us on similar reefs of misfortune and dishonor; hence, we must seek a mean between them. . . .

By the nature of their geographic location, wealth, population, and character, I expect that the Mexicans, at the outset, intend to establish a representative republic in which the executive will have great powers. These will be concentrated in one person who, if he discharges his duties with wisdom and justice, should almost certainly maintain his authority for life. If through incompetence or violence he should excite a popular revolt and it should be successful, this same executive power would then, perhaps, be distributed among the members of an assembly. If the dominant party is military or aristocratic, it will probably demand a monarchy that would be limited and constitutional at the outset, and would later inevitably degenerate into an absolute monarchy; for it must be admitted that there is nothing more difficult in the political world than the maintenance of a limited monarchy. Moreover, it must also be agreed that only a people as patriotic as the English are capable of controlling the authority of a king and of sustaining the spirit of liberty under the rule of scepter and crown.

The states of the Isthmus of Panama, as far as Guatemala, will perhaps form a confederation. Because of their magnificent position between two mighty oceans, they may in time become the emporium of the world. Their canals will shorten distances throughout the world, strengthen commercial ties between Europe, America, and Asia, and bring to that happy area tribute from the four quarters of the globe. There some day, perhaps, the capital of the world may be located. . . .

New Granada will unite with Venezuela, if they can agree to the establishment of a central republic. Their capital may be Maracaibo or a new city to be named Las Casas (in honor of that humane hero) to be built on the borders of the two countries, in the excellent port area of Bahía-Honda. This location, though little known, is the most advantageous in all respects. It is readily accessible, and its situation is so strategic that it can be made impregnable. It has a fine, healthful climate, a soil as suitable for agriculture as for cattle raising, and a superabundance of good timber. The Indians living there can be civilized. . . . This nation should be called Colombia as a just and grateful tribute to the discoverer of our hemisphere. Its government might follow the English pattern, except that in place of a king there will be an executive who will be elected, at most, for life, but his office will never be hereditary, if a republic is desired. There will be a hereditary legislative chamber or senate. This body can interpose itself between the violent demands of the people and the great powers of the government during periods of political unrest. The second representative body will be a legislature with restrictions no greater than those of the lower house in England. The Constitution will draw on all systems of government, but I do not want it to partake of all their vices. As Colombia is my country, I have an indisputable right to desire for her that form of government which, in my opinion, is best. It is very possible that New Granada may not care to recognize a central government, because she is greatly addicted to federalism; in such event, she will form a separate state which, if it endures, may prosper, because of its great and varied resources. . . .

Surely unity is what we need to complete our work of regeneration. The division among us, nevertheless, is nothing extraordinary, for it is characteristic of civil wars to form two parties, conservatives and reformers. The former are commonly the more numerous, because the weight of habit induces obedience to established powers; the latter are always fewer in number although more vocal and learned. Thus, the physical mass of the one is counterbalanced by the moral force of the other; the contest is prolonged, and the results are uncertain. Fortunately, in our case, the mass has followed the learned.

I shall tell you with what we must provide ourselves in order to expel the Spaniards and to found a free government. It is *union*, obviously; but such union will come about through sensible planning and well-directed actions rather than by divine magic. America stands together because it is abandoned by all other nations. It is isolated in the center of the world. It has no diplomatic relations, nor does it receive any military assistance; instead, America is attacked by Spain, which has more military supplies than any we can possibly acquire through furtive means.

When success is not assured, when the state is weak, and when results are distantly seen, all men hesitate; opinion is divided, passions rage, and the enemy fans these passions in order to win an easy victory because of them. As soon as we are strong and under the guidance of a liberal nation which will lend us her protection, we will achieve accord in cultivating the virtues and talents that lead to glory. Then will we march majestically toward that great prosperity for which

South America is destined. Then will those sciences and arts which, born in the East, have enlightened Europe, wing their way to a free Colombia, which will cordially bid them welcome. . . .

16. BOLIVARIAN NAVAL DOMINANCE (1818)[16]

From Jamaica, Bolivar went to Haiti and sought aid from Pétion. In addition to receiving military support from the Haitian President (in exchange for a promise to abolish slavery in liberated Venezuela), Bolivar also enlisted Luis Brión in his cause. A merchant from the Dutch colony of Curacao, Brión commanded a fleet of privateers (officially sanctioned private warships). The naval power provided by Brión— and dozens of other foreign privateer captains who eventually joined the cause of independence—gave the insurgents command of the sea. In addition to blockading the ports of Spain itself, the privateers played a key role in shipping arms to the Latin American insurgents, isolating Spanish strongpoints in America, and giving the insurgent armies strategic mobility. These naval factors contributed significantly to the ultimate victory of Latin American independence. This was clearly understood by expert observers at the time. The following document is the assessment of the admiral in charge of the British naval squadron in the West Indies.

Spain, during her contest with France, was not able to divert any very great proportion of her military force from the immediate object against which she was employing her best efforts. An opportunity was therefore afforded to the disaffected in her South American colonies to make an effective stand against the colonial government in certain places, and at length to succeed in establishing at Cartagena and in the provinces of Caracas and Venezuela, governments independent of the Mother Country. These governments, though pursuing the same object, had but little connection with each other, and were governed, or rather conducted, by different chiefs, assuming and exercising distinct and independent powers; and in the exercise of such functions, commissions of war were granted to vessels commanded by officers embracing the independent cause, for the purpose of cruizing against vessels the property of the subjects of the King of Spain. . . .

At this period the independent governments bore a form and feature which identified their chiefs and principal functionaries as persons . . . duly exercising the authority they assumed, and under this system matters remained without anything material taking place until Spain, being enabled by the peace with France to turn her attention to her disaffected colonies; and the forces of the independent governments beings partially defeated, the persons exercising the powers of government were compelled to abandon the places over which they previously had control to the possession and administration of the royal forces.

---

[16]British National Archives, Admiralty, Series 1, Box 269.

Upon this change in affairs of the independents, such of their governments as suffered from disaster were either annihilated altogether, or the chiefs and principal officers were compelled to move from place to place for refuge and protection.

It appears that the partisans of the independents, notwithstanding their calamities, contrived to ingratiate themselves with the subjects of Great Britain and America to such a degree as to create a considerable spirit of enterprize in their favor, and, without any other resources in themselves than the popularity of their cause, induced subjects of both countries to embrace it and to adventure their lives in its support, in the ardent hope of raising their fame and fortune by flattering expectations which it held out to them.

From this period, the spirit of adventure in favor of the insurgents increased, which gave a more flattering aspect to their affairs, for instead of finding the vessels which were sailing under the independent colors, manned as heretofore entirely or chiefly so by Spaniards, we had daily experience of vessels commanded and manned by any other than the people of that nation.

These adventurers increased in numbers and enterprize. . . .

The force under General Aury consists of 17 sail, vessels with strong crews, chiefly English . . . and is in every respect well-provided with ammunition and stores of every description.

Admiral Brion has lately left the Orinoco River and joined Aury in the Mona [Passage] with about eight sail of vessels, making altogether 25 sail.

17. ROUSSIN, "REPORT ON VENEZUELA AND NEW GRANADA" (JULY 30, 1820)[17]

The following is a later assessment by a French captain who had been ordered to gather intelligence on the independence movement. His conclusion—that Spain had no hope of reimposing its authority—carries weight because, as a royalist Bourbon naval officer of Restoration France, he was not sympathetic to the independence movement.

The experience of nearly five years of war has shown [the Spanish] the absolute impossibility of penetrating and occupying the interior. The nature of the terrain, crisscrossed with inaccessible mountains, vast plains, and rivers alternately dried up and flooded; the devastation of the country; the total lack of everything a European army needs to subsist; the insalubrity of the climate; and, above all, the continual attacks of an indomitable cavalry formed of people who live on horseback—all this has come together to prove to the Spaniards that they cannot go far from the sea without running the risk of certain ruin. Your Excellency will see from the account of the conversations I had with General Morillo that he

---

[17]Service Historique de la Défense, Series BB4, Box 14.

himself is now entirely convinced of this, although his position does not permit him to admit it openly.

But the facts speak for themselves. The Spaniards have been forced to restrict themselves to the coastal provinces, or rather (to be exact) cities on the coast; for, given the instability of most of their conquests, it seems clear that they control only the ground they occupy and that the population is almost unanimously against them. . . .

Masters of the interior, the patriots no longer fear being attacked. Their possession of the near-totality of the provinces of New Grenada gives them an immense advantage. It gives their federal government a consistency, a density that they did not have before. This conquest, which is the result of extremely remarkable military plans and operations, does great honor to Bolivar, even in the opinion of his enemies. In the middle of winter, when enormous rains and storms make it almost impossible to cross the Andes, Bolivar arrived with 1,000 men at the foot of the slope of the Andes and, joined by the guerrilla forces of General Paez, crossed the San Cristobal in early July and fell upon Santa Fe de Bogota . . . without anyone dreaming that such a feat was even possible. . . .

Now, using the rivers they control, the independents are perfectly organizing themselves [for a final offensive]. Thanks to the ease of communications, they are revivifying all branches of their army. It takes them only 20 days to go from Angostura to Santa Fe by the Meta River. This position allows them to cut all communication between the maritime provinces and those of the interior. They intercept the flow of all provisions from the plain . . . leaving the coastal cities occupied by the Spaniards with no way of supplying themselves except by sea. But this of no use to them, because they have no navy, and Brion's corsairs are blockading their ports.

During this time, the [independent] government is acquiring stability. The certitude that it cannot be attacked gives it the time to perfect its institutions, fill gaps in its legal system, and form national establishments. In a word, each day adds a new degree of stability to this government. . . .

Bolivar's army is composed of 16,000 mostly Creoles and Indians. He has few foreign troops except for the British Legion. . . . This Legion is very costly to the Republic because it must be supplied and equipped in European fashion; many officers have told me that it would be very advantageous to disband it. But when it entered into service, it was highly regarded in public opinion; moreover, it was armed, and, at that time, arms were totally lacking. Today, there is no longer a shortage; the conquest of New Grenada has given them the means to purchase weapons. Despite official prohibitions, the United State[s] and England export them as contraband, depositing them on Haiti or St. Thomas. They are then transshipped via the Orinoco and Rio Hacha, which explains the importance of these points to the Republic.

There are few Frenchmen in Bolivar's army. Many officers of that nation had joined it in the beginning, but they quickly became disgusted with a type of war so different from that to which they were accustomed. Brion's crews, however, are composed of foreigners, among whom, it is aid, there are many French sailors. . . .

From all the facts and intelligence I have gathered on the current state of affairs in America, [one must conclude] that Spain has lost forever most of its colonies in these parts. Each day makes this truth more obvious and increases the imbalance in power [between the two sides]. This imbalance is already immense. It is no longer an uncoordinated insurrection of a few scattered provinces; it is no longer the sedition of a few turbulent men. . . . The Republic of Columbia has taken its place among the nations of the earth, and its people is demonstrating the firm resolution to never cease to be free.

18. STATE OF REVOLUTION IN SOUTH AMERICA (1817–1818)[18]

By 1817–1818, the tide had also turned decisively in favor of independence in the southern part of South America. After Argentina's formal declaration of independence (July 9, 1816), its leading general, Jose de San Martin, launched a daring military offensive. Leading his troops over the Andes, he surprised the royalist forces in Chile; and after the Battles of Chacabuco (1817) and Maipu (1818), he drove them out of the country. Then, using the strategic mobility afforded him by a powerful naval force under the renegade British Admiral Cochrane, he leapfrogged his army north along the Pacific coast to the vicinity of Lima. By 1821, he had entered Lima and declared Peruvian independence. The following year, he met with Bolivar to coordinate operations with him. Over the next several years (1822–1824), Bolivar's northern army—and the southern army from Argentina, Chile, and Peru—crushed the remaining royalist forces in a vice. These were decisively defeated by Bolivar at the Battle of Junín (August 1824) and by Bolivar's lieutenant Sucre at the Battle of Ayacucho (December 1824). After Ayacucho, there were no Spanish royalist forces left in America except in a handful of fortified coastal points, all of which were blockaded by insurgent naval forces. The confidence of the Argentinians shines through in these documents, designed to secure U.S. recognition.

Most Excellent Sir: Three centuries of colonial oppression by a corrupt, superstitious, and ignorant nation, whose obstinate and iniquitous policy ever has been to vilify the inhabitants of South America, *as being destined to vegetate in obscurity and abasement* (such are the expressions of the viceroy Albancos); the violent system of keeping them in ignorance of all information incompatible with its principles of colonial dependence; the perverse policy of denying to the children of the mother country and their lawful descendants on the American continent the rights of citizens in the exercise of a practical equality; the exclusive monopoly of commerce despotically exercised, regulated by the laws solely in favor of the mother

---

[18]"Manuel H. de Aguirre, Agent of the United Provinces of South America to the United States, to James Monroe, President of the United States" (Washington, October 29, 1817), in Manning, *Diplomatic Correspondence*, vol. 1, 357–358, 362–365.

country, and maintained by force at the price of the blood of innocent victims, natives of the country; the black ingratitude with which it has conducted itself towards the capital of Buenos Ayres, after having so gallantly and energetically defended the Spanish dominion against the English army under General Beresford in 1806, and the army of 12,000 men of the same nation, commanded by General Whitelock in 1807; finally, the infamous engagement to force them against their consent to submit to the yoke which the Emperor Napoleon (an instrument, as it were, of divine justice for the chastisement of thrones) imposed upon Spain, to avenge the bloody usurpations of the empires of Mexico and Peru, prepared these people, on the 25th of May, 1810, for their separation from the Spanish nation, already conquered by the French, not to admit the additional circumstance that the inhabitants of these provinces preserved them for the captive King Don Ferdinand VII and his lawful successors.

On the restoration of the King of Spain to his throne, a sufficient time was afforded to give him the opportunity of correcting his counsels, stating the grievances and injuries he complained of, and finally of proposing an honorable termination of these differences. Although the deputy had not yet arrived at the court of Madrid, the King had already despatched his inexorable and bloody decrees; and the expedition under General Morillo crossed the seas to wage a war of devastation on these countries. The natural right of self-defence imposed the necessity of taking measures to repel force by force. Hostile armies were the worst means which could be employed to bring about an accommodation.

When the deputy of the court of Madrid informed this Government that the King of Spain insisted on leaving no other alternative than the most abject submission, and that he claimed these provinces as the property of his crown (doubtless to make them victims to Spanish vengeance), then it was that the sovereign Congress of these provinces having assembled did, in imitation of the example of their brethren and natural friends of North America, unanimously proclaim in the city of Tucuman, on the 9th day of July, 1816, the solemn act of their civil independence of the Spanish nation, of the King of Spain, his heirs and successors, and did swear together with the people represented by them, to support their political emancipation at the risk of their lives and honor.

"Manuel H. de Aguirre, Agent of the United Provinces of South America to the United States, to John Quincy Adams, Secretary of State of the United States" (Washington, December 16, 1817)

. . . Almost eighteen months have passed since this declaration; eighteen months, during which the King's forces have had no other object in view than to rivet anew the chains which Spanish America had burst asunder and shaken off! If such an undertaking had been within the power of Spain, she never could have had a more favorable opportunity than at present, when she has had at her disposal, disengaged from any other calls of service, an army numerous and warlike, and the aids of all who interest themselves in perpetuating the monopoly and subjection of our country. It is true that Spain proceeded to fit out an expedition the most brilliant that was ever employed in the subjugation of our continent; but this expedition, although repeatedly reinforced, has scarcely been able to maintain its ground with honor in a single province; consumed as it has been by the dreadful phenomena of nature, and, above all, by a six years' war of the most sanguinary and exasperated character; while the provinces of Rio de la Plata have not only been able, during all that time, to preserve the precious treasure of their liberty, but to bestow it, without foreign aid, on their brethren of Chili, and to force the King's troops to retire towards Peru, which, having been reinforced by fresh detachments, had ventured to show themselves on our territory. It is under such circumstances, it is after having shown and proven the grounds and motives of its declaration, and the means it possesses to support it, that my Government has thought it conformable to the respect due to nations to make it known to them, and to solicit their acknowledgement of its sovereignty.

My Government, considering that of the United States as one of the first of whom it ought to solicit this acknowledgment, believed that the identity of political principles, the consideration of their inhabiting the same hemisphere, and the sympathy so natural to those who have experienced similar evils, would be so many additional reasons in support of its anxiety. There still exist, there still preside over the councils of the nation, many of those who supported and sealed here with their blood the rights of man; their wounds, permit me to say so, are so many powerful advocates here for the Spanish Americans. The recollection that it was these States which first pointed out to us the path of glory, and the evidence that they are enjoying most fully the blessed effects of liberty, inspire me with the conviction that it is for them also to show that they know how to appreciate our efforts, and thereby animate the other provinces which, less fortunate, have not yet been able to put an end to the sanguinary struggle.

I cannot close this communication without requesting you to make known to the President the wishes of the United Provinces in South America; and also to represent to him their earnest desire to see firmly established, between these States and those Provinces, relations mutually beneficial, suited to Governments and people whose institutions are so analogous, and all whose interests invite them to promote and maintain a close and permanent friendship.

"Manuel H. de Aguirre, Agent of the United Provinces of South America to the United States, to John Quincy Adams, Secretary of State of the United States" (Washington, December 26, 1817)

Sir: I had the honor to inform you, on the 16th of this month, that the United Provinces of South America, having declared themselves free and independent, had made a request to be considered as such by the United States; and, as you expressed a desire . . . to be more fully informed of the grounds on which those provinces formed their request, I now comply. . . .

In my said note, I particularly stated the circumspection with which my Government had proceeded, and the precautions it had taken from a sense of its own honor, and the respect due to other nations, before it required to be considered by them as a sovereign Power. You were pleased to remark on the uncertainty of establishing a new Government, and the hesitation naturally produced by such a request; and you preferred that it should be delayed, or not made until all doubt was removed of the real existence and duration of their sovereignty, and they had given a pledge to foreign nations that there existed no intention to commit them by making this request.

For more than seven years have these provinces carried on, alone, an active and successful war. The evidences of their successes have been witnessed in the capture of the royal squadron, the occupation of Montevideo, the numerous prisoners of war who fertilize our fields, the chastisement of the King's forces in Peru, and the recovery of the provinces of Chili. Meanwhile, our interior organization has been progressively improving. Our people have made an essay in the science of government, and have appointed a congress of representatives which is engaged in promoting the general weal. A plan of military defence has been formed, in which we were before deficient, and a system of revenue organized that has hitherto been competent to provide for our numerous wants; finally, public opinion is daily gaining ground, unsupported by which the Government would have been unable to undertake the enterprises which have distinguished it.

The strength of our oppressors diminishing with the increase of our means of defence, their hopes declining of longer tyrannizing over us, a regular system of government, the decision of our citizens, the competent revenue, an organized force sufficiently strong for the defence of the country, a squadron afloat, a disposable army in Chili, and a second operating in Peru—all of this must surely undeceive our enemies, even if the habit of authority should still flatter them with hopes.

Notwithstanding the professions of neutrality, on the part of the United States, towards the contending parties in Spanish America; notwithstanding the indifference, if I may say so, with which the United States have looked on a country deluged with blood by its tyrants, I would not offend you, Sire, by the idea that you consider it necessary that we should offer proofs of the justice of our cause. The few of our sufferings that have come to the knowledge of foreign nations have filled them with horror and indignation; never was the human race so debased elsewhere as we have been; never did men draw their swords in a more sacred cause. But the provinces of Rio de la Plata mean not to excite the sensibility of the United States. They only call upon their justice. The contest in South America can be viewed in no other light than as a civil war; and I have proven to you, sir, the prosperous and respectable attitude of those provinces. Are they then to be thought worthy of being ranked among nations? Do their full enjoyment of all the rights of sovereignty for more than seven years, their successes, and present position give them a right to become one?

The apprehension that this acknowledgment might involve the United States in a war with the chief of the adverse party could not be justly considered by my Government as a sufficient motive to prevent their soliciting it; since, however, little of justice or prudence may be found in the councils of the King of Spain, even that would suffice to prove that other nations have distinct and fixed rules whereby to estimate political successes; that, practically, they acknowledge no other sovereign power than that which is so *de facto*; that they can inquire no further without interfering with the internal concerns of other nations; and that, when a nation is divided into two parties, or the bonds of the political compact between the monarch and the people happen to be otherwise broken, they have equal rights, and owe the same obligations to neutral nations. It follows, therefore, that the contending parties in Spanish America are not subjected to different rules.

If these rules may sometimes be varied, or admit of any alteration, the exception should always be in favor of the oppressed against the oppressor. It is therefore strongly contended by many of the most celebrated civilians, "that in all revolutions produced by the tyranny of the prince, foreign nations have a right to assist an oppressed people," a right dictated by justice and generosity. Now it cannot be supposed that the observance of justice ever gave a pretext for war to the party or nation most interested in a different conduct. Since, therefore, my Government has limited its pretensions to the acknowledgment of its real and effective sovereignty, which even our adversary himself would not call in question, it considers itself authorized to take this step, by the practice of nations, by public opinion, and the sanction of eternal justice. . . .

You also remarked that similar pretensions had been formed by other provinces of Spanish America now contending for their liberties. Would to Heaven that they all could now offer to this Government the same proofs of their effective sovereignty, and equal pledges of their respective preponderating power! Humanity would then have much fewer evils to deplore, and all America would exhibit a united people, only rivalling with each other in the art of improving their civil institutions, and extending the blessings and enjoyment of social order.

When I contemplate the distinguished part the United States may take in realizing this grand enterprise, and consider how much it is in their power to hasten this happy period, only by giving an example of national justice, in acknowledging the independence of those Governments who so gloriously and by so many sacrifices have known how to obtain it, my reason persuades me that the wishes of the United Provinces cannot fail to be speedily accomplished.

CHAPTER 10

The Contours of Independence

Achieving independence from Spain was a major feat. But independence itself left two major issues unresolved: the political structure of the new Latin American states and their place within the international community.

Surprisingly, the first issue was decided almost everywhere in favor of liberal republicanism. What makes this surprising is that the new states had been ruled for three centuries by monarchs before achieving independence. They had been subjects, not citizens, and thus had little direct experience with republican government. However, they had the intellectual tradition of the Enlightenment to draw from, as well as precedents furnished by the recent Atlantic Revolutions. What ultimately appealed to Latin American political elites was the moderate liberalism of Montesquieu (rather than the more purist, unitary approach of Rousseau) and the concrete examples of British parliamentarianism and U.S. constitutionalism (rather than the centralized democracy of Revolutionary France). With the short-lived exception of Mexico and somewhat more durable one of Brazil, Latin America adopted liberal republican forms of government.

Carving out a place in the world for themselves proved more difficult. This is because the European powers and the United States hovered over the disintegrating Spanish empire like vultures around carrion. Each power had its own, specific agenda, but all aimed to profit from Spain's loss. The United States and Great Britain sought to pry open and dominate the Latin American economy, previously closed to foreign trade by the exclusionary, mercantilist policies of Spain. Spain and the conservative powers of continental Europe eyed Latin American independence and the republics it spawned with deep suspicion, considering them as yet another manifestation of the worldwide revolutionary epidemic that had broken out in 1789. Consequently, the threat of foreign military intervention (sometimes actually carried out) hung heavily over the young Latin American republics. These two liabilities—economic dependence on the Anglo-American powers and political hostility from conservative Europe—were a crippling burden for the new republics.

I. A New World of Republics?

By 1819, with Bolivar's victory at Boyacá and San Martin's consolidation of Chilean independence, it was clear that the tide had turned. By 1821, with Bolivar's victory at Carabobo and San Martin's entry into Lima, it was evident that the cause of independence would triumph. But even before the last royalist bastions surrendered, Spanish America's liberators were already considering the new political order they wanted to create. With a few notable exceptions, the monarchist San Martin foremost among them, they advocated republican government.

1. BOLIVAR, "ANGOSTURA ADDRESS" (FEBRUARY 15, 1819)[1]

Bolivar's "Angostura Address," in which he shared his notion of republicanism with the Angostura Congress (which was meeting to give the new republic of Columbia a constitution), is the most complete expression of this brand of republicanism. Bolivar's debt to the Enlightenment (particularly Montesquieu's tripartite typology of governments, as well as its historical-political current) and the actual examples of the United States and Great Britain, is clear. One distinct feature, however, is Bolivar's insistence on the abolition of formal racial distinctions—necessary, in his view, to create a sense of national community from the diverse and hierarchically divided elements of Spanish American colonial society. With this notable exception, Bolivar's exposé offers a classic example of elite, liberal republicanism.

Fortunate is the citizen who, under the emblem of his command, has convoked this assembly of the national sovereignty so that it may exercise its absolute will! I therefore place myself among those most favored by Divine Providence, for I have had the honor of uniting the representatives of the people of Venezuela in this august Congress, the source of legitimate authority, the custodian of the sovereign will, and the arbiter of the Nation's destiny.

In returning to the representatives of the people the Supreme Power which was entrusted to me, I gratify not only my own innermost desires, but also those of my fellow-citizens and of future generations who trust to your wisdom, rectitude, and prudence in all things. Upon the fulfillment of this grateful obligation, I shall be released from the immense authority with which I have been burdened and from the unlimited responsibility which has weighed so heavily upon my slender resources. Only the force of necessity, coupled with the imperious will of the people, compelled me to assume the fearful and dangerous post of *Dictator and Supreme Chief of the Republic*. But now I can breathe more freely, for I am returning to you this authority. . . .

---

[1]Simon Bolivar, *"Address Delivered at the Inauguration of the Second National Congress of Venezuela in Angostura,"* ed. Harold A. Bierck (New York: Colonial Press, 1951), vol. 1, 173–196.

Legislators! I deliver into your hands the supreme rule of Venezuela. Yours is now the august duty of consecrating yourselves to the achievement of felicity of the Republic; your hands hold the scales of our destiny, the measure of our glory. They shall seal the decrees that will insure our liberty. At this moment the Supreme Chief of the Republic is no more than just a plain citizen, and such he wishes to remain until his death. I shall, however, serve as a soldier so long as any foe remains in Venezuela. . . .

Let us review the past to discover the base upon which the Republic of Venezuela is founded.

America, in separating from the Spanish monarchy, found herself in a situation similar to that of the Roman Empire when its enormous framework fell to pieces in the midst of the ancient world. Each Roman division then formed an independent nation in keeping with its location or interests; but this situation differed from America's in that those members proceeded to reestablish their former associations. We, on the contrary, do not even retain the vestiges of our original being. We are not Europeans; we are not Indians; we are but a mixed species of aborigines and Spaniards. Americans by birth and Europeans by law, we find ourselves engaged in a dual conflict: we are disputing with the natives for titles of ownership, and at the same time we are struggling to maintain ourselves in the country that gave us birth against the opposition of the invaders. Thus our position is most extraordinary and complicated. But there is more. As our role has always been strictly passive and our political existence nil, we find that our quest for liberty is now even more difficult of accomplishment; for we, having been placed in a state lower than slavery, had been robbed not only of our freedom, but also of the right to exercise an active domestic tyranny. Permit me to explain this paradox.

In absolute systems, the central power is unlimited. The will of the despot is the supreme law, arbitrarily enforced by subordinates who take part in the organized oppression in proportion to the authority that they wield. They are charged with civil, political, military, and religious functions; but, in the final analysis, the satraps of Persia are Persian, the pashas of the Grand Turk are Turks, and the sultans of Tartary are Tartars. China does not seek her mandarins in the homeland of Genghis Khan, her conqueror. America, on the contrary, received everything from Spain, who, in effect, deprived her of the experience that she would have gained from the exercise of an active tyranny by not allowing her to take part in her own domestic affairs and administration. This exclusion made it impossible for us to acquaint ourselves with the management of public affairs; nor did we enjoy that personal consideration, of such great value in major revolutions, that the brilliance of power inspires in the eyes of the multitude. In brief, Gentlemen, we were deliberately kept in ignorance and cut off from the world in all matters relating to the science of government.

Subject to the threefold yoke of ignorance, tyranny, and vice, the American people have been unable to acquire knowledge, power, or virtue. The lessons we received and the models we studied, as pupils of such pernicious teachers, were most destructive. We have been ruled more by deceit than by force, and we have been degraded more by vice than by superstition. Slavery is the daughter of Darkness: an ignorant people is a blind instrument of its own destruction. Ambition and intrigue abuse the credulity and experience of men lacking all political, economic, and civic knowledge; they adopt pure illusion as reality; they take license for liberty, treachery for patriotism, and vengeance for justice. This situation is similar to that of the robust blind man who, beguiled by his strength, strides forward with all the assurance of one who can see, but, upon hitting every variety of obstacle, finds himself unable to retrace his step.

If a people, perverted by their training, succeed in achieving their liberty, they will soon lose it, for it would be of no avail to endeavor to explain to them that happiness consists in the practice of virtue; that the rule of law is more powerful than the rule of tyrants, because, as the laws are more inflexible, everyone should submit to their beneficent austerity; that proper morals, and not force, are the bases of law; and that to practice justice is to practice liberty. Therefore, Legislators, your work is so much the more arduous, inasmuch as you to reeducate men who have been corrupted by erroneous illusions and false incentives. Liberty, says Rousseau, is a succulent morsel, but one difficult to digest. Our weak fellow-citizens will have to strengthen their spirit greatly before they can digest the wholesome nutrient of freedom. Their limbs benumbed by chains, their sight dimmed by the darkness of dungeons, and their strength sapped by the pestilence of servitude, are they capable of marching toward the august temple of Liberty without faltering? Can they come near enough to bask in its brilliant rays and to breathe freely the pure air which reigns therein?

Legislators, meditate well before you choose. Forget not that you are to lay the political foundation for a newly born nation which can rise to the heights of greatness that Nature has marked out for it if you but proportion this foundation in keeping with the high plane that it aspires to attain. Unless your choice is based upon the peculiar tutelary experience of the Venezuelan people—a factor that should guide you in determining the nature and form of government you are about to adopt for the well-being of the people—and, I repeat, unless you happen upon the right type of government, the result of our reforms will again be slavery.

The history of bygone ages affords you examples of thousands of governments. Visualize the nations that have shone in brightest splendor and you will be grieved to see that virtually all the world has been, and still is, the victim of its governments. You will note numerous systems of governing men, but always their purpose has been to oppress them. If our habit of looking upon the human species as being led by its own shepherds did not diminish the horror of so distressing a spectacle, we should be stunned to see our docile species grazing upon the surface of the earth, like meek flocks destined to feed their cruel keepers. Nature, in truth, endows us at birth with the instinctive desire for freedom; but, be it laziness or some tendency inherent in humanity, it is obvious that mankind rests unconcerned and accepts things as they are, even though it is bound forcibly in fetters. As we contemplate humanity in this state of prostitution, it would appear that we have every right to persuade ourselves that most men hold this humiliating maxim to be the truth: it is harder to maintain the balance of liberty than to endure the weight of tyranny. . . .

Many ancient and modern nations have shaken off oppression; yet those who have enjoyed even a few precious moments of liberty are rare, as they have speedily returned to their old political vices; because peoples rather than governments repeatedly drag tyranny in their train. The habit of being ruled makes them insensible to the attractions of honor and national prosperity, and they regard with indifference the glory of living in the free sway of liberty, under the protection of laws dictated by their own free will. The records of the universe proclaim this awful truth.

Only democracy, in my opinion, is amenable to absolute liberty. But what democratic government has simultaneously enjoyed power, prosperity, and permanence? On the other hand, have not aristocracy and monarchy held great and power empires together century after century? Is there any government older than that of China? What republic has lasted longer than Sparta or Venice? Did not the Roman Empire conquer the earth? Has not France had fourteen centuries of monarchy? Is there any nation greater than England? Yet these nations have been or still are aristocracies and monarchies.

Despite these bitter reflections, I experience a surge of joy when I witness the great advances that our Republic has made since it began its noble career. Loving what is most useful, animated by what is most just, and aspiring to what is most perfect, Venezuela, on breaking away from Spain, has recovered her independence, her freedom, her equality, and her national sovereignty. By establishing a democratic republic, she has proscribed monarchy, distinctions, nobility, prerogatives, and privileges. She has declared for the rights of man and freedom of action, thought, speech, and press. These eminently liberal acts, because of the sincerity that has inspired them, will never cease to be admired. The first Congress of Venezuela has indelibly stamped upon the annals of our laws the majesty of the people, and, in placing its seal upon the social document best calculated to develop the well-being of the nation, that Congress has fittingly given expression to this thought. . . .

[But] the more I admire the excellence of the federal Constitution of Venezuela, the more I am convinced of the impossibility of its application to our state. And, to my way of thinking, it is a marvel that its prototype in North America endures so successfully and has not been overthrown at the first sign of adversity or danger. Although the people of North America are a singular model of political virtue and moral rectitude; although that nation was cradled in liberty, reared on freedom, and maintained by liberty alone; and—I must reveal everything—although those people, so lacking in many respects, are unique in the history of mankind;, it is a marvel, I repeat, that so weak and complicated a government as the federal system has managed to govern them in the difficult and trying circumstances of their past. But, regardless of the effectiveness of this form of government with respect to North America, I must say that it has never for a moment entered my mind to compare the position and character of two states as dissimilar as the

English-American and the Spanish-American. Would it not be most difficult to apply to Spain the English system of political, civil, and religious liberty? Hence, it would be even more difficult to adopt to Venezuela the laws of North America. Does not *L'Esprit des Laws* state that laws should be suited to the people for whom they are made; that it would be a major coincidence if those of one nation could be adapted to another; that laws must take into account the physical conditions of the country, climate, character of the land, location, size, and mode of living of the people; that they should be in keeping with the degree of liberty that the Constitution can sanction respecting the religion of the inhabitants, their inclinations, resources, number, commerce, habits, and customs? This is the code we must consult, not the code of Washington!

The Venezuelan Constitution, although based upon the most perfect of constitutions from the standpoint of the correctness of its principles and the beneficent effects of its administration, differed fundamentally from the North American Constitution on one cardinal point, and, without doubt, the most important point. The Congress of Venezuela, like the North American legislative body, participates in some of the duties vested in the executive power. We, however, have subdivided the executive power by vesting it in a collective body. Consequently, this executive body has been subject to the disadvantages resulting from the periodic existence of a government which is suspended and dissolved whenever its members adjourn. Our executive triumvirate lacks, so to speak, unity, continuity, and individual responsibility. It is deprived of prompt action, continuous existence, true uniformity, and direct responsibility. The government that does not possess these things which give it a morality of its own must be deemed a nonentity.

Although the powers of the President of the United States are limited by numerous restrictions, he alone exercises all the governmental functions which the Constitution has delegated to him; thus there is no doubt but that his administration must be more uniform, constant, and more truly his own than an administration wherein the power is divided among a number of persons, a grouping that is nothing less than a monstrosity. The judicial power in Venezuela is similar to that of North America: its duration is not defined; it is temporary and not for life, and it enjoys all the independence proper to the judiciary.

The first Congress, in its federal Constitution, responded more to the spirit of the provinces than to the sound idea of creating an indivisible and centralized republic. In this instance, our legislators yielded to the ill-considered pleadings of those men from the provinces who were captivated by the apparent brilliance of the happiness of the North American people, believing that the blessings they enjoy result exclusively from their form of government rather than from the character and customs of the citizens. In effect, the United States' example, because of their remarkable prosperity, was one too tempting not to be followed. Who could resist the powerful attraction of full and absolute enjoyment of sovereignty, independence, and freedom? Who could resist the devotion inspired by an intelligent government that has not only blended public and private rights but has also based its supreme law respecting the desires of the individual upon common consent?

Who could resist the rule of a beneficent government which, with a skilled, dexterous, and powerful hand always and in all regions, directs its resources toward social perfection, the sole aim of human institutions?

But no matter how tempting this magnificent federal system might have appeared, and regardless of its possible effect, the Venezuelans were not prepared to enjoy it immediately upon casting off their chains. We were not prepared for such good, for good, like evil, results in death when it is sudden and excessive. Our moral fiber did not then possess the stability necessary to derive benefits from a wholly representative government; a government so sublime, in fact, that it might more nearly benefit a republic of saints. . . .

Permit me to call the attention of the Congress to a matter that may be of vital importance. We must keep in mind that our people are neither European nor North American; rather, they are a mixture of African and the Americans who originated in Europe. Even Spain herself has ceased to be European because of her African blood, her institutions, and her character. It is impossible to determine with any degree of accuracy where we belong in the human family. The greater portion of the native Indians has been annihilated; Spaniards have mixed with Americans and Africans, and Africans with Indians and Spaniards. While we have all been born of the same mother, our fathers, different in origin and in blood, are foreigners, and all differ visibly as to the color of their skin; a dissimilarity which places upon us an obligation of the greatest importance.

Under the Constitution, which interprets the laws of Nature, all citizens of Venezuela enjoy complete political equality. Although equality may not have been the political dogma of Athens, France, or North America, we must consecrate it here in order to correct the disparity that apparently exists. My opinion, Legislators, is that the fundamental basis of our political system hinges directly and exclusively upon the establishment and practice of equality in Venezuela. Most wise men concede that men are born with equal rights to share the benefits of society, but it does not follow that all men are born equally gifted to attain every rank. All men should practice virtue, but not all do; all ought to be courageous, but not all are; all should possess talents, but not everyone does. Herein are the real distinctions which can be observed among individuals even in the most liberally constituted society. If the principle of political equality is generally recognized, so also must be the principle of physical and moral inequality. Nature makes men unequal in intelligence, temperament, strength, and character. Laws correct this disparity by so placing the individual within society that education, industry, arts, services, and virtues give him a fictitious equality that is properly termed political and social. The idea of a classless state, wherein diversity increases in proportion to the rise in population, was an eminently beneficial inspiration. By this step alone, cruel discord has been completely eliminated. How much jealousy, rivalry, and hate have thus been averted!

Having dealt with justice and humanity, let us now give attention to politics and society, and let us resolve the difficulties inherent in a system so simple and natural, yet so weak that the slightest obstacle can upset and destroy it. The diversity of racial origin will require an infinitely firm hand and great tactfulness in order to manage this heterogeneous society, whose complicated mechanism is easily damaged, separated, and disintegrated by the slightest controversy.

The most perfect system of government is that which results in the greatest possible measure of happiness and the maximum of social security and political stability. The laws enacted by the first Congress gave us reason to hope that happiness would be the lot of Venezuela; and, through your laws, we must hope that security and stability will perpetuate this happiness. You must solve the problem. But how, having broken all the shackles of our former oppression, can we accomplish the enormous task of preventing the remnants of our past fetters from becoming liberty-destroying weapons? The vestiges of Spanish domination will long be with us before we can completely eradicate them: the contagion of despotism infests the atmosphere about us. . . .

Venezuela had, has, and should have a republican government. Its principles should be the sovereignty of the people, division of powers, civil liberty, proscription of slavery, and the abolition of monarchy and privileges. We need equality to recast, so to speak, into a unified nation, the classes of men, political opinions, and public customs. Let us now consider the vast field of problems yet to be traversed. . . . Let history serve us as a guide in this survey. First, Athens affords us the most brilliant example of an absolute democracy, but at the same time Athens herself is the most melancholy example of the extreme weakness of this type of government. The wisest legislator in Greece did not see his republic survive ten years; and he suffered the humiliation of admitting that absolute democracy is inadequate in governing any form of society, even the most cultured, temperate, and limited, because its brilliance comes only in lightning flashes of liberty. We must recognize, therefore, that, although Solon disillusioned the world, he demonstrated to society how difficult it is to govern men by laws alone.

The Republic of Sparta, which might appear to be but a chimerical invention, produced more tangible results than all the ingenious labors of Solon. Glory, virtue, morality, and, consequently, national felicity, were the results of Lycurgus' legislation. Although two kings in one state meant two monsters to devour it, Sparta had little to regret because of its dual throne; whereas Athens promised itself a most brilliant future replete with absolute sovereignty, free and frequent election of magistrates, and moderate, wise, and politic laws. Pisistratus, the usurper and tyrant, accomplished more for Athens than did her laws; and Pericles, although also an usurper, was her most useful citizen. . . . Codes, systems, statutes, wise as they may be, are useless works having but small influence on societies; virtuous men, patriotic men, learned men make republics.

The Roman Constitution brought power and fortune such as no other people in the world have ever known. It did not provide for an exact distribution of powers. The consuls, senate, and people were alternately legislators, magistrates, and judges; everyone participated in all powers. The executive, comprising two consuls, was subject to the same weakness as was that of Sparta. Despite this weakness, the Republic did not experience the disastrous discord that would appear to have been unavoidable in a magistrature composed of two individuals with equal authority, each possessing the powers of a monarch. A government whose sole purpose was conquest would hardly seem destined to insure the happiness of a nation; but an enormous and strictly warlike government lifted Rome to the highest splendor of virtue and glory, and made of this earth a Roman dominion, thereby demonstrating to man what political virtues can accomplish and the relative unimportance of institutions.

Passing from ancient to modern times, we find England and France attracting the attention of all nations and affording them a variety of lessons in matters of government. The evolution of these two great peoples, like a flaming meteor, has flooded the world with such a profusion of political enlightenment that today every thinking person is aware of the rights and duties of man and the nature of the virtues and vices of governments. All can now appreciate the intrinsic merit of the speculative theories of modern philosophers and legislators. In fact, this political star, in its illuminating career, has even fired the hearts of the apathetic Spaniards, who, having also been thrown into the political whirlpool, made ephemeral efforts to establish liberty; but recognizing their incapacity for living under the sweet rule of law, they have returned to their immemorial practices of imprisonment and burnings at the stake.

Here, Legislators, is the place to repeat what the eloquent Volney says in the preface of his *Ruins of Palmyra*: "To the newborn peoples of the Spanish Indies, to the generous leaders who guide them toward freedom; may the mistakes and misfortunes of the Old World teach wisdom and happiness to the New." May the teachings of experience not be lost; and may the schools of Greece, Rome, France, England, and North America instruct us in the difficult science of creating and preserving nations through laws that are proper, just, legitimate, and, above all, useful. We must never forget that the excellence of a government lies not in its theories, nor in its form or mechanism, but in its being suited to the nature and character of the nation for which it is instituted.

Among the ancient and modern nations, Rome and Great Britain are the most outstanding. Both were born to govern and to be free and both were built not on ostentatious forms of freedom, but upon solid institutions. Thus I recommend to you, Representatives, the study of the British Constitution, for that body of laws appears destined to bring about the greatest possible good for the peoples that adopt it; but, however perfect it may be, I am by no means proposing that you imitate it slavishly. When I speak of the British government, I only refer to its republican features; and, indeed, can a political system be labelled a monarchy when it recognizes popular sovereignty, division and balance of powers, civil liberty, freedom of conscience and of press, and all that is politically sublime? Can there be more liberty in any other type of republic? Can more be asked of any society? I commend this Constitution to you as that most worthy of serving as a model for those who aspire to the enjoyment of the rights of man and who seek all the political happiness which is compatible with the frailty of human nature.

Nothing in our fundamental laws would have to be altered were we to adopt a legislative power similar to that held by the British Parliament. Like the North Americans, we have divided national representation into two chambers: that of Representatives and the Senate. The first is very wisely constituted. It enjoys all its proper functions, and it requires no essential revision, because the constitution, in creating it, gave it the form and powers which the people deemed necessary in order that they might be legally and properly represented. If the Senate were hereditary rather than elective, it would, in my opinion, be the basis, the tie, the very soul of our republic. In political storms this body would arrest the thunder-bolts of the government and would repel any violent popular reaction. Devoted to the government because of a natural interest in its own preservation, a hereditary senate would always oppose any attempt on the part of the people to infringe upon the jurisdiction and authority of their magistrates. It must be confessed that most men are unaware of their best interests and that they constantly endeavor to assail them in the hands of their custodians—the individual clashes with the mass, and the mass with authority. It is necessary, therefore, that in all governments there be a neutral body to protect the injured and disarm the offender. To be neutral, this body must not owe its origin to appointment by the government or to election by the people, if it is to enjoy a full measure of independence which neither fears nor expects anything from these two sources of authority. The hereditary senate, as a part of the people, shares its interests, its sentiments, and its spirit. For this reason, it should not be presumed that a hereditary senate would ignore the interests of the people or forget its legislative duties. The senators in Rome and in the House of Lords in London have been the strongest pillars upon which the edifice of political and civil liberty has rested.

At the outset, these senators should be elected by Congress. The successors to this Senate must command the initial attention of the government, which should educate them in a special school designed especially to train these guardians and future legislators of the nation. They ought to learn the arts, sciences, and letters that enrich the mind of a public figure. From childhood they should understand the career for which they have been destined by Providence, and from earliest youth they should prepare their minds for the dignity that awaits them.

The creation of a hereditary senate would in no way be a violation of political equality. I do not solicit the establishment of a nobility, for, as a celebrated repub-lican has said, that would simultaneously destroy equality and liberty. What I pro-pose is an office for which the candidates must prepare themselves, an office that demands great knowledge and the ability to acquire such knowledge. All should not be left to chance and the outcome of elections. The people are more easily deceived than is Nature perfected by art; and, although these senators, it is true, would not be bred in an environment that is all virtue, it is equally true that they would be raised in an atmosphere of enlightened education. Furthermore, the lib-erators of Venezuela are entitled to occupy forever a high rank in the Republic that they have brought into existence. I believe that posterity would view with regret the effacement of the illustrious names of its first benefactors. I say, moreover, that it is a matter of public interest and national honor, of gratitude on Venezuela's part, to honor gloriously, until the end of time, a race of virtuous, prudent, and persevering men who, overcoming every obstacle, have founded the Republic at the price of the most heroic sacrifices. And if the people of Venezuela do not applaud the elevation of their benefactors, then they are unworthy to be free, and they will never be free.

A hereditary senate, I repeat, will be the fundamental basis of the legislative power, and therefore the foundation of the entire government. It will also serve as a counterweight to both government and people; and as a natural power, it will weaken the mutual attacks of these two eternally rival powers. In all conflicts the calm reasoning of a third party will serve as the means of reconciliation. Thus the Venezuelan senate will . . . be the mediator . . . and maintain harmony between the head and the other parts of this political body.

No inducement could corrupt a legislative body invested with the highest honors, dependent only upon itself, having no fear of the people, independent of the government, and dedicated solely to the repression of all evil principles and to the advancement of every good principle—a legislative body that would be deeply concerned with the maintenance of a society, for it would share the consequences, be they honorable or disastrous. . . .

The British executive power possesses all the authority properly appertaining to a sovereign, but he is surrounded by a triple line of dams, barriers, and stockades. He is the head of the government, but his ministers and subordinates rely more upon the law than upon his authority, as they are personally responsible; and not even decrees of royal authority can exempt them from this responsibility. The executive is commander in chief of the army and navy; he makes peace and declares war; but Parliament annually determines what sums are to be paid to these military forces. While the courts and judges are dependent on the executive power, the laws originate in and are made by Parliament. To neutralize the power of the King, his person is declared inviolable and sacred; but, while his head is left untouched, his hands are tied. The sovereign of England has three formidable rivals: his Cabinet, which is responsible to the people and to Parliament; the Senate [House of Lords] which, representing the nobility of which it is composed, defends the interests of the people; and the House of Commons, which serves as the representative body of the British people and provides them with a place in which to express their opinions. Moreover, as the judges are responsible for the enforcement of the laws, they do not depart from them; and the administrators of the exchequer, being subject to prosecution not only for personal infractions but also for those of the government, take care to prevent any misuse of public funds. No matter how closely we study the composition of the English executive power, we can find nothing to prevent is being judged as the most perfect model for a kingdom, for an aristocracy, or for a democracy. Give Venezuela such an executive power in the person of a president chosen by the people or their representatives. . . .

No matter what citizen occupies this office, he will be aided by the Constitution, and therein being authorized to do good, he can do no harm, because his ministers will cooperate with him only insofar as he abides by the law. If he attempts to infringe upon the law, his own ministers will desert him, thereby isolating him from the Republic, and they will even bring charges against him in the Senate. The ministers, being responsible for any transgressions committed, will actually govern, since they must account for their actions. . . .

Although the authority of the executive power in England may appear to be extreme, it would, perhaps, not be excessive in the Republic of Venezuela. Here the Congress has tied the hands and even the heads of its men of state. This deliberative assembly has assumed a part of the executive functions, contrary to the maxim of Montesquieu, to wit: a representative assembly should exercise no active function. It should only make laws and determine whether or not those laws are enforced. Nothing is as disturbing to harmony among the powers of government as their intermixture. Nothing is more dangerous with respect to the people than a weak executive; and if a kingdom has deemed it necessary to grant the executive so many powers, then in a republic these powers are infinitely more indispensable.

If we examine this difference, we will find that the balance of power between the branches of government must be distributed in two ways. In republics the executive should be the stronger, for everything conspires against it; while in monarchies the legislative power should be superior, as everything works in the monarch's favor. . . .

A republican magistrate is an individual set apart from society, charged with checking the impulse of the people toward license and the propensity of judges and administrators toward abuse of the laws. He is directly subject to the legislative body, the senate, and the people: he is the one man who resists the combined pressure of the opinions, interests, and passions of the social state and who, as Carnot states, does little more than struggle constantly with the urge to dominate and the desire to escape domination. He is, in brief, an athlete pitted against a multitude of athletes.

This weakness can only be corrected by a strongly rooted force. It should be strongly proportioned to meet the resistance which the executive must expect from the legislature, the judiciary, and from the people of a republic. Unless the executive has easy access to all the [administrative] resources, fixed by a just distribution of powers, he inevitably becomes a nonentity or abuses his authority. By this I mean that the result will be the death of the government, whose heirs are anarchy, usurpation, and tyranny. Some seek to check the executive authority by curbs and restrictions, and nothing is more just; but it must be remembered that the bonds we seek to preserve should, of course, be strengthened, but not tightened.

Therefore, let the entire system of government be strengthened, and let the balance of power be drawn up in such a manner that it will be permanent and incapable of decay because of its own tenuity. Precisely because no form of government is so weak as the democratic, its framework must be firmer, and its institutions must be studied to determine their degree of stability. Unless this is done . . . we will have to reckon with an ungovernable, tumultuous, and anarchic society. . . .

Legislators, we should not be presumptuous. We should be moderate in our pretentions. It is not likely that we will secure what mankind has never attained or that which the greatest and wisest nations have not acquired. Complete liberty and absolute democracy are but reefs upon which all republican hopes have foundered. . . . Only angels, not men, can exist free, peaceful, and happy while exercising every sovereign power.

The people of Venezuela already enjoy the rights that they may legitimately and easily exercise. Let us now, therefore, restrain the growth of immoderate pretentions which, perhaps, a form of government unsuited to our people might excite. Let us abandon the federal forms of government unsuited to us; let us put aside the triumvirate which holds the executive power and center it in a president. We must grant him sufficient authority to enable him to continue the struggle against the obstacles inherent in our recent situation, our present state of war, and every variety of foe, foreign or domestic. . . . Let the legislature relinquish the powers that rightly belong to the executive; let it acquire, however, a new consistency, a new influence in the balance of authority. Let the courts be strengthened by increasing the stability and independence of the judges and by the establishment of juries and civil and criminal codes. . . .

My desire is for every branch of government and administration to attain that degree of vigor which alone can insure equilibrium, not only among the members of the government, but also among the different factions of which our society is composed. . . . All the peoples of the world have sought freedom, some by force of arms, others by force of law, passing alternately from anarchy to despotism, or from despotism to anarchy. Few peoples have been content with moderate aims, establishing their institutions according to their means, their character, and their circumstances. We must not aspire to the impossible, lest, in trying to rise above the realm of liberty, we again descend into the realm of tyranny. Absolute liberty invariably lapses into absolute power, and the mean between these two extremes is supreme social liberty. Abstract theories create the pernicious idea of unlimited freedom. Let us see to it that the strength of the public is kept within the limits prescribed by reason and interest; that the national will is confined within the bonds set by a just power; that the judiciary is rigorously controlled by civil and criminal laws, analogous to those in our present Constitution—then an equilibrium between the powers of government will exist, the conflicts that hamper the progress of the state will disappear, and those complications which tend to hinder rather than unite society will be eliminated.

The formation of a stable government requires as a foundation a national spirit, having as its objective a uniform concentration on two cardinal factors, namely, moderation of the popular will and limitation of public authority. . . .

Love of country, love of law, and respect for magistrates are the exalted emotions that must permeate the soul of a republic. The Venezuelans love their country, but they cannot love her laws, because these, being sources of evil, have been harmful; neither can they respect their magistrates, as they have been unjust, while the new administrators are scarcely known in the calling which they have just entered. Unless there is a sacred reverence for country, laws, and authority, society becomes confused, an abyss—and endless conflict of man versus man, group versus group.

All our moral powers will not suffice to save our infant republic from this chaos unless we fuse the mass of the people, the government, the legislation, and the national spirit into a single united body. Unity, unity, unity must be our motto in all things. The blood of our citizens is varied; let it be mixed for the sake of unity. Our Constitution has divided the powers of government; let them be bound together to secure unity. Our laws are but a sad relic of ancient and modern despotism. Let this monstrous edifice crumble and fall; and having removed even its ruins, let us erect a temple of Justice; and guided by its sacred inspiration, let us write a code of Venezuelan laws. Should we wish to consult monuments of legislation, those of Great Britain, France, and the United States of North America afford us admirable models. . . .

Legislators! In the plan of a constitution that I most respectfully submit to your better wisdom, you will observe the spirit in which it was conceived. In proposing to you a division of citizens into active and passive groups, I have endeavored to promote the national prosperity. . . . By setting just and prudent restrictions upon the primary and electoral assemblies, we can put the first check on popular license, thereby avoiding the blind, clamorous conventions that have in all times placed the stamp of error on elections, an error that consequently carries over to the magistrates and in turn to the conduct of the government; for the initial act of election is the one by which a people creates either liberty or slavery. . . .

In seeking to vest in the executive authority a sum total of powers greater than that which it previously enjoyed, I have no desire to grant a despot the authority to tyrannize the Republic, but I do wish to prevent deliberative despotism from being the immediate source of a vicious circle of despotic situations, in which anarchy alternates with oligarchy and monocracy. In requesting tenure for judges and the establishment of juries and a new code of law, I have asked the Congress to guarantee civil liberty, the most precious, the most just, the most necessary, in a word, the only liberty, since without it the others are nothing. . . .

Horrified by the disagreement that has reigned and will continue to reign among us owing to the subtle nature which characterizes the federal government, I am impelled to request that you adopt a central form of government, uniting all the states of Venezuela into a republic, one and indivisible. This measure, which I regard as urgent, vital, and redeeming is of such a nature that, unless it is adopted, death will be the fruit of our rebirth. . . .

I would not dwell upon the most notable acts of my command did they not concern the majority of Venezuelans. I refer, Gentlemen, to the more important resolutions of this most recent period. The dark mantle of barbarous and profane slavery covered the Venezuelan earth, and our sky was heavy with stormy clouds, which threatened to rain a deluge of fire. I implored the protection of the God of Humanity, and redemption soon dispersed the tempests. Slavery broke its fetters, and Venezuela was filled with new sons, grateful sons who have forged the instruments of their captivity into weapons of freedom. Yes, those who once were slaves are now free; those who once were the embittered enemies of a stepmother are now the proud defenders of their own country. To describe the justice, the necessity, and the beneficent results of this measure would be superfluous, for you know the history of the Helots, of Spartaco, and of Haiti; and because you know that one cannot be both free and enslaved at the same time, without simultaneously violating every natural, political, and civil law, I leave to your sovereign decision the reform or the repeal of all my statutes and decrees; but I plead for the confirmation of the absolute freedom of the slaves, as I would plead for my very life and for the life of the Republic. . . .

I pray you, Legislators, receive with indulgence this profession of my political faith. . . . Grant to Venezuela a government preeminently popular, preeminently just, preeminently moral; one that will suppress anarchy, oppression, and guilt—a government that will usher in the reign of innocence, humanity, and peace; a government wherein the rule of inexorable law will signify the triumph of equality and freedom.

II. Mexico Achieves Independence

Although South America was well on the way toward winning independence in 1819, this was not the case in Mexico. There, creole elites, horrified by the specter of Indian insurgency, servile uprising, and race war, had rallied to the royal banner. Staffing the royal army, they had ruthlessly crushed the movements of Hidalgo and Morelos and had reduced what was left of the insurgency to a few scattered bands of hunted guerillas. This creole–royalist alliance had kept Mexico firmly within the Spanish orbit. But events in Spain changed all this. In January 1820, a bored, underpaid Spanish expeditionary army waiting at Cadiz for transportation to America rose up and demanded that Fernando VII accept the constitution of Cadiz and become a limited, constitutional monarch. This liberal revolution spread throughout civil society, and Fernando was forced to accede— thus beginning a three-year period of liberalism in Spain.

In Mexico, news of the liberal revolution in Spain frightened the conservative creole elites. Confident that they could handle the remnants of local insurgency, which they had well in hand, they now came to see the liberal Cortes reinstalled in Madrid as the greater danger. Afraid that it would force unwanted reforms on Mexico, the creole commander of the royalist forces, Augustin Iturbide, acted. In early 1821, he made peace with the rebel leader, Vincente Guerrero; and in February, the two men issued a joint proclamation of independence, the *Plan de Iguala*. In contrast to the revolutions of South America, Mexican independence was in many ways a conservative reflex against liberalism.

2. ADDRESS OF COLONEL QUIROGA TO
FERDINAND VII (JANUARY 7, 1820)[2]

*In January 1820, officers of the ragged Spanish expeditionary force at Cadiz, which
had been waiting for years for ships (which nearly bankrupt Spain did not possess)
to take them to America to fight the independence movements, rose in frustration.
They demanded that Fernando VII accept the 1812 Constitution of Cadiz and rule
as a constitutional monarch. The uprising spread to civil society, and Fernando was
forced to acquiesce. This rising (known as the Riego Revolt, after one of its leaders)
not only dashed Spanish hopes of subjugating Spanish America by military force. It
also had far-reaching consequences in both the New World (where it prompted Iturbide to proclaim Mexican independence) and Old (where it served as an inspiration
for further liberal risings in Latin Europe, notably Portugal). The following document
is the declaration issued by another leader of the revolt.*

Sire, the Spanish Army, by whose blood and unheard of sacrifices your Majesty
was restored to the throne of your ancestors, the Spanish Army under whose auspices the nation sanctioned, by means of its representatives, the code of laws which
were to have fixed forever its happy destiny, saw its honor and ardent patriotism
affected the day on which Your Majesty, in defiance of the laws of gratitude and of
justice, overturned that monument of wisdom and declared that to be an offence,
which was an expression of the most legit rights.

Six years have not been able to alter such deeply engraved sentiments. The
several insurrections which have broken out at different periods and in different
places will have convinced your Majesty that they are still fostered by the whole
nation, as well as that if your Majesty's person has been the object of general ado-
ration, neither is so the system which you have adopted, nor the persons who
surround you, so unworthy of your favor and confidence. The genius of ill has
hitherto suppressed a cry to generous and respectable, and the brave men who
raised it have fallen victims to that iniquity which pardons not him who removes
the veil by which it fascinates an easy and ignorant people.

So disastrous a fate has not intimidated the corps of the Expeditionary Army
who again raise a cry so sweet to every Spaniard who knowns the value of that appellation. They, Sire, raised it and swore to it solemnly on the 1st day of January.
They swore to it with the firm and decided determination to be faithful to an oath
to which the country hearkened. Nothing can render them false to it and the last
drop of their blood appears to them but a paltry sacrifice when compared with the
grand enterprise which they have undertaken. To revive the Constitution of Spain is
their object. To decide that it is the nation legitimately represented that alone has the
right to give itself laws is the end which inspires them with the purest ardor, the sub-
limest enthusiasm. The enlightened state of Europe does not now, Sire, permit that

[2]British National Archives, Foreign Office, Series 72, Box 234.

nations should be governed as the absolute property of kings. The people require other institutions and the representative form of government is that which seems most analogous to vast societies, the individuals of which cannot assemble in mass for the promulgation of their laws. It is this form of government which the wisest of nations have adopted, that which all covet, and that the possession of which has cost so much blood and of which no nation is more worthy than the people of Spain.

Why is this nation, the most favored by nature, to see itself deprived of the greatest gift which man can bestow? Why is this nation unworthy to breathe the air of civil liberty which alone vivifies the body of a state? Ancient prejudices, systems enforced by violence, frivolous and vain prerogatives which only flatter the folly of pride, and the treacherous suggestions of favorites who oppress today to be oppressed tomorrow—are these just motives for violating the laws of reason, humanity and justice? Kings are from the people. Kings are kings because the people will it so. The information now generally diffused has rendered these truths incontrovertible, and if governments follow other principles, their language is that of deceit and hypocrisy, not of error and ignorance. It is the desire and the determination of the Army that such language should exist no longer. The nation has the same feelings, but habits of obedience and the laws of fear have opposed a dike to the general declaration of them, but this will be broken when it shall be known that the brave have overcome it. The country occupied by the Army already breaks out in acclamations upon the promulgation of a Code which ought to have been proclaimed but once.

Their cries will spread throughout the Peninsula, which shall again be the theatre of virtue and heroism. But should these sweet hopes not be realized, should Heaven not grant such ardent wishes, not on this account will they look upon their labors as lost and to die in behalf of liberty will appear to them far sweeter than to live so long under the laws and exposed to the caprices of those who seduce the heart of your Majesty and will lead you to your infallible ruin.

3. PLAN OF IGUALA (FEBRUARY 24, 1821)[3]

In February 1821, the leader of the royalist army in Mexico, Augustin de Iturbide (1783–1824), met with the head of the insurgency, Vincente Guerrero, in the town of Iguala. There they proclaimed the independence of Mexico and established three fundamental principles—Catholicism, independence, and racial equality—to govern the new polity. These guarantees were enshrined in the Plan de Iguala. The document also proclaimed that independent Mexico would be a constitutional monarchy and that Fernando VII would be invited to occupy the throne. In the actual event, Fernando never came; and the following year, Iturbide proclaimed himself Emperor Augustin I. The Mexican Empire lasted less than a year. Iturbide was overthrown by his generals in early 1823, and Mexico became a republic.

[3]British National Archives, Foreign Office, Series 72, Box 234, 8–13. http://www.constitucion1917 .gob.mx/es/Constitucion1917/Plan_de_Iguala. Translation by Daniel Arenas.

Americans! That name includes not only those born in America, but also the Europeans, Africans, and Asians who reside there. Have the kindness to listen to me. All of today's great nations were once dominated by others. Until their leaders permitted them to form their own opinions, they did not emancipate themselves. The Europeans who have today reached the highest status were once slaves to the Romans. Their empire, the greatest that history has ever known, is like the father of a family who, in antiquity, saw his sons and grandsons leave his household once they reached an age to establish their own, . . . while maintaining respect, veneration, and love for their origin.

For three hundred years Mexico has been under the tutelage of the most Catholic, pious, heroic, and magnanimous nation. Spain nurtured it and encouraged its growth, founding those opulent cities, those beautiful villages, these kingdoms and provinces more distinguished than any others in the universe. The population and its leaders have grown. All branches of its agriculture and mineral wealth have developed. . . . The branch is now equal to the tree trunk. Public opinion and the majority of the people call for absolute independence from Spain and any other nation. . . .

In 1810 this same cry echoed in the village of Dolores. The many horrors that ensued . . . convinced public opinion that the general union of Europeans and Americans, Indians and Natives was the only solid foundation on which our common happiness could rest. Who could doubt that after the horrible experience of so many disasters. . . . European Spaniards! Your homeland is America. That is where you live, where you have your loving wives, your tender sons, your lands, your commerce, and your goods. Americans! Who among you can say that he is not descended from a Spaniard? Behold the sweet chain that unites us. Add the other links of friendship, shared interest, common education and language, and the similarity of feelings, and you shall see that it is strong and that the common happiness of the kingdom is necessary, that it brings you all together in one sole opinion, one sole voice.

It is time to show that our sentiments are the same and that our union shall be the powerful hand that frees all of America without foreign help. At the head of a valiant and resolute army, I proclaim the independence of Mexico. She is now free, lord of her own destiny, and no longer recognizes or depends upon Spain or any other nation. . . .

The army is animated by no other desire than to preserve in all its purity the holy religion we profess and to ensure general happiness. Hear the solid bases upon which its resolution is founded.

1. The Catholic, Apostolic, and Roman Religion, without tolerance for any other.
2. The absolute independence of this kingdom.
3. A monarchical government tempered by a constitution suitable to this country.
4. Fernando VII or members of his dynasty shall be our emperors, to forestall the fatal designs of the ambitious.
5. There shall be an interim Junta that shall convoke the Cortes and execute this plan.

6. This Junta shall be called Governing and shall be composed of those ministers and honorable men already proposed to the Lord Viceroy.
7. It shall govern in the name of the king. . . .
8. If Fernando VII does not decide to come to Mexico, the Junta or regency shall reign in the name of the nation while the question of who shall be crowned is resolved.
9. This government shall be sustained by the Army of the Three Guarantees.
10. The Cortes shall decide if this Junta shall continue or if a regency shall be established until the Emperor takes the throne.
11. From their first meeting, they shall work on a Constitution for the Mexican Empire.
12. All resident inhabitants are eligible for any kind of employment, without any distinction but merit and virtue.
13. Their persons and property shall be respected and protected.
14. The regular and secular clergy shall retain all of their privileges and properties.
15. All branches of the state and their public employees shall be retained. Only those who oppose this plan shall be removed. . . .
21. Whoever conspires against independence shall go to prison, with no recourse until the Cortes establishes a punishment for the crime of high treason.
22. A vigilant watch will be kept for those who intend to sow division, and they shall be declared as conspirators against independence. . . .

III. Brazilian Independence

Brazil's path to independence was unique. In 1808, when Napoleon invaded Iberia, the Portuguese royal family escaped to Brazil, to which they transferred the seat of the Portuguese Empire. Because of this, Brazil was not separated from its king, as were the Spanish colonies. At first, the king and his government regarded the wars of Latin American independence as an opportunity to grab territory from the crumbling Spanish empire and occupied the Banda Oriental (modern-day Uruguay). But in 1820, a liberal revolution in Portugal (inspired by the one in Spain) imposed a constitution and required the king to return. He complied, but left his eldest son to rule Brazil as Prince Regent. The reforms of the liberal Portuguese Cortes frightened the Brazilian elite—particularly its plans to reassert direct Portuguese control over the Brazilian provinces and reimpose onerous trade monopolies, as well as its hostility toward slavery and the slave trade. Prompted by Brazilian mercantile and planter elites, the Prince Regent declared independence in 1822 with himself as Emperor Pedro I. After Mexico, Brazil thus became the second independent monarchy in the New World. And also like Mexico, Brazilian independence can be regarded as a conservative, creole reaction against metropolitan-imposed liberalism.

4. MANIFESTO OF THE PRINCE REGENT TO THE PEOPLE OF BRAZIL (AUGUST 1, 1822)[4]

The following document is a manifesto issued by the Prince Regent, shortly before his formal declaration of independence. It lays out Brazil's grievances against the liberal reforms of the Lisbon Cortes and offers justifications for independence.

Brasilians. The time for deceiving mankind is at an end. The Governments that still wish to found their Power upon the pretended Ignorance of the People, or upon ancient Errors and Abuses, will see the Colossus of their Greatness fall from the fragile Base on which it was built in other Times. For want of thinking in this manner, it has been that the Cortes of Lisbon have driven the Provinces of the South of Brasil to shake off the yoke that was preparing for them: From thinking in this manner, it is, that I now see all Brasil united round Me, requiring of me the Defence of Her Rights, and the Maintenance of her Liberty, and Independence. It behooves Me therefore to speak the Truth to you, Brasilians! Hear Me then.

The Congress of Lisbon arrogating to itself the Tyrannical Right to impose upon Brasil an Article of new Belief, founded upon a partial and promissory Oath, which could in no way involve the Approbation of her own Ruin, compelled Her to examine that assumed Authority, and to recognize the Injustice of such unbecoming Pretensions. This Examination, which insulted Reason recommended and required, shewed the Brasilians that Portugal, destroying all established Forms, changing all the ancient and respectable Institutions of the Monarchy, passing the Sponge of ridiculous Forgetfulness over all its Relations, and reconstituting itself anew, could not compel Them to accept a dishonourable and degrading System without attacking those very principles, whereon She founded her Revolution, and the Right to change her Political Institutions; without destroying that Basis whereon were established her new Rights, the unalienable Rights of the People, without embarrassing the March of Reason and of Justice, whose Laws are derived from the very Nature of Things, and never from the private Caprices of Men.

Then the Southern Provinces of Brasil, uniting together, and taking the Majestick Attitude of a People, which distinguishes amongst its Rights those of Liberty, and its own Happiness, cast their Eyes upon Me, the Son of their King, and their Friend, who looking at this rich and great Portion of our Globe in its true point of view; who, knowing the Talents of its Inhabitants, and the immense Resources of its Soil, saw with Pain the erroneous and tyrannical proceedings of those who so falsely and prematurely had taken the Name of Fathers of the Country, leaping from Representatives of the People of Portugal, to Sovereigns of all the vast Portuguese Monarchy; then I judged it unworthy of Me, and of the Great King whose Son and Delegate I am, to disregard the Wishes of such Faithful Subjects, who repressing perhaps Republican Desires, and Propensities, have turned from the

---

[4]British National Archives, Foreign Office, Series 63, Box 246.

fascinating Example of some neighbouring People, and have deposited in Me all their Hopes, in this manner preserving Royalty in this Great American Continent, and the acknowledged Rights of the August House of Braganza.

I acceded to their generous and sincere Wishes, and have remained in Brasil, making our Good King acquainted with this My firm Resolution, in the Persuasion that this Step would be for the Cortes of Lisbon the Thermometer of the Disposition of Brasil, of her well understood Dignity, and of the new Elevation of Her Sentiments; that it would make them stop in the Career they had begun, and return to the path of Justice, from which they had strayed. Thus Reason commanded; but the wild Views of Egotism continued to suffocate her Cries, and Precepts, and Discord pointed out new Deceits: Then, as was to have been expected, the Resentment and Indignation of the Leagued Provinces rose, and, as if by a sort of Magick, all Ideas and Sentiments converged towards the same point—were directed to one single End. Without the Noise of Arms, without the Cries of Anarchy, They requested of Me, as the Guarantee of their precious Liberty and National Honour, the speedy Installation of a General Constituent and Legislative Assembly in Brasil. Much did I desire to defer that Moment to see whether the Vanity of the Cortes of Lisbon would give way to the Voice of Reason, of Justice, and of their own Interests; but the Order suggested by them, and transmitted to the Portuguese Consuls, to prohibit the Clearing out of Arms and Ammunition for Brasil, was a Signal for War, and a real Commencement of Hostilities.

This Kingdom, which had already declared Me her Perpetual Defender, then insisted that I should provide in the most prompt and energetick Manner for her Security, Honour, and Prosperity. Had I delayed in My Resolution, I should have betrayed on one side My Sacred Promises, and, on the other, who could have been able to stay the Evils of Anarchy, the Dismemberment of the Provinces, and the Frenzy of Democracy?

What an obstinate Struggle between the inveterate and bloody parties, between a thousand successive and opposing Factions? To whom would have belonged the Gold and Diamonds of our inexhaustible Mines, the mighty Rivers which are the Strength of States, that prodigious Fertility, the inexhaustible Fountain of Riches, and Prosperity? Who could have calmed so many dissenting Parties, who would have civilized our widespread Population, separated by so many Rivers, which are Seas? Who would have sought after our Indians in the Centre of their impenetrable Forests, across the highest and most inaccessible Mountains? Certainly, Brasilians, Brasil would have been torn in pieces. This Great Work of Beneficent Nature, which is the Envy and Admiration of the Nations of the World, and the benevolent Views of Providence, would be destroyed, or at least retarded for many years.

I was responsible for all these Evils, for the Blood that was about to be spilled, and for the Victims that would infallibly be sacrificed to the Passions, and to private Interests: I formed my Resolution therefore; I took the Part the People desired; and I ordered the Assembly of Brasil to be convoked in order to cement the Political Independence of this Kingdom; without, however, breaking the Ties of

Portuguese Fraternity; harmonizing, with Decorum and Justice, the whole United Kingdom of Portugal, Brasil, and Algarve, and preserving under the same Chief, two Families, separated by immense Seas, who can only live united by the bonds of Equality of Rights, and reciprocal Interests.

Brasilians! For you it is unnecessary to call to mind all the Evils to which you were subject, and which impelled you to the Representation made to me by the Camara, and People of this City, on the 24th of May, which gave rise to My Royal Decree of the 3rd of June, of the present Year: but the Respect We owe to Mankind requires that We give the Reasons of your Justice, and of My Behaviour. The History of the Acts of the Congress of Lisbon towards Brasil is a History of incessant Injustice and Unreasonableness. Their Object was to paralize the Prosperity of Brasil, to consume all her Vitality, and to reduce her to such a state of Inanition and Weakness that her Ruin and Slavery should be inevitable. That the World may be convinced of what I say, let us enter upon the simple Exposition of the following Facts.

The Congress of Lisbon legislated for Brasil without waiting for her Representatives, putting thus aside the Sovereignty of the Majority of the Nation.

It denied her a Delegation of the Executive Power, of which she stood so much in need, to bring forth all the forces of her Virility, considering the great distance that separates her from Portugal, leaving her without Laws suitable to her Climate, and her local Circumstances; without ready Resources in her Necessities.

It refused her a Centre of Union and Strength, to weaken her, previously inciting her Provinces to separate themselves from that they fortunately had within themselves.

It decreed Governments without Stability, and without Connection, with three Centres of differing Action, insubordinate, rival, and contradictory, destroying by these means her Category of Kingdom, undermining the Basis of her future Greatness and Prosperity, and only leaving her all the Elements of Disorder and Anarchy.

It excluded, de facto, all Brasilians from every honourable Employment, and filled your Cities with European Bayonets, commanded by rude, cruel, and immoral Chiefs.

It received with Enthusiasm and lavished Praises upon all those Monsters who had inflicted painful Wounds in your Hearts, as promised not to cease tearing them open.

It laid violent Hands upon the Resources applied for the Bank of Brasil, overloaded with an enormous National Debt, with which the Congress never troubled itself; although the Credit of the Bank was intimately connected with the Publick Credit of Brasil, and its Prosperity.

It opened Negociations with Foreign States for the Alienation of Portions of your Territory, to weaken and enslave you.

It disarmed your Fortresses, emptied your Arsenals, left your Ports without defence, and called all your Navy to the Ports of Portugal. It drained your Treasuries with repeated Drafts for the Expence of Troops who came, without your asking, to spill your Blood, and destroy you; at the same time that you were prohibited the Introduction of Foreign Arms and Ammunition wherewith you might arm your avenging Hands, and support your Liberty.

It presented a Project of Commercial Relations, which, under the false appearance of a Chimerical Reciprocity, and Equality, monopolized your Riches, shut your Ports to Foreigners; thus destroying your Agriculture and Industry, and reducing the Inhabitants of Brasil again to the State of Wards and Colonists.

It treated from the Beginning, and still continues to treat, with unworthy Degradation and Contempt, the Representatives of Brasil, when these have the courage to insist upon their Rights, and even (who will dare to speak it) threatened you with giving Liberty to the Blacks, and turning them against their Masters.

To put an End to this long Narration of appalling Injustice, when for the first time the Sound of your just Indignation was heard in the Congress, They doubled their Mockery. Oh! Brasilians! Trying to disculpate their attempts under the plea of your own Will and Desire.

The Delegation of the Executive Power, which the Congress rejected as Anti-Constitutional, is now offered to us by a Commission from the bosom of this Congress, and with so much Liberality, that instead of one Centre of Power, which alone we wanted, they wish to give you two, or more. What unheard of Generosity! But who does not see that its object is to destroy your Strength, and Integrity; to arm Province against Province; Brothers against Brothers.

Let us awake therefore, Generous Inhabitants of this vast and powerful Empire, the Great Step of your Independence and Happiness, so many times foretold by the Great Politicians of Europe, is taken. Already you are a Sovereign People; already you have entered into the great Society of Independent Nations to which you had every right. Honour and National Dignity, the Desire to be prosperous, the Voice of Nature itself, order that Colonies cease to be Colonies when they arrive at a State of Manhood, and although treated as Colonies, you really were not so; but in fact a Kingdom. Besides; the same Right that Portugal had to overthrow her ancient Institutions and reconstitute herself, with much more Reason do you possess you inhabit a vast and extensive Country, with a Population (altho' wide spread) already greater than that of Portugal, and which will go on increasing with the same Rapidity as heavy Bodies that fall through Space. If Portugal deny you this Right, Let Her renounce herself the Right She can advance to have her new Constitution acknowledged by Foreign Nations, who thereupon might allege just motives for interfering in her Domestick Concerns, and for violating the Attributes of the Sovereignty and Independence of Nations.

What remains for you, then, Brasilians? It remains for you, to be all united in Interests, in Love, in Hope: to cause the August Assembly of Brasil to enter upon the Exercize of its Functions, in order that steered by Reason and Prudence, you may avoid the Shoals, which in the Sea of Revolution, France, Spain, and even Portugal unfortunately present: that You may mark with a sure and wise hand, the Separation of Powers, and found the Code of your Legislation in sound Philosophy, and apply it to your peculiar Circumstances.

Doubt it not, Brasilians: Your Representatives occupied, not in overcoming Renetencies, but in settling Rights, will support yours, trodden under foot and disregarded for three Centuries: They will consecrate the true principles of the Brasilian Representative Monarchy: They will declare Lord Don John the sixth, My August Father, of whose Love you are in the highest degree possessed, King of this fine Country: They will sever all the heads of the Hydra of Anarchy and of Despotism. They will impose the necessary Responsibility upon all Publick Functionaries and Employments: and the legitimate and just Will of the Nation will never more see its Majestick Flight continually impeded. . . .

Behold, Inhabitants of Brasil, Behold the perspective of Glory and Greatness which is before you: Be not alarmed at the backwardness of your actual Situation. The Flow of Civilization already begins to run impetuous from the Deserts of California to the Straights of Magellan. A Constitution, and a Lawful Liberty, are inexhaustible Springs of Wonders, and will by the Bridge over which, what is good of old and convulsed Europe, will pass to our Continent. Fear not Foreign Nations. Europe, which acknowledged the Independence of the United States of America, and remained neutral during the Struggle of the Spanish Colonies, cannot but acknowledge that of Brasil, who, with so much justice, and so many Means, and Resources, endeavour also to enter into the Great Family of Nations. We will never involve ourselves in their private Affairs, and they also will not wish to disturb the Peace and free Commerce we offer them, guaranteed by the Representative Government we are about to establish.

Let no Cry be heard amongst you but Union: From the Amazons to the Plata, let no other Echo resound but Independence. Let all our Provinces form the Mysterious Faggot which no Force can break. Let old prejudice disappear for ever, and the Love of the General Good be substituted for that of any one Province, or of any one City. Regard not what obscure Libelers send forth against you, against Me, against our Liberal System, Injuries, Calumnies, and Invectives. Recollect that, had they praised you, Brasil was lost. Let them say that our Attempts are against Portugal, against the Mother Country, against our Benefactors: By preserving our Rights, but punishing by our Justice, by consolidating our Liberty, We wish to save Portugal from a new Class of Tyrants.

Regard not their Cry that we are rebelling against our King. He knows that we love him, as a Citizen King, and wish to rescue him from the insulting State of Captivity to which they have reduced him by tearing the Mask of Hypocrisy from infamous demagogues and marking with true Liberalism the just Limits of Political Powers. Let them talk, in the Wish to persuade the World, that we are breaking all the Ties of Union with our European Brethren. No. We wish to establish it upon a solid Basis, without the Influence of a Party, who has villainously despised our Rights, and who, openly shewing itself, by so many facts, that they can no longer be concealed, to be tyrannical and domineering, to our Dishonour and Prejudice, weakens and destroys irremediably that moral power so necessary in a Congress, and which is wholly supported by Publick Opinion and Justice.

IV. Latin American Independence and the Atlantic Powers

The struggle for Latin American independence was both a civil war and a revolution. But it was not a purely Latin American event, for it had important international dimensions. For Great Britain, the breakup of the Spanish and Portuguese empires in America meant an end to the mercantilist regulations that had closed those markets to British trade. For the United States, it also represented a commercial opportunity; but it had strong ideological valence, for it signaled the weakening of European colonialism in the western hemisphere and the rise of republicanism. For Spain, however, the fragmentation of the empire was an unmitigated catastrophe, an end to all hope of ever again figuring on the world stage as a first-rate power. Lacking sufficient financial and military power to subdue its rebellious colonies, it sought the intervention of other European powers. All of Europe—and especially the three arch-conservative countries that composed the Holy Alliance (Austria, Prussia, and Russia)—thus found itself involved in the fate of Spanish America.

5. CIRCULAR OF SPAIN TO THE EUROPEAN GOVERNMENTS (DECEMBER 10, 1817)[5]

Spain had been devastated by Napoleonic occupation and did not have the resources to restore its authority over its American colonies. It had managed to equip and dispatch Morello's expeditionary force in 1815, but this was the last significant effort it could muster. It therefore turned to the European powers for help. But this was a tough sell. Most of them had no direct interest in America. The one that did, Great Britain, saw Spanish America as a potential market for its commerce and industry. Because of this, Britain actually had an interest in seeing that Spain did not regain control, for that would mean the reimposition of trade barriers. With most of continental Europe unconcerned with American affairs and Great Britain actually hostile to Spain's aim of reconquest, Spain was in a weak position. But it did have one strong argument: that the contagion of revolution sweeping through its American colonies would, if not eradicated, eventually cross the Atlantic and infect Europe itself. From this perspective, the revolutions of Spanish America did not just threaten Spain; as a manifestation of dangerous principles that had appeared in 1789, they were a menace to monarchy, religion, and aristocracy in Europe itself. The following document is a declaration to this effect circulated by Spanish diplomats in preparation for a Great Power meeting at the Congress of Aix-la-Chapelle (1818).

The repeated efforts of Europe for destroying the empire of arbitrary power reestablished the doctrine of legitimacy as the essential basis of public order and

---

[5]British National Archives, Foreign Office, Series 82, Box 204a.

of the tranquility of the world. A general subversion which lasted for upwards of 25 years amid the confusion of war, of progressive irreligion, of revolutionary maxims, and of violent measures, adopted by the despotism of vengeance and ambition, could not disappear all of a sudden or render practicable the restoration of the public edifice of Europe to the same solidity that it enjoyed previous to this period of disorder and misfortunes. The Congress of Vienna undertook the grand task of arranging the interests of all, in a manner the most convenient and the best adapted to circumstances; and His Catholic Majesty by acceding to the Act of that Congress with a noble frankness, a generous disinterestedness, and the purest desire of diffusing the blessings of peace, evinced how willing he is to concur with his generous Allies in their intentions. The same spirit prevails in all the treaties which now bind the illustrious confederation of Europe. But it must be allowed that legitimacy ought not to consist only in the upholding of sovereign families, but also in the integrity of their dominions; an integrity which can never be violated without simultaneously trenching upon the rights of legitimacy, property, and sovereignty, that alone are capable of maintaining peace and that much desired equilibrium which serves as a bulwark against the caprices of ambition. It was on these principles that the cabinet of Madrid directed the attention of its allies to the state of the Spanish provinces in America, a state involving not a mere rebellion against the Mother Country but a pernicious asylum to the tremendous revolution which has desolated the old world. The war kindled in those regions has a character decidedly inimical to Europe whether it be viewed in its moral, political, or commercial tendency. There is not description of extravagance, the coinage of revolutionary spirits in the present day, but what has been transferred to the new world; and on that, as on this side of the Atlantic, the vaunted doctrine of liberty and equality is cried up by all the means of violence, terror, and prejudice. It is impossible to calculate the consequences that would result from the triumph of such principles disseminated in that vast hemisphere, and their influence upon the future lot of Europe herself. The independence of those dominions would lead to a numerous progeny of democratic states, since not one of the chiefs is sufficiently popular to seize upon absolute power; and neither could such absolute authority be anyways recognized without attacking the rights of all legitimate sovereigns, nor do the morality and prudent policy of European monarchs justify the plan of personal aggrandizement by usurping and taking advantage of the revolt of those provinces.

Nothing can more evidently prove this position than the powerful mediation which they interpose with a view of terminating the differences which have arisen between their Catholic and most Faithful Majesties, on account of the occupation of the eastern bank of the River Plate by the Portuguese forces. Another proof of it is the reception which the powers have given to the information furnished by Spain on this important subject and the result being connected with the glory and common interest of Europe, now better understood than heretofore, will depend on the manner in which the wisdom of the powers shall construe that information, and on the light in which they shall consider it.

The establishment of so extensive a democratic government in countries so opulent and so much frequented for their great commercial advantages would even in anticipation be a continual incentive to those restless and turbulent spirits who, in Europe, avail themselves of every opportunity to revive the days of bloodshed and devastation; it would form the sanctuary of all the seditious; the point of union for fresh attempts on their part as in the case at present in the U.S., and in other quarters, whither daily resort all the querulous, all the malcontents, the turbulent and the misguided, it being notorious that incessant endeavors are making in various parts of Europe to inveigle and persuade to emigration all that present themselves. The complication of independent governments on so large a scale and in the present order of things would produce this effect, that all lawful means to repress such great evils would prove abortive and as one state would be supported by the other, all remonstrances would be without effect, and impunity but the more certain. Such governments, precarious in their very essence, immoral upon principle and from necessity, and versible in their policy on account of the influence of jarring passions, would offer no guarantee for commercial treaties and Europe could, on this point, never look for the same probity that is presented by Spain in a frank and advantageous commercial system, such as she has laid down in her various communications relative to the mediation solicited in order to effect the general pacification of America.

The seas, by this time, swarm with knots of pirates under the unrecognized flag of the insurgents; already do they colleague with the Negroes off St. Domingo, already do they rival in their conduct the very Barbary Corsairs. No European flag is exempt from their rapacity, not even the powerful cross of England; and what must excite still greater surprise, the very vessels of the U.S. in whose bosom, under shelter of the facilities or restrictions of their constituent government, the insurgents find means, encouragement, and permission to sail on such expeditions, are not free from the outrages of these public enemies.

Such proceedings ought at length to stimulate the governments, thus offended, to come to some resolution, and if their measures were taken impartially, they would doubtless be productive of that unanimity which is so desirable and so consistent with the general interest.

Another of the evils to which the insurrection has given rise and which would acquire more extent if the independence of those countries should be consolidated is the emigration of so many Europeans who, pining under the misery produced by the calamities and habits of protracted warfare, yield imprudently to illusion and go to seek an imaginary happiness in the new world, where they encounter likewise hunger, war, revolutions, despair, and ultimately death.

In a word, the present posture of affairs cannot be of any duration. Unless an enlightened and powerful mediation, which is desired both by sound policy and humanity contribute towards the redress of those evils, the sanguinary contest now maintaining must end either in the emancipation of those provinces or in their subjugation, in both which cases their destruction will be the direct consequence. Subjugation, the least of the two inconveniences, would always be purchased at the price of blood and sacrifices, which the allies of His Catholic Majesty cannot view with indifference; and emancipation would be attended by all the mischiefs indicated. Besides, so considerable an alteration in the territorial integrity of Spain would infallibly change the political system of Europe, which at present is founded on the proportionate distribution of strength and power. The restless ambition of nations does not in such cases admit of calculation, nor are governments themselves always strong enough to repress it, as might be proved by a variety of examples; for political and commercial combinations take then an unexpected direction, the relations between governments change, rivalries increase rapidly, fears and suspicions augment together with rancor and distrust, and only a new period of war and disaster is capable to restore peace by producing a new order of things.

If Europe were to experience another such violent crisis, the most powerful states might sustain very rude shocks, and the result of such extraordinary convulsions would not only be the freedom of some few provinces that should make themselves independent, but a general overthrow of the political, legislative, and commercial principles of the world.

His Majesty deemed these truths to be so clear and evident as not to require fresh demonstrations and under this impression, he had submitted them to the consideration of his allies, without giving them all the extension of which they are capable. Unfortunately, a positive enterprise which might easily have been anticipated has verified the prognostics of the Spanish Government and established as a fact what some might or were disposed to consider as merely put forth by the Cabinet of Madrid because it was apt, from mistaking its true interests, to impose restrictions that could only originate in ill-judged policy.

The discontented and the guilty of Europe who have made their escape to the U.S. and entered into a confederacy with Joseph Bonaparte seek to continue in the new world their plans, which have uniformly for their object ambition, usurpation and disorder; and they now attempt to establish in those countries the reign of tyranny which has so happily been destroyed in Europe by the effective union of sovereigns and the efforts of nations. This is substantiated by the inclosed copies.[6]

This incident, the subject of the interesting communication with which the undersigned is charged, presents to the Governments of Europe a new field for observation, and while it gives a formidable aspect to the affairs of America, affects respectively their most immediate and intimate interests, frustrates their best founded hopes, and threatens destruction to all their adjustments and to the system of Europe, which was obtained through immense sacrifices. A similar attempt could not excite a moment's alarm if we had the good fortune to be assured that the flames of civil discord and rebellion against the legitimate monarch had not burst forth in those dominions and that they did not contain any partisans of

---

[6]These were mysterious (and utterly impractical) plans for a "Napoleonic Confederation" of America that supposedly involved French exiles who had sought refuge in the United States after the fall of Napoleon's empire.

anarchy, the tools of usurpation who are ever prepared and formidable; but, fatally, such is not the case. The least progress, the slightest advantage of these daring adventurers would be an insult to the dignity of all sovereigns and to the authority of all governments. These would expose themselves to a kind of imputation on the part of the people who, in return for their respect, their attachment, and their sacrifices, expect from their rulers continued vigilance, provident anticipation, and vigorous exertions for the maintenance of tranquility, and the steady preservation of their laws, their properties, and their independence.

On the other hand, the plots and views of such men must, as is affirmed by some, have an intimate reference to the destiny of Napoleon himself; and perhaps there subsist even dangerous communications with him; all which suffices to inflame anew the imagination of his rash votaries and precipitate them into fresh conspiracies and outrages, wherever usurpation sets up her throne, wherever the sacred principle of legitimacy is profaned, it becomes necessary to stifle the evil in its very bud. The interest is general, the cause is common, and the means ought to be uniform, expeditious, and decisive. Even the government of the U.S., knowing as it does, the extent of the evil, ought to convince itself that there can exist no solid increase of states, nor any frank, amicable, and lasting communication among nations at the expense of morality.

The wisdom of the allies cannot but be aware that this circumstance gives a new aspect to the whole question concerning the American Revolution [of Spain's colonies], an aspect which certainly has nothing new for Spain, who never for one moment diverted her attention from the real bearing of the momentous events that have occurred in Europe and America, but who, nevertheless, received on the present occasion and irresistible ray of light from the detailed accounts adverted to.

After thus setting forth, in part, the inconveniences that would accrue to the stability and even to the commerce of all Europe from the supposed independence of a portion of America under Republican governments, it would appear, in this point of view alone, that its pacification involves considerations of direct and general interest, and that the whole cause becomes eminently European; wherefore a stop is put at once to the illusions of the liberal system which is rendered impossible in those dominions, and it is an easy task to demonstrate that the commerce and preponderance of Europe can only be advantaged by the submission of the trans-Atlantic provinces to and by their well arranged union under the political sway of their monarch. This interest greatly increases by the reflection that America will be metamorphosed by the proceedings referred to on the theatre of organized subversion, usurpation, and domination, and under the auspices of that hateful family who have carried the destruction of legitimate thrones and of public welfare through all the recesses of Europe. Can therefore the case of America be called the cause of independence and liberty, when both of them are illusory and impossible? Certainly not. It is the case of Napoleon's preponderance, the case that labors to restore the immoral and destructive order of things to which that person served as a motto. Such are its objects.

The same chief, the same generals, the same Machiavellian principles are about to reorganize the same cause, that proved so detrimental to Europe, by means of the physical resources which abound in a fertile country, and by those moral ones which seduction meets with in the innocence and unsuspecting inexperience of the people in South America. It is of no avail to Europe to have freed herself from that domestic and terrible enemy, she is on the point of being attacked even more directly than before, by the same foe, in the very foundation of her prosperity.

The Continental System, which was ridiculous in Europe, because impracticable, would speedily acquire a fatal reality. In a word, as the misguided Americans cannot possibly consolidate a system of liberty, of which they want the most necessary elements, it is very clear that the enterprises of those refugees, defrayed out of the product of their robberies in Europe, sustained by the military talents of known and skillful generals, recommended by the illusion (as yet untried in those countries) of the chief, whose exploits are known while his crimes and faults have never been brought under the public view, and propped up by a name, whose spell for a long time Europe was unable to break or to resist, must meet with more countenance in a country as yet new to political experience and where, besides, the Imposter is aided by so many elements analogous to his nature in all the noted criminals, bandits, adventurers, malcontents, and speculators of all the states of Europe.

His Catholic Majesty flatters himself by hoping that his august allies will take advantage of the present moment to unite their powerful influence and put a period to the evils which threaten the world, should the American continent be suffered to become a prey to a revolution so antisocial in its spirit and so dangerous to governments. The Revolution of America is the Revolution of Europe. In order to prove this position, nothing was required than that the Bonaparte family should personally figure in it, which, unfortunately, has come to pass.

6. CANNING'S MEMORANDUM TO THE CABINET ON SPANISH AMERICAN POLICY (NOVEMBER 15, 1822)[7]

Britain pursued two nearly irreconcilable objectives. It sought to trade with Spain's insurgent colonies while at the same time maintaining good relations with Spain itself. During the Napoleonic Wars and for some time thereafter, this had been accomplished through an informal agreement: Spain would tolerate British trade, and in return, Britain would not recognize Latin American independence. But in 1820, Spanish royal privateers began to seize British merchant ships trading with the insurgents. The capture of one British vessel, the Lord Collingwood, *gave Britain's foreign minister, George Canning, a pretext to move toward open recognition of Latin American independence. Many factors influenced this shift, including a desire to warn off the Holy Alliance from intervention, as well as to dissuade the United States from encroaching on Cuba. Canning's memorandum to the British Cabinet analyzes the complex interplay of these factors.*

---

[7]British National Archives, Foreign Office, Series 72, Box 266.

Important as the interests may be which are now in discussion at Verona, yet in the present state of the world no question relating to continental Europe can be more immediate and vitally important to Great Britain than those which relate to America.

Our commerce is exposed to daily depredations in the American seas; and the accustomed awe of our maritime preponderancy is daily diminished in the eyes of all nations by a series of outrages perpetrated not wholly by pirates and marauders who bear no national character and for whom no government is answerable, but by the subjects of that very nation against the invasion of whose territory, by the arms of the allies, as well as against their interference in its political dissentions, the Duke of Wellington is contending at Verona.

If any reliance were to be placed on a sentiment of national gratitude, it would seem incredible that Spain, after the obligations heaped upon her by this country in the late war for her liberation and independence, should not have been cautious to avoid giving just cause of offence to Great Britain; or at least to abstain from inflicting injury upon her benefactress; and it might have been expected that in any case in which such injury might have been unintentionally done to the interests of British subjects by the agents, whether civil or military, of the Spanish government, the utmost promptitude would have been evinced by that government to offer redress.

So far, however, is this from being a true picture of the conduct of the Spanish government that before two years had elapsed from the restoration of Ferdinand VII to his throne, instances occurred of vexation, fraud, and violence towards the persons of British subjects resident in Spain; and by the beginning of the year 1819 a list of grievances, of these various kinds, had accumulated upon the hands of our ambassador and remained, in spite of urgent and repeated remonstrances, unredressed; such as in times of a quieter character when the resentment of national injustice was not checked by the fear of shaking the peace of Europe to its foundations, would not only have justified but have called for avengement by reprisal or by war.

A despatch of Sir Henry Wellesley's of March 1819 contains an enumeration of these grievances, coupled with an avowal of the utter fruitlessness of all his endeavors to obtain acknowledgment or reparation for them.

And a list is subjoined completing the series, from that time to the present; when the government of the Spanish West Indian islands that have not thrown off their allegiance to the mother country appear to vie with the commander of the only remaining maritime post on the continent of America still occupied by a Spanish force, in carrying on against British commerce a direct and undisguised hostility.

Not to weary the Cabinet with the specification of many instances, Mr. Canning selects the case of the *Lord Collingwood*, British merchant ship captured by the *Panchita*, royal Spanish privateer, and condemned in the courts of Porto Rico; because the instrument of that condemnation brings the ground of the capture distinctly into view; and also because this particular case, having already been mentioned in Parliament (while the fact of the condemnation though asserted was not officially known) it is one upon which His Majesty's government will undoubtedly be called upon to show what course they have taken and what reparation they have obtained.

And he subjoined a report received at the Admiralty of the instructions issued to Spanish ships of war by the commander of Porto Cabello.

In consequence of this report, the Admiralty have determined upon giving convoy to merchant vessels trading to the ports of the Columbian Republic. . . .

Convoy in time of peace! And against the attacks of a nation with which we are professedly in amity!

Our commerce with the late Spanish colonies is one which we either claim a right to carry on or carry on knowing it to be illegitimate.

If the former, ought we to need convoy?

If the latter, ought we not either to abandon the commerce or to make it lawful?

The means of doing the latter are in our own hands. Nothing but the excess of our forbearance has prevented us from resorting to them; and when that forbearance is thus requited, surely it is time to consider a system at once so romantick and so thankless with regard to Spain and so ruinous and so disparaging to ourselves.

It is not intended to hold out the example of the United States, as recommending a decision to which their very origin must necessarily have inclined them with so strong a bias.

But it can hardly be denied that the United States government, recognizing the de facto independence of the Spanish colonies, claiming a right to trade with them, and avenging the attempted interruption of the exercise of that right by capturing the *Panchita* and carrying her into a harbor of the United States, pursues upon the whole a more straightforward course and presents itself before the world in a more intelligible position than Great Britain, forbearing, for the sake of Spain, to acknowledge the separate existence of her colonies; trading with those colonies by their sufferance, and in faith of the continued connivance of Spain; apprized of the discontinuance of that connivance by the *Panchita's* depredations upon her commerce; and taking refuge from similar depredations not in reprisal but in convoy.

If, in pursuance of this contrast, the government of the U.S., not contented with punishing the capturing vessel with capture, shall insist upon taking security against the like attacks upon the commerce of its citizens in the future; and shall make the military occupation of Cuba a part of that security; while we, continuing on the best possible terms with Spain, fighting her political battles in Europe, acknowledging (what none else can see) the continuance of her supremacy in America; acquiesce in the unredressed condemnation of the *Lord Collingwood*, and venture only to warn off, or at most to repel the royal privateers of Porto Cabello, it may perhaps (when Parliament meets) be mooted as a question in which of these two opposite lines of policy, the policy of England such as it was in older times, is most discernable.

That the U.S. have such an acquisition in view, has been suggested for some time by the common rumours of Havana; but the accompanying extract of a letter from that place (with the paper which it incloses) appears to give to those rumours a degree of countenance and probability, which entitle the supposed project to our serious reflection.

It may be questioned whether any blow that could be struck by any for power in any part of the world would have a more sensible effect on the interests of this country, and on the reputation of its government.

The possession by the U.S. of both shores of the channel through which our Jamaica trade must pass would, in time of war with the U.S.; or indeed of a war in which the U.S. might be neutral, but in which we continued (as we must do) to claim the right of search and the Americans (as they would do) to resist it; amount to a suspension of that trade and to a consequent total ruin of a great portion of the West Indian interests.

The cure for all the evils and dangers of the present state of things in the West Indian seas is to be found (if at all) not in a perseverance in that system of forbearance and submission which we have hitherto observed towards Spain; but in a prompt and vigorous vindication of our rights by the means which Providence has placed in our power. . . .

It is not necessary to declare war against Spain. Spain and her colonial empire are altogether separated de facto. She has perhaps as little direct and available power over the colonies which she nominally retains as she has over those which have thrown off her yoke.[8]

Let us apply therefore a local remedy to the local grievance and make the ships and harbors of Cuba, Porto Rico and Porto Cabello answerable for the injuries which have been inflicted by those ships and the perpetrators of which found shelter in those harbors. . . .

[Canning then offered a detailed plan for sending a large British naval force to the West Indies. It mission would be to demand the release of the *Lord Collingwood* from Spanish authorities, seize Spanish merchant vessels if the blockade of Columbia were not lifted, pursue Spanish royal privateers at sea, and threaten the Spanish authorities of Cuba and Porto Rico with military action if they did not halt their privateering campaign. He then turned to the question of recognizing Latin American independence.]

The immediate object of safety to British commerce and navigation being provided for by the measures here suggested towards the Spanish authorities and towards the de facto states of America, remains the great question of a more suitable arrangement of our relations with those states, with a view both to the regularity of commercial intercourse and to the settlement of the political difficulty of which we can no longer defer the solution.

---

[8]This is largely because conservative colonial elites in loyal colonies like Cuba viewed the liberal, constitutional government that ruled Spain from 1820 through 1823 with deep suspicion. As we have seen, this dynamic was one of the important factors that motivated Mexican independence in 1821.

The partiality which has unquestionably been shewn by this country to Spain in the contest between her and her colonies has not excited any hostile feeling in the latter.

They have looked forward patiently to the time when the force of circumstances must lead to our recognition of them; and it would be difficult to conceive under what circumstances such a recognition is ever to take place if the present crisis does not incline us to consider of it.

In the first place, the very explanations to which the exercise of our just rights of self defence must lead, recommend, if they do not absolutely require, the residence of civil agents at the principal ports of each of the states of Spanish America.

Secondly, the merchants of the United Kingdom pray for such protection for their commerce.

The overbearing arrogance of Spain no longer acquiesces in our neutrality.

Our ships are seized and confiscated, not because they violate blockade or have enemy's goods on board, but simply because they trade with the colonies.

The tacit compact which subsisted for years, by which Spain was to forbear from interrupting our trade, in compensation for our forbearance to recognize her colonies, is now forgotten or renounced by Spain; and the old colonial system is revived in as full vigor as if she had still a practical hold over her colonies and had a navy to enforce her pretentions.

What resource have we but to take away all pretext for the enforcement of these absurd and obsolete pretentions against us, by conferring on the colonies, so far as our recognition can do it, an independent instead of a colonial character; thus cutting short all dispute as to Spain's colonial jurisdiction?

No man will say that there is a reasonable hope of her recovering that jurisdiction.

No man will say that, under such circumstances, our recognition of these states can be indefinitely postponed.

The question is therefore entirely of time and degree.

And no man surely will say that we should pass by an opportunity, when all things conspire to render this step at once most justifiable towards Spain and most acceptable to her late colonies, and most beneficial to ourselves, in the vain hope that we may, some time or other, act in this matter with the concurrence of the Spanish government.

From no government that Spain ever saw or is ever likely to see, despotick or constitutional, monarchical or republican, is such concurrence to be expected. Nor can a moment (it is to be hoped) ever arrive when our wrongs from Spain will set us more entirely free to take that course with respect to her colonies, which our own interests proscribe.

The degree of recognition must of course be proportioned to the degree of force and stability which the several states may have respectively acquired; and to the absence of struggle for ascendency on the part either of the mother country or of the parties into which each state may be divided.

Neither in Buenos Aires nor in Chile is there any vestige of Spanish force.

In Columbia, the single point occupied by Spain is Porto Cabello.

Nor is there in either of these three states such a contest for power, as either to endanger its independence, or to disqualify it for maintaining external relations.

Peru, not entirely cleared of Spanish troops, is also torn by conflicting parties; and in Mexico, though Spain has but one inconsiderable post, the newly settled government may be considered as not out of the reach of revolution.

But in Peru and even in Mexico, there are British commercial interests which require the superintendence of some civil agency on the part of the British government.

In both these states, as well as in all the others, the government of the U.S. has established the means of national intercourse; and France has avowedly sent to most if not to all of them commissions of enquiry which may, at any time, be matured into resident missions.

Our conduct hitherto towards Spain has already been described in general terms.

To say nothing of the mediation so frequently offered on our part and rejected by Spain.

To say nothing of our own voluntary engagement to forbid the purchase of arms in this country for the colonies; one single fact speaks volumes as to our disposition towards Spain. It is this: that in the very Spring (perhaps the very month) in which the list of unredressed grievances . . . came under the observation of the Cabinet, the Cabinet nevertheless consented to propose to Parliament the Foreign Enlistment Bill; a measure professedly impartial indeed, but one of which the especial benefit to Spain, as against her colonies, could not be disguised.

But such refinements must have an end.

The practical business of the world does not admit of a perpetual exchange of benefit for injury and it is surely sufficient to acquit us of harshness or precipitancy towards Spain that we do not recognize her late colonies, till we are compelled to resort, in our defence against her aggressions, to measures little short of war, and in a case in which the very want of that recognition is the main justification of those aggressions.

It is no fault of ours that Spain at the same moment that her agents are insulting our flag and preying upon our commerce in America, is involved in a revolution at home. Her condition in that respect is not a motive for our hastening our measures, but neither can it be held a reason for retarding them. . . .

Spain has been already apprized that some steps must soon be taken to vindicate the honor of our flag and the security of our commerce.

An intimation of the probability of our recognizing, in a more or less qualified manner, the independent states of Spanish America has already been conveyed to her through Mr. Onis.[9] She is therefore prepared for the more direct communication of our purpose.

Mr. Canning will prepare a paper to this effect which may take the form of a note or declaration; and submit it to the Cabinet by the time of the Duke of Willington's return from Verona.

---

[9]Spain's ambassador to the United States.

7. THE "POLIGNAC MEMORANDUM"
(OCTOBER 23, 1823)[10]

The so-called Polignac Memorandum was an informal agreement over Latin American policy between the British foreign minister Canning and the French ambassador to Britain, Jules de Polignac. They agreed that Spain could never reimpose its authority, that neither Britain nor France had any desire to intervene, and that both countries wanted the new republics to be open to the trade of all nations. The Polignac Memorandum amounted to a French declaration that it would not intervene in Latin America on behalf of Spain or the Holy Alliance. Given that France was the only continental European country with sufficient naval power to have undertaken such an expedition, the Memorandum ensured the triumph of Latin American independence.

[Mr. Canning stated:]

That the near approach of a crisis, in which the affairs of Spanish America must naturally occupy a great share of the attention of both Powers, made it desirable that there should be no misunderstanding between them on any part of a subject so important.

That the British Government were of opinion, that any attempt to bring Spanish America again under its ancient submission to Spain, must be utterly hopeless; that all negotiation for that purpose would be unsuccessful; and that the prolongation or renewal of war for the same object would be only a waste of human life, and an infliction of calamity on both parties, to no end.

That the British Government would, however, not only abstain from interposing any obstacle, on their part, to any attempt at negotiation, which Spain might think proper to make, but would aid and countenance such negotiation, provided it were founded upon a basis which appeared to them to be practicable; and that they would in any case, remain strictly neutral in a War between Spain and the Colonies, if war should be unhappily prolonged.

But that the junction of any Foreign Power in an enterprize against the Colonies, would be viewed by them as constituting an entirely new question; and one upon which they must take such decision as the Interests of Great Britain might require.

That the British Government absolutely disclaimed not only, any desire of appropriating to itself any portion of the Spanish Colonies, but any intention of forming any connexion with them, beyond those of Amity and Commercial Intercourse.

That in those respects so far from seeking an exclusive preference for its subjects over those of Foreign states, it was prepared and would be contented, to see the Mother Country (by virtue of an amicable arrangement) in possession of that

---

[10]*Diplomatic Correspondence of the United States Concerning the Independence of the Latin-American Nations*, ed. William R. Manning (New York: Oxford University Press, 1925), vol. 3, 1496–1499.

preference; and to be ranked, after her, equally with others, only on the footing of the most favoured nation.

That, completely convinced that the ancient system of the Colonies could not be restored, the British Government could not enter into any stipulation binding itself either to refuse or to delay its Recognition of their Independence.

That the British Government had no desire to precipitate that Recognition, so long as there was any reasonable chance of an accommodation with the Mother country, by which such a recognition might come first from Spain.

But that it could not wait indefinitely for that result; that it could not consent to make its Recognition of the New States *dependent* upon that of Spain; and that it would consider any Foreign Interference, by force or menace, in the dispute between Spain and the Colonies, as a motive for recognizing the latter without delay. . . .

That the old pretension of Spain to interdict all trade with [the revolted colonies], was, in the opinion of the British Government, altogether obsolete; but that, even if attempted to be enforced against others, it was, with regard to Great Britain, clearly inapplicable.

That permission to trade with the Spanish Colonies had been conceded to Great Britain in the year 1810, when the mediation of Great Britain between Spain and her Colonies was asked by Spain, and granted by Great Britain; that this mediation, indeed, was not afterwards employed, because Spain changed her Counsel; but that it was not therefore practicable for Great Britain to withdraw Commercial Capital once embarked in Spanish America, and to desist from Commercial Intercourse once established. . . .

That Great Britain, however, had no desire to set up any separate right to the free enjoyment of this Trade; that she considered the force of circumstances, and the irreversible progress of events, to have already determined the question of the existence of that freedom for all the world; but that, for herself, she claimed and would continue to use it; and should any attempt be made to dispute that claim, and to renew the obsolete interdiction, such attempt might be best cut short by a speedy and unqualified Recognition of the Independence of the Spanish American States.

That, with these general opinions, and with these peculiar claims, England could not go into a joint deliberation upon the subject of Spanish America, upon an equal footing with other Powers; whose opinions were less formed upon that question, and whose interests were less implicated in the decision of it. . . .

The Prince de Polignac declared:

That his Government believed to be utterly hopeless to reduce Spanish America to the state of its former relation to Spain;

That France disclaimed, on her part, any intention or desire to avail herself of the present state of the Colonies, or of the present situation of France towards Spain, to appropriate to herself any part of the Spanish possessions in America; or to obtain for herself any exclusive advantages; and that like England, she would willingly see the Mother country in possession of superior commercial advantages, by amicable arrangements; and would be contented, like her, to rank after the Mother country, among the most favoured nations. Lastly that she abjured, in any case, any design of acting against the Colonies by force of arms.

The Prince de Polignac proceeded to say that, as to what might be the best arrangement between Spain and Her Colonies, the French Government could not give, nor venture to form, an opinion until the King of Spain should be at Liberty; that they would then be ready to enter upon it, in concert with their allies, and with Great Britain among the number.

In observing upon what Mr. Canning had said, with respect to the peculiar situation of Great Britain, in reference to such a Congress;

The Prince de Polignac declared that he saw no difficulty to prevent England from taking part in the Congress, however she might now announce the difference in the view which she took of the question from that taken by the Allies. The refusal of England to cooperate in the work of reconciliation might afford reason to think, either that she did not really wish for that reconciliation, or that she had some ulterior object in contemplation; two suppositions equally injurious to the honour and good faith of the British Cabinet. The Prince de Polignac further declared, that he could not conceive what could be meant, under the present circumstances, by a pure and simple acknowledgment of the Independence of the Spanish Colonies; since, those Countries being actually distracted by civil wars, there existed no government in them which could offer any appearance of solidity; and that the acknowledgment of American Independence, so long as such a state of things continued, appeared to him to be nothing less than a real sanction of Anarchy.

The Prince de Polignac observed that, in the interest of humanity, and especially in that of the Spanish Colonies, it would be worthy of the European Governments to concert together the means of calming in those distant and scarcely civilized regions, passions blinded by party spirit, and to endeavour to bring back to a principle of Union in Government, whether Monarchical or Aristocratical, people among whom absurd and dangerous theories were not keeping up agitation and disunion.

Mr. Canning, without entering into any discussion upon these abstract principles, contented himself with saying that however desirable the establishment of a Monarchical form of Government in any of those Provinces might be, he saw great difficulties in the way of it; nor could his Government take upon itself to put it forward as a condition of their Recognition.

Mr. Canning further remarked, that he could not understand how an *European* Congress could discuss Spanish American affairs, without calling to their Councils a Power so eminently interested in the result, as the United States of *America*; Austria, Russia, and Prussia being Powers comparatively so much less concerned in the subject.

The Prince de Polignac professed himself unprovided with any opinion of his Government upon what respected the United States of America; but did not *for himself* see any insuperable difficulty to such an association. . . .

8. MONROE DOCTRINE (DECEMBER 2, 1823)[11]

The United States began to recognize the Latin American republics in 1822. The following year, in his seventh State of the Union address, President James Monroe announced a new policy toward them. Known as the Monroe Doctrine, it warned European powers not to intervene in the affairs of the Western Hemisphere, nor to try to acquire new colonies there. Although it carried a powerful symbolic charge, the doctrine had no discernable impact at the time. Given American military weakness in 1823, there was no way at that time that the United States could have enforced it. In fact, it was British naval power and its understanding with France that kept the Holy Alliance from intervening in Latin America. But as U.S. power grew during the nineteenth century, it began to apply the Monroe Doctrine—and reinterpreted it as a license to intervene in Latin America.

The American continents, by the free and independent condition which they have assumed and maintain, are henceforth not to be considered as subjects for future colonization by any European powers. . . .

It was stated at the commencement of the last session that a great effort was then making in Spain and Portugal to improve the condition of the people of those countries, and that it appeared to be conducted with extraordinary moderation. It need scarcely be remarked that the results have been so far very different from what was then anticipated. Of events in that quarter of the globe, with which we have so much intercourse and from which we derive our origin, we have always been anxious and interested spectators. The citizens of the United States cherish sentiments the most friendly in favor of the liberty and happiness of their fellow-men on that side of the Atlantic. In the wars of the European powers in matters relating to themselves, we have never taken any part, nor does it comport with our policy to do so. It is only when our rights are invaded or seriously menaced that we resent injuries or make preparation for our defense. With the movements in this hemisphere we are of necessity more immediately concerned, and by causes which must be obvious to all enlightened and impartial observers. The political system of the allied powers is essentially different in this respect from that of America. This difference proceeds from that which exists in their respective Governments; and to the defense of our own, which has been achieved by the loss of so much blood and treasure, and matured by the wisdom of their most enlightened citizens, and under which we have enjoyed unexampled felicity, this whole nation is devoted. We owe it, therefore, to candor and to the amicable relations existing between the United States and those powers to declare that we should consider any attempt on their part to extend their system to any portion of this hemisphere as dangerous to our peace and safety. With the existing colonies or dependencies of any European

---

[11]James Monroe, "Monroe Doctrine; December 2 1823" *The Avalon Project*, http://avalon.law.yale.edu/19th_century/monroe.asp.

power we have not interfered and shall not interfere. But with the Governments who have declared their independence and maintain it, and whose independence we have, on great consideration and on just principles, acknowledged, we could not view any interposition for the purpose of oppressing them, or controlling in any other manner their destiny, by any European power in any other light than as the manifestation of an unfriendly disposition toward the United States. In the war between those new Governments and Spain, we declared our neutrality at the time of their recognition, and to this we have adhered, and shall continue to adhere, provided no change shall occur which, in the judgement of the competent authorities of this Government, shall make a corresponding change on the part of the United States indispensable to their security.

The late events in Spain and Portugal shew that Europe is still unsettled. Of this important fact no stronger proof can be adduced than that the allied powers should have thought it proper, on any principle satisfactory to themselves, to have interposed by force in the internal concerns of Spain. To what extent such interposition may be carried, on the same principle, is a question in which all independent powers whose governments differ from theirs are interested, even those most remote, and surely none of them more so than the United States. Our policy in regard to Europe, which was adopted at an early stage of the wars which have so long agitated that quarter of the globe, nevertheless remains the same, which is, not to interfere in the internal concerns of any of its powers; to consider the government de facto as the legitimate government for us; to cultivate friendly relations with it, and to preserve those relations by a frank, firm, and manly policy, meeting in all instances the just claims of every power, submitting to injuries from none. But in regard to those continents, circumstances are eminently and conspicuously different.

It is impossible that the allied powers should extend their political system to any portion of either continent without endangering our peace and happiness; nor can anyone believe that our southern brethren, if left to themselves, would adopt it of their own accord. It is equally impossible, therefore, that we should behold such interposition in any form with indifference. If we look to the comparative strength and resources of Spain and those new Governments, and their distance from each other, it must be obvious that she can never subdue them. It is still the true policy of the United States to leave the parties to themselves, in hope that other powers will pursue the same course. . . .

9. LATIN AMERICAN CRITICISM OF THE MONROE DOCTRINE[12]

Latin American reaction to the Monroe Doctrine was mixed. One critic was Juan-Bautista Alberdi (1810–1884), an Argentinian political theorist, diplomat, and constitutional scholar. The following is an excerpt from his critique.

---

[12]Juan-Bautista Alberdi, "Against the Monroe Doctrine," in *La Doctrina de Monroe y la America Espanola*, ed. R. Rodriguez (Buenos Aires, Argentina: Nuevo Meridion, 1987), 103–104, 117–118.

The independence revolution has not rid the new world of civilization, which resulted from European action upon America; it has only changed its form. What exists in America remains an extension of what exists in Europe. An intimate community of interests and destinies links the peoples of both continents.

They are neither two worlds . . . nor two planets with beings from different races; rather, they are two parts of one single geographical and political world.

Seas bring people closer to each other. . . .

Without the sea, there would be no communication between Chile and Europe. The notion of an overland voyage of three thousand leagues is absurd. The community of commercial interests proves the general community of interests and destinies linking both continents. The doctrine attributed to Monroe is a nonsensical product of egotism. While the United States owes everything to Europe, it seeks to insulate America from Europe, except through the intermediary of the United States, which would thus become the sole entry point for transatlantic civilization. Monroe wanted to make his country the Porto-Bello[13] of American liberty. . . .

Although it is the antithesis of the doctrines attributed to the Holy Alliance . . . the Monroe doctrine is just as threatening to Latin America as the Holy Alliance. The goal of both is the conquest of Spanish America: the one for the benefit of Spain, the other for the benefit of the United States. . . .

What is the difference between the colonial annexation of South America by European nation and annexation by the United States? What is preferable for South America? Neither: independence is better. This is to say, neither Monroism nor Holy Alliance.

But let us compare the result of both types of annexation through the practical examples of Havana and Texas. Though a colony, Havana is a Spanish land. Although free, Texas is no longer a part of the Spanish race. Havana lives, albeit enslaved; as for Texas, nothing remains but the soil.

Thus, colonial annexation to Europe means the conservation of the race and species, but with the loss of liberty. Annexation to the United States means the loss of the race, but the acquisition of liberty. . . .

10. BERNARDO MONTEAGUDO, "ESSAY ON THE NEED FOR A GENERAL FEDERATION BETWEEN THE HISPANO-AMERICAN STATES" (1824)[14]

For decades after independence, the republics of Latin America remained dependent on European powers and the United States. One solution to this might have been a general federation of the Latin American countries. By uniting their political,

---

[13]This is the rich commercial town in Panama that had historically linked the Atlantic and Pacific sides of Spain's American dominions.

[14]Fabian Herrero, ed., *Monteagudo: Revolucion, Independencia, Confederacionismo* (Buenos Aires, Argentina: Ediciones Cooperativas, 2005), 183–193.

economic, and military power, they might have been able to resist outside pressure more effectively. This dream of unity had a respectable pedigree—including Aranda from a royalist perspective and Miranda from a revolutionary one. The principle of Latin American unity was also dear to Simon Bolivar. In 1826, he came close to achieving it in practice when he convened a meeting of representatives from the Latin American republics (with the exception of Argentina and Chile, who distrusted his power and refused to participate) in Panama. The Panama Congress was intended to create a structure of united political and military action. Its resolutions, however, were never ratified by the new republics and thus never implemented. The following is an essay by Bernardo Monteagudo (1789–1825), an associate of Bolivar, in preparation for the Congress.

Each century carries within it the germs of the events that will occur in the one that follows. . . . The Revolution of the American World grew from eighteenth century ideas. . . .

Our newly gained independence is an event that, by changing our very being and place in the universe, cancels all the obligations that have been dictated to us by the spirit of the fifteenth century and signals to us the new relations into which we are about to enter . . . and the principles we must follow to establish the public rights that govern independent states. Their federation is the object of this essay . . .

For those who directed public affairs during the revolution, nothing has been nearer and dearer to them than the formation of a general league against the common enemy. . . . But the immense distance that separates the sections [of former Spanish America] that are now independent, the difficulties in establishing communications and coordinating their activities, all this diminishes the prospect of realizing a General Federation. Until recently, those in the sections to the south of Ecuador were completely ignorant of what was happening to the north. . . . Each setback that our armies suffered made us feel more acutely the need for union. But the obstacles remained greater than this necessity.

In the year 1821, this design appeared practicable for the first time. Although most of it was occupied, Peru nonetheless entered into the American system. Guayaquil and other Pacific ports were opened to foreign commerce; Mexico and Columbia were victorious. The genius who directed and still directs the war . . . has undertaken to make the plan for a Hispano-American confederation a reality. . . .

The President of Columbia [Bolivar] took the initiative in this most important affair, and he sent plenipotentiaries to the governments of Mexico, Peru, Chile, and Buenos Aires, to prepare the general union of our continent. In Peru and Mexico, the proposed agreements were put into effect; with slight modifications, treaties with both governments have already been ratified by their respective legislatures. In Chile and Buenos Aires, unavoidable obstacles have arisen. . . . But the general tone of public discourse and the situation of the independence movement lead us to believe that in 1825 a Hispano-American federation will be established under the auspices of an assembly based on the rights of the people, not those of select noble families. . . .

Independence, peace, and security are the eminently national interests of the new-born republics of the New World. Each of these interests requires the formation of a political system that supposes the preexistence of an assembly or congress where ideas are discussed. . . .

Independence is the primary interest of the New World. To throw off the yoke of Spain, to erase the last vestiges of its dominion, and to exclude any other [imperial dominion] are enterprises that demand—and will demand for a long time—the concentration of all our capacities and a uniform impulse to direct them. It is true that the continental war with Spain ended at Ayacucho[15] . . . and that there remain only three isolated points where one sees the arms of Castile. . . .

San Juan de Ulloa, Callao, and Chiloe are the last bastions of Spanish power. It shall not be long before the first two surrender or are liberated by force of arms. Even though its reduction requires a combination of [naval and ground] forces, and even though there is only small period of several months in which the climate permits offensive operations, the Chiloe archipelago shall follow them this year. . . .

Yet vengeance lives in the hearts of the Spaniards. Their hatred for us has not been defeated. And even though they no longer have force to fight us, they have the pretention, to which they give the name of "rights," to invoke in their favor the aid of the Holy Alliance. . . .

Since we triumphed alone over superior Spanish armies during the first years of our political being, it is easy to suppose that we can hope for victory now that we possess the totality of our countries' resources, and especially since our warriors have more than fourteen years' experience on the field of battle. But it is also necessary to keep in mind that, whereas our fight up to now has been against an impotent nation . . . the danger now threatening us is war with the Holy Alliance. . . .

This matter raises two questions: the probability of a new war and the force that could be employed against us in that event. Even discounting the continuing rumors of hostility and the quasi-official information we have concerning the views of the Holy Alliance on the political organization of the New World, . . . the reestablishment of legitimacy . . . has been their aim. . . . Their interest is the same in Europe as in America. And if in Naples and Spain the shadow of the throne has not been enough to prevent the invasion of both countries,[16] the force of our governments shall certainly not be the best guarantee against the system of the Holy Alliance.

As for the mass of power that will be employed against us, it shall be proportionate to the respective influence of the courts of St. Petersburg, Berlin, Vienna, and Paris. It would not be prudent to doubt that they have more than enough to undertake the reconquest of America—though not for the benefit of Spain, which

---

[15]The battle of Ayacucho was the decisive battle in Peru (December 9, 1824) that destroyed the last royalist army in the Americas.

[16]The Holy Alliance intervened in Naples and Spain in the early 1820s to restore absolute power to kings who had been forced to accept liberal constitutions.

will never recover its former possessions, but for the principle of legitimacy, that modern talisman that today serves as the emblem of those who condemn popular sovereignty....

It is true that the first ship to sail from Europe against the liberty of the New World shall raise the alarm among liberals in both hemispheres. Great Britain and the United States shall take their rightful places in this universal contest. Public opinion, that new power that now presides over the destinies of nations, shall offer its alliance to us. Victory ... will choose the side of justice and force the partisans of absolute power to seek salvation in the representative system.

In the meantime, we must not hide the fact that our new republics ... will experience in this contest immense dangers that will be difficult to foresee and avoid if there is a lack of uniform action or will stemming from a previously-settled agreement and an assembly that extends or modifies it according to circumstances....

In surveying the potential dangers of the future, we must not view with complacency the new Empire of Brazil. It is true that the throne of Pedro I has arisen from the same ruins as those from which liberty has elevated itself in the rest of America. It was necessary to make the same transition that we had made ourselves from colony to independent nation. But it is also true that that sovereign does not respect the liberal institutions whose spirit put the scepter in his hands, so that those hands would become an instrument of liberty, but never of oppression....

Everything makes me think that the imperial cabinet of Rio de Janeiro would tend to share the views of the Holy Alliance against the republics of the New World; and that Brazil might become the headquarters of the party of servitude....

This rapid description of pitfalls and dangers demonstrates the need to form an American league.... All the human foresight in the world is not enough to grasp the accidents and vicissitudes that our republics will suffer until they consolidate their existence. Among the possible consequences of military defeat would be the effects of any treaty concluded in Europe between the powers that maintain the current equilibrium, domestic disturbances, and the resulting corruption of principles. These might eventually favor the pretentions of the party of legitimacy if we do not form an active and uniform resistance, if we do not hasten to conclude a true pact ... that guarantees our independence....

This requires a congress of plenipotentiaries of each State to determine the quantity of troops and the amount of subsidies that must be granted by each confederate. The more we contemplate the vast distances that separate us, the great delays that will afflict any joint enterprise requiring the simultaneous approval of the governments of the Rio de la Plata, Mexico, Chile, Columbia, Peru, and Guatemala, the more it appears necessary to form a congress to be the repository of all the strength and will of the confederated states....

This Hispano-American assembly should come together to end the war with Spain, consolidate independence, and face the tremendous threat posed by the Holy Alliance.

Conclusion

The movement of republican revolution that began to sweep through the Atlantic world in the 1760s effected a paradigm shift that redefined political concepts, vocabulary, and norms across the globe. Everywhere—even in places barely touched by it at the time—we now see republics populated by citizens and governed by laws that are the same for all.[1] Individual freedoms (of assembly, conscience, and expression, as well as from arbitrary arrest) are everywhere considered basic rights—even though they are often violated. Private property, one of the freedoms considered most essential by the original generation of republican revolutionaries, is ubiquitous. With the exception of the few surviving monarchies of the world, sovereignty and the subordinate public powers are everywhere understood as a delegation to, not the private property of, those in office. In practice, there are many breaches of these principles. But they all appear as exceptions, not the norm, and are routinely denounced by international bodies as violations of human rights (themselves an outgrowth of the revolutionary age).[2]

In the immediate aftermath of colonial independence, attempts were made in some places—Mexico, Brazil, Haiti, and France—to establish monarchies and empires, rather than republics. These all proved unstable and short-lived, lasting at most several decades. When they fell, they were replaced by republics. And when Europe's second imperial age came to an end in the decolonization movements of 1945–1960, most of the sovereign states that emerged were also republics. It is true that dictators, tyrants, and one-man rulers of all stripes have

---

[1]Although recent research is revealing that important parts of Asia and the Middle East felt its ripples as well. See C. A. Bayly, "The 'Revolutionary Age' in the Wider World, c. 1790–1830," in *War, Empire and Slavery, 1770–1830*, eds. Richard Bessel, Nicholas Guyatt, and Jane Rendall (Basingstoke, England: Palgrave-Macmillan, 2010), 21–43; and *The Age of Revolutions in Global Context, c. 1760-1840*, eds. David Armitage and Sanjay Subrahmanyam.

[2]Lynn Hunt, *Inventing Human Rights: A History* (New York: Norton, 2007).

often tried to make their power hereditary, to perpetuate their grasp on sovereignty down through their family line. But these experiments—such as the Central African Empire of Jean-Bédél Bokassa (1966–1979) or the Kingdom of Albania of Zog I (1928–1939)—seem downright bizarre. Even the decades-long reign of the Kim family of North Korea (whose official name is, significantly, "The People's Democratic Republic of Korea") has avoided the language of hereditary power. Each of the Kims has ruled as some form of "Chairman" of the republic's single party and paid lip service to the idea of popular sovereignty by holding referenda.

The example of totalitarian North Korea shows that republics can take a wide range of concrete forms. Rather than being a specific form of administration, the republic is a set of concepts that define political modernity itself and can thus be used to construct different types of regime. The United States is a republic, but so too was the Union of Soviet Socialist Republics and its Warsaw Pact allies. Militantly secular France is a republic, but so too is the Republic of Iran (which actually has a more generous definition of suffrage than France). What these contrasting republics have in common is that they are founded on the principle that sovereignty is considered a public good, not a private, patrimonial possession. With this republican understanding of sovereignty dominating the globe today, it is easy to overlook what a monumental transformation it was when first introduced by the Atlantic revolutions. In the eighteenth century, nearly every country was ruled by a hereditary sovereign. Today there are very few, and most of those appear as quaint relics, cherished national symbols of a bygone age.

Curiously, the greatest concentration of monarchies today is found in Europe, one of the geographical zones most directly affected by the revolutionary republican movement. But all are actually republics, with elected, representative assemblies, written constitutions, codes of human rights, and all the rest. Even the oldest in form (and arguably most potent in reality), Great Britain was already widely regarded in the eighteenth century as a republic in all but name. The displacement of the ideal of hereditary sovereignty by the concept of public power was the great transformation wrought by the Atlantic republican revolutions.

This collection of primary sources has focused on the four most influential of these revolutions. The American Revolution popularized the idea of republican revolution and showed that republics could work in reality. The United States Declaration of Independence, its states' constitutions and bills of rights, and the United States Constitution of 1787 all served as models for various revolutionary movements and independent republican governments.[3] The French Revolution

---

[3]David Armitage, *The Declaration of Independence: A Global History* (Cambridge, MA: Harvard University Press, 2008). On the global influence of Tory exiles, see Maya Jasanoff, *Liberty's Exiles: American Loyalists in the Revolutionary World* (New York: Knoph, 2011).

popularized the vocabulary of revolution and came to be considered as establishing a script that revolutionaries of other countries and centuries consciously (even slavishly) followed. This influence was particularly evident in the socialist and communist revolutions.[4] During the nineteenth century, the Haitian Revolution was a great source of inspiration to those—the enslaved and their allies—who wanted to destroy the institution of slavery and institute racial equality. In the twentieth century, it took on a new significance—as a beacon of hope to the emerging movement of decolonization in Africa. "If we live in a world in which democracy is meant to exclude no one," Laurent Dubois has observed, "it is in no small part because of the actions of those slaves in Saint-Domingue who insisted that human rights were theirs too."[5] The Latin American revolutions, including Brazil's, ended the first period of European colonization by destroying the two great Iberian Atlantic empires and replacing them with a hemisphere of new republics. Not until the decolonization movement of 1945–1960 would there be such a wholesale creation of new republics. Each of the four revolutions discussed in this book made its own distinctive contribution to the values and norms of the world we inhabit. Collectively, their impact was to create a set of concepts, liberty and equality, at the forefront, which define our political hopes and expectations. These ideals set loose an expansive dynamic of inclusion that shows no sign of slowing.

---

[4]François Furet, *Interpreting the French Revolution*, trans. Elborg Forster (Cambridge, England: Cambridge University Press, 1981).

[5]Laurent Dubois, *Avengers of the New World* (Cambridge, MA: Harvard University Press, 2004), 3.